MW01641346

ROUTLEDGE HANDBOOK OF GLOBAL HEALTH SECURITY

This new handbook presents an overview of cutting-edge research in the growing field of global health security.

Over the past decade, the study of global health and its interconnection with security has become a prominent and rapidly growing field of research. Ongoing debates question whether health and security should be linked; which (if any) health issues should be treated as security threats; what should be done to address health security threats; and the positive and negative consequences of "securitizing" health. In academic and policy terms, the health security field is a timely and dynamic one and this handbook is the first work to comprehensively address this agenda.

Bringing together leading experts and commentators on health security issues from across the world, the volume comprises original and cutting-edge essays addressing the key issues in the field and also highlighting currently neglected avenues for future research. The book provides an accessible yet sophisticated introduction to the key topics and debates and is organized into four key parts:

- Health Securities: the fundamental conceptual issues, historical links between health and security, and the various ways of conceptualizing health as a security issue;
- Threats: those health issues that have been most frequently discussed in security terms;
- Responses: the wide range of contemporary security-driven responses to health threats; and
- Controversies: the securitization of health, its impact on rights and justice, and the potential distortion of the global health agenda.

This book will be of great interest to students of global health security, public health, critical security studies, and international relations in general.

Simon Rushton is a Faculty Research Fellow in the Department of Politics at the University of Sheffield, UK. He is editor of the journal *Medicine, Conflict & Survival* and an Associate Fellow of the Centre on Global Health Security at the Royal Institute of International Affairs, Chatham House.

Jeremy Youde is an associate professor of political science at the University of Minnesota Duluth, USA. He is author of three books on global health issues and on the editorial board of the journal *Global Health Governance*.

ROUTLEDGE HANDBOOK OF GLOBAL HEALTH SECURITY

Edited by Simon Rushton and Jeremy Youde

LONDON AND NEW YORK

First published 2015
by Routledge
2 Park Square, Milton Park, Abingdon, Oxon OX14 4RN

and by Routledge
711 Third Avenue, New York, NY 10017

Routledge is an imprint of the Taylor & Francis Group, an informa business

British Library Cataloguing-in-Publication Data
A catalogue record for this book is available from the British Library

Library of Congress Cataloging-in-Publication Data
Routledge handbook of global health security / edited by Simon Rushton and Jeremy Youde.
pages cm
Includes bibliographical references and index.
1. World health. 2. Public health—International cooperation. 3. Medical policy. 4. National security. I. Rushton, Simon, 1978– editor of compilation. II. Youde, Jeremy R., 1976– editor of compilation.
RA441.R68 2015
616.1'32—dc 3 2014008106

ISBN: 978-0-415-64547-8 (hbk)
ISBN: 978-0-203-07856-3 (ebk)

Typeset in ApexBembo
by Apex CoVantage, LLC

Printed and bound in the United States of America by
Edwards Brothers Malloy on sustainably sourced paper

CONTENTS

List of tables and figures *viii*
Notes on contributors *ix*

Introduction 1
Jeremy Youde & Simon Rushton

PART I
Health securities **5**

1 The many meanings of health security 7
Colin McInnes

2 Inventing global health security, 1994–2005 18
Lorna Weir

3 Health and human security: Pathways to advancing a human-centered approach to health security in East Asia 32
Mely Caballero-Anthony & Gianna Gayle Amul

4 Gender, health, and security 48
Colleen O'Manique

5 The politics of health security 60
João Nunes

6 The medicalization of insecurity 71
Stefan Elbe & Nadine Voelkner

PART II
Threats **81**

7 Pandemics and security 83
Yanzhong Huang

8 Emerging infections: Threats to health and economic security 92
David L. Heymann & Alison West

9 AIDS as a security threat: The emergence and the decline of an idea 105
Pieter Fourie

10 Biological weapons and bioterrorism 118
Gregory D. Koblentz

11 Life science research as a security risk 130
Christian Enemark

12 Conflict, instability, and health security 141
Frank L. Smith III

13 Health security and environmental change 151
Robert L. Ostergard Jr. & Derek Kauneckis

14 Malaria and security: More than a matter of health 163
Nicholas Knowlton

15 Noncommunicable disease as a security issue 175
Christopher Benson & Sara M. Glasgow

PART III
Responses **187**

16 Health, security, and diplomacy in historical perspective 189
Adam Kamradt-Scott

17 Preparedness and resilience in public health emergencies 201
Rebecca Katz & Erin Sorrell

18 Medical countermeasures and security 215
Kendall Hoyt

19 Internet surveillance and disease outbreaks 226
Sara E. Davies

20 Making the international health regulations matter: Promoting compliance through effective dispute resolution 239
Steven J. Hoffman

21 Biosecurity education for life scientists: The missing past, inadequate present, and uncertain future 252
Malcolm Dando

22 Health security and foreign policy 265
Joshua Michaud

23 NGOs and health security: Securing the health of people living with HIV/AIDS 277
Amy S. Patterson

PART IV
Controversies **291**

24 Health security and/or human rights? 293
Joseph J. Amon

25 Reevaluating health security from a cosmopolitan perspective 304
Garrett Wallace Brown & Preslava Stoeva

26 Indonesia, power asymmetry, and pandemic risk: The paradox of global health security 318
William L. Aldis & Triono Soendoro

27 Health security and the distortion of the global health agenda 328
Michael A. Stevenson & Michael Moran

28 Whose interests is the securitization of health serving? 339
Debra L. DeLaet

Select bibliography *349*
Index *355*

TABLES AND FIGURES

Tables

3.1 Regional Health Frameworks and Areas of Cooperation 40
8.1 Breeches in the Species Barrier: Selected Emerging Infections since 1976 93
10.1 Properties of Biological Warfare Agents 119
17.1 Public Health Preparedness Capabilities, as Defined by the U.S. Centers for Disease Control and Prevention 203
17.2 Select Legislation and Presidential Directives in Support of Public Health Emergency Preparedness and Resilience in the United States 205
17.3 Checklist and Indicators for Monitoring Progress in Meeting Capacity on Preparedness 209
20.1 Goals for IHR Dispute Resolution 241
20.2 Advisory and Adjudicative Dispute Resolution Processes 246
22.1 Top Recipients of U.S. Bilateral Foreign Assistance, Fiscal Year 2012 269

Figures

3.1 Prioritization of Health Security Issues in East Asia 38
8.1 Rapid Spread of Influenza A (H1N1) after Emergence, 2009 96
8.2 International spread of SARS, 2003 98
8.3 Passenger Movement, Hong Kong International Airport, March–July 2003 99
8.4 Revenue in Commercial Sector, Hong Kong, 2002–2003 100
13.1 The Indirect Effect of Climate Change on Health Security 154
14.1 Malaria and State Capacity 170
19.1 Timeline of Key Events in MERS-CoV Outbreak, June 2012 234
20.1 Proposed Multitiered IHR Dispute Resolution Process and its Shadow System 247

NOTES ON CONTRIBUTORS

William L. Aldis is Assistant Professor in the School of Global Studies, Thammasat University, Thailand. His interests include policy on access to medicines, child survival in low-income countries, health care during war and civil unrest, and preparedness for pandemics. In the World Health Organization he served as Country Representative in Sierra Leone, Malawi, and Thailand; as Regional Advisor of Emergency and Humanitarian Action in WHO's African Region and as Coordinator for Health Policy and Research in WHO's Regional Office for South-East Asia. He is a graduate of the Johns Hopkins University and Harvard Medical School.

Joseph J. Amon is the Director of the Health and Human Rights Division at Human Rights Watch. Before joining Human Rights Watch in 2005, he worked for more than 15 years conducting epidemiological research, designing programs, and evaluating interventions related to HIV, malaria, hepatitis and Guinea Worm disease for a range of governmental and nongovernmental organizations. He is also a lecturer at the Woodrow Wilson School of Princeton University and an associate in the Department of Epidemiology at the Bloomberg School of Public Health at Johns Hopkins University.

Gianna Gayle Amul is Senior Analyst at the Centre for Non-Traditional Security (NTS) Studies in the S. Rajaratnam School of International Studies (RSIS), Nanyang Technological University, Singapore. She is co-author of *Promoting Peace, Development and Human Security: The Mining Act of 1995 and the Indigenous People's Rights Act (IPRA)* published for the UNDP Conflict Prevention and Peacebuilding Programme. Her research interests are primarily in health security issues, particularly global and regional health governance, health diplomacy, and noncommunicable diseases, as well as climate change, environmental security, and natural disasters.

Christopher Benson is currently an advanced undergraduate at the University of Montana Western, where he is completing his B.A. in Global Politics and Psychology. He plans on pursuing graduate studies after completing his degree.

Garrett Wallace Brown is Reader in Political Theory and Global Ethics in the Department of Politics at the University of Sheffield, UK. His publications include work on cosmopolitanism, globalization theory, global justice, and global health governance. He has published widely on issues in global health and has recently published *Grounding Cosmopolitanism: From Kant to the Idea of a Cosmopolitan Constitution* (Edinburgh University Press 2009), co-edited *The Cosmopolitanism Reader* (Polity 2010) with David Held, and is currently publishing *Global Health Policy* (Wiley-Blackwell 2014). His latest IDRC funded research is examining the practice of performance based funding in global health.

Mely Caballero-Anthony is Associate Professor and Head of the RSIS Centre for Non-Traditional Security (NTS) Studies at the S. Rajaratnam School of International Studies (RSIS), Nanyang Technological University, Singapore. Until May 2012, she served as Director of External Relations of the ASEAN Secretariat. Dr. Anthony serves on the UN Secretary General's Advisory Board on Disarmament Matters and the UN Academic Advisory Council on Mediation and Conflict Prevention. She is also a member of the World Economic Forum (WEF) Global Agenda Council on Conflict Prevention. Since 2008, she has served as the Secretary-General of the Consortium of Non-Traditional Security Studies in Asia (NTS-Asia).

Malcolm Dando is Professor of International Security at the University of Bradford, UK. Originally trained as a zoologist, he joined Bradford in 1979 and since then has worked on issues of WMD, arms control, and disarmament. In recent years his work has focused on the life sciences community and how they might be better engaged in protecting their benignly intended work from misuse. His recent books include *Preventing a Biochemical Arms Race* (Stanford University Press 2012, with Alexander Kelle & Kathryn Nixdorff) and *Deadly Cultures: Biological Weapons Since 1945* (Harvard University Press 2006, coedited with Mark Wheelis & Lajos Rozsa).

Sara E. Davies is an ARC Future Fellow at the Health Law Resource Center in the Faculty of Law at Queensland University of Technology, Australia. Her research is concerned with global health governance, specifically the relationship between health security and health diplomacy. She has published two sole authored books – *Global Politics of Health* (Polity Press 2010) and *Legitimising Rejection: International Refugee Law in South East Asia* (Martinus Nijhoff 2008) – and has authored a number of articles on international refugee law and global health governance.

Debra L. DeLaet is Professor of Politics & International Relations at Drake University. Her areas of scholarly expertise include human rights, global health, and gender issues in world politics. She has published three books: *U.S. Immigration Policy in the Age of Rights* (Praeger 2000), *The Global Struggle for Human Rights*, 2nd ed. (Cengage 2015 2006), and (coauthored with David E. DeLaet) *Global Health in the 21st Century: The Globalization of Disease and Wellness* (Paradigm Publishers 2012). In addition to these books, she has published numerous articles and book chapters in her areas of interest.

Stefan Elbe is Professor of International Relations and Director of the Centre for Global Health Policy at the University of Sussex, UK. He has published widely on the international politics of health, including *Security and Global Health: Towards the Medicalization of Insecurity* (Polity Press 2010), *Virus Alert: Security, Governmentality and the AIDS Pandemic* (Columbia University Press 2009), *Strategic Implications of HIV/AIDS* (Oxford University Press 2003), and articles both in leading international relations and medical journals. He is currently Principal Investigator on a 4-year research project funded by the European Union on "Pharmaceuticals and Security: The Role of Public-Private Collaborations in Strengthening Health Security."

Christian Enemark is Reader in Global Health and International Politics at Aberystwyth University, UK. He is the author of *Disease and Security: Natural Plagues and Biological Weapons in East*

Asia (Routledge 2007) and *Armed Drones and the Ethics of War: Military Virtue in a Post-Heroic Age* (Routledge 2013), and the coeditor of *Ethics and Security Aspects of Infectious Disease Control: Interdisciplinary Perspectives* (Ashgate 2012). His research on disease, security, and ethics has been sponsored by the Australian Research Council.

Pieter Fourie is an Associate Professor of Political Science at Stellenbosch University, South Africa, and was trained at the universities of Stellenbosch, Paris, London, and Johannesburg. He has worked for UNAIDS, the Australian Department of Foreign Affairs & Trade, in civil society, and has taught International Relations at universities in South Africa and Australia. His research focuses on global health governance, health diplomacy, and the political economy of development. His book *The Political Management of HIV and AIDS in South Africa* (Palgrave Macmillan 2006) was longlisted for the Alan Paton Award. He coauthored *The Politics of AIDS Denialism* (Ashgate 2010).

Sara M. Glasgow is Professor of Political Science at the University of Montana Western, where she specializes in health politics – especially those surrounding noncommunicable disease, discursive frames of illness, and comparative public health policy. She has published articles in such journals as *International Studies Perspectives, Global Health Governance*, and *Journal of Human Security* and provided a chapter for the *Ashgate Research Companion to the Globalization of Health* and review pieces for *Critical Public Health*.

David L. Heymann is a medical doctor, currently Chair of the Advisory Board of Public Health England, Head of the Centre on Global Health Security at Chatham House, and Professor of Infectious Disease Epidemiology at the London School of Hygiene and Tropical Medicine. Before joining his current positions in the UK in 2009, he held various senior positions at the World Health Organization, and prior to that worked for 15 years as a medical epidemiologist in sub-Saharan Africa and Asia on assignment from the U.S. Centers for Disease Control and Prevention (CDC).

Steven J. Hoffman is an Assistant Professor of Clinical Epidemiology and Biostatistics at McMaster University, an adjunct faculty with the McMaster Health Forum, and a visiting assistant professor of Global Health at the Harvard School of Public Health. An international lawyer by training, his research integrates analytical, empirical, and big data methods to study global health decision-making and to evaluate international strategies for addressing health threats and social inequalities. He previously worked for the Alliance for Health Policy & Systems Research, the UN Secretary-General's Office, and the World Health Organization.

Kendall Hoyt is an Assistant Professor at the Geisel School of Medicine and a Lecturer at the Thayer School of Engineering at Dartmouth College. She serves on the National Academy of Sciences Committee on the Department of Defense's Programs to Counter Biological Threats and on the advisory board of the Vaccine and Immunotherapy Center at Massachusetts General Hospital. She received her Ph.D. in the History and Social Study of Science and Technology at the Massachusetts Institute of Technology in 2002.

Yanzhong Huang is Associate Professor at the School of Diplomacy and International Relations, Seton Hall University, and Senior Fellow for Global Health at the Council on Foreign Relations. He is the founding editor of *Global Health Governance: The Scholarly Journal for the New Health Security Paradigm*. His research interests cover global health governance, health security, and health diplomacy. He obtained his Ph.D. in political science from the University of Chicago.

Adam Kamradt-Scott is Senior Lecturer in International Security at the Centre for International Security Studies, University of Sydney, Australia, and Coconvenor of the Humanities Division of the Marie Bashir Institute for Infectious Diseases and Biosecurity. He previously worked as a health-care professional, political adviser, and public servant in Australia before joining the ranks of academe. He joined the Centre for International Security Studies in November 2011. His research interests include health security and diplomacy, securitization theory, and civil–military relations.

Derek Kauneckis is an Associate Professor in the Department of Political Science at the University of Nevada, Reno where he teaches environmental policy and policy analysis. He holds a Ph.D. from Indiana University at Bloomington. He specializes in policy analysis, institutional analysis, and policy design. His research examines the evolution of governance arrangements as they relate to environmental and natural resources. Current work focuses on climate change adaptation and resilience, the emergence and enforcement of property rights institutions, and environmental innovation policy.

Rebecca Katz is an Associate Professor at The Milken Institute School of Public Health at the George Washington University and co-director of the Global Health Security Program. She is also a public health expert consultant to the U.S. Department of State. Dr. Katz received her undergraduate degree in Political Science and Economics from Swarthmore College, an MPH in International Health from Yale University, and a PhD in Public Affairs from Princeton University.

Nicholas Knowlton is a Ph.D. candidate in the Department of Political Science at the University of Florida. His research investigates the relationship between malaria and the state in sub-Saharan Africa, with additional studies in post-Cold War transitions to democracy in Africa. He was named as a Boren Fellow for 2013/2014 and has conducted research in Ghana.

Gregory D. Koblentz is an Associate Professor in the Department of Public and International Affairs and Deputy Director of the Biodefense Graduate Program at George Mason University. He is also a research affiliate with the Security Studies Program at MIT and a member of the Scientists Working Group on Chemical and Biological Weapons at the Center for Arms Control and Non-Proliferation in Washington, DC. He received his Ph.D. from MIT, his M.P.P. from the Harvard Kennedy School, and his B.A. from Brown University.

Colin McInnes is the UNESCO Chair of HIV/AIDS Education and Health Security in Africa and the Director of the Centre for Health and International Relations at Aberystwyth University, UK, where he also holds a professorial chair in International Politics. He has written extensively on global health security, especially relating to HIV/AIDS, and is currently leading a major project on global health governance funded by the European Research Council. His most recent book (with Kelley Lee) is *Global Health and International Relations* (Polity Press 2012).

Joshua Michaud is an Associate Director for Global Health Policy at the Kaiser Family Foundation, and a Professorial Lecturer at the Johns Hopkins University School of Advanced International Studies (SAIS) in Washington, D.C. His research, teaching, and analytical work focus on global health policy and financing, global health diplomacy, health security and emerging diseases, and the links between health and development. He holds a Ph.D. in International Health Policy from Johns Hopkins SAIS, an M.A. in Applied Economics from Johns Hopkins University, and an M.H.S. in Epidemiology from the Johns Hopkins University Bloomberg School of Public Health.

Michael Moran is a research fellow at the Asia-Pacific Centre for Social Investment and Philanthropy at Swinburne University, Australia. He was awarded his Ph.D. from the University of Melbourne. An edited version of his thesis, which examined private foundations and public–private partnership formation in health and agriculture, was published as *Private Foundations and Development Partnerships: American Philanthropy and Global Development Agendas* (Routledge 2013).

João Nunes is a Leverhulme Trust Early Career Fellow at the University of Warwick, UK. His research interests are in security theory, global health governance, and the politics of food. He is the author of *Security, Emancipation and the Politics of Health: A New Theoretical Perspective* (Routledge 2013) and one of the editors of *Critical Theory in International Relations and Security Studies* (Routledge 2011). His work has also been published in the journal *Security Dialogue*.

Colleen O'Manique is an Associate Professor in the departments of International Development Studies, and Gender & Women's Studies at Trent University, Canada, where she teaches courses on gender, health, globalization, and world politics. Her research and publications have been broadly focused on the gender dimensions of health and health policy under neoliberal globalization and the intersections of health and security. She is currently the principle investigator on a research project funded by SSHRC (Canada) that examines the ways that "women's empowerment" and gender justice are addressed in the consultative global process to replace the Millennium Development Goals.

Robert L. Ostergard Jr. is Associate Professor of Political Science at the University of Nevada, Reno. His research focuses on global health, the political economy of intellectual property rights, human rights, and international security issues, particularly within sub-Saharan Africa. His current research includes projects on global health and human rights and the impact of women's rights on the HIV/AIDS epidemics in Africa. He has served as a consultant for the UN Economic Commission for Africa (UNECA), the Commission on HIV/AIDS and Governance in Africa (CHGA), the Council on Foreign Relations, UNAIDS, the U.S. Department of Defense and the Canadian Ministry of Defense.

Amy S. Patterson is Professor of Politics at University of the South. She is editor of *The African State and the AIDS Crisis* (Ashgate 2005) and author of *The Politics of AIDS in Africa* (Lynne Rienner 2006) and *The Church and AIDS in Africa: The Politics of Ambiguity* (Lynne Rienner 2010). She has published in *Africa Today*, *Journal of Modern African Studies*, *Canadian Journal of African Studies*, *African Journal of AIDS Research*, *Contemporary Politics*, and *African Studies Review*. In 2011, she was a Fulbright Scholar to Zambia. She serves on the Governing Board of the International Research Network on AIDS and Religion in Africa.

Simon Rushton is a faculty research fellow in the Department of Politics at the University of Sheffield, UK. He has written widely on international responses to HIV/AIDS and other diseases; the links between health and security; the changing nature of global health governance; and issues surrounding health, conflict, and post-conflict reconstruction. He edits the journal *Medicine, Conflict & Survival* (with Maria Kett at UCL) and is an associate fellow of the Centre on Global Health Security at the Royal Institute of International Affairs, Chatham House.

Frank L. Smith III is a lecturer with the Centre for International Security Studies and the Department of Government and International Relations at the University of Sydney, Australia.

His teaching and research focus on science, technology, and international security. Among other topics, he has published work on biodefense in the United States and global governance during transnational outbreaks of infectious disease.

Triono Soendoro is Senior Adviser to the Minister, Ministry of Health, Republic of Indonesia. Previously he served as Director General of Indonesia's National Institute for Health Research and Development (NIHRD). Dr. Soendoro has coordinated research projects in collaboration with Johns Hopkins, the World Health Organization, and several Indonesian universities; and has numerous publications in the international literature on reproductive health and on health systems and policy issues. He was a Gates fellow at the Johns Hopkins, and holds a Ph.D. and master's degrees from Yale University and an M.D. from the Faculty of Medicine, Airlangga University, Surabaya, Indonesia.

Erin Sorrell is a Senior Research Scientist at The Milken Institute School of Public Health at the George Washington University. Prior to joining George Washington, she worked at the Department of State as a American Association for the Advancement of Science (AAAS) Science and Technology Policy Fellow. She received her MS and PhD in Molecular Virology from the University of Maryland and a BS in Animal Science from Cornell University. Her research focused on the molecular mechanisms behind the adaptation and interspecies transmission of influenza A viruses.

Michael A. Stevenson recently completed a doctorate in Global Governance at the University of Waterloo, Canada. His thesis examined the agency of the Rockefeller and Bill and Melinda Gates Foundations in the governance of global health and agricultural development. Previously, he worked as a senior policy analyst within the British Columbia Ministry of Health Services and as an instructor at Outward Bound Canada.

Preslava Stoeva is a lecturer in the Department of Global Health and Development at the London School of Hygiene and Tropical Medicine, UK. Her research interests include global governance, the role of non-state actors in global politics, international law including human rights, and most recently security politics. She is the author of *New Norms and Knowledge in World Politics* (Routledge 2010). With a background in international relations theories, her research now focuses on understanding health security politics and the global governance of health.

Nadine Voelkner is Assistant Professor in International Relations at the University of Groningen in the Netherlands and Associate Researcher at the Centre for Global Health Policy at the University of Sussex, UK. She is coauthor of *Critical Security Methods: New Frameworks for Analysis* (Routledge 2013) that resulted from the Economic & Social Research Council-funded "International Collaboratory on Critical Methods in Security Studies." Her research has revolved around understanding the global politics of human security, including the governance of health security in relation to Burmese migrant communities in Thailand. Her current work investigates the role of the medical sciences and advances in medical knowledge in the medicalization of insecurity.

Lorna Weir is Professor of Sociology at York University, Toronto, Canada. She specializes in health and social theory. Her books include *Pregnancy, Risk and Biopolitics: On the Threshold of the Living Subject* (Routledge 2006) and *Global Public Health Vigilance: Creating a World on Alert* (Routledge 2010, with Eric Mykhalovskiy). Her current research is on biopolitics, technology and the proper (with an empirical focus on the integration of security into genomics), and sacrifice in biopolitics.

Alison West is a Junior Honours undergraduate pursuing a degree in Modern and Mediaeval History at the University of St. Andrews. In 2013, she worked as a research intern at the Centre on Global Health Security at Chatham House. Previously, she has held positions with Organizing for America and Democrats of Washington. Currently, in addition to her studies, she holds the position of Gender Equality officer within the St. Andrews Students' Association.

Jeremy Youde is Associate Professor of Political Science at the University of Minnesota Duluth. He previously taught at San Diego State University and Grinnell College. He has written on topics such as global health governance, disease surveillance systems, the intersections of human rights and global health, and health policies in southern Africa. He is the author of *AIDS, South Africa, and the Politics of Knowledge* (Ashgate 2007), *Biopolitical Surveillance and Public Health in International Politics* (Palgrave Macmillan 2010), and *Global Health Governance* (Polity 2012).

INTRODUCTION

Jeremy Youde & Simon Rushton

As is so often the case, clichés can obscure the existence of a deeper truth. It has become traditional for books examining the global dimensions of health to begin with a statement to the effect that "pathogens do not respect national borders." In reality, of course, they never did – as is shown by the countless examples of deadly diseases that have swept across entire continents throughout human history. Yet it is undoubtedly true that something fundamental has changed as a result of globalization. Diseases have long spread along trade and travel routes, but the SARS outbreak in 2003 and the global spread of H1N1 "swine flu" in 2009 demonstrated the rapidity with which germs and viruses can disseminate as a result of the rapid movement of people and goods around the planet. At the same time other globalization-related processes – including migration, urbanization, climate change, and global markets in food and other goods – have increased the possibilities of local epidemics becoming global pandemics. Diseases have never been containable, but health is undoubtedly more global now than ever before.

Just as the (global) public health community has its clichés, so too does the security studies community. From the early 1990s onwards we heard much about the redefinition of the "post-Cold War security agenda" and how security policy communities were now alert to a far broader range of security threats than ever before. No longer did the threat of thermonuclear war between the superpowers dominate security policy. The "new security challenges" posed by transboundary issues such as climate change, energy and natural resource availability, information technology, and disease have become increasingly apparent in the national and international security discourse, and they require global collaboration and cooperation to address them in any meaningful manner. Over the same period we have seen human security emerge as a challenge to the traditional state-centric approach, again bringing with it a willingness to take into account a far wider range of threats to human well-being. It should come as no surprise that health, which is at the heart of human well-being, has been prominent in human security discussions.

Disease, then, has increasingly found its way onto the agendas of both policymakers and academics concerned with human, national, international, and global security. In January 2000 the UN Security Council declared HIV/AIDS to be a threat to international peace and security (United Nations Security Council 2000). The World Health Organization devoted its 2007 World Health Report to the theme of "Global Public Health Security in the 21st Century" (WHO 2007). In September 2011, the United Nations General Assembly convened the High Level Meeting on Non-Communicable Diseases. The UK government's National Risk Register of Civil Emergencies identifies pandemic influenza as "the most significant civil emergency risk" facing the UK (Cabinet Office 2012: 6). The potential threat posed by pandemics has assumed a similarly prominent place in U.S. national security policy (e.g., Homeland Security Council 2006; National Intelligence Council 2003).

In tandem with these policy developments around the security implications of health issues has grown a burgeoning academic literature on the subject. Scholars from a range of backgrounds including International Relations/Security Studies, Medicine, and Public Health have examined the security implications of a range of health issues. Some have seen the "securitization" of health as having the potential to improve responses to global health problems, bringing much-needed attention and resources to bear on infectious diseases and other health threats that pose a danger to individuals and communities. Others have been concerned that linking health and security could bring negative side effects. It could promote anti-democratic responses to health challenges, it might lead to attacks on the human rights and civil liberties of individuals suffering from a particular disease, or it might distort the global health agenda in inequitable ways. As a result, as Stefan Elbe (2011) rightly noted in *The Lancet*, health professionals face a difficult dilemma in deciding whether or not to "play the global health security card."

Looking across the field of global health and security as a whole, *The Routledge Handbook of Global Health Security* does not take a position on the desirability or otherwise of addressing health in security terms. Rather, we deliberately invited authors with different perspectives on health and security to contribute to the volume, leaving each author free to approach their topic in line with their own approach and normative position. This stridently agnostic position allows the chapters to fully explore and examine the myriad dimensions of the intersections between health and security in the global realm. Chapters in the first section of the book, "Health Securities," reflect upon the various ways in which health can be (and has been) conceptualized as a security issue, including debates over the appropriate referent object (should the focus be on national security? Human security?) and what including health on the security agenda may mean for security discourses and practices. The second section of the book, "Threats," examines some of the health issues that have been most frequently discussed in security terms but also draws attention to others (such as malaria and noncommunicable diseases) that have not yet come to be widely viewed in security terms but that share some of the features of established health security issues.

Under the heading of "Responses," Part III of the handbook examines the measures that have been put in place at both the national and supranational levels to address health security challenges, including attempts to foster international cooperation to enhance health security in a globalized world and the various technological and political strategies that have been adopted to address the threat posed by infectious diseases. Finally, Part IV of the book examines some of the controversies that have emerged around the linking of health and security, including the implications for human rights, the potential distortion of the global health agenda, and the possible obstacles to cooperation that can emerge as states increasingly come to view diseases in national security terms.

In compiling the chapters included in this Handbook, we drew on a wide range of academics and policy specialists from political science, international relations, medicine, and other fields. The authors do not share a common outlook on the value or desirability of linking health and security, but they do share a background in examining this nexus and a status as the some of the leading scholars in the field.

Readers of this handbook will, we hope, find it a wide ranging and accessible, yet sophisticated, introduction to the contemporary debates around global health security. We cannot provide definitive answers about the right relationship between health and security in the global realm, just as we cannot predict the next pandemic that will threaten the international community.

Instead, we hope that readers will understand the contours of the debates as they currently exist and use the insightful chapters by the various authors as the basis for future studies.

References

Cabinet Office. (2012) *National Risk Register of Civil Emergencies: 2012 Update*, London: HMSO. Online. Available HTTP: <http://www.cabinetoffice.gov.uk/sites/default/files/resources/CO_NationalRiskRegister_2012_acc.pdf> (accessed 16 December 2013).

Elbe, S. (2011) 'Should health professionals play the global health security card?' *Lancet*, 378: 220–221.

Homeland Security Council. (2006) *National Strategy for Pandemic Influenza: Implementation Plan*, Washington, DC: Homeland Security Council. Online. Available HTTP: <http://www.flu.gov/planning-preparedness/federal/pandemic-influenza-implementation.pdf> (accessed 13 December 2013).

National Intelligence Council. (2003) *SARS: Down but Still a Threat*. Intelligence Community Assessment NIC ICA 2003–09, Washington: National Intelligence Council. Online. Available HTTP: <http://www.fas.org/irp/nic/sars.html> (accessed 16 December 2013).

United Nations Security Council. (2000) S/RES/1308 (17 July 2000). Online. Available HTTP: <http://daccess-dds-ny.un.org/doc/UNDOC/GEN/N00/536/02/PDF/N0053602.pdf?OpenElement> (accessed 25 February 2014).

World Health Organization (WHO). (2007) *World Health Report 2007. Global Public Health Security in the 21st Century: A Safer Future*, Geneva: World Health Organization.

PART I

Health securities

1
THE MANY MEANINGS OF HEALTH SECURITY

Colin McInnes

The link between security and health is not new, but has traditionally been seen in narrow, albeit bidirectional, terms: the manner in which disease may affect military capacity and especially military operations and the impact of conflict on health and health care. By the turn of the millennium, however, this link was broadening and its significance to national and international agendas rising. The rationale for this was constructed along fairly consistent lines: that new global health risks had appeared as a result of emerging and reemerging diseases, increased population mobility, spreading transnational crime, environmental change, and bioterrorism; and that these posed new security dangers (see for example Brundtland 2003; CIA 2000; WHO 2007c; Yuk-ping & Thomas 2010). Moreover, this was a period when security audiences had been sensitized to the idea of new risks following the "bonfire of the certainties" at the end of the Cold War. The attempt to construct health as a security issue (to "securitize" it) therefore fell on more fertile ground than might previously have been the case. Beyond "real world" concerns, however, were political considerations, with some within the public health community recognizing that the security label was a potentially effective means of elevating global health issues on the national and global stage.

"Security," however, is not a straightforward concept but "essentially contested" – that is, a concept that generates unsolvable debates about its meaning and application (Buzan 1991: 7). This chapter focuses on four terms widely used in debates over health security in this global context. It does this to illustrate how health security is similarly essentially contested. These terms are global (public) health security, national security, human security, and biosecurity. Crucially the chapter suggests that these are not mutually transferable terms but have different implications both for the range of health issues involved and for whose security is at risk. The meaning of each term is constructed for a particular purpose including promoting a certain agenda and privileging certain interests over others. The object of this chapter, therefore, is not to suggest that there are criteria whereby a health issue may or may not be considered a security issue or that there is a single agreed definition of health security when used in the global context. Instead, it is to reveal how, like other forms of security, it is essentially contested and not amenable to a single set of agreed criteria. The lack of an agreed definition is not due to lack of effort but because in its different uses and terms it reflects different interests and agendas.

National and international security

National security is often characterized in a narrow manner: that the referent object of security is the state; that the main concerns are direct threats, usually military in nature; that the context is one of an anarchic international states system where self-help is the order of the day; and that stability (both state and international) is privileged over issues such as rights and justice. Security therefore depends on the state protecting itself from threats, and a social contract is entered into whereby citizens forsake some of their individual freedoms to secure the greater collective good. The risk, however, is that the social contract is undermined by the increasing power of the state, which may become willing to sacrifice the freedoms and rights of the people it is supposed to protect in order to preserve its own power. It is this fear that has led to many health practitioners – concerned with protecting and promoting the well-being of individuals and communities – to be wary of national security.

National security's traditional focus on military threats however has been replaced by a more diverse range of risks. This broadening of the security agenda has created a space where issues such as health can be considered part of national security. But understandings of the state and state power have also changed. Of particular significance for health security is the shift away from sovereign power and towards governmentality. Drawing on the work of French philosopher Michel Foucault, both Stefan Elbe and Alan Ingram have argued that power is no longer oriented self-referentially towards preserving the power of the state (sovereign power) but rather towards improving the welfare of citizens (governmentality). Both Elbe and Ingram accept that this shift applies predominantly to Western states; but as these states have set the agenda for health security, the significance is considerable (Elbe 2009: 86–107; Ingram 2010).

National security's interest in health has been longstanding in that the physical condition of military troops affects their operational performance. Diseases such as cholera and dysentery have historically caused significant numbers of casualties during military campaigns. From the late 1990s on, however, interest in a broader range of health concerns began to develop within a number of key policy circles. In so doing, the foreign and security policy community maintained a robustly state-centric approach in prioritizing the national interest and international stability when discussing health security issues (for example Cook 2000: 2; Downe 2003; FCO 2003: 13; U.S. State Department 2004: 76). Two examples of this are the 1999 U.S. National Intelligence Estimate on the global threat of infectious disease to the United States and the January 2000 meeting of the UN Security Council. On the first, in 1999 the Central Intelligence Agency (CIA) identified a number of risks to U.S. security arising from infectious disease, risks exacerbated by rapid globalization and the increased worldwide movement of goods and people. These included not only risks to U.S. citizens traveling abroad but to citizens at home given the potential for certain infectious diseases to spread globally. Crucially, however, the CIA went further than this, arguing that infectious disease also posed a risk to international stability and even economic growth, thus placing it firmly in the territory of national security (CIA 2000). On the second, at its first meeting of the new millennium, the UN Security Council discussed the threat of HIV/AIDS to Africa and, in Resolution 1308, warned "that the HIV/AIDS pandemic, if unchecked, may pose a risk to stability and security" (UNSC 2000a; see also McInnes & Rushton 2010; UNSC 2000b). In particular, the Security Council drew attention to the effects of HIV/AIDS on social stability and on peacekeeping missions. In both the interests of the state appeared paramount, whether in terms of stability or the protection of its citizens or soldiers (peacekeepers).

Three issues have dominated national security's interest in and engagement with health: acute and severe infectious diseases of epidemic potential; HIV/AIDS; and bioterrorism (for an overview, see McInnes 2012). What is missing, however, is a rationale as to why some health issues might be considered national security problems but not others. Health issues are not identified as national security risks by reference to an explicit set of criteria but rather have arisen in an ad hoc manner and been agreed to intersubjectively by key national and international actors. Although it is possible to identify three broad sets of reasons suggesting an implicit agenda, these are also problematic, as will be seen below. The first of these reasons is the potential of a health issue to threaten international stability. Four possible arguments can, in turn, be identified as supporting this:

1 Health crises may have dramatic effects on the global economy. That health crises may have detrimental economic effects has been long understood. Globalization has not only increased this sensitivity but has also broadened the geographical territory potentially affected. An epidemic may lead to reduced economic growth in areas not directly affected by the disease or even in worst case scenarios trigger a global recession, increasing levels of poverty and creating stresses on lifestyle and livelihood amongst even the wealthy states.
2 Poverty and poor health may lead to migration as people seek a better, safer life elsewhere. Migration flows risk spreading disease and may act as destabilizing forces in a region.
3 Militaries may be at increased risk from some diseases, such as HIV/AIDS, impacting upon their operational capabilities with potential effects on national security and thereby international stability.
4 Finally, risks from certain diseases (and in particular HIV/AIDS) may affect the willingness of states to send troops on peacekeeping missions. Concerns have also been expressed at the willingness of countries to receive peacekeepers if they fear that troops may bring high rates of HIV infection into a country with them.

The problem with these four arguments is that the causal relationship between an adverse health effect and international stability is questionable, and/or the empirical evidence to support the claim is suspect or missing. For example there is no credible evidence that international stability is affected by the macroeconomic effects of health crises. Neither sudden outbreak events such as SARS and pandemic influenza nor chronic diseases such as malaria and (increasingly) HIV/AIDS have affected international stability because of their macroeconomic effects; nor have SARS and pandemic influenza demonstrated significant long-term macroeconomic effects. Similarly, although there is an awareness of migration as a security issue (for example, see Huysmans 1997; Weiner 1992–1993; in contrast see Graham & Poku 2000), health status does not appear to be a key driver in people leaving their homes. Rather, poverty, famine, and conflict appear to be much more significant causes of mass migration. Although there was some evidence in the early years of the millennium that militaries were more susceptible to HIV infection, the empirical evidence is no longer so clear cut, while HIV/AIDS awareness campaigns have helped to reduce the risk of infection (ASCI 2009; McInnes 2006). Equally, the link between a military weakened by disease and state instability/insecurity is also unclear and lacking empirical evidence, while research on the global spread of HIV/AIDS does not support the argument that peacekeeping is an important vector in the transmission of the disease or that peacekeepers are especially susceptible (UNAIDS 2005; UN DPKO 2005).

The second broad set of reasons offered as to why health issues might be a national security problem concern their ability to affect the internal security of a state (see for example CIA 2000; ICG 2001). If the domestic economy is damaged, then divisions between rich and poor may be exacerbated. Increased levels of poverty may, in turn, breed social discontent and provide a fertile ground for entrepreneurs of violence. Moreover, confidence in the government, or in the state more generally, may be damaged if public health services are unable to cope. What is again lacking, however, is the empirical evidence to support these arguments. With HIV/AIDS, in particular, a number of states have had very high levels of infection for more than a decade, especially in sub-Saharan Africa. These are also among some of the poorest countries on earth. Yet there is little evidence to date that high HIV/AIDS prevalence has created destabilizing pressures threatening the security of the state.

The third set of reasons concerns high morbidity and mortality rates. When the number of people at risk reaches exceptional levels, then this moves into the realm of national security, both because of the responsibility of the state to protect its citizens and because the effective operation of the state may be at risk. The level at which an event becomes sufficiently extraordinary to be considered a security issue, however, is not definable for example as a percentage of the population; rather it is determined intersubjectively on a case-by-case basis. But a key feature, for the purposes of this section, is that the cause can be represented as an exogenous threat. Three health issues seem both to meet this necessary condition of externality and breach the threshold of being outside the ordinary: the spread of existing diseases such as Ebola or West Nile virus to new geographies; the emergence of new, potentially pandemic, diseases such as SARS or a novel strain of influenza; and bioterrorism. Of these, probably only the second has the potential to kill very large numbers of people within a state. But it is not only the level of morbidity that matters, but the sense of risk felt within high-income countries. Thus in the 1990s, when the Ebola virus first appeared in the United States, the level of concern and attention far outran what might have been assumed from the number of people realistically at risk from the disease (see for example CIA 2000; Garrett 1994). Similarly, concerns over bioterrorism may be overstated with doubts over how easy it is for sub-state groups to gain access to, or produce, effective weapons and over how easy it is to use them in a manner that might cause significant loss of life. But this does not mean that the threat is not *considered* to be very real and of high political salience, resulting in substantial resources being allocated to allay those fears (see for example Graham 2008).

Global public health security

The term *global public health security* (sometimes abbreviated to *global health security*) is largely associated with the WHO and its interest in how risks to public health have been globalized (e.g., Baker & Forsyth 2007; Rodier 2007; WHO 2002). Although the impact on public health is not WHO's only concern here – "global health security, or lack of it, may also have an impact on economic or political stability, trade, tourism, access to goods and services and, if they occur repeatedly, on demographic stability" (WHO 2007c: 1) – it is the main focus. In its 2007 *World Health Report* (WHO 2007c), WHO discussed its understanding of global health security explicitly in terms of public health security. For the WHO, "Public health security is defined as the activities required, both proactive and reactive, to minimize vulnerability to acute public health events that endanger the collective health of national populations. Global public health security widens this definition to include acute public health events that endanger the collective health of populations living across geographical regions and international boundaries . . . [it] embraces a wide range of complex and daunting issues, from the international stage to the individual household, including the health consequences of human behaviour, weather-related events and infectious diseases, and natural catastrophes and man-made disasters" (WHO 2007c: 1).

The background document accompanying the 2007 *World Health Report* provides a list of eight health security *issues* as identified by WHO: emerging diseases; economic stability; international crises and humanitarian emergencies; chemical, radioactive, and biological terror threats; environmental change; HIV and AIDS; building health security; and strengthening health systems (WHO 2007b: 3). This list, and the manner in which WHO then describes each of the issues, is important to this chapter because it reflects a perspective of health security as being primarily a public health concern rather than, for example, a threat to the state. More generally, WHO's identification of global health security *risks* may be placed into three somewhat broad categories:

- Infectious disease, motivated not so much by the continued existence of diseases, such as malaria, which are endemic to large parts of the world, but by new diseases or new variants of known diseases that pose new risks and hazards;
- Food safety, especially risks arising from the industrialization of agriculture exacerbated by the global nature of the food industry, as seen for example in the 2011 outbreak of *e. coli* in Germany; and
- Catastrophes affecting the natural environment, whether deliberate, accidental, or natural in origin. These include industrial accidents (such as toxic spills, the dumping of chemicals, and nuclear incidents such as Chernobyl and Fukushima); the release of pathogens through breaches of laboratory safety protocols or their deliberate use by terrorists; and extreme natural events (such as the European heat wave in 2003 or the Japanese earthquake and tsunami of 2011).

What is interesting here is the manner in which health security is broadened to include food safety and industrial issues, concerns traditional to public health but that do not feature in other understandings of health security in this chapter.

What is also clear is that, from WHO's perspective, global health security is a call for action. Its analysis of global health risks leads to a very clear prescription to develop "collective international public health action [to] build a safer future for humanity" (WHO 2007c: ix; see also Wilson et al. 2008: 48). Indeed WHO *defines* global health security in terms of actions:

> global health security is defined as the activities required, both proactive and reactive, to minimize vulnerability to acute public health events that endanger the collective health of populations living across geographical regions and international boundaries.
>
> (WHO 2007c: ix)

This prescriptive dimension can also be seen in some of the academic literature on global health security. Collier and Lakoff (2008: 7), for example, talk of an attempt to bring together previously distinct fields of health and politics to effect change. Fidler writes of a "transformational moment" in public health as a governance activity (Fidler 2006: 196). Because of this, the use of the term *security* begins to appear less of an analytical tool and more of a strategic or pragmatic practice. In other words, the term is used not to describe a condition but to increase awareness and encourage action for change by adding a sense of urgency and importance (Balzacq 2005: 172; Vuori 2008). If so, then global health security is not an objective condition, but something constructed to promote health, a traditional task of health services nationally but now taken by WHO onto a global stage with added urgency.

Human security

Although the contemporary origins of human security lie in the 1990 and 1994 Reports of the UN Development Programme (UNDP 1990, 1994), its roots lie much deeper in classical liberalism's emphasis upon the individual. The 1994 Report in particular argued that security:

> has for too long been interpreted narrowly: as security of territory from external aggression, or as protection of national interests in foreign policy. . . . Forgotten were the

> legitimate concerns of ordinary people who sought security in their daily lives. . . . For many of them, security symbolized protection from the threat of disease, hunger, unemployment, crime, social conflict, political repression and environmental hazards. . . . For most people, a feeling of insecurity arises more from worries about daily life than from the dread of a cataclysmic world event.
>
> (UNDP 1994: 22).

The 1994 Report explicitly identified health in general as a component of human security (UNDP 1994: 24), while disease in particular runs through the report as a threat to human security. By the turn of the millennium, human security was receiving considerable attention, not least because of the efforts of a small number of key advocates including then Canadian Minister of Foreign Affairs Lloyd Axworthy (1997, 2001), Nobel laureate Amartya Sen (2000), and academics Lincoln Chen and Caroline Thomas (Chen 2004; Chen et al. 2003; Thomas 2000). The high point perhaps came in 2003 with the report of the Commission on Human Security, an initiative supported by UN Secretary General Kofi Annan and chaired by Sen and former UN High Commissioner for Refugees, Sadako Ogata (Ogata & Sen 2003). In this report, Ogata and Sen argued that human security was about freedom from want, freedom from fear, and the capacity of individuals to take action on their own behalf.

At the heart of human security is a shift in the focus of security from the state to people. A strong and often explicit normative bias is common – that the world can and should be run in a different, better way by putting people first. Perhaps unsurprisingly then it is strongly linked to the promotion of human rights (for example, Ogata & Cels 2003: 274) and is also emancipatory in that it attempts to free people whether from fear, want, or other forms oppression. However, most advocates of human security do not see it as replacing, but complementing, state security, not least because a stable state may be a prerequisite for human security (Ogata & Cels 2003: 275). Thus human security *expands on* rather than replaces the idea of security as threats to the state. It addresses those risks and actors that threaten individuals and communities, and includes the idea of "empowering people to fend for themselves" (Ogata & Sen 2003: 4).

That health is a human security issue appears to be unchallenged (see also Cabellero-Anthony & Amul, chapter 3 in this volume). To some extent, this is because health fits into human security's view of the emergence of transnational threats that states are no longer able to mediate but that affect the lives of individuals (Curley & Thomas 2004: 19–20). However, not all health issues are also risks to human security. Rather the Commission on Human Security suggested four criteria:

- "The scale of the disease burden now and into the future;
- The urgency for action;
- The depth and extent of the impact on society; and
- The interdependencies or "externalities" that can exert ripple effects beyond particular diseases, persons or locations." (Ogata & Sen 2003: 97)

More commonly, commentators have tended to focus on two of human security's key freedoms: freedom from want and freedom from fear. On the former, the link is not only about the manner in which health is fundamental to an individual's quality of life and dignity; it is also and more importantly about the relationship between health and poverty (Ogata & Cels 2003: especially 278–279). This relationship may be characterized as a feedback loop: poverty leads to poor health, which in turn increases levels of poverty. In contrast, improved health may lead to economic growth as people become better able to work and less dependent upon health services.

A generally good standard of health among the population may lead to economic stability and development that, in turn, would feed back into individual security through reduced fears over health and economic survival (WHO 2001). On the second of human security's key freedoms, the freedom from fear, for health security this has been constructed in terms of more traditional state stability and military security (for example, Brower & Chalk 2003: 8–9; Chen 2004: 4–5; Ogata & Sen 2003: 97). Three concerns are commonly raised: that health crises may affect confidence in a state and the social order if the state is failing in its duty to protect its citizens from health threats; health crises may affect regional stability if they prompt population movements, either due to large-scale migration or the spread of disease via migration; and finally military security may be affected by placing troops at risk from disease, including sexually transmitted infections (STIs).

Despite the interest generated in human security in some quarters, and its apparent complementarities with the increased interest in humanitarianism and poverty relief at the turn of the millennium, human security has failed over the last decade to establish itself as the main security narrative. To a significant extent, this may be due to the manner in which Western governments have been able to construct terrorism both as the dominant security concern after 9/11 and as a national security problem. This, in turn, suggests the continued power of states to construct the dominant security narratives – in spite of human security's emphasis on states being as much the problem as the solution and the inability of states to deal with new risks. Yet it is also, to some extent, the product of human security's vagueness as a concept. As Roland Paris comments:

> everyone is for it, but few people have a clear idea of what it means . . . [definitions] tend to be extraordinarily expansive and vague, encompassing everything from physical security to psychological well-being, which provides policymakers with little guidance in the prioritization of competing policy goals.
>
> (Paris 2001: 88)

For critics such as Paris, human security is "slippery by design" (2001: 88), a concept that is kept deliberately vague to ensure maximum support from diverse constituencies but that then makes it ultimately little more than a slogan. Moreover, in its expansive articulation of security as encompassing social, economic, and cultural well-being, it becomes difficult to see the difference between cause and effect: the causes of insecurity (poverty, poor health, economic deprivation) are also the effects of insecurity (Paris 2001: 93). As a consequence, human security has not had the impact that its proponents have hoped for.

Biosecurity

Although *biosecurity* has become an increasingly common term over the past 15 years, its meaning remains vague covering almost everything from threats arising from biological weapons (e.g., Fidler & Gostin 2008) to more general risks to public health (e.g., Collier & Lakoff 2008). This creates no small amount of confusion since the first is clearly suggestive of a national security approach, while the second appears almost identical to global health security. This section however focuses on a narrow and specific use of the term concerning the risks posed by the development of new micro-organisms in science laboratories. These risks include both the deliberate and the inadvertent release of pathogens outside controlled laboratory environments. Enemark (2010; see also Enemark, chapter 11 in this volume) points out that even trusted laboratory scientists may pose security risks: the main suspect of the U.S. Federal Bureau of Investigation (FBI) for the 2001 release of anthrax spores in letters addressed to U.S. congressmen and the media was Bruce Ivins, a government scientist with high security clearance levels who committed suicide before his arrest. As the numbers of these laboratories and scientists involved increases, matched by increases in the numbers of biological agents and potential pathogens held in such locations and in the movement of these pathogens internationally, the risks appear to escalate.

This creates what is known as the "dual use dilemma" where research and techniques developed in laboratories for medical benefit may also be used for harmful purposes (WHO 2007a: 4). In 2005 for example, *Science* and *Nature* published research conducted by, amongst others, the U.S. Centers for Disease Control (CDC), which successfully reconstructed the highly pathogenic 1918 Spanish Flu virus. CDC acknowledged that this research might be used for bioterrorist purposes but justified its publication on the grounds that it made health interventions easier should the disease recur. Similarly in 2001 the *Journal of Virology* published results of an Australian attempt to produce an infectious contraceptive for mice but that had the unforeseen side effect of increasing the virulence of mousepox. The publication of the technique used by the Australian team alerted others engaged in similar work to these possible side effects, but also raised concerns over whether it might be deliberately used on other orthopox viruses such as smallpox for harmful purposes (WHO 2007b).

This use of the term biosecurity is important to this chapter because it suggests two things. First, it highlights the continuing potential for tension between health and security as well as its complementarity. The dual use dilemma demonstrates that, for all of the initiatives and discussion over the past decade and a half, the two remain uncomfortable bedfellows and at times in opposition. Second, that the focus of health security can be very narrowly defined – in this instance on the security of laboratories handling or developing dangerous pathogens and on the right to publish these results. The wider risks to populations if these pathogens are used for harmful purposes gives the issue salience but are not the primary security concern.

Conclusion

This chapter has shown how the links between health and security now encompass a wider range of issues and vulnerabilities than previously. This new development is generally cast in terms of a response to exogenous developments, that new risks have emerged and have acquired added salience in the context of accelerated globalization. At the same time the broadening of security's horizons beyond the narrow defense of the state against (usually) military threats to include a more diverse range of risks from novel directions has created a space whereby health issues can more easily become a part of the security agenda. That much of the discussion over health and security focuses on a similar range of issues – usually severe and acute epidemic infectious diseases, HIV/AIDS, and bioterrorism – has helped to create the sense that this is a coherent picture where there is agreement over the landscape. What differences do emerge are therefore deemed second-order issues concerning how to respond to such risks, rather than the first-order scene-setting issues of what is being discussed within the realm of health security in the first place.

This chapter, however, suggests that health security is essentially contested with a number of identifiable terms each reflecting a particular perspective and with its own narrative of health security. Crucially these narratives, which attempt to explain the social world, are not objective accounts of observed phenomena, but help to construct social reality by promoting particular understandings. In this context, the health–security nexus is not a coherent field but one where there are key differences that are obscured by superficial commonalities. This chapter identifies four distinct ways of seeing the health-security nexus, each of which is different in what it privileges. Health issues tend to figure on the *national security* agenda if they are seen as a potential threat to the internal security of the state, have an impact on international stability, or cause exceptional levels of morbidity and/or mortality. Its perspective remains heavily state-centric with the interests of the state (and indeed certain powerful states) privileged over those of individuals or communities within the state. What is notably important is how the national security agenda on health has been constructed with limited empirical evidence to support it, suggesting the ability of narratives to construct social realities based on discourse and intersubjective understandings. The fact that there has been no health crisis leading to state failure has not prevented health issues appearing on certain national security agendas. *Global (public) health security* is concerned with health promotion on a global scale. It is motivated by a belief that risks to public health have been globalized, requiring a response beyond that which individual states are capable of. Its focus is on the emergence of global threats to public health and security, and its primary goal is therefore the well-being of individuals and populations in the face of these threats. *Human security* appears similar in that it is concerned with individuals and communities. Its focus however is not on health but on freedom from fear and from want. Health is thus only a part of the human security agenda, not the focus of it, and other issues may be prioritized, especially poverty alleviation. Both human security and global health security privilege individuals and populations, but they differ over what they are protecting them from. Finally, although *biosecurity* is used in a number of different ways, when referring to the risk of laboratory-created pathogens becoming more widespread it demonstrates not only how definitions can be dramatically narrowed but also how tensions between different perspectives remain.

References

AIDS, Security and Conflict Initiative (ASCI). (2009) *HIV/AIDS, Security and Conflict: New Realities, New Responses*, New York: Social Science Research Council. Online. Available HTTP: <http://www.ssrc.org/workspace/images/crm/new_publication_3/%7Be2090d2b-72a8-de11-9d32-001cc477ec70%7D.pdf> (accessed 20 January 2014).

Axworthy, L. (1997) 'Canada and human security: the need for leadership', *International Journal*, 52: 183–196.

Axworthy, L. (2001) 'Human security and global governance: putting people first', *Global Governance*, 7: 19–24.

Baker, M.G. and Forsyth, A.M. (2007) 'The new International Health Regulations: a revolutionary change in global health security', *New Zealand Medical Journal*, 120 (1267). Online. Available HTTP: <http://journal.nzma.org.nz/journal/120-1267/2872/> (accessed 20 January 2014).

Balzacq, T. (2005) 'The three faces of securitization: political agency, audience and context', *European Journal of International Relations*, 11: 171–201.

Brower, J. and Chalk, P. (2003) *The Global Threat of New and Re-emerging Infectious Diseases: Reconciling US National Security and Public Health*, Santa Monica, CA: RAND Corporation.

Brundtland, G.H. (2003) 'Global health and international security', *Global Governance*, 9: 417–423.

Buzan, B. (1991) *People, States and Fear*, 2nd ed. Hemel Hempstead: Harvester Wheatsheaf.

Central Intelligence Agency (CIA). (2000) *The Global Infectious Disease Threat and Its Implications for the United States*, National Intelligence Estimate NIE99-17D. Online. Available HTTP: <http://www.fas.org/irp/threat/nie99-17d.htm> (accessed 20 January 2014).

Chen, L.C. (2004) 'Health as a human security priority for the 21st century', paper for Helsinki Process Human Security Track III. Online. Available HTTP: <http://citeseerx.ist.psu.edu/viewdoc/download?doi=10.1.1.176.681&rep=rep1&type=pdf> (accessed 28 January 2014).

Chen, L.C., Leaning, J. and Narashimhan, V. (eds.) (2003) *Global Health Challenges for Human Security*, Cambridge, MA: Harvard University Press.

Collier, S.J. and Lakoff, A. (2008) 'The problem of securing health', in S.J. Collier and A. Lakoff (eds.) *Biosecurity Interventions: Global Health and Security in Question*, New York: Columbia University Press.

Cook, R. (2000) 'Foreign policy and national interest', speech delivered to the Royal Institute of International Affairs, Chatham House, London, 28 January.

Curley, M. and Thomas, N. (2004) 'Human security and public health in Southeast Asia: the SARS outbreak', *Australian Journal of International Affairs*, 58: 17–32.

Downer, A. (2003) 'Why health matters in foreign policy', speech delivered to the UK-Australia Seminar: Health and Foreign Policy Seminar, Canberra, 16 September.

Elbe, S. (2009) *Virus Alert: Security, Governmentality and the AIDS Pandemic*, New York: Columbia University Press.

Enemark, C.P. (2010) 'Law in the time of anthrax: biosecurity lessons from the United States', *Journal of Law and Medicine*, 17: 748–760.

Fidler, D.P. (2006) 'Biosecurity: friend or foe for public health governance?', in A. Bashford (ed.) *Medicine at the Border: Disease Globalization and Security from 1859 to the Present*, Basingstoke: Palgrave Macmillan.

Fidler, D.P. and Gostin, L. (2008) *Biosecurity in the Global Age: Biological Weapons, Public Health and the Rule of Law*, Stanford, CA: Stanford University Press.

Garrett, L. (1994) *The Coming Plague: Newly Emergent Diseases in a World Out of Balance*, New York: Farrar, Straus and Giroux.

Graham, B. (2008) *World at Risk: The Report of the Commission on the Prevention of WMD Proliferation and Terrorism*, New York: Vintage.

Graham, D.T. and Poku, N. (eds.) (2000) *Migration, Globalisation and Human Security*, London: Routledge.

Huysmans, J. (1997) 'Revisiting Copenhagen, or, about the creative development of a security studies agenda in Europe', *European Journal of International Relations*, 4: 488–506.

Ingram, A. (2010) 'Governmentality and security in the US President's Emergency Plan for AIDS Relief (PEPFAR)', *Geoforum*, 41: 607–616.

International Crisis Group (ICG). (2001) *HIV/AIDS as a Security Issue*, Brussels: ICG.

McInnes, C. (2006) 'HIV/AIDS and security', *International Affairs*, 82: 315–326.

McInnes, C. (2012) 'Health and national security', in Paul Williams (ed.) *Security Studies*, London: Routledge.

McInnes, C. and Rushton, S. (2010) 'HIV, AIDS and security: Where are we now?', *International Affairs*, 86: 225–245.

Ogata, S. and Cels, J. (2003) 'Human security – protecting and empowering the people', *Global Governance*, 9: 273–282.

Ogata, S. and Sen, A. (2003) *Human Security Now: Commission on Human Security*, New York: Commission on Human Security.

Paris, R. (2001) 'Human security: paradigm shift or hot air?', *International Security*, 26: 87–102.

Rodier, G. (2007) 'New rules on international public health security', *Bulletin of the World Health Organization*, 85: 428–430.

Sen, A. (2000) 'Why human security?', text of presentation at the International Symposium on Human Security, Tokyo, 28 July. Online. Available HTTP: <http://www.unocha.org/humansecurity/chs/activities/outreach/Sen2000.html> (accessed 20 January 2014).

Thomas, C. (2000) *Global Governance, Development and Human Security: The Challenge of Poverty and Inequality*, London: Pluto.

UK Foreign and Commonwealth Office (FCO). (2003) *UK International Priorities: A Strategy for the FCO, Cm 6052*, London: HMSO.

UNAIDS. (2005) *AIDS Epidemic Update: December 2005*, Geneva/New York: UNAIDS.

UN Department of Peace Keeping Operations (UN DPKO). (2005) *Background Note: 31 December 2005*. Online. Available HTTP: <http://www.un.org/en/peacekeeping/archive/2005/bn1205e.pdf> (accessed 20 January 2014).

UN Security Council (UNSC). (2000a) *Resolution 1308 on the Responsibility of the Security Council in the Maintenance of International Peace and Security: HIV/AIDS and International Peacekeeping Operations.* Online. Available HTTP: <http://daccess-dds-ny.un.org/doc/UNDOC/GEN/N00/536/02/PDF/N0053602.pdf?OpenElement> (accessed 20 January 2014).

UN Security Council (UNSC). (2000b) *UN Security Council Press Release SC/6781*, 10 January. Online. Available HTTP: <http://www.un.org/News/Press/docs/2000/20000110.sc6781.doc.html> (accessed 20 January 2014).

United Nations Development Programme (UNDP). (1990) *Human Development Report 1990*, New York: Oxford University Press. Online. Available HTTP: <http://hdr.undp.org/en/reports/global/hdr1990> (accessed 20 January 2014).

United Nations Development Programme (UNDP). (1994) *Human Development Report: New Dimensions of Human Security*, New York: Oxford University Press.

U.S. State Department. (2004) *Strategic Plan Fiscal Years 2004–2009: Security, Democracy, Prosperity*, Washington, DC: US Department of State and US Agency for International Development.

Vuori, J.A. (2008) 'Illocutionary logic and strands of securitization: applying the theory of securitization to the study of non-democratic political orders', *European Journal of International Relations*, 14: 65–99.

Weiner, M. (1992–1993) 'Security, stability, and international migration', *International Security*, 17: 91–126.

WHO. (2001) *Macroeconomics and Health: Investing in Health for Economic Development, Report of the Commission on Macroeconomics and Health*, Geneva: WHO.

WHO. (2002) *Global Defense against the Infectious Disease Threat*, Geneva: WHO.

WHO. (2007a) *Scientific Working Group on Life Science Research and Global Health Security: Report of First Meeting Geneva Switzerland, 16–18 October 2006*, Geneva: WHO.

WHO. (2007b) 'World health day: high level debate tackled need for improved international health security'. Online. Available HTTP: <http://www.who.int/world-health-day/previous/2007/activities/global_event/en/> (accessed 20 January 2014).

WHO. (2007c) *The World Health Report 2007 – A Safer Future: Global Public Health Security in the 21st Century*, Geneva: WHO.

Wilson, K, Von Tigerstrom, B. and McDougall, C. (2008) 'Protecting global health security through the International Health Regulations: requirements and challenges', *Canadian Medical Association Journal*, 179: 44–48.

Yuk-ping, C.L. and Thomas, N. (2010) 'How is health a security issue? Politics, responses and issues', *Health Policy and Planning*, 25: 447–453.

2
INVENTING GLOBAL HEALTH SECURITY, 1994–2005

Lorna Weir[1]

Global health security was formed by linking together two previously separate policy fields: health and national/international security. The linkage has resulted in diverse institutional forms of global health security with differing practices, meanings, and effects. In this chapter I provide a pocket genealogy of global health security organized through the World Health Organization (WHO) in the period from 1994 to 2005, one of the many global securities that were first invented in the 1990s. The approach is genealogical in the sense that it provides an historical account of the power/knowledge relations of expertise, combined here with a concern for broader geopolitical relations. It differs from those accounts that implicitly assume "global health security" began only when the phrase entered routine WHO usage from 2001, with scattered preconditions in the 1990s. I show that "global health security" names a governance apparatus, a sociotechnical one, in formation from 1994 by WHO, a process instigated by the United States and its Northern allies. An apparatus rather than a phrase, global health security conjoins human actors, objects, statements, and technical devices in networks formed through authorized expertise. I show that while the phrase "global health security" was used by WHO from 2000 onwards, it referred to a global outbreak detection and rapid response apparatus that had begun to take organizational form from 1995. "Global health security" and "global alert and response" remain synonymous in WHO usage to date.

The chapter is structured around two intersecting themes, each with an active history of scholarship: North–South relations and international security. A number of studies have suggested that the global North has been the main beneficiary of global health security (Aldis 2008; Davies 2010; McInnes & Lee 2006; Rushton 2011). Drawing on and extending previous work with my colleague Eric Mykhalovskiy (Mykhalovskiy & Weir 2006; Weir & Mykhalovskiy 2006, 2010),[2] I further this line of interpretation by investigating two intersections of the global health security project with North–South geopolitics: the first at its inception between 1992 and 1995 and the second in the political debates about its legal form in 2004–2005. First, I show that the global North, mobilizing in the name of new, emerging, and reemerging diseases (EID), initiated and gave programmatic form to global health security at WHO. Second, I demonstrate that the global South by at least 2004 accepted in principle that EID should be addressed by WHO but objected to the international security elements, especially related to chemical, biological, radiological, and nuclear CBRN incidents, that were attached to global alert and response in the draft revisions to the International Health Regulations (1983) (the main international health law related to mandatory infectious disease control). Discussion begins here with an outline of how global health security took programmatic form at the WHO, moves to a sketch of the technoscientific apparatus that realized that program, and ends with a discussion of the North–South political struggle around the international security elements in the draft revisions to the International Health Regulations (IHR). In the conclusion I take up the question of global health security in world order.

The program

The impetus for the formation of global health security came from a 1992 national policy report, the U.S. Institute of Medicine's *Emerging Infections: Microbial Threats to Health in the United States* (Lederberg et al. 1992). *Emerging Infections* reframed contagious disease prevention and control through the invention of a new disease concept, EID, that was cast as the most significant problem for public health in the United States and, by extension, the world. The Institute of Medicine (IOM) report first defined the EID concept as "clinically distinct conditions whose incidence in humans has increased" and then spatialized EID in nationally specific terms as "diseases that have emerged in the United States within the past few decades" (Lederberg et al. 1992: 34). As used in *Emerging Infections*, the EID concept implicitly rendered endemic disease with constant or falling incidence as nonthreatening for public health and thus of secondary importance to national and global public health systems. The action lay instead with EID, posed as a national threat to the United States. The report framed EID control as an international problem and recommended that the United States approach WHO to implement a global surveillance system with the capacity to detect and respond to EID outbreaks (Lederberg et al. 1992: 6), a difficult recommendation since EID included novel and previously unknown diseases that would be challenging for public health surveillance to detect.

The United States then sought to export the EID concept. In December 1993, the Canadian federal government's Laboratory Center for Disease Control convened a workshop to discuss Canadian public health policy as it pertained to EID. The report of that workshop, the Lac Tremblant Declaration (1994), signals the formation of a U.S.–Canadian alliance to persuade WHO to act on global surveillance of EID. Dr. Robert Shope, coauthor of the 1992 IOM report, led off the workshop's reports with a summary of *Emerging Infections* and concluded by asking for Canadian support in approaching WHO to undertake global surveillance of EID. Dr. Giorgio Torrigiani (Director, Division of Communicable Diseases, WHO) supported the need for an "early warning system" and "an active global surveillance program" in order to "define existing patterns of diseases and identify new diseases that represent a threat to global public health" (Lac Tremblant Declaration 1994: 5). The first recommendation of the Lac Tremblant Declaration (1994: 18) suggests that Canada develop "a national strategy for surveillance and control of emerging and resurgent infections" (Lac Tremblant Declaration 1994: 18) and that Canada participate with WHO in establishing global surveillance of EID.

Two subsequent ad hoc meetings on emerging infectious diseases were held at WHO Headquarters in Geneva on 24–26 April 1994 and 12–13 January 1995. The first WHO meeting in April 1994 was thick on the ground with U.S. expertise. Joshua Lederberg, coauthor of the IOM's *Emerging Infections*, acted as chair. In the discussion that followed reports presented by the United States, Canada, and the IOM, participants remarked that there was a "need to 'internationalize' the efforts described during these first presentations, since the focus had been towards the developed world" (WHO 1994: 5). Unnamed participants also observed that, in the context of EID, "[f]or many African nations, this means specifically addressing malaria, tuberculosis and yellow fever" (WHO 1994: 5). The discussion addressed a point untheorized in the IOM Report and the Lac Tremblant Declaration: lists of emerging diseases would vary across nations and world regions. The comments also revealed that the IOM's approach to EID was situated in a solidly Northern protectionist project to which Southern nations would respond by expanding the range of EID to include infectious diseases significant in their regions. At the second ad hoc meeting in January 1995, WHO staff applied the EID concept to a long history of WHO programming in communicable disease surveillance and control: antimicrobial resistance, tuberculosis, malaria, influenza, polio, arboviruses, HIV, leishmaniasis, foodborne disease, and a variety of initiatives to digitize knowledge of infectious diseases (WHO 1995: 2–6). In so doing, WHO implicitly reframed EID as a problem for all world regions, although only the European Union joined the United States and Canada in providing national/regional reports at the January 1995 meeting.

The IOM's program for dealing with the problem of EID through rapid detection and response (that is, a control rather than a prevention strategy) was carried forward by the World Health Assembly (the legislative body of WHO) in May 1995 when it approved WHA Resolution 48.13, *Communicable Disease Prevention and Control: New, Emerging and Re-emerging Infectious Diseases.* That resolution directed WHO to "improve recognition and response to new, emerging, and reemerging infectious diseases" (World Health Assembly 1995). This resolution translates EID, the IOM's novel disease concept together with its surveillance and response strategy for EID control, into the normative discourse of international public health endorsed by the WHO's highest political and legislative body.

Thus the Lac Tremblant Declaration, the reports of the 1994 and 1995 WHO meetings, and WHA Resolution 48.13 formed a discourse chain that recontextualized the EID concept from U.S. domestic public health into international public health at WHO. The actors accomplishing the recontextualization were the United States, Canada, and the European Union, which formed an alliance around EID as a need of the global North. The main technical goals of public health action around EID remained constant: early detection of EID outbreaks and rapid response to contain them. But for WHO, programming related to EID demanded a renewal of its presence in communicable disease prevention and control, an area in which the WHO had first made its reputation during the 1950s and 1960s, but that had declined during the period 1970–1995, with the exception of the HIV pandemic (Amrith 2006; WHO 1994: 1). WHO's renewed interest in communicable diseases was not done in the name of integrating health into national development by lowering the incidence of regionally/nationally endemic diseases but in the name of preventing international disease transmission.

Despite its sense of a nation beleaguered by disease threats, *Emerging Infections* nowhere dealt with public health in relation to "traditional" national or international security threats, nor did it discuss CBRN incidents. Its one glancing reference to security explained that the Report "did not address biological warfare because this issue is already under study by another panel within the National Academy of Sciences" (Lederberg et al. 1992: R6). Across the Lac Tremblant Declaration and the reports of the two ad hoc WHO meetings discussed above there occurs only one reference to security: when the ProMED representative remarked that his organization "[i]ncluded in their areas of interest . . . the threats of biological warfare" (WHO 1994: 5). Global health security in its early programmatic form was not on record integrated with international security.

Forming a technoscientific apparatus

In October 1995 a new WHO division called Emerging and Other Communicable Diseases (EMC) was established, with David Heymann as Founding Director, to lead WHO's work in developing global alert and response. None of the WHO personnel from the former Division of

Communicable Diseases were appointed to the new division. EMC quickly developed a strategic plan, "The World on Alert" (WHO 1996), to carry forward WHA Resolution 48.13 and the recommendations of the two ad hoc WHO meetings on emerging infectious diseases. Its strategic vision projects a particular temporal standard, "real time": public health knowledge is to coincide with the time of outbreak in order to facilitate flexible responses while it is taking place (Weir & Mykhalovskiy 2010: 148–149). Field response was to occur within 24 hours of outbreak alert.

The world on alert was enacted brilliantly in the period 1995–2000 through the formation of a sociotechnical apparatus for early outbreak detection and rapid response.

Building on prior WHO success in organizing international collaborative networks of partners, EMC began from 1997 to develop the Global Outbreak Alert and Response Network (GOARN). In April 2000 the WHO Division of Communicable Diseases Surveillance and Response (the successor to EMC) convened an international meeting "to discuss the challenge of epidemic-prone and emerging diseases faced by the world as we enter the 21st century and the need to build a global network on existing partnerships to deal with these threats" (WHO 2000b: 1). The resulting network, GOARN, was institutionally tasked with "maintaining global health security by ensuring mechanisms for outbreak alert and response" (WHO 2000b: 17). Formalized in 2000, the GOARN partnership was designed to have response capacity for three differing types of outbreak: EID, well-characterized infectious diseases, and accidental or deliberate spread of biological agents (WHO 2000a: 3–4). GOARN thus had (and has) an international security dimension that was integrated into its operations from the late 1990s.

In WHA Resolution 48.13 the World Health Assembly had called for the development of international public health surveillance systems capable of detecting EID. To do this, between 1995 and 2000 WHO experimented with event-based monitoring sourced in nondiagnostic databases such as news, consumer spending, and stock market trends. The databases were thought to be indicators of health practices evident during infectious disease outbreaks. Previous forms of public health surveillance had been based on the case report, that is, an authorized disease diagnosis. Under the IHR (1969), member states were obligated to notify WHO of all cases of cholera, plague, and yellow fever in their territories: specific disease notification. Notification was an official case-based knowledge limited by the fact that sovereign states were regularly unaware of outbreaks occurring in their territories and, even when aware, sometimes did not report due to economic repercussions and national stigma. Event-based monitoring was sourced in unofficial, digitally mediated information that flowed across national borders. Through providers such as ProMED-mail[3] and the Global Public Health Intelligence Network (GPHIN)[4] WHO had access to faster and more complete information than had previously been possible about disease outbreaks and other public health events (see also Davies, chapter 19 in this volume).

Event-based monitoring, however, is an indicative form of knowledge; an outbreak alert shows the likelihood of outbreak, not its actual occurrence. Between 1998 and 2000, EMC developed the Outbreak Verification Team at WHO Headquarters (Geneva) as a social and political solution to aligning unofficial, indicative outbreak alerts with sovereign confirmation of an outbreak. In 2001 WHO and Health Canada formally agreed that GPHIN would supply outbreak alerts to WHO that would in turn undertake to verify the outbreak alerts through its Member States (Mykhalovskiy & Weir 2006: 43).

The technoscientific apparatus known as "global outbreak alert and response" was increasingly also called "global health security" after the May 2001 approval of WHA Resolution 54.14, *Global Health Security: Epidemic Alert and Response* (World Health Assembly 2001). Its title rendered "global health security" equivalent to "epidemic alert and response." WHA Resolution 54.14 additionally configured global health security to encompass "the risks posed by biological agents," a phrase that intended both naturally occurring disease and biological weapons.

WHA 54.14, occurring several months before the events now known as 9/11, did no more than authorize the broad surveillance and response already given de facto to GOARN between 1997 and 2000. The international security mandate of global health security was further extended under WHA Resolution 55.16, *Global Public Health Response to Natural Occurrence, Accidental Release or Deliberate Use of Biological and Chemical Agents or Radionuclear Material that Affect Health*, which called on member states to "treat any deliberate use, including local, of biological and chemical agents and radionuclear attack to cause harm also as a global public health threat" (World Health Assembly 2002). This "all-risks" approach to detection and response was designed to address the complete range of transborder events that have acute effects on population health. Chemical, biological, radiological, and nuclear (CBRN) incidents, formerly an international security matter outside WHO's remit, fell squarely within this all-risks approach. WHA Resolution 55.16 was passed in May 2002 in an international political context affected by U.S. protectionist reactions to the destruction of the World Trade Center and the intentional spread of anthrax in the United States during the fall of 2001. So it came to pass that the powers exercised by WHO from the late 1990s in global alert and response, powers clearly in excess of those mandated under the IHR (1969) (Fidler 2006: 188), were deemed politically acceptable by the World Health Assembly.

Meanwhile, endemic communicable diseases, that is diseases with a high and constant prevalence in a region, were not inscribed within the all-risks framework because they are only rarely associated with transborder epidemics. WHO documentation on the 1998 draft revision to the IHR[5] explicitly addressed the exteriorization of endemic diseases from global health security: "[i]t is proposed that regularly occurring endemic diseases should not be notified unless an outbreak occurs having particular features that would indicate urgent international importance" (WHO. Regional Office for South-East Asia 1998: 4). Global health security had been fashioned in an experimental space protected by resolutions of the World Health Assembly[6] and with the full knowledge of WHO Member States, a process that I have elsewhere called "pure governance" (Weir 2012).

Revising the IHR: International security and resistance from the global south

WHO had been institutionally aware from the beginning of its work on global health security that the legal framework of the IHR (1969) was inadequate, embarking on a 10-year revision process in 1995. After an abortive early draft of the IHR in 1998, the final revision process was to wait until 2003–2005. On 12 January 2004 the Intergovernmental Working Group on the Revision of the International Health Regulations, the body WHO tasked with producing a final draft of the IHR for the May 2005 meeting of the World Health Assembly, released a Working Paper (WHO 2004b) (hereinafter "January 2004 IHR Draft") containing a draft of the IHR. The January 2004 IHR Draft became the basis for consultations organized during 2004 in the six geographical regions of WHO together with comments by its member states and other international organizations. WHO released two further drafts of the IHR on 30 September 2004 (WHO 2004a; hereinafter "September 2004 IHR Draft") and 24 January 2005 (WHO 2005; hereinafter "January 2005 IHR Draft"). It conducted another round of regional consultations in January and February 2005, but only two reports of those consultations are presently available: the Montevideo Document (2005) and the Third Consultation of the South-East Asia Regional Organization (SEARO) (WHO Regional Office for South-East Asia 2005). As the documentation from the 2004 and 2005 regional consultations and other comments comprises the only publicly available record to date of the positions taken by regions and national governments during the final revision process of the IHR, it provides the basis of analysis here. My comments draw on articles by David Fidler (2005), Alexander Kelle (2007), and the late Jonathan Tucker (2005), which examine the role international security played in the final IHR negotiations, but my analysis is framed in terms of North–South relations and uses the 2004–2005 reports and comments to characterize regional and national positions.

Although the EID concept originated in the United States, it had achieved strong acceptance across South and North by the time the revisions to the IHR were being considered in 2004–2005. The Eastern Mediterranean Regional Organization (EMRO) and SEARO made statements strongly supporting the integration of EID within the scope of the IHR:

> The current International Health Regulations require the reporting of cholera, plague and yellow fever only. This not only stigmatizes those diseases but does not provide for the emergence of new infectious diseases, such as severe acute respiratory syndrome (SARS) which afflicted the world in 2003.
>
> (WHO Regional Office for the Eastern Mediterranean 2004)

> The present regulations were issued 35 years ago, in 1969. Increasing globalization and the emergence of new diseases such as severe acute respiratory syndrome (SARS) have highlighted the importance of establishing a more effective basis for coordinating the response to international threats to human health.
>
> (WHO Regional Office for South-East Asia 2004)

No region or member state spoke out against the expansion in the scope of the IHR to cover EID.

There were areas of common concern for Northern and Southern states with respect to the January 2004 IHR Draft. The issue of sovereignty was raised, surprisingly gently, with regional groups and member states maintaining that WHO should have no right of entry into their territories, except by invitation. North and South also called attention to the extensive work and resources that would be required in order to develop the core capacity requirements for their public health systems mandated under the January 2004 IHR draft (Mexico 2004; PAHO 2004a, 2004b; Samoa 2004; WHO Regional Office for Africa 2004; WHO Regional Office for the Western Pacific 2004). The Government of Mexico's comments were straightforward in observing that the burden of implementing the IHR should not fall on the poorest countries:

> Updating systems of surveillance and adapting means of notification and response calls for considerable investment in terms of both money and human resources. This may be an obstacle for many countries when it comes to implementing the new Regulations. A study is needed of the investment Members States will need to make in their territory and plans should be drawn up to provide support to those countries whose resources are limited. A policy whereby the wealthy countries provide subsidies or support to the poorest countries needs to be drawn up in order to ensure that international health truly is a global public good.
>
> (Mexico 2004)

EMRO (WHO Regional Office for the Eastern Mediterranean 2004: 11) and SEARO (WHO Regional Office for South-East Asia 2004: 28) noted that they would need external financial support for capacity strengthening related to laboratory facilities, epidemiological and environmental surveillance, communications infrastructure, and emergency preparedness and response.

International security elements were incorporated in the three drafts of the IHR, concentrated in its definitions, notification criteria, and the article (variously numbered 41 and 45 across the drafts) entitled *Information Sharing During a Suspected Intentional Release. Disease* was defined as "caused by biological, chemical or radionuclear sources" (WHO 2004b, 2004d: Art. 1). This amounted to an international security conception of disease, as distinct from medical conceptions that conventionally focus on pathology present in the human body (rather than weapons classifications). The September 2004 and January 2005 IHR Drafts also contained a concept of "public health threat" as "a serious and direct danger to the health of human populations" (WHO 2004d: Art. 1; WHO 2005: Art. 1). This definition introduced a threat-defense logic into the IHR drafts. Moreover, all three of the 2004–2005 IHR drafts proposed that WHO member states be required to notify WHO about CBRN events (WHO 2004b, Annex 2; WHO 2004d, Annex 2; WHO 2005, Annex 2). Lastly, Article 41 in the January 2004 IHR (renumbered as Article 45 in the September 2004 and January 2005 IHR Drafts), *Information Sharing During a Suspected Intentional Release*, proposed that each member state be required to notify WHO if it suspected intentional CBRN weapons use in its territory whether or not the incident had any public health impact. This article further required states to give WHO all pertinent information, materials, and samples related to CBRN releases.

The United States supported strengthening the international security elements of the IHR drafts. In its initial comments (United States of America 2004a) on the January 2004 IHR Draft, the United States suggested that the definitions be revised to include "suspected intentional release" and that the definition of "public health risk" be modified "to include the possibility that an event may be intentional as well as a natural occurrence." The United States offered further comments on 27 April 2004 (United States of America 2004b) that sought to strengthen WHO's powers under Article 41, *Information Sharing During a Suspected Intentional Release*, to provide for "a consultative/facilitative role for the WHO Secretariat through which it could, if asked, assist Member States in their recognition or detection of 'suspected intentional releases,' and their investigation, confirmation, and public health response to such releases" (United States of America 2004b: 1). In other words, it was the U.S. government that proposed that WHO have the power to conduct field investigations for suspected intentional CBRN use.

Granting WHO the power to undertake field investigations for suspected treaty violations involving weapons of mass destruction was read by WHO member states in the context of the close connection between WHO and the U.S. Centers for Disease Control and Prevention (CDC). Due to CDC's leading technical skills in epidemiological investigations, it had become closely associated with WHO's global health security networks (Calain 2007: 6). Alexander Kelle (2007: 228) observes that the United States and other participants at the intergovernmental negotiations around the revisions to the IHR wished to give WHO the power of investigating CBRN weapons use because they "believed the IHR could be utilized to gather information not otherwise obtainable on such incidents." One might also remember that the 2004–2005 negotiations around the IHR occurred after the second War in Iraq had begun in 2003 under the pretext of an Iraqi arsenal of bioweapons that UN field investigations had been unable to find. Under these combined conditions, certain WHO members in the global South were concerned that field investigations during suspected intentional CBRN releases would result in espionage within their territories.

It was unsurprising, then, that the proposed integration of CBRN agents into the IHR regime was questioned by some WHO regions, although others, notably the Regional Office for Africa and EMRO, remained silent. The Western Pacific Regional Office (WPRO) noted that its consultation participants had been divided with respect to "[t]he scope of the IHR as it relates to nonbiological hazards (chemical and radiological) . . . some participants believe the scope should be limited to infectious diseases and diseases of unknown aetiology" (WHO Western Pacific Regional Office 2004: 16). The SEARO consultation reported the same range of divided opinion as the earlier WPRO consultation (WHO Regional Office for South-East Asia 2004: vi). Japan, a member of WPRO from the global North, spoke out against the all-risks approach and noted that, although the sensitivity of global event monitoring would necessarily result in alerts regarding CBRN weapons use, "we do not think it is practical to design the IHR to detect and respond to known chemical and radionuclear incidents" (Japan 2004). Other regions and Member States accepted the all-risks approach to detection and notification (e.g., PAHO 2004b: 1), but were concerned that WHO's powers of response be restricted so that a conflict of jurisdiction with other international agencies did not arise (Norway 2004; Switzerland 2004; WHO 2004a: 1–2; WHO Regional Office for Europe 2004). The International Atomic Energy Agency (2004) was scathing in its comments on the January 2004 IHR Draft, speaking from the position of an international security agency objecting to what it clearly saw as the incompetent drafting of the IHR with respect to radiological and nuclear materials and weapons use.

The January 2005 IHR draft showed little change in response to these concerns, other than to modify the text of Article 45 to enable each member state to apply its provisions "consistent with its security and law enforcement requirements" (WHO 2005: Art. 45) and to add a definition of "public health risk" as "an event posing a probability of international spread of disease" (January 2005: Art. 1). The governments of Argentina, Bolivia, Brazil, Chile, Colombia, Ecuador, Paraguay, Peru, Uruguay, and Venezuela responded by issuing a consensus statement, the Montevideo Document (2005), which gave a strong and systematic critique of international security in the January 2005 IHR Draft. The Montevideo Document began with a recommendation that affirmed the use of public health concepts over threat-defense discourse in the draft IHR: "[w]e propose to replace the concept of *threat* with *risk throughout* the document, especially in the definition of *public health emergency of international concern (PHEIC)*" (Montevideo Document 2005: 1; emphasis in original). In understated language, the Montevideo Document recommended the deletion of Article 45 on the grounds it did not "currently specify the relationship between the notification of an event of an intentional nature and an international public health risk. This broad language exceeds the scope of the IHR" (Montevideo Document 2005: 13). This reasoning accepted the all-risks approach but limited the scope of the IHR to international public health risk. The backers of the Montevideo Document won these points in subsequent negotiations.

During the February 2005 intergovernmental meeting on the revision of the IHR, the international security elements in the January 2005 Draft were debated without resolution. The meeting adjourned, deadlocked, and a final round of negotiations was scheduled for 12–13 May 2005 just prior to the 16–25 May Session of the World Health Assembly (where the revised Regulations were approved unanimously). Alexander Kelle's (2007: 227) interview research with delegates who had attended the May 2005 negotiations shows that regional groups from EMRO and SEARO, led by delegates from Pakistan and Iran, successfully opposed the inclusion of Article 45. David Fidler (2005: 356, N. 183) notes that Brazil and Iran, acting on behalf of EMRO, had proposed an amendment to the September 2004 IHR Draft deleting Article 45. These negotiations also agreed on deleting explicit mention of CBRN from the final text (Tucker 2005: 342).

The opposition to the international security elements in the draft regulations thus included the EMRO and SEARO together with the majority of South American states that had signed the Montevideo Document and, as I have shown, some members states in WPRO: a Southern bloc. Whether the signers of the Montevideo Document intentionally acted in coordination with EMRO, SEARO, and some member of WPRO is presently unknown. It is likely that at least one power from the global North allied with the Southern bloc: Japan, given the strength of its previous refusal of the international security elements in the IHR Drafts. While the evidence clearly indicates the existence of a Southern bloc, it is not clear to date whether the United States acted alone or in concert with its Northern allies.

This Southern bloc produced a complex compromise in the IHR (2005), which retains an all-risks scope while stripping all references to CBRN from the final text.[7] The result is a masterpiece of oblique diplomacy. "Public health threat" disappears from the definitions (Article 1), resulting in a general weakening of the threat-defense framing present in 2004–2005 IHR drafts. The definition of disease, however, is sufficiently broad to include harm from CBRN incidents. A similar move occurred in the notification criteria (Annex 2) that includes a reference to "spread of toxic, infectious, or otherwise hazardous materials that may be occurring naturally or otherwise" (IHR 2005; Annex 2, I, 2).[8] The powers of the WHO are restricted under the IHR (2005) to providing public health responses in the case of international public health emergencies, inclusive of CBRN weapons use (Fidler 2005: 366). If an outbreak is suspected or discovered to be intentionally or unintentionally caused, WHO is obligated to inform the UN Security Council, which would then conduct the investigation, although WHO would be authorized to deal with the public health aspects of the emergency, including the support of UN field investigations (Hjalmarsson et al. 2010: 73–74).

As a result of this compromise, WHO has an international security mandate under the IHR (2005), but one narrower than the United States had desired. The acceptance of all-risks detection and response is binding on the design of national public health systems among WHO members and on WHO. The result is an ongoing integration of all-risks emergency management into public health at a planetary level.

Global health security in world order

The genealogy of global health security has shown its history as shaped by the geopolitical division between the United States and the global South. We have seen that global health security was a strategic initiative initiated and given programmatic form between 1992–1995 by an alliance between the United States, Canada, and the European Union. During the final revision process of the IHR in 2004–2005, there was strong support across North and South for extending the scope of the IHR to encompass EID, but some in the global South objected to the proposed inclusion of CBRN releases in the IHR. The final draft of the IHR became the subject of a sharp geopolitical struggle between South and the United States over the extent of its articulation to international security. Where the United States favored more international security in the IHR, the global South favored less. A Southern bloc with middle power allies limited the extension of WHO's powers to the public health aspects of international emergencies, regardless of source or origin, but defeated the proposal to grant WHO the more general power of doing field investigations, with mandatory member state cooperation in providing information and samples, for treaty violations involving CBRN releases.

Global health security represents a novel technical division of world order that reiterates the North-South divide. More than half the verified alerts between 1996 and 2009 occurred in sub-Saharan Africa, followed by Southeast Asia, South America, and Latin America (Chan et al. 2010: Fig. 1, 21702). Few verified alerts involved the global North. Now the global South is also subject to a far higher incidence of endemic diseases than the global North. Global health security constitutively excludes epidemically stable endemic disease but reintroduces the excluded spaces of endemic disease as the primary location of verified alerts. Global health security reinscribes the geopolitical divide between North and South, with confirmed outbreaks, and by logical extension international public health emergencies, being primarily located in the global South. In this space of global division, global health security concerts Northern protectionism with the stabilization of international trade relations that benefits the South as the main site of verified alerts and international public health emergencies.

Global health security reinscribes world order geopolitically, but it also revises the governance of world order. From the beginnings of global health security in 1994, WHO consistently took the position that, to be effective, it would require the strengthening of national and local public health systems. Yet the goal of strengthening national core public health capacity in surveillance and response for the sake of preventing and controlling the international spread of disease exists in tension with national and local public health goals. The all-risks standard for alert and response also strains the alignment between global health security and national public health systems. The all-risks standard is governed by what WHO terms a "dual use" strategy that aims to harmonize international security with (what are now) other public health functions. In WHO usage, "dual use" signifies the benefits to both civilian public health and international security thought to arise from strengthening local, national and global surveillance and response capacities (WHO 2007: 17–33. See Kinderhauser 2003: 17). In addition, "dual use" operates strategically as a claim that improved civilian public health surveillance will detect any unusual outbreak, including those related to CBRN agents, and is thus to be preferred to a surveillance system dedicated solely to detecting CBRN incidents (Heymann 2004: vii). In its support of dual use, WHO has been concerned to develop global health security as a program that does not divert scarce public health resources into separate CBRN detection and response systems at the expense of public health needs in the global South, where one in two deaths are from naturally caused infectious diseases. Global health security is thus characterized by internal tensions in its goals and governing strategies in need of empirical investigation to see their effects and how the divisions are symbolically disappeared.

Global health security is characterized by a harmonian ethos of borderlessness that places its actions above the petty divisions of geopolitical world order. *Emerging Infections*, the 1992 IOM report, framed EID as a transborder global microbial threat that would require equally transborder human cooperation in the name of health. The subsequent alert and response apparatus assembled at the turn of the 21st century lightened the significance of national borders and sovereign knowledge for international public health. Event-based monitoring is a phenomenon of the Internet with its capacity to source and circulate electronic data across national borders (particularly weakly encrypted internet borders). Borderlessness seeks to trump geopolitics through inflated universalistic claims that disguise the situatedness of those making them. The humanist value of borderlessness seeks to repeat the control Euroamerican colonialism exercised over public health in the colonial world that was only shaken by decolonization in the second half of the twentieth century (Weir & Mykhalovskiy 2010: 65–77). Limits to borderlessness were raised by the global South during the revision of the International Health Regulations in 2004–2005, an assertion of borders to block field investigations that could well have been used for U.S. intelligence purposes in ways that might damage national security in the South. Borderlessness is a lullaby for Northern hegemony.

Global health security thus inevitably raises questions of global justice. Its apparatus mainly acts to prevent the diseases of poor people in the South from spreading to the North and laterally to other areas in the South. Bracketing off endemic disease to construct the domain of global health security is a constitutive exclusion that violates the principles of cosmopolitanism and borderlessness. If and when the levels of endemic disease in the global South converge with those in the global North, the sociotechnical apparatus now known as global health security would have the possibility of becoming a practice of international solidarity. In this imaginable utopia, global health security would become an apparatus through which differing political regions of the world defended themselves against each other with respect to international public health emergencies. This line of reasoning would lead from the primarily genealogical framing found in my writing here to a philosophical argument focused on the normative question of a just world order on the terrain of human health.

Notes

1 Many thanks to Eric Mykhalovskiy with whom I first began research on global public health surveillance and to Frank Pearce for his power of listening. This research was partially funded by SSSHRC Standard Grant 41020071414.

2 For further information about research methods, including key informant interviews with members of GPHIN (Public Health Agency, Ottawa), ProMED-mail, the Department of Communicable Diseases Surveillance and Response at WHO Headquarters (Geneva), and the Archives of WHO (Geneva), see Weir and Mykhalovskiy (2010: 27–28).

3 Established in 1994 as an email list, Pro-MED-mail used the fast pace of internet communications and the low cost of email to internationally exchange information on local outbreaks (Madoff & Woodall 2005).

4 GPHIN was a partnership established between WHO and the government of Canada to develop another form of event-based monitoring, one sourced in online news (Weir & Mykhalovskiy 2010: 79–88). GPHIN was designed to operate as a secure, Internet-based global monitoring system that retrieved and analyzed online news, sending alerts to WHO, Health Canada, and its international subscribers. Officially launched by Health Canada in 1998, GPHINs software categorized news articles according to a six-part typology: animal, plant, and human diseases, biologics (such as vaccines and pharmaceuticals), natural disasters, chemical incidents, radiological incidents, and unsafe products (Keller et al. 2009). GPHINs design thus incorporated the detection of CBRN incidents.

5 The 1998 Draft IHR is not presently publicly available.

6 The WHA resolutions authorizing the alert and response apparatus include WHA48.13, *Communicable Disease Prevention and Control: New Emerging and Re-emerging Infectious Diseases*, WHA48.7, *Revision and Updating of the International Health Regulations*, and WHA54.14, *Global Health Security: Epidemic Alert and Response.*

7 See Fidler (2005: 358–379) for a careful discussion of the scope of the IHR (2005).

8 The 2007 World Health Report (WHO 2007: 17–33) interprets public health emergencies of international concern to include naturally, accidentally, or deliberately caused foodborne illness, chemical, environmental, natural, nuclear, and radiological disasters, and industrial accidents. These are in addition to outbreaks of known and unknown infectious diseases.

References

Aldis, W. (2008) 'Health security as a public health concept: a critical analysis', *Health Policy and Planning*, 23: 369–373.

Amrith, S.S. (2006) *Decolonizing International Health: India and Southeast Asia, 1930–65*, Cambridge: Cambridge University Press.

Calain, P. (2007) 'Exploring the international arena of global public health surveillance', *Health Policy and Planning*, 22: 2–12.

Chan. E.H., Brewer, T.F, Madoff, L.C., Pollack, M.P., Sonricker, A.L., Keller, M., Freifeld, C.C., Blench, M., Mawudeku, A. and Brownstein, J.S. (2010) 'Global capacity for emerging infectious disease detection', *PNAS*, 107: 21701–21706.

Davies, S. (2010) *Global Politics of Health*, Cambridge: Polity Press.

Fidler, D. (2005) 'From International Sanitary Conventions to global health security: the new International Health Regulations', *Chinese Journal of International Law*, 4: 325–392.

Fidler, D. (2006) 'International law, infectious diseases, and globalization', in S. Kobler, A. Mahmoud and S. Lemon (eds.) *The Impact of Globalization on Infectious Disease Emergence and Control*, Washington, DC: The National Academies Press: 181–196.

Heymann, D. (2004) 'Foreword', in *Public Health Response to Biological and Chemical Weapons, WHO Guidance*, Geneva: World Health Organization. Online. Available HTTP <http://www.who.int/csr/delibepidemics/biochemguide/en/> (accessed 28 August 2013): vi-vii.

Hjalmarsson, K., Isla, N., Kraatz-Wadsack, G. and Barbeschi, M. (2010) 'Global watch: the state of biological investigations', *Bulletin of the Atomic Scientists*, 66: 70–76.

International Atomic Energy Agency. (2004) *Comments of the International Atomic Energy Agency on the draft revised International Health Regulations, 9 November.* Online. Available HTTP < http://www.who.int/ihr/iaea2004_11_09.pdf > (accessed 20 January 2014).

International Health Regulations. (1983) *International Health Regulations (1969)*, 3rd ed. Geneva: World Health Organization. Online. Available HTTP <http://whqlibdoc.who.int/publications/1983/9241580070.pdf> (accessed 6 September 2013).

International Health Regulations. (2008) *International Health Regulations (2005)*, 2nd ed. Geneva: World Health Organization. Online. Available HTTP <http://www.who.int/csr/ihr/en/> (accessed 3 September 2013).

Japan. (2004) *Japan's Comments on the First Draft of the Proposed Revision of the International Health Regulations (IHR), 15 September.* Online. Available HTTP <http://www.who.int/ihr/revisionprocess/japan2004_09_15.pdf?ua=1> (accessed 20 January 2014).

Kelle, A. (2007) 'Securitization of international public health: implications for global health governance and the biological weapons prohibition regime', *Global Governance*, 13: 217–235.

Keller, M., Blench M., Trolentino H., Clark C., Freifeld C.C., Mandl K.D., Mawudeku A., Eysenbach G. and Brownstein J. (2009) 'Use of unstructured event-based reports for global infectious disease surveillance', *Emerging Infectious Disease*, 15. Online. Available HTTP <http://wwwnc.cdc.gov/eid/article/15/5/08-1114_article.htm> (accessed 20 January 2014).

Kinderhauser, M.K. (ed.) (2003) *Global Defence against Infectious Disease Threat*, Geneva: WHO.

Lac Tremblant Declaration. (1994) 'Proceedings and recommendations of the expert working group on emerging infectious disease issues: Lac Tremblant declaration', *Canada Communicable Disease Report*, 20S2: 1–21.

Lederberg, J., Shope, R.E. and Oaks, S.C. (Eds.) (1992) *Emerging Infections: Microbial Threats to Health in the United States*, Washington, DC: National Academy Press.

Madoff, L.C. and Woodall, J.P. (2005) 'The internet and the global monitoring of emerging diseases: lessons from the first 10 years of ProMED-mail', *Archives of Medical Research*, 36: 724–730.

McInnes, C. and Lee, K. (2006) 'Health, security and foreign policy', *Review of International Studies*, 32: 5–23.

Mexico. (2004) *General Comments by Mexico on the Draft International Health Regulations*, 10 August. Online. Available HTTP <http://www.who.int/ihr/revisionprocess/mexicoenglish2004_08_07.pdf?ua=1> (accessed 20 January 2014).

Montevideo Document. (2005) *Considerations and Points of Consensus between Argentina, Bolivia, Brazil, Chile, Colombia, Ecuador, Paraguay, Peru, Uruguay, and Venezuela with Regard to Document A/IHR/IGWG/2/2, of 24 January 2005 (Review and Approval of Proposed Amendments to the IHR – Proposal by the Chair).* Online. Available HTTP <http://www.who.int/ihr/revisionprocess/englishmontevideo.pdf?ua=1> (accessed 20 January 2014).

Mykhalovskiy, E. and Weir, L. (2006) 'The global public health intelligence network and early warning outbreak detection: a Canadian contribution to global health', *Canadian Journal of Public Health*, 97: 42–44.

Norway. (2004) *Revision of the International Health Regulations, Comments by the Government of Norway, 31 August.* Online. Available HTTP <http://www.who.int/ihr/revisionprocess/norway2004_08_31.pdf?ua=1> (accessed 20 January 2014).

Pan American Health Organization (PAHO). (2004a) *Report of the Consultation Meeting for the English Speaking Caribbean Countries for the Revision of the International Health Regulations (IHR), 19–20 April.* Online. Available HTTP <http://www.who.int/ihr/revisionprocess/grenada2004_09_06.pdf> (accessed 20 January 2014).

Pan American Health Organization (PAHO). (2004b) *Report of the North American Consultation Meeting of the Revision of the International Health Regulations (IHR), 2–3 June.* Online. Available HTTP <http://www.who.int/ihr/revisionprocess/canada12004_09_06.pdf> (accessed 20 January 2014).

Rushton, S. (2011) 'Global health security: Security for whom? Security from what?' *Political Studies*, 59: 779–796.

Samoa. (2004) *Revision of the International Health Regulations, Initial Comments by the Government of Samoa, 12 October.* Online. Available HTTP <http://www.who.int/ihr/revisionprocess/Samoa.pdf?ua=1> (accessed 20 January 2014).

Switzerland. (2004) *Revision of the International Health Regulations: Comments by the Swiss Government, 3 June.* Online. Available HTTP <http://www.who.int/ihr/revisionprocess/swissIHR.pdf?ua=1> (accessed 20 January 2014).

Tucker, J. (2005) 'Updating the International Health Regulations', *Biosecurity and Bioterrorism: Biodefense Strategy, Practice, and Science*, 3: 338–347.

United States of America. (2004a) *Initial U.S. Government Comments on the First Draft of the Proposed Revision of the International Health Regulations,* 5 March. Online. Available HTTP <http://www.who.int/ihr/revisionprocess/usacomments.pdf?ua=1> (accessed 20 January 2014).

United States of America. (2004b) *Second U.S. Government Comments on the First Draft of the Proposed Revision of the International Health Regulations (IHRs),* 27 April. Online. Available HTTP <http://www.who.int/ihr/revisionprocess/ihruscomments.pdf> (accessed 20 January 2014).

Weir, L. (2012) 'A Genealogy of global health security', *International Political Sociology*, 6: 322–325.

Weir, L. and Mykhalovskiy, E. (2006) 'The geopolitics of global public health surveillance in the twenty-first century', in A. Bashford (ed.) *Medicine at the Border: Disease, Globalization and Security, 1850 to the Present*, New York: Palgrave Macmillan: 240–263.

Weir, L. and Mykhalovskiy, E. (2010) *Global Public Health Vigilance: Creating a World on Alert*, New York: Routledge.

WHO. (1994) *Report of WHO Meeting on Emerging Infectious Diseases*, Geneva: World Health Organization. Online. Available HTTP <http://whqlibdoc.who.int/hq/1994/CDS_BVI_94.2.pdf> (accessed 2 August 2013).

WHO. (1995) *Report of the Second WHO Meeting on Emerging Infectious Diseases*, Geneva: World Health Organization. Online. Available HTTP <http://whqlibdoc.who.int/HQ/1995/WHO_CDS_BVI_95.2.pdf> (accessed 10 August 2013).

WHO. (1996) *Emerging and Other Communicable Disease: Strategic Plan 1996–2000* (WHO/EMC/96.1). Geneva: World Health Organization. Online. Available HTTP <http://whqlibdoc.who.int/hq/1996/WHO_EMC_96.1.pdf> (accessed 29 April 2012).

WHO. (2000a) *A Framework for Global Outbreak Alert and Response*. Online. Available HTTP: <http://www.who.int/csr/resources/publications/surveillance/WHO_CDS_CSR_2000_2/en/> (accessed 6 August 2013).

WHO. (2000b) *Global Outbreak Alert and Response: Report of a WHO Meeting*. Online. Available HTTP <http://www.who.int/csr/resources/publications/surveillance/whocdscsr2003.pdf> (accessed 3 August 2013).

WHO. (2004a) *Intergovernmental Working Group on Revision of the International Health Regulations: Summary Report of Regional Consultations, 14 September* (A/IHR/IGWG/2). Online. Available HTTP <http://apps.who.int/gb/ghs/pdf/IHR_IGWG_2-en.pdf> (accessed 20 January 2014).

WHO. (2004b) *International Health Regulations: Working Paper for Regional Consultations* (IGWG/IHR/Workingpaper/12.2003, 12 January). Online. Available at HTTP: <http://www.who.int/csr/resources/publications/IGWG_IHR_WP12_03-en.pdf> (accessed 20 September 2013).

WHO. (2004c) *Public Health Response to Biological and Chemical Weapons*, Geneva: World Health Organization. Online. Available HTTP <http://www.who.int/csr/delibepidemics/biochemguide/en/> (accessed 28 August 2013).

WHO. (2004d) *Review and Approval of Proposed Amendments to the International Health Regulations: Draft Revision* (A/IHR/IGWG/3). Online. Available HTTP <http://apps.who.int/gb/ghs/pdf/A_IHR_IGWG_3-en.pdf> (accessed 20 September 2013).

WHO. (2005) *Review and Approval of Proposed Amendments to the International Health Regulations: Proposal by the Chair* (A/IHR/IGWG/2/2, 24 January). Online. Available HTTP <http://apps.who.int/gb/ghs/pdf/IHR_IGWG2_2-en.pdf> (accessed 20 September 2013).

WHO. (2007) *A Safer Future: Global Public Health Security in the 21st Century*. Geneva: World Health Organization. Online. Available HTTP <http://www.who.int/whr/2007/en/index.html> (accessed 20 August 2013).

WHO Regional Office for Africa. (2004) *Regional Consultation on the Revised International Health Regulations, Harare, Zimbabwe, 1–3 June*. Online. Available HTTP <http://www.who.int/ihr/revisionprocess/harareenglish2004_09_14.pdf> (accessed 20 January 2014).

WHO Regional Office for the Eastern Mediterranean. (2004) *International Health Regulations – Update on the Revised Version. Fifty-first Session, Agenda item 8* (EM/RC51/6, August). Online. Available HTTP <http://applications.emro.who.int/docs/em_rc51_6_en.pdf> (accessed 20 January 2014).

WHO Regional Office for Europe. (2004) *European Regional Consultation on Revision of the International Health Regulations, Copenhagen, Denmark*. Online. Available HTTP <http://www.who.int/ihr/revisionprocess/eucomments2004_08_31.pdf> (accessed 20 January 2014).

WHO Regional Office for South-East Asia. (1998) *Revision of the International Health Regulations, Regional Committee, Fifty-first Session, Provisional Agenda Item 15* (SEA/RC51/11 Add.1). Online. Available HTTP: <http://repository.searo.who.int/bitstream/123456789/5318/42/rdr98_RIHR.pdf> (accessed 6 September 2013).

WHO Regional Office for South-East Asia. (2004) *Second Regional Consultation on the Proposed Revised International Health Regulations*. Online. Available HTTP <http://www.searo.who.int/entity/ihr/topics/Communicable_Diseases_Surveillance_and_response_CD-135.pdf> (accessed 20 January 2014).

WHO Regional Office for South-East Asia. (2005) *Revision of the International Health Regulations: Report of the Third Regional Consultation*. Online. Available HTTP: <http://www.searo.who.int/entity/ihr/topics/Communicable_Diseases_Surveillance_and_response_CD-140.pdf> (accessed 20 January 2014).

WHO Regional Office for the Western Pacific. (2004) *Consultation on the Revision of the International Health Regulations (IHR) in the Western Pacific Region*. Online. Available HTTP <http://www.who.int/ihr/revisionprocess/wpro2004_09_10.pdf> (accessed 20 January 2014).

World Health Assembly. (1995) *Communicable Disease Prevention and Control: New, Emerging and Re-emerging Infectious Diseases*, WHA 48.13, 12 May.

World Health Assembly. (2001) *Global Health Security: Epidemic Alert and Response*, WHA54.14, 21 May. Online. Available HTTP: <http://apps.who.int/medicinedocs/documents/s16356e/s16356e.pdf> (accessed 30 August 2013).

World Health Assembly. (2002) *Global Public Health Response to Natural Occurrence, Accidental Release or Deliberate Use of Biological and Chemical Agents or Radionuclear Material that Affect Health*, WHA55.16, 18 May. Online. Available HTTP <http://apps.who.int/gb/archive/pdf_files/WHA55/ewha5516.pdf> (accessed 20 January 2014).

3

HEALTH AND HUMAN SECURITY

Pathways to advancing a human-centered approach to health security in East Asia

Mely Caballero-Anthony & Gianna Gayle Amul

The concept of human security was an outcome of several significant developments after the end of the Cold War. States and societies were faced with new risks as a result of the structural changes brought on by rapid globalization and their consequences. Poverty and marginalization increased. Ecosystems deteriorated, plagued by the impacts of climate change, pollution, and environmental degradation. The last three decades saw intrastate conflicts outpace interstate ones. At the same time, there was a rise in security threats with transboundary implications such as cybercrime, terrorism, pandemics, irregular migration, and resource scarcity. These challenges significantly transformed the global security environment, such that security can no longer be conceptualized merely in terms of the protection of the territorial borders of states. To navigate the changed landscape, security has to also be about protecting individuals and human collectivities from harm, fear, and want.

This chapter examines the significance of human security as a conceptual framework in understanding and addressing one of the most urgent security challenges in recent history – health security. Using East Asia as a case study, the chapter argues that health security is an integral part of the human security agenda and demands no less than a human-centered approach to address the complex array of health security challenges, particularly for the most vulnerable sections of society. East Asia presents a gamut of diverse societies, a region dotted with both developed and developing economies where health security is prioritized at the domestic level to varying degrees. East Asia also encapsulates various shades of integration of human security at subregional levels (Northeast and Southeast Asia) whether in principle, policy, or practice. The region thus offers an interesting case in examining how broadly (and how deeply) human security and health security has been incorporated in the regional security agenda.

This chapter sets out to frame health security from a human security perspective. The first section takes into account how human security has been interpreted. It then discusses how human security entered the security lexicon in East Asia and how health security and human security have been conceptualized. It then highlights the possible convergence, complementarities, and interdependencies that exist between health and human security. The rest of the chapter briefly examines the official regional bodies and frameworks including the networks of non-state actors engaged in various aspects of health security in East Asia.

The concept of human security

The ascendance of the human security perspective is captured in various UN documents, the most referenced of which are the UN Development Programme's (UNDP) 1994 *Human Development Report* (HDR) on "New Dimensions of Human Security" and the 2003 Commission on Human Security's report titled *Human Security Now: Protecting and Empowering People*. The 1994 HDR sparked a new wave of security discourse with its promotion of a universal, interdependent, prevention-based, and people-centered approach to security.

Mahbub ul Haq, the scholar whose seminal work on 'New Imperatives of Human Security' influenced the 1994 HDR, best encapsulated the new security thinking when he called for a security concept "that is reflected in the lives of our people, not in the weapons of our country" (Ul Haq 1994: 2). Ul Haq became an influential figure in the production of the human development index (HDI), which was included in the 1994 HDR on the basis that any formulation of development thinking and policies should put the welfare of individuals – and not a state's macroeconomy – first.

The 1994 HDR outlined seven key elements of human security: economic security, food security, health security, environmental security, personal security, community security, and political security. Aside from identifying these elements, the report highlighted four essential characteristics of human security: (1) it is a universal concern; (2) the components are interdependent; (3) it is best ensured through early prevention rather than later intervention; and (4) it is people-centered (UNDP 1994: 22–23).

Since the introduction of the concept, human security has generated tremendous interest as well as vigorous debates among scholars and policy makers (Hampson et al. 2001), leading some authors to refer to human security's conceptual journey as one of "dizzying complexity" (Rothschild 1995: 55; see also Alkire 2001; Paris 2001: 93).[1] Notwithstanding the challenges that usually follow a new concept, human security was embraced by many scholars, development economists, and security specialists for its potential to re-envision and broaden security. Human security unravels the very premise of what security means and its security referent, going to the heart of the question: *security for whom, and whose security*? Under traditional security precepts, the state is the main object of security. Human security, by contrast, positions individuals and human collectivities at the center of security concerns. As the concept evolved, human security zeroed in on two main aspects of security: "safety from chronic threats such as hunger, disease and repression" and "protection from sudden and hurtful disruptions in the patterns of daily life" (UNDP 1994: 23). In its current iteration, human security is often understood as "freedom from want" and "freedom from fear" (UNDP 1994: 24).

The 2003 report by the Commission on Human Security further set the tone and agenda for a human security approach by highlighting not only the insecurities of people in vulnerable situations but also, more importantly, how to respond to these insecurities (Commission on Human Security 2003). Sadako Ogata, Co-chair of the Commission on Human Security (2001–2003) pointed out that the concept of human security should provide a solid framework for crafting international responses and should serve as a guiding principle for addressing security threats (Ogata 2003). In this regard, a human security approach should be inherently people-centered, and governance should entail participatory decision-making processes that are inclusive and bring together a number of actors, state as well as non-state. Given the complexity of the many human security challenges, it becomes equally important that policy responses are imbued with the principles of transparency and accountability if dialogue and cooperation are to be encouraged among actors that are involved in and have a stake in providing security. It is this multi-actor, multisectoral, and multilateral approach that makes up one of the distinctive facets of a human security framework.

Locating human security in the security lexicon of East Asia

It has been observed that "comprehensive security" had been used as an organizing concept in East Asia even before "human security" was promoted in the international discourse. Comprehensive security is the "pursuit of sustainable security in all fields (personal, political, economic, social, cultural, military, environmental) in both the domestic and external spheres, essentially through cooperative means" (CSCAP 1995: 2). Given that comprehensive security, like human security, covers a wide range of security concerns and emphasizes cooperation, it would have been expected that human security would readily gain traction in the region. Yet, in East Asia, human security in fact experienced a fairly long gestation period. One explanation for this is that comprehensive security was initially conceptualized with regime stability and economic development in mind. In this formulation, the state remained the main security referent as well as the main actor that defines and provides security. Unlike human security, which upholds individuals and human collectivities as the main referents of security, comprehensive security reifies the role of the state.

The dual focus on "freedom from fear" and "freedom from want" promoted by human security represents another barrier to its adoption. States in East Asia were reluctant to endorse the concept given their reservations about the implications of "freedom from fear." Many states in East Asia feared that that the two-pronged focus could be used as a Trojan horse for the West to interfere in their domestic affairs given that issues under "freedom from fear" include violence and displacement from internal conflicts (Acharya 2001: 442–460). Indeed, when Japan adopted human security as one of the pillars of its foreign policy, it emphasized "freedom from want," and so-called developmental challenges like poverty and health.

It took the disastrous impact of the 1997 Asian financial crisis on states and societies – which "unravelled the role of the state as the only provider of security, as well as the legitimation that economic development had as a means to security" (Caballero-Anthony 2004: 173) – to pave the way for human security in East Asia. The crisis brought to the fore two critical points. First, the "emergence of non-traditional security threats reaffirmed the close nexus between economics and security" (Caballero-Anthony 2004: 175). Second, the "complexity of the problems that emerged and the way that they unfolded" suggested that arguments for regime security were inadequate against the new types of security threats that did not recognize borders and that tested the limited capacities of state authorities (Caballero-Anthony 2004: 175–176).

Consequently, Asian intellectuals[2] began to champion human security as a "tool for acknowledging that even two decades of economic growth and state building had not eliminated severe vulnerabilities for large numbers of Asians" (Evans 2004: 269). This rising tide of opinion developed in parallel with increasing recognition of the role of non-state actors as "alternate service providers" to the state and as "participants in the policy process" (Evans 2004: 269). Track two regional processes such as the ASEAN Institutes of Strategic and International Studies (ASEAN ISIS), the Council for Security Cooperation in the Asia-Pacific (CSCAP), and the East Asia Vision Group used human security in either its narrower or broader formulations, ingraining human security in their security lexicons. The vibrant and emergent human security discourse from these actors served as the foundation for promoting the viability of human security as a common framework for advancing both security and development in the region (Caballero-Anthony 2004: 183–185).

The human security framework also slowly seeped into the security lexicon of official regional frameworks. The ASEAN Plus Three[3] heads of governments as well as the East Asia Study Group have been using it since 2001 in the context of "non-traditional security" issues, including communicable diseases, environmental degradation, and illegal migration. "Human security" was first used in the Asia-Pacific Economic Cooperation (APEC) forum in 2002 and eventually made its way into the 2003 APEC Leaders' Declaration that laid out prescriptions for "enhancing human security." By 2004, a decade after human security entered the security lexicon, the term was found within the vocabulary of regional governmental institutions, albeit with different formulations of what it stands for (Evans 2004: 270).

The second tipping point for human security's entry into the East Asian security lexicon was the health crisis that confronted the region with the sudden onset of the severe acute respiratory syndrome (SARS) pandemic in 2003. SARS not only highlighted public health vulnerabilities but also the interlinked socioeconomic and political risks that went beyond national borders (see Heymann, chapter 8 in this volume). It is important to note that until SARS, East Asia was still focused on the notion that economic security and development is integral to national security. Health security was also not part of the discourses on the complex and contemporary security challenges facing the region. The health crisis caused by the SARS pandemic jolted governments in the region and compelled them to recognize that health issues could have a significant impact on security. The SARS crisis and its cross-cutting effects gave impetus to a rethinking of security by governments in East Asia and compelled them to expand the scope of their security concerns to reflect current and emerging threats on various fronts, in effect introducing a less static formulation of the comprehensive security approach (Caballero-Anthony 2005: 475–495).

Health security and human security: Never the twain shall meet?

Today, various demographic changes and development trends (such as urbanization), "uneven health transitions" (poverty-linked diseases, chronic and degenerative diseases), and emerging epidemiological threats (emerging and reemerging infectious diseases, environmental threats, behavioral pathologies) can impact an individual's vulnerability and exposure to health insecurities (Støre et al. 2003: 69–71). Thus, it would seem logical for health security to be conceptualized from a human security perspective.

As noted earlier, the 1994 HDR in fact highlights health security as an element of human security, identifying as fundamental threats communicable and noncommunicable diseases as well as the links between health, poverty, and inequality (UNDP 1994). The 2003 report by the Commission on Human Security takes this further: health is seen to be a "vital core of human security" (Commission on Human Security 2003: 96). Illness, disability, and preventable death are identified as "critically pervasive threats" to human security (Commission on Human Security 2003: 96). Significantly, good health is seen not as the mere absence of disease but as a "state of complete physical, mental and social well-being" (Commission on Human Security 2003: 96). The report laid out the strong links between health and human security, raising concerns over the "the scale of the disease burden now and into the future," "the depth and extent of the impact on society," and "the interdependencies or externalities that create ripple effects beyond particular diseases, persons or locations" (Commission on Human Security 2003: 97). With this, the Commission identified three health-related threats to human security: global infectious diseases, poverty-related issues, and violence and crises that threaten survival, dignity, and livelihoods (Commission on Human Security 2003: 97–101).

In practice, however, there are major differences in how health security, and its relationship to human security, is defined. In particular, the health security literature suggests a tension between "statist" and "globalist" perspectives (Davies 2010; O'Manique & Fourie 2010). The statist perspective, which is founded on traditional notions of national and international security, is predominantly aligned towards how states as the provider of security can *contain* health threats that could have direct economic, political, and military impact on their territory such as the cross-border spread of infectious diseases with pandemic potential. The globalist perspective, on the other hand, is grounded on the well-being and rights of individuals and veers towards an individual's health concerns. It focuses on examining how states as well as other actors – both local and global – act to the benefit or detriment of an individual's health security (Davies 2010: 1167–1190). These two perspectives mirror to a large extent the tension between traditional security and human security, and the same argument applies here. Statist perspectives result in narrowly focused policies that are not able to adequately address the complexities of the health security issues seen today or the cross-linkages between poverty, health, and development.

The current global health security regime continues however to be dominated by statists. Health may be securitized, but it is a narrow, state-centric version of health security, preoccupied with acute, transboundary public health emergencies (Weir & Mykhalovskiy 2010: 150–151) rather than with problems of chronic diseases or social determinants of health. This is evident in the 2007 World Health Report entitled *A Safer Future: Global Public Health Security in the 21st Century.* The report focused on minimizing vulnerabilities to public health emergencies of international concern (PHEIC) that threaten the collective health of populations across geographic regions and political boundaries (WHO 2007: 17–33). One could argue, however, that the privileging of public health emergencies caused by highly pathogenic diseases like SARS overlooks the many other health challenges faced by the more vulnerable groups who are among those most affected by the burden of diseases. This skewed priority presents a real challenge to advancing a more human-centered approach of human security. Thus, the political conundrum that follows from the persistence of statist perspectives is this: how can the inequities in the burden of costs be addressed and who benefits from such inequities (Hoffman 2010; Lo & Thomas 2010; O'Manique & Fourie 2010; Rushton 2011)?

Such dilemmas are compounded by the impacts of the process of health securitization. Securitizing health involves not only the use of speech acts but also the building of political networks and the implementation of relevant policies, which could themselves bring about inequities. For example, when SARS broke out in East Asia, official statements and press briefings were peppered with declarations that SARS is a "national security concern." Crisis management measures such as mandatory and voluntary quarantine, closure of schools, entertainment centers, and other public areas, and border and immigration controls, were implemented in affected countries in the region. At the regional level, the coordination efforts initiated through the ASEAN Plus Three mechanism focused on the short- to mid-term solutions through information sharing, cooperation among "frontline enforcement agencies," and the harmonization of travel procedures for health screening. Such limited responses make it vital that the health security agenda should go beyond merely securitizing health, and move towards recognizing and understanding the nexus of health and human security.

The study and practice of health security also reflects traditional security politics. This is perhaps most visible in the emerging research on the securitization of pandemics and their implications for global health diplomacy. Health diplomacy has been said to be "most effective when narrowed to a set of health security topics – especially outbreak containment and biosecurity preparedness" while "broader issues such as health equality, access to medicines, and health system strengthening receive less sustained high-level political attention and are vulnerable to funding cuts" (Davies 2012: 316–320). The "medicalization of insecurity," that is, the increasing level and depth of involvement of medical and health professionals in the analysis and formulation of security policy (see Elbe & Voelkner, chapter 6 this volume), could also sideline human security perspectives in the health security discourse (Elbe 2012: 320–322).

Health and human security: Convergence, complementarities, and interdependencies

Convergence and complementarities

Despite the debates on definition and the lack of consensus on what threats health security should address, health and human security discourses, particularly those on approaches to communicable diseases, appear to have converged along two streams. One stream focuses on the individual as the referent of security such that "state security resides in the security of the individual" (Curley & Thomas 2004: 17). Another stream sees states as core actors advancing the goal of "health as a foreign policy issue" (Davies 2010: 1177). Within this stream, "security and equity arguments" capture the interests of both "developed states (as donors, inventors and beneficiaries) and developing states (as recipients, investors and beneficiaries)" (Davies 2010: 1168). The UN Secretary-General's High-level Panel on Threats, Challenges and Change (2004), the UN Millennium Development Goals, and the 2008 One World, One Health strategic framework are part of this latter stream.

Some convergence, and complementarity, between health and human security is also observed in the Asian view of "comprehensive security" that is characterized by a multidimensional and holistic approach to security that at the same time looks beyond the boundaries of state security to the individual and communal nature of threats and insecurities (Caballero-Anthony 2003).

Another point of convergence between health and human security is in the development of health governance norms. Health governance requires addressing questions of who provides security and who benefits from health security. Issues such as human rights, equity, and human development – the same concerns highlighted by the human security concept – are thus salient (Harman 2012: 1–26, 139–145). To effectively address such issues, norms of health governance would need to evolve towards inclusive and multilevel decision making; engaging not only medical professionals or public health bureaucrats but also nongovernmental actors, individuals, and communities, from local to regional to global levels (Harman 2012: 1–26, 139–145).

The link between health security and human security is further reinforced by the global public goods approach. Health security is a global public good owing to the fact that benefits from realizing it can "reach across borders, generations and population groups" (Caballero-Anthony 2006: 110). The global public goods approach advances a governance perspective shared by human security, in that it underscores the "shared responsibility among various actors: responsible and transparent governments, active and engaged civil society and socially concerned businesses" (Caballero-Anthony 2006: 111).

The rights-based approach to health also furthers the cause of health and human security. The right to health and the principles of "availability, accessibility, acceptability and quality of goods and services" (Gruskin et al. 2012: 340) are valuable for advancing health security, particularly with respect to primary health care, health systems strengthening, and universal health coverage. Primary health care is considered one of the "surest routes to health security" as long as it operates on principles of fairness, efficiency, and affordability (Chan 2009: 1586–1587). This can only be done through health systems strengthening based on "a renewed ethic of human rights" (Frenk 2009: 2181–2182). These principles also underpin the argument for universal health coverage that can affect access to appropriate health care (Anand 2012: 9–10). Promoting the right to health (as the UN and the WHO have done) may have heightened the politicization of health, but rights-based approaches emphasize many of the critical elements of human security: equality and nondiscrimination, participation, accountability, and the legal and policy context (Gruskin et al. 2010: 129–145).

Regional approaches and interdependencies

Health and human security could also converge through regional approaches, which can provide a middle path by recognizing the interdependencies of systems involved in addressing health risks, vulnerabilities, and threats. Ideally, regional approaches to health security would not be so global that they skew the focus towards pandemics, nor so local that they neglect the potential spillover and transfer of the burden of health insecurities to those already vulnerable. They would also be more able to address context-specific conditions so as to reach the poor and vulnerable members of populations most likely to be affected by disease.[4]

How is this balance played out in the regional frameworks that had evolved in East Asia? To date, current frameworks manifest an uneven approach and a tiered securitization of health issues. Figure 3.1 reflect the kinds of priorities given by governments in addressing health challenges in the region. At the apex are the most securitized health threats, including SARS and strains of avian and human influenza, such as H1N1, H5N1, and possibly H7N9 (if not successfully contained in China). The middle layer includes HIV/AIDS, malaria, and tuberculosis.

The lowest layer includes a whole swathe of health concerns: noncommunicable diseases, primary health care, health systems strengthening, and universal health coverage. Yet there can be no doubt that health issues intersect with poverty, humanitarian emergencies (such as famine, flooding, natural disasters), illiteracy, and environmental degradation (Caceres 2011: 1962). The interdependencies of poverty, malnutrition, and chronic and infectious diseases are silent killers that claim more lives than conflicts and violence (Caballero-Anthony 2003). The poor are subject to the financial risks of paying for health care. They are also highly vulnerable to catastrophic illness, which can deplete their meager financial assets and deprive entire households of daily income. As the pyramid of priorities shows, however, such social, political, and economic determinants of health are often neglected or given a lower priority. Resources necessary to control epidemics or respond to humanitarian emergencies may even be taken from resources for national development or poverty reduction.

The pyramid of priorities also reflects the academic discourse on health security. Such distribution of priorities suggests that there is a gap in the academic and policy understanding of the

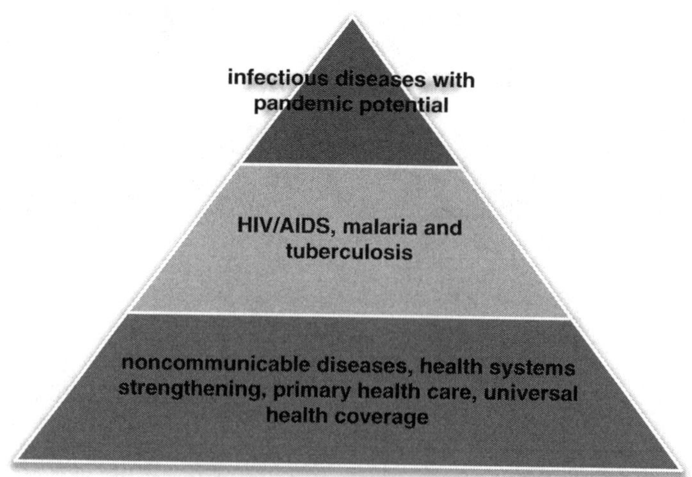

Figure 3.1 Prioritization of Health Security Issues in East Asia
Source: Authors' own data

interdependencies between health and human security and a need to develop capacity in this area. There are some signs that this is happening. UN guiding documents, such as the 2009 UN Office for the Coordination of Humanitarian Affairs (OCHA) handbook called *Human Security in Theory and Practice*, have highlighted such interdependencies. The handbook identified three main strategies for health security: (1) "access to basic health care and services"; (2) "risk sharing arrangements that pool membership funds and promote community-based insurance schemes"; and (3) "interconnected surveillance systems to identify disease outbreaks at all levels" (Human Security Unit UNOCHA 2009: 16).

One of the direct challenges to regional health security is the pandemic potential of emerging and reemerging infectious diseases. These can spread quickly and are hard to stop, creating unpredictable stresses on national public health systems (Campbell 2012: 175). The 2003 SARS episode demonstrated that an outbreak of that magnitude not only threatens health security but also severely affects regional economic development and stability (Caballero-Anthony 2012: 13). Problems such as lack of access to essential medicines worsened the pressure on health systems during the outbreak and highlighted basic health system deficiencies such as poor health infrastructure, lack of technical assistance, and even questionable quality of pharmaceuticals (Campbell 2012: 176, 178).

The SARS crisis in many ways defined the contours of the regional health security agenda in East Asia, spurring the establishment of a number of regional health security frameworks. While it is clear from the discussion here that there are critical interdependences between health and human security, the question is whether such interdependencies are incorporated into policy and practice.

Regional health security: Frameworks, networks, actors

Health security and governance in East Asia are defined by a number of frameworks, networks, and actors, including actors within and beyond the state. The official regional approaches remain explicitly statist (though they border on being globalist in some respects, such as engaging other multilateral actors for support and espousing objectives beyond communicable or infectious diseases). It thus stands to reason that resources have been heavily invested in pandemic preparedness and response, particularly in surveillance and monitoring. In fact, most of the current regional health security initiatives started off as responses to the SARS and avian influenza outbreaks, which explains the high number of frameworks addressing emerging and reemerging infectious diseases with pandemic potential (Fidler 2013: 208), including but not limited to SARS (2003), H5N1(2005–2006), H1N1 (2009), and possibly H7N9 (2013). Many of these initiatives have been implemented through technical and financial support from developed East Asian countries and are concentrated on developing ASEAN countries.

Despite the fact that increasing drug resistance and increasing rates of malaria, tuberculosis, and AIDS represent some of the most serious infectious disease threats in the region, the burden of combatting this host of diseases is taken more seriously by non-state actors. Funding for primary health care and health systems strengthening, and for addressing the political, economic, and social determinants of health, remains limited. This is not to say that there is no official support at all for such priorities. It is regularly emphasized in regional agendas that health system strengthening is critical to regional health security, not only in addressing the containment of a possible pandemic but also in preventing noncommunicable diseases. Table 3.1 shows that priorities other than pandemics have at least appeared on the agenda of many regional cooperative frameworks, though at a lower priority level than would be preferred.

There are also increasing pathways for the human security perspective to embed itself in regional health security agendas with the rise in the number and diversity of the frameworks,

Table 3.1 Regional Health Frameworks and Areas of Cooperation

Regional Frameworks	*Areas of Health Security Cooperation*			
	Emerging infectious diseases with pandemic potential	*Infectious diseases: HIV/AIDS, malaria and tuberculosis*	*Noncommunicable diseases*	*Health systems strengthening*
ASEAN-China	√		√	
ASEAN-Japan	√		√	√
ASEAN-Korea	√	√	√	√
ASEAN Plus Three Health Cooperation Framework	√	√		
East Asia Summit	√	√		

Source: Authors' own.

networks, and actors (particularly non-state actors) involved in health security in the region. The more promising of them are outlined in the next section.

Intergovernmental networks and actors

- *WHO regional bodies*

The World Health Organization (WHO) presence in the region is spearheaded by its regional offices, the Western Pacific Regional Office (WPRO) and the South-East Asia Regional Office (SEARO). These offices have initiatives spanning communicable diseases, family health and research, health systems development, and sustainable development and healthy environment. East Asia also houses 177 WHO Collaborating Centers, the majority of which are based in China and Australia, while others are based in Japan, South Korea, Singapore, Malaysia, New Zealand, the Philippines, and Vietnam (WHO WPRO 2012).

- *DAH initiatives*

China, Japan, and South Korea have been supportive in terms of development assistance for health (DAH) to developing countries (Pilcavage 2013; Qu Wang et al. 2013) but it was only in the last decade that cooperation on regional health matters materialized in East Asia. The Trilateral Cooperation between China, Japan, and South Korea extended its areas of cooperation to health only in 2007. In 2009, they committed to strengthening communication and consultation on public health as a regional and international concern (Joint Statement, 2009). In 2012, the Trilateral Summit recognized the importance of regular meeting mechanisms and cooperation between their health ministries on various health issues (Joint Declaration, 2013).

The three countries also cooperate with ASEAN on a range of health-related issues. The ASEAN-Japan High Level Officials Meeting on Caring Societies, which has met annually since 2003, and the initiatives to prevent communicable diseases under the ASEAN-Japan Plan of Action (2011–2015) are a case in point (ASEAN Secretariat 2012a). The ASEAN-China Health Ministers Meeting has met every two years since 2006. In 2012, the level of engagement was further strengthened through the ASEAN-China MOU on Health Cooperation. The ASEAN-Korea Plan of Action (2011–2015) also includes cooperation on health (ASEAN Secretariat 2012b).

- *ASEAN Plus Three*

ASEAN Plus Three has strongly supported an Emerging Infectious Diseases (EID) framework, a legacy of the urgency of developing effective responses after the region's experience with SARS. The APT Partnership Laboratories, for example, aims to strengthen the capacity of APT countries to "respond appropriately to infectious diseases through regional laboratory networking" (Joint Statement 2010). The APT also established a Field Epidemiology Training Network (FETN) in 2011. It has also been involved in specific disease interventions (including malaria, rabies, and dengue) and in animal and human health collaboration spurred by the outbreak of highly pathogenic avian influenza (HPAI) virus.

- *East Asia Summit*

Another forum for health security though a relatively young one is the East Asia Summit. Health was an agenda item right from the first EAS Summit in 2005, where the EAS Declaration on Avian Influenza Prevention, Control and Response acknowledged the impact of the avian influenza outbreak not only on the regional poultry industry but also on public health, livestock production, trade, tourism, and economic and social development. It aimed to enhance capacity to tackle avian influenza and its potential transformation into human influenza through collaboration and coordination among governments, communities and businesses, and regional and international organizations and mechanisms (East Asia Summit Declaration 2005). In 2012, the EAS expanded its areas of focus to malaria through the Declaration on Regional Responses to Malaria Control and Addressing Resistance to Antimalarial Medicines (Declaration of the 7th East Asia Summit 2012).

Non-state actors and networks

- *Donors and financial institutions*

Most regional WHO bodies are dependent on donor contributions, from developed member countries, foundations, and dedicated multilateral funds such as the Global Alliance for Vaccines and Immunization (GAVI Alliance) and the Global Fund to Fight AIDS, Tuberculosis, and Malaria. The GAVI Alliance for example has disbursed approximately U.S. $1.6 billion[5] while the Global Fund has committed approximately U.S. $2.97 billion[6] to developing East Asian countries.

Aside from the WHO and UN bodies with specific health agendas (Harman 2012: 40–46)[7], a few major organizations are involved in securing health as part of their other priorities, for example, the World Bank, through its poverty reduction programs and human development and social protection and risk management projects (World Bank 2013a) and the World Trade Organization (WTO) because of its interest in intellectual property and public health (WTO 2013). From 1986 to 2013, 128 of the World Bank's projects were focused on the health sector in East Asia and the Pacific (particularly in Indonesia, Vietnam, China, the Philippines, and Laos), amounting to U.S. $7.235 billion (World Bank 2013b).[8]

At the regional level, the Asian Development Bank (ADB) supports various projects with health implications. They include: (1) infrastructure development, particularly water supply and sanitation and transportation; (2) economic governance and public expenditure management for the cost-effective delivery of health programs and services, which includes health care financing; (3) regional public goods including the prevention and control of HIV/AIDS (Cooperation Fund for Fighting HIV/AIDS in Asia and the Pacific) and other communicable diseases (e.g., avian influenza), regional communicable disease control (Greater Mekong Subregion Projects), and a regional health observatory (Asia Pacific Observatory on Health Systems and Policies); (4) knowledge management and knowledge products; and (5) its Health Community of Practice for health sector development and advocacy in the region (ADB 2013). From 2003 to 2012, the ADB financed health projects amounting to U.S. $718 million.

- *CSOs and NGOs*

Civil society organizations (CSOs) in the region have been increasingly instrumental in complementing and supporting if not substituting for (the lack of) state-driven health security activities. CSOs driven by health agendas are considerable contributors to human security at the individual, regional, and global levels as direct service providers; alternative sources of information; providers of material and human resources for mobilization; and as transnational networks to combat common health threats (Huang 2013: 40).

Most of the health-promoting CSOs in East Asia work on HIV/AIDS prevention and control. There are some working on infectious diseases and health system capacity building, and a relatively few working on noncommunicable diseases. In terms of development and engagement, which is dependent on the political opportunity structures for CSOs to operate in, CSOs have more clout in health security promotion in Japan, Thailand, and Indonesia than in China, Vietnam, and Laos (Huang 2013: 36–37).

International NGOs have been critical in building networks bringing together different sectors, policy actors, and stakeholders on health issues. The AIDS Society of Asia and the Pacific (ASAP) (ASAP 2013) and the Health Action International Asia-Pacific (HAIAP), which focuses on increasing access to essential medicines (HAI AP August 2012), are examples of such collaborative networks. Some of the regional cooperative networks focus on a specific policy intervention to address noncommunicable diseases, an example of which would be the Southeast Asian Tobacco Control Alliance (SEATCA), a multisectoral alliance comprising representatives from government, the WHO, and leading tobacco control NGOs from across Southeast Asia (SEATCA 2012; SEATCA 2013). There are also networks focused on women's sexual and reproductive rights, for example, the Asian-Pacific Resource and Research Centre for Women (ARROW) (ARROW 2012a, 2012b) and the Asia Pacific Alliance for Sexual and Reproductive Health and Rights (APA), a network of NGOs, donors, and other stakeholders (APA 2013).

- *Research entities*

Research communities – including think tanks and non-state organizations involved in research and advocacy on public health, health governance, health diplomacy, "health as foreign policy," and health security – are also part of the spectrum of actors involved in developing and supporting regional health security frameworks in East Asia.

The Southeast Asian Ministers of Education Organisation (SEAMEO) Tropical Medicine network has since 1993 expanded its scope from tropical medicine research, education, and training to include health and development with increasing collaborations with other institutions in developed countries as well as the developing countries of the Asia-Pacific (Bennett et al. 2013: 172–173). One of the by-products of the avian influenza outbreak in 2005, for example, was the establishment of the Asia Partnership on Emerging Infectious Diseases Research (APEIR), which is made up of more than 30 partner institutions from Cambodia, China, Laos, Indonesia, Thailand, and Vietnam. By 2009, its agenda has been expanded to include all emerging infectious diseases (APEIR 2013).

Another regional health research initiative is the World Bank-WPRO-ADB-supported Asia Pacific Observatory on Health Systems and Policies (APO) established in 2011, which can be considered as part of a trend towards increased multisectoral and interagency collaboration on health security. Described as a "partnership of governments, development agencies and the research community," it involves 31 different institutions across the Asia Pacific and aims to be a "knowledge broker between researchers and policy makers" and to advance "evidence-based health policy-making in the region" (APO 2013). A recent addition is the ASEAN Non-Communicable Diseases (NCD) Network (Philips 2013), an informal network of "healthcare experts and thought leaders." Interestingly, this is supported by Philips (Philips 2013).

These regional non-state networks, despite not being able to outweigh official regional health security frameworks, have the potential to advance a human security approach to health security by virtue of their role in widening the spectrum of actors engaged in advancing health security, even if in a fragmentary way.

The way forward

The process of securitizing health in East Asia has not been a smooth or a straight path. The tipping points for securitization were rooted in the region's own internal conceptualizations of security as comprehensive and broad and in the intricacies of the principles of sovereignty and noninterference in pushing forward a more human-centered security agenda. This experience could be different in other parts of the world. Nonetheless, the securitization of health in East Asia was triggered by specific events – the outbreak of infectious diseases with pandemic potential in particular. And while responses still remain state-centered and are still limited in relation to noncommunicable diseases or strengthening health systems, the push for a human security approach is notable.

The current regional health security regime is in effect characterized by: (1) the possibilities of convergence of the "health and security" and "health and human security" discourses; (2) the development of frameworks as responses to developments in the discourses; and (3) the rise of non-state actors and networks engaged in health security.

The various regional frameworks and the proliferation of non-state regional health security actors have provided more channels for advancing the human security agenda, given that they have increasingly adopted principles of inclusive participation and cooperation among diverse actors at different levels of health governance. This trend shows the slow, more often implicit, but recognizable path towards a conceptualization of health security rooted in a more globalist and human-centered security agenda. The avenues for multisectoral collaboration have increased and the opportunities for deeper and expanded cooperation for a health and human security agenda need to be harnessed.

The discussion above has shown how the development of parallel tracks in scholarship, policy, and praxis has paved the way for institutionalizing health and human security in East Asia, albeit at different rates of progress. The increasing scholarship in health security in the interrelated fields of international relations, development, and security has also pushed the agendas of health diplomacy and global health governance, which in turn had advanced the cause of health and human security. These developments were concurrent with the progress in policy spurred on by the 1994 HDR that espoused health security as a component of human security.

Hence, while progress in practice is slow and can be seen to be more reactive than preventive, the increasing number of official regional bodies engaged in health security is a positive step in the right direction. And, while the approach that informs these official frameworks are still largely confined to the securitization of infectious diseases, the rising number of non-state actors that focus on health and human security issues will hopefully tip the balance in favor of health and human security.

Notes

1 As the debates around human security swirled, some questioned the viability of the concept given its conceptual ambiguity. Some scholars have criticized the broad definition of human security. Roland Paris (2001), for instance, has argued that the seven elements comprising human security in the 1994 report makes it difficult to determine which can be excluded. He raised the analytical value of human security, pointing out that if "human security means almost anything, then it effectively means nothing."

2 Evans (2004: 269) noted the likes of Tadashi Yamamoto of the Japan Centre for International Exchange, the ASEAN Institute of Strategic and International Studies (ASEAN ISIS) group, and political figures such as Obuchi Keizo, Surin Pitsuwan, and Kim Dae-Jung who promoted human security.

3 ASEAN Plus Three heads bring together 10 ASEAN states with China, Japan, and South Korea.

4 This was highlighted by Caceres (2011: 1962–1963) who also argued that global health security "lacks the drive and speed needed to make proposals materialize and operationalize ideas in the geographic areas where they are most desperately needed."

5 This is an approximate amount derived from GAVI disbursements as of March 2013 to the following East Asian countries: Cambodia, China, Laos, Papua New Guinea, Vietnam, Indonesia, Korea DPR, Myanmar, and Timor Leste. See: GAVI (2013) http://www.gavialliance.org/results/disbursements/

6 This is an approximate amount derived from Global Fund Portfolio as of June 2013, to the following East Asian countries: China, Indonesia, Myanmar, Philippines, Cambodia, DPRK, Laos, Malaysia, Papua New Guinea, Thailand, Timor Leste, and Vietnam. See: Global Fund Portfolio Downloads (2013) http://portfolio.theglobalfund.org/en/Downloads/DisbursementsInDetail

7 Within the UN system, there are three main bodies that explicitly recognize the linkages between health and development and focus on the social determinants of health including the United Nations Children's Fund (UNICEF), the United Nations Population Fund (UNFPA), and the United Nations Development Programme. For more discussion on their roles, see Harman (2012).

8 This data was generated from the World Bank database, using the following search criteria: East Asia and Pacific (region), Health (sector). See: http://www.worldbank.org/projects/search?lang=en&searchTerm=&mjthemecode_exact=8 (accessed 27 June 2013).

References

Acharya, A. (2001) 'Human security: East versus West', *International Journal*, 56: 442–460.

AIDS Society of the Asia and the Pacific (ASAP). (2013) *About ASAP: Major Activity Areas*. Online. Available HTTP: <http://www.aidssocietyap.org/major_activities.php> (accessed 27 June 2013).

Alkire, S. (2001) *Conceptual Framework for the Commission on Human Security* (Working Manuscript, 6 December 2001).

Anand, S. (2012) 'Human security and universal health insurance', *The Lancet*, 379: 9–10.

ASEAN Secretariat. (2012a) *The ASEAN-Japan Plan of Action*. Online. Available HTTP: <http://www.asean.org/news/item/the-asean-japan-plan-of-action> (accessed 21 June 2013).

ASEAN Secretariat. (2012b) *Plan of Action to Implement the Joint Declaration on ASEAN-ROK Strategic Partnership for Peace and Prosperity (2011–2015)*. Online. Available HTTP: <http://www.asean.org/news/item/plan-of-action-to-implement-the-joint-declaration-on-asean-republic-of-korea-strategic-partnership-for-peace-and-prosperity-2011–2015> (accessed 21 June 2013).

Asian Development Bank (ADB). (2013) *Health: Core Areas*. Online. Available HTTP: <http://www.adb.org/sectors/health/core-areas> (accessed 27 June 2013).

Asian Pacific Research and Resource Centre for Women (ARROW). (2012a) *About Us: Strategies*. Online. Available HTTP: <http://www.arrow.org.my/?p=strategies> (accessed 27 June 2013).

Asian Pacific Research and Resource Centre for Women (ARROW). (2012b) *ARROW and Herstory*. Online. Available HTTP: <http://www.arrow.org.my/?p=arrow-herstory> (accessed 27 June 2013).

Asia Pacific Alliance (APA). (2013) *About APA*. Online. Available HTTP: <http://www.asiapacificalliance.org/about-apa-54.html#> (accessed 27 June 2013).

Asia Pacific Observatory on Health Systems and Policies (APO). (2013) *About Us*. Online. Available HTTP: <http://www.wpro.who.int/asia_pacific_observatory/about/en/> (accessed 27 June 2013).

Asia Partnership on Emerging Infectious Diseases Research (APEIR). (2013) *Partnership*. Online. Available HTTP: <http://www.apeiresearch.net/smenupage.php?menuid=3> (accessed 27 June 2013).

Bennett, S., Pang, T., Chunharas, S. and Sakhunpanit, T. (2013) 'Global health research governance: an Asian perspective on the need for reform', in K. Lee, T. Pang and Y. Tan (eds.) *Asia's Role in Governing Global Health*, London and New York: Routledge.

Caballero-Anthony, M. (2003) 'Human security and primary health care in Asia: realities and challenges', in L. Chen, J. Leaning and V. Narasimhan (eds.) *Global Health Challenges for Human Security*, Cambridge and London: Global Equity Initiative, Asia Center, Harvard University/Harvard University Press.

Caballero-Anthony, M. (2004) 'Revisioning human security in Southeast Asia', *Asian Perspective*, 28: 155–189.

Caballero-Anthony, M. (2005) 'SARS in Asia: crisis, vulnerabilities and regional responses', *Asian Survey*, 45: 475–495.

Caballero-Anthony, M. (2006) 'Combating infectious diseases in East Asia: securitization and global public goods for health and human security', *Journal of International Affairs*, 59: 105–127.

Caballero-Anthony, M. (2012) 'Health and human security in Southeast Asia: issues and challenges', in C.G. Hernandez (ed.), *Mainstreaming Human Security in ASEAN Integration, Volume I: Regional Public Goods and Human Security*, Quezon City: Institute for Strategic and Development Studies.

Caceres, S.B. (2011) 'Global health security in an era of global health threats', *Emerging Infectious Diseases*, 17: 1962–1963.

Campbell, J.R. (2012) 'Human health threats and implications for regional security in Southeast Asia', in B. Teh Cheng Guan (ed.), *Human Security: Securing East Asia's Future*, New York: Springer: 173–191.

Chan, M. (2009) 'Primary health care as a route to health security', *The Lancet*, 373: 1586–1587.

Commission on Human Security. (2003) *Human Security Now: Protecting and Empowering People*, New York: Commission on Human Security.

Council for Security Cooperation in the Asia-Pacific (CSCAP). (1995) *CSCAP Memorandum No.3: The Concepts of Comprehensive and Cooperative Security*, Kuala Lumpur: Council for Security Cooperation in the Asia-Pacific.

Curley, M. and Thomas, N. (2004) 'Human security and public health in Southeast Asia: the SARS outbreak', *Australian Journal of International Affairs*, 58: 17–32.

Davies, S.E. (2010) 'What contributions can International Relations make to the evolving global health agenda?', *International Affairs*, 86: 1167–1190.

Davies, S.E. (2012) 'The healthy trends of International Relations research', *International Political Sociology*, 6: 316–320.

Declaration of the 7th East Asia Summit. (2012) *Declaration of the 7th East Asia Summit on Regional Responses to Malaria Control and Addressing Resistance to Antimalarial Medicines, 20 November 2012, Phnom Penh, Cambodia.* Online. Available HTTP: <http://www.dfat.gov.au/asean/eas/121120_declaration_7th_eas_regional_responses.html> (accessed 21 June 2013).

East Asia Summit Declaration. (2005) *East Asia Summit Declaration on Avian Influenza Prevention, Control and Response, 14 December 2005, Kuala Lumpur, Malaysia.* Online. Available HTTP: <http://www.dfat.gov.au/asean/051214_avian_influenza_prevention.html> (accessed 17 June 2013).

Elbe, S. (2012) 'Bodies as battlefields: toward the medicalization of insecurity', *International Political Sociology*, 6: 320–322.

Evans, P.M. (2004) 'Human security and East Asia: in the beginning', *Journal of East Asian Studies*, 4: 263–284.

Fidler, D. (2013) 'Asia and global health governance: power, principles and practice', in K. Lee, T. Pang and Y. Tan (eds.) *Asia's Role in Governing Global Health*, London and New York: Routledge: 198–214.

Frenk, J. (2009) 'Strengthening health systems to promote security', *The Lancet*, 373: 2181–2182.

GAVI. (2013) *Disbursements by Country as of March 2013.* Online. Available HTTP: <http://www.gavialliance.org/results/disbursements/> (accessed 27 June 2013).

Global Fund. (2013) *Portfolio Downloads as of June 2013.* Online. Available HTTP: <http://portfolio.theglobalfund.org/en/Downloads/DisbursementsInDetail> (accessed 27 June 2013).

Gruskin, S., Ahmed, S., Bogecho, D., Ferguson, L., Hanefeld, J., Maccarthy, S., Raad, Z. and Steiner, R. (2012) 'Human rights in health systems frameworks: what is there, what is missing and why does it matter?', *Global Public Health: An International Journal for Research, Policy and Practice*, 7: 337–351.

Gruskin, S., Bogecho, D. and Ferguson, L. (2010) 'Rights-based approaches to health policies and programs: articulations, ambiguities and assessment', *Journal of Public Health Policy*, 31: 129–145.

Hampson, F.O., Daudelin, J., Hay, J., Reid, H. and Martin, T. (2001) *Madness in the Multitude: Human Security and World Disorder*, New York and Oxford: Oxford University Press.

Harman, S. (2012) *Global Health Governance*, London and New York: Routledge.

Health Action International Asia Pacific (HAI AP). (2012) *HAI AP News, August 2012*. Online. Available HTTP: <http://www.haiweb.org/08082012/HAIAPNews3August2012.pdf> (accessed 27 June 2013).

Hoffman, S.J. (2010) 'The evolution, etiology and eventualities of the global health security regime', *Health Policy and Planning*, 25: 510–522.

Huang, Y. (2013) 'Global health, civil society and regional security', in R. Sukma and J. Gannon (eds.) *A Growing Force: Civil Society's Role in Asian Regional Security*, Tokyo: Japan Center for Economic Research.

Human Security Unit, UN Office for the Coordination of Humanitarian Affairs (UNOCHA). (2009) *Human Security in Theory and Practice: Application of the Human Security Concept and the United Nations Trust Fund for Human Security*, New York: United Nations.

Joint Declaration. (2013) *Joint Declaration on the Enhancement of Trilateral Comprehensive Cooperative Partnership, 13 May 2012, Beijing, China*. Online. Available HTTP: <http://www.mofa.go.jp/region/asia-paci/jck/summit1205/joint_declaration_en.html> (accessed 27 June 2013).

Joint Statement. (2009). *Joint Statement on the Tenth Anniversary of Trilateral Cooperation among the People's Republic of China, Japan, and the Republic of Korea, 10 October 2009, Beijing, China*. Online. Available HTTP: <http://www.mofa.go.jp/region/asia-paci/jck/meet0910/joint-1.pdf> (accessed 27 June 2013).

Joint Statement. (2010) *Joint Statement of the Fourth ASEAN Plus Three Health Ministers Meeting, Singapore, 23 July 2010*. Online. Available HTTP: <http://www.asean.org/news/item/joint-statement-of-the-4th-asean3-health-ministers-meeting-singapore-23-july-2010> (accessed 21 June 2013).

Lo, C.Y. and Thomas, N. (2010) 'How is health a security issue? Politics, responses and issues', *Health Policy and Planning*, 25: 447–453.

Ogata, S. (2003) 'Empowering people for human security', Payne Lecture, Stanford University, 28 May 2003. Online. Available HTTP: <http://www.unocha.org/humansecurity/chs/newsandevents/payne.html> (accessed 20 January 2014).

O'Manique, C. and Fourie, P. (2010) 'Security and health in the twenty-first century', in M. Duan Cavelty and V. Mauer (eds.) *The Routledge Handbook of Security Studies*, London and New York: Routledge: 243–253.

Paris, R. (2001) 'Human security: paradigm shift or hot air?', *International Security*, 26: 87–102.

Philips. (2013). *ASEAN Non-Communicable Diseases (NCD) Network Launched*. Online. Available HTTP: <http://www.newscenter.philips.com/main/standard/news/press/2013/20130408-asean-ncd-network.wpd#.U3I-joFdV7c> (accessed 13 May 2014).

Pilcavage, C. (2013) 'Japan's overseas development assistance in the health sector and global health governance' in K. Lee, T. Pang and Y. Tan (eds.) *Asia's Role in Governing Global Health*, London and New York: Routledge.

Qu Wang, J., Liu, M., Liu, A., Wei, T. and Li, H. (2013) 'Global health governance in China: the case of China's health aid to foreign countries', in K. Lee, T. Pang and Y. Tan (eds.) *Asia's Role in Governing Global Health*, London and New York: Routledge.

Rothschild, E. (1995) 'What is security?', *Daedalus*, 124: 53–98.

Rushton, S. (2011) 'Global health security: security for whom? Security from what?', *Political Studies*, 59: 779–796.

Southeast Asian Tobacco Control Alliance (SEATCA). (2012) *Catalyst for Change: Towards a Healthy and Tobacco-Free ASEAN*, Bangkok: SEATCA. Online. Available HTTP: <http://seatca.org/dmdocuments/catalyst%20for%20change%202012.pdf> (accessed 27 June 2013).

Southeast Asian Tobacco Control Alliance (SEATCA). (2013) *About SEATCA*. Online. Available HTTP: <http://seatca.org/?page_id=2> (accessed 27 June 2013).

Støre, J., Welch, J. and Chen, L. (2003) 'Health and security for a global century', in L. Chen, J. Leaning and V. Narasimhan (eds.) *Global Health Challenges for Human Security*, Cambridge and London: Global Equity Initiative, Asia Center, Harvard University/Harvard University Press: 69–71.

Ul Haq, M. (1994) 'New imperatives of human security', *RGICS Paper No. 7*, New Delhi: Rajiv Gandhi Institute for Contemporary Studies (RGICS), Rajiv Gandhi Foundation.

United Nations Development Programme (UNDP). (1994) *Human Development Report 1994*, New York and Oxford: Oxford University Press.

Weir, L. and Mykhalovskiy, E. (2010) *Global Public Health Vigilance: Creating a World on Alert*, London and New York: Routledge.

World Health Organization (WHO). (2007) *The World Health Report: A Safer Future: Global Public Health Security in the 21st Century*, Geneva: World Health Organization.

World Health Organization Western Pacific Regional Office (WHO WPRO). (2012) *WHO Collaborating Centres*. Online. Available HTTP: <http://www2.wpro.who.int/sites/whocc/home.htm> (accessed 27 June 2013).

World Bank. (2013a) *Projects and Operations: By Theme*. Online. Available HTTP: <http://www.worldbank.org/projects/theme?lang=en> (accessed 27 June 2013).

World Bank. (2013b) *World Bank Database*. Online. Available HTTP: <http://www.worldbank.org/projects/search?lang=en&searchTerm=&mjthemecode_exact=8> (accessed 27 June 2013).

World Trade Organization (WTO). (2013) *Specific TRIPS Issues*. Online. Available HTTP: <http://www.wto.org/english/tratop_e/trips_e/trips_e.htm#issues> (accessed 27 June 2013).

4 GENDER, HEALTH, AND SECURITY

Colleen O'Manique

Feminist perspectives remain on the borders of the evolving body of scholarship that situates global health within a security frame. Yet social and political life is profoundly gendered and feminist scholarship has a critical role to play in illuminating both the foundations of health insecurities and the effects of insecurities on differently gendered and located bodies. We need only look to some of today's sites of conflict to see the ubiquity of sexual violence as part of militarized violence, to the structural violence of the austerity response that has undermined basic health care and has left women struggling to fill the care gap, or the deaths of hundreds of young Bangladeshi women, the result of the absence of the most basic occupational health conditions in the factory where they produced clothing for multinational buyers. One's experience of "health security" has much to do with gender to the extent that specific vulnerabilities are located in culturally defined gender roles, and one's sex and gender can circumscribe one's access to health care and health's social determinants. Furthermore, in/security is constituted through and by gender as a key component of the matrix of power that governs the life economy. Within most scholarship of global health and accounts of health's social determinants, gender tends to be seen as one of a collection of variables, with sex and gender often conflated. The reality is more complicated.

The purpose of this chapter is to illuminate some of the intersections between gender, health, and security. A feminist perspective on health security leads us to ask different questions about health and in/security and to problematize some of the "common sense" assumptions that underlie much of the discourse in this area. Critical feminist perspectives go beyond an analysis of the relationship between health and state and global security concerns, expanding the parameters of health security to consider the power relations – the norms, ideologies, vested interests – that determine which diseases are framed as threats and to whom and impact policy responses. A feminist lens casts a light on the root causes and the social determinants of health insecurity, foregrounding the role that hegemonic masculinity plays in constructing and responding to health threats, as well as the role of unequal gender relation in shaping access to the basic constituents of health and medicine.

While feminist perspectives on the "health and security" question are scant, feminist perspectives have much to offer the discussion. The first section of this chapter will provide a brief overview of the main challenges of feminist international relations (FIR) scholars to "mainstream" security studies. Within the field of FIR, feminist security studies (FSS) and feminist political economy (FPE) have challenged the normative assumptions of mainstream IR and constructions of security, FSS mostly focused on the gender dimensions of war and peace and FPE on insecurities arising from the contemporary governance of the global economy. The second section introduces the robust body of scholarship on transnational women's health and rights and addresses the ways in which feminist scholars of global health have taken up gender as a central determinant of health, again, just skimming the surface. The third section casts a feminist light on health security through the window of the securitization of the AIDS pandemic in sub-Saharan Africa, an issue that has received some attention from a feminist perspective. The chapter concludes with some reflections on future directions for research.

Feminist approaches to security

Security studies is ostensibly the most masculine of subfields within the discipline of political science. The variety of feminist approaches to security share the common project of transforming the field to take gender relations seriously, whether the focus is security in the military sense or the broader view of human security that transcends the pragmatic orthodoxy of the narrow state-centric definition of national security. Feminist international relations scholars have exposed the ways in which gendered power relations, articulating with other hierarchical axes of differentiation such as race, ethnicity, class, and sexuality, operate to produce discourses and practices that render invisible many of the insecurities experienced in the daily lives of people. This short section cannot do justice to the variety and breadth of feminist contributions to security. What I want to do is to highlight the overarching feminist critiques of conventional security studies and the general directions in which scholars have taken the security question. Elisabeth Prügl (2011) summarizes the theoretical insights of feminist international relations scholars in these words:

> [they] problematize foundational concepts in security and political economy, provide new insights into the link between war and gender, re-conceptualize the global economy and show how it is governed, analyze feminist strategies in international organizations, and explore the way in which international gender norms travel.
>
> (Prügl 2011)

Feminist voices in IR appeared in the 1980s, around the same time as the critical turn. Both critical and feminist IR are explicitly normative in their commitment to a transformative constructivist theory and practice of security, and both challenge the hegemonic "common sense" of mainstream security studies, rooted in political realism. Although there are various schools within the dominant neo/realist tradition, its adherents share a commitment to its foundational premises; a fixed understanding of the human subject as rational, autonomous, driven by self-interest, and existing in an unstable and anarchic world; politics as primarily conflictual; and the main concern of the state to enforce order (Wohlforth 2010). Whether materialist, post-structural, or post-colonial in orientation, critical security scholars interpret security and the pathways for its achievement in ways that challenge the supposed objectivity and political/normative neutrality of the security studies mainstream. A recognition of the complicated and constructed nature and variety of human experience, which includes relationships based on self-interest and autonomy but also dependence, interdependence and cooperation, is at the center of critical security studies' commitment to a scholarship that informs a politics of transformation. The abstract model of human nature and the nation-state is replaced with the messy reality of human agency and political struggle in the unfolding of history, while the decentering of the state acknowledges the wide-ranging effects of historical legacies of colonization and the current global geopolitical context in shaping local conditions of in/security.

Sylvester describes the scholarship of international relations today as a "capricious field of camps" rather than a state-centric narrative with one of its central tensions, the tendency to ignore, or fail to consider the knowledge that the other camps produce (Sylvester 2010: 608). Certainly this is true of feminist perspectives; they remain on the margins of the field while interrogating the androcentrism of many of IR's subfields, both mainstream and critical. While feminist scholars share the critical IR challenge to the foundations of mainstream security studies, they center gender as a structure of power in its intersections with class, race, nation, sexuality, and other dimensions of stratification and difference. Gender pervades language and divisions of authority that determine whose voices and experiences dominate, and it structures divisions of labor, dictating what counts as work, who does what kinds of work, and how work is valued (Peterson 2003: 21). While acknowledging the importance of other dimensions of social identity and stratification, feminist perspectives recognize that the differentiation between and relative positioning of women and men is a fundamental ordering principle that pervades the system of power in all societies and that other dimensions of social identity are shaped by gender (Cockburn 2001: 15). Gender relations are highly variable and subject to dramatic shifts; discourses of masculinity and femininity and the meanings of differently located and classified bodies are in fairly constant flux. But much evidence points to the pervasive dominance of men and masculinity across time and cultures despite the variability of gender relations and other axes of power such as ethnicity and class (Cockburn 2001). Mounting evidence demonstrates that gender relations magnify other dimensions of social inequality, yet the invisibility of gender as a "governing code" (Peterson 2012) and the consequences of that invisibility remain pervasive. Feminist IR scholarship acknowledges the diversity and difference amongst women and challenges the a priori privileging of any specific axis of power including gender. But as Wilchins recognizes, the control of bodies, genders, and desires is as close as we have to a universal constant; it is common to all cultures. He argues that this is the case of gender in its widest sense, including sexual orientation, because underpinning homophobia is the notion that gay men are insufficiently masculine and lesbian women insufficiently feminine. "I take it as obvious that what animates sexism and misogyny is gender, and our astounding fear and loathing around issues of vulnerability or femininity" (Wilchins 2002: 11).

With its central concerns of the military, war, and peace, FSS scholars such as Cockburn (2001), Korac (2006), Moser and Clark (2001), Steans (2006), and Tickner (2001, 2011) have uncovered the gendered dynamics of power in the construction of the theories and practices of security and in the concrete material effects on people that emerge from conflict and war. The hierarchical, hypermasculine, and sexualized cultures of militarism play out in ways that show similar patterns the world over; for example, rape and sexual violence have always and everywhere been a part of war. But it is only in recent history that sexual violence in conflict situations has been taken up as a legitimate focus of inquiry and policy intervention. That being said, mainstream accounts of gender based-violence in war have failed to address the various structural and systemic factors that have shaped war and conflict in preconflict, conflict, and post-conflict situations (Moser & Clarke 2001). Feminist scholars of war uncover the specific meanings of security and insecurity in military and conflict discourse, the role of militarized masculinity in strategic thinking and in military practices, and the far-reaching effects and impacts of war on military and civilian populations, acknowledging the multiple roles of women as not just victims but as active agents: as participants in war and as perpetrators/supporters of violence, and as critical actors in processes of peace and reconciliation (Cohn 2012). They also recognize that gender relations condition the variable and shifting subject positions of boys and men in situations of conflict, who are not simply the aggressors. Investigations guided by a feminist ethos center the voices of the people in conflict situations, while uncovering the foundations of in/security in their communities and in the wider geopolitical environment.

Feminist scholarship has also been central to bridging the historical separation between the traditional concerns of security and the concerns of political economy (Sjoberg 2011: 600). As global economic restructuring has taken a stronger hold, neoconservative militarization and neoliberal globalization have converged to realign "developmental" and "fragile" states to conform to the "good governance" and free market dictates of the international financial institutions (IFIs) (Marchand & Runyan 2011: 4). Feminist International Political Economy (IPE) has illuminated how the tight alliance between corporate and state interests and the structural privileging of men and masculinity operates to shape what are commonly understood as "gender neutral" policies. They demonstrate the pathways between contemporary neoliberal governance at both supranational and state levels and the local conditions that underpin poverty and deepen insecurities (Cohen & Brodie 2007; Gill & Roberts 2011; Griffin 2009; Marchand & Runyan 2011; Peterson & Runyan, 2010; Young et al. 2011).

Feminist analyses of the global political economy denaturalize global capitalism and challenge the idea that security can be realized within the current climate of neoliberal globalization. A central focus of feminist political economy has been the historical and cultural separation within the disciplines and practices of economics and politics into public and private spheres. While the "productive" economy is privileged, the household realm of social reproduction remains invisible as an economic unit where a growing range of unpaid and informal activities that sustain capital accumulation are carried out, essentially absorbing the costs of reproducing laboring bodies. This invisibility is made possible only through the "common sense" notion that the state is there to secure the economy, abstractly understood as economic growth. Post-2008 austerity has further intensified the 1980s policies of structural adjustment, evacuating the state from responsibility for maintaining many of the basic conditions of social reproduction, which has in essence consolidated the state's role in guaranteeing the security of capital at the expense of human security (Bakker & Gill 2003). The same sets of policy prescriptions responsible for the soaring rise in global income inequality and environmental degradation underpin the persistent trends of the hollowing out of the middle class in the global north, the integration of (mostly racialized) women into feminized and informal wage economies, and the increasing feminization of male labor (Braunstein 2006; Grown 2006; Peterson 2010).

Feminist scholars of globalization have contributed to understanding the relationship between the geopolitical dimensions of global health and the local conditions that circumscribe health security, the ideologies and practices of governance that determine the existence of the underlying determinants of health in communities, and the power relations that shape one's access to those determinants. In the last three decades, the theory and praxis of global women's health has evolved into a broad based and heterogeneous transnational network that continues the struggle for global health and rights. According to Petchesky, the three major drivers of the transnational women's health movement have been the negative impacts of global capitalism and macroeconomic restructuring on poverty levels and health, the rise of explicitly antifeminist, fundamentalist politico-religious forces, and the HIV/AIDS pandemic, which significantly challenged prior discourses of sexuality and the meaning of a human right to health (Petchesky 2003: 1). Rights-based discourses have been a key source of political mobilization, providing a distinct counter to the dominant neoliberal normative and policy approach to health, with their recognition of the inherent dignity and worth of all human persons (Chapman 2012: 274).

Transnational feminism, health, and security

Women's health arrived on the global governance agenda in the mid-1990s at the 1993 Vienna Human Conference on Human Rights, the 1994 International Conference on Population and Development in Cairo, and in the 1995 Beijing Plan of Action. The concept of human rights embraced by transnational feminist activists at the time was consistent with so-called second generation rights codified in the International Covenant on Economic, Social and Cultural Rights in 1976 that included the "right to health" as an essential part of basic citizenship rights (Nowicka 2011). Despite the critique of the rights framing of the movement as re-inscribing the power of the global north, the meaning of human rights was reconfigured to challenge the boundaries of the public/private spheres to encompass a conception of bodily integrity that made human rights violations actionable within international human rights frameworks (Hawkesworth 2006: 80–83). As with all social movements, there were tensions and debates around ownership and agenda setting, and it was when leadership from the global south stepped up that an expansive and inclusive view of sexual and reproductive rights emerged (Petchesky 2003). The "right to health" for women encompasses a broad range of protections and entitlements: freedom from coerced contraception and forced sterilization, unwanted sexual relations, involuntary maternity (including access to safe abortion), sexual and domestic violence, and rights to comprehensive health services including maternal and child health care, and access to health's social determinants including proper nutrition, water and sanitation, and shelter (Hawkesworth 2006; Nowicka 2011; Petchesky 2003).

The broad sexual and reproductive rights frame of the transnational health movement was a response to the initial invisibility of women and gender in human rights instruments and conventions that addressed the right to health, and the understanding that girls' and women's health rights could only be achieved in the context of economic, gender, and racial justice and poverty alleviation. In many ways, it was consistent with the human security frame that gained prominence in the 1990s that was based on the idea that the individual is the only irreducible focus of security and that the claims of other referents, whether communities, states, or the globe, emerge from the individual's right to dignity and security of person (McFarlane & Khong 2006). But as Hoogensen and Stuvøy have demonstrated (2006), feminist perspectives were only marginally embraced within the human security debates, despite the centrality of gendered power relations in shaping the security of individuals. Although their experiences show great variation depending on location and subjectivity, the bodily autonomy of girls and women is subject to ideologies, laws, and customs that can drastically limit their ability to make choices around sex and fertility. Girls and women are far more likely to be the victims of domestic and sexual violence while the perpetrators are overwhelmingly men. Cultural practices that exist to restrict women's mobility, bodily autonomy, and reproductive freedom are perceived to be natural and benign and, in some places, are codified in law and justified on religious or cultural grounds (Sen & Ostlin 2008: 4). Gender relations also shape boys' and men's health. The current hegemonic definitions of manhood and masculinity hurt men and boys who are also the victims of sanctioned and nonsanctioned forms of violence, including sexual violence (Katz 2012). Cultures of gender depend on the performance of a particular type of masculinity that often stands in the way of boys and men seeking the care that they need when they are injured or sick, and that encourages risk-taking behaviors such as the excessive consumption of alcohol and drug taking, unsafe sexual practices, and violence (Hearn 2010: 169). The heteronormative assumptions of both manhood and womanhood have serious implications for the health of gay, lesbian, and transgendered people, who experience stigma and discrimination in their daily lives with consequences for both physical and emotional health. Hegemonic forms of masculinity devalorize not only females but also males who don't live up to masculine ideals, including racially, culturally, and economically marginalized men (Peterson 2003: 14). Scott-Samuel et al. understand contemporary masculinity as an underlying cause of health inequalities: "To summarize this phenomenon in simple language: tough aggressive and unemotional models of manhood generate tough, aggressive and unemotional politics and public policies" (Scott-Samuel et al. 2009: 288). Today's hegemonic masculinity mirrors the assumptions of contemporary neoliberalism and is reproduced within institutions of governance (Scott-Samuel et al. 2009: 289).

The discursive field of racialized and gendered global capital shapes how rights are taken up in different contexts at different times (Petchesky 2003). While major successes with regard to women's health rights have taken place in a number of countries since Beijing and Cairo, the detrimental impact on human rights standards globally post-9/11 has meant holding the line, or the erosion of some of the gains of the past decades (Nowicka 2011). Nowicka maintains that in the era of the Bush administration, and particularly since the 9/11 attacks and the launch of the "War on Terror," the detrimental impact on human rights globally meant a shift in the political climate around women's health with a growing conservatism around any reference to rights, and a gradual depoliticization of the women's health agenda (Nowicka 2011: 120–121). Another significant moment rolling back the right to health was the 2008 financial crisis that pulled the global economy into recession, imperiling the economic security of large segments of the global population. Cause marketing and corporate philanthropy have mushroomed to fill the gap resulting in a renewed emphasis on vertical single disease campaigns that focus on technological quick fixes. The increased incidence and prevalence of cancers, diabetes, and heart disease in the global South has further entrenched the behavioral model of health prevention in which the maintenance of a healthy body involves self-regulation in the context of self-reliance, with scant attention to the sociopolitical and economic environments that are detrimental to health (Glasgow 2012). While health has, at the level of the biological body, become increasingly depoliticized, at the state and intrastate level, it has become firmly established as a security issue.

Gender and the securitization of HIV/AIDS

The HIV/AIDS pandemic is one of a number of health issues that have been constructed as a security threat over the past two decades, alongside other cross-border health emergencies such as biological and chemical "terrorism," pandemic influenza, and tainted food scandals. The meanings of health security and the practices to secure health reflect a tension between health as a basic human right linked to broader rights of citizenship and health's social determinants and health as an instrumental condition for securing geopolitical and economic interests, principally of states of the global North. The securitization of HIV/AIDS in Africa provides one example of the health security discourse. Its beginnings are dated to January 2000 with the UN Security Council's designation of HIV/AIDS as a security threat, the first time in its history that their interpretation of a threat fell outside the domain of armed security. In May of the same year, the Clinton Administration declared HIV/AIDS a threat to United States national security. As Pieter Fourie discusses in this volume in chapter 9, the initial concerns were for the prevalence of HIV in soldiers and their ability to maintain security with the potential hollowing out of the military, and the spread of HIV to the civilian population in contexts of civil unrest and low-intensity conflict. Other concerns were for state capacity and the potential economic impact of high levels of mortality amongst the most productive members of the population. What was at stake was stable governance, economic growth, and, potentially, the security of northern geostrategic interests, with oil security and terrorism at the top of the list.

The initial claims about the "threat" HIV/AIDS epidemics posed to national and global security were overstated but discursively shaped the AIDS security nexus while drawing attention away from many of the underlying drivers of HIV spread and the real impacts on people, households, and communities. The predictions of state failure were not borne out; as Fourie explains, there has been "no significant co-variation between HIV/AIDS prevalence and military insecurity, social uprising, macroeconomic failure, electoral instability or democratic consolidation" (Fourie, chapter 9 in this volume). But the securitization frame had the effect of placing emphasis on policies to secure states instead of the provision of better health systems and addressing the longer term realities and impacts of HIV/AIDS (Fourie in this volume). A careful reading of documents produced by the U.S. Department of Defense on their programs in Africa by Alan Ingram describes a military strategy in which concerns for disease control and the provision of health services, counterterrorism and counterinsurgency, and energy and resource security converged to set fragile states on the path to "normal healthy market-based growth, inclusion in the global economy and responsible self-management" (Ingram 2011: 656). Anne-Emmanuelle Birn reminds us that throughout history, international health has always focused on disease control to facilitate conquest and colonization, to increase labor productivity, and to fend off social unrest (Birn 2012), a focus that seemingly continues in the form of 21st century health securitization.

A feminist perspective on the AIDS and security polemic helps to illuminate two broad concerns. The first is the problematic nature and impacts of the military security framing of HIV/AIDS on communities and particularly women in conflict and post-conflict contexts. The second concern is for the consequences of the realist conception of security that undergirds the construction of the securitization of HIV/AIDS. Both the gendered and the structural analysis of the spread of HIV infection and its impacts are invisible in the AIDS and security frame. When women and gender have been named in the security polemic, it has been in regard to their heightened risk of sexual violence or their links to prostitution without consideration of the underlying drivers (Seckinelgin et al. 2010). Indeed, FSS scholars have drawn attention to the ubiquity of sexual violence in conflict situations but call for a gender sensitive analysis of the communities in which the conflict is unfolding, including the power relations that shape individual and collective gendered and ethnic/racialized identities, alliances, and behaviors (Korac 2006: 511). While some have seen in the securitization of health the elevation of the importance of global public health, citing in particular the increase in global spending on the HIV/AIDS pandemic following the UN Security Council's declaration of the pandemic as a security threat, others have raised the question of whose health has been secured and for what purpose.

The issue of the military framing in the AIDS and securitization discourse was addressed in a joint multidisciplinary project of the Social Science Research Council and the Cligendael Institute, the "AIDS, Security and Conflict Initiative." It set out to analyze the links between HIV/AIDS and a variety of security concerns in relation to fragile states, uniformed services, humanitarian crises and post-conflict situations (ASCI 2010: 11). Consistent with Fourie's analysis, the evidence base challenged the predictions of HIV/AIDS-related state collapse but illuminated other largely neglected challenges to the security of individuals and the spread of HIV in conflict situations shaped by historically rooted and deeply entrenched gendered and ethnicized power relations (de Waal et al. 2010: 24). As part of this project, Seckinelgin et al. (2010, 2011) carried out ethnographic field research that involved the collection of life histories amongst a broad section of the population in Burundi, a small landlocked country in the Great Lakes region of Africa that had a troubled history of protracted civil war from its independence in 1962 until 2004. The extreme racism and violent masculinity of Belgian colonization was the slate upon which sexual and structural violence in the post-independence period was written (Daley 2008). The research aimed to uncover the manner in which existing gender relations created insecurities including risk of HIV for women, how these were magnified during the conflict, and how women fared in the post-conflict reconstruction.

This small space cannot do justice to their detailed analysis. Broadly, the research uncovered how patterns of conflict articulated with existing gender orders, undermining the foundations of women's security and increasing their vulnerability to HIV infection as well as other health conditions. They describe a patrilineal and patrilocal familial structure within which girls and women were typically dependent upon their relationship to their father or husband in a legal marriage for access to a house and land to secure their livelihoods. Coupled with an absence of legal rights and protections (such as rights to own and inherit property), limited control over material resources, and a culture of compliant behavior vis-à-vis men and in-laws, women's security was bound up in existing social/familial networks (Seckinelgin et al. 2010, 2011). Underpinning the specific vulnerabilities of women were ethnicity, regional origin, age, marital, and educational status (Seckinelgin 2010: 526). The authors describe a context in which large numbers of men in military and rebel groups mobilized for long periods away from families. The conflict's duration, and the extensive mobility it created in both military and rebel camps, disrupted familial structures, undermining the security of girls and women no longer protected in patrilineages when husbands died or did not return home after a long time away. A range of survival strategies were employed by women: some became support personnel carrying out domestic tasks for the rebels or "bush wives"; some formed relationships with the brothers of their husbands to secure their continued access to resources in their husband's home; others moved in search of resources, making them vulnerable to sexual violence or transactional sex as a means of survival; while others ended up as refugees, subject to sexual violence in camps. The conflict situation was one in which sexual exploitation of women became the norm and went unpunished and access to women's bodies was instrumentalized within the military to assert hierarchical power among ranks (Seckinelgin 2011: 69). In the process of disarmament, demobilization, and reintegration (DDR) that began in December 2004, women fared poorly. Some were infected with HIV by returning husbands during the post-conflict period, the spread of the virus exacerbated by men's silence about HIV, their low participation in sensitization efforts and HIV testing, and their blaming women for bringing disease into the family. Many women were forced to leave. The reintegration of men into their communities ignored women's heightened insecurities emerging from the conflict, and women who were combatants, personnel, or "bush wives" were simply left out of the DDR process. Many women who participated in the rebellion, even involuntarily, faced stigma and were disowned by parents and forced into precarious livelihoods including begging and transactional sex, putting them at further risk of HIV in the post-reconstruction period.

Another case study by D'Errico et al. (2013) questions the dominant narratives of gender-based violence associated with high levels of conflict in the Democratic Republic of Congo (DRC) since 1996. While acknowledging the critical importance of international attention to rape in the war-torn DRC, the authors interrogate the simplistic "rape-minerals" narrative produced in the process of documenting and bringing global attention to rape. Through survey and narrative data on the social determinants of health, they reported that for Congolese women, gender-based violence and rape was central to damaging women's health, but it was not the only factor, and the single focus on rape obscured the other health insecurities that women were experiencing (D'Errico et al. 2013: 53). Western narratives created by international organizations had the effect of removing women's agency to define their own vulnerabilities and solutions to the crisis and diverted resources from other urgent determinants of health and sexual violence as defined by the women. For decades, women had been organizing in their own spaces to address their insecurities. In the context of the general breakdown of the health system during the conflict, solutions that women prioritized focused on strengthening the health care system and health care provider capacity, reducing women's barriers to access services, integrating soldiers into community life, and strengthening legal rights and livelihood options for women (D'Errico et al. 2013).

Both cases advance an argument for placing the voices of ordinary people who are living the insecurity within the understanding of the "security crisis" of HIV/AIDS. While states and economies continue to carry on during and after protracted low-intensity war, the physical and psychological trauma of sexual violence, malnutrition, and disease in the absence of basic health services and livelihood options is naturalized and normalized. They both point to the consequences of the underlying "realist" conception of health security in the construction of the securitization of HIV/AIDS. On a more general level it can be argued the initial polemic of HIV/AIDS and security was framed within a traditional paradigm that privileged military and economic interests, discursively aligning these with liberal developmental concerns that included scant concern for the actual health of affected people. While the subjects of health security are human bodies, the objects of the "health threat" to be secured are militaries, states, or economies. Policies that emerged from the securitization of AIDS skewed responses in some regions toward armed forces and away from the real security crisis of HIV/AIDS, a significant one, the crisis at the household level that is experienced largely by women who have shouldered the main care burdens and multiple impacts (O'Manique & Fourie 2010: 250). This is where a consideration of the invisibility of feminized reproductive labor is important. Research carried out in rural and urban Zimbabwe in 2005–2006 by Grant and Papart (2010) paints a similar picture to that found in previous accounts of the gendered burden of caregiving earlier in the epidemic. The broader impacts for women included physical and emotional strain and exhaustion, time poverty from home-based care and trips to hospital, time away from cultivating or wage labor, and difficulty in providing food for patients and other household members. How caregivers fared depended upon degree of illness, financial and material status, and extended family, and predictably, the poorest households shouldered the most difficult burdens. Addressing the needs of people with HIV/AIDS in their households and communities will require an understanding of the broad health requirements of those most at risk and the least resilient and placing those needs at the front and center of health priorities. A serious consideration of gender, not simply referring to male–female relations and women's status but to all whose activities are devalued as feminized, can potentially describe and specify more precisely the evidence base required if policy responses are to meet the specific needs of girls, with regard to both the exercise of their right to health and as those socially constructed as feminized, free, or cheap labor in local and global economies of care.

But a gendered health security must also address the broader context. Mirroring the security agenda of the colonial era, the security practices of many African states have their roots in a model of governance that transferred power at independence to a small elite for the purposes of population and resource control for the benefit of their security only, a model that has persisted through the Cold War and to this day with the complicity of foreign governments, and donors (Olonisakin 2011: 17–22). While women have become increasingly vocal in the security dialogue, drawing attention to the vacuum for their claims to security in both formal and informal institutions of security governance, peace settlements are products of elite bargains rather than civil society struggles, leaving the human security concerns of the population unaddressed. States Olonisakin (2011: 25):

> Women's security and justice concerns are not high on the agenda of either state or non-state security actors. Indeed, the treatment of women's security concerns in existing security arrangements, whether in the formal or informal realm is perhaps the most glaring indicator of whether or not the governance of security in any given context has been transformed.

The costs of armed conflict on the continent between 1990 and 2005 were reportedly $300 billion, with Oxfam reporting that 95% of licit and illicit arms originate from every major arms producing country in the world (Oxfam 2007). The estimated direct health costs of conflict: 50% more infant deaths, 15% more undernourished, life expectancy reduced by 5 years, 2.5 fewer doctors per patient, and 12.4% less food per person (Oxfam 2007: 6). The indirect costs include the diversion of resources from investments essential to health and well-being. The first effects of war are effects on health.

Conclusion

Competing conceptions of in/security reflect the tension between the conception of health as a security issue linked to the exercise of human rights and a broader analysis of the ideological and structural forces shaping both the governance of global health and the conditions that shape human health, and the focus on a cluster of specific issues as potential sources of instability that need to be contained in an increasingly globalized economy. Critics (cf. Anand et al. 2006; Daniels 2008; Hilts 2005) have responded to the way that health has been understood as a security issue by pointing to the silence within the dominant polemic about the structural inequalities emerging from the contemporary governance of the global economy and its role in creating new health "threats," undermining people's access to the social determinants of health and limiting access to health care and medicines. The mortality and morbidity that emerges from poverty and structural violence is not disruptive to Northern states and material interests nor does it pose a threat to the lives of the rich.

What general insights can a feminist IR lens on the securitization of HIV/AIDS provide for how we more broadly understand the relationship between security and health? It draws our attention to how human health is entwined with the conditions and contexts within which our lives unfold. It demonstrates how hierarchies of class, gender, and ethnicity shape the communities and the physical environments in which we seek to secure our health. And it illuminates how national security policies and strategies are imprinted on the body.

A holistic understanding of the conditions necessary to secure health – clean air and water, healthy food, physical security and bodily autonomy, rest and leisure, access to health knowledge, health care, and medicines – continues to evolve, but has little influence on policy perspectives and politics. The structural underpinnings of new trans-border threats to health – conflict, climate change, loss of biodiversity, the consolidation of the global industrial food industry, the unregulated nature of biotechnology – emerge from the neoliberal governance of the global economy, which takes as its security referent the interests of the wealthy and powerful. The kind of social transformation necessary to genuinely secure health will emerge from a human-centered, rather than a market-centered, security, an acknowledgement of the basic human rights and dignity of all people, and a valorization of the feminine in all of humanity.

References

AIDS, Security and Conflict Initiative (ASCI). (2010) *HIV/AIDS, Security and Conflict: New Realities, New Responses,* New York: Social Science Research Council. Online. Available HTTP: <http://www.ssrc.org/workspace/images/crm/new_publication_3/%7Be2090d2b-72a8-de11-9d32-001cc477ec70%7D.pdf> (accessed 13 May 2014).

Anand, S., Peter, F. and Sen, A. (2006) *Public Health, Ethics and Equity*, Oxford: Oxford University Press.

Bakker, I. and Gill, S. (2003) 'Ontology, method and hypotheses', in I. Bakker and S. Gill (eds.) *Power, Production and Social Reproduction,* Basingstoke: Palgrave Macmillan.

Birn, A. (2012) 'From plagues to peoples: health on the modern/global international agenda', in T. Schrecker (ed.) *Ashgate Research Companion to the Globalization of Health*, Farnham: Ashgate Publishing Ltd.: 39–59.

Braunstein, E. (2006) 'Women's work, autonomy and reproductive health: the role of trade and investment liberalization', in C. Grown, E. Braunstein and A. Malhorta (eds.) *Trading Women's Health and Rights? Trade Liberalization and Reproductive Health in Developing Countries*, London: Zed Books: 69–86.

Chapman, A. (2012) 'The contribution of a human rights approach to health', in T. Schrecker (ed.) *Ashgate Research Companion to the Globalization of Health*, Farnham: Ashgate Publishing Ltd.

Cockburn, C. (2001) 'The gendered dynamics of armed conflict and political violence', C. Moser and F. Clarke (eds.) in *Victims, Perpetrators or Actors? Gender, Armed Conflict and Political Violence*, London: Zed Books: 13–29.

Cohn, C. (ed.) (2012) *Women and Wars: Contested Histories, Uncertain Futures.* Cambridge: Polity Press.

Cohen, M.G. and Brodie, J. (2007) 'Remapping gender in the new global order', in M.G. Cohen and J. Brodie (eds.) *Remapping Gender in the New Global Order*, London and New York: Routledge: 1–12.

Daley, P.O. (2008) *Gender and Genocide in Burundi: The Search for Spaces of Peace in the Great Lakes Region*, Oxford: James Currey.

D'Errico, N., Tshibang, K., Nzigire, L.B, Maisha, F. and Kalisya, L.M. (2013) "You say rape, I say hospitals. But whose voice is louder?' Health, aid and decision-making in the Democratic Republic of Congo', *Review of African Political Economy*, 40: 51–66.

de Waal, A., Klot, J., Mahajan, M., Huber, D., Frerks, G. and M'Boup, S. (2010) *HIV/AIDS, Security and Conflict: New Realities, New Responses.* Brooklyn, NY: Social Science Research Network. Online. Available HTTP: <http://www.ssrc.org/workspace/images/crm/new_publication_3/%7Be2090d2b-72a8-de11-9d32-001cc477ec70%7D.pdf> (accessed 15 May 2014).

Daniels, N. (2008) *Just Health: Meeting Health Needs Fairly*, Cambridge: Cambridge University Press.

Gill, S. and Roberts, A. (2011) 'Macroeconomic governance, gendered inequality, and global crises', in I. Bakker, D. Elson and B. Young (eds.) *Questioning Financial Governance from a Feminist Perspective*, London and New York: Routledge: 155–172.

Glasgow, S. (2012) 'The politics of non-communicable disease policy', in T. Schrecker (ed.) *The Ashgate Research Companion to the Globalization of Health*, Farhnam: Ashgate: 61–77.

Grant, M. and Parpart, J.L. (2010) 'Gender based care for HIV/AIDS and TB patients in rural and urban Zimbabwe', *Canadian Journal of African Studies*, 4: 503–523.

Griffin, P. (2009) *Gendering the World Bank: Neoliberalism and the Gendered Foundations of Global Governance*, Basingstoke: Palgrave Macmillan.

Grown, C. (2006) 'Trade liberalization and reproductive health: understanding the linkages', in E. Braunstein, C. Grown and A. Malhorta (eds.) *Trading Women's Health and Rights? Trade Liberalization and Reproductive Health in Developing Countries*, London: Zed Books.

Hawkesworth, M.E. (2006) *Globalization and Feminist Activism*, Oxford: Rowman and Littlefield.

Hearn, J. (2010) 'Reflecting in men and social policy: contemporary critical debates and implications for social policy', *Critical Social Policy*, 30: 165–188.

Hilts, P.J. (2005) *RX for Survival: Why We Must Rise to the Global Health Challenge.* New York: Penguin.

Hoogensen, G. and Stuvøy, K. (2006) 'Gender, resistance and human security', *Security Dialogue*, 37: 207–228.

Ingram, A. (2011) 'The Pentagon's HIV/AIDS programmes: govermentality, political economy, security', *Geopolitics*, 16: 655–674.

Katz, J. (2012). *Ted Talk: Violence Against Women: It's a Men's Issue.* Online. Available HTTP: <http://www.ted.com/talks/jackson_katz_violence_against_women_it_s_a_men_s_issue.html> (accessed 15 May 2013).

Korac, M. (2006) 'Gender, conflict and peace building: Lessons from the conflict in the former Yugoslavia', *Women's Studies International Forum*, 29: 510–520.

Marchand, M.H. and Runyan, A.S. (2011) 'Introduction: feminist sightings of global restructuring: old and new conceptualizations', in M.H. Marchand and A.S. Runyan (eds.) *Gender and Global Restructuring: Sightings, Sites and Resistances*, London and New York: Routledge.

McFarlane, N. and Khong, Y.F. (2006) *Human Security and the UN: A Critical History.* Bloomington: Indiana University Press.

Moser, C. and Clark, F. (2001) *Victims, Perpetrators or Actors? Gender, Armed Conflict and Political Violence*, Basingstoke: Palgrave Macmillan.

Nowicka, W. (2011) 'Sexual and reproductive rights and the human rights agenda: controversial and contested', *Reproductive Health Matters*, 19: 119–128.

Olonisakin, F. (2011) 'Evolving narratives of security governance in Africa', in F. Olonisakin and A. Okech (eds.) *Women and Security Governance in Africa*, Cape Town: Pambazuka Press: 16–29.

O'Manique, C. and Fourie, P.P. (2010) 'Security and health in the 21st century' in M.D. Cavelty and V. Mauer (eds.) *The Routledge Handbook of Security Studies*, New York: Routledge: 243–254.

OXFAM, International Action Network on Small Arms, and Saferworld (Oxfam). (2007) *Africa's Missing Billions: International Arms Flows and the Cost of Conflict*. Online. Available HTTP: <http://www.oxfam.org/en/policy/bp107_africas_missing_billions> (accessed 4 June 2013).

Petchesky, R. (2003) *Global Prescriptions: Gendering Health and Human Rights*, London: Zed Books.

Peterson, V.S. (2003) *A Critical Re-writing of Global Political Economy: Integrating Reproductive, Productive and Virtual Economies*, New York: Routledge.

Peterson, V.S. (2012) 'Inequalities, informalization and feminist quandaries', *International Feminist Journal of Politics*, 14: 5–35.

Peterson, V.S. and Runyan, R.S. (2010) *Global Gender Issues in the New Millennium*, Philadelphia: Westview Press.

Prügl, E. (2011) 'Feminist international relations', *Politics and Gender*, 7: 111–116.

Scott-Samuel, A., Stanistreet, D. and Crawshaw, P. (2009) 'Hegemonic masculinity, structural violence and health inequalities', *Critical Public Health*, 19: 287–292.

Seckinelgin, H., Bigirumwami, J. and Morris, J. (2010) 'Securitization of HIV/AIDS in context: gendered vulnerability in Burundi', *Security Dialogue*, 41: 515–535.

Seckinelgin, H., Bigirumwami, J. and Morris, J. (2011) 'Conflict and gender and the implications of the Burundian conflict on HIV/AIDS Risks', *Conflict, Security and Development*, 11: 55–77.

Sen, G. and Ostlin, P. (2008) 'Gender inequity in health: why it exists and how we can change it', *Global Public Health*, 3: 1–12.

Sjoberg, L. (2011) 'Looking forward: conceptualizing feminist security studies' *Politics and Gender*, 7: 600–604.

Steans, J. (2006) *Gender and International Relations*, Oxford: Polity Press.

Sylvester, C. (2010) 'Tensions in feminist security studies', *Security Dialogue*, 41: 607–614.

Tickner, J.A. (2001) *Gendering World Politics: Issues and Approaches in the Post- Cold War Era*, New York: Columbia University Press.

Tickner, J.A. (2011) 'Feminist security studies: celebrating an emerging field', *Politics and Gender*, 7: 576–581.

Wilchins, R.A. (2002) 'A continuous nonverbal communication', in J. Nestle, C. Howell and R.A. Wilchins (eds.) *Genderqueer: Voices from Beyond the Sexual Binary*, Los Angeles: Alyson Books: 11.

Wolforth, W.C. (2010) 'Realism and security studies', in M.D. Cavelty and V. Mauer (eds.) *The Routledge Handbook of Security Studies*, London and New York: Routledge.

Young, B., Bakker, I. and Elson, D. (2011) 'Introduction', in B. Young, I. Bakker and D. Elson (eds.) *Questioning Financial Governance from a Feminist Perspective*, London and New York: Routledge.

5
THE POLITICS OF HEALTH SECURITY

João Nunes

Security is now a central dimension of the global governance of health. Explicit articulations of the health–security nexus can be traced back to the post-WWII period when the Constitution of the World Health Organization (WHO) presented health as a basic principle of the "security of all peoples" (Harman 2011: 20). Nonetheless, recent years have witnessed a new sense of urgency to the connection between health and security. The United States of America has a National Health Security Strategy (United States Department of Health and Human Services 2009) based upon the assumption of an "interdependent relationship between national security, homeland security, and national health security." The European Commission has its own Health Security Committee, equipped with "mechanisms and tools for Europe-wide coordination of prevention, preparedness and response to health security threats" (Commission of the European Communities 2009: 3). The WHO is now part of a Global Health Security Initiative aimed at strengthening preparedness and response to threats of biological, chemical, radio-nuclear terrorism, and pandemic influenza.

Academics have considered different aspects of the connection between health and security. Some have looked at how security (in the physical sense) is important for a healthy life (Coupland 2007). Others have argued that the occurrence of disease may impact upon social stability, national security, and international security (Price-Smith 2009). Health has also been approached as one of the core components of human security (Chen & Narasimhan 2003). An influential strand of the literature (discussed in more detail below) has considered the securitization of health issues, that is, their framing as existential threats demanding extraordinary measures. Overall, there is a growing recognition that approaching health through the prism of security changes things. Indeed, Jeremy Youde (2012: 132) argues that seeing "health threats as security problems has affected how global governance structures have responded to them and the sorts of interventions and coordinated responses planned."

In policy statements, the notion of health security is very often presented as a self-evident response to threats that are seen to be "out there" – threats demanding the allocation of resources, the redefinition of policy priorities, and, sometimes, new institutional architectures. The self-evident status of health security is also assumed by some scholarly contributions, which study the development of the health security regime without defining health security or without considering why health has been conjoined with security in the first place, what the consequences of doing so are, and whether it should be done at all. We do not know enough about the processes through which diseases are framed as problems of security – and the conditions that allow for this framing to take place. We also need to know more about the impact of health security upon the political sphere. Put differently, we need to understand how health security "is made" politically, and what it "does" to politics.

This chapter speaks to a burgeoning literature that has sought to examine the nature and implications of the health–security nexus. It starts with the observation that health security is normally presented as a natural evolutionary step that has led to a transformation in policy and governance. Going beyond this "technical" approach that sees health security mechanisms as straightforward responses to new challenges or threats, this chapter engages with more basic questions. Why has the health–security nexus gained so much traction, and why is it so often presented as self-evident? How does health security impact upon the political sphere? Could the situation be conceived otherwise?

In sum, then, this chapter looks at what is *political* about health security. This question, neglected in policy debates and in much academic literature, is deceptively simple. Engaging with it requires one to consider the conditions in which health security emerges. It also leads one to investigate the deeper political processes, challenges, and transformations that health security reveals and foregrounds, and that go well beyond resource allocation and policy prioritization. Finally, this question invites one to think of alternative, more desirable, ways of approaching health security. In line with this tripartite line of inquiry, this chapter teases out and explores three dimensions of the politics of health security: its political nature; its political impact; and its political potential.

The political nature of health security

The *Oxford English Dictionary* defines health as the "general condition of the body with respect to the efficient or inefficient discharge of functions." Disease is a "morbid physical condition" of the body, "or of some part or organ of the body, in which its functions are disturbed and deranged."[1] Health and disease are thus defined as bodily states or conditions. However, when linked to security, health and disease become something more. After all, being ill is not the same as being insecure; by conceiving disease as a threat we are implicitly bringing forth a set of assumptions about what insecurity means and what the achievement of more security would require. The health–security nexus is not a natural state of affairs (according to which diseases are threats "out there in the world") but rather a particular interpretation of physical phenomena, events, and conditions. In other words, health security is not a fact of life, but rather a process through which disease is defined as a problem – a process that involves interaction, negotiation, and sometimes struggle between actors.

It thus becomes important to recognize that, whilst disease may ultimately be a bodily condition, when conjoined with security it becomes a political assemblage of practices of problem-definition and problem-resolution – an assemblage that is supported by assumptions and perceptions, and that in turn contributes to reproducing them. This recognition allows us to explore the nature of health security in a different way: instead of seeking to identify health threats in a top-down manner, the focus is shifted to an investigation of the ideas, actions, and processes, as well as the underlying conditions (both enabling and constraining), that allow for health issues to emerge as security problems.

In this context, analysis of the securitization of health issues has become increasingly popular (Davies 2008; Elbe 2006). Indeed, securitization theory provides a very useful starting point for the analysis of the political nature of health security. As is well known, the original formulation of securitization theory holds that threats are constituted via security speech-acts that portray issues as existential threats, calling for an exceptional politics in response (Wæver 1995).

A successful securitization requires that an audience accepts securitizing processes as necessary and/or desirable. However, it is important to note that focusing merely on speech-acts is not enough. Indeed, the words "security" or "threat" need not be present for a security rationale to be in place. Moving beyond the original formulations of the so-called Copenhagen School (Buzan et al. 1998), the securitization literature has considered underlying processes and conditions that are not dependent on the explicit utterance of security or on specific securitizing intentions. Examples include the work on the management of "unease" (Bigo 2002; Huysmans & Buonfino 2008) and the notion of "macrosecuritization" (Buzan & Wæver 2009). The latter refers to an overarching securitization that structures identities and relations around a particular issue area, thus "pre-conditioning" discursive connotations and, hence, social reactions.

These theoretical developments suggest that looking at the nature on health security requires us to go beyond merely seeking and identifying overt attempts to portray health issues as security threats. Rather, acknowledging that the construction of security can work at a deeper level – and often in surreptitious ways – opens up a new line of investigation.

As Mika Aaltola (2012) has argued, today's globalized world is prone to pandemic scares. Understanding the climate of anxiety and dread that surrounds health issues requires that one looks at trends that run deeper than specific securitizing moves. Lorna Weir and Eric Mykhalovskiy (2010) have provided such an analysis by studying some of the discursive connections and practices that have been mobilized in relation to health issues in recent years. Specifically, they studied the development of an "emerging infectious disease" concept in public health knowledge from the end of the 1980s onwards. This concept was originally put forward in U.S. public health circles as a challenge to diminished funding for infectious disease control before being internationalized and taken up by the WHO (see also Weir, chapter 2 in this volume). The infectious disease paradigm emphasizes the potentially catastrophic dangers of "new" or "emerging" viruses that threaten to turn into devastating pandemics and disrupt human society as we know it. As Weir and Mykhalovskiy note, an important component of this paradigm is the idea of "emergency vigilance," that is, the focus not only on actual diseases but also on any other events that create the potential for disease. In their view, there has been a shift in public health from actual diseases to a broader, precautionary engagement with a "microbial world full of potential and surprise" (Weir and Mykhalovskiy 2010: 62), which requires the constant monitoring of phenomena that may trigger catastrophic events. This permanent watchfulness has become more pressing with the intensification of flows of people, information, and goods, which allows for constant updates about outbreaks in other parts of the world and threatens to bring these diseases very close to home in only a few hours.

When studying the origins of health security we thus need to look not only at explicit attempts to securitize disease through speech-acts but also at the linkages that are established between health and other issue areas, as well as to the connotations that are attached to health and disease. Mark W. Zacher and Tania J. Keefe (2008) have studied this process. They identify a concern with disease containment in global health governance, which has resulted in the development of surveillance systems and emergency response programs. For Zacher and Keefe, the framing of health issues as potential emergencies shapes the recent trajectory of health governance. This idea of disease as emergency renders possible and even natural a series of mechanisms of response that draw on institutions and procedures used for dealing with other security issues. It is no surprise that bioterrorism looms large in their analysis as a "bridging issue" between health security and more traditional security concerns. Other authors have followed up on the "militarization" of health governance, that is, the establishment of linkages between health issues and military threats. David P. Fidler (2005: 363) suggested that the global health security regime should be understood as a "more comprehensive governance strategy that applies to significant international threats to public health emanating from biological, chemical or radiological sources." A similar observation is made by William Aldis (2008), for whom the health security regime also results from the convergence of public health and biodefense. Aldis (2008: 373) writes:

> Taken together, the introduction of a threat protection mentality, foreign policy agendas, military interests and bioterrorism concerns into global public health, under the concept of global public health security, have subtly altered our understanding of global public health.

These accounts illustrate the processes through which diseases have come to acquire connotations of actual or potential emergency and danger. They reveal the contemporary reproduction in policymaking circles of an anxiety surrounding health – a state of alert and anticipation of the next pandemic scare. SARS, "avian flu," and "swine flu" are recent examples of how this fear-based modality for dealing with disease outbreaks has become dominant. In order to make sense of this dominance, and of the contemporary traction of these processes, it is important to take into account the underlying conditions that make them appear as possible and natural. In this context, it becomes useful to think of the politics of health security in terms of a broader social imaginary. Charles Taylor (2004: 23) has defined a social imaginary as incorporating:

> the ways people imagine their social existence, how they fit together with others, how things go on between them and their fellows, the expectations that are normally met, and the deeper normative notions and images that underlie these expectations.

For Taylor, an imaginary can be conceived as a shared set of meanings, expectations, and assumptions regarding what is natural, necessary, and legitimate in a society. Although they do not need to be translated into written norms, these meanings help to define the boundaries of political imagination – the conditions of possibility of thought and action in a given context.

Conceiving health as shaped by a fear-based imaginary helps to explain its emergence as a site of societal concern and a domain of intervention for policymakers. The contemporary emergence of health security draws on a history of meanings and connotations attached to health and disease. Specifically, health security is underpinned by a long-standing anxiety over the integrity of the political community in the face of disease cast as invasion and corruption.

The connection between disease and immigration offers a powerful illustration of the long-term political dynamics underpinning the connection between health and security. The development of contagionist views of disease, particularly from the 19th century onwards, was connected to an increasing concern with the identification and isolation of foci of infection. Disease came to be conceived as something external to communities, which is introduced by population movements. The result is an anxiety towards foreign bodies that threaten to bring infection. Immigrants are identified as risky in a process that draws on, and interacts with, other anxieties in society. Whilst studying the association between immigration and disease in the United States of America, Howard Markel (1997) argued that ideas about the health risks of immigration cannot be separated from economic concerns – the fear that immigrants will take up existing jobs, drive down wages, and constitute a burden for the public welfare system. Equally important are anxieties about the integrity of the political system. In the United States, prejudice against foreigners was often intertwined with suspicions regarding their "untoward political (e.g., anarchist, socialist, or communist) beliefs and the fear of the immigrants' collective potential somehow to taint the American political process" (Markel 1997: 9). Finally, there were fears related to the moral and social degeneracy that supposedly would be introduced by immigrants. One thus sees how the connection between immigration and disease mobilized security-related ideas about the integrity of the American self. Indeed, in a time of Cold War ideological confrontation, immigrants were identified as subversive elements that endangered the national security of the United States – security being understood not only as strategic advantage vis à vis the Soviet Union, but also in terms of the self-understanding of the United States as a society and political system.

This brief foray into the case of immigration suggests the presence of an imaginary that predates contemporary iterations of health as a security issue. It provides further proof that the nature of health security must not be taken for granted but rather conceived as the result of long-standing political processes. Health security has been "made" politically in a certain way by being enveloped with fear. What are the consequences of seeing health security in this way?

The political impact of health security

Health is an important component of the day-to-day of policymaking. For example, disease outbreaks call for the implementation of strategies of response. Sometimes, health issues are of such magnitude that states are forced to alter their priorities. Mechanisms and institutions for dealing with health issues are now an intrinsic part of the bureaucratic apparatus of most states. The policy-making impact of health is heightened when the latter is framed as a security issue. As securitization theory reminds us, framing issues as threats to security entails the establishment of a political modality for dealing with them; this modality is normally predicated upon the circumvention of democratic policy-making procedure (Buzan et al. 1998).

However, the political impact of health security can also be witnessed beyond the surface level of specific policies of response – such as inoculation campaigns or embargoes on imports. This is because "security" is not only a label attached to health, supposedly reflecting a certain reality, but also a register of meaning that helps to constitute the reality it purports to describe. As authors like Michael Dillon (1996) and Jef Huysmans (1998) have argued, security is a signifier in the sense that it not only names something but also does certain things or allows for certain things to be done. Invoking security or drawing on a security rationale allows for problems to be framed in certain ways and for certain responses to appear as natural and desirable. It thus becomes important to acknowledge the deep political work of security. The question becomes one of inquiring into the political consequences of attaching health issues to a security signifier that, as was argued above, is intimately linked with a politics of fear. What does health security, as a broader register of meaning, do to our understanding of the political?

The previous section suggested that when considering its origins, health security can be defined as an assemblage of perceptions, meanings, and practices. When it comes to scrutinizing its effects, health security can also be conceived as a political experience. This view has been advanced by Michel Foucault (1977), who suggests that diseases call for interventions that should not be seen merely as medical or therapeutic, insofar as they are also concerned with the organization of the political sphere. Foucault looked at different models of medical organization in order to chart a transformation of the nature of power in Western societies during the 18th and 19th centuries. The first example analyzed by Foucault is leprosy. Leprosy provided the opportunity for the emergence of a political problematization focused on the viability of excluding diseased elements from the healthy social body or the pure community. Some historians (Edmond 2006; Watts 1997) have questioned the idea that there was a "Great Exile" of lepers. Nonetheless, the political problem posed by leprosy remains important. Lepers represented a threat to the purity of the social body; the aim of protecting the integrity of the latter calls for the mobilization of power that seeks to establish borders and distinctions, upholding the boundaries of political community and preventing the diseased from spreading pollution. This is where leprosy emerges as a political problematic – an opportunity for a reflection on the configuration of the political sphere.

Another example considered by Foucault is the plague, a disease that requires a distinct political problematization because of its different nature. Whilst leprosy could be easily identified and contained, the plague struck entire populations very quickly and the exclusion of affected individuals did not stop the spread of the disease. For Foucault, the challenge provided by the plague thus called for a different political problematization. To begin with, the victims of plague are not simply excluded from society; rather, they need to be "placed at the centre of an administrative system to control and render calculable the scale of the disease" (McKinlay 2009: 168). Political power thus assumes the responsibility of care for the sick and for the management of disease. At the same time, the power that the plague model calls for is not one that merely exiles the sick; it is one that actively produces health. Producing a healthy population requires a form of power that is able to reach the minutiae of bodily life. The smallest details of everyday life must be observed and regulated; patterns must be identified and trends calculated; dynamics must be steered towards desirable ends. As Foucault (2007: 10) puts it:

> [t]hese plague regulations involve literally imposing a partitioning grid on the regions and towns struck by plague, with regulations indicating when people can go out, how, at what times, what they must do at home, what type of food they must have, prohibiting certain kinds of contact, requiring them to present themselves to inspectors, and to open their homes to inspectors.

As a political experience, the plague represents the utopia of a perfectly governed town: the ordering of space by opening up new streets and waterways, the partitioning of the population, the control of movements and contacts by imposing quarantines and curfews, the standardization of bodily circulation according to a desirable norm. Thus, for Foucault, more than a concrete reality – an actual epidemic affecting a given city – the plague constituted a horizon of possibility and the motivation for rulers and political theorists to envision an exhaustive kind of power.

Seeing diseases as political experiences, as Foucault does, highlights the ways in which health issues may pose problems to the configuration of the political sphere, calling for the reconfiguration of power. Indeed, ideas and practices of health can be considered as political in and of themselves. This is particularly discernible when they are conjoined with something as powerful as a security-dominated, fear-based imaginary – one that is concerned with the containment of possible threats to the integrity of a political group or community. A good example is the case of colonial medicine. Since the beginning of the European expansion in the 15th century, colonial medicine evolved as a response to the political problematic stemming from the increased contact between Westerners and non-Westerners in colonial settings. Medicine assumed the role of a boundary-drawing and boundary-maintaining device, "a fence around Europe and around the European in the tropics" (Edmond 2006: 141). More than merely re-inscribing the difference between colonizers and colonized, tropical medicine shaped it in important ways. As Rod Edmond (2006: 141) writes:

> [h]ealth and disease were an important element in this refashioned grammar of difference, and tropical medicine played a significant role in naturalizing the basis upon which difference was constructed.

Health and disease constituted the backdrop for a reconfiguration of the social and political space of the colony. The distinction between civilized and uncivilized, clean and unclean, rational and irrational, developed and backward was imbued with medical vocabularies and rationales. Medicine provided legitimacy and conceptual support for a process in which social differentiation served as a means of political control.

Colonial medicine helped to define the self-understandings of colonizers vis à vis the colonized and the territory. It informed their relative positions, the nature of their interactions and the space in which these interactions occurred. As Warwick Anderson (1992: 526) argued in relation to North American colonialism in the Philippines, the colonized "were construed as a collection of hygienically degenerate types, requiring constant surveillance, instruction, and sometimes isolation." Medicine spoke to the anxiety regarding the protection of the Western self in a "hostile" environment, with the colonized being portrayed as the major threat for the health of colonizers. More importantly, their position as potential *foci* of contamination, combined with their habits and hygiene, were seen as threats to the colonial project.

A security imaginary was thus in place as the backdrop of colonial medicine. The fear of the "native body" and the deployment of measures to ensure the colonizers' invulnerability provided the incentive and the legitimization for a transformation of the ways in which life in the colony was managed. By providing the occasion for colonial power to reassert itself, ideas and practices of health security became an intrinsic part of empire, one that contributed decisively to the expansion and consolidation of political rule in the colony.

Colonial medicine provides an illustration of how ideas and practices of health have profound political effects – effects that go well beyond the allocation of resources or policy prioritization. Importantly, the colonial medical experience still shapes the political work of health and is relevant to the analysis of contemporary global health governance. Anderson (2006) has made the case for the continuity between the intervention models of colonial medicine and the regulation of international health, especially after World War II. Indeed, it can be argued that a colonial mentality is still present in the way health is perceived and dealt with at the international level. The agenda and concerns of developed countries in the West are still privileged (McInnes & Lee 2006). This means that global health governance strategies are still geared towards the containment of those issues – namely infectious diseases – that pose a threat to the populations of richer nations. The (security-based) political work of health that assumed such an important role in the colonial period is still part of the contemporary imaginary.

The political potential of health security

This chapter has so far presented a pessimistic picture of the politics of health security. When conjoined with security, ideas and practices of health have often been shaped by an anxiety in relation to the integrity of a political group or community (such as the West or the developed world) vis à vis threats (primarily infectious diseases) that are seen as "invasions." This anxiety has resulted in a fear-based politics that mobilizes mechanisms of containment of external elements that threaten to disrupt an orderly "inside." But does this mean that health security is determined once and for all? Or is it possible to conceive health security in a different way? The identification of alternative meanings – and of alternative political possibilities deriving from these meanings – is an important dimension of the politics of health security.

In recent years, security has been identified with a dangerous logic. It is claimed that mobilizing security in public debate and policy-making entails a politics of calculability, exclusion and violence. For Dillon (1996: 130), the Western understanding of security makes "politics a matter of command; membership of a political community a matter of obedience; love synonymous with a policing order; order a function of discipline; and identity a narcissistic paranoia." Claudia Aradau (2008: 72) writes of an "exclusionary logic of security" underpinning and legitimizing "forms of domination." Mark Neocleous (2011: 186) goes as far as linking security to fascism. This logic of security can be gleaned in the portrayal of immigrants as threats to security, as well as in colonial medicine.

However, it would be essentialist to claim that security has an inescapable logic. The exclusionary and violent meanings that have been attached to security in recent years are themselves the result of social and historical processes. Moreover, they are only real inasmuch as actors believe them to be natural and act on those assumptions. This means that current ideas and practices of health security may be changed if actors start from different assumptions regarding what security is and what should be done to achieve it.

The literature provides alternative understandings of the politics of security. Some authors have argued that, rather than opening the way for an undemocratic politics, security actually makes democratic politics possible by providing individuals with the ability to make decisions and act on matters pertaining to their own lives (Booth 2007). In other words, security is not a blueprint of absolute invulnerability requiring forceful measures for its achievement but rather the alleviation of specific constraints and vulnerabilities that prevent individuals and groups from having a life with well-being and dignity.

This perspective dovetails with other views that have focused on the positive impact of security. Ian Loader and Neil Walker (2007), for example, have argued that security is an essential element of the social relations that constitute a society. For Loader and Walker (2007: 8), security is "the producer and product of forms of trust and abstract solidarity between intimates and strangers that are prerequisite to democratic political communities." The existence of a public sphere and of meaningful social bonds depends upon the existence of stable social expectations. Security, and the expectation of future security, helps to maintain the sense of commonality and publicness that is essential to society. As a result, security is "implicated in the very process of constituting the 'social' or 'the public'" (Loader & Walker 2007: 162).

In these accounts, one can see an understanding of security that is remarkably different from the one described above, in which security was paradoxically fuelled by an ever-present anxiety. Here, security is conceived as a condition characterized by the absence of anxiety, the predictability of expectations and a degree of individual control over one's own surroundings. On the basis of this understanding, it is possible to begin to reconsider the connection between security and health. Specifically, one can begin to recognize the positive effects that ideas and practices of health security can have on the political realm.

For example, the "health as a bridge for peace" literature has investigated the role that health initiatives and health professionals can play in situations of conflict or post-conflict reconstruction. The main theme of this literature has been the question of whether health can be considered a factor in pacification, political reconciliation, or avoidance of conflict. The idea that health can be a bridge for peace began to be espoused in an explicit manner during the 1980s (Beigbeder 1998; Garber 2002). The underlying rationale was that health constituted a superordinate goal – that is, one that transcends political and ethnic divisions – and that cooperation in the field of health could in turn promote solidarity and further dialogue.

In this context, Graeme MacQueen and Joanna Santa Barbara (2000) have distinguished five main mechanisms through which health may contribute to peace. The first is conflict management: conflicts can be "resolved, lessened or contained through the use of 'medical diplomacy' or health oriented superordinate goals" (MacQueen & Santa Barbara 2000: 294). Second, health may contribute to peace because of the solidarity of health workers to people and groups that are themselves involved in peacebuilding. Next, the delivery of healthcare can contribute to transcending social differences, thus rebuilding or strengthening the social fabric. The fourth way in which health can contribute to peace is by dissent, that is, by encouraging views that depart from the prevailing ones. Health knowledge and provision can provide the expertise or legitimacy with which people express their disagreement or seek to redefine a situation. The final contribution of health to peace is the possibility of reducing the destructiveness of war: the expertise and legitimacy of health workers can contribute to the restriction or abolition of policies or weapons that are particularly destructive.

Simon Rushton (2005) has offered a more cautious reflection on the peace-impact of health. He argues that health-sector initiatives can only by effective when they are "part of a broader agenda encompassing democracy, good governance, the availability of the necessary financial resources . . . and the infrastructure to deliver improvements in services on the ground' (Rushton 2005: 451–452). The potential that health holds for long-term change thus resides in its ability to strengthen the social contract and to interact with other developments in the social and economic sphere.

Important lessons can be drawn from this discussion. Whilst it is true that ideas and practices of health security have impacted upon the social and political sphere in problematic ways, this is not inescapable. Rather, the present nature and implications of health security are underpinned by a certain set of assumptions and practices. They are political and, therefore, contingent and open to contestation. Health security has no inherent logic and it is thus possible to conceive it outside the register of fear. An alternative understanding of security – for example, one based on the emancipatory and democratic effects of security – may well yield new ideas and practices of global health governance. The idea of "health as a bridge for peace" serves as a reminder that the politics of health security is not predetermined.

Conclusion

This chapter began with the observation that being ill is not the same as being insecure. It investigated the different political dimensions of health security, with the objective of showing how health insecurity is different from disease. It was argued that health security is a political category: it emerges out of political assumptions and processes; it has political consequences that go well beyond the surface level of policymaking; and it is fundamentally open to contestation and change.

When looking at global health governance, it is crucial to consider these facets of the politics of health security. They help us to understand how the governance of health came to be understood and practiced in this way: the connotations that surround health issues, the assumptions that underlie current practices, how these have evolved, and how they are reproduced. The political dimensions of health security also help us to gauge the impact of doing health governance like this: what it does to political community, to the relations between groups, countries, and regions. Knowing how health security has been "made" and what it "does" politically also allows for the identification of alternative views, as well as sites where transformative practices can be deployed.

Put differently, a better understanding of these political dimensions may well be the first step towards a new vision of health security. Such a vision should start from an acknowledgment of real situations of health insecurity: the structures and relations that lead to an unequal provision of, and access to, affordable health care, and to situations of systematic harm and vulnerability to disease. Achieving more health security is not merely about providing health care when people fall ill. Ultimately, striving for more health security entails transforming the global relations and structures that are at the heart of the systematic production of ill health. This is not the same as saying that we should seek total immunity or invulnerability to disease but rather that it is possible to be more secure, in the sense of being able to deal with disease and to take meaningful decisions and actions when it occurs.

Note

1 Entries "health" and "disease" in the *Oxford English Dictionary*. Online. Available HTTP: <http://www.oed.com> (accessed 3 May 2013).

References

Aaltola, M. (2012) *Understanding the Politics of Pandemic Scares: An Introduction to Global Politosomatics*, London and New York: Routledge.

Aldis, W. (2008) 'Health security as a public health concept: a critical analysis', *Health Policy and Planning*, 23: 369–375.

Anderson, W. (1992) "Where every prospect pleases and only man is vile': laboratory medicine as colonial discourse', *Critical Inquiry*, 18: 506–529.

Anderson, W. (2006) *Colonial Pathologies: American Tropical Medicine, Race, and Hygiene in the Philippines*, Durham and London: Duke University Press.

Aradau, C. (2008) *Rethinking Trafficking in Women: Politics out of Security*, Houndmills: Palgrave Macmillan.

Beigbeder, Y. (1998) 'The World Health Organization and peacekeeping', *International Peacekeeping*, 5: 31–48.

Bigo, D. (2002) 'Security and immigration: towards a critique of the governmentality of unease', *Alternatives*, 27: 63–92.

Booth, K. (2007) *Theory of World Security*, Cambridge: Cambridge University Press.

Buzan, B. and Wæver, O. (2009) 'Macrosecuritisation and security constellations: reconsidering scale in securitisation theory', *Review of International Studies*, 35: 253–276.

Buzan, B., Wæver, O. and de Wilde, J. (1998) *Security: A New Framework for Analysis*, Boulder, CO and London: Lynne Rienner Publishers.

Chen, L. and Narasimhan, V. (2003) 'Human security and global health', *Journal of Human Development and Capabilities*, 4: 181–190.

Commission of the European Communities. (2009) *Health Security in the European Union and Internationally*, Brussels: Commission of the European Communities.

Coupland, R. (2007) 'Security, insecurity and health', *Bulletin of the World Health Organization*, 85: 181–184.

Davies, S.E. (2008) 'Securitizing infectious disease', *International Affairs*, 84: 295–313.

Dillon, M. (1996) *Politics of Security: Towards a Political Philosophy of Continental Thought*, London and New York: Routledge.

Edmond, R. (2006) *Leprosy and Empire: A Medical and Cultural History*, Cambridge: Cambridge University Press.

Elbe, S. (2006) 'Should HIV/AIDS be securitized? The ethical dilemmas of linking HIV/AIDS and security', *International Studies Quarterly*, 50:119–144.

Fidler, D.P. (2005) 'From International Sanitary Conventions to global health security: the new International Health Regulations', *Chinese Journal of International Law*, 4: 325–392.

Foucault, M. (1977) *Discipline and Punish: The Birth of the Prison*, trans. A. Sheridan, London: Allen Lane.

Foucault, M. (2007) *Security, Territory, Population: Lectures at the Collège de France, 1977–1978*, trans. G. Burchell, New York: Palgrave Macmillan.

Garber, R. (2002) 'Health as a bridge for peace: theory, practice, and prognosis – reflections of a practitioner', *Journal of Peacebuilding and Development*, 1: 69–84.

Harman, S. (2011) *Global Health Governance*, Abingdon: Routledge.

Huysmans, J. (1998) 'Security! What do you mean? From concept to thick signifier', *European Journal of International Relations*, 4: 226–255.

Huysmans, J. and Buonfino, A. (2008) 'Politics of exception and unease: immigration, asylum, and terrorism in parliamentary debates in the U.K.', *Political Studies*, 56: 766–788.

Loader, I. and Walker, N. (2007) *Civilizing Security*, Cambridge: Cambridge University Press.

MacQueen, G. and Santa Barbara, J. (2000) 'Peace building through health initiatives', *British Medical Journal*, 321: 293–296.

Markel, H. (1997) *Quarantine!: East European Jewish Immigrants and the New York City Epidemics of 1892*, Baltimore and London: The Johns Hopkins University Press.

McInnes, C. and Lee, K. (2006) 'Health, security, and foreign policy', *Review of International Studies*, 32: 5–23.

McKinlay, A. (2009) 'Foucault, plague, Defoe', *Culture and Organization*, 15: 167–184.

Neocleous, M. (2011) 'Inhuman security', in D. Chandler and N. Hynek (eds.) *Critical Perspectives on Human Security: Rethinking Emancipation and Power in International Relations*, London and New York: Routledge.

Oxford English Dictionary. (2010) Oxford: Oxford University Press.

Price-Smith, A.T. (2009) *Contagion and Chaos: Disease, Ecology, and National Security in the Era of Globalization*, Cambridge, MA: The MIT Press.

Rushton, S. (2005) 'Health and peacebuilding: resuscitating the failed state in Sierra Leone', *International Relations*, 19: 441–456.

Taylor, C. (2004) *Modern Social Imaginaries*, Durham: Duke University Press.

United States Department of Health and Human Services. (2009) *National Health Security Strategy of the United States of America*, Washington, DC: United States Department of Health and Human Services.

Wæver, O. (1995) 'Securitisation and desecuritisation', in R.D. Lipschutz (ed.) *On Security*, New York: Columbia University Press.

Watts, S. (1997) *Epidemics and History: Disease, Power and Imperialism*, New Haven and London: Yale University Press.

Weir, L. and Mykhalovskiy, E. (2010) *Global Public Health Vigilance: Creating a World on Alert*, Abingdon: Routledge.

Youde, J. (2012) *Global Health Governance*, Cambridge: Polity Press.

Zacher, M.W. and Keefe, T.J. (2008) *The Politics of Global Health Governance: United by Contagion*, Houndmills: Palgrave Macmillan.

6

THE MEDICALIZATION OF INSECURITY

Stefan Elbe & Nadine Voelkner

As the contributions to this volume demonstrate, the notion of "health security" is increasingly shaping the formulation and implementation of international health policy (Bell 2012; Davies 2008, 2010; Weir & Mykhalovskiy 2010). This "securitization" of health has given rise to a growing number of studies drawing upon securitization theory (Buzan et al. 1998) in order to analyze the act of labeling health issues as security threats and to further trace how this security framing shapes their contemporary governance. David Fidler has even suggested that global health governance has entered a "post-securitization" phase, in the sense that it is now widely taken for granted that health issues constitute a security problem (2007:41). Whilst much of the security studies literature on health security has so far righty focused on the dynamics of securitization, the rise of health security should be seen as a more complex social phenomenon – and one that cannot be reduced solely to the latest example of securitization in world politics. From a sociological point of view, this chapter suggests, the rise of health security also represents a critical instance of "medicalization" insofar as the discourse of health security is a site where the social forces of medicine are further expanding and intensifying in international politics – to the point that they are now also beginning to shape a range of security discourses and practices. This chapter therefore advances an alternative reading of the rise of health security as marking what we might call the "medicalization of insecurity." It traces, in other words, the process through which the problem of security in global politics is itself coming to be partially framed and treated broadly as a medical problem through ongoing efforts to strengthen health security.

The notion of medicalization first appeared in the 1960s when sociologists began analyzing the increasing tendency in American society to view deviant behavior in terms of "sickness" rather than "badness." Since then, the concept of medicalization has been adopted in a variety of other disciplines including anthropology and history examining a wide range of processes of medicalization through which social issues become framed as medical problems and treated through medical frameworks. In these works, medicalization has been shown to consist of three elements. First, it is a process through which nonmedical problems become redefined and treated as illnesses or disorders. According to a leading scholar, Peter Conrad, the crux of medicalization lies precisely in this process of definition: "the key to medicalization is the definitional issue. Medicalization consists of defining a problem in medical terms, using medical language to describe a problem, adopting a medical framework to understand a problem, or using a medical intervention to 'treat' it" (1992: 211).

Second, the process of medicalization involves an increased social influence and standing of the medical professions, elevating medicine to the status of a powerful social institution. According to Irving Zola "medicine is becoming a major institution of social control, nudging aside, if not incorporating, the more traditional institutions of religion and law. It is becoming the new repository of truth, the place where absolute and often final judgements are made by supposedly morally neutral and objective experts" (1972: 487). One of the consequences of medicalization, therefore, is that doctors and medical professionals are asked to address a growing number and range of issues that have become redefined as medical.

Third, and an element less appreciated in the general medicalization literature, scholars influenced by Michel Foucault's genealogical studies of medicine argue that medicalization also involves the adoption of a variety of strategies of disease management common in modern medicine to wider issues of public health. This has been referred to as "social" medicine where measures are aimed not just at the individual patient but also at the general population. As Foucault pointed out in relation to the European context, the rise of private medical practices in the eighteenth century "cannot be divorced from the concurrent organization of a politics of health." In fact, "'private' and 'socialized' medicine, in their reciprocal support and opposition, both derive from a common global strategy" (2000: 91). Put differently, modern medicine is a double-sided phenomenon incorporating measures aimed at both the individual and the population as a whole.

Crucially, medicine is understood here not just as a set of complex technical procedures but as a broad system of knowledge used to understand and experience our bodies. Medical discourses and practices are thus seen to shape the very understanding of who we are, and how our lives ought to be lived. As Nikolas Rose has suggested in this regard:

> we relate to ourselves and others, individually and collectively, through an ethic and in a form of life that is inextricably associated with medicine in all its incarnations. In this sense, medicine has done much more than define, diagnose and treat diseases – it has helped make us the kinds of living creatures that we have become at the start of the 21st century.
>
> (Rose 2007: 701)

Modern individuals today understand themselves and their existence through a range of medical categories, effectively rendering medicine a social practice.

By way of extension, we can see how ongoing efforts to strengthen global health security similarly begin to infuse the domains of national and international security policy much more deeply with medical modes of thinking and acting. Just as securitization theory directs one to think about the effects of securitizing international health issues, so too medicalization theory encourages reflection on how practices of security are changing as a result of their growing association with pressing international diseases.

In line with other medicalization processes, at least three such changes to the understanding and practice of security can be identified. First, we can trace how – definitionally – health security discourses are subtly reshaping our understanding of insecurity in world politics in a way that broadens and expands its boundaries to include a number of disease-based threats. Second, we can analyze how health security discourses are leading to a greater role for medical professionals in the discussions and decision making of global security policy, representing a further overall enhancement in the societal role and influence of a range of medical professionals. Third, we can examine how health security discourses are even transforming the way security is practiced: rather than just forming military forces and accumulating weapons as has traditionally been the principal way of security professionals, security practice now also comes to involve a growing number of "medical countermeasures" – including developing, procuring, and stockpiling medical equipment and new pharmacological products.

Collectively, these three transformations to the practice of security constitute what we might call the "medicalization of insecurity" (Elbe 2010) – raising new questions about the close association between health and security. How, for example, are medical knowledge and practices shaping the practice of military intervention and security more broadly? What kinds of pharmacological interventions are being developed to enhance the capacity of soldiers in combat and to protect populations against a range of deliberately released or naturally occurring biological threats? What, moreover, is the role of political economy in the emergence of health security? And to what extent does the medicalization of insecurity also give rise to new security fears?

Insecurity as a medical problem

Ongoing efforts to strengthen health security encourage a subtle change to our understanding of insecurity in global politics. Previously considered largely a nonmedical issue (with the possible exception of military medicine), insecurity is becoming understood more broadly as being linked to problems of health and disease and becoming partially redefined as broadly a medical problem requiring medical expertise and interventions. With the rise of health security, insecurity is no longer understood as originating predominantly from the military capabilities and hostile political intentions of other states. Rather, a disease itself can also be understood as a source of insecurity. In fact, insecurity can now be caused by a range of medical conditions presenting in the population such as a rapidly emerging lethal infectious diseases like H5N1 influenza, a disease intentionally unleashed by terrorists such as anthrax, a disease that is already endemic in many developing countries like malaria or tuberculosis, or even a new lifestyle disease such as obesity that is taking on epidemic proportions. Crucially, by presenting the cause of these securitized issues as the underlying physiological processes and dysfunctions of a population, insecurity in global politics comes to be understood as partly arising from medical problems presenting within the bodies of citizens. Simply put, insecurity comes to be seen as a "disorder" caused by disease. In this way, health security discourses are subtly altering our understanding of security and insecurity in global politics by providing them with a more explicit medical dimension.

This transformation can be seen across a range of contemporary health security discourses. For one, health security discussions about the threat posed by pandemic infectious diseases construe a range of infectious diseases as threats to national security. Here, insecurity is no longer seen as being a quintessentially military and political problem but seen to stem from the proliferation of medical conditions brought about by the rapid spread of potentially lethal infectious diseases within the population. One of the most significant contributing factors for this microbial anxiety is the substantial expansion of civilian air travel around the world in recent history. The growth in air travel compresses both space and time in a way that makes many Western governments feel more vulnerable to the spread of infectious diseases. Air travel reduces the significance of geographical space in that it creates connections between places, populations, and microbes that would previously only rarely, if ever, come into direct physical contact with one another because they are located in different countries or continents. Aircraft thus generate what is an increasingly global epidemiological space, making even geographically distant infectious diseases a matter of concern. Examples of this have been the concerns with the international spread of HIV/AIDS and SARS.

Indeed, HIV/AIDS became the first infectious disease to be singled out in the 21st century as representing more than just an important international public health or development problem. The AIDS pandemic was also considered a threat to national security because it could threaten vital organs of the state, such as the military, and in the worst-case scenario might even cause some states to collapse. This relates to U.S. government estimates that pointed to staggering levels of HIV prevalence in some African armed forces in 1999. Though since contested and disputed, these figures were widely cited at the time and formed one of the core arguments for establishing that national security could be threatened by the spread of a new infectious disease. Additionally, the spread of HIV/AIDS was claimed to further threaten national security by the possible longer term ramifications for social and political stability that it could have in the worst-affected countries. Notwithstanding persisting concerns with the accuracy of claims about the link between AIDS and national security, these arguments were widely accepted for several years. They created a crucial precedent by establishing that the national security of a country could be threatened by the spread of a new and lethal infectious disease.

The experience of SARS advanced the scope of the medical redefinition of insecurity beyond where the AIDS pandemic had initially taken it. It showed that an infectious disease other than HIV/AIDS could also threaten national security. It also demonstrated that those threats were relevant beyond the African continent, and certainly beyond the borders of developing countries with comparatively weak public health infrastructures. SARS is believed to have emerged in Guangdong province in China in 2002. In early 2003, a local Chinese doctor by the name of Dr. Liu Jianlun travelled from Guangdong province to Hong Kong. He stayed in the Metropole Hotel, spreading the infection to other guests residing in the same hotel. Dr. Jianlun would later become identified by public health officials as a "super-spreader," in that those who became infected by him subsequently traveled as far as Singapore, Vietnam, Ireland, Canada, and the United States. The World Health Organization ultimately attributed more than 4,000 worldwide cases of SARS to this doctor alone. If one person's fate exemplifies the links between infectious diseases and security in the era of international tourism and air travel, it is his. The national security threat posed by infectious disease thus emerged as a geographically much wider – if not planetary – phenomenon. The case of SARS established that lethal infectious diseases presenting in the population could threaten a country's national security, solely by virtue of the mortality and serious economic disruptions they cause. In this way, the concern over SARS gave the medicalization of insecurity greater scope in that it now became possible legitimately to view any infectious disease with the potential to cause significant mortality and economic damage as a national security threat.

In these national security discussions, then, the meaning of insecurity in global politics begins to undergo a subtle but significant change. And this subtle process of redefinition is not restricted to pandemic preparedness; it also occurs in discussions about biosecurity and about human security concerns with improving health in developing countries. Biosecurity discussions, for example, focus on the possibility of an infectious disease being intentionally released for hostile political purposes. Within this context, the so-called War on Terror is being fought not only through recourse to military force but also through the development of new vaccines and pharmacological treatments to counter the effects of the security threat of a biological attack. In this way, biosecurity discussions too construe and redefine insecurity as a medical problem caused by the rapid and unexpected onset of a lethal disease within the population. Similarly, human security activities devoted to global health focus on endemic diseases in developing countries, reminding us that these diseases have a plethora of wider social, political, and economic ramifications that can adversely affect other dimensions of human security too. Through these processes, medicine begins to define not only who the population is and how human beings relate to one another; it is also shaping assessments of whether or not human existence is considered secure.

To be clear, this reference to the "medicalization" of security is not meant to imply that the medical redefinition of insecurity in global politics is total and complete. Traditional conceptions of insecurity certainly continue to be highly influential in international relations. There remains a formidable concern about military developments across the globe, and war continues to be a perennial activity in the international system. Yet it is a well-documented characteristic of medicalization processes more generally that they usually come in different degrees and are frequently partial – especially when important social phenomena are simultaneously handled through competing frameworks. Insecurity is a case in point. Here is a broader social issue that has not been completely medicalized in all of its manifestations, but there are at least four significant sites in international relations where insecurity is becoming redefined as a medical problem caused by the onset of disease. First, a redefinition of security can be traced in the debate about the threat that pandemics pose to national security. Second, it can be located in the debate about biosecurity and the weaponization of disease such as in the case of bioterrorism. Third, it can be found in the debate about the endemic threat to the human security of populations in developing countries. Finally, it can be traced to the debate about smoking, fat, and alcohol as lifestyle "timebombs." At a broader level, then, how we think about security has begun to change and has expanded to include a range of medical conditions and threats.

Medical security professionals

Efforts to strengthen health security also involve changes to *who* practices security. Indeed, the rise of health security has been accompanied by a further increase in the social influence and status of a wide range of medical experts in deliberations about – and the provision of – security. That is part of a wider social process of medicalization that is seeing medicine emerge as an increasingly powerful sociopolitical institution in global politics. As sociologists have shown, that wider process of medicalization can be driven directly by medical professionals themselves or by social groups other than those directly involved in clinical settings. Indeed, medicalization is "a broad definitional process, which may or may not directly include physicians" (Cornwell 1984, cited in Conrad 1992: 211).

Yet even more important from the medicalization perspective is the overall social and political effect that such processes of medical redefinition have. In the context of health security, the effect has been to increase the social jurisdiction of a range of medical professionals working in both clinical and wider settings. The rise of health security adds the analysis and provision of security to the long list of social activities that a broad range of different medical professionals are seen to be legitimately engaged in today.

For one, medical and health professionals are becoming more closely involved in the analysis and formulation of security policy with the result that their social jurisdiction is rising. That expansion in the social influence and jurisdiction of doctors and physicians echoes many earlier medicalization processes. For example, medical professionals with a variety of expertise in clinical practice, epidemiology and microbiology increasingly form part of the new health security programs established over the past decade by influential policy and security think tanks. In the United States, they include the Global Health Program at the Council on Foreign Relations in New York; the HIV/AIDS Task Force and the Global Health Policy Center at the Center for Strategic and International Studies in Washington, DC, and both the Global Health Center and the Center for Domestic and International Health Security at the RAND Corporation in Arlington, VA. In the United Kingdom, it also includes the Centre on Global Health Security housed at the Royal Institute of International Affairs in London (Chatham House). These programs analyze the ways in which infectious disease, and other global health issues, impact upon security and foreign policy. Many of the programs are run by, or at least rely upon the close involvement of, people trained in the medical and related professions. They thus mark one area where the societal jurisdiction of medical professionals is expanding through their more intimate involvement in discussions of security and foreign policy.

Responding to the threat of bioterrorism similarly required opening up a domestic medical "front" in the War on Terror. That medical front is made up, on the one hand, of terrorists potentially weaponizing a range of infectious diseases. On the other hand, it consists of sustained efforts by a range of biomedical researchers and institutions to rapidly develop new medical countermeasures to protect their populations against possible attacks. This inevitably requires the greater involvement of a swath of different medical professionals. For example, biomedical experts and researchers need to become involved in mapping out how doctors and hospitals will respond in the event of an attack and how to liaise with the relevant government authorities. Public health experts, in turn, will also be required for designing and running surveillance systems that would detect the release of those agents within the proximity of human populations. Biosecurity concerns about biological weapons too, therefore, encourage a further augmentation in the societal jurisdiction of a broad array of medical professionals by involving them much more closely in biodefense and biosecurity policy.

In fact, the push for health security has prompted the establishment of entire new organizations and emergency response initiatives dealing with the threat of infectious diseases. In 2005, following the realization that the European Union was ill-prepared to deal with emerging infectious diseases in the region, the European Centre for Disease Prevention and Control (ECDC) was created in Stockholm. This center carries out disease surveillance on behalf of EU member states. The ECDC is mandated to identify, assess, and communicate existing, as well as emerging, threats to human health. That also makes the ECDC an important example of a new regional health organization created partially in response to the growing concern about the threat posed by infectious diseases. The UN itself established the Global Outbreak Alert and Response Network (GOARN) in 2000 in which member states agree to pool some of their resources at the international level, to be able to mount a rapid and effective response to the outbreak of a new infectious disease irrespective of where it first emerges. GOARN helps to respond to over 50 outbreaks of disease annually such as cholera, meningitis, yellow fever, plague, Ebola, etc. It serves to minimize the international spread of dangerous microbes. For example, it helped to detect the SARS outbreak, but also showed that this disease was spreading beyond Asia, and linked scientists and laboratories around the world as they sought to detect the causative agents and transmission patterns of SARS.

The rise of health security and the imperative to manage disease is also leading to the growing influence of other professions involved in a wide range of institutions outside of a hospital or clinical setting. That extended list of actors includes public health institutions such as the Centers for Disease Control and Prevention in the United States, various national health ministries around the world, international initiatives like the Global Health Security Initiative, and intergovernmental institutions such as the World Health Organization as mentioned earlier. But it also includes nongovernmental organizations such as Médecins Sans Frontières and philanthropic institutions devoted to global health like the Gates Foundation. So far these wider groups have received far less attention in the existing literature on medicalization because the latter has tended to focus on the "private" arm of medicine and the doctor–patient relationship. Yet these too represent important "medical" actors in the broader sense of being similarly engaged in the modern prevention and treatment of disease. They are the institutions of what Foucault earlier referred to as "social" medicine. The fact that their social and political role is also enhanced by the rise of health security constitutes additional evidence of how health security discussions are today extending the social jurisdiction of a wide range of different medical professionals.

In the United States, for example, fears of infectious disease "outbreaks" in the context of globalization led to the creation of a new post of Senior Advisor for International Health, sitting at the National Security Council under the Clinton administration. In a different way, human security discourses around HIV/AIDS similarly commanded the presence of the Executive Director of UNAIDS in New York to extensively brief the United Nations Security Council when drafting its resolution on the threat HIV/AIDS poses to international peace and security in Africa. Indeed, the broader human security concern with global health has triggered an explosion in the number of new governmental and nongovernmental initiatives devoted to endemic diseases in the global South. Many of these are aimed at procuring new kinds of medical interventions and distributing them to people living in developing countries. The Global Alliance for Vaccines and Immunization (GAVI), launched in 2000, is a prominent case in point. As an international public–private health partnership, GAVI focuses on HIV/AIDS, tuberculosis, and malaria, as well as a range of other diseases in the developing world. The Geneva-based alliance consists of governments, research institutes, international organizations (including WHO, UNICEF, the World Bank), and nongovernmental organizations and the vaccine industry in both developed and developing countries. Whilst many health professionals also express considerable reservations about linking their work with security, health security discourses have already opened up this additional – and some would say paramount – domain of politics to the increased influence of a variety of medical experts and knowledges.

Medical countermeasures

The rise of health security is also changing *how* security is practiced – as enhancing the security of populations against the new sources of insecurity entails recourse to an extensive range of medical interventions. The quest for health security thus broadens the range of instruments for security policy to include a growing number of pharmaceutical interventions – or what the literature now refers to as "medical countermeasures" (see also Hoyt, chapter 18 in this volume). Here, health security debates expand the available arsenal of security policy and strategy to include not just the amassing of military capabilities but also the development, procurement, and stockpiling of medical equipment and new pharmacological products. The medical countermeasures range from new antiviral medications, antibiotics, and medical equipment through to various medicines for treating HIV/AIDS, malaria, and tuberculosis. The tendency of modern medicine to prescribe a "pill for every ill" – so widely noted in the existing medicalization literature – is also at play in health security debates. Perhaps this multifaceted tendency is best exemplified by the manner in which many governments have sought to proactively acquire and stockpile billions of pills of antiviral medications such as Tamiflu for their populations (as well as other medications and pandemic vaccines). Within the context of health security, pills and other pharmaceutical interventions have become crucial policy instruments for strengthening national, international, and human security. This has expanded the range of options in the toolkit of security policy and opened up new avenues for medical intervention in the pursuit of security.

Yet, other types of medical intervention simultaneously pursued by the "social" arm of modern medicine at the population level must be noted here too. Vaccines in particular continue to be particularly important medical interventions that repeatedly surface in a variety of different health security deliberations. The World Health Organization points out that "vaccines are among the most important medical interventions for reducing illness and deaths" available today (WHO 2009). Whereas pills and other therapies mark the tools of clinical medicine, vaccines play a crucial part in the arsenal of "social" medicine and public health. Developing and rolling out new vaccines against a range of current (and future) diseases therefore represents further evidence of how the rise of health security is also encouraging security to be practiced through the introduction of new medical interventions in society.

For example, the pandemic preparedness plans drawn up by governments are multifaceted and often contain a range of wider public health measures in the event of a new pandemic. Yet for most governments the crucial means of securing their populations against the threat of infectious diseases remains the stockpiling of medical interventions like vaccines and treatments. The international response to the security threat posed by HIV/AIDS already foreshadowed this move, with antiretroviral programs being initiated in the armed forces, and later rolled out more generally to civilian populations in Africa through unprecedented initiatives such as the U.S. President's Emergency Plan for AIDS relief (PEPFAR). That medical response model was subsequently also adopted in the development of domestic pandemic preparedness in many Western countries. This focus on developing pharmacological countermeasures became even more important when, in 2006, the U.S. Congress adopted the Pandemic and All-Hazards Preparedness Act. That Act established the Biomedical Advanced Research and Development Agency and tasked it with developing and acquiring new medical "countermeasures" to protect the population against pandemic threats (as well as bioterror threats).

Emphasis on medical interventions has also been evident in the ways in which governments have been responding to the specific threat of avian influenza (H5N1). Governments with the requisite resources have been encouraging companies to rapidly develop and produce new vaccines and antivirals to reduce the spread and impact of a potential human H5N1 (or other highly pathogenic) pandemic. Since concern about H5N1 first emerged, manufacturers have effectively been in a race to develop a new H5N1 vaccine. Recognizing the widespread desire for vaccines amongst many governments around the world, the World Health Organization in turn issued its Global Pandemic Influenza Action Plan to Increase Vaccine Supply in 2006 and has been working with vaccine manufacturers to create a global stockpile of vaccine for the H5N1 influenza virus since 2007. Several pharmaceutical companies have contributed to such a stockpile, whilst the United States government has also donated millions of doses. This push for a stockpile shows just how widespread and pervasive the desire to have access to such medical interventions has become amongst many governments – even beyond wealthy Western states.

Human security concerns with global health encompass not just major outbreak events but also those diseases that are causing significant morbidity and mortality on a daily basis around the world. That lengthens the list of diseases that can be considered as security threats further still. Indeed, human security has given rise to a virtual explosion in the range of new governmental and nongovernmental initiatives devoted to endemic diseases. Many of the human security initiatives are geared towards procuring new kinds of medical interventions and distributing them to people living in developing countries. A case in point is the already mentioned Global Alliance for Vaccines and Immunization (GAVI). In fact, there are now a wide range of other organizations devoted to specific diseases that are similarly trying to develop new vaccines and treatments or making existing ones more widely available around the world. To varying degrees, all of the initiatives place a strong emphasis on eradicating or minimizing human insecurities through better, newer, or cheaper medical interventions, like vaccines and other medical treatments. Human security will only be achieved by greater recourse to medical interventions. In all of these different ways, health security discourses end up creating social and political pressure to develop a range of medical interventions – both at the individual and population level – in order to enhance the security of populations.

Conclusion

How does our thinking about health security begin to change when approached from the perspective of medicalization – rather than just securitization? One of the most significant consequences of the medicalization of insecurity outlined above is that it renders the provision of security increasingly somatic. With the rise of health security, in other words, security begins to function by intervening medically in the inner workings of the human organism. Health security thus takes the provision of security beyond distant warzones and also brings it to bear directly on – and indeed inside – the human body. Efforts to enhance health security thus render the inner biological processes of our bodies – metaphorically and materially – new "battlefields" of security policy.

A poignant example of this occurred between 2009 and 2010 in the UK, where protecting the population against pandemic threats involved the creation of the National Pandemic Flu Service. This service oversaw the distribution of over one million treatment courses of Tamiflu to the UK population. It remains one of the most spectacular examples in recent history where government policy for securing the nation required the collective mass ingestion of a pharmaceutical substance. Nor is the story of Tamiflu simply an isolated case. Within the domain of bioterrorism, the primary focus of the multibillion dollar Project BioShield, in the United States, has similarly been to develop a range of new "medical countermeasures" and to amass them in the Strategic National Stockpile so that they can be rapidly deployed in the event of an attack. Before that, international and human security debates about HIV/AIDS also saw the mass delivery of millions of antiretroviral therapies to people living in sub-Saharan Africa and other developing countries. Nor will this tendency disappear anytime soon, as current anxieties about a range of noncommunicable lifestyle "time bombs" are also increasingly managed by resorting to surgeries and pills (obesity), as well as nicotine replacement therapy (smoking). In the end, the medicalization of insecurity demands of citizens that in order to be secure, one must first become a patient.

Finally, the medicalization perspective also raises a range of new questions about the rise of health security. How, for example, are medical knowledges and metaphors shaping the practice of military intervention and counterinsurgency practice? What new medicines are being developed to make soldiers less fearful in combat or to tire less quickly? What, moreover, are the legal and political strategies through which citizens are persuaded to consume medical countermeasures? Why and how are these new political rationalities resisted? How does this medicalization of insecurity also create new anxieties, especially around the emergence of diseases for which there are no drugs, or indeed around diseases that are becoming drug resistant? These are some of the new lines of inquiry emerging from the medicalization perspective on health security.

References

Bell, C. (2012) 'Hybrid warfare and its metaphors', *Humanity: An International Journal of Human Rights, Humanitarianism and Development*, 3: 225–247.

Buzan, B., Waever, O. and De Wilde, J. (1998) *Security: A New Framework for Analysis*, Boulder and London: Lynne Rienner.

Conrad, P. (1992) 'Medicalization and social control', *Annual Review of Sociology*, 18: 209–232.

Davies, S. (2008) 'Securitizing infectious disease', *International Affairs*, 84: 295–313.

Davies, S. (2010) *Global Politics of Health*, Cambridge: Polity Press.

Elbe, S. (2010) *Security and Global Health: Towards the Medicalization of Security*, Cambridge and Malden: Polity.

Fidler, D. (2007) 'A pathology of public health securitism: approaching pandemics as security threats', in A.F. Cooper, J.J. Kirton and T. Schrecker (eds.) *Governing Global Health: Challenge, Response, Innovation*, Aldershot: Ashgate.

Foucault, M. (2000) 'The politics of health in the eighteenth century', in *Essential Works of Foucault, Vol. III: Power*, trans. Robert Hurley and others, New York: The New Press: 90–105.

Rose, N. (2007) 'Beyond medicalization', *The Lancet*, 369: 700–702.

Weir, L. and Mykhalovskiy, E. (2010) *Global Public Health Vigilance: Creating a World on Alert*, New York: Routledge.

World Health Organization (WHO). (2009) *Safety of Pandemic Vaccines*, Geneva: World Health Organization. Online. Available HTTP: <http://www.who.int/csr/disease/swineflu/notes/h1n1_safety_vaccines_20090805/en/index.html> (accessed 21 January 2014).

Zola, I. (1972) 'Medicine as an institution of social control', *Sociological Review*, 20: 487–503.

PART II

Threats

7
PANDEMICS AND SECURITY

Yanzhong Huang

Infectious disease has influenced world history more deeply and profoundly than most of us would imagine (McNeill 1976; Sherman 2007); its impact is usually maximized in a pandemic – a worldwide spread of a new disease. The term *pandemic* is derived from the combination of Greek word *pan* – meaning "all" – and *demos* – meaning "people." The 1918 "Spanish Flu," which killed up to 50 million people worldwide, including 675,000 in the United States (Crosby 2003), certainly qualifies as a pandemic. At the beginning of the 21st century, the spread of SARS and H5N1 avian flu highlighted the potentially devastating impact of pandemics. In 2009, a new strain of H1N1 virus began to quickly spread to all regions of the world, prompting the World Health Organization (WHO) to pronounce the virus a full-blown pandemic on June 11. By August 2010, most countries had been hit by the virus, which led to more than 18,000 laboratory-confirmed fatalities worldwide (WHO 2010b). While the pandemic eventually burned out, the subsequent rise of other lethal viral strains, including H7N9 avian flu and the Middle East respiratory syndrome coronavirus (MERS-CoV), have again sparked fears of a new pandemic (Builder & Garrett 2013; Chan 2013).

The threat posed by the emergence of new virus strains with pandemic potential eventually galvanized global efforts to tackle the challenge. In 2000, the United Nations Security Council unanimously adopted Resolution 1308 to address the impacts of the HIV/AIDS pandemic. It is the first resolution in the history of the Security Council to address a health issue and it views public health through the lens of security, which has become an integral aspect of public health governance in the 21st century (Fidler 2007: 41). In 2002, the Global Health Security Initiative broadened its health security remit beyond the threat of terrorism to include public health threats posed by pandemic influenza. This helped broaden the recognized scope of health threats beyond HIV/AIDS and expanded the geographic focus beyond Africa (Elbe 2010b: 5). The SARS and H5N1 outbreaks reinforced the linkage between pandemics and security. Hard on the heels of the H5N1 outbreak, then Senators Barack Obama and Richard Lugar argued that pandemics were a major threat to national security because "an outbreak could cause millions of deaths, destabilize Southeast Asia (its likely place of origin), and threaten the security of governments around the world" (Obama & Lugar 2005).

This chapter provides an overview of the pandemics–security nexus. It begins with a discussion of the nature of the threat pandemics pose in the 21st century, followed by an illustration of the potential links between pandemics and security. The security implications of pandemics will then be evaluated through a case study of the 2009 H1N1 outbreak, which points to some of the downsides of the securitizing pandemics.

Why should we be concerned?

Flu pandemics are the most common form of pandemic, typically originating from animal influenza viruses. Such a pandemic occurs when a novel virus emerges for which most of the population has little or no immunity. A novel flu strain can be created in two separate ways – through antigenic drift and antigenic shift (CDC 2011). Seasonal flu epidemics are the result of antigenic drift, in which two key viral genes "drift" and are internally mutated due to its error-prone RNA polymerase. At least two major pandemics in the 20th century (1957 "Asian Flu" and 1969 "Hong Kong Flu") were the result of antigenic shift, in which humans are infected with novel "shift" viruses arising from either avian origin or from viruses that contain a combination of genes from human and avian sources (Clancy 2008).

These pandemics inflicted a heavy toll on human beings. During 1918–1919, approximately one quarter of the world's population was infected and nearly 50 million people are thought to have died. Compared to "attrition epidemics" such as HIV/AIDS, flu pandemics can generate significant shocks over a very short period. As John Barry noted in his 2004 book *The Great Influenza*, the 1918 Spanish influenza pandemic "killed more people in 24 weeks than AIDS has killed in 24 years" (Barry 2004).

The impact of pandemic flu can be amplified by globalization. As Singapore's former prime minister Lee Kuan Yew observed, historically new viruses would have killed nearby villagers but then the danger would have passed. As people and goods can now move more quickly, viruses can now also travel swiftly across long distances (Lee 2004). For example, the SARS virus arrived in Toronto before it first appeared in Beijing in 2003. Virtually any city in the United States can today be reached from anywhere in the world by a commercial flight within 36 hours – less than the incubation period for most infectious diseases. As the distinction between domestic and international public health is blurred, so are the differences between national and international economies. Indeed, globalization and growing economic interdependence means that even countries with few to no cases of a disease have to deal with the economic shocks caused by the spread of infections within a region. The economies of Cambodia and Myanmar, for example, suffered in 2003 even though they were epidemiologically spared by SARS (Huang 2010: 130). This negative impact can be reinforced by the so-called "just-in-time economy." Because food, medicines, and equipment parts are shipped for immediate consumption and less likely to be warehoused, we could quickly become overwhelmed by a flu pandemic (Osterholm 2007).

Despite the potentially devastating impact of pandemics, many countries have not met the International Health Regulations (IHR) requirements in core capacity building to combat pandemics. In Southeast Asia, seven countries thus far have requested and been granted extensions to put in place the IHR core capacities. A preliminary estimate of a "model" Southeast Asian country found that while it met 74% of IHR surveillance targets, only 31% of human resources targets, 53% of laboratory targets, and 62% of response targets were met.[1] To some extent, the capacity gap can be attributed to increasingly demanding international health rules and norms regarding response to public health emergencies. By June 2009, for example, Thailand had only 5% of the population covered by government antiviral stockpiles, which was far below the recommended stockpile sufficient to cover 20% of the population. Most other Asian countries had only 1% of their population covered. In addition, despite the recognition of the importance of a multisectoral approach in coping with health security threats, there is still inadequate national support and coordination for response activities. This is certainly a major concern in politically decentralized states, such as Indonesia, but even countries that have strong state capacities, such as China, face challenges of interdepartmental coordination in capacity building (Huang 2013a).

The securitization of pandemics

The threat of pandemics and lack of surge response capacity have led to efforts to "securitize" pandemics, as evidenced by the 2002 decision to broaden the Global Health Security Initiative. The securitization of pandemics is not a new phenomenon, however. When the bubonic plague engulfed Europe in the 14th and 15th centuries, rulers in European city-states did not hesitate to employ military forces to enforce draconian disease prevention and control measures (Price-Smith 2009). Ironically, such quarantinist ideologies mandated harsh laws that inflamed tensions between state and society, threatening the very security rulers sought to maintain (Guillemin 2005: 22). Beginning in the 18th century, the security aspect of health was largely forgotten as attention and commitment were increasingly redirected toward the goal of enhancing the welfare of population a whole (Elbe 2009).

It was not until after the end of the Cold War that health was rediscovered as a "non-traditional" security challenge. The post-Cold War era re-legitimized the role of human beings in pursuing security, leading to the rise of a new security paradigm – human security (see Cabellero-Anthony & Amul, chapter 3 in this volume). In 1994, the United Nations Development Programme (UNDP) characterized human security as the "freedom from fear and freedom from want" and "safety from chronic threats such as hunger, disease, and repression as well as protection from sudden and harmful disruptions in the patterns of daily life – whether in homes, in jobs or in communities" (UNDP 1994). Pandemics become a human security challenge due to their ability to cause "sudden and harmful disruption in in the patterns of daily life." Indeed, an argument can be made that threats to human security from pandemics are "far more immediately destructive" than many other nontraditional security threats such as immigration and resource scarcities (Price-Smith 2002: 118).

What differentiates pandemics from other human security threats is that they are also considered a national security challenge. As Ullman noted, "A threat to national security is an action or sequence of events that (1) threatens drastically and over a relatively brief span of time to degrade the quality of life for the inhabitants of a state, or (2) threatens significantly to narrow the range of policy choices available to the government of a state or to private, nongovernmental entities (persons, groups, corporations) within the state" (Ullman 1983: 133). This definition is sufficiently broad to cover health-related human security threats, given its focus on the potential for a particular threat to degrade the quality of life and narrow the range of policy choices. But pandemics may also be viewed as a threat to national security even if we adopt a narrower and more traditional definition of security, which focuses on the use of military power to protect national borders and interests abroad and targets interstate conflicts as the main threat. For example, pandemics could affect military operations, even war outcomes by compromising combat capabilities. As Jared Diamond has noted, "The winners of past wars were not always the armies with the best generals and weapons, but were often merely those bearing the nastiest germs to transmit to their enemies" (Diamond 1999: 197). A similar argument was made by the historian William McNeill when he described the Spanish conquest of the New World: "If smallpox had not broken out when it did, Cortez's victory would have been more difficult, and perhaps impossible" (McNeill 1976: 216). Arno Karlen went as far as to call the Fourth Horseman in the form of Old World epidemics the Spaniards' "strongest ally and "deadliest weapon" in conquering the Aztec and Inca empires (Karlen 1996: 103). In a more recent study, Price-Smith pointed to evidence that the differential impact of the Spanish Flu on the military capabilities of the warring nations might have contributed to the defeat of Germany in World War I (Price-Smith 2009).

Pandemics could also generate dynamics that directly threaten the state's ability to project power abroad. As a scholar at the U.S. Naval War College has pointed out, the U.S. military cannot afford to be immobilized by pandemic influenza in light of its substantial global responsibilities, but the extensive deployment of U.S. forces and the sheer scope of U.S. military operations also increases the likelihood for pandemic influenza to compromise the operational capabilities of U.S. forces by infecting troops, civilians, and dependents (Erickson 2007).

According to a recent assessment of health security threat in Southeast Asia conducted by the U.S. Armed Forces Health Surveillance Center (AFHSC), health threats such as pandemic flu not only threaten U.S. military forces in the region, but could also "overwhelm host country and regional response capacity" and even "undermine short- or long-term host country or regional stability" (AFHSC 2012). This assessment implies that pandemics not only compromise military readiness but also affect state capacity and regional stability. Pandemics can affect state capacity by weakening national economy, social stability, and political institutions. Historical examples of the impact of pandemics on national economies abound. The bubonic plague in the 14th century, for example, resulted in drastic depopulation and decades of crop and livestock deficiencies across the European continent (Herlihy 1997).

Like SARS, a contemporary flu pandemic will affect consumer confidence and alter consumption and social patterns. Yet unlike SARS, whose main impact was on the demand side (Fan 2003), a flu pandemic can cause supply shocks by also affecting the health of the labor force. U.S. Health and Human Services officials predicted that during the peak of an influenza pandemic as many as 40% of workers in U.S. firms could be absent, including those who are sick, people who need to care for others, and people who are just plain scared to come to work (Reuters 2005). Depending on the epidemiological features and the psychological impact of the pandemic, the demand and supply shocks will vary. In general, the more pathogenic and contagious the virus, the greater the supply shock (due to higher level of absenteeism of otherwise healthy workers) and demand shock (due to reduced consumer confidence and activities).

The onset of a flu pandemic will work in combination with economic instability and other factors to create volatile social and political situations. Uncertainty about the nature of the disease could produce significant worry, anxiety, fear, panic, even mass hysteria in an affected society. Because of its psychological effect, an infectious disease outbreak often acts as a catalyst for social instability. During the plague outbreak in Surat, India, in 1994, the fear of an epidemic was so intense among the city residents that within 4 days, one quarter of the populace had fled the city (World Resources Institute 1996).

The fear factor could be amplified in future pandemics because people will be advised to minimize if not avoid social interactions. As pandemics become part of a national lexicon, rumor, suspicion, and misinformation could lead to profiling and discrimination against people associated with or from an affected region. The psychological impact and changing social patterns could increase the likelihood of lawlessness and violence by fostering more intense rivalries between different ethnic/religious groups, between the socially privileged and the marginalized, and between the state and society. The Bubonic Plague, for example, increased the tensions between the rich and poor in Europe, leading to peasant riots in England, France, Belgium, and Italy (Hays 1998). At the same time, the pandemic may be so overwhelming that people with shortened time horizons could engage in all kinds of risky behaviors (e.g., crimes and riots). As documented by Thucydides, the Plague of Athens in the 5th century BCE triggered "a state of unprecedented lawlessness" because "men, not knowing what would happen next to them, became indifferent to every rule of religion or law" (Thucydides 1980: 155).

Pandemics affect not only the power of the state over its people (the "first face of power") but also the power of a state relative to its sovereign rivals (the "second face of power") (Price-Smith 2009: 193). The proliferation of a virus can lead to power shifts in both absolute and relative terms. In absolute terms, the pandemic-induced effect on physical and human capital as well as on fighting capabilities will change a state's level of power over the long run, if power is measured in terms of GDP or military strength. In relative terms, since the economic and sociopolitical impact varies across states and economies, some states will suffer less damage than others, therefore gaining an advantage in the relative distribution of power amongst states.

Again, history abounds with cases of pandemics that have unsettled the balance of power and change the international and strategic landscape. By affecting manpower, imperial finance, and morale of the empire, the Plague of Justinian in the 6th century – the first known pandemic on record – greatly weakened the Byzantine Empire and shifted political power to the relatively unaffected peoples of northern Europe (Russell 1968: 174–184). Similarly, the Bubonic Plague disrupted trade flows and ultimately shifted regional balances of economic power from the affected city-states to unaffected regions (Watts 1997: 20–21).

Assessing the security impact of the 2009 H1N1 pandemic

The 2009 H1N1 outbreak provides the most recent example of the security implications of a flu pandemic. According to the WHO, more than 213 countries and overseas territories reported laboratory confirmed cases of pandemic influenza H1N1, including over 17,483 deaths (WHO 2010a). A subsequent study estimated that the virus killed approximately 284,500 people (Dawood et al. 2012: 687–695).

As the H1N1 influenza virus spread rapidly to all parts of the globe, countries sought to combat the virus by intensifying their efforts to safeguard public health and minimizing any potential impact on society and economy (Leung & Nicoll 2010: 1–6). Most countries, especially those in Europe and North America, quickly focused their energies and resources on preparing to treat the increasing number of cases and scaling up for mass vaccination (Nicoll & Coulombier 2009). In contrast, many East Asian and Southeast Asian countries implemented strict containment measures, despite the limited benefit of such an approach in stopping the spread of the virus. The H1N1 "witch hunt" in some of these countries inevitably led to breaches of privacy and human rights – fear and pressure were so intense that the father of the boy who was China's second confirmed H1N1 case made a public apology on the local television for his son's illness. The Egyptian government ordered all pigs in their country – 300,000 – be slaughtered, even though the country did not have a single case of H1N1 (ABC News 2009).

Given its sudden and harmful disruptions of the patterns of our daily lives, as well as the fear associated with the virus, the H1N1 pandemic was undoubtedly a human security problem. That said, the connection between pandemics and human security itself is not analytically interesting – in the words of Stefan Elbe, the link is just a "definitional fiat" (Elbe 2009: 34). What is more interesting is that the H1N1 pandemic also compromised national security through its impact on state capacity. It took a heavy toll on some countries' national economies. The pandemic and the drastic social distancing measures enforced in Mexico, for example, cost the country U.S. $2.3 billion in the first week after the outbreak. In China, fear mongering and self-serving protectionism hurt its domestic pork industry and discouraged tourism and international trade. For fear of being quarantined, many political and business leaders canceled their trips to China and the impact on tourism was probably even more significant.

On the sociopolitical front, the virus set off widespread fear and panic, resulting in outsize impact that changed the political landscape in many countries, including those in Eastern

Europe and Central Asia. In the Ukraine, the president and prime minister accused one another of exploiting the crisis for their own advantage ahead of the January 2010 presidential election (Pan 2009). A lack of core response capacities also narrowed the policy choices of affected governments and encouraged them to react defensively to disease outbreaks, disrupting trade and travel as well as international markets. Since policy measures were often undertaken without addressing the needs or concerns of other countries, they became a source of foreign policy disputes. China's quarantine measures initially targeted Mexican nationals, which immediately triggered a diplomatic row between the two countries. Calling Chinese measures "discriminatory and ungrounded," Mexican Foreign Minister Patricia Espinosa even advised Mexicans to stay away from China. On May 3, Mexico's president lashed out at countries he said were "acting out of ignorance and disinformation" and taking "repressive, discriminatory measures" (Lacey & Jacobs 2009). The H1N1 pandemic was also used by some governments to justify protectionism. During the outbreak, 20 countries banned the import of pork products from Mexico, Canada, and the United States. These bans occurred despite the WHO's advice that pork products handled in a hygienic way were not a source of the H1N1 virus (FAHO/WHO/OIE/WTO 2009; Gostin 2009).

In addition, the pandemic exacerbated the North–South conflict over access to vaccines and medicines. Manufacturing capacity for influenza vaccines is limited and concentrated in the developed world. For poorer countries that did not have vaccine development capabilities or could not afford to order vaccines from overseas manufacturers, access to the vaccine had to be made possible through a WHO-coordinated donation, which turned out to be too little, too late (Huang 2013b). This "vaccine apartheid" sent a chilling message to the developing world. Prior to the H1N1 outbreak, Indonesian Health Minister Siti Fadilah Supari (who coined the term "viral sovereignty") had refused to share H5N1 samples with the WHO, arguing that big pharmaceutical companies in industrialized nations would develop vaccines using the samples the country provided free of charge, yet market the vaccine with prices too high for sufficient distribution in Indonesia (see Aldis & Soendoro, chapter 26 in this volume). The continuous failure of the United States and other industrialized nations to adequately address the concerns of poorer countries during the H1N1 outbreak only encouraged Supari to ramp up the rhetoric, accusing the United States of genetically engineering H1N1 and H5N1 as biological weapons. She then cut off cooperation with NAMRU-2, the U.S. Naval Medical Research Unit in Jakarta (Ricks 2009: 40–74). The facility was closed in 2010.

Despite the foreign policy conflicts and the increased political bickering, there is no evidence to support the view that the pandemic significantly undermined short- or long-term stability in affected countries or regions. There were outbreaks in the military, but the impacts on fighting capabilities were negligible. There is also no indication that the pandemic significantly affected global or regional balances of power.

The downsides of securitizing pandemics

The securitization of pandemics raises political awareness and helps free up resources to more effectively combat them. Fear of future pandemics not only led to strong political commitment to building national surveillance and response capacities but also gave rise to international cooperation that enhanced surveillance and response capacities at regional and global levels.

But the same mode of discourse may also structure global health debates in ways that are not conducive to achieving higher levels of international health cooperation. First, it implies that health is less important than security and that health interventions can only be justified in terms of their impact on security. This causes an internal contradiction in securitization efforts: advocates of human security argue against thinking in purely national terms, but they appeal to nationalism to achieve their goals (Peterson 2002/2003: 51). Incoherence in public health as security has negative implications for international cooperation over health. As implied in the accusations Supari levied at the U.S. government, purely national and bilateral efforts to address pandemics as a national security threat may arouse suspicion in other states, exacerbating the security dilemma.

Moreover, the emphasis on national security (which by definition is state-centric) could relieve developed countries (which do not face as many public health threats as developing countries) of any moral obligation to respond to the immediate needs of the developing world during a pandemic. Such nonchalance could be reinforced by the competitive rush amongst countries to secure access to pharmaceutical countermeasures when a pandemic is imminent (Elbe 2010a: 477). Given the North–South gap in access to life saving drugs and vaccines, these competitive dynamics could exacerbate conflicts between the "haves" and "have-nots." Not surprisingly, developing countries have begun "to openly question the value of maintaining existing forms of international health cooperation which appeared to be mostly benefiting developed countries" (Elbe 2010a: 480).

Paradoxically, high-level concern about pandemic flu in the West has also rendered the viruses circulating in certain front line countries (e.g., Indonesia) very "valuable" (Elbe 2010a: 477). As the virus became a precious resource, international health cooperation is increasingly subject to the logic of realpolitik, which could lead to efforts to use virus samples as diplomatic bargaining chips for pursuing national interest. Indonesia's decision not to participate in the existing global virus-sharing mechanism, for example, caused "one of the most substantial setbacks in international health cooperation of the past decade" (Elbe 2010a: 477).

Equally important, the pandemics–security relationship may imply that a national military response to pandemics is required. First, it presumes that in "fighting" pandemic flu, the enemy is sick or exposed individuals, not the virus. Second, it could reinforce the misperception that forced quarantine is the appropriate response to all disease outbreaks, which could compromise capacity building efforts (e.g., addressing the shortage of health personnel, hospitals, ventilators, etc.). Third, effective public health policy must be built on social capital (i.e., trust), not public fear. In a "securitized" public health atmosphere, fear and panic could create a society less willing to cooperate with the enforcement of public health measures; draconian quarantine measures would probably have the unintended effect of encouraging people to shun public health officials or health workers. Finally, when the military is involved in enforcing quarantines, it could cause confusion concerning the chain-of-command in health matters, complicating communication and coordination problems between civilian public health institutions and military/law enforcement agencies.

Conclusion

Pandemics are historically rare events, but their devastating impact on humankind is well documented and can be amplified by globalization and growing economic interdependence. This chapter based its analysis on the redefined post-Cold War security framework and provided the analytical tools to examine the security implications of pandemics. While historical studies suggest a strong relationship between pandemics and security, security implications can vary depending on the nature of the pandemic. Despite the positive outcomes that can result from making health a security priority, there are limits and incoherencies to such securitization efforts, which could potentially undermine government capacity building efforts as well as deter international cooperation to cope with the pandemic threat.

Note

1 Communication with a CDC official, December 19, 2012.

References

ABC News (2009, April 30) 'Egypt orders pig cull'. Online. Available HTTP: <http://www.abc.net.au/news/2009-04-30/egypt-orders-pig-cull/1667152> (accessed 21 January 2014).

AFHSC. (2012, December 19) 'Health Threats in Southeast Asia: Armed Forces Health Surveillance Center (AFHSC) Perspective', paper for the Second Meeting of Health Smart Power in Asia Task Force, CSIS Global Health Policy Center, Washington, DC.

Barry, J. (2004) *The Great Influenza: The Epic Story of the Deadliest Plague in History*, New York: Penguin Books.

Builder, M. and Garrett, L. (2013, July 28) 'The Middle East plague goes global', *Foreign Policy*. Online. Available HTTP: <http://www.foreignpolicy.com/articles/2013/06/28/the_middle_east_plague_goes_global?page=full> (accessed 21 January 2014).

CDC. (2011) *How Viruses Can Change: "Shift" and "Drift"*. Online. Available HTTP: <http://www.cdc.gov/flu/about/viruses/change.htm> (accessed 21 January 2014).

Chan, M. (2013, July 9) 'Middle East respiratory syndrome coronavirus (MERS-CoV)', World Health Organization. Online. Available HTTP: <http://www.who.int/ihr/procedures/statements_20130709/en/index.html> (accessed 21 January 2014).

Clancy, S. (2008) 'Genetics of the influenza virus', *Nature Education*, 1: 83.

Crosby, A. (2003) *America's Forgotten Pandemic: The Influenza of 1918*, New York: Cambridge University Press.

Dawood, F.S., Iuliano, A.D., Reed, C., Meltzer, M.I., Shay, D.K., Cheng, P-Y., Bandaranayake, D., Breiman, R.F., Brooks, W.A., Buchy, P., Feikin, D.R., Fowler, K.B., Gordon, A., Hien, N.T., Horby, P., Huang, S., Katz, M.A., Krishnan, A., Lal, R., Montgomery, J.M., Mølbak, K., Pebody, R., Presanis, A.M., Razuri, H., Steens, A., Tinoco, Y.O., Wallinga, J., Yu, H., Vong, S., Bresee, J. and Widdowson, M-A. (2012) 'Estimated global mortality associated with the first 12 months of 2009 pandemic influenza A H1N1 virus circulation: a modelling study', *Lancet Infectious Diseases*, 12: 687–695.

Diamond, J. (1999) *Guns, Germs, and Steel: The Fates of Human Societies*, New York: WW Norton & Company.

Elbe, S. (2009) *Virus Alert: Security, Governmentality, and the AIDS Pandemic*, New York: Columbia University Press.

Elbe, S. (2010a) 'Haggling over viruses: the downside risks of securitizing infectious disease', *Health Policy and Planning*, 25: 476–485.

Elbe, S. (2010b) *Security and Global Health: Toward the Medicalization of Insecurity*, Malden, MA: Polity Press.

Erickson, A. (2007) 'Combating a collective threat: prospects for Sino-American cooperation against avian influenza', *Global Health Governance*, 1. Online. Available HTTP: <http://ghgj.org/Erickson_1.1_Combating.htm> (accessed 21 January 2014).

Fan, X.E. (2003) 'SARS: economic impacts and implications', *ERD Policy Brief* No. 15, Asian Development Bank. Online. Available HTTP: <http://www.adb.org/sites/default/files/pub/2003/PB015.pdf> (accessed 21 January 2014).

FAO/WHO/OIE/WTO. (2009) *Joint FAO/WHO/OIE/WTO Statement on Influenza A (H1N1) and the Safety of Pork*. Online. Available HTTP: <http://www.who.int/mediacentre/news/statements/2009/h1n1_20090502/en/index.html> (accessed 21 January 2014).

Fidler, D. (2007) 'A pathology of public health securitism: approaching pandemics as security threats', in A.F. Cooper, J.J. Kirton, and T. Schrecker (eds.) *Governing Global Health: Challenge, Response, Innovation*, Aldershot: Ashgate Publishers.

Gostin, L. (2009) 'Influenza A (H1N1) and pandemic preparedness under the rule of international law', *Journal of the American Medical Association*, 301: 2376–2378.

Guillemin, J. (2005) *Biological Weapons*, New York: Columbia University Press.

Hays, J.N. (1998) *The Burdens of Disease*, New Brunswick, NJ: Rutgers University Press

Herlihy, D. (1997) *The Black Death and the Transformation of the West*, Cambridge: Harvard University Press.

Huang, Y. (2010) 'Pursuing health as foreign policy: the case of China', *Indiana Journal of Global Legal Studies*, 17: 105–146.

Huang, Y. (2013a) *Governing Health in Contemporary China*, London and New York: Routledge.

Huang Y. (2013b) 'The 2009 H1N1 flu pandemic and the policy response in East Asia', in R.M. Hathaway and M. Wills (eds.) *New Security Challenges in Asia*, Washington, DC: Woodrow Wilson Center Press/ Johns Hopkins University Press: 121–143.

Karlen, A. (1996) *Man and Microbes: Diseases and Plagues in History and Modern Time*, New York: Touchstone.

Lacey, M. and Jacobs, A. (2009, May 4) 'Even as fears of flu ebb, Mexicans feel stigma', *New York Times:* A1.

Lee, K.Y. (2004, April 14) 'New viruses in Asia', *Forbes.*

Leung, G. and Nicoll, A. (2010) 'Reflections on pandemic (H1N1) 2009 and the international response', *PLoS Medicine*, 7. Online Available HTTP: <http://www.plosmedicine.org/article/info%3Adoi%2F10.1371%2Fjournal.pmed.1000346> (accessed 21 January 2014).

McNeill, W. (1976) *Plagues and Peoples*, New York: Anchor Press.

Nicoll, A. and Coulombier D. (2009) 'Europe's initial experience with pandemic (H1N1) 2009', *Eurosurveillance*, 14. Online. Available HTTP: <http://www.eurosurveillance.org/images/dynamic/EE/V14N29/art19279.pdf> (accessed 21 January 2014).

Obama, B. and Lugar, R. (2005, June 6) 'Grounding a pandemic', *New York Times.*

Osterholm, M. (2007) 'Unprepared for a pandemic', *Foreign Affairs*, 86: 47–57.

Pan, P. (2009, November 21) 'In Ukraine, H1N1 pandemic sets off panic and politicking', *Washington Post.*

Peterson, S. (2002/2003) 'Epidemic disease and national security', *Security Studies*, 12: 43–81.

Price-Smith, A. (2009) *Contagion and Chaos: Disease, Ecology, and National Security in the Era of Globalization*, Cambridge: MIT Press.

Price-Smith, A.T. (2002) *The Health of Nations: Infectious Disease, Environmental Change, and Their Effects on National Security and Development*, Cambridge: MIT Press.

Reuters. (2005, December 6) '40 percent absenteeism seen for flu pandemic', *Arizona Daily Star.*

Ricks, D. (2009) 'Flu wars', *Discover*, 30(11).

Russell, J.C. (1968) 'That earlier plague', *Demography*, 5: 174–184.

Sherman, I. (2007) *Twelve Diseases That Changed Our World*, Washington, DC: ASM Press.

Thucydides. (1980) *History of the Peloponnesian War*, New York: Penguin.

Ullman, R. (1983) 'Redefining security', *International Security*, 8: 129–153.

United Nations Development Program (UNDP). (1994) *Human Development Report 1994 – New Dimensions of Human Security*, New York: Oxford University Press.

Watts, S. (1997) *Epidemics and History: Disease, Power, and Imperialism*, Great Britain: Redwood Books.

World Health Organization (WHO). (2010a) 'Pandemic (H1N1) 2009: update 94'. Online. Available HTTP: <http://www.who.int/csr/don/2010_04_01/en/> (accessed 21 January 2014).

World Health Organization (WHO). (2010b) 'Pandemic (H1N1) 2009: update 112'. Online. Available HTTP: <http://www.who.int/csr/don/2010_08_06/en/index.html> (accessed 21 January 2014).

World Resources Institute. (1996) *World Resources 1996–97: The Urban Environment*, New York: Oxford University Press.

8

EMERGING INFECTIONS

Threats to health and economic security

David L. Heymann & Alison West

Emerging infections provide a clear example of how infectious diseases cause a threat not only to human health but also to economic security. Emerging infections are caused by microbes that were not known previously to infect humans, or by microbes that were known to infect humans, but have begun to infect persons in a geographic area where they had previously not been seen. They cause human suffering, illness, and death; and they require medical care – sometimes costly because of the requirement for special procedures and protracted hospitalization. Their control may require culling of animals being raised commercially for food or other animal products, with loss of profit. And finally, emerging infections sometimes cause economic loss because of barriers to trade and travel when there is a perceived, often misguided, fear of their international spread.

A report published by the United States Institute of Medicine in 1992 first called attention to emerging infectious diseases as evidence that the fight against infectious diseases was far from won, despite great advances in the development of anti-infective drugs and vaccines (Lederberg et al. 1992). Since then, emerging infections have been identified at an average rate of one per year, sometimes in pandemic proportion when they spread throughout the world in a matter of weeks or months, placing millions of persons, or entire populations, at risk.

It is estimated that up to 70% or more of all emerging infections have a source in animals. Bats are particularly important carriers of infections that emerge in humans, and are often the source of emergence that leads to major outbreaks (Table 8.1).

Once an emergence has occurred there are three possible outcomes. Some emerging infections do not spread from person to person, and then disappear from human populations, but may reemerge when conditions are right. Others spread from human to human and cause an outbreak, then disappear when the outbreak is over, but may likewise appear again under the right conditions. Still others spread indefinitely, remaining in human populations as endemic infectious diseases for generations to come.

One of the most important recent emerging infections is AIDS, first identified in the early 1980s. AIDS is now an endemic disease, a human infection that continues to spread among humans, and from genetic study of the Human Immunodeficiency Virus (HIV) that causes AIDS, it is estimated that it actually emerged sometime during the late 19th or early 20th century from a nonhuman primate in the African rain forest, and then continued to spread from

Table 8.1 Breeches in the Species Barrier: Selected Emerging Infections since 1976

Infection	*Animal linked to transmission*	*Year infection first reported*
Ebola virus	Bats	1976
HIV-1	Primates	1981
E. coli 0157:H7	Cattle	1982
Borrelia burgdorferi	Rodents	1982
HIV-2	Primates	1986
Hendra virus	Bats	1994
BSE/vCJD	Cattle	1996
Australian lyssavirus	Bats	1996
Influenza A(H5N1)	Chickens	1997
Nipah virus	Bats	1999
SARS coronavirus	Palm civets	2003
Influenza (H1N1)	Swine	2009
MERS coronavirus	Possibly camel	2012
Influenza A(H7N9)	Chickens	2013

Source: Authors

human to human. Its emergence was likely caused by exposure of a hunter, or hunters, to the blood of an animal killed for food, and the virus was either able to easily transmit from human to human at the start, or it developed this capacity as it mutated during reproduction in the first humans infected. After its emergence, HIV continued to spread in human populations as a sexually transmitted infection. Sometime in the latter part of the 20th century, an infected human or humans carried the virus from rural areas where it had emerged and continued to spread at low levels, to urban areas where risky sexual behavior amplified the possibilities for it to spread, and to infect persons who then spread it from continent to continent as they traveled in an interconnected world.

Other recent emerging infections include Ebola, Marburg, variant Creutzfeldt-Jakob Disease (vCJD), Severe Acute Respiratory Syndrome (SARS), and avian and swine influenza. Each of these infections is thought to have infected humans by breeching the species barrier between animals and humans in whom they caused illness and were able to spread. Some of them, such as Ebola and Marburg, cause highly lethal outbreaks, then disappear from humans but reemerge at a later time when conditions, that are not yet clearly understood, are right. Others – such as SARS and swine influenza (influenza A – H1N1) – have the potential to cause a pandemic and spread throughout the world following major international airline routes.

This chapter will first examine the human health and economic consequences of emerging infections. It will then present in more detail the health and economic impact of two recent high profile emerging infection events – SARS and influenza. Finally it will briefly review measures that have been undertaken by countries to prevent the cross-border spread of emerging infections in the past, and describe the International Health Regulations (2005), the current global framework designed to prevent the international spread of emerging infections that are of international concern because of their potential to spread internationally and cause severe human and economic consequences.

The impact of emerging infections on humans and economies

Emerging infections cause human sickness and death, and they often pose a threat to economic security. During 2011, HIV was estimated to have caused 2.5 million new human infections and 1.7 million AIDS deaths worldwide, placing it high on the list of causes of human sickness and death (UNAIDS 2012). HIV is a chronic infection, and because of its long incubation period and the use of antiretroviral medicines to prolong life, persons infected with HIV accumulate in the population. By the end of 2011, therefore, it was estimated that 34 million persons were living with HIV infection, and that HIV infection had killed over 25 million people since AIDS was first identified in 1981. The sickness and death from HIV infection and AIDS have caused a direct and indirect negative economic impact, particularly in the poorest countries. The estimated direct costs in 2009 to achieve universal access to treatment and care for persons with HIV infection in developing countries was U.S. $7 billion, and reductions of 2%–4% in national GDP have been estimated across a range of African countries, mainly the result of lost human contribution to the work force because of sickness and death.

Variant Creutzfeldt-Jakob disease (vCJD) is a human infection that emerged in the United Kingdom (UK) in the mid-1990s. It spread to humans from cattle, or meat and other cattle products that were infected with the causative agent of Bovine Spongiform Encephalopathy (BSE), also known as Mad Cow Disease. vCJD does not spread from one human to another, and each human infection is thought to occur independently, either from infected cattle or products made from cattle. Since first being identified, 225 cases of vCJD have been reported from 12 countries, and each case has been fatal within a short period from onset. BSE was first identified in cattle in the UK during the 1980s. In order to rid cattle of infection, culling of herds with infected cattle was required. When it was understood that humans could be infected with BSE from cattle and cattle products in 1996, culling activity increased, and the economic loss in the UK during the following year was estimated to be U.S. $1.5 billion (Atkinson 1996). Trade of British beef and other cattle products was banned in many countries, markedly decreasing British exports, and adding greatly to the costs already associated with culling. In the 11 countries where BSE and vCJD had spread from the UK with cattle or bovine products, herds of cattle infected with BSE were culled at a considerable economic loss to each of these countries as well (Diack et al. 2012).

An extensive 2012 World Bank study estimated that economic losses from six major outbreaks of highly fatal emerging infections between 1997 and 2009 amounted to at least U.S. $80 billion. These infections include Nipah Virus (Malaysia), West Nile Fever (USA), SARS (Asia, Canada, others), Highly Pathogenic Avian Influenza (Asia, Europe), Bovine Spongiform Encephalopathy (US, UK), and Rift Valley Fever (Tanzania, Kenya, Somalia).

Case studies of emerging infectious diseases

Influenza

One infectious organism that is often able to spread easily from human to human after it emerges, or after it mutates, is the influenza virus (see Huang, chapter 7 in this volume). There are many different influenza viruses that live in aquatic birds, and these birds are thought to serve as the reservoir of human influenza infections. The influenza viruses in aquatic birds occasionally emerge in human populations, and while some of them are able to spread from human to human, others are not.

Some of those influenza viruses that spread from human to human eventually become endemic and cause seasonal influenza outbreaks each winter. A vaccine has been developed to protect against seasonal influenza, and it is provided to persons at risk of influenza each year before the influenza season. The vaccine is prepared from the influenza virus, but it becomes less effective as the virus mutates as it reproduces in humans. Because seasonal influenza viruses mutate frequently, there is a need for a change in influenza vaccine each year to match the mutated viruses so that the vaccine continues to protect humans against seasonal influenza. The Global Influenza Surveillance Network studies influenza viruses, and each year makes recommendations for the necessary changes in influenza vaccine 6 months before the influenza epidemic season, so that a new vaccine can be developed.

In addition to the influenza viruses that are circulating among humans and cause annual seasonal influenza outbreaks, other influenza viruses occasionally breech the species barrier between aquatic birds and animals such as pigs and poultry. Such was the case in 2009, when Mexico first reported human infections with the H1N1 (swine) influenza virus. This virus is thought to have undergone several different mutations in pigs and finally mutated in such a manner that it could then breech the species barrier between pigs and humans. Because it spread easily from human to human, it caused a major influenza outbreak in Mexico that then spread globally within weeks to cause a pandemic (Figure 8.1).

A total of 70,715 Mexicans were reported with confirmed H1N1 infection in the initial outbreak, of whom 1,316 (˜ 5%) had died. By the end of 2009, more than 208 countries and territories had reported laboratory confirmed cases of pandemic influenza (H1N1) to WHO, and there had been at least 12,799 deaths.

Countries mobilized during 2009, and put into action their influenza pandemic plans after the World Health Organization (WHO) declared a public health emergency of international concern, and later WHO declared that H1N1 influenza had become pandemic. Though at no time did WHO recommend any decreases in pork trade and travel, there were major economic losses related to H1N1 in Mexico in both these sectors. They occurred because of an unwarranted perception among tourists and travel agencies that the risk of becoming infected with H1N1 was somehow greater in Mexico than elsewhere, even though the virus had spread throughout the world; and by a misunderstanding among pork markets that the pandemic was being amplified by infected pigs, despite the fact that it was being caused by human to human transmission, in which pigs no longer played a role.

Because of the resulting decrease in overseas visitors to Mexico, thought to be approximately 1 million, there was an estimated economic loss of approximately U.S. $2.8 billion. Because of unnecessary trade bans on Mexican pork products there was a major decrease in demand from the pork industry that contributed to a pork trade deficit of an estimated U.S. $27 million. In countries other than Mexico there were official recommendations, apparently based on this same misunderstanding, that likewise caused negative economic impact. In Egypt, for example, slaughter of pigs was ordered by the Egyptian Government early in the pandemic, even though the H1N1 virus had already been demonstrated to be highly transmissible from human to human, and despite the recommendation of the World Organization for Animal Health (OIE) that culling of pigs was not scientifically justifiable.

Countries around the world were affected as the H1N1 pandemic spread, and most economies suffered. In Spain, for example, the direct economic impact of illness from H1N1 influenza on health services utilization, and indirect costs from work absenteeism, has been estimated at €6,236 per hospitalized patient. In Canada, it is estimated that the cost of the increased patient load to hospitals caused by H1N1 between April and December 2009 was Canadian $200 million.

At the same time, other influenza viruses from aquatic birds continue to occasionally infect humans directly, or indirectly from intermediary animal populations that have been infected by these birds. The H5N1 avian influenza virus was first identified in Hong Kong as the cause of human illness in 1997. It was thought to have spread from migrating shorebirds to ducks, and

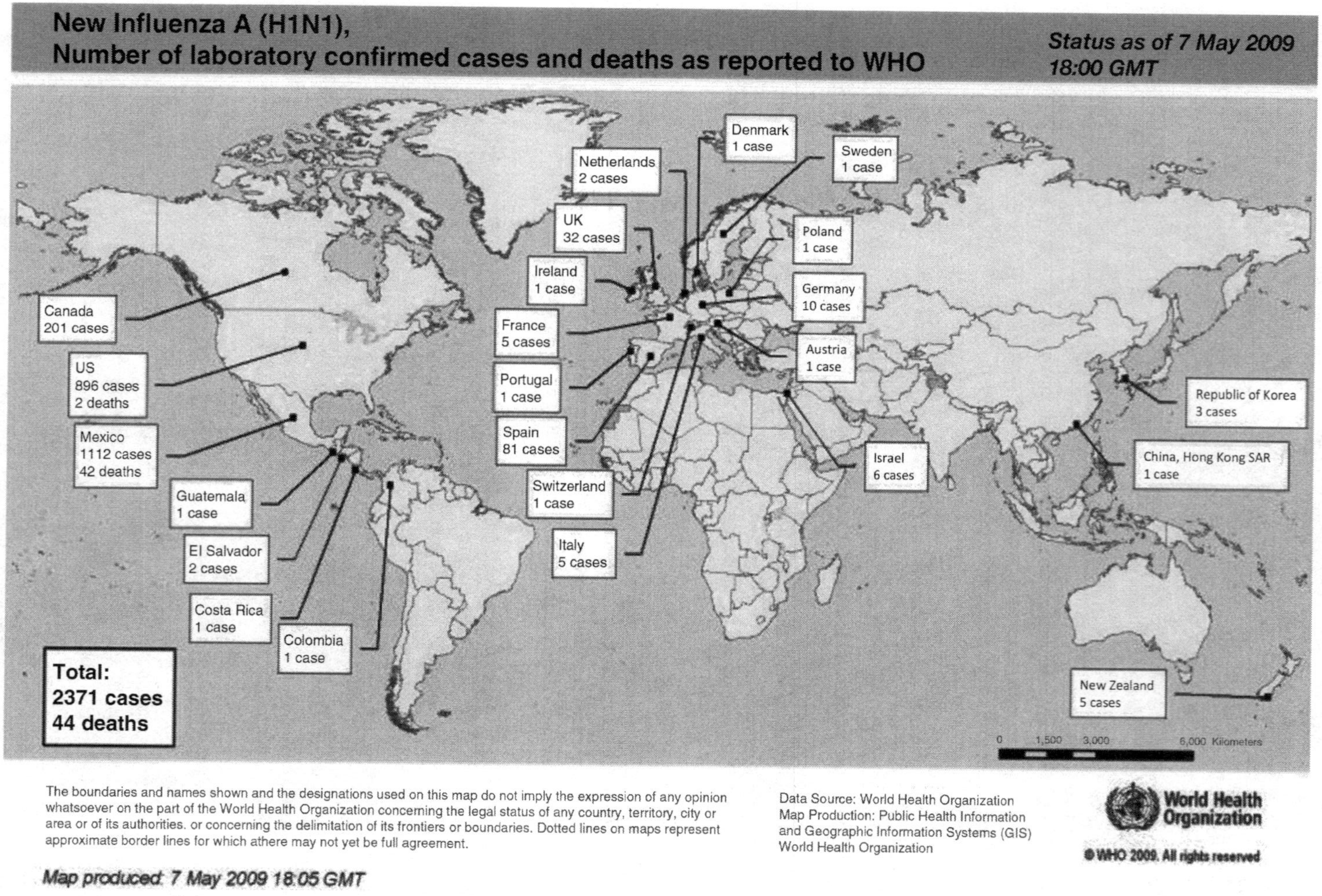

Figure 8.1 Rapid Spread of Influenza A (H1N1) after Emergence, 2009

Source: WHO.

then spread from ducks to chickens that were sold in live bird markets. Humans then became infected by exposure to infected chickens.

H5N1 has now spread to chickens in many parts of Asia, and the virus continues to cause occasional severe and fatal infections in humans when it breeches the animal/human species barrier, but it remains an endemic infection of poultry and does not transmit easily from person to person. The Global Influenza Surveillance Network continuously monitors H5N1, however, because like all influenza viruses, it has the potential to mutate into a form that could spread easily among humans. The highly fatal 1918 influenza pandemic is thought to have originated from an influenza virus that had spread from aquatic birds to pigs where it mutated in such a way that when it breached the species the animal/human species barrier it caused the highly lethal pandemic (Taubenberger & Morens 2006).

The World Bank predicts that a pandemic caused by a highly infectious and virulent influenza virus such as H5N1 could cost the world economy as much as U.S. $800 billion a year from direct patient costs, and indirect costs from lost lives, travel and trade (World Bank 2005). In order to prevent such a scenario related to the H5N1 influenza virus, attempts are being made to eliminate the H5N1 virus by culling entire flocks of infected poultry, mainly chickens. This precautionary measure, recommended by the World Health Organization and the Food and Agriculture Organization (FAO) in order to stop periodic emergence in humans, is causing lost revenue and poultry-replacement costs that have been estimated to be in the billions of U.S. dollars.

Severe acute respiratory infection (SARS)

An outbreak caused by another breech in the animal/human species barrier occurred in the Guangdong Province of China in late 2002. The initial cases in the outbreak of SARS in China spread from human to human. Infected persons passed the infection to other family members and to health workers, and they in turn spread it to others in the community, causing an outbreak associated with severe illness and death.

In February 2003, when SARS was still unrecognized as a new and emerging infection in China, it crossed the border from the Guangdong Province to Hong Kong in a doctor who had been treating patients with SARS. He himself had become sick, and during a one-night stay in a Hong Kong hotel spread SARS to other hotel guests. Before they had any major symptoms, infected individuals travelled by plane to other Asian countries, North America, and Europe where they became sick and spread infection to others (Figure 8.2).

SARS had never before been seen in humans. There were thus no vaccines, medicines, or predetermined measures that could be used for its control. Because the virus continued to spread from human to human, there was concern that, like HIV, it would become an endemic infection, sustaining itself indefinitely in humans.

Precautionary measures to prevent international spread of the infection were immediately recommended by WHO – and there was an immediate decrease in international travel and tourism, most dramatic in Asian countries, and in Canada where major outbreaks had begun after tourists returned from Hong Kong where they had been infected by the infected medical doctor staying in the same hotel.

These precautionary measures caused a decrease in international air travel from geographic areas where outbreaks were occurring. Concern and panic ensued, however, among populations from other geographic areas as well – clearly demonstrated in a decrease in passenger movements through international airports. The precautionary prevention measures recommending that persons who were ill with SARS-like symptoms postpone travel resulted in a decrease of passengers who were ill, but many well passengers perceived the risk of travel as being great. This resulted

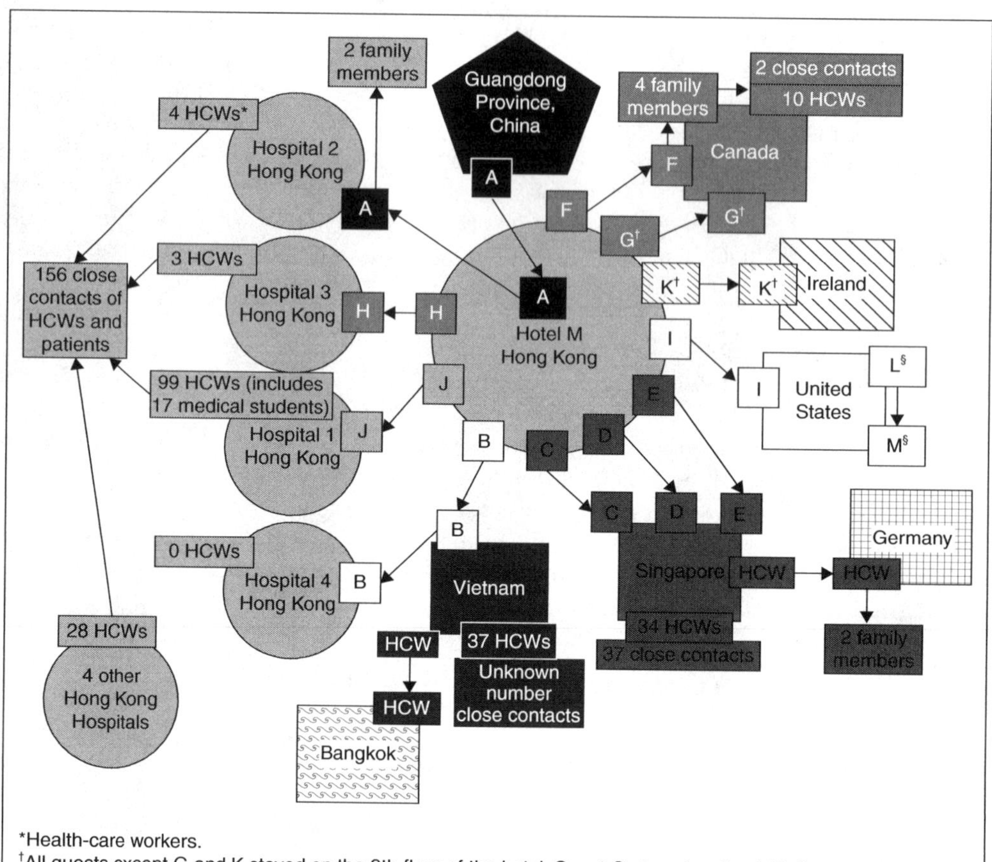

Figure 8.2 International Spread of SARS, 2003
Source: CDC/MMWR March 28, 2003 / 52(12): 241–248.

in a steady decrease in airline travel as in Hong Kong, where passenger movements at the international airport decreased soon after the outbreak was announced.

Figure 8.3 shows passenger movement through the Hong Kong Airport from March 16, 2003, the day after the announcement of the SARS outbreak, to July 2003 when the outbreak was declared over. Passenger movement decreased immediately after the epidemic was announced on March 15, continued to decrease after a travel advisory to postpone travel was made by WHO, but increased again beginning May 23 when WHO lifted the travel advisory.

Overall, Hong Kong International airport had had an approximate decrease of 70% in passenger movements in April 2003 compared with April 2002, and aircraft movements decreased by an estimated 30%. In April 2003, the number of flights canceled each day in and out of Hong Kong was around 164, representing more than 30% of all daily flights, and resulting in an estimated loss in landing fees in Hong Kong of a minimum of $3.5 million per day.

During this same period, income from restaurants, hotels, and retail sales decreased because of panic and misperception of the risk among the Hong Kong population that resulted in decreased

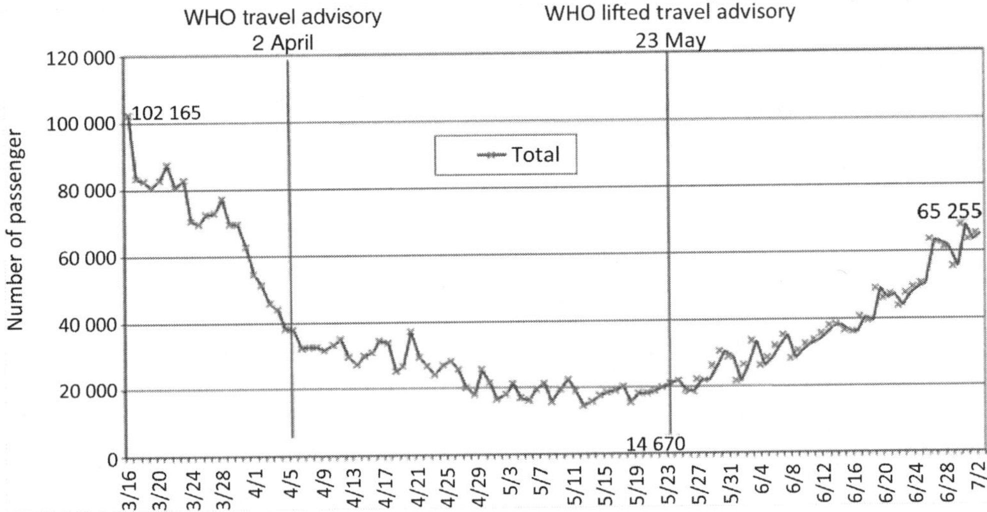

Figure 8.3 Passenger Movement, Hong Kong International Airport, March–July 2003
Source: Hong Kong International Airport.

consumer activity. Figure 8.4 provides clear examples of the decreases in economic activity that occurred.

The SARS outbreak ended in July 2003, and during the period 1 November 2002–7 August 2003, 8422 cases, of which 916 (11%) were fatal, were reported to WHO from 32 countries. The Asian Development Bank estimated the economic impact of SARS at approximately U.S. $18 billion in East Asia – around 0.6% of gross domestic product. But fortunately economic recovery was rapid once international spread had been stopped.

The International Health Regulations and international spread of infectious diseases

The International Health Regulations (IHR) are a global framework agreement of all Member States of the World Health Organization, and are designed to limit the international spread of public health emergencies, including emerging infections, with minimal interruption to travel and trade. They were first developed in 1969, and after the SARS outbreak in 2003 a process of updating and revision that had begun in 1996 was completed, broadening their disease coverage and setting up a process for more evidence-based recommendations for prevention and control. The concerns about the international spread of emerging infections that led to the development of the IHR in 1969 were not new (see Kamradt-Scott, chapter 16 in this volume). By the 14th century, governments clearly recognized the capacity for diseases to spread internationally. This was most clearly demonstrated in the city-state of Venice where quarantine measures were developed to attempt to stop the spread of bubonic plague. Ships arriving in the harbor of Venice were not permitted to dock for 40 days, and people at land borders were held in isolation, also for 40 days – one of the earliest well documented attempts to keep an infectious disease from crossing international borders.

By the mid-19th century, governments had become concerned that quarantine measures were not preventing the importation of another disease – cholera – and that the risk of plague remained. They recognized that better cooperation between countries was required in order to decrease the

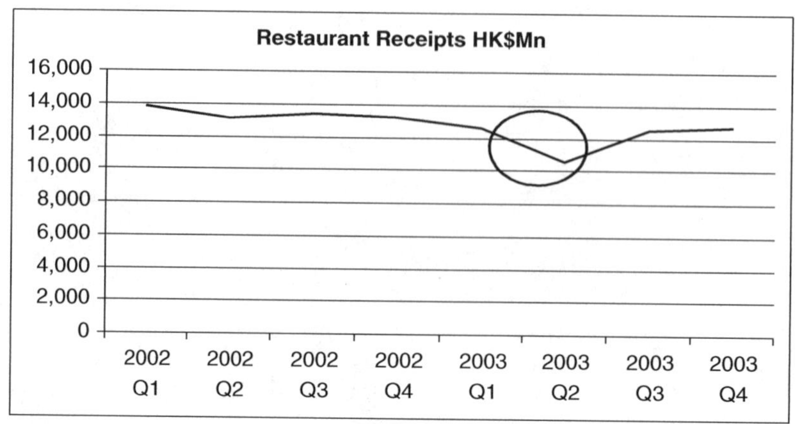

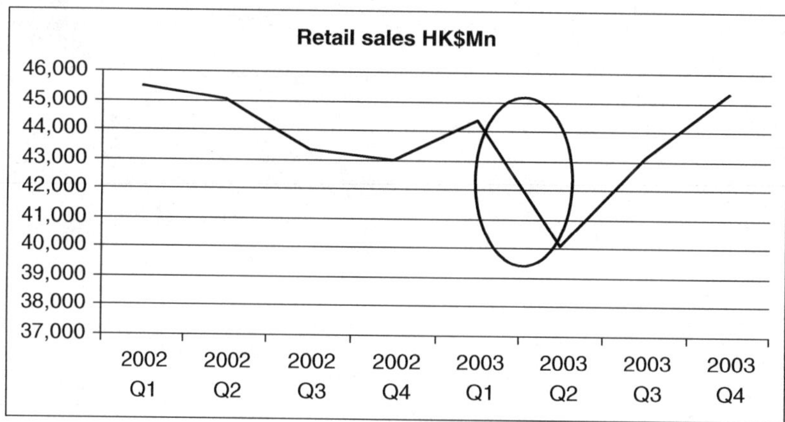

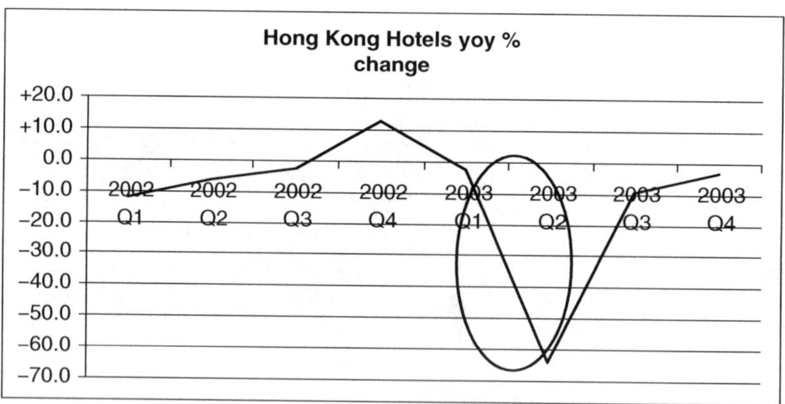

Figure 8.4 Revenue in Commercial Sector, Hong Kong, 2002–2003
Circles indicate period of SARS outbreak.
Source: Smith R, LSHTM.

risk of international spread of these diseases, and a series of international conventions were developed, aimed at stopping the spread of cholera and plague by applying certain measures at international borders.

During the 19th century, most international agreements to control the international spread of cholera and plague were among European countries. They began in 1851 in Paris, followed in 1892 by the first International Sanitary Convention that dealt with cholera. Five years later, at the 10th International Sanitary Conference, a similar convention was signed to prevent the spread of plague.

As communications technology developed, obligatory telegraphic notification of first cases of cholera and plague was begun among countries in the Americas, and these notifications soon included yellow fever as well. Because cholera and plague were often carried to the Americas by European immigrants, international agreements were broadened to include both Europe and the Americas.

During the early 20th century two major international sanitary bureaus were created to support the development of regional public health capacity against infectious diseases – one in the Washington for the Americas called the Pan American Sanitary Bureau (now called the Pan American Health Organization) and one in Paris for European countries, called the Office International d'Hygiène Publique. Cooperation between these two sanitary bureaus continued through the early part of the 20th century, and in 1951, after the creation of WHO, broad International Sanitary Regulations were developed as a means of fostering international cooperation in the control of cholera, plague, yellow fever, and smallpox.

In 1969, after over 20 years of implementation of the International Sanitary Regulations, WHO developed the International Health Regulations (IHR) – specifically aimed at better ensuring public health security with minimal interruption in travel and trade. In addition to requiring reporting of four infectious diseases – cholera, plague, yellow fever, and smallpox – the IHR were aimed at stopping the spread of these four diseases by the application of preestablished control measures at international borders. When a country reported one of these diseases, it triggered these standardized measures at border posts such as the requirement for yellow fever vaccination of passengers arriving from countries where yellow fever outbreaks had been reported. The international vaccination certificate, recognized by most countries, serves as official certification of vaccination under the IHR.

The IHR thus provided a legal framework for global surveillance and response, with the potential to decrease the world's vulnerability to four infectious diseases that were known to cross international borders. It soon became evident, however, that countries often reported late, or not at all, because of fear of stigmatization and economic repercussions. It was likewise understood by 1996 that the IHR did not meet the challenges caused by emerging infectious diseases and their rapid global transit, often crossing borders while still in the incubation period in humans, or silently in nonhuman hosts – insects, animals, and food and agriculture goods.

Therefore, from 1996 until 2005, the Member States of WHO undertook a process to examine and revise the IHR. The result – the IHR (2005) – provides a more up-to-date legal framework requiring reporting of any public health emergency of international concern (PHEIC) and the use of real-time evidence to recommend measures to stop their international spread. A PHEIC is defined as an extraordinary event that could spread internationally or might require a coordinated international response, and each newly identified outbreak is evaluated for its potential to become a PHEIC by the country in which it is occurring, even though reporting might legitimately come from elsewhere, using a decision tree instrument developed for this purpose.

Once a potential PHEIC is identified and reported to WHO by the country or countries concerned, the revised IHR require that an ad hoc Emergency Committee be set up to review the evidence available to WHO and conduct a risk assessment. A recommendation is then made to the WHO Director General as to whether or not the criteria for a PHEIC are met, and the Director General uses this recommendation, and other sources of information, to decide the course of action.

The Emergency Committee has met several times under the revised IHR, first when Influenza A (H1N1) was reported as a PHEIC by Mexico in 2009 when its risk assessment suggested that a pandemic would occur, after which the Director General declared a pandemic; and in 2012, 2013, and 2014 to conduct risk assessments of the newly emerging Middle East Respiratory Syndrome coronavirus (MERSCoV) that continues to sporadically infect humans, but has not been declared a global emergency by the Director General as of June 2014. WHO has continuously sought additional information about the MERSCoV from the countries in which is appears to be emerging in order that the Emergency Committee risk assessment can be more complete, but some of this information has not been forthcoming, and there is no enforcement mechanism within the revised IHR that can be used to obtain it.

Under the revised IHR countries are also required to notify WHO for even a single occurrence of a disease that would always threaten global public health security – smallpox, poliomyelitis caused by a wild-type poliovirus, human influenza caused by a new virus subtype, and SARS. In addition, there is a second list that includes diseases of documented – but not inevitable – international impact. An event involving a disease on this second list, which includes cholera, pneumonic plague, yellow fever, Ebola, and the other haemorrhagic fevers, still requires the use of the decision tree instrument to determine if it is a PHEIC. Thus, two safeguards create a baseline of public health security by requiring countries to respond, in designated ways, to well-known threats.

In contrast to the IHR of 1969 that only attempted to stop the spread of infections by action across international borders, the IHR (2005) have introduced a requirement that each country develop and maintain a set of core capacities for surveillance and response in order to rapidly detect, assess, notify, report, and contain the events covered by the regulations so that their potential for international spread and negative economic impact can be minimized. Countries are being monitored as to whether they have developed these core capacities by annual voluntary reports to the World Health Organization, based on a standardized self-assessment tool. Several countries have recently asked for an extension of the time period during which this core capacity strengthening must be accomplished, initially decided as 2007–2015. These extensions are being granted, but as for reporting of evidence required for risk assessment, there has been no enforcement mechanism established to ensure that core capacities are actually developed.

The IHR (2005) also require collective action by all WHO Member States in the event that an emerging or reemerging infectious disease begins to spread internationally, and the free-sharing of information pertaining to this threat. They thus provide a safety net against the international spread of emerging or reemerging infections, requiring collaboration between all countries to ensure the timely availability of surveillance information and technical resources that better guarantee international public health security.

Other international frameworks have also been developed to contain and curtail the international spread of emerging infections. Among them are the WHO Global Strategy for the Containment of Antimicrobial Resistance (World Health Organization 2001). Antimicrobial resistance – the acquired ability of microbes to resist treatment with antibiotics and other anti-infective drugs, is one of the most important emerging infectious disease problems of the 21st century. Resistant microbes can emerge anywhere where infections are present, including at the animal/human interface in shared human and animal ecosystems. Though not legally binding, this framework calls on countries to work across the human health, animal health, agricultural, and trade sectors to ensure more rational use of anti-infective drugs in order to limit the factors that accelerate the emergence and proliferation of anti-infective-drug-resistant microbes.

Conclusion

Emerging infectious diseases, most of which emerge at the animal/human interface, are clearly complex, dynamic, and constantly evolving. When they emerge, they have the potential for a major negative impact on economic security. At the same time however, efforts to prevent their international spread – either precautionary, evidence-based, or reactionary – can also have damaging economic repercussions because of measures such as culling and decreased travel and/or trade.

In 1969 the Member States of the World Health Organization put in place a global framework agreement, the International Health Regulations, in an attempt to ensure continued functioning of the global economy, international travel, and cross-border trade when three infectious diseases that had the potential to spread internationally were reported by the countries in which they were occurring. The IHR were based on the premise that international spread of these infectious diseases could be stopped by instituting predetermined measures at international border posts.

The International Health Regulations were revised and broadened in scope after the SARS outbreak in 2003 to include all public health emergencies of international concern, and the IHR are now based on the understanding that measures at international borders are not sufficient to decrease the risk of international spread of emerging infections – and that the best possible prevention is linked to rapid detection and response where and when infections emerge.

Under the revised IHR, WHO member states are now being monitored on the development of core capacities against a set of predetermined core capacities required to accomplish this. Monitoring is based on voluntary country reporting after having used a standardized self-assessment tool, but questions have arisen whether self-assessment is the best means of holding countries accountable and whether an external assessment is required.

Should country efforts to stop an emerging infection be unsuccessful, the revised IHR also provide a safety net for collective international action. An international Emergency Committee is now required under the IHR, and it is convened under the IHR to make recommendations to the Director General of WHO as to whether an event is a PHEIC, and if so what measures should be taken based on existing evidence. Limitations however, remain. Though the Emergency Committee requires best possible evidence for risk assessment, there is no enforcement mechanism that can be called into action if countries fail to collect and report the necessary information (see Hoffman, chapter 20 in this volume). This in fact, as for the SARS outbreak in 2003, requires additional international, sometimes political, pressure from the global community.

In summary, over the centuries the world has collectively made great advances in decreasing the risk of international spread of infectious diseases, including those that are emerging. International agreements have been regularly revised as better understanding of the dynamics of infectious, and emerging infectious diseases have been understood. Whereas in the past it was felt that international borders could effectively stop international spread when countries voluntarily reported, it is now understood that the best defense is rapid detection and response when and where infectious diseases occur or emerge.

At the same time, because the majority of emerging infections occur as breeches in the species barrier between animals and humans occur, there is growing understanding that the animal health and human health communities must work closer together under what is now called a "one health" framework. Challenges in working together are obvious: human concerns are about health and cost is often secondary, while animal health concerns are about making a profit on animals sold for food. The way forward includes understanding of the cost-effectives of intervening earlier at the animal health level and continuing to use, assess, and revise international agreements such as the IHR.

References

Atkinson, N. (1996) 'The impact of BSE on the UK economy', Online. Available HTTP: <http://www.veterinaria.org/revistas/vetenfinf/bse/14Atkinson.html> (accessed 17 January 2014).

Diack, A.B., Ritchie, D., Bishop, M., Pinion, V., Brandel, J-P., Haik, S., Tagliavini, F., Van Duijn, C., Belay, E.D., Gambetti, P., Schonberger, L.B., Piccardo, P., Will, R.G. and Manson, J.C. (2012) 'Constant transmission properties of variant Creutzfeldt-Jakob Disease in 5 countries', *Emerging Infectious Diseases*, 18. DOI:10.3201/eid1810.120792

Lederberg, J., Shope R.E. and Oaks S.C., Jr. (eds.) (1992) *Emerging Infections: Microbial Threats to Health in the United States*, Washington, DC: National Academy Press.

Taubenberger, J. and Morens, D. (2006) '1918 influenza: the mother of all pandemics', *Emerging Infectious Diseases*, 12. DOI: 10.3201/eid1201.050979

UNAIDS. (2012) *World AIDS Day Report – Results,* Geneva: UNAIDS. Online. Available HTTP: <http://www.unaids.org/en/media/unaids/contentassets/documents/epidemiology/2012/gr2012/JC2434_WorldAIDSday_results_en.pdf> (accessed 17 January 2014).

World Bank. (2005) *Avian Flu: Economic Losses Could Top US$800.* Online. Available HTTP: <http://go.worldbank.org/5KMZGBOTE0> (accessed 14 May 2014).

World Health Organization. (2001) *WHO Global Strategy for Containment of Antimicrobial Resistance*, Geneva: WHO. Online. Available HTTP: <http://www.who.int/drugresistance/WHO_Global_Strategy_English.pdf> (accessed 14 May 2014).

9

AIDS AS A SECURITY THREAT

The emergence and the decline of an idea[1]

Pieter Fourie

This chapter explores the historical development of multilateral efforts in global health governance to frame HIV/AIDS as a security issue to be included on national and international political agendas.

With the complexities brought about by globalization and the emergence of new, more virulent pathogens, health challenges have increasingly been labeled as security issues or as exemplars of collective insecurity for sovereign states in particular. This frame presents effective health governance as a matter of national and international security that demands sophisticated surveillance, institutionalization, and health policy prescriptions crafted at the multilateral level and then applied to the whole world. In so doing, public health challenges, which are usually discussed as "low" politics, focusing on soft issues including social justice, human rights, and the general delivery of services, are legitimized as security challenges, which are thus rendered exceptional, as "high" politics.

This security framework has placed emphasis on a process to secure *states*, instead of prioritizing *people* by providing better health systems around the world and dealing with the long-term reality of AIDS. However, hard evidence has shown no significant covariation between AIDS prevalence and military insecurity, social uprising, macroeconomic failure, electoral instability, or democratic consolidation – in short, there is no empirical proof to support the hypothesis that AIDS, even in the context of mature, high-prevalence epidemics, poses any significant threat to state survival.

Instead of a knee-jerk, high political response, appropriate intervention to assist with AIDS epidemics should focus on better healthcare, not security; on health systems, tailored to each different context. In this way AIDS governance should be done in a more conscious manner to facilitate public health interventions, mobilize funds, and create institutions with a long-term agenda. Multilateral consensus on the effective governance of HIV/AIDS should be mindful of the systemic and temporal realities of the pandemic, such as long-term changes required in gender relations, sustainable behavior change, and cultural adaptation. This would be a more appropriate and sustainable response to the epidemic, rather than feeding an AIDS-security complex, which does more harm than good.

The chapter proceeds by explaining in the first instance how health and international security came to be associated with one another and then institutionalized over the past two centuries. The chapter then explains how AIDS specifically came to be crafted as an international security threat, and how the three master narratives in international relations contributed to such a conceptualization. Third, the decline of the AIDS security frame is discussed, and the chapter ends with an appeal to a different, more appropriate perspective on the kinds of challenges that the pandemic poses.

Security and health: past is prologue

Until the Industrial Revolution of the 19th century, state-centered interventions to limit the spread and impact of disease focused mostly on isolated epidemic outbreaks. This was the case with the quarantining of people and goods suspected of carrying infectious disease, a practice that originated in the Port of Venice during the plague epidemics of the 14th century (King 2002: 764).

According to Zacher (2007: 15–29), global health collaboration has evolved through three historical periods. First, from the mid-19th century to the early 20th century, a treaty to control the international spread of epidemic disease was negotiated, mostly by European states. This happened in parallel with the Industrial Revolution, as colonial masters interacted more frequently with and were more exposed to the diseases of other parts of the world. The negotiations followed on a conference held in Paris in 1851 to address the threat of cholera. The negotiations culminated in the acceptance of the International Sanitary Regulations of 1903, which were later renamed the International Health Regulations (the IHRs are continuously updated and remain active today).

The second major development in the search for an international health regime was the establishment of the World Health Organization (WHO) in 1948 under the aegis of the UN. The WHO championed and approved revised versions of the IHR in 1951, 1969, 1973, and 1981. International relations (which refer to interactions between states) thus became institutionalized via multilateral (and not bilateral) channels and actors; this presaged a move from international health governance to global health governance.

Lastly, since 1990, there has been a dramatic expansion in multilateral efforts at global health cooperation. After the Severe Acute Respiratory Syndrome (SARS) scare of 2003, the IHR was again amended. The revised version was formally adopted in May 2005 and came into force in June 2007. A key thrust of this evolving health regime is health surveillance (Davies 2008: 308–13), along with emergency interventions to control epidemic outbreaks. Fidler and Gostin (2006: 86) argue that the new IHR is a paradigm shift compared to the old version, to the extent that it will transform and expand "the scope of the IHR's application, incorporate international human rights principles, contain more demanding obligations for states parties to conduct surveillance and response, and establish important new powers for WHO."

Fidler (2007: 41–66) points out that this regime is noted for its embrace of health problems as security issues. He remarks that the world now operates in a "post-securitization phase," in which "[v]iewing public health through the lens of security has become an integral aspect of public health governance in the 21st century" (Fidler 2007: 41). He further argues that the contemporary securitization of health is the result of post-Cold War fears regarding the proliferation of bioweapons and the global spread of communicable diseases (especially HIV/AIDS, but also the SARS and H5N1 scares of recent years), as well as mounting sensitivities regarding the vulnerability of populations in both rich and poor countries in the context of rapid globalization. Zacher (2007) contends that there is no simple explanation for the change in the international health regime, but that a contributing factor has been the emergence of new and more virulent pandemic diseases, the greater understanding of the costs of disease to economies and societies that are more deeply linked through processes of globalization, the expanding participation of civil society and private actors (many via public–private partnerships) in global health governance, and the improvement of disease detection and surveillance via the internet (pp. 21ff).

Health has thus come to be viewed as an exemplar of humanity's "new collective insecurity" (Shaw et al. 2006: 5). According to Pirages (2007: 625), such "growing complexity requires more sophisticated forms of governance," as well as the move from a state-centric to a supranational level of global public health governance to address what are, in essence, health issues that transcend national borders. Significantly, emerging from these new realities is the tension between the broader people-centric perspective on health, which views health as a basic individual human right linked to broader rights of citizenship and health's social determinants, and the understanding of health that links it to securitization. We have thus witnessed the complication of individual human health, its rapid evolution to a state-centric conception, then demanding supra- and multilateral responses, and the concomitant institutionalization that his allowed.

Why securitize an epidemic?

On 5 June 1981 the Centers for Disease Control and Prevention (CDC) published its *Weekly Morbidity and Mortality Report*, chronicling for the first time the symptoms amongst a few urban gay men of what was set to become the most deadly plague known to humanity. The HIV/AIDS pandemic has since killed over 30 million individuals worldwide. Globally, 34 million people were living with HIV at the end of 2011. An estimated 0.8% of adults aged 15–49 years worldwide are living with HIV, although the burden of the epidemic continues to vary considerably between countries and regions. Sub-Saharan Africa remains most severely affected, with nearly 1 in every 20 adults (4.9%) living with HIV and accounting for 69% of the people living with HIV worldwide. Although the regional prevalence of HIV infection is nearly 25 times higher in sub-Saharan Africa than in Asia, almost 5 million people are living with HIV in South, Southeast, and East Asia combined. After sub-Saharan Africa, the regions most heavily affected are the Caribbean, Eastern Europe, and Central Asia, where 1% of adults were living with HIV in 2011 (UNAIDS 2012).

To make matters worse, epidemiologists say that the AIDS epidemic (since it results from HIV, a *lentivirus*, meaning that it acts slowly) is a "long-wave event." Amongst other implications, this means that it is an insidious phenomenon that might take up to 50 or even 120 years to play itself out (Barnett 2006: 304). Humanity has never experienced anything comparable in its history. The world does not know what the long-term impact of the pandemic will be.

How does one respond to such a threat in an effective and appropriately scaled way? There have been several attempts to make sense of the global epidemic and to propose appropriate responses to it. The following short list is incomplete, and only illustrative of the main discourses that have emerged; one often finds a hybrid of their individual narrative elements:

- *Medicalization*: viewing AIDS strictly as a biological event, driven by a pathogen, and applying epidemiology and medical science to craft responses, focusing on biomedical interventions. Randomized controlled trials are the gold standard for finding out what works to combat the virus that causes AIDS;
- *Moralization*: viewing AIDS as a punishment, or as the result of objectionable (often "sinful") behavior of individuals or groups of immoral people (in particular gays, promiscuous people, and prostitutes; often particular cultural practices are also blamed). The appropriate response to HIV in this frame ranges from behavior change to social sanctions, legislation, and punishment;
- *Monetization*: viewing AIDS as the result of unequal or unfair distribution of material means. There are two main schools of thinking here: 1) a developmental set, which emphasizes

structural impediments and the dynamics of poverty/inequality in particular in determining the manifestation of the pandemic; the appropriate response to AIDS in this conception would be to work for greater global justice and the elimination of material and structural inequalities generally (blaming the Global North, the legacies of colonialism, and pharmaceutical companies are particularly seductive narratives here), and 2) a neoliberal response, which stresses market imperfections and interference as the main factor driving the pandemic; an appropriate response according to neoliberal proponents would be to allow the invisible hand of the market to generate efficient economies of scale around the pandemic.

Another key response has been to polemicize the epidemic; a master narrative has been created to "securitize" AIDS. McInnes and Rushton (2010: 226) point out that "[t]he idea that AIDS poses a potential threat to security has been around for a surprisingly long time. As early as 1987 – at which time only eleven sub-Saharan African states had reported over 100 cases. . . . A US Special National Intelligence Estimate examined the implications of the AIDS pandemic for the region in detail . . . [and] there were clear concerns about the strategic and security implications of AIDS."

By making appeals to *states'* security, and by crafting AIDS as an "enemy" that needs to be "battled" and "defeated," a number of effects can be achieved (also see Fourie & Follér 2013):

- An issue can be moved from the domain of "normal" and low politics to "exceptional" and high politics – according to McInnes and Rushton (2011: 121) "[t]he securitization of HIV/AIDS was an explicit attempt to change the status of the disease, moving it from the realm of 'normal' politics to that of an exceptional issue posing as existential threat to states";
- A sense of imminent danger or threat is evoked;
- There is an increase in the political commitment to addressing the issue, domestically, multilaterally, as well as globally;
- An identifiable and common villain becomes apparent;
- It allows mythmaking around who the saviors or victors might be – according to Roe (2012: 250) "securitization inevitably produces categories of 'haves' and 'have-nots' – those that belong to the political community and those that do not. . . . [W]e cannot all be equal sharers of security";
- Institutions, budgets, and manpower can be provided to combat the spread of the epidemic;
- Public health interventions can be activated, and human rights concerns can take a backseat;
- Interfering laws, rules, and regulations can be suspended to enable rapid intervention. Elbe (2006: 128) reminds us that security "pushes responses to the disease away from civil society towards the much less transparent workings of military and intelligence organizations, which also possess the power to override human rights and civil liberties";
- "[Securitization] enabled the argument that HIV/AIDS should be ex-cepted [sic] from the actually existing neoliberal regime for dealing with infectious disease. . . . HIV/AIDS thus became a prime candidate for . . . 'market foster care', where . . . limited, targeted (or exceptional) aid is justified to save populations and enable countries to join in the neoliberal growth paradigm" (Ingram 2013: 441).

Since AIDS first made newspaper headlines in the early 1980s this narrative or culture of securitization has come to be associated with the epidemic. In the context of the "war against terror" after 11 September 2001 many are becoming increasingly familiar with the super-patriotic proclivities and nationalistic pathologies that securitization can enable. Thus a closer look at the powerful ways that the AIDS pandemic has been constructed as a threat is in order. At the zenith of the George W. Bush administration in the US, Laurie Garrett (2005: 64) observed that:

> in the aftermath of September 11, 2001, the United States tends to define all national security concerns through the prism of terrorism. That framework is overly limited even for the United States, and an absurdly narrow template to apply to the security of most other countries. The HIV/AIDS pandemic is aggravating a laundry list of underlying tensions in developing, declining, and failed states. As the burden of death due to HIV/AIDS skyrockets around the world over the next five to ten years, the disease may well play a more profound role on the security stage of many nations, and present the wealthy world with a challenge the likes of which it has never experienced. How countries, rich and poor, frame HIV/AIDS within their national security debates today may well determine how well they respond to the massive grief, demographic destruction, and security threats that the pandemic will present tomorrow.

Since the late 1990s there has been significant academic interest in the construction of metaphors and myths (including the securitization) of disease and even of the AIDS epidemic in recent years – for instance, see Altman and Buse (2012), Elbe (2006, 2009), World Health Organization (2008), Ingram (2007), Poku et al. (2007), United Nations (2004), Altman (1999, 2003), Sontag (1989, 2002), and Fourie and Schönteich (2002). This analysis has been happening within the context of a mostly discreet yet exceedingly influential battle between individual state sovereignty and its concomitant epidemic response imperatives on the one hand, and the multilateralization of the pandemic on the other. This multilateralization happens via the World Bank's Multi-Country HIV/AIDS Program (MAP), Global Fund initiatives, and UNAIDS.

Potentially the scene is set for either tension between autonomous, state-centered interventions on the one hand, and multilateral initiatives on the other, or large-scale and mostly coercive policy transfer from well-resourced multilateral agencies to poor countries. Discursively, one of the ways in which this tension has been playing itself out has been through appeals to either a (hard) securitization agenda that make appeals to the dangers that AIDS implies for state survival, or an agenda that appeals more directly to a softer, human security approach that underlines the nefarious implications of the epidemic for individual human rights to health. The latter approach has been most closely associated with a developmental agenda. Either way, global AIDS governance has become supremely political.

Security narratives in international relations

Securitization was formally problematized in Political Science discourse in the 1990s, when Ole Wæver, Barry Buzan, and other members of the so-called Copenhagen School coined the term to advance discourse regarding security "beyond a focus on the nation-state and on the provision or analysis of military security issues only" (Kelle 2007: 218). Buzan and Wæver (quoted in Cook 2008: 6) summarize the securitization process as follows:

> A security issue is posited (by a securitizing actor) as a threat to the survival of some referent object (nation, state, the liberal economic order, the rain forests), which is claimed to have a right to survive. Since a question of survival necessarily involves a point of no return at which it will be too late to act, it is not defensible to leave this

> issue to normal politics. The securitizing actor therefore claims a right to use extraordinary means or break normal rules, for the reasons of security.

Since 11/9 (9 November 1989: the fall of the Berlin Wall) and 9/11 (the terrorist attacks on the United States in September 2001), the nations of the G-8 and UN agencies in particular have been in the throes of what could potentially be an interesting marriage between a traditional, militaristic way of thinking about security and the more contemporary, human security perspective alluded to above. The war on terror and the war on AIDS are seen as two sides of the same coin. Both have been constructed by the U.S. State Department as risks requiring the rapid mobilization of resources and have become a central subject of foreign policy requiring U.S. leadership and international collaboration.

In terms of power politics – politically as well as economically – words and institutions matter. They have had significant impacts on the manner in which ideologies have shaped elites' mental maps, descriptions, and prescriptions about the allocation of scarce resources in broader society. The multilateralization of AIDS as a security issue peaked in the first decade of the 21st century: "the intervention of the Security Council in 2000 was a critical move in securitizing HIV/AIDS, *constructing* the disease as something extraordinary which demanded international attention and action" [emphasis added] (McInnes 2006: 315).

In these terms, the current global order is the result of three major ideological developments that inform everything from international law to the manner in which multilateral institutions and states conceptualize and respond to new threats such as HIV/AIDS. The first major ideological development was the Treaty of Westphalia of 1648, which ended the 30-year religious war in Europe and established the modern state system. Modern notions of state sovereignty and the search for a global balance of power in the absence of a global government resulted from this development. It continues to permeate the way in which states relate to each other. Normatively, the Realist ideology that emanated from the Treaty of Westphalia of 1648 emphasizes the centrality of state autonomy and security – notions that have become embedded in international law and inform the ways in which governments in particular respond to external and other threats.

This Realist notion of traditional security has since been questioned and in some ways challenged by Liberal notions regarding global power. The French revolution in 1789 shifted the state-centric view towards greater empathy for a humanistic and individually based level of analysis. The state was now seen as secondary or complementary to the interests of its citizens, whose rights it was obligated to protect. These notions have also become embedded in international law and other conventions – amongst them UN conventions on individual human rights (amongst these are rights to health and other forms of security).

This human-centered approach was supported by a greater developmental focus emphasized by Marxian thinkers, who base their ideological prescriptions on notions of security and what it is that humans need to be "safe from" in the original writings of Karl Marx and others in the mid-to-late 19th century. Rather than focusing on the individual unit of analysis, as the Liberals would, proponents underline the importance of economic class and exploitation resulting from material inequalities and structural deficiencies at the national and global levels.

This ideological history is important, as it has had a direct impact on the evolution of the multilateral custodians of peace and security after World War II, as well as the ideological underpinnings informing perspectives of health as a security issue in the 21st century. The victors at the end of the war wanted to create an organization that would assist in establishing a global order based on the notion of "collective security" (Nye 2000). States would become each other's keepers, not allowing any individual member of the UN to abuse economic or politically nationalistic notions to drag the world into a third world war.

This new system of collective security was entrenched institutionally through the creation of the UN. It was in turn couched in the context of an evolving global legal system based broadly on guarantees of state sovereignty, collective state security, and individual human rights. The ideal thus became a rather interesting hybrid of Realist and Liberal discourses applied within the multilateral organization, with members of especially the new second and third worlds emphasizing (discursively at least) notions of greater global class equity and fairness. The post-World War II multilateral context thus created a political arena in which the three main ideologies (Realism, Liberalism, and Marxism) pertaining to evolving notions of "security" could be tested and played out.

After 1989 and the end of that ideological conflict, however, conceptions of "security" were reconsidered. No longer was the world subject to conventional notions of conflict; new/other threats would come to permeate the orthodox description of *realpolitik*. The global context had moved on from narrow notions regarding an ideological battle between the first and the second worlds played out through proxy wars in mainly the developing/third world. After 1989 nationalism was reasserting itself: from intra-state conflicts in the Balkans and in Africa to the appearance of a new kind of terrorism wrought of fundamentalist or politicized religion. It was also around this same time (in 1990) that the U.S. Central Intelligence Agency (CIA) for the first time added HIV/AIDS to its list of variables that might cause greater state fragility and eventual failure, particularly in the developing world (Fourie & Schönteich 2002: 8). As the traditional military notions of security threats started to recede in the early 1990s, the UN Development Program (UNDP) released a report in 1994, coining the phrase "human security." It referred to any threat (military or other) that threatened the well-being of humans (see Caballero-Anthony & Amul, chapter 3 in this volume).

Academia responded predictably, by commencing an abstract, semantic game of establishing what the implications might be of a human security versus a military security agenda. These debates crystallized around two main positions. Most argued that the securitization of an issue is useful by forcing states to put an issue such as AIDS on the public agenda. By applying the language of wars or imminent threat a polemic is presupposed, and states respond to crises by mobilizing resources – "there is more than a suspicion that the securitizing move was part of an attempt to gain greater political attention for the HIV/AIDS crisis" (McInnes 2006: 326). Other analysts warned that securitization might actually have a counter-productive effect: by "othering" and "enemizing" selective aspects of the pandemic (e.g., homosexuality, commercial sex workers, intravenous drug users, insidious big pharma, and so on), a dangerous space could be created for increased stigmatization, especially of persons living with HIV (see Elbe 2006; Sontag 2002).

In the short term the securitization of AIDS achieved exactly what many said it needed to: after a visit by the U.S. ambassador to the UN, Richard Holbrooke, to Africa in December 1999 to personally witness the impact of the growing AIDS epidemic, on 10 January 2000 the UN Security Council (UNSC) for the first time in its history debated what was ostensibly a health issue in terms of security (Behrman 2004: 158–165). This meeting was followed in July 2000 by UN Resolution 1308, which formalized the securitization of HIV/AIDS. It is important that these developments took place within the UNSC: in the days of the Cold War this was the UN body where global powers could do their posturing; the UNSC is a state-centric vehicle par excellence. However, in terms of how Resolution 1308 formally securitized the pandemic, the language of human security was to a large extent evoked. One year after Resolution 1308, in mid-2001, the UN General Assembly held a special session on HIV/AIDS (UNGASS), which went even further to putting the pandemic on the multilateral agenda. During the special session, former U.S. Military Chief of Staff and then Secretary of State General Colin Powell declared that "there is no enemy in war more insidious than AIDS" (Behrman 2004: 266).

The ideological and instrumental utility of securitizing AIDS

AIDS only became a biomedical issue in the 1980s, and then only appeared on the global public agenda in the 1990s. As a result, this context of normative contestation regarding the securitization of AIDS is a very recent phenomenon. The consequence has been that various AIDS watchers have been making claims and counter-claims regarding the link between the pandemic and its impacts. This discourse is constantly revised – a process that takes place in an increasingly political global and particularly multilateral environment. This is understandable, given the high stakes: billions of dollars have been made available to counter AIDS and other chronic diseases. This has given rise to an AIDS industry (in both financial and ideological terms) as the battle for the control over who can and should shape global efforts to combat AIDS has taken hold (Garrett 2007). In the high political discursive environment regarding the purported link between AIDS and state security there have been significant developments.

As mentioned above, in 1990 the CIA added HIV to its "state failure watchlist" as a variable that contributes to state collapse (CIA 1991). In 2002 the U.S. National Security Strategy identified failing states as the United States' main threat, arguing that failed or failing states provide a fertile breeding ground for terrorism and also lead to regional spillover effects (Wolff 2006), dragging more than only the failing states into a condition of anarchy – this conclusion was reiterated by the 2006 U.S. National Security Strategy document (Carment 2003: 407; Patrick & Brown 2006: 2).

But then something strange happened. Security professionals and academics appeared to change their minds about the purported link between AIDS and security. In 2005 the U.S. National Intelligence Council (NIC) stated that "it is not clear if AIDS can be directly tied to state collapse in the way that was feared and anticipated a few years ago" (NIC 2005: 2). Even in the U.S. homeland security environment there thus appears to be no consensus regarding the link between AIDS and state fragility. This in itself is not problematic, given that Kuhnian scientific revolutions are based on the testing and revision of theses. However, what is problematic is that it became apparent that the AIDS-security discourse had been shaped by a surprising lack of attention to conceptual clarity and, importantly, empirical enquiry. The result was that the debates about the supposed link between AIDS and state fragility came to be informed by (mostly unsubstantiated) normative and ideological agendas.

The central polemic can be summarized as follows. First, loose and unsubstantiated statements were made about the covariance of mature AIDS epidemics on the one hand and state fragility on the other. In other words, there was an assumption that state fragility itself creates an enabling environment for the vectoring of HIV. Rising prevalence levels in turn were seen to be contributing to state fragility and ultimate state collapse. This first polemic was for the most part untested.

Integrated with this first polemic was an implied polemic that provided the ideological environment for a broader *problematique*: state fragility in itself was seen as contributing to global insecurity (particularly as it is seen to act as a vector for terrorism) (Krasner & Pascual 2005). In turn it was argued that this global insecurity provided an enabling environment for further instances of state fragility and eventual collapse.

Given the obfuscation and contestation associated with these arguments and the general AIDS-state failure discourse thus far, it is worth exploring what states are, in fact, supposed to do, as well as what is meant by state fragility. Once this has been more firmly established one should be able to speak more confidently to the possible causal links between AIDS and state stability.

Testing the polemics: states and fragility

Essentially the core functions of the state are 1) to provide physical security to everyone living in its area of jurisdiction; 2) to build and maintain legitimate political institutions to implement government programs and sustain the whole; 3) to provide sound and consistent economic management; and 4) to provide mechanisms of social welfare to those who need them (Eisenstat et al. 2005: 136; Patrick 2006).

Analysts of state fragility stress a number of qualifications to be borne in mind. For instance, one should not assume that the weakest states are necessarily the poorest; weak states tend to have bouts of political instability in common; state weakness spillovers are not linear, but vary by threat (Patrick 2006: 31–32). In other words, any analysis of state fragility as an independent variable is contingent; except for the manifestation of political instability, state fragility manifests in exceedingly granular ways. It is thus easier to initially describe fragile states in terms of what they are not: stable or resilient states have effective institutions, the political will and capacity to fulfill the core functions referred to above, achieve and maintain an adequate degree of social cohesion, social equality, and the ability to withstand exogenous and endogenous shocks. Fragile states on the other hand are broadly associated with social dissent, lack of border control, predation by the state on their own constituents, flawed institutions, deteriorating infrastructure, endemic corruption, a declining gross domestic product, food shortages, loss of legitimacy, an increase in infant mortality, a closed economic system, and a general informalization of the economy towards localized subsistence rather than commercial surplus production (Patrick 2006: 45–49; Vallings & Moreno-Torres 2005: 4).

In this logic those who argue that AIDS threatens security by weakening the state should be able to demonstrate that the pandemic is directly eroding and reversing the very existence and effectiveness of the state functions described above. However, amongst those states about which there is general consensus regarding their fragility or their danger of failing, AIDS does not appear as a common feature. In fact, for the most part AIDS is not an issue in most of these states. Recent studies have shown that there are no empirically demonstrable data that prove any significant covariation between AIDS prevalence and military insecurity, social uprising, macroeconomic failure, electoral instability, or democratic consolidation (De Waal 2006; Fourie 2009; O'Keefe 2012). This is the case even in national contexts of high-prevalence, mature epidemics.

Given this reality, it is prudent to ask whether the link between AIDS and state fragility in general is not more a matter of ideology than description:

> At bottom, the entire literature on fragile or failed states assumes a particular normative model of the state – a liberal democratic state that is market-friendly, transparent, and accountable, with very specific institutional requirements – without analysing that model at all. It is a given in identifying failure
>
> (Woodward 2004:6).

Significantly, policy or programmatic prescriptions resulting from this ideological model also form the basis of an evolving multilateral or "Geneva Consensus" for not only good governance but also for good AIDS governance. In other words, the political values associated with the institutions that are set up to address the challenges of AIDS have implications for how those institutions should be managed, and how individual countries should be governed. This has exceedingly political implications for the supposed links between HIV and democracy, democratic remedies/vaccines against HIV, the inferred links between HIV and fragile states, and the evolution of the discourse of securitization around both state failure and HIV post-9/11.

The future of the AIDS and security agenda

This chapter emphasizes two critical lessons, complemented by a number of implications as to a required future research agenda.

The first lesson is that precise Words Matter. How HIV/AIDS – the "problem" – is defined, and by whom, will make a fundamental difference in terms of how responses to the pandemic are conceptualized and implemented (Ostergard & Barcelo 2005). This is the case on a national as well as on a global level. The AIDS policy environment in South Africa was in disarray for years because of contending and contested problem definition spaces (Fourie & Meyer 2010). As demonstrated above, states as well as multilateral institutions are working towards coming to grips with the rapidly shifting ontological demands that the pandemic implies. On a continental level, Africa needs to find its own voice regarding perceptions and conceptualizations of the purported links between AIDS and security (De Waal 2003).

The second lesson is that reliable numbers matter. Inductive research can all too quickly lead intellectual elites into a trap of "wag-the-dog" result-seeking. Malleable conceptual clarity requires action based on reliable empirical evidence – and the AIDS research community has seen precious little of that. In fact, as McInnes and Rushton (2011: 120) point out, "[w]hat we find is a phenomenon whereby the securitizing move [in the case of AIDS] used a series of claims for which little hard 'evidence' was needed (or, indeed, offered)." The result has been that scholars have been at war with each other over semantics and dollars rather than with the HI virus. Researchers everywhere need greater accountability to the clients implied by contemporary conceptions of the marriage between heterodox conceptions of security. Such accountability should galvanize the move towards evidence-based policy making, rather than an ongoing tolerance for policy-based evidence making.

With these two insights at the macro level in mind, a number of specific research areas requiring urgent enquiry vis-à-vis the link between AIDS and security present themselves (also see Barnett & Prins 2006; Benatar 2005).

This first is the search for better data. Given the dearth of AIDS-related data relating to issues of security, there is a need to establish an integrated surveillance system for recording rates of HIV and AIDS in uniformed services globally within obvious constraints of confidentiality and security. To complement such a system, it is necessary to establish a data base of the demographic structure of armies and other uniformed services, their experiences with anti-retroviral medicines, terms of access for serving members and their households, and service policies in relation to HIV/AIDS issues in general, to include: testing, treatment, care while in and after leaving the service. Also empirically based analysis is needed of the role of HIV/AIDS in relation to the issue of force/mission ratios that cannot be met.

The second area is the relationship between AIDS and evolving conceptions of "security." Scholars need much more careful testing of the hypothesis that in situations of civil disorder the isolation of civil populations may reduce rates of transmission. AIDS analysts need to move beyond orthodox qualitative and empirical data-gathering methodologies and include the innovative use of scenarios and other futures methodologies to explore the possible impact and expand thinking about this and other long-wave events.

The third area is the relationship between AIDS and governance. Scholars need to recognize the new type of challenge that AIDS poses in high prevalence countries and develop policies and programs designed to counter this trend as well as to mitigate the impact on communities, service providers and vital public sector functions. Comparative studies are needed of HIV/AIDS in irregular forces and in situations of civil peace, with particular emphasis on potential development of appropriate prevention measures and programs.

The fourth area is the relationship between AIDS and uniformed services. New research needs to explore the relationships between uniformed services and their host environments, whether at home or on overseas deployment. This should include the integration of prevention, diagnostic, treatment, and care services for households and families of military and other uniformed service personnel, paying particular attention to gender issues. There has been a particular research silence on the impact of AIDS in police services, so a comparative study of HIV/AIDS and police forces in a range of countries to assess the availability of services for these forces would be timely. To facilitate this, detailed ethnographic studies of uniformed service behaviors in peace-keeping operations are required. This context is compounded by the rising threat of TB and especially multiple-drug resistant TB in high-AIDS prevalence areas. This can only add to the weight of the problem, and the incremental effect of parallel epidemics should be explicated. At the behavioral level, research is needed regarding the relationship between sexual risk taking and training with the aim of exploring the hypothesis that risk taking in combat training results in sexual risk taking behaviors among military personnel. Institutionally there also needs to be more examination of the question of how HIV/AIDS is being addressed in the context of security sector reforms, rule of law, and sexual violence in relation to concentrations of uniformed service populations.

Conclusion

In addressing these issues, one should be wary of notions invoking any so-called "tyranny of best practice." AIDS is not a monolithic epidemic; it has a variety of impacts in different localities. Thus "intervention can move away from a 'one size fits all' approach into much smarter and more targeted policies and programs" (Dutch Ministry of Foreign Affairs 2005: 2). That said, the global AIDS pandemic offers an enormous opportunity for societal and intellectual learning – in that way it can go beyond an assemblage of tragic anecdotes and become a truly transformational social agent.

But in order to get there, one must heed this chapter's most basic message: the securitization of AIDS needs to be done in a conscious and nuanced manner. Securitization comes with significant normative and ideological baggage, and it has become fashionable to securitize everything from the "war on terror" to global water scarcity and famine. Securitization has significant implications as an enabling tool – it can determine who is demonized, who the enemy is, who is excluded or included in decision-making, who the saviors are, the creation of myths regarding guilt and exculpation, as well as serve a multitude of industries.

It is true that securitization can be remarkably effective for public health interventions in particular, for mobilizing money, creating institutions, galvanizing a sense of crisis, and implementing short-term, rapid responses. However, given the long-wave reality of the global AIDS crisis and the multilateral consensus regarding a global human rights-based response, such securitization and a focus on quick fixes may actually blind those in power to the more systemic and temporal realities of the pandemic. The proactive, long-term changes required in gender relations, sustainable behavior change, and cultural adaptation are not served by the knee-jerk reactivity and short-termism of recent AIDS securitization.

Note

1 This is a revised and updated version of a contribution which first appeared in J. Kirton, A. Cooper, F. Lisk, and H. Besada (eds.) (2014). *Moving Health Sovereignty in Africa: Disease, Governance, Climate Change*, Farnham: Ashgate.

References

Altman, D. (1999) 'AIDS and questions of global governance', *Pacifica Review*, 11: 195–211.

Altman, D. (2003) 'HIV and security', *International Relations*, 17: 417–427.

Altman, D. and Buse, K. (2012) 'Thinking politically about HIV: political analysis and action in response to AIDS', *Contemporary Politics*, 18: 127–140.

Barnett, T. (2006) 'A long-wave event. HIV/AIDS, politics, governance and "security": sundering the intergenerational bond?', *International Affairs*, 82: 297–313.

Barnett, T. and Prins, G. (2006) 'HIV/AIDS and security: fact, fiction and evidence – a report to UNAIDS', *International Affairs*, 82: 359–368.

Behrman, G. (2004) *The Invisible People: How the US Has Slept through the Global AIDS Pandemic, the Greatest Humanitarian Catastrophe of Our Time*, New York/London: Free Press.

Benatar, S. (2005) 'The HIV/AIDS pandemic: a sign of instability in a complex global system', in A. Van Niekerk and L. Kopelman (eds.) *Ethics and AIDS in Africa: the Challenge to Our Thinking*, Claremont: David Philip Publishers.

Carment, D. (2003) 'Assessing state failure: implications for theory and policy', *Third World Quarterly*, 24: 407–427.

CIA. (1991) 'The global AIDS disaster', Interagency Intelligence Memorandum 91-10005, Washington, DC: CIA.

Cook, A. (2008) 'Securitization of disease in the US: globalisation, public policy, and pandemics', Unpublished thesis, East Carolina University.

Davies, S. (2008) 'Securitizing infectious disease', *International Affairs*, 84: 295–313.

De Waal, A. (2003) 'Human rights organizations and the political imagination: how the west and Africa have diverged', *Journal of Human Rights*, 2: 475–494.

De Waal, A. (2006) *AIDS and Power: Why There is No Political Crisis – Yet*, London/New York: Zed Books.

Dutch Ministry of Foreign Affairs. (2005) *AIDS, Security and Conflict Initiative*, briefing held on 3 June, New York.

Eisenstat, S., Porter, J. and Weinstein, J. (2005) 'Rebuilding weak states', *Foreign Affairs*, 84: 134–46.

Elbe, S. (2006) 'Should HIV/AIDS be securitized? The ethical dilemmas of linking HIV/AIDS and security', *International Studies Quarterly*, 50, 119–144.

Elbe, S. (2009) *Virus Alert: Security, Governmentality and the AIDS Pandemic*, New York: Columbia University Press.

Fidler, D. (2007) 'A pathology of public health securitism: approaching pandemics as security threats', in A. Cooper, J. Kirton and T. Schrecker (eds.) *Governing Global Health – Challenge, Response, Innovation*, Altershot: Ashgate Publishing.

Fidler, D. and Gostin, L. (2006) 'The new International Health Regulations: an historic development for international law and public health', *Journal of Law, Medicine and Ethics*, 34: 85–94.

Fourie, P. (2009) 'The relationship between the AIDS pandemic and state fragility' in P. Fourie, S. Maclean, and S. Brown (eds.) *Health for Some: The Political Economy of Global Health Governance*, Basingstoke and New York: Palgrave Macmillan.

Fourie, P. and Follér, M. (2013) 'AIDS hyper-epidemics and social resilience: theorising the political', in K. Buse and D. Altman (eds.) *Thinking Politically About HIV*, Abingdon: Routledge.

Fourie, P. and Meyer, M. (2010) *The Politics of AIDS Denialism: South Africa's Failure to Respond*, Farnham: Ashgate.

Fourie, P. and Schönteich, M. (2002) 'Africa's new security threat', *African Security Review*, 10: 29–44.

Garrett, L. (2005) 'The lessons of HIV/AIDS', *Foreign Affairs*, 84: 551–564.

Garrett, L. (2007) 'The challenge of global health', *Foreign Affairs*, 86: 14–38.

Ingram, A. (2007) 'HIV/AIDS, security and the geopolitics of US-Nigerian relations', *Review of International Political Economy*, 14: 510–534.

Ingram, A. (2013) 'After the exception: HIV/AIDS beyond salvation and scarcity', *Antipode*, 45: 436–454.

Kelle, A. (2007) 'Securitization of international public health: implications for global health governance and the biological weapons prohibition regime', *Global Governance*, 13: 217–235.

King, N. B. (2002) 'Security, disease, commerce: ideologies of postcolonial global health', *Social Studies of Science*, 32: 763–789.

Krasner, S. and Pascual, C. (2005) 'Addressing state failure', *Foreign Affairs*, 84: 153–163.

McInnes, C. (2006) 'HIV/AIDS and security', *International Affairs*, 82: 125–141.

McInnes, C. and Rushton, S. (2010) 'HIV, AIDS and security: where are we now?', *International Affairs*, 86: 225–245.

McInnes, C. and Rushton, S. (2011) 'HIV/AIDS and securitization theory', *European Journal of International Relations*, 19: 115–138.

NIC. (2005) 'Mapping Sub-Saharan Africa's future: conference summary', National Intelligence Council, CR 2005–02, March. Online. Available HTTP: <http://www.au.af.mil/au/awc/awcgate/nic/africa_future.pdf> (accessed 14 May 2014).

Nye, J. (2000) *Understanding International Conflict*, New York: Longman.

O'Keefe, M. (2012) 'Lessons from the rise and fall of the military AIDS hypothesis: politics, evidence and persuasion', *Contemporary Politics*, 18: 239–253.

Ostergard, R. and Barcelo, C. (2005) 'Personalist regimes and the insecurity dilemma: prioritizing AIDS as a national security threat in Uganda', in A. Patterson (ed.) *The African State and the AIDS Crisis*, Aldershot: Ashgate.

Patrick, S. (2006) 'Weak states and global threats: fact or fiction?', *The Washington Quarterly*, 29: 27–53.

Patrick, S. and Brown, K. (2006) 'Fragile states and US foreign assistance: show me the money', Center for Global Development, Working Paper no. 96, August. Online. Available HTTP: <http://www.cgdev.org/sites/default/files/9373_file_WP96_final.pdf> (accessed 21 January 2014).

Pirages, D.C. (2007) 'Nature, disease, and globalization: an evolutionary perspective', *International Studies Review*, 9: 616–628.

Poku, N., Renwick, N. and Porto, J. (2007) 'Human security and development in Africa', *International Affairs*, 83: 1155–1170.

Roe, P. (2012) 'Is securitization a "negative" concept? Revisiting the normative debate over normal versus extraordinary politics', *Security Dialogue*, 43: 249–266.

Shaw, T., Maclean, S. and Black, D. (2006) 'Introduction: a decade of human security: what prospects for global governance and new multilateralisms?', in S. Maclean, D. Black and T. Shaw (eds.) *A Decade of Human Security: Global Governance and New Multilateralisms*, Altershot: Ashgate Publishing.

Sontag, S. (1989) *AIDS and Its Metaphors*, New York: Farrar Straus and Giroux.

Sontag, S. (2002) *Illness as Metaphor and AIDS and Its Metaphors*, London: Penguin Classics.

UNAIDS. (2012) *Report on the Global AIDS Epidemic*, Geneva: UNAIDS.

United Nations. (2004) *A More Secure World: Our Shared Responsibility*, Report of the Secretary-General's High-Level Panel on Threats, Challenges and Change. UN, A/59/565, December. Online. Available HTTP: <http://www.un.org/en/peacebuilding/pdf/historical/hlp_more_secure_world.pdf> (accessed 21 January 2014).

Vallings, C. and Moreno-Torres, M. (2005) 'Drivers of fragility: what makes states fragile?' DFID PRDE Working Paper no. 7, April.

Wolff, S. (2006) 'State failure in a regional context', Unpublished research report, University of Bath, United Kingdom.

Woodward, S. (2004) 'Fragile states', paper presented at meeting of the Ford Foundation, Rio de Janeiro, Brazil, 29 November.

World Health Organization. (2008) *World Health Report 2007: A Safer Future: Global Public Health Security in the 21st Century*, Geneva: WHO.

Zacher, M. (2007) 'The transformation in global health collaboration since the 1990s', in A. Cooper, J. Kirton and T. Schrecker (eds.) *Governing Global Health – Challenge, Response, Innovation*, Aldershot: Ashgate Publishing.

10
BIOLOGICAL WEAPONS AND BIOTERRORISM

Gregory D. Koblentz

One of the earliest recognitions of the connection between health and security can be found in the domain of biological warfare. Biological warfare has been described as "public health in reverse" (Rosebury 1949), Historically, state-based biological warfare programs have been viewed as posing the only biological threat to international security. More recently, non-state actors such as terrorists and criminals have also demonstrated an interest in acquiring and using biological agents as weapons (Koblentz 2010). This chapter reviews the threat posed by biological weapons in the hands of states and terrorists and describes international efforts to control the proliferation of biological weapons.

Biological warfare

Biological warfare is the use of microorganisms, toxins derived from living organisms, or bioregulators to deliberately cause the death or illness of humans, plants, or animals. Biological weapons are unique among the instruments of warfare because they are composed of, or derived from, living organisms. This feature of biological weapons has several important implications for their use as weapons by states and non-state actors.

Disease-causing microorganisms such as bacteria, viruses, and fungi are called pathogens. Pathogens require a human, plant, or animal host in order to multiply and cause disease. Because these organisms are self-reproducing, a small dose can initiate an infection. Once a pathogen infects a host, its effects are determined by a complex interaction between the microorganism and the host's immune system. The time between infection and the onset of disease symptoms is called the incubation period, and it can last for days or weeks. Pathogens also vary in their level of virulence, the severity of the disease they cause. Some pathogens kill only a low percentage of those infected and instead cause temporary incapacitation or long-term illness. Other pathogens have high levels of lethality. If the disease is transmissible from person to person, a small number of infections could spark an epidemic. Table 10.1 lists the key attributes of some pathogens and toxins that have been developed or used as biological weapons.

Since toxins and bioregulators are nonliving molecules that do not replicate in the body, the initial exposure dose is what causes the illness. This means that toxins tend to be faster acting than pathogens, causing effects within hours or at most a day or two. Their effects are still slower than some chemical weapons, such as nerve agents, which can kill victims within minutes.

Table 10.1 Properties of Biological Warfare Agents

Agent	*Disease*	*Infective Dose (Aerosol)*	*Incubation Period*	*Lethality (% if Untreated)*	*Duration of Illness*	*Person-to-Person Transmission*
Bacteria						
Bacillus anthracis	Anthrax	8,000–50,000 spores	1–6 days (up to 60)*	High (>90)	3–5 days	No
Yersinia pestis	Plague	500–15,000 organisms	2–3 days	High (>90)	1–6 days	Moderate
Francisella tularensis	Tularemia	10–50 organisms	3–6 days	Moderate (35)	>2 weeks	No
Brucella spp.	Brucellosis	10–100 organisms	5–60 days	Low (<5)	Weeks–months	No
Burkolderia mallei	Glanders	Unknown, potentially low	10–14 days	Moderate (>50)	7–10 days	Low
Burkholderia pseudomallei	Melioidosis	Unknown, potentially low	1–21	Moderate (19–50)	2–3 days	Low
Coxiella burnetii	Q Fever	1–10 organisms	7–41 days	Low (5)	2–14 days	Rare
Viruses						
Variola	Smallpox	Assumed low (10–100 organisms)	7–17 days	Moderate (30)	4 weeks	High
Venezuelan Equine Encephalitis	Viral Encephalitis	10–100 organisms	2–6 days	Low (1)	1–2 weeks	Low
Ebola	Viral Hemorrhagic Fever	Unknown, potentially low	4–21 days	Moderate to High (50–90)	7–16 days	Moderate
Toxins						
Clostridium botulinum	Botulism	.003 μg/kg	12 hours–5 days	High (>90)	24–72 hours	No
Ricin		3–5 μg/kg	18–24 hours	High	Days	No
Staphylococcus aureus	Staph Enterotoxin B	.003 μg/person	3–12 hours	Low (1)	2 weeks	No

Source: Jon B. Woods, et al. (eds.) *USAMRIID's Medical Management of Biological Casualties Handbook*, 6th ed. (Frederick: U.S. Army Medical Research Institute of Infectious Diseases, 2005).

*Laboratory experiments and the 1979 outbreak of inhalation anthrax in Sverdlovsk, USSR demonstrated that spores of *B. anthracis* in the lungs can remain dormant for several weeks before causing illness. Jeanne Guillemin, *Anthrax: Investigation of a Deadly Outbreak* (Berkeley: University of California Press, 1999, 189, 237).

Toxins can be derived from a variety of sources such as plants (ricin from the castor bean), animals (saxitoxin from shellfish), fungi (aflatoxin from *Aspergillus flavus*), or bacteria (botulinum toxin from *Clostridium botulinum*). The number of toxins that are highly lethal and easily obtainable in large quantities, however, is far more limited than the number of pathogens with these attributes (Koblentz 2009).

Bioregulators are a recent addition to the traditional definition of biological weapons. Bioregulators are chemicals normally produced in the human body that control communication between cells and play a crucial role in governing the nervous, endocrine, and immune systems. Small imbalances in the level of bioregulators can have dramatic effects on cognition, emotion, and physiological processes. (Tucker 2008)

Biological weapons present both attackers and defenders with some unique challenges and opportunities. Biological weapons, whether pathogens, toxins, or bioregulators, are selective in their targets. They affect only living things and do not damage or destroy vehicles, buildings, or machinery. Most biological agents are also fragile creatures that require special measures to keep them alive or stable during production, storage, delivery, and dissemination. There are several ways to disseminate biological agents. The most primitive tactics use fomites (a physical object that serves to transmit an infectious agent) or vectors (a living organism such as a human or insect that transmits disease) as crude munitions. The most effective means of disseminating a biological agent to infect a large population is by dispersing the agent as an aerosol or cloud of microscopic droplets in the size range of 1–5 microns. Aerosols composed of particles in this size range have several advantages: they can stay airborne longer, require a smaller dose to cause an infection, the severity of the resulting disease is typically more severe, and they are invisible to the human senses. Creating an aerosol containing viable organisms and particles of the correct size is difficult. In addition, most biological warfare agents will die if exposed to sunlight or extremes of temperature or humidity and aerosol clouds of biological agents are subject to the vagaries of meteorological conditions. Thus, the use of biological agents as weapons is fraught with uncertainties for the attacker.

Defending against biological weapons is complicated by the range of available agents, the agent-specific nature of most defenses, and the time lag required to develop new vaccines and treatments (see Hoyt, chapter 18 in this volume). Biological weapons, however, are in some ways more susceptible to countermeasures than high explosives, chemical weapons, or nuclear weapons. They are unique among weapon systems in that vaccines can protect soldiers and civilians before an actual attack. The incubation period following infection with a pathogen provides a window of opportunity for a well-prepared defender to detect an attack and launch a public health and medical intervention to mitigate the consequences of an attack. For these reasons, a strong public health system is the best defense against a biological attack.

Another key aspect of biological weapons is the multiuse dilemma: the skills, materials, and technology needed to produce biological weapons are also necessary to develop defenses against them and to conduct civilian activities such as biomedical research and pharmaceutical production. Many of the raw materials and equipment required for the research, development, production, and weaponization of biological weapons are used in civilian industries or in biodefense programs. The multiuse property of biotechnology allows a nation developing biological weapons to hide its activities in civilian institutes that appear to be, or actually are, conducting legitimate pharmaceutical or medical research. This exacerbates the difficulty in determining the true purpose behind suspicious activities or facilities through intelligence and verification. The rapid pace of innovation in the life sciences and the globalization of biotechnology have exacerbated this dilemma (Koblentz 2009).

History of biological warfare

Biological warfare has been practiced since ancient times, though the number of actual attacks is small. Greek and Roman armies contaminated water supplies using toxic plants or dead animals, the Mongols catapulted plague-infected corpses into the besieged city of Kaffa in 1346, British soldiers at Fort Pitt gave blankets contaminated with smallpox virus to hostile Native American tribes in 1763, and British forces may have tried to infect the Continental Army with smallpox during the Revolutionary War by sending infected individuals behind enemy lines. Given the prevalence of these diseases at the time and the lack of authoritative records, it is difficult to determine if any of these attacks was successful.

The development of germ theory, which identified microorganisms as the causative agent of disease, enabled the emergence of the discipline of microbiology, which allowed scientists to isolate pathogens and cultivate them in small quantities. During World War I, Germany applied this new knowledge to conduct an extensive, although ultimately ineffective, sabotage campaign against cavalry and draft animals being shipped from neutral countries to the Allies. By the beginning of World War II, most of the great powers, including Britain, France, Japan, the Soviet Union, and the United States, had offensive and defensive biological warfare (BW) programs.

Japan's aggressive BW program, launched in 1931 under the leadership of the military scientist Ishii Shiro, was the largest of its kind during this era. Japanese scientists conducted gruesome experiments on thousands of prisoners and used biological weapons against Chinese civilians and soldiers on multiple occasions. The Japanese, however, never developed an efficient means for delivering biological agents. Instead, the Japanese relied on fomites, vectors such as fleas, and the contamination of food and water supplies to spread disease. Although the Japanese succeeded in causing widespread epidemics, the techniques proved unreliable, caused Japanese casualties as well, and did not provide Japan with a significant advantage over the Chinese opposition forces. These attacks are the only confirmed large-scale use of biological weapons in the 20th century (Harris 2002).

During World War II, the United States and Britain collaborated on the development of biological weapons. After the war, the British gradually phased out their program while the United States continued to develop lethal, incapacitating, and anticrop agents for use against the Soviet Union and its allies. The United States conducted research and development at Camp (later Fort) Detrick in Maryland, produced biological agents at Pine Bluff Arsenal in Arkansas, and tested biological weapons at Dugway Proving Ground in Utah and overseas locations. In 1969, after a comprehensive review of U.S. chemical and biological weapons policy, President Richard M. Nixon decided to unilaterally renounce the use of biological weapons, terminate the offensive BW program, and destroy existing stockpiles of biological agents and munitions. Since that time, the United States military has conducted only defensive research and development (Koblentz 2009).

The Soviet Union launched a biological weapons program in the 1920s. During the Cold War, the Soviet military ran biological weapon facilities at Zagorsk, Sverdlovsk, and Kirov as well as a testing facility on Vozrozhdenie Island in the Aral Sea. In 1973, the Soviet Union created a new organization, Biopreparat, whose purpose was to apply advances in biotechnology to create new and improved biological weapons. The Scientific-Research Institute of Applied Microbiology in Obolensk and the Scientific-Research Institute of Molecular Biology (also called Vector) in Koltsovo were tasked with engineering pathogens to be more lethal. The Institute of Ultra-Pure Biological Preparations in Leningrad was dedicated to developing improved methods for stabilizing, drying, milling, and disseminating BW agents. Biopreparat also maintained a network of six standby production plants that could be mobilized during wartime to produce thousands of tons of BW agents a year. By the time the Soviet Union collapsed, Biopreparat had become a massive complex of 50 research and production facilities with over 30,000 employees (Leitenberg & Zilinskas 2012).

In the late 1970s, Rhodesian counterinsurgency units used various pathogens and poisons to contaminate clothing, food, drinks, and water supplies used by guerilla groups and their supporters. During the 1980s, South Africa's apartheid-era chemical and biological weapons program, Project Coast, supplied members of the South African security services with small quantities of poisons, toxins, and pathogens to contaminate food and beverages and assassinate anti-apartheid activists. (Gould & Folb 2002)

Iraq launched a biological warfare program in 1985 at the height of the Iran–Iraq War and made significant progress over the next 6 years. By the 1991 Persian Gulf War, Iraq had mass-produced *B. anthracis* (the bacterium that causes the disease anthrax), botulinum toxin, and aflatoxin and filled these agents into Scud missile warheads and aerial bombs. Iraq secretly destroyed its biological agents and weapons during the summer of 1991 out of fear that they would be discovered by the United Nations Special Commission (UNSCOM), which was charged with disarming Iraq of its nuclear, biological, and chemical weapons. Iraq denied the existence of its BW program until July 1995 when UNSCOM's detective work forced Iraq to admit that it had used unaccounted-for growth media to produce biological agents for military purposes at a facility called Al Hakam. Following the defection of the high-ranking Iraqi official Hussein Kamal in August 1995, Iraq further revealed that it had produced biological agents at additional facilities, filled these agents into bombs and missile warheads, and destroyed them in 1991. In 1996, UNSCOM destroyed Iraq's main BW production facility at Al Hakam. The inspectors, and their successors in the United Nations Monitoring and Verification Commission (UNMOVIC), were unable to fully verify Iraq's account of its past BW work. In 2003, the United States accused Iraq of possessing mobile biological agent production trucks and a stockpile of biological weapons. An independent bipartisan commission later found the intelligence supporting these assessments was deeply flawed. Following the U.S. invasion of Iraq, the Iraq Survey Group determined that Iraq had indeed given up the last residues of its BW program in 1995 and had not subsequently resumed its work on those weapons. (Koblentz 2009)

Currently, the United States is concerned that China, Iran, North Korea, Russia, and Syria are developing biological weapons (Department of State 2012; Director of National Intelligence 2012).

International efforts to control the proliferation of biological weapons

The use of disease as a weapon has long been considered taboo. This taboo can be found in ancient Indian, Greek, Roman, and Muslim traditions, so it is multicultural and has existed since antiquity. This sense of revulsion at using poison or disease as an instrument of war has been codified in national legal prohibitions for centuries and in international law in the 20th century. The two primary treaties relating to biological weapons are the 1925 Geneva Protocol and the 1972 Biological Weapons Convention. In addition, a multilateral export control arrangement called the Australia Group has played an important role in stemming the proliferation of biological weapons.

1925 Geneva Protocol

In response to the horrors of chemical warfare during World War I, the use of chemical and biological weapons was banned in 1925 under the Geneva Protocol. The Geneva Protocol does not prohibit the development or possession of chemical and biological weapons so it did not restrain the proliferation of biological weapons during the interwar period. In addition, since most of the signatories to the treaty reserved the right to retaliate with these weapons if they were attacked first, it was really a "no first use" treaty. As of May 2013, 137 nations had ratified the treaty.

1972 Biological Weapons Convention (BWC)

The Convention on the Prohibition of the Development, Production, and Stockpiling of Bacteriological (Biological) and Toxin Weapons and on their Destruction, also known as the Biological Weapons Convention (BWC), opened for signature in 1972 and entered into force in 1975. As of May 2013, 170 nations had become parties to the treaty and another 10 had signed but not ratified it.

The BWC was a groundbreaking treaty, the first international treaty to outlaw an entire class of weapons. The drafters of the treaty capitalized on the preexisting stigma against using disease as a weapon to further reinforce this norm. The preamble states that the use of biological weapons is "repugnant to the conscience of mankind" and that the prohibition of these weapons is "for the sake of all mankind." The heart of the treaty is Article 1, which states:

> Each State Party to this Convention undertakes never in any circumstances to develop, produce, stockpile or otherwise acquire or retain:
>
> (1) Microbial or other biological agents, or toxins whatever their origin or method of production, of types and in quantities that have no justification for prophylactic, protective or other peaceful purposes;
> (2) Weapons, equipment or means of delivery designed to use such agents or toxins for hostile purposes or in armed conflict.
>
> (*Convention on the Prohibition of the Development, Production and Stockpiling of Bacteriological (Biological) and Toxin Weapons and on their Destruction* 1972)

The language in this article walks a fine line between the aspirations of the drafters to achieve a clear and unequivocal prohibition against biological weapons and the reality of the multiuse nature of biological agents and biological research. As a result, while state parties are obligated "never in any circumstances" to develop, produce, or possess biological weapons, the borders demarcating prohibited and legitimate activities are either vague or undefined. The convention does not prohibit research on biological weapons in recognition of the great difficulty in determining whether such activities are being undertaken for permitted or prohibited purposes. Furthermore, the convention does not define what activities are considered research, and therefore fall outside the scope of the treaty, and what activities constitute development, and are therefore subject to the treaty's provisions. In addition, the treaty allows the development, production, and stockpiling of biological agents of appropriate "types and quantities" so long as they have "prophylactic, protective or other peaceful purposes." However, the types, quantities, and purposes that are permitted are not further defined in the treaty. This ambiguous wording and lack of definition was required to allow states to continue conducting medical, scientific, public health, commercial, and defensive work with organisms that could also be used as BW agents. The multiuse dilemma resulted in a treaty that places a heavy burden on interpreting the intent of an activity to determine whether or not it is in compliance with Article I.

Although the BWC was written before the advent of the biotechnology revolution, its drafters were aware of the amazing advances that had already taken place in the life sciences and fully expected further such advances in the future. The inclusion of the phrases "other biological agents" and "whatever their origin or method of production" in Article I was intended to provide as broad as possible coverage of biological threats. The parties to the BWC have reaffirmed at each of the treaty's review conferences, held once every 5 years, that Article I covers all recent developments in science and technology relevant to biological weapons.

The BWC has two notable differences from the other international nonproliferation treaties: the Nuclear Non-Proliferation Treaty (NPT), the Chemical Weapons Convention (CWC), and the Comprehensive Test Ban Treaty (CTBT). First, the BWC does not contain any verification provisions. As a result, the international community has been engaged in an ongoing effort since 1975 to strengthen the treaty. State parties have adopted several voluntary confidence-building measures (CBMs) designed to improve the transparency of civilian and defensive biological activities. International negotiations to devise stronger mandatory measures to further improve transparency and provide greater confidence that all state parties were in compliance with the treaty began in 1995. These negotiations ended in 2001 after the United States rejected a draft verification protocol. A new process began in 2002 that features annual meetings of nongovernment experts and state parties to exchange ideas and proposals on a wide array of national and international measures to improve implementation of the treaty.

The second major difference between the BWC and the other nonproliferation treaties is that the BWC lacks an international organization to support its implementation. When the NPT was signed in 1968, the International Atomic Energy Agency was charged with ensuring that nonnuclear states did not divert nuclear material into a weapons program. When the CWC was signed in 1993, the Organization for the Prohibition of Chemical Weapons was created to oversee the destruction of existing chemical weapons and to monitor civilian chemical facilities to ensure that they were not utilized for military purposes. The Comprehensive Test Ban Treaty Organization was created in 1996 to oversee a global verification regime for the test ban treaty including an international monitoring system. In 2007, a three-person Implementation Support Unit (ISU) for the BWC was created to administer the CBMs, the annual meetings, and the review conferences. While the creation of a dedicated group to assist with the implementation of the BWC was a long overdue measure, the authority and capability of the ISU are severely limited.

The BWC remains the cornerstone of the BW nonproliferation regime and has played a vital role in reinforcing the norm against the use of disease as a weapon. The treaty's CBMs increase transparency of BW-related activities and facilities and help states demonstrate their compliance with the treaty. Although efforts to strengthen the treaty through a legally binding verification protocol have halted, parties to the treaty are continuing to explore other means of reducing the threat posed by biological weapons during their annual meetings.

Australia Group

The Australia Group is an informal multilateral arrangement used by 42 states to harmonize national export control policies regarding dual-use equipment and materials that could be used to produce chemical and biological weapons. The Australia Group was created in 1985 by 15 Western countries in response to Iraq's use of chemical weapons during its war against Iran. In 1991, the group expanded its mandate to include biological weapon nonproliferation as well. The group maintains a control list of dual-use items that are subject to licensing for export. In addition, the members of the group meet annually to exchange intelligence, provide briefings on best practices in export control compliance and enforcement, and discuss new proposals for improving the implementation of national export controls. Beginning in 2001 the Australia

Group expanded the scope of its control lists to include pathogens and dual-use items, such as small fermenters, that might be sought after by terrorist groups.

Biological terrorism

The prospect of terrorists acquiring and using biological weapons emerged as a security threat during the mid-1990s. The terrorist attacks on September 11, 2001 and the anthrax letter attacks that fall elevated biological terrorism to the top of the international security agenda. This section reviews the four most important cases of bioterrorism and provides an assessment of the current threat of biological terrorism.

Biological terrorism has been exceedingly rare. During the 20th century, only eight terrorist groups succeeded in acquiring a biological agent. Prior to the anthrax letter attacks in 2001, only one group, the disciples of guru Bhagwan Shree Rajneesh in Oregon, managed to cause any casualties with a biological agent (Carus 2001). Although terrorists have fewer resources to develop biological weapons compared to states, their needs are more limited. Unlike states, terrorists can achieve their objectives without developing BW agents that can be produced in large quantities, stored for lengthy periods of time, disseminated by highly efficient and reliable devices, and delivered by systems designed for use under battlefield conditions. Nevertheless, terrorists who seek to inflict mass casualties still face significant hurdles in acquiring and producing virulent agents and designing effective dissemination devices. Terrorists whose interest is limited to causing a small number of casualties or mass disruption face fewer obstacles. As the proliferation of anthrax hoax letters since 2001 has demonstrated, individuals interested in causing terror and disruption at a local level can achieve their objectives with nothing more than a powdery substance and a threatening note.

Rajneeshees

In 1984, members of the Rajneeshee cult poisoned salad bars in The Dalles, Oregon with *Salmonella Typhimurium*, sickening 751 townspeople. From the establishment of their ranch in The Dalles in 1981, the Rajneeshee found themselves in a series of disputes with state and local authorities. As part of a strategy to influence a local election, the cult contaminated 10 salad bars in the town with *S. Typhimurium* that they had produced in their medical clinic. Public health officials believed that the cause of the mass food poisoning was unsanitary practices by food handlers at the restaurants. The identities of the perpetrators weren't revealed until the mastermind of the attack had a falling out with other members of the cult and the group's leader publicly accused her of poisoning local officials and the townspeople. (Carus 2000)

Aum Shinrikyo

The Japanese cult Aum Shinrikyo is the only group that is known to have tried to create an aerosolized biological weapon to cause mass casualties. Aum's efforts, however, were unsuccessful due to scientific, technical, operational, and organizational deficiencies. Aum, led by its guru Shoko Asahara, was characterized by an apocalyptic ideology that justified the murder of nonbelievers.

Although Aum was motivated by a mix of religious beliefs, it also had an extremely ambitious political objective: the overthrow of the Japanese government. Despite its significant financial resources, the scientific backgrounds of many of its members, and its ability to operate unmolested by Japanese authorities, none of Aum's 10 attempted BW attacks conducted between 1990 and

1995 resulted in any casualties. Aum's inability to develop an effective aerosolized biological weapon led the cult to turn to chemical weapons. The group released the nerve gas sarin in Matsumoto in June 1994 and on the Tokyo subway system in March 1995, killing a total of 19 and injuring over 1,000.

Aum's experience sheds some light on the difficulties that terrorists face in developing biological weapons. Although Aum was well funded and well equipped, their BW effort suffered several handicaps. At the scientific level, Aum's program was not run by a microbiologist who knew how to work with bacteria. As a result, Aum was unable to cultivate a lethal strain of botulinum toxin from the wild, and the only strain of *B. anthracis* it could acquire was a vaccine strain used for animals. At the technical level, the slurry of *B. anthracis* that was produced was very low quality. Aum also lacked the engineering capability to disseminate a liquid slurry of *B. anthracis*. Their rooftop sprayer was prone to breaking down, leaking, clogging, and was either incapable or highly inefficient at producing particles in the 1–5 micron size. At the operational level, Aum did not demonstrate an understanding of the proper environmental conditions conducive to a BW attack. Aum attempted to disseminate its biological agents during the day, which exposed the agents to UV radiation and thermal updrafts, reducing the viability of the agents and the area covered by the aerosol (Rosenau 2001).

Aum's failure indicates that biological terrorism capable of causing mass casualties through an aerosolized agent is not as easy as commonly portrayed. Developing biological weapons requires the right strain of a pathogen, the ability to produce the organism in a form suitable for dissemination, and a means of effectively disseminating the agent at the desired location. Aum failed on all of these levels. Aum's experience demonstrates that money, equipment, and educated personnel alone are not sufficient to produce biological weapons; scientific and organizational skills are needed as well.

Anthrax letters

In September and October 2001, envelopes containing a dry powder of *B. anthracis* spores were mailed to Senators Thomas Daschle (D-SD) and Patrick Leahy (D-VT) and five media outlets in Florida and New York City. The letters caused 22 cases of anthrax, including 11 cases of cutaneous (on the skin) anthrax and 11 cases of inhalation anthrax. Five of the inhalation anthrax cases were fatal. The anthrax letter attacks also had pervasive ripple effects, forcing thousands of people to take antibiotics as a precaution, disrupting the U.S. Postal Service, temporarily shutting down the U.S. Senate, causing nationwide anxiety about the safety of the mail, and triggering a flood of false alarms and hoaxes involving white powders. All told, the cost of the incident was estimated at $6 billion. The anthrax letter attacks were dubbed Amerithrax by the FBI.

In August 2008 the FBI announced that its sole suspect in the Amerithrax case was Bruce E. Ivins, a microbiologist and anthrax vaccine researcher with the United States Army Medical Research Institute for Infectious Diseases (USAMRIID) at Fort Detrick, Maryland. Only days earlier, Ivins, who had been under investigation for over a year and knew he was about to be indicted for the anthrax letter attacks, killed himself with an intentional drug overdose. The strongest evidence presented by the FBI links the *B. anthracis* used in the attacks to a flask of *B. anthracis* in Ivins's lab at USAMRIID. The FBI established this link using the new discipline of microbial forensics that employs powerful analytical techniques to determine the genetic, chemical, and physical properties of a pathogen or toxin agent used as a weapon. Ivins also spent extended periods of unsupervised time in his lab on nights and weekends immediately before the anthrax letters were mailed to the senators and media outlets (Koblentz & Tucker 2010).

Ivins's motive for sending the anthrax letters was possibly his frustration with the slow pace of anthrax vaccine development. By the fall of 2001, this work had virtually ground to a halt due to technical, bureaucratic, political, and financial problems. According to the FBI, Ivins was also suffering at this time from serious mental health problems. In the aftermath of September 11, Ivins may have feared that the next attack could be with biological weapons that could cause even more harm than 9/11 had. Ivins may have intended the anthrax letters as a warning to the nation about the dangers posed by biological weapons and the need for stronger defenses against these weapons.

Notwithstanding the important unanswered questions regarding whether, how, and why Ivins conducted the anthrax letter attacks, it is possible to make several observations about the implications of this case for assessing the threat posed by bioterrorism. The Amerithrax case indicates that the current level of concern about the capabilities of non-state actors to develop sophisticated biological weapons on their own is overstated. Ivins possessed a level of experience, set of skills, and extensive tacit knowledge that could only be found in an individual affiliated with a state-run biodefense program. Ivins was a PhD microbiologist with over 20 years of experience working with *B. anthracis*, was considered an expert in the growth, sporulation, and purification of the bacteria, and had extensive experience preparing liquid anthrax spore preparations for animal aerosol challenges.

Ivins's employment at USAMRIID also afforded him advantages such as access to a highly virulent strain of *B. anthracis,* a well-equipped biocontainment laboratory, experience working in such a lab, immunization against anthrax, and knowledge of decontamination procedures. These are resources that a terrorist group would find difficult to acquire on its own.

The high concentration and very good aerosolization properties of the *B. anthracis* spores sent to Senators Daschle and Leahy led many to assume that the powder was produced using sophisticated equipment and/or the use of special additives or coatings. The FBI's contention that Ivins was able to produce such high-quality powder of *B. anthracis* spores with standard laboratory equipment and without the use of any special additives has raised concern that the technical threshold for sophisticated biological weapons is lower than commonly assumed. This inference, however, ignores the high level of tacit knowledge that Ivins possessed about *B. anthracis*. Even if Ivins employed a low-tech method to produce the powder in the anthrax letters, it does not mean that this method did not require a high level of skill to apply successfully (Koblentz 2009).

Al Qaeda

Al Qaeda is commonly viewed as the terrorist group most likely to develop both the motivation and the capability to cause mass casualties with biological weapons. In December 1998 Osama bin Laden declared it a "religious duty" to acquire nuclear, biological, and chemical weapons. In May 2003 a Saudi cleric issued a fatwa legitimating the use of nuclear, biological, and chemical weapons against infidels.

Al Qaeda's chemical and biological weapon program, code-named Project al-Zabadi (Arabic for yogurt), was created in 1999 and headed by Ayman al-Zawahiri, the second-ranking official in al Qaeda. Zawahiri was attracted to biological weapons because he believed that these weapons were as lethal as nuclear weapons, that they could be produced simply, that the delayed effects of a biological attack would increase the number of casualties, and that defending against these weapons was very difficult. By 2001 the group had established two laboratories in Afghanistan, obtained scientific literature on several bacterial pathogens, procured dual-use production equipment, recruited microbiologists, and had a small cell dedicated to producing *B. anthracis*. Al Qaeda's progress was stymied by its inability to obtain a virulent strain of *B. anthracis* or to master the techniques necessary to aerosolize a biological agent. According to captured al Qaeda operatives, the group's BW efforts were in the early "conceptual stage" when it was disrupted by the United States invasion of Afghanistan. Al Qaeda's BW ambitions were set back further by the death or arrest of most of the key participants in the program. Although al Qaeda's aspirations in this area far outstripped its capabilities, the fact that this group has been as interested in these weapons for as long as it has sets them apart from other terrorist organizations.

In addition to the bioterrorist threat posed directly by al Qaeda, there is growing concern that al Qaeda–trained or inspired cells could also launch bioterrorist attacks. One factor driving this concern is the wide availability of recipes in al Qaeda training manuals and online jihadist chat rooms that purportedly describe how to produce biological weapons. The second factor is the emergence of a new generation of terrorists who are inspired by al Qaeda's narrative that the West is waging a war against Islam. These self-radicalized jihadists form small cells or loose networks that do not receive support or commands from al Qaeda or its affiliates, making it difficult for law enforcement or intelligence agencies to identify them before an attack.

The threat of "do-it-yourself" jihadi bioterrorism, however, is overstated. The jihadist BW recipes and manuals are rudimentary, lack important details or include incorrect information, and are unsuited for producing pathogens or toxins of sufficient quantity or quality to cause mass casualties. At best, the recipes might be suitable for producing small, crude quantities of certain toxins. None of these recipes describe techniques for disseminating biological agents, thereby limiting their utility to assassinations or the contamination of food or beverages. Although the phenomenon of "leaderless jihad," with its fluid networks and lack of connections to existing terrorist groups, does increase the difficulty of preventing attacks, it also limits the sophistication of such attacks. The small size and limited resources of most such cells will limit their ability to engage in the long-term, expensive, technically demanding, and multidisciplinary work needed to develop a biological weapon capable of causing mass casualties (Koblentz 2009).

Conclusion

The development of biological weapons by states and terrorists has lagged far behind the number of countries and groups capable of producing such weapons. The magnitude of the future threat posed by biological weapons will be determined by two poorly understood and difficult to influence variables. The first variable is the net impact of the biotechnology revolution on the balance between offense and defense in biological warfare. While advances in the life sciences strengthen the defender and provide new capabilities to verify biological arms control agreements, they also enable attackers to develop more sophisticated weapons and the means of concealing them. This type of assessment is complicated by the accelerating pace of innovation in the life sciences, the inevitable global diffusion of these technologies, and the multiuse nature of biotechnology. In addition, social factors such as tacit knowledge and communities of practice can mediate the capability of a state or terrorist group to transform scientific or technical breakthroughs into weapons (Vogel 2013). An unfortunate by-product of the multiuse dilemma is that investing in biodefense research also generates new knowledge that could be applied to the development of biological weapons.

The second key variable is the level of interest of states and non-state actors in developing biological weapons. Since the capabilities to develop these weapons are already widespread, the main factor driving the pursuit of these weapons will be intent. Will the norm against BW continue to limit the appeal of these weapons or will security concerns or the bureaucratic ambitions of scientific and military leaders overwhelm this inhibition? What is the likelihood that non-state actors will emerge that combine technical acumen, a desire to cause mass casualties, and an interest in biological weapons? Thus far, no terrorist group has combined both the capability and motivation to use biological weapons to cause mass death. Terrorists still overwhelmingly prefer to use guns and bombs to wreak havoc. While this history is reassuring, the events of September 11, 2001, are a reminder that past experience is not always a reliable predictor of future threats. Given the difficulty in tracking terrorist groups and detecting activities to develop biological weapons, it is possible that such a group will arise with little or no warning. Preventing the emergence of such groups and the misuse of the biotechnology revolution will be major security challenges for the 21st century.

References

Carus, W.S. (2000) 'The Rajneeshees (1984)', in J.B. Tucker (ed.) *Toxic Terror: Assessing Terrorist Use of Chemical and Biological Weapons*, Cambridge: MIT Press: 115–137.

Carus, W.S. (2001) *Bioterrorism and Biocrimes: The Illicit Use of Biological Agents in the 20th Century*, Washington, DC: National Defense University.

Convention on the Prohibition of the Development, Production and Stockpiling of Bacteriological (Biological) and Toxin Weapons and on their Destruction. (1972) Online. Available HTTP: http://www.unog.ch/bwc (accessed 14 May 2014).

Department of State. (2012) *Adherence to and Compliance with Arms Control, Nonproliferation and Disarmament Agreements and Commitments*, Washington, DC: Department of State.

Director of National Intelligence. (2012) *Unclassified Report to Congress on the Acquisition of Technology Relating to Weapons of Mass Destruction and Advanced Conventional Weapons Covering 1 January to 31 December 2011*, Washington, DC: Office of Director of National Intelligence.

Gould, C. and Folb, P. (2002) *Project Coast: Apartheid's Chemical and Biological Warfare Programme*, Geneva: United Nations Publications.

Harris, S.H. (2002) *Factories of Death: Japanese Biological Warfare, 1932–45, and the American Cover-up*, 2nd ed. London: Routledge.

Koblentz, G.D. (2009) *Living Weapons: Biological Warfare and International Security*, Ithaca: Cornell University Press.

Koblentz, G.D. (2010) 'Biosecurity reconsidered: calibrating biological threats and responses', *International Security*, 34: 96–132.

Koblentz, G.D. and Tucker, J.B. (2010) 'Tracing an attack: the promise and pitfalls of microbial forensics', *Survival*, 52: 159–186.

Leitenberg, M. and Zilinskas, R.A. (2012) *The Soviet Biological Weapons Program: A History*, Cambridge: Harvard University Press.

Rosebury, T. (1949) *Peace or Pestilence: Biological Warfare and How to Avoid It*, New York: McGraw-Hill.

Rosenau, W. (2001) 'Aum Shinrikyo's biological weapons program: why did it fail?' *Studies in Conflict and Terrorism*, 24: 289–301.

Tucker, J.B. (2008) 'The body's own bioweapons', *Bulletin of the Atomic Scientists*, 64: 16–22, 56–57.

Vogel, K.M. (2013) *Phantom Menace or Looming Danger? A New Framework for Assessing Bioweapons Threats*, Baltimore, Johns Hopkins University Press.

11

LIFE SCIENCE RESEARCH AS A SECURITY RISK

Christian Enemark

Laboratory research on pathogenic (disease-causing) micro-organisms is in two ways relevant to the relationship between health and security. First, such research informs medical and public health measures to protect individuals and populations against infectious diseases. A disease outbreak almost always occurs as a result of natural processes, but microorganisms have been and can be used deliberately to harm people. In either event, knowledge of how various bacteria and viruses behave inside the human body enables life scientists to develop remedies like antibiotics, antiviral drugs, and vaccines. Such knowledge is particularly valuable for disease-control purposes in circumstances where a disease outbreak causes widespread disruption and anxiety along with illness and death. A scientist who knows what makes pathogens dangerous (and what could make them more dangerous) is someone whose skills could also manifest at the nexus of health and security in precisely the opposite way: he or she could instead apply that knowledge to the design, development, and use of biological weapons. The potential for biotechnology (along with virtually all other technologies) to be used for both benign and malign purposes presents dual-use dilemmas for scientists and policymakers. In practical terms, the challenge when conducting or governing research is to maximize the health benefits to be derived from the life sciences while minimizing the security risks.

This chapter discusses benefits and risks in three overlapping contexts. The first is pathogen research conducted by states for the purpose of biodefense. Such research can help defend against biological attacks, but it can also generate pressure towards biological weapons proliferation. The second context is the imposition of biosecurity regulations on individual scientists engaged in research on particular microorganisms. Regulations of this kind can reduce the likelihood of laboratory-based biological materials being used to cause harm, but they can also inhibit the pursuit of life-saving scientific discoveries. Finally, by reference to recent research on the transmissibility of an influenza virus, the chapter discusses health benefits and security risks associated with experimentally applying genetic modification techniques and publishing the results.

Biodefense research

A useful starting point for discussing dual-use research is Article I of the 1972 Biological Weapons Convention (BWC) that provides:

> Each State Party to this Convention undertakes never in any circumstances to develop, produce, stockpile or otherwise acquire or retain:
>
> (1) Microbial or other biological agents, or toxins whatever their origin or method of production, of types and in quantities that have no justification for prophylactic, protective or other peaceful purposes;
> (2) Weapons, equipment or means of delivery designed to use such agents or toxins for hostile purposes or in armed conflict.
>
> (*Convention on the Prohibition of the Development, Production and Stockpiling of Bacteriological (Biological) and Toxin Weapons and on their Destruction* 1972)

The Convention does not mention "research," although research involving the development, production, etc. of biological agents could reasonably be characterized as having a "protective . . . purpose" if it is intended to improve a state's defenses against biological attacks. Most state-run biodefense projects and capabilities are obviously defensive and clearly benign in nature. For example, acquiring pharmaceutical resources (antibiotic and vaccines) to cure or prevent known diseases is a measure aimed directly at reducing the human cost of a deliberately caused (or naturally occurring) outbreak. There are other forms of biodefense, however, the purpose of which is harder to justify as essentially peaceful. If laboratory research is aimed at deliberately creating novel (i.e., hitherto nonexistent) biological agents, this could serve to anticipate future defense requirements. Yet it could also amount to the creation of a powerful new "type" of biological agent against which defense was previously unnecessary. Research into "means of delivery designed to use [biological] agents . . . for hostile purposes" could inform the design or improvement of such countermeasures as protective body-suits and pathogen detection devices. Equally, however, it could guide the planning and execution of a biological attack. Thus, although the health benefits to be derived from genuinely peaceful biodefense research are valuable, there is a countervailing security risk associated with external perceptions of that research. A familiar phenomenon in international relations is "the security dilemma [that] arises from states' accumulation of more and more power for their own security due to fear and uncertainty about other states' intentions" (Tang 2009: 591). If biodefense research by one state generates feelings of doubt and insecurity on the part of other states, this has the potential to cause horizontal proliferation (i.e., an increase in the number of states possessing biological weapons) and a worsening of the very threat to be defended against.

In 1969, U.S. President Richard Nixon announced his decision to abandon biological warfare, and this paved the way for the BWC to be opened for signature in 1972. The following year, the Soviet Union established Biopreparat, which, to the outside world, was a state-owned pharmaceutical complex developing vaccines for the civilian market. It was later revealed that Biopreparat was a military-funded program for developing new types of biological weapons (Tucker 2001: 145). A likely explanation for this deception is that the Soviets believed the United States intended also to maintain a secret program of biological research for offensive purposes. In his 1999 memoir *Biohazard*, Soviet defector Ken Alibek reflected: "We didn't believe a word of Nixon's announcement . . . we thought the Americans were only wrapping a thicker cloak around their activities" (Alibek 1999: 234). Today, the same kind of suspicion is likely felt by the U.S.

government itself, although the dual-use nature of life science research makes it extremely difficult sometimes to establish whether or not weapons-relevant activities have a genuinely offensive purpose. A 2012 report by the U.S. State Department assessed the BWC compliance of various countries, and the language used reflects the deep uncertainty that exists over the marrying of research capabilities with hostile intentions. It remained "unclear," according to the report, whether any Iranian and Russian activities were inconsistent with the BWC (U.S. State Department 2012). The assessment of North Korea was that it "*may* still consider the use of biological weapons as an option," and the Department expressed concern that Syria "*may* be engaged in activities that would violate . . . the BWC" (US State Department 2012, emphasis added).

Because the degree of official transparency on the part of these countries is insufficient to allay U.S. government suspicion, pessimistic uncertainty is probably a strong driver of U.S. biodefense efforts. The security risk, however, is that international uncertainty about the true purpose of those efforts will in turn drive other countries to increase their own biodefense capabilities. The result would be a dangerous spiral of mutual suspicion based on the dual-use nature of pathogen research. Of particular concern, in terms of generating proliferation pressure, are U.S. military research projects conducted for "threat assessment" purposes. These purportedly investigate possible offensive applications of pathogenic micro-organisms so as to determine appropriate countermeasures. Large-scale experimentation with biological aerosols, for example, can appear to be exactly the kind of research that would guide a biological attack, even if such experiments are also useful for testing detection devices and protective equipment. The U.S. government operates at least two facilities that conduct outdoor aerosol studies. One is the U.S. Army's Edgewood Chemical and Biological Center in Maryland, which receives annual funding of over U.S. $22 million from the Defense Department. The other is the Lothar Salomon Test Facility in Utah, which receives annual funding of U.S. $4.3 million jointly from the Departments of Defense, Justice, and Homeland Security (United States of America 2012: 92–95). The Maryland facility has "[a]erosol simulation chambers and the Aerodynamic Research Laboratory, comprising approximately 11,000 ft^2 of experimental aerodynamic facilities that include four wind tunnels for component and materials tests" (Federation of American Scientists 2006: 69). And the Utah facility has as one of its objectives: "Testing of battlefield detection and identification methods, protective equipment, and decontamination systems, to include interferent testing of biological detectors and to develop/validate *aerosol particle dispersion models*" (United States of America 2012: 71–72, emphasis added).

Such activity, if conducted by another state, would almost certainly be of concern to the U.S. government. For example, when a 2005 State Department report assessed that "China maintains some elements of an offensive BW [biological weapons] capability in violation of its BWC obligations," it warned that:

> From 1993 to the present, [Chinese] military scientists have published in open literature the results of studies of aerosol stability of bacteria, models of infectious virus aerosols, and detection of aerosolized viruses using polymerase chain reaction technology. Such advanced biotechnology techniques could be applicable to the development of offensive BW agents and weapons.
>
> (U.S. State Department 2005)

By the same process of reasoning, the Chinese government itself could plausibly characterize U.S. development of "aerosol particle dispersion models" at an outdoor facility in Utah as the maintenance of "some elements of an offensive BW capability." China, suspicious of U.S. intentions, could justify its own biodefense research as being "protective," and U.S. suspicions of

Chinese intentions could in turn perpetuate a competition to acquire more and better knowledge of weaponization techniques.

One way to short-circuit the mutual suspicion and reduce the proliferation risk associated with biodefense programs might be to establish an international regime for increasing transparency and verifying states' compliance with the BWC. For more than 40 years, however, the challenge of BWC verification has been to achieve an adequate level of information exchange while overcoming the tendency of many governments to assume that security is enhanced by secrecy. Prior to 2001, BWC member states had been negotiating a legally binding verification regime for the Convention. Broadly speaking, greater confidence in states' compliance was to be generated by: declarations of facilities with the potential to engage in research and production relevant to biological weapons; routine and unannounced visits to such facilities; and investigations of suspicious disease outbreaks. The negotiations quickly unraveled after mid-2001 when the U.S. government announced it would not support a draft verification scheme. The basis for this decision was a concern (shared by some other states) that opening up national facilities to international inspection teams would compromise confidential commercial and military information. A biological attack involving anthrax bacteria in the United States occurred later the same year, and this confirmed the George W. Bush administration in its view that America had to rely less upon international law and more upon its own resources. The subsequent expansion in U.S. biodefense capabilities has brought increased health benefits in the form of more and better ways of preventing and curing infectious disease. At the same time, however, it has generated another kind of proliferation risk: vertical proliferation (i.e., a numerical increase within one state) of laboratories containing hazardous pathogens and of scientists with expertise applicable to biological weapons.

Following the 2001 anthrax attacks, annual U.S. government spending on biodefense programs increased enormously, from a total of U.S. $569 million in FY2001 to over U.S. $4 billion in FY2002 (Franco 2009: 292). At the time of writing, the budgeted amount for FY2013 was more than U.S. $5.5 billion, bringing the total allocation over the previous 13 years to almost U.S. $72 billion (Franco & Sell 2012: 164). Multiple government agencies, universities, and commercial enterprises have participated in research and development activities. On one view, this multi-billion dollar enterprise reduces the U.S. population's vulnerability to biological attacks (and infectious disease threats more generally) by investigating and producing countermeasures. Another view is that the risk of biological attacks from within is higher because of the large number of American scientists now working with hazardous pathogens. Over 15,000 personnel in nearly 1,500 laboratories reportedly have authorization to work with one or more of the "select [biological] agents" officially identified as being of bioterrorist concern (Gottron & Shea 2009: 3; Kaiser 2011: 1215). With so many people and places engaged in biodefense work, there is an increased chance that pathogenic microorganisms might be deliberately misused.

Laboratory biosecurity and export controls

On 29 July 2008 a microbiologist named Bruce Ivins, employed for 28 years at a U.S. Army laboratory in Maryland, committed suicide before he could be charged in connection with the anthrax attacks of 2001 (Johnson, Leonnig & Wilbur 2008). Ivins was a recently published expert on anthrax vaccines (Hewetson et al. 2008), and in 2003 he had received the U.S. Defense Department's highest civilian honor for his work in this area (Dance 2008). Affidavits for search warrants published by the U.S. Justice Department in August 2008 showed that part of Ivins' job was to prepare "large batches" of aerosolized anthrax bacteria, and he would then subject animals to "aerosol challenges" to test the effectiveness of anthrax vaccines (Dellafera 2008). Ivins knew how to use laboratory devices such as lyophilizers, incubators, and centrifuges, which are "considered essential for the production of the highly purified, powdered anthrax used" in 2001 (Dellafera 2008). The Justice Department's conclusion was that this scientist had made and used biological weapons (Johnson, Wilbur & Eggen 2008); an American had attacked Americans using American anthrax. If this is correct, it is ironic that the expansion of U.S. biodefense research has since 2001 provided a great many more American scientists with access to and knowledge of dangerous microorganisms. The U.S. government's response to the risk of biological attacks from within has been to impose stricter controls on the workplaces and behavior of scientists. However, when laboratory biosecurity mechanisms are used to manage the security risks of life science research, a potential downside is a diminution of scientists' ability to discover new and better responses to infectious disease threats of deliberate or natural origin.

Four years before Bruce Ivins' suicide in connection with the anthrax attacks, an expert on a different bacterium – *Yersinia pestis* (plague) – was sentenced to 2 years in prison. Thomas Butler, formerly chief of the infectious diseases division at Texas Tech University, was the first U.S. scientist to be tried for biosecurity offences under the federal Public Health Security and Bioterrorism Preparedness and Response Act of 2002. This legislation strengthened preexisting laws regulating the storage, handling, transfer, and disposal of listed microorganisms, and the charges brought against Butler included smuggling (i.e., transferring without government permission) *Yersinia pestis*. In December 2003 a Texas jury found Butler guilty on three charges related to the shipment of plague samples to a Tanzanian researcher without the proper permit, the package having been labeled merely as "laboratory materials" (Chang 2004; Piller 2003). In sentencing Butler the following year, the judge cut 7 years off a possible 9-year sentence, citing testimony that the bacteria shipment was done for humanitarian reasons and that the U.S. Commerce Department would have issued a transport permit had Butler applied for one. Significantly, the judge also cited Butler's early work on treatment of diarrheal diseases and oral rehydration as having "led to the salvage of millions of lives throughout the world" (Federation of American Scientists 2004). Here was a life scientist who manifested both as a bringer of health benefits and as a security risk. But to what extent does Butler's brush with the law discourage other scientists from engaging in risky behavior, and to what extent does it act as a disincentive to engage in pathogen research at all?

Biosecurity regulations have the potential to reduce the likelihood of a scientist misusing biological materials and technologies to cause harm. If regulation becomes widely regarded as too onerous, however, there is a danger that too many career scientists will simply opt out of particular lines of research and that students will be deterred from entering the scientific profession. In the United States, the likelihood of such an outcome might be reduced by the existence of a well-funded biodefense industry attracting talent and dispersing grants for research on organisms that humans might encounter in a biological attack or a natural disease outbreak. However, in other countries that maintain strict biosecurity regulations, scientists may find that there is little or no incentive to work with microorganisms deemed to be of bioterrorism concern. The diseases caused by those microorganisms could (with the exception of the eradicated smallpox virus) still pose a public health risk in the form of a naturally occurring outbreak. Thus, the health benefit to be derived from keeping scientists happy and preserving research capacity is an important factor weighing against the need to manage security risks in the laboratory. On this point it is also worth noting the warning in a 2009 report by the U.S. National Science Advisory Board for Biosecurity (NSABB) that "the institution of onerous [personnel] reliability measures could isolate select agent researchers from the mainstream scientific community, isolation that might inhibit research and paradoxically increase the risk of the insider threat" (NSABB 2009: iv). Such measures could include, for example, criminal history checks, financial background assessments, and psychological screening. The report concluded, moreover, that "a PRP [personnel reliability program] is likely to have unintended and detrimental consequences for the scientific enterprise that in the future could result in more harm to public health and safety and to national security than an insider threat poses" (NSABB 2009: v).

Regulating the work carried out by life scientists can extend beyond the laboratory in a way that further affects the potential beneficiaries of their scientific discoveries. Export controls, as a means of preventing or restricting the international transfer of technology, are aimed at reducing biological weapons risks. The rationale is that fewer people with access to potentially dangerous materials and information equates to a lower likelihood of harmful misuse. Under Australia's Defence Trade Controls Act of 2012, for example, a person commits an offence (and may be imprisoned for 10 years) if he or she "supplies DSGL [Defence and Strategic Goods List] technology to another person . . . outside Australia" without a permit issued by the Minister for Defence. The minister may issue a permit if he or she is "satisfied that the supply would not prejudice the security, defence or international relations of Australia" (Australian Government 2012b). A regulatory impact statement attached to the original legislation included an assessment that "this provision should have minimal impact on . . . research programs as these controls will not apply to broad discussions of research projects or experiments that do not discuss or transfer technology listed in the DSGL" (Australian Government 2011). The critical point about what scientists might "discuss or transfer," however, is that the DSGL itself includes more than 100 human, animal, and plant pathogens, and it also covers "genetically modified organisms or genetic elements that contain nucleic acid sequences associated with pathogenicity of organisms" (Australian Government 2012a). Some Australian researchers have reportedly expressed fears that the requirement for an export permit will inhibit their ability to publish and to communicate with international colleagues by email or even in person at scientific conferences (Dayton 2013).

To the extent that export controls inhibit openness among scientists, this is a problem for two reasons. First, the free exchange of research findings allows for the quality and reliability of research methods to be tested by other scientists. Second, the overall health benefit derived from scientific discoveries is increased by sharing them more widely. When a government chooses to address infectious disease threats by imposing restrictions on scientists' communications, the challenge is somehow to satisfy non-proliferation and technology-transfer imperatives concurrently. Adding to this challenge is the growing potential for security risks and health benefits to arise in relation to technology that is essentially intangible. The virtual traffic of biotechnology techniques, as distinct from the physical traffic of biological materials, is increasingly a source of both hope and concern.

Research and publication

Due to advances in gene modification and synthesis technologies, it is now possible to make dangerous microorganisms (and to make microorganisms dangerous) in a laboratory setting. The main reason scientists apply such technology is to investigate the potential for a microorganism's genome to mutate naturally and so present a new threat to human health. By anticipating that threat, research findings on the nature and behavior of a mutated microorganism can then inform the preparation of medical and public health responses. A scientist might, for example, set out deliberately to generate a bacterium resistant to a certain class of antibiotics to determine whether it could become resistant to that class through natural processes. Such information would be relevant to recommendations on how best to administer the antibiotic and could help guide clinical infectious disease management. It is in the nature of scientific inquiry, however, that results cannot be perfectly predicted; surprises can and do arise.

In Australia, where periodic mouse plagues impose huge agricultural costs, a group of scientists in the late 1990s attempted to address this problem by producing an infectious contraceptive for mice. The scientists first spliced the zona pellucida glycoprotein 3 (ZP3) gene into a mild *ectromelia* virus

(EV) – the organism that causes mousepox – in the hope that injecting mice with that virus would induce antibodies with a sterilizing effect (Jackson et al. 1998). They subsequently inserted the interleukin-4 (IL-4) gene in order to boost this effect, but the actual result of *ectromelia* virus expressing the interleukin-4 gene (EVIL-4) was a strain of mousepox so virulent that it killed mice that were vaccinated against ordinary mousepox (Jackson et al. 2001). A disturbing implication of this result was that adding an IL-4 gene might similarly allow the smallpox virus (or some other poxvirus that infects humans) to circumvent vaccination. Such a microorganism would arguably constitute a powerful biological weapon. When project leader Ron Jackson was questioned by the *New York Times* on the decision to publish his team's findings in the *Journal of Virology*, his comment on the associated security risk was: "We thought it was better that the information came out in case somebody constructed something more sinister. . . . We felt we had a moral obligation because it is existing technology" (Broad 2001). The justification for publishing dual-use technology for making a virus more dangerous was, in other words, that the potential benefits of doing so outweighed the potential harms.

Raising awareness about a newly discovered disease threat can indeed spur the timely preparation of medical and public health responses, although publication also carries the risk of enabling malicious actors to bring that very threat to fulfillment. A decade after Jackson's mousepox findings were published, and at a time of heightened concern worldwide about pandemic influenza, scientists researching influenza viruses found themselves in the security spotlight. In 2011, researchers in the Netherlands and in the United States had been investigating whether the H5N1 avian influenza virus (the "bird flu" that emerged in Asia in 2003) could mutate into a human-to-human transmissible (pandemic) form. Both teams conducted laboratory experiments in which, by applying genetic modification techniques, they gradually induced the mutation of H5N1 into a form directly transmissible between ferrets (and, therefore, between humans, given the similarity of both mammals' respiratory systems). The virologists led by Ron Fouchier (Erasmus Medical Center in Rotterdam) and those led by Yoshihiro Kawaoka (University of Wisconsin-Madison) submitted their findings for publication in *Science* and *Nature* respectively. The manuscripts immediately raised concerns that the altered viruses themselves or the methodologies being reported could be misused to cause a highly damaging influenza pandemic. Accordingly, the editors of each journal passed the papers to the NSABB, which, in late 2011, unanimously called for the researchers to redact the "materials and methods" section of their manuscripts. This sparked an intense and global debate among scientists and the general public over whether or the extent to which publication of particular research findings should be restricted. Fouchier and Kawaoka asked the NSABB to reconsider its decision, arguing that publication of the full results would make a significant contribution to global public health. In early 2012 a meeting organized by the World Health Organization produced a recommendation that the two sets of results be published in full, the NSABB reversed its earlier decision, and articles duly appeared in June 2012 (InterAcademy Council and InterAcademy Panel 2012: 15).

Only after the Dutch and U.S. teams' findings were published did it become generally apparent that the risks of publication had probably been overstated. Regarding the risk that another scientist would misuse a published "recipe" for a pandemic virus, the assumption was often made that the new form of H5N1 virus was both human-transmissible *and* highly virulent. At the time of writing, the global average case-fatality rate among human cases of H5N1 illness since 2003 stood at 59% (World Health Organization 2013). If such a rate were maintained during the human-to-human spread of the virus, the death toll would indeed be devastating. However, in the Dutch experiments conducted in 2011, "[n]one of the recipient ferrets died after airborne infection with the mutant A/H5N1 viruses" (Herfst et al. 2012). This is consistent with the generally observed phenomenon that a virus's virulence decreases as its transmissibility increases. Another factor mitigating the "recipe" risk is that published methodologies are not certain to produce the same results when applied by other scientists. As Sonia Ben Ouagrham-Gormley has argued, although "globalization of the pharmaceutical and biotechnology industries has enabled an increasingly widespread diffusion of information, materials, and equipment," these inputs are "hardly sufficient [for a state or terrorist group] to produce a significant [biological] weapons capability" (Ouagrham-Gormley 2012: 112–113). Importantly, she has found, "such intangible factors as organizational makeup and management style greatly affect the use of acquired knowledge [and] the creation of tacit knowledge," and these factors "cannot be easily transferred among individuals or from one place to another" (Ouagrham-Gormley 2012: 112–113).

If the risks of publishing the H5N1 experiment results were overstated, so too were the benefits. The Dutch and U.S. teams, like many influenza researchers before them, couched the benefit in terms of providing advance warning of a pandemic. The article by Fouchier's team stated that the experiments were conducted to "address the concern that the virus could acquire this ability [airborne transmission between humans] under natural conditions" (Herfst et al. 2012: 1534). Similarly, Kawaoka's team argued (Imai et al. 2012: 420):

> Our findings emphasize the need to prepare for potential pandemics caused by influenza viruses . . . and will help individuals conducting surveillance in regions with circulating H5N1 viruses to recognize . . . pandemic potential . . . which will inform the development, production and distribution of effective countermeasures.

In assessing the benefit (to be weighed against the risk) of publishing these H5N1 mutation findings, it is important to note that such information would not in itself solve the well-known problem of inadequate response capacity. The value of advance warning is low given that, as shown during the 2009 H1N1 ("swine flu") pandemic, the extreme difficulty of containing influenza transmission is clear. It is common knowledge also that there is insufficient global capacity for the timely production and universal distribution of influenza vaccine. In such circumstances, there is little benefit to be derived from research results that raise awareness of an influenza problem of which people and political leaders are already well aware. Thus, if even a low-level security risk could be shown to outweigh the health benefit of publication, a journal editor or a government might have a justification for deciding not to publish those results at all. At the same time, it needs to be acknowledged, firstly, that the benefits of sharing the results of particular experiments are often not obvious or immediate. Secondly, life-saving scientific discoveries can be and are built upon earlier findings emanating from other areas of biotechnology and even from other branches of science. Over the long term, repeatedly privileging security at the expense of scientific freedom could increasingly inhibit the ability of those who rely on that freedom to protect populations against pandemic influenza and other infectious diseases.

Conclusion

Biological weapons are a problem that most scientists would probably rather not contemplate, but there is a clear need for greater awareness and more discussion of this problem. Future controversies like that generated by the H5N1 transmissibility experiments could damage the reputation of the scientific profession and undermine support for much life-saving laboratory research. It was an unfortunate feature of the debate over the health benefits and security risks of those experiments that it occurred only after the research had been completed. Under sudden pressure to assuage public concern about scientists deliberately causing viral mutation, 39 of the world's leading influenza researchers took the drastic and reactive step of committing to a moratorium, which lasted for more than a year, on "any research involving highly pathogenic avian influenza

H5N1 viruses leading to the generation of viruses that are more transmissible in mammals" (Fouchier et al. 2012). A better approach would be for life scientists rather to be proactive in anticipating and managing dual-use dilemmas encountered in their work.

It is in the nature of dilemmas that straightforward solutions are not available. Nevertheless, the process of assessing research risks and benefits would be enhanced if it was systematically incorporated into the education, training, and everyday practices of life scientists (see Dando, chapter 21 in this volume). Laws to regulate behavior have the potential to reduce biological weapons risks, but there is a danger that top-down approaches to governance will undervalue the health benefits to be derived from laboratory research. Imposing and tightening biosecurity regulations could also adversely affect scientists' ability and willingness to address infectious disease threats of natural or deliberate origin. An alternative approach, and one that is perhaps more likely to succeed, is a bottom-up fostering of awareness of the need for individual scientists to consider carefully the potential downsides of their research. Collectively, scientists could achieve this by establishing and maintaining their own frameworks for decision making: professional codes of conduct. These would fall short of actual law, but no law could anticipate every pathway and outcome of pathogen research anyway. Moreover, existing biosecurity and export control laws that contemplate physical materials are becoming obsolete. Knowledge of techniques, rather than mere possession of microorganisms, is increasingly the critical factor when it comes to the use and misuse of biotechnology.

The fundamental aim of a code of conduct for life scientists would be to prevent the direct or indirect application of biotechnology to the development, production, or use of biological weapons. A code need not be a detailed and lengthy document but rather could serve two basic functions. First, from school through to university and beyond, a code would educate present and future scientists about the ongoing problem of biological weapons. Second, it would put researchers on notice to insert an extra step – consideration of the potential for harmful misuse of biotechnology – in their processes for deciding what, how, and why pathogen research will be conducted. All life scientists working in all laboratory settings – academic, commercial, and military – would be ethically bound to adhere to such a code, and a number of reinforcement mechanisms could be built around it. For example, university scientists seeking public or philanthropic funding for research could first be required to demonstrate commitment to a code of conduct by completing a short course on dual-use challenges. Commercial scientists who are not dependent on external funding could receive special government recognition of their personal commitment to a code, and their employers could derive a market advantage from such recognition.

In the case of scientists working in a military setting, however, a code of conduct would need to be supplemented by a strict and legally enforceable rule. Even if a code had an in-built presumption in favor of freedom of scientific inquiry, fulfillment of the code's fundamental aim would require that research on microorganism delivery systems be expressly forbidden. In a biodefense context, and consistent with the spirit of the BWC, this would render the "biological" separate from the "weapon," always and entirely. By conspicuously eschewing experiments involving large-scale dissemination of aerosolized microorganisms, for example, a government would reduce the risk of biological attacks against it. Laboratory insiders like Bruce Ivins would be deprived of access to weaponization technologies, and foreign governments would have fewer reasons to suspect that biodefense activities disguise offensive intent.

References

Alibek, K. (1999) *Biohazard*, London: Arrow.

Australian Government. (2011) *Regulation Impact Statement: Defence Trade Controls Bill 2011*, Department of Finance. Online. Available HTTP: <http://ris.finance.gov.au/files/2011/11/03-Defence-Export-Controls-RIS.pdf> (accessed 21 January 2014).

Australian Government. (2012a) *Defence and Strategic Goods List*, Department of Defence, 5 December. Online. Available HTTP: <http://www.defence.gov.au/deco/DSGL.asp> (accessed 14 May 2014).

Australian Government. (2012b) *Defence Trade Controls Act 2012*. Online. Available HTTP: <http://www.comlaw.gov.au/Details/C2012A00153> (accessed 21 January 2014).

Broad, W.J. (2001) 'Australians create a deadly mouse virus', *New York Times*, 23 January. Online. Available HTTP: <http://www.nytimes.com/2001/01/23/health/23MOUS.html> (accessed 21 January 2014).

Chang, K. (2004) 'Scientist in plague case is sentenced to two years', *New York Times*, 11 March: A18.

Convention on the Prohibition of the Development, Production and Stockpiling of Bacteriological (Biological) and Toxin Weapons and on their Destruction. (1972). Online. Available HTTP: http://www.unog.ch/bwc (accessed 14 May 2014).

Dance, A. (2008) 'Death renews biosecurity debate', *Nature*, 454: 672.

Dayton, L. (2013) 'Australian researchers rattled by export control law', *Science*, 339: 1263.

Dellafera, T.F. (2008) *Affidavit in Support of Search Warrant*, U.S. Department of Justice. Online. Available HTTP: <http://www.justice.gov/archive/amerithrax/docs/07-524-m-01.pdf> (accessed 14 May 2014).

Federation of American Scientists. (2004) *United States v Butler*, 5:03-CR-037-C, U.S. District Court, Northern District of Texas, 10 March. Online. Available HTTP: <http://www.fas.org/butler/sentence.html> (accessed 21 January 2014).

Federation of American Scientists. (2006) *Department of Defense Chemical and Biological Defense Program Annual Report to Congress*, March. Online. Available HTTP: <https://www.fas.org/irp/threat/cbdp2006.pdf> (accessed 21 January 2014).

Fouchier, R.A.M., Garcia-Sastre, A., Kawaoka, Y. and 36 co-authors. (2012) 'Pause on avian flu transmission studies', *Nature*, 481: 443.

Franco, C. (2009) 'Billions for biodefense: federal agency biodefense funding, FY2009-FY2010', *Biosecurity and Bioterrorism*, 7: 291–309.

Franco, C. and Sell, T.K. (2012) 'Federal agency biodefense funding, FY2012-FY2013', *Biosecurity and Bioterrorism*, 10: 162–181.

Gottron, F. and Shea, D.A. (2009) *Oversight of High-Containment Biological Laboratories: Issues for Congress*, Washington DC: Congressional Research Service.

Herfst, S., Schrauwen, E.J.A., Linster, M., Chutinimitkul, S., de Wit, E., Munster, V.J., Sorrell, E.M., Bestebroer, T.M., Burke, D.F., Smith, D.J., Rimmelzwaan, G.F., Osterhaus, A.D.M.E. and Fouchier, R.A.M. (2012) 'Airborne transmission of influenza A/H5N1 virus between ferrets', *Science*, 336: 1534–1541.

Hewetson, J.F., Little, S.F., Ivins, B.E., Johnson, W.M., Pittman, P.R., Brown, J.E., Norris, S.L. and Nielsen, C.J. (2008) 'An in vivo passive protection assay for the evaluation of immunity in AVA-vaccinated individuals'', *Vaccine*, 26: 4262–4266.

Imai, M., Watanabe, T., Hatta, M., Das, S.C., Ozawa, M., Shinya, K., Zhong, G., Hanson, A., Katsura, H., Watanabe, S., Li, C., Kawakami, E., Yamada, S., Kiso, M., Suzuki, Y., Maher, E.A., Neumann, G. and Kawaoka, Y. (2012) 'Experimental adaptation of an influenza H5 HA confers respiratory droplet transmission to a reassortant H5 HA/H1N1 virus in ferrets', *Nature*, 486: 420–428.

InterAcademy Council and InterAcademy Panel. (2012) *Responsible Conduct in the Global Research Enterprise: A Policy Report*, Amsterdam. Online. Available HTTP: <http://www.interacademycouncil.net/24026/GlobalReport.aspx> (accessed 21 January 2014).

Jackson, R.J., Maguire, D.J., Hinds, L.A. and Ramshaw, I.A. (1998) 'Infertility in mice induced by a recombinant ectromelia virus expressing mouse zona pellucida glycoprotein 3', *Biology of Reproduction*, 58: 152–159.

Jackson, R.J., Ramsay, A.J., Christensen, C.D., Beaton, S., Hall, D.F. and Ramshaw, I.A. (2001) 'Expression of mouse interleukin-4 by a recombinant ectromelia virus suppresses cytolytic lymphocyte responses and overcomes genetic resistance to mousepox', *Journal of Virology*, 75: 1205–1210.

Johnson, C., Leonnig, C.D. and Wilber, D.Q. (2008) 'Scientist set to discuss plea bargain in deadly attacks commits suicide', *Washington Post*, 2 August: A01.

Johnson, C., Wilber, D.Q. and Eggen, D. (2008) 'Evidence against scientist detailed', *Washington Post*, 7 August: A01.

Kaiser, J. (2011) 'Taking stock of the biodefense boom', *Science*, 333: 1214–1215.

NSABB. (2009) *Enhancing Personnel Reliability Among Individuals with Access to Select Agents*, Washington DC: National Science Advisory Board for Biosecurity.

Ouagrham-Gormley, S.B. (2012) 'Barriers to bioweapons: intangible obstacles to proliferation', *International Security*, 36: 80–114.

Piller, C. (2003) 'Plague expert cleared of serious charges in bioterror case', *Los Angeles Times*, 2 December: A16.

Tang, S. (2009) 'The security dilemma: a conceptual analysis', *Security Studies*, 18: 587–623.
Tucker, J.B. (2001) *Scourge: the Once and Future Threat of Smallpox*, New York: Atlantic Monthly Press.
United States of America. (2012) *Confidence Building Measure Return Covering 2011*, United Nations: Geneva. Online. Available HTTP: www.unog.ch/bwc/cbms (accessed 21 January 2014).
U.S. State Department. (2005) *2005 Adherence to and Compliance with Arms Control, Nonproliferation, and Disarmament Agreements and Commitments*, 30 August. Online. Available HTTP: <http://www.state.gov/t/avc/rls/rpt/51977.htm> (accessed 21 January 2014).
U.S. State Department. (2012) *2012 Adherence to and Compliance with Arms Control, Nonproliferation, and Disarmament Agreements and Commitments*. Online. Available HTTP: <http://www.state.gov/t/avc/rls/rpt/197085.htm#part3a> (accessed 21 January 2014).
World Health Organization. (2013) *Cumulative Number of Confirmed Human Cases of Avian Influenza A(H5N1) Reported to WHO*. Online. Available HTTP: <http://www.who.int/influenza/human_animal_interface/H5N1_cumulative_table_archives/en> (accessed 26 April 2013).

12

CONFLICT, INSTABILITY, AND HEALTH SECURITY

Frank L. Smith III

Health and security both involve survival and so these concepts are deeply intertwined; they probably have been since our ancestors first started to fear death. While we each may experience health most acutely as individuals, the association between individual health and the well-being of social groups – including the metaphorical "body politic" – is also ancient and powerful. Sometimes this association is no mere metaphor. Infectious diseases have threatened national and international security throughout our history, just as conflict and instability have long spread diseases and threatened human health in other ways. These interactions have been documented at least since Thucydides described the Plague of Athens during the Peloponnesian War.

Because health and security are so deeply intertwined, it can be difficult to distinguish between them in order to critically analyze how they affect each other. As a result, both concepts are frequently defined in excessively broad or overly narrow terms. Unfortunately, this makes some claims about the causal relationships between health, conflict, and instability either imprecise or, alternatively, so tenuous as to defy deductive logic and common sense.

For example, while it may be normatively pleasing, there is little analytical utility in defining "health" as "a state of complete physical, mental, and social wellbeing" (WHO 1978), or in defining "human security" as "freedom from fear and freedom from want" (UNDP 1994: 24). By including everything, these excessively broad definitions run the risk of explaining nothing (Paris 2001). Conversely, it is not realistic to define security only in terms of military force or to claim that including health in security studies "would destroy its intellectual coherence" (Walt 1991: 213). Even if we accept the core tenets of realist theory, which tend to be narrowly applied to armed conflict, there is nothing inherent in realist assumptions about anarchy, uncertainty, or rationality to suggest that military force is the only threat to state survival and thus national security.

In order to avoid these errors and pitfalls, I adopt a pragmatic approach to analyzing health security in the context of conflict and instability. First, this chapter examines the extreme case of war and how it threatens human health through infectious diseases. Of course, infectious diseases are far from the only way that conflict and instability might harm health. War also causes trauma, and it can adversely affect food, water, and the environment as well as infrastructure, all of which impact health. Even so, pathogens often play an intervening role (e.g., exploiting the immunosuppression caused by malnutrition), and therefore the threat of infectious disease provides an important proxy for health throughout this chapter. In the second section, I flip the causal arrow and examine the ongoing debate over how health might affect conflict and instability.

The impact of conflict and instability on health

Health security rarely benefits in a direct or immediate fashion from conflict and instability. For instance, war represents conflict and instability in the extreme and, not surprisingly, war is hell for health. Regardless of whether armed conflict is between states or within them, the political ends of war are pursued through violent means that are intended to disable or destroy people and matériel. Many of the direct effects of war on health are therefore painfully obvious, such as injury and death among armed forces and civilian populations. Granted, the number of battle deaths around the world is thought to be in decline (Lacina et al. 2006). But warfare remains a quintessentially unhealthy feature of the human condition.

Furthermore, the direct and indirect effects of war are far more varied and, at times, far more significant than injury or death on the battlefield. Until World War II, for example, more American soldiers, sailors, and marines died from infectious diseases during war than those that perished in battle (Cirillo 2008). Rarely if ever were these deaths from disease due to biological weapons – namely the deliberate use of pathogens for warfare or terrorism (although some evidence suggests that the British spread smallpox to thwart the American Revolution). Instead, war usually served as what Andrew Price-Smith calls a "disease amplifier" (Price-Smith 2009), and the instability of armed conflict helped to catalyze contagion with devastating effects.

What is it about war that helps spread disease? "The causal relationship between conflict and infectious disease is rather complex" (Price-Smith 2009: 160), and it includes "a broad range of social, physical, psychological, and environmental considerations" (Smallman-Raynor & Cliff 2004: 4). That being said, key features of this relationship can be summarized in overlapping terms of displacement and concentration, as well as disruption and destruction – each of which indicates how crisis and instability can affect health security.

Depravation through disruption and destruction

War disrupts and destroys people and places, including the medical personnel and health infrastructure that might otherwise be available. This impedes or eliminates access to essential services and thus deprives people of health care. On the one hand, "international legal standards for the protection of health in armed conflict have been in place for 150 years" (Rubenstein & Bittle 2010: 330). These standards draw on humanitarian law and medical ethics; they are codified in the Geneva Conventions; and they are embodied in the work of nongovernmental organizations like the International Committee of the Red Cross, as well as the United Nations (UN) and other international organizations.

On the other hand, however, "international laws are not respected" (Rubenstein & Bittle 2010: 329). As a result, "in certain conflicts, attacks on medical workers and facilities seem to be part of generalised violence," while, in other instances, "destabilization tactics included targeted attacks on physicians as community leaders," as well as "attacks on medical facilities, personnel, or patients . . . to prevent enemy combatants from receiving care and re-entering battle" (Rubenstein & Bittle 2010: 329). Even when health care is not deliberately targeted, indiscriminate attacks can still disrupt or destroy it, as evident in armed conflicts ranging from Sri Lanka to Iraq. All of this suggests that "security is a prerequisite for health" (Coupland 2007: 181), regardless of international law, and that "conflict, violence, and insecurity are more than constraints on the delivery of health care in many parts of the world: they are showstoppers" (Coupland 2013: 1076).

The adverse effects of disruption and destruction extend beyond the depravation of intensive care in clinical settings. War can also break down the health systems used for infection control, treatment, and surveillance. This is argued to have amplified outbreaks of viral hemorrhagic fever in central Africa, for example, and enabled the persistence of malaria in central Asia (Gayer et al. 2007). Like malaria itself, the collapse of health systems can persist long after conflict and instability have passed their peak, and, by impeding data collection on threats like infectious disease, war can also interfere with the very record of its own effect on health (Murray et al. 2002). Health systems are rarely if ever disrupted or destroyed on their own; war also deprives people of food, water, shelter, and other basic requirements for health security. Moreover, by disrupting social norms and order, conflict can change behavior and thus harm health through sexual violence (e.g. Elbe 2002: 167; MacKenzie 2012: 100), and even help spread infectious diseases through commercial sex and drug abuse.

Displacement and concentration

Like disruption and destruction, another hallmark of war is that it can both displace and concentrate large numbers of people. This is true for the military and civilians alike. People are displaced as they move around to either engage in armed conflict or attempt to avoid it. Often, in the process of moving, these people also end up concentrated in locations like military barracks and refugee camps. When coupled with the depravation caused by war, the dynamics of displacement and concentration are usually destabilizing and rarely benign.

People on the move carry infectious diseases with them and, through the mixing of different populations that often accompanies displacement, they are sometimes exposed to diseases that they may not have previously encountered. By moving and mixing large numbers of people, military and civilian, war can therefore amplify disease by increasing the rate and range over which it spreads. This ancient process has shaped human history. For instance, the Peloponnesian War may have helped spread typhus – the probable cause of what Thucydides described as the Plague of Athens. European conquest of the New World introduced smallpox into the Americas, which subsequently decimated the indigenous population (Diamond 1999), and one theory is that Columbus introduced syphilis into Europe upon return from what is now Haiti (Singh & Romanowski 1999: 188).

As significant as war, displacement, and disease have been in the past, scholarship is now divided over the extent to which armed conflict contributes to the spread of HIV. The conventional view is that "armed conflicts and their participants constitute an important vector of HIV/AIDS" (Elbe 2002: 174), and UN Security Council Resolution 1308 recognized "that the HIV/AIDS pandemic is also exacerbated by conditions of violence and instability, which increase the risk of exposure to the disease through large movements of people" (UN Security Council 2000: 1–2). Some evidence supports this view. According to Matthew Smallman-Raynor and Andrew Cliff, for example, "the spread of HIV infection in the 1980s, and the subsequent development of AIDS to its 1990 spatial pattern, were significantly and positively correlated with ethnic patterns of recruitment into the Ugandan Liberation Army" (Smallman-Raynor & Cliff 2004: 549). Similarly, statistical analysis beyond Uganda indicates that "both international and domestic conflict are consistently associated with substantially higher adult HIV infection rates," and "large influxes of migrant populations accelerate" the spread of this disease (Iqbal & Zorn 2010: 159).

But just as war can drive displacement, it can also restrict mobility, and, according to Paul Spiegel, "whether or not conflict and displacement affect HIV transmission depends upon numerous competing and interacting factors" (Spiegel 2004: 322). Furthermore, Spiegel and his colleagues find "insufficient evidence that HIV transmission increases in populations affected by conflict," as well as "insufficient data to conclude that refugees fleeing conflict have a higher prevalence of HIV infection than do their surrounding host communities" (Spiegel et al. 2007: 2192). Contributing to this empirical critique is the fear that the conventional view of conflict and HIV/AIDS might portray refugees as a vector for contagion and thus security threat (McInnes 2011: 487), increasing social stigma and worsening their plight. Yet even critics of the conventional view do not deny a possible link between displacement and this disease, arguing instead for a more nuanced view that acknowledges that "the extent to which conflict is a vector for HIV depends on the specificities of both the conflict and the epidemic in that state" (McInnes & Rushton 2010: 239).

Here, as elsewhere, HIV/AIDS is not the only disease that warrants consideration, nor is war the only source of instability that might drive displacement. Following the Haiti earthquake in 2010, for instance, UN peacekeepers carried cholera from Nepal into Haiti: a location where that disease had never been recorded. This compounded the damage wrought by the earthquake, creating one of the worst cholera epidemics in modern history, infecting more than 500,000 people, and causing more than 7,000 deaths (Frerichs et al. 2012). Along with displacement, concentration was likely a contributing factor in this outbreak. First, the peacekeepers deployed from Nepal were concentrated at the United Nations Stabilization Mission in Haiti (MINUSTAH) camp – which had poor sanitation – near the town of Mirebalais, where the first cases of cholera emerged. Second, the concentration of displaced earthquake victims in squalid and overcrowded refugee camps probably helped cholera spread down the Artibonite River and ultimately into the devastated capital of Port-au-Prince.

As devastating as it is, however, the cholera epidemic in Haiti is an exceptional case. Large populations are rarely displaced following acute natural disasters (at least, they are rarely displaced very far), which is one reason why "outbreaks are less frequently reported in disaster-affected populations than in conflict affected populations" (Watson et al. 2007: 1). War displaces more people and, for those who flee their country of origin, "the most common reported causes of death among refugees during the influx phase have been diarrheal diseases, measles, acute respiratory infections, malaria, and other infectious diseases" (Toole & Waldman 1997: 292). These diseases are amplified by crowding in refugee camps, as well as by inadequate shelter, sanitation, food, water, and medical care. Moreover, "the health status of the internally displaced may be worse" (Toole & Waldman 1997: 286), since they usually remain closer to conflict.

And civilians do not suffer alone. For military personnel, "the general problem of camp epidemics has extended beyond the initial massing of unseasoned recruits in barracks and tent camps on home soil to include the field camps, siege camps, and bivouacs of deployed armies, as well as temporary and makeshift military settlements such as prisoner of war (POW) and concentration camps" (Smallman-Raynor & Cliff 2004: 416). In these settings, large numbers of people are quickly concentrated, often without adequate shelter, sanitation, supplies, or support. These conditions sometimes mirror those found in civilian camps and, at least historically, so too do some of the diseases. This is why it was not until World War II that battle started to kill more troops than contagion.

Finally, because the relationship between war and disease is complex, one implication is that not every aspect of this relationship is bad for health security. While troops are concentrated in barracks, for example, military recruits may also receive vaccinations and health care that they might not have otherwise had. Likewise, while concentrating people into refugee camps increases some health risks, it might also increase their access to humanitarian aid, which may result in "elevated mortality, followed by rapid declines with the arrival of assistance and a modicum of stable and safe living conditions" (Reed & Keely 2001: 12). Even when the tradeoff between investment in the military versus healthcare appears stark, it is incorrect to imply that reduced military spending can simply be redirected to increase funding for public health (e.g., Levy & Sidel 1997). Therefore, a nuanced view of how conflict and instability affect health must acknowledge the complex interplay between them, despite the fact that potentially beneficial outcomes do little to counterbalance the overwhelmingly harmful effects of war.

The impact of health on conflict and instability

So conflict and instability often – though not always – hurt health security, as illustrated by the complex relationship between war and infectious disease. Might the reverse be true as well? Namely, can health affect the course of political conflict or social instability?

These questions are typically debated in terms of HIV/AIDS (see Fourie, chapter 9 in this volume). This is understandable. With 35 million people having died from AIDS and a similar number living with HIV today, the social and political effects of this disease are hugely significant. Initially, it was argued that these effects would be acute, particularly in Africa, where it was feared that institutions like the military might collapse alongside the economy and society at large. However, subsequent research has called some of these initial arguments into question and suggested that the timeframe, causal pathways, and institutional effects of this disease maybe longer, more complicated, and more localized or variable than originally assumed. This is not to say that HIV/AIDS does not contribute to conflict and instability. But it is only one of many diseases, and health is only one of many factors that influence stability. Careful research and better theories are therefore needed to understand the impact of disease on politics and, relatedly, the effect that health interventions might have on political conditions.

HIV and the military

In 2000, UN Security Council Resolution 1308 stressed "that the HIV/AIDS pandemic, if unchecked, may pose a risk to stability and security." According to the Security Council, one prominent way that stability and security were threatened was through "the potentially damaging impact of HIV/AIDS on the health of international peacekeeping personnel." First, countries with high rates of HIV/AIDS might be unable to provide peacekeepers for missions abroad. Second, other countries might be unwilling to contribute to missions in locations where the disease is prevalent. Third, countries in need of peacekeepers may nevertheless object to hosting them for fear of spreading infection (Feldbaum et al. 2006). Assuming that peacekeepers provide peace, stability would suffer as a result.

Along with the impact on UN peacekeepers, several scholars and policymakers argued that HIV/AIDS also threatened the armed forces, thereby destabilizing these national institutions and, with them, international security more broadly. Although evidence was limited, HIV was initially thought to be as much as two to five times more prevalent inside the military than in the general population of some African states (UNAIDS 1998: 2). Treating and replacing sick soldiers was expected to strain defense budgets; "hollow out" command structures through the loss of experienced, trained, and specialized staff; and weaken unit cohesion and morale (Elbe 2002; Elbe & Ostergard 2007; Feldbaum et al. 2006). These effects might not destroy the afflicted military's operational capacity, but they were expected to significantly reduce combat readiness and effectiveness, compromising the state's ability to defend itself against internal and external attack. While these effects were expected to be most acute in Africa, it was feared that a "second wave" of HIV might also destabilize Russia, India, and China in years ahead.

The future remains uncertain, of course, but recent scholarship suggests that many of the acute effects of HIV/AIDS on the armed services and peacekeepers have not materialized (McInnes & Rushton 2010). While some evidence indicates that, in Africa, "HIV prevalence within the military is elevated compared to the general population" (Ba et al. 2008: 88), this is not always the case. As Alan Whiteside, Alex de Waal, and Tsadkan Gebre-Tensae argue, "the oft-cited claim that soldiers have prevalence rates two to five times higher than the civilian population is unsustainable and should no longer be cited" (Whiteside et al. 2006: 216). Just as there are reasons to hypothesize a high prevalence of HIV in the military (e.g., machismo culture that promotes promiscuity, long periods of deployment, ready access to prostitution, etc.), there are also plausible reasons why the opposite might be true (e.g., recruits drawn from demographic categories with low prevalence, as well as the military's hierarchical structure that can implement screening, awareness programs, medical treatment, and other interventions). Even if the prevalence of disease is higher among older and thus more experience service members, the armed forces have built-in redundancy to cope with some loses, regardless of whether attrition is caused by combat or disease. Moreover, "it is highly improbable that one nation will see that its neighbour's military has been heavily hit by AIDS and decide this is the opportunity to invade" (Whiteside et al. 2006: 216; similarly, Price-Smith 2009: 160, 200).

This does not mean that HIV/AIDS does not destabilize the military – along with the police and other security services – in important ways, including their operational capabilities. But these effects vary as a function of other factors. Perhaps more important, the most significant effects may not be acute; to some extent, this disease was initially mischaracterized as a short-term "emergency" (De Waal et al. 2009: 28). Plus, though it tends to dominate the discussion, HIV is neither the only infectious disease that might harm the military nor is it the fastest. According to Price-Smith, for example, the 1918 influenza pandemic quickly killed or debilitated large swaths of military personnel, "undermined force cohesion, planning, and execution, and reduced the capacity for effective reinforcement of divisions in the midst of battle," particularly among the Central Powers. This pandemic might even have been the "straw that broke the camel's back," helping to shatter Austria-Hungary and prevent a German victory (Price-Smith 2009: 64, 76). Even if it was not a deciding factor during World War I, the acute shock of a lethal influenza pandemic may be more destabilizing for the military than the slow grind of HIV/AIDS, at least in the short term.

Political and economic stability

The military and police are far from the only institutions whose contribution to stability might be threatened by infectious disease. Poor health is also argued to undermine most other political and economic institutions, damaging the performance of governments and markets along with confidence in them. Despite the grim toll of HIV/AIDS, however, most of the broad effects of this disease on political and economic stability are indirect and they are yet to cause state failure. Furthermore, it remains to be proven how the provision of healthcare in the midst or aftermath of armed conflict might increase stability through peacemaking and peace building.

"There is an inexorable link between issues of health and political legitimacy and stability" (Youde 2007: 197). The poor health caused by infectious diseases can threaten political stability in several ways. For example, HIV/AIDS has killed tens of millions of people, many of them between 20 and 50 years old. This crippling blow to populations stands to diminish states' latent power (Mearsheimer 2001: 61), and, in those states hardest hit, the disease is also changing the demographic distribution. According to Laurie Garrett, this demographic shift creates a "youth-bulge" that is "at greater risk of civil disturbances, conflict, and disorder" (Garrett 2005: 11). Similarly, most commentators argue that HIV/AIDS destabilizes states by destroying human capital, including civil servants, healthcare providers, teachers, and other skilled professionals. Their labor and talents are necessary in order for political institutions to provide public goods and services, civil society to function, and private industry to contribute to economy development and productivity.

Estimates of the economic impact of HIV/AIDS vary considerably, depending on factors ranging from sector and gender to geographic scope and timescale. With few exceptions, the effects are bad because of the damage to economic development and productivity caused by sickness and death, as well as the additional demand for scarce resources like drugs and medical care. Furthermore, if markets and governments are unable or unwilling to provide these resources, then the resulting disparities might undermine the legitimacy of these institutions and thus feed discontent, unrest, or even violence. In other words, politics and the economy are linked, which is why Jeremy Youde argues that because of HIV/AIDS, "economic factors will work to undermine the stability and legitimacy of the democratic regimes of Botswana, Lesotho, South Africa, Zambia, and Zimbabwe" (Youde 2007: 210). The economic and political threats from infectious diseases are neither limited to HIV/AIDS nor democratic regimes. After all, China's authoritarian regime interpreted the outbreak of Severe Acute Respiratory Syndrome (SARS) as a threat to its economic development and political stability as well (Huang 2004).

Despite these potential sources of instability, however, HIV/AIDS is yet to cause an acute crisis of state failure. "Those countries with the highest HIV prevalence are not ranked among the most fragile, and those considered most fragile do not report the highest rates of HIV" (De Waal et al. 2009: 35; also Barnett & Dutta 2008). Granted, "fragility" and "state failure" are contested concepts and so their lack of correlation with HIV prevalence may be due in part to macroeconomic indicators that underestimate or ignore important costs and consequences of this extraordinarily complex disease. But the lack of correlation between HIV and state failure should not be dismissed. As with this disease's effect on the military, several countervailing factors might also be at work.

For instance, the HIV/AIDS pandemic did not rage unchecked as initially feared because state and non-state actors eventually intervened. Along with nonmedical interventions, antiretroviral therapies in particular have saved and extended many lives. This is at least one reason why the U.S. President's Emergency Plan for AIDS Relief (PEPFAR) is said to have "helped to prevent instability and societal collapse in a number of at-risk countries" (Lugar, quoted in McInnes & Rushton 2010: 241).

Perhaps more important, HIV/AIDS demonstrates that states are remarkably resilient. Therefore, "some aspects of state functioning can remain robust even while communities are plunged into protracted crises" (De Waal et al. 2009: 44). Ironically, this finding mirrors insights from security studies on why punishing civilians through strategic bombing is often ineffective during war. "States have extremely high pain thresholds," their economies do not have a breaking point because "they deteriorate incrementally by a process of successive substitution," and, for the people under assault, "heavy bombardment produces apathy, not rebellion" (Pape 1996: 316, 24).

As with strategic bombing, this resilience does not mean that infectious diseases do not threaten national security. But the rate at which HIV/AIDS destabilizes states can be overstated and the mechanisms involved may be more indirect and complicated that originally assumed. On the one hand, complex causal chains provide multiple opportunities for intervention. Fortunately, this means that the political and economic effects of infectious diseases are not deterministic because they vary as a function of other factors, some of which might dampen the impact on stability.

On the other hand, the efficacy of some celebrated interventions is also open to question, since it is wrong to simply assume that providing health care will result in peace and stability. For instance, the World Health Organization promoted the idea of "health as a bridge for peace," at least until initial support from the United Kingdom disappeared (Rushton & McInnes 2006). Illustrated by cease-fires in Afghanistan and elsewhere that were brokered to permit immunization campaigns, this "approach to conflict management" assumes that "the medical community is particularly well placed to forge co-operation between communities in conflict," since health can be a common goal and health care professionals have special skills, stature, education, empathy, and access (Gutlove 1998: 12). These heroic assumptions mirror those found in the literature on science diplomacy, which also argues that scientific and technical exchanges – in medicine, as well as physics and other fields – can build cooperation between countries where trust is otherwise lacking (AAAS 2009; Royal Society 2010).

Unfortunately, like science diplomacy, most literature on "health as a bridge for peace" is dominated by advocacy rather than analysis and so the only empirical evidence is anecdotal. "It is not clear from the literature the conditions under which health interventions can facilitate these types of ceasefires, or whether health co-operation itself was a causal factor in the ceasefire or a symptom of something else." As a result, "it is difficult to find any evidence that credibly portrays health co-operation as the principal driver or initiator of a peace process" (Gordon 2011: 50).

While empirical analysis of healthcare as a causal factor in peacemaking is almost totally lacking, there is slightly more support for the relationship between health and post-conflict peace-building, due in part to the significance of nation-building during and after wars in Iraq and Afghanistan. For example, based on comparative case studies ranging from Afghanistan and Iraq to Germany and Japan, one RAND report argues that "nation-building efforts cannot be successful unless adequate attention is paid to health," since "health can have an important independent impact on nation-building and overall development." Providing health is argued to help win "hearts and minds," but "policymakers often fail to adequately coordinate and plan health reconstruction and to provide sufficient infrastructure and resources" (Jones et al. 2006: xvi, xvii, xxi).

These findings are not above reproach. In particular, the efficacy and appropriateness of health interventions for nation-building and stabilization are often questioned when they involve the military. This is not only because "the evidence of stabilization benefits appears slim," according to Stuart Gordon, but also because of the supposed "potential for the stabilization and counter insurgency agendas to change conventional health priorities through introducing political distortions" (Gordon 2011: 61). While the evidence of stabilization may warrant critique, arguments about political distortions are often predicated on the assumption that healthcare somehow occupies a "politically neutral space" (Kruk et al. 2010: 94). But healthcare is politically contentious even in stable countries like the United States, so to suggest that it – or any other collective, consequential, and expensive endeavor – is apolitical in conflict zones strains belief. For instance, "effort by humanitarian actors to restore health to at least one million Rwandan refugees . . . had the unfortunate effect of helping to restore the capacity of Hutu militias to fight," according to Sara Davies. "Medical assistance may have been delivered with neutral intentions but it had political consequences" (Davies 2010: 94). Tragically, even the Red Cross has been attacked in Afghanistan, Iraq, and Syria, despite its renowned neutrality. To therefore assume that healthcare is apolitical and incapable of producing winners and losers may undermine our ability to better understand the conditions under which health might actually help build peace and stability.

Conclusion

More often than not, the relationships between conflict, instability, and health security are complex. While it is simple – and not surprising – to see that the depravation caused by war is bad for human health (and correspondingly good for infectious disease), depravation and disease interact with the displacement and concentration that also accompany war in complicated ways. This is true for both military personnel and civilian populations. When coupled with limited data, this complexity helps explain why the impact of armed conflict on the spread of infectious disease is still debated to this day.

Even greater debate surrounds the reverse relationship, namely, how health might affect conflict and instability. Concerns about HIV/AIDS typically dominate this debate but, contrary to initial fears, the direct effects of this disease are yet to destroy key political, economic, or military institutions. In part, this is because HIV/AIDS is a long-term disaster rather than an acute emergency. Unlike a lethal influenza pandemic, which might deliver a more abrupt and destabilizing blow, HIV/AIDS is a relatively slow grind and many of its most significant effects are indirect and complicated as a result. In addition, state institutions are more resilient than is often assumed and, because the social effects of infectious diseases are not deterministic, interventions by state and non-state actors can shape important outcomes. Given the complex interplay of actors and factors, it is doubtful that simplistic assumptions about health being apolitical provide plausible predictions for how healthcare might be used to reduce armed conflict or build peace. Therefore, the complexity and significance of all these relationships demand careful consideration.

Note

Special thanks to James Goymour for his research assistance on this chapter.

References

AAAS. (2009) *Science and Diplomacy: A Conceptual Framework.* Online. Available HTTP: <http://www.aaas.org/sites/default/files/scidip_framework_aaas_2009.pdf> (accessed 21 January 2014).

Ba, O., O'Regan, C., Nachega, J., Cooper, C., Anema, A., Rachlis, B. and Mills, E.J. (2008) 'HIV/AIDS in African militaries: an ecological analysis', *Medicine, Conflict and Survival*, 24: 88–100.

Barnett, T. and Dutta, I. (2008) *HIV and State Failure: Is HIV a Security Risk?* ASCI Research Report 7, New York: AIDS, Security, and Conflict Initiative.

Cirillo, V.J. (2008) 'Two faces of death: fatalities from disease and combat in America's principal wars, 1775 to present', *Perspective in Biology and Medicine*, 51: 121–133.

Coupland, R. (2007) 'Security, insecurity and health', *Bulletin of the World Health Organization*, 85: 181–184.

Coupland, R. (2013) 'Security of health care and global health', *New England Journal of Medicine*, 368: 1075–1076.

Davies, S.E. (2010) *Global Politics of Health*, Cambridge: Polity Press.

De Waal, A., Klot, J.F., Mahajan, M., Huber, D., Frerks, G. and M'boup, S. (2009) *HIV/AIDS, Security and Conflict: New Realities, New Responses*, New York: Social Science Research Council.

Diamond, J. (1999) *Guns, Germs, and Steel*, New York: W. W. Norton & Company.

Elbe, S. (2002) 'HIV/AIDS and the changing landscape of war in Africa', *International Security*, 27: 159–177.

Elbe, S. and Ostergard, R.L. (2007) 'HIV/AIDS, the military, and the changing landscape of Africa's security', In R.L. Ostergard (ed.) *HIV/AIDS and the Threat to National Security*, New York: Palgrave Macmillan.

Feldbaum, H., Lee, K. and Patel, P. (2006) 'The national security implications of HIV/AIDS', *PLoS Medicine*, 3. doi:10.1371/journal.pmed.0030171

Frerichs, R.R., Keim, P.S., Barrais, R. and Pairroux, R. (2012) 'Nepalese origin of cholera epidemic in Haiti', *Clinical Microbiology and Infection*, 18: E158–E163.

Garrett, L. (2005) *HIV And National Security: Where Are The Links?* New York: Council on Foreign Relations.

Gayer, M., Legros, D., Formenty, P. and Connolly, M.A. (2007) 'Conflict and emerging infectious diseases', *Emerging Infectious Diseases*, 13: 1625–1631.

Gordon, S. (2011) 'Health, stabilization and securitization: towards understanding the drivers of the military role in health interventions', *Medicine, Conflict and Survival*, 27: 43–66.

Gutlove, P. (1998) 'Health bridges for peace: integrating health care with community reconciliation', *Medicine, Conflict and Survival,* 14: 6–23.

Huang, Y. (2004) 'The SARS epidemic and its aftermath in China: a political perspective', in S. Knobler, A. Mahmoud, S. Lemon, A. Mack, L. Sivitz, K. Oberholtzer (eds.) *Learning from SARS: Preparing for the Next Disease Outbreak*, Washington, DC: National Academies Press.

Iqbal, Z. and Zorn, C. (2010) 'Violent conflict and the spread of HIV/AIDS in Africa', *Journal of Politics*, 72: 149–162.

Jones, S.G., Hilborne, L.H., Anthony, C.R., Davis, L.M., Girosi, F., Benard, C., Swanger, R.M., Garten, A.D. and Lsina, A.T. (2006) *Securing Health: Lessons from Nation-Building Missions*, Santa Monica, CA: RAND Corporation.

Kruk, M.E., Freedman, L.P., Anglin, G.A. and Waldman, R.J. (2010) 'Rebuilding health systems to improve health and promote statebuilding in post-conflict countries: a theoretical framework and research agenda', *Social Science and Medicine*, 70: 89–97.

Lacina, B., Gleditsch, N.P., and Russett, B. (2006) 'The declining risk of death in battle', *International Studies Quarterly*, 50: 673–680.

Levy, B.S. and Sidel, V.W. (1997) 'The impact of military activities on civilian populations', in B.S. Levy, V.W. Sidel (eds.) *War and Public Health*, Oxford: Oxford University Press.

Mackenzie, M. (2012) *Female Soldiers in Sierra Leone: Sex, Security, and Post-Conflict Development*, New York, New York: University Press.

McInnes, C. (2011) 'HIV, AIDS and conflict in Africa: why isn't it (even) worse?' *Review of International Studies*, 37: 485–509.

McInnes, C. and Rushton, S. (2010) 'HIV, AIDS and security: where are we now?' *International Affairs*, 86: 225–245.

Mearsheimer, J.J. (2001) *The Tragedy of Great Power Politics*, New York: W. W. Norton & Company.

Murray, C.J.L., King, G., Lopez, A.D., Tomijima, N. and Krug, E.G. (2002) 'Armed conflict as a public health problem', *British Medical Journal*, 324: 346–349.

Pape, R.A. (1996) *Bombing to Win*, Ithaca: Cornell University Press.

Paris, R. (2001) 'Human security: paradigm shift or hot air?' *International Security*, 26: 87–102.

Price-Smith, A.T. (2009) *Contagion and Chaos: Disease, Ecology, and National Security in the Era of Globalization*, Cambridge, MA: MIT Press.

Reed, H.E. and Keely, C.B. (2001) *Forced Migration & Mortality*, Washington DC: National Academy Press.

Royal Society. (2010) *New Frontiers in Science Diplomacy: Navigating the Changing Balance of Power*, London: The Royal Society, Science Policy Centre.

Rubenstein, L.S. and Bittle, M.D. (2010) 'Responsibility for protection of medical workers and facilities in armed conflict', *Lancet*, 375: 329–340.

Rushton, S. and McInnes, C. (2006) 'The UK, health and peace-building: the mysterious disappearance of health as a bridge for peace', *Medicine, Conflict and Survival*, 22: 94–109.

Singh, A.E. and Romanowski, B. (1999) 'Syphilis: review with emphasis on clinical, epidemiologic, and some biologic features', *Clinical Microbiology Reviews*, 12: 187–209.

Smallman-Raynor, M.R. and Cliff, A.D. (1991) 'Civil war and the spread of AIDS in Central Africa', *Epidemiology and Infection*, 107: 69–80.

Smallman-Raynor, M.R. and Cliff, A.D. (2004) *War Epidemics: An Historical Geography of Infectious Diseases in Military Conflict and Civil Strife, 1850–2000*, Oxford: Oxford University Press.

Spiegel, P.B. (2004) 'HIV/AIDS among conflict-affected and displaced populations: dispelling myths and taking action', *Disasters*, 28: 322–339.

Spiegel, P.B., Bennedsen, A.R., Claass, J., Bruns, L., Patterson, N., Yiweza, D. and Schilperoord, M. (2007) 'Prevalence of HIV infection in conflict-affected and displaced people in seven sub-Saharan African countries: a systematic review', *Lancet*, 369: 2187–2195.

Toole, M.J. and Waldman, R.J. (1997) 'The public health aspects of complex emergencies and refugee situations', *Annual Review of Public Health*, 18: 283–312.

UN Security Council. (2000, July 17) *Resolution 1308 (2000)*. Online. Available HTTP: <http://daccess-dds-ny.un.org/doc/UNDOC/GEN/N00/536/02/PDF/N0053602.pdf?OpenElement> (accessed 14 May 2014).

UNAIDS. (1998) *AIDS and the Military*, Geneva: UNAIDS. Online. Available HTTP: <http://data.unaids.org/Publications/IRC-pub05/militarypv_en.pdf> (accessed 21 January 2014).

UNDP. (1994) *Human Development Report 1994: New Dimensions of Human Security*, New York: Oxford University Press. Online. Available HTTP: <http://hdr.undp.org/en/reports/global/hdr1994/chapters/> (accessed 21 January 2014).

Walt, S.M. (1991) 'The renaissance of security studies', *International Studies Quarterly*, 35: 211–239.

Watson, J.T., Gayer, M. and Connolly, M.A. (2007) 'Epidemics after natural disasters', *Emerging Infectious Diseases*, 13: 1–5.

Whiteside, A., de Waal, A. and Gebre-Tensae, T. (2006) 'AIDS, security, and the military in Africa: a sober appraisal', *African Affairs*, 105: 201–218.

WHO. (1978) *Declaration of Alma-Ata*. Online. Available HTTP: <http://www.who.int/publications/almaata_declaration_en.pdf> (accessed 21 January 2014).

Youde, J. (2007) 'HIV/AIDS and democratic legitimacy and stability in Africa', in R.L. Ostergard (ed.) *HIV/AIDS, the Military, and the Changing Landscape of Africa's Security*, New York: Palgrave Macmillan.

13
HEALTH SECURITY AND ENVIRONMENTAL CHANGE

Robert L. Ostergard Jr. & Derek Kauneckis

The implications of climate change for human health security are wide-ranging and profound. Because climate plays a central aspect in so many of the ecological systems on which human systems rely – from hydrological systems that provide the quantity and quality of water we have come to expect, to stable spatial distributions of species and their associated pathogens, and even the predictability of the timing and severity of extreme weather events – changes to the climate cycle will impact a broad range of human activities and have associated health impacts. However, determining the influence of a changing climate challenges both our understanding of health security risks as well as the complex interactions between climatic, natural, and human systems. As an emerging area of research focused on potential future conditions it is a literature filled with debate and contestation. This chapter reviews the current state of research on climate change impacts to human health security. Health security in this chapter has two interpretations, which are common themes in the discussion of health security. First is the notion of "health security" that refers to securing health itself. The second are the notions of "health and security" that refers to the contributions of health to global security (Aldis 2008). We address both concepts in this chapter. The chapter begins with an overview of climate science, moves on to examine research on the influence of climate change on a variety of aspects of health security, and concludes with a discussion of climate change policy and human health.

The climate change picture: perceptions and complexities

On November 6, 1965, President Lyndon Johnson accepted a report from the President's Science Advisory Committee on Pollution, of Air, Soil, and Waters. The committee had set off alarms with regard to what would later be known as climate change. In its report, the committee highlighted what we now understand as one of the base problems associated with climate change: "Carbon dioxide is being added to the earth's atmosphere by the burning of coal, oil, and natural gas at the rate of 6 billion tons a year. By the year 2000 there will be about 25 percent more carbon dioxide in our atmosphere than at present. Exhausts and other releases from automobiles contribute a major share to the generation of smog" (Johnson 1965). In accepting the committee's report, Johnson pointed to the one factor that would set off a public controversy that now extends into its fifth decade:

> Pollution now is one of the most pervasive problems of our society. With our numbers increasing, and with our increasing urbanization and industrialization, the flow of pollutants to our air, soil, and waters is increasing. This increase is so rapid that our present efforts in managing pollution are barely enough to stay even, surely not enough to make the improvements that are needed.
>
> (Johnson 1965)

Millions of dollars and years of research since have given us a clearer picture of the problem, though research has not clarified the precise impact of climate change to human and ecological systems. While the current discourse may still question the problem of climate change as a human induced (anthropogenic) process, the scientific community has generally accepted the basic principle that the recent warming trend is mostly due to anthropogenic forcing of the atmosphere by human activity and greenhouse gas emissions (Oreskes 2004).

What is climate change?

In understanding what climate change is, it is just as important to understand what climate change is not. Climate change does not refer to weather, though day-to-day weather is a component of climate change as an indicator of the phenomena rather than as *the* phenomena itself. Weather is the short termed fluctuations of climate that we see on a day-to-day basis. But this has problems as it implies that climate, over a long period, is a constant when scientists understand climate as constantly changing. Hence, any reference to climate change generally has to have not just a geographical reference attached to it, but also an historical time period.

As such, we can think of climate as the *average* weather over a long period of time in a particular region or zone (Reiter 2001: 141). As the Intergovernmental Panel on Climate Change noted, climate change is characterized by "significant variations that persist for an extended period, typically decades or longer. It includes shifts in the frequency and magnitude of sporadic weather events as well as the slow continuous rise in global mean surface temperature" (Watson et al. 2003: 43). Historically, weather has been the indicator of what people perceive as the immediate conditions that affect them. This perception becomes an important matter because one of the factors that contributes to debate around climate change is our inability to detect and identify definitively climate change. We see weather every day and tend to place emphasis on weather as it affects our immediate condition. To put it more directly, no human ever lives long enough to perceive climate change in a meaningful way. We can understand this better if we look at what scientists studying the phenomena examine in time frames for climate change. For instance, while climate scientists have documented a significant rise in global temperatures since the beginning of the Industrial Revolution, it is likely that the current levels of carbon dioxide gases (CO_2, a major greenhouse gas that helps to retain heat inside the atmosphere) have not existed at least for the past 400,000 years and most likely for the past 20 million years (Houghton et al. 2001: 7; Petit et al. 1999).

Scientists also have attached a host of indicators to climate change. These indicators fall into three basic categories: atmospheric concentration indicators (such as concentrations of carbon dioxide (CO_2), nitrous oxide (N_2O), ozone (O_3), and hydrofluorocarbons); weather indicators (such as global mean surface temperatures, heat indexes, frost days, drought, and precipitation); and biological and physical indicators (such as measures of sea levels, ice covers, glaciers, permafrost, plant and animal ranges, and coral reef bleaching) (Watson et al. 2003: 45–46). These indicators are just a sample of those that scientists use to paint a collective picture of climate change. In this sense, climate change is really a syndrome that displays a pattern of symptoms characterizing the climate change condition.

Beyond the problem of the imperceptible changes over time, climate change has proven to be one of the most complex problems that humans have confronted in terms of how climate change works and the eventual impact of climate change on natural and human systems. Such complexities mean that natural, social and behavioral scientists engaged in this research will *never* be able to account for every detail of these changes and will often find contradictory evidence across disciplinary boundaries and regions of the world. These natural problems of a long-term evolving agenda that moves slowly towards scientific consensus mean that policymakers and the public writ large will be more prone to debate the problem than to act towards policies to mitigate it (Moser 2010). Hence, a key factor in understanding climate change is realizing that its complexity as a natural, social, and behavioral phenomenon entails research that comes in smaller, isolated pieces that contribute to a larger image of the problem collectively. Taken alone, research on any particular aspect of climate change may have isolated meaning or implications, leading to limited understandings within a particular area.

Seeing the direct impact of climate change on natural and social systems is exceedingly difficult as most studies rely on indirect causality that attempts to link any impact or outcome back to climate change. Consequently, synthesizing the importance and meaning of the research has been daunting and even subject to ridicule. For instance, when animal science researchers linked agriculture-related methane emissions (cow flatulence) to increased atmospheric methane levels (Houghton et al. 2001: 44; Johnson & Johnson 1995; Kurihara et al. 1999), instead of placing the findings into the larger issue of developmental problems and agricultural systems, policy makers and even the public at large either ridiculed the findings, used it as an opportunity to cast doubt on the larger phenomena of climate change or raised fears of perceived government overreach (Corley 2009; O'Brien 2009). Media reporting on the issue couched the problem in the context of a humorous story rather than within the broader implications of the story. The complex nature of climate change means that linking climate change to health security is a difficult task that involves a corpus of literature that crosses disciplines and methodologies and provides, at best, a mixed picture on how climate change will affect the health security of large populations.

Climate change and the health security nexus

The difficulty in establishing the causal links between climate change and health security is that there are few, if any, direct causal links between them. Climate change operates *through* environmental conditions that can then lead to changes in processes that have an impact on health security. Moreover, as climatologists point out, climate change is a natural process and an evolving condition. Making progress towards policies to mitigate the impact of climate change and its impact on health security can be difficult if the natural processes of climate change cannot be separated from the anthropogenic causes of climate change. As Figure 13.1 shows, atmospheric conditions that induce macro level climate change affects localized environmental factors. This relationship highlights the specific regional and time periods that are associated with the differential impacts that climate change can have. The regional and localized impacts of climate change can be delimited into three categories that affect health security: 1) shifting patterns in bio organism behavior and patterns; 2) changing agricultural growth and food supply patterns; and 3) altered patterns of social interactions. Each of these dynamic relationships has differential impacts on local conditions that can affect health security.

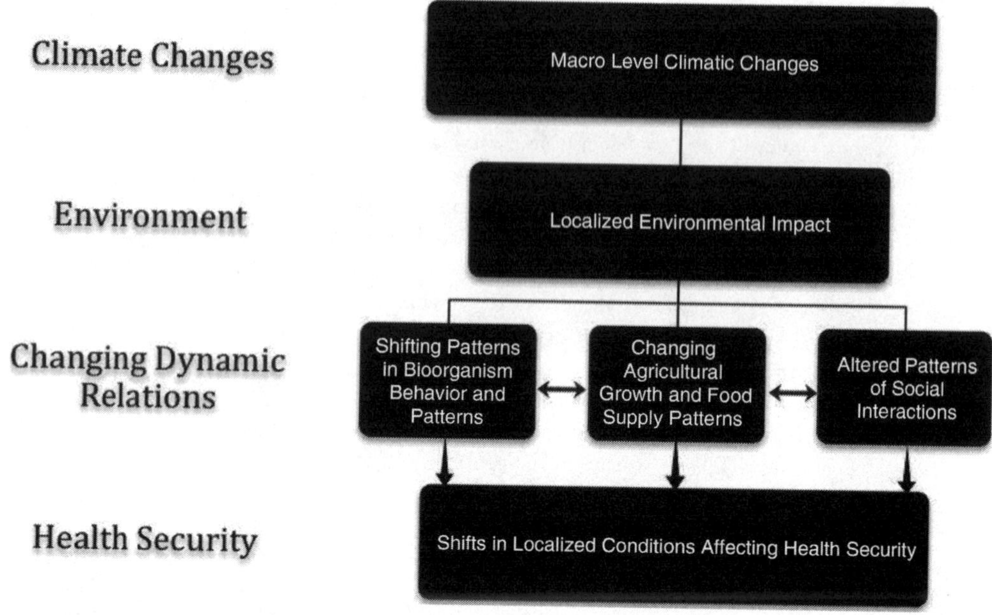

Figure 13.1 The Indirect Effect of Climate Change on Health Security

Behavior and patterns of bioorganisms

The difficulty in establishing the link between climate change and the patterns of bioorganisms, particularly those related to viruses and diseases that affect human health and security, is in the ecological complexity that affects the survival of specific bioorganisms. This complexity makes causality difficult to establish between the larger macro phenomena of climate change and the more localized problem of conditions that affect bioorganisms. Ecological complexity makes it difficult to rule out alternative explanations for any pattern changes. This problem is crucial because policy solutions may not be sufficient if they are unidimensional approaches that address only factors contributing to climate changes (treating the symptoms as opposed to the cause of the syndrome). As such, Kovats et al. (2001) have suggested three requirements before accepting causal linkages between climate change and shifting patterns of disease or processes that affect disease prevalence:

1 Basic evidence of biological sensitivity to climate – this is usually met through strong evidence that emerges from laboratory or field work.
2 Meteorological evidence of climate change – significant geographical variation exists in pattern changes of climate change, making data from a single site or over a short period a reason for caution.
3 Evidence of entomological and/or epidemiological change associated with climate change – changes in vectors and diseases observed in association with changing meteorological conditions must be couched within standardized monitoring practices of disease patterns. The degree of change attributed to climate change should be consistent with the known climate sensitivity of the vector.

Given these conditions, the link between climate change and changing patterns of disease is tentative, though better analysis, instruments and modeling are making the connections clearer.

For our purposes it makes sense to review the relationship between climate change and bioorganisms that affect human health through diseases and vectors that transmit those diseases.

Vector-borne diseases have been shown to be sensitive to changes in humidity, temperatures, and precipitation (Kiska 2000). What may be thought of as short-term weather conditions can have an influence over vectors' survival and reproduction rates, intensity and behavioral patterns (such as biting or feeding rates), and rates of growth and development (Semenza & Menne 2009: 366). While these principles are understood, it is also the case that a host of other conditions, such as habitat destruction, land use patterns, pesticides, population movements, and drug and pesticide resistance, amongst other factors, can affect vector and pathogen patterns (Gage et al. 2008; Lafferty 2009; Semenza & Menne 2009).

Research on how climate change affects vectors and their pathogens has focused on a number of specific pathogens, though this list is not exhaustive. These pathogens include:

- Mosquito vectors: malaria, dengue fever, yellow fever, Chikungunya fever, West Nile virus, Rift Valley Fever, and Ross River Virus;
- Tick vectors: tick borne encephalitis, lyme borreliosis, tularemia, human granulocytic anaplasmosis, human monocytic ehrlichiosis, and plague (Gage et al. 2008: 437).

Because of its endemic nature in many developing countries and mosquitos' high sensitivity to temperature change, researchers and policy makers have given significant attention to how climate change may affect malaria (see also Knowlton, chapter 14 in this volume).

About 3,500 species of mosquitos are found throughout the world with most native to tropical and subtropical regions (Reiter 2001). Malaria is caused by one of four parasites transmitted by the female of about 60 species of anopheles mosquitos (Reiter 2001; Semenza & Menne 2009). Females feed on blood to obtain protein needed for feeding eggs. Salivary excretions help the feeding process but also provide a means by which to transmit viruses, protozoa, and nematode worms (Reiter 2001). Malarial transmission occurs during this feeding stage of reproduction.

Recent research has focused on the potential for climate change to spread malaria to areas where it was previously rare or unknown. However, the historical record of malaria shows the difficulty in linking its spread to climate change solely. Malaria was common in ancient Greece and imperial Rome, with a wealth of authors making reference to fever areas and attributing the disease to animals too small to be seen (Lafferty 2009; Reiter 2001). The Dark Ages saw malaria strike the invading Visigoths, Vandals, Ostrogoths, and other barbarian armies. The medieval warm period and the great economic growth that accompanied it also saw periods of malarial outbreak. Despite a severe cooling trend in the 15th century, malaria persisted. The Little Ice Age that ensued over the next 200 years still saw persistent malarial infection. Beyond the Little Ice Age, temperatures generally returned to pre-16th century levels normal in Europe. During the 18th and 19th centuries, malaria was still common, but its geographic limits were becoming known. In Britain, malaria moved as far north as Inverness (Scotland) and it was endemic in Denmark, coastal areas of Norway, southern Sweden, and Finland. In Russia, it was common through the Baltic areas and along the same latitudinal lines through Siberia (Reiter 2001). During the second half of the 19th century as industrialization and economic development began to occur in many areas, malaria began to decline. After the 1880s, cases of malaria became rare in England and Germany with similar experiences occurring across a number of European countries (Reiter 2001). By 1975, malaria had been eradicated from Europe.

What this long history indicates is that there are two instructive factors about malaria and climate change. Long-term climate and short-term weather patterns can affect malarial transmission (Gage et al. 2008; Lafferty 2009). Researchers have highlighted this relationship particularly in cases of highland malaria, which has experienced increases in regional occurrences since the 1980s (Kovats et al. 2001; Reiter 2001). Because of this trend, speculation on the role that climate change may be playing in the malarial outbreaks has grown. Given the altitudinal range in which highland malaria thrives and because temperatures negatively correlate with altitude, this would appear to be a natural laboratory for examining the linkages amongst vectors, vector transmission and climate change. However, as Kovats et al. (2001) argue, there are complicating issues that again compromise the ability to link climate change to health security. Seasonal and annual fluctuations in temperatures and precipitation contribute to malaria patterns, with precipitation being an important constraint on malarial transmission in highland areas (Kovats et al. 2001). The dominant factor for malarial transmission is the presence of a breeding ground for mosquitos. So even if temperatures are increasing, the lack of precipitation and particularly bodies of water where mosquitos breed means that there may be limitations of using climate change as an explanatory factor in malarial transmission in highland areas. The relationship between altitude and temperature is affected by other conditions such as latitude and continentality, which exemplifies the degree to which climate in a region reflects interior areas of a large land mass (Kovats et al. 2001: 1064). The correlation between altitude and rainfall is significant but it is highly variable and weak. Moreover, understanding what is the historical "norm" or establishing a baseline for malarial transmission to start from has been subject to expert opinion and systematic survey bias (Kovats et al. 2001: 1065). Finally, it is also the case that vectors do not neatly conform to simple cutoff markers attitudinally and that subtle seasonal and annual variations make malaria patterns difficult to shift. Thus while anecdotal evidence shows that climate change affects vectors and pathogens, as the historical case of malaria demonstrates, the linkages are a complex interaction that involves endogenous social and natural factors as well.

Changing agricultural growth and food supply patterns

While infectious disease transmission has been a central concern in the climate change and health security discussions, a secondary condition that could have an impact on health security is climate change's impact on agricultural production and food supplies or food security. However, again, the connections amongst all these processes are difficult to predict and evidence may be more localized.

Research on the links between climate change and food security has been lacking. Some studies have assessed the impact of climate change as increasing the number of undernourished people by 5%–26% (Schmidhuber & Tubiello 2007: 19705). However, many studies predicate these numbers within the context of existing and future economic development, which may decrease undernourishment over the long term. As such, these studies may in fact underestimate the number of undernourished people in some cases, and in other cases overestimate the numbers as the numbers are based upon an assumed economic performance. Researchers contend that the impact of climate change on food safety and security can be direct by affecting conditions that promote crop failure and indirect where food security can affect the conditions that promote infectious diseases that cause or extend hunger, which can further lead to other infectious diseases (Schmidhuber & Tubiello 2007). Crops, in this sense, can also include global fish production. Moreover, climate change, by affecting supplies of food, could further threaten food security through rising food prices (Schmidhuber & Tubiello 2007: 19705).

The notion of food security has specific connotations. The Food and Agriculture Organization (FAO) defines food security as "a situation that exists when all people, at all times, have physical, social and economic access to sufficient, safe and nutritious food that meets their dietary needs and food preferences for an active and healthy lifestyle" (Schmidhuber & Tubiello 2007: 19708). According to Schmidhuber and Tubiello, the definition comprises four dimensions:

(a) availability – how available food is, which is affected by agricultural and climatic conditions and socio-economic conditions and cultural factors that affect farming practices;
(b) stability – refers to people who are susceptible to losing access to food through a lack of resources from income issues that hinder acquisition of food or a consistent and adequate supply of food;
(c) access – entails having appropriate entitlements to acquire appropriate food. Entitlements in this sense refers to commodities in that a person can command through social, political, legal and economic arrangements of individuals' communities. This factor is a critical point for capability theorists in economic development, who focus on entitlements and needs that affect a person's capacities through formal and informal institutional arrangements (Sen 2001); and
(d) utilization – includes food safety and nutrition that affects health security through the inclusion of sanitation issues.

These dimensions of food security demonstrate the complex relationship that food security has with climate change. Most importantly, as Brown and Funk point out, food insecurity is just a byproduct of climatic factors, but is strongly affected by prevailing economic, agricultural, and political policies (Brown & Funk 2008).[1]

Conventional wisdom amongst policy makers and activists is that climate change could lead to increases in crop failure at a time when the earth's population is set to exceed 11 billion people this century. Such concerns are real but may be empirically inconsistent across crops and regions, as it is unlikely that all crops and regions would be affected equally by climate change. Brown and Funk contend that rising temperatures and declining precipitation will likely reduce primary crop yields over the next two decades. Others concur with this assessment, but assert that the impact on food production will likely be small (Tubiello et al. 2007: 19689).

Agricultural research seems to have pinpointed a dual impact of climate change on crops. The gradual change in temperatures and precipitation levels could lead to increased crop yields in some areas. In temperate latitudes, higher temperatures may generally benefit agriculture, but arid and semiarid regions may see localized conditions worsen, which would include detrimental impacts to livestock (Schmidhuber & Tubiello 2007). Adding to this mixture is the overlying impact that greenhouse gasses have on crop yields. As Coakley et al. find, researchers reviewing hundreds of CO_2 enrichment studies have reported a consensus that an increase in atmospheric CO_2 will most likely have "growth-enhancing effects" (Coakley et al. 1999). Additional research suggests that the CO_2 effect may be contingent upon latitude (Coakley et al. 1999: 402).

While research suggests a mixed, and in some cases, positive impact, on crop yields, these findings must also be placed in the context of the other impact of rising temperatures, fluctuating precipitation, and rising CO_2 levels – namely the likely increase in crop destroying insects, plant pathogens, and weeds that compete for water, light, soil, nutrients, and land space. Weeds can also harbor crop diseases and destructive insects.

Plant pathogens may experience the same type of fluctuations that vector borne diseases in humans may experience. Coakley et al. report while studies generally are limited to fungal diseases, under rising CO_2 conditions, fungal infections in plants were initially delayed and more difficult to establish; however, once established, fungal colonies grew much faster under increased CO_2 conditions (Coakley et al. 1999: 405). Research in general on plant pathogens is severely lacking, so the applicability of such findings must be explained across a spectrum of plants and pathogens. Moreover, changing temperatures may activate dormant pathogens that crops and plants harbor, leading to diseases in warmer climates. Despite these suggested findings, drawing definitive causal links has been difficult because of the complex factors and, in the case of the impact on plant pathogens, the lack of research (Coakley et al. 1999; Luck et al. 2011) makes drawing any generalizable conclusions about how crops will fare under climate change difficult to assess.

The impact of climate change on food security also extends to aquaculture and global fish production. With captured production of fish and other ocean fare declining since 1989, aquaculture has become an important outlet in fish supplies and communities that rely on those supplies for their own food security. According to Brander, climate change will have direct and indirect effects on the commercialization of fish stocks (Brander 2007). Increasing temperatures already are producing shifts in fish migration and locations. Where some fish stocks may migrate and increase, other areas may experience local species extinctions (Brander 2007: 19710). The migration may see fish leave but allow other species to move into an area possibly as a competitor species. Climate change's impact in this regard has already been felt with areas experiencing species mortalities (Brander 2007: 19710). Coral destruction through bleaching may further reduce species variety and contribute to reduced fishing capacities locally (Brander 2007: 19711). Inland fish production is also threatened with the potential disappearance of lakes and rivers (Lake Chad's demise being one of the most dramatic examples of this).

The impact of climate change on food security is again a puzzle that has a mixed set of propositions in the relationship. Research shows that some areas may benefit from climate change's impact on agriculture, while other areas will suffer greater food insecurity. In areas where food security becomes unstable, disease-related malnutrition may increase. Such effects might include impaired physical growth, increased respiratory infections, malabsorption, and impaired organ and immune functions, making people more susceptible to other diseases.

Altered patterns of social interactions

As a result of the potential impact on short-term weather conditions, the long-term ecological conditions and the concurrent impacts on pathogens, vectors, and food security, researchers have postulated that climate change may have implications for social interactions, broadly construed to include both states and their populations. The implication for the changes to social interaction patterns is that health security may be affected as well, particularly through the other two avenues of bioorganisms and food security, though other effects may materialize outside these avenues.

While social scientists have long debated the role of the state in the global political system, it remains a central element of the system, strongly tied to the populations over which they govern. Historically as states expanded in power and wealth, the global system, through complex political, economic and social interactions amongst states, also began to divide on those lines of power and wealth. Today, the global system has two key features that will produce differential impacts on states within the climate change debate. The first is the long-standing principle of sovereignty and the second is the global inequality that has emerged within the system over its long history.

State sovereignty is a central component to issues of security for states, with states focused on protecting or compensating for weaknesses that make them vulnerable or heighten their perceptions of threats to their sovereignty and security. Climate change presents unique problems for the state as issues related to the climate change can transcend state borders. Even those issues that do not transcend borders may still be problematic as states may be reluctant to deal with the problem or to cooperate with other states. Moreover, the geography of climate change and the associated costs of its large-scale impacts mean that climate change will be a differential problem for the global state system. Climate change for most developed, wealthy states may be a matter of adaptation; for poorer, developing states particularly in the south and in low-lying coastal areas, there are few feasible adaptation options with many considered highly vulnerable to moderate temperature increase scenarios. These states also possess the most vulnerable populations and low state capacity and already confront significant challenges to human security.

As Buzan (1983: 132) has pointed out, climate change has the potential to change the very geography of human habitation, leading to fundamental changes in the social and political interactions within the global system. As early as 1971, after the release of President Johnson's Science Advisory Committee report, Falk recognized the problem of climate change through what he termed "the first law of ecological politics"; specifically, "there exists an inverse relationship between the interval of time available for adaptive change and the likelihood and intensity of violent conflict, trauma and coercion accompanying the process of adaptation" (Falk 1972: 353 in Barnett 2003: 3). Falk's proposition focuses on two issues: the rapidity of change and reaction time to that change and the probability of social interaction becoming more intense and violent. In this vein, researchers have focused on two areas of social interaction that may evolve from climate change with direct implications for health security – violent conflict and mass migration.

Researchers focusing on climate change's impact on violent conflict draw upon issues of state survival that are linked to growing resource scarcity and competition to sustain population livelihoods (Salehyan 2008: 316). Through changes in desertification, sea levels, spreading disease vectors, and natural disasters, resources will become scarcer putting states into direct competition with each other. Moreover, disruptions to economic systems and patterns of sustainability will lead to mass migration out of areas, subsequently placing people in greater violent competition for scarcer resources (Salehyan 2008: 315). The implications of such connections are significant with some even attributing genocides (i.e., Rwanda and Darfur) to ecological changes and ecologically induced migrations. The connections to health security follow the long line of research that links conflict and migration to increased violent deaths, potential for disease outbreaks (particularly in refugee camps), conflict induced food scarcity, and sanitation issues (Barnett 2003; Brown & Funk 2008; Cresswell et al. 2009; Epstein 2005; Gleditsch 1998, 2010; Jones et al. 2008; Patz et al. 2005; Salehyan 2008; Schmidhuber & Tubiello 2007).

The general problem in this body of literature is the same problem confronting our understanding of climate change and its relationship to bioorganisms and food security – causality and differentiated impacts. The research into climate change and violent conflict has little empirical support overall (Barnett 2003; Gleditsch 1998), which may also be linked to the general problem of international relations research into violent conflict that has not generally pinpointed a coherent explanation of the origins of conflict and war by itself (Barnett 2003: 5). Thus claims linking violent conflict to climate change and ultimately to health security are, at best, weak and more often speculative as the issue of causality has not been dealt with sufficiently on an empirical or theoretical level.

The same problem of causality shadows the link between climate change and mass migration. Migration tends to be mostly intrastate and not interstate. In cases of reported environmentally induced migration, often times other factors contributed to the ensuing violence (Barnett 2003). Reuveny (2007) shows this multiple factor issue in research on migration and violent conflict. In examining 38 cases of climate-induced migrations, 19 of the 38 had no significant violence attached to them. Of the 19 that did not have a violent component, eight involved intrastate (civil) wars, three involved interstate conflicts, and eight involved intercommunal conflicts (Reuveny 2007: 662). At best, it would appear that environmental degradation linked to climate change does not always lead to conflict. When it does, it is usually a stressor factor that adds to preexisting conditions that may make violent conflict more likely and more intense (Reuveny 2007: 668).

Conclusion

Climate change policy has generally focused on two fundamental categories of activities: mitigation and adaptation. Mitigation activities are those directed at reducing the level of greenhouse gases in the atmosphere, whereas adaptation policies focus on how to respond to changing conditions and maintain the various ecological and human systems expected to be impacted by climate change (Schneider et al. 2009). The impacts of climate change on health security are most closely associated with adaptation policy and will involve managing existing health security risks that may be compounded by climate change as well as new health risks that may emerge. Existing health security risks, such as malnutrition or limited access to health care, will likely increase with extreme weather events such as drought, floods, and heat waves. New health risks may include increased exposure to new zoonotic diseases as habitats and species adjust to new climate conditions and as the range of existing disease vectors increases (Patz et al. 2005). While the complexity of interactions across climatic, natural, and social systems make it difficult to anticipate the potential increased health risks, most of the sources of these new risks are already managed within current health policies. The challenge is likely to be greatest in those regions where even well-understood health risks go unmanaged.

The health security impact of climate change will be determined not by the natural systems that generate exposure to risk, but rather by the ability of social and political systems to respond rapidly enough to minimize current climate related health impacts as well as react to new risks. While significant work has been done examining the social vulnerability of populations to climate changes (see Brooks et al. 2005), perhaps a better conceptualization of the problem is to examine the vulnerability of the various political and policy systems to be able to respond adequately. Such an approach would reemphasize some of what has been written in the vulnerability literature already, such as poverty as a key limitation of an individual's ability to cope with health threats and the pivotal role of poor governance in not reducing risk at the national and regional levels (Mearns & Norton 2010). However it would also highlight aspects of health security and climate that are often overlooked. The emphasis on the level of economic development at a national level as a rough proxy measure for capacity to deal with climate change impacts often glosses over policy subsystems even in wealthy nations that may be too inflexible to respond to new risk or ineffectual when they do respond. The response by the national government to Hurricane Katrina in the United States remains a lingering reminder that the potential capacity to respond does not equal the effectiveness of the response (Brodie et al. 2006). Likewise, the large number of deaths associated with the 2003 heat wave in France was due not to the event itself, but due to a large number of medical staff being on vacations during the period and inadequate monitoring of high-risk populations (Vandentorren et al. 2006). Health care access by low-income populations may be a more significant driver of the level of risk than climate induced changes to the environment.

A focus on the social systems that produce risk-reducing strategies and improve the resilience of local communities and regions will also likely help illuminate the factors in many low capacity states that can help minimize the impacts of climate change on health security. Local social capital and the ability to pool resources when needed offer existing social structures on which to build improved local capacity to adapt to new climate conditions or respond to extreme weather events (Adger 2003). Since there are few altogether new health security risks that climate change poses, effective policy responses will entail better diffusion of existing practices that have worked and adapting lessons from elsewhere to a local context, rather than a need for radically new approaches. The policy tools to deal with most of the climate-induced health security threats already exist; however, they will require faster deployment to new areas and ideally better peer-to-peer communications among the communities most affected. This does assume mitigation policy that begins to produce a reduction of greenhouse gas emission and that the worst-case scenarios of climate change do not come into effect. There are limits to the speed at which any system can adapt and the worse climate scenarios would exceed the capacity of most local, community, and national policy systems.

Note

1 This point is made most strongly by Sen. As he notes, in the worst instances of food insecurity, famines, no historical example of famine has ever occurred in a stable democracy. Famines have been prevalent in dictatorships and politically unstable countries where food has been used as a weapon against political enemies (Sen 2001). Marcus highlights this problem further by examining what he refers to as faminogenocides in the context of Russia, Ethiopia, and North Korea (Marcus 2003).

References

Adger, W.N. (2003) 'Social capital, collective action, and adaptation to climate change', *Economic Geography*, 79: 387–404.

Aldis, W. (2008) 'Health security as a public health concept: a critical analysis', *Health Policy and Planning*, 23: 69–378.

Barnett, J. (2003) 'Security and climate change', *Global Environmental Change*, 13: 7–17.

Brander, K.M. (2007) 'Global fish production and climate change', *Proceedings of the National Academy of Sciences*, 104: 19709–19714.

Brodie, M., Weltzien, E., Altman, D., Blendon, R.J. and Benson, J.M. (2006) 'Experiences of Hurricane Katrina evacuees in Houston shelters: implications for future planning', *American Journal of Public Health*, 96: 1402–1408.

Brooks, N., Neil Adger, W. and Mick Kelly, P. (2005) 'The determinants of vulnerability and adaptive capacity at the national level and the implications for adaptation', *Global Environmental Change*, 15: 151–163.

Brown, M.E. and Funk, C.C. (2008) 'Food security under climate change'. Online. Available HTTP: <http://digitalcommons.unl.edu/nasapub/131/> (accessed 26 May 2013).

Buzan, B. (1983) *People, States, and Fear: The National Security Problem in International Relations*, Brighton: Wheatsheaf Books.

Coakley, S.M., Scherm, H. and Chakraborty, S. (1999) 'Climate change and plant disease management', *Annual Review of Phytopathology*, 37: 399–426.

Corley, M. (2009) 'Boehner: it's "almost comical" to say carbon dioxide and climate change are dangerous since cows fart a lot,' *ThinkProgress,* 20 April. Online. Available HTTP: <http://thinkprogress.org/politics/2009/04/20/37669/boehner-carbon-cow-fart/?mobile=nc> (accessed 16 June 2013).

Cresswell, W., Clark, J.A. and Macleod, R. (2009) 'How climate change might influence the starvation–predation risk trade-off response,' *Proceedings of the Royal Society B: Biological Sciences*, 276: 3553–3560.

Epstein, P.R. (2005) 'Climate change and human health', *New England Journal of Medicine*, 353: 1433–1436.

Falk, R.A. (1972) *This Endangered Planet: Prospects and Proposals for Human Survival*, New York: Vintage Books.

Gage, K.L., Burkot, T.R., Eisen, R.J. and Hayes, E.B. (2008) 'Climate and vectorborne diseases', *American Journal of Preventive Medicine*, 35: 436–450.

Gleditsch, N.P. (1998) 'Armed conflict and the environment: a critique of the literature', *Journal of Peace Research*, 35: 381–400.

Gleditsch, N.P. (2010) 'Climate change and conflict', lecture at the University of Greifswald, 12 July. Online. Available HTTP: <http://www.phil.uni-greifswald.de/fileadmin/mediapool/histin/Neuzeit/Gleditsch_Climate_Change_Security.pdf> (accessed 17 June 2013).

Houghton, J.T., Ding, Y., Griggs, D.J., Noguer, M., van der Linden, P.J., Dai, X., Maskell, K. and Johnson, C.A. (2001) *Climate Change 2001: The Scientific Basis*, Cambridge: Cambridge University Press. Online. Available HTTP: <http://www.acrim.com/%5C/Reference%20Files/CLIMATECHANGE%202001%20-%20The%20Scientific%20Basis.pdf> (accessed 16 June 2013).

Johnson, K.A. and Johnson, D.E. (1995) 'Methane emissions from cattle', *Journal of Animal Science*, 73: 2483–2492.

Johnson, L. (1965) 'Lyndon B. Johnson: Statement by the President in Response to Science Advisory Committee Report on Pollution of Air, Soil, and Waters', November 6. *The American Presidency Project*. Online. Available HTTP: <http://www.presidency.ucsb.edu/ws/?pid=27355> (accessed 16 June 2013).

Jones, K.E., Patel, N.G., Levy, M.A., Storeygard, A., Balk, D., Gittleman, J.L. and Daszak, P. (2008) 'Global trends in emerging infectious diseases', *Nature*, 451: 990–993.

Kiska, D.L. (2000) 'Global climate change: an infectious disease perspective', *Clinical Microbiology Newsletter*, 22: 81–86.

Kovats, R.S., Campbell-Lendrum, D.H., McMichel, A.J., Woodward, A. and Cox, J.S.H. (2001) 'Early effects of climate change: do they include changes in vector-borne disease?', *Philosophical Transactions of the Royal Society of London. Series B: Biological Sciences*, 356: 1057–1068.

Kurihara, M., Magner, T., Hunter, R.A. and McCrabb, G.J. (1999) 'Methane production and energy partition of cattle in the tropics', *British Journal of Nutrition*, 81: 227–234.

Lafferty, K.D. (2009) 'The ecology of climate change and infectious diseases', *Ecology*, 90: 888–900.

Luck, J., Spackman, M., Freeman, A., Griffiths, W., Finlay, K. and Chakraborty, S. (2011) 'Climate change and diseases of food crops', *Plant Pathology*, 60: 113–121.

Marcus, D. (2003) 'Famine crimes in international law', *American Journal of International Law*, 97: 245–281.

Mearns, R. and Norton, A. (2010) *Social Dimensions of Climate Change: Equity and Vulnerability in a Warming World*, Washington: World Bank. Online. Available HTTP: <https://openknowledge.worldbank.org/bitstream/handle/10986/2689/520970PUB0EPI11C010disclosed0Dec091.pdf?sequence=1> (accessed 16 September 2013).

Moser, S.C. (2010) 'Communicating climate change: history, challenges, process and future directions', *Wiley Interdisciplinary Reviews: Climate Change*, 1: 31–53.

O'Brien, M. (2009) 'GOP congressman warns against "cow fart tax"', *The Hill*, June 9. Online. Available HTTP: <http://thehill.com/blogs/blog-briefing-room/news/lawmaker-news/34900-gop-congressman-warns-against-cow-fart-tax> (accessed 1 June 2013).

Oreskes, N. (2004) 'The scientific consensus on climate change', *Science*, 306: 1686.

Patz, J.A., Campbell-Lendrum, D., Holloway, T. and Foley, J.A. (2005) 'Impact of regional climate change on human health', *Nature*, 438: 310–317.

Petit, J.R., Jouzel, J., Raynaud, D., Barkov, N.I., Barnola, J-M., Basile, I., Bender, M., Chappellaz, J., Davis, M., Delaygue, G., Delmotte, M., Kotlyakov, V.M., Legrand, M., Lipenkov, V.Y., Lorius, C., Pépin, L., Ritz, C., Saltzman, E. and Stievenard, M. (1999) 'Climate and atmospheric history of the past 420,000 years from the Vostok ice core, Antarctica', *Nature*, 399: 429–436.

Reiter, P. (2001), 'Climate change and mosquito-borne disease', *Environmental Health Perspectives*, 109: 141–161.

Reuveny, R. (2007) 'Climate change-induced migration and violent conflict', *Political Geography*, 26: 656–673.

Salehyan, I. (2008), 'From climate change to conflict? No consensus yet', *Journal of Peace Research*, 45: 315–326.

Schmidhuber, J. and Tubiello, F.N. (2007) 'Global food security under climate change', *Proceedings of the National Academy of Sciences*, 104: 19703–19708.

Schneider, S.H., Rosecranz, A., Mastrandrea, M. and Kuntz-Duriseti, K. (2009), *Climate Change Science and Policy*, Washington: Island Press.

Semenza, J.C. and Menne, B. (2009), 'Climate change and infectious diseases in Europe', *Lancet Infectious Diseases*, 9: 365–375.

Sen, A. (2001), *Development as Freedom*, New York: Alfred A. Knopf.

Tubiello, F.N., Soussana, J.-F. and Howden, S.M. (2007) 'Crop and pasture response to climate change', *Proceedings of the National Academy of Sciences*, 104: 19686–19690.

Vandentorren, S., Bretin, P., Zeghnoun, A., Mandereau-Bruno, L., Croisier, A., Cochet, C., Ribéron, J., Siberan, I., Declercq, B. and Ledrans, M. (2006) 'August 2003 heat wave in France: risk factors for death of elderly people living at home', *European Journal of Public Health*, 16: 583–591.

Watson, R.T., Albritton, D.L. and Dokken, D.J. (2003) *Climate Change 2001: Synthesis Report*, Geneva: World Meteorological Organization. Online. Available HTTP: <http://www.ipcc.ch/ipccreports/tar/vol4/english/> (accessed 16 June 2013).

14
MALARIA AND SECURITY
More than a matter of health

Nicholas Knowlton

It is rather surprising to consider how one of the oldest and biggest threats to humanity could be found in something as small as the mosquito. Indeed, for hundreds of thousands of years mosquitoes, and the malaria parasites residing within them, have exacted a toll so high that it compelled the human body to evolve – including Duffy negativity and sickle cell, two types of genetic mutations on an individual's red blood cells – in order to endure its consequences (Packard 2007: 29–31). And yet, for as much attention as the subject of malaria has gained within the public sphere, there remains a void concerning its effects and implications beyond individual health.

With origins dating back as far as three million years ago (Webb 2009: 20–21), malaria continues to be a pervasive feature in the world, with a particular impact in sub-Saharan Africa (Africa). In 2010, there were an estimated 219 million cases of malaria reported around the world, accounting for approximately 660,000 deaths (most of which were of children under 5 years old in Africa) (WHO 2012: 59). In Africa, malaria accounts for approximately 15% of all childhood deaths and stands as the second highest single cause of child mortality (WHO 2013). In addition, in tropical regions where malaria remains endemic, the economic impacts of the disease have been estimated to affect overall gross domestic product (GDP) by as much as 1.3% (Sachs & Malaney 2002).

Malaria has long held prominence in the fields of international and public health, but as the disease has gained increased publicity, one area that has remained underexamined is the manner in which this disease is more than a problem of public health. This chapter examines the ways in which malaria constitutes a threat to the security of the state and those living within its borders. Placing the disease within a context of state building and state capacity, it highlights the security implications of malaria, as well as the direct and indirect costs this disease imposes at an aggregate level. In short, this chapter explains why malaria is a threat to international security and furthermore explains how its burden in sub-Saharan Africa poses an even more distinct threat. Beyond a matter of human security for those afflicted with the disease, malaria at the aggregate level affects communities, regions, as well as the state. Affecting a range of issues, from whether people are healthy enough to contribute to the productivity of the economy to the ability of the state to protect those residing within its borders, malaria makes its presence known across all levels of analysis, producing a sincere threat to security deserving scholarly attention.

Background

Before elaborating upon malaria's challenges to security, it is first necessary to provide a brief background on the disease. First, malaria refers to a (plasmodium) parasite existing within a self-contained system between its mosquito and human hosts.[1] As a previously uninfected female anopheles mosquito takes a blood meal from an infected individual, the mosquito ingests the parasite in the form of *gametocytes* (sexually differentiated versions of the malaria parasite). After ingestion, male and female *gametocytes* combine and develop into cysts within the infected mosquito's gut; upon rupturing these cysts produce *sporozoites* that travel into the mosquito's salivary glands. When the infected mosquito eventually takes another blood meal, these *sporozoites* are transmitted through the mosquito and into the individual's bloodstream. After initially entering an individual's liver, *sporozoites* later reemerge as *merozoites* that attack and replicate within an individual's red blood cells. The cycle of red blood cell infection continues within an infected individual, generally within intervals of 3–4 days (depending on the type of parasite), producing additional *merozoites*. Lastly, rather than continuing to produce additional *merozoites* ad infinitum, some parasites instead form *gametocytes* where, upon being ingested by another female anopheles mosquito, the cycle completes itself.

Unlike other diseases, malaria refers to a family of parasites (genus plasmodium). Variants that afflict humans include *P. falciparum*, *vivax*, *ovale*, and *malariae*. As transmitted by female anopheles mosquitoes, these different types of parasites attack and multiply within an individual's red blood cells, which not only destroy the host's red blood cells as a result of the reproductive process but additionally release toxic byproducts, thus bringing about the symptoms commonly associated with malaria, including fever, chills, headaches, nausea, lethargy, anemia, and even death in severe cases. It is important to note that different forms of plasmodium exhibit different symptoms in infected persons. *Vivax* and *ovale*, for example, only infect a limited number of red blood cells and additionally exhibit a dormant period, where the parasite produces *hypnozoites* that enter into an infected individual's liver (CDC 2012b; Packard 2007: 23; Shah 2010: 23; Webb 2009: 4). An individual may not experience malarial symptoms until much later – sometimes months or even years – when these *hypnozoites* reemerge from the liver and resume attacking an individual's red blood cells (Packard 2007: 23). In contrast, *P. falciparum* does not undergo any type of dormant period, yet attacks red blood cells in a more voracious and indiscriminate manner than other forms of the parasite, sometimes as much as 80% of an infected individual's red blood cells (Packard 2007: 23; Webb 2009: 5).

Not every type of mosquito transmits malaria to humans. Only female anopheline mosquitoes are known to carry and transmit malaria, as only female mosquitoes take blood meals (CDC 2012b; Packard 2007: 24; Shah 2010: 15). Anopheline mosquitoes possess a much greater general susceptibility to the malaria parasite than other species, making it a much likelier vector for malaria transmission (Packard 2007: 24–25; Service & Townson 2002: 59; Shah 2010: 15;).[2]

In sum, malaria may be best conceived as a sophisticated system composed of multiple parts. On its surface, malaria transmission appears so complex as to be improbable: only one genus of mosquito generally transmits the disease; such a mosquito must ingest infected blood containing *both* male and female *gametocytes*; then, even after ingesting both male and female gametocytes, the reproduction and development of *sporozoites* must occur within a stable climate (between 16 and 35 degrees centigrade), and must furthermore occur within the infected mosquito's life span, typically only 2 weeks (CDC 2012a; Packard 2007: 24; Snow & Gilles 2002: 91–92).[3] Finally, the mosquito must take another blood meal after the parasite's *sporozoites* have traveled to the mosquito's salivary glands, ready to be transmitted to another human host. It is only through the large numbers of malaria-transmitting mosquitoes, and the large numbers of people living within endemic zones, that this process has managed to sustain itself for thousands of years.

In terms of controlling malaria, interventions traditionally include preventive measures – such as taking antimalarial medications, using (insecticide-treated) bed nets, and covering exposed extremities – as well as reactive measures including treating the disease through in- or outpatient medical treatment.[4] However, each type of intervention contains its own inherent challenges and limitations. For example, although malaria is widely treatable, resistance to antimalarial medications has been an ongoing challenge for health professionals (WHO 2010). Chloroquine, once considered the premier antimalarial treatment, has over time lost much of its effectiveness against many strains of malaria (Garrett 1994: 442; Webb 2010: 176–177).[5] While alternative medications are available, fears about whether they too will lose effectiveness against malaria remain.

In addition to these concerns, the availability and affordability of antimalarial drugs remains a barrier. For example, while artemisinin combination therapy (ACT) is considered to be the most effective means for treating malaria, its cost has remained out of the reach of many afflicted with the disease (Shah 2010: 115). Issues concerning the cost of development, as well as maintaining intellectual property rights on such treatments, have made the cost of ACT many times higher than cheaper, though less effective treatments. Although measures have been taken to decrease the price of ACT therapies, such as extending artemisinin formulas without patent restrictions, black markets in antimalarial drugs have already emerged (Shah 2010: 116–117). While less expensive, these black market drugs are widely known to contain varying amounts of antimalarial medicine, as well as inappropriate dosing instructions. Many countries in malaria endemic regions have witnessed an alarming rise in fake or weak malaria drugs that not only fail to effectively treat those afflicted with the disease but furthermore increase the risk that the disease will develop resistance.

Lastly, there is a concern that interventions against the disease may do more harm than good, especially if such interventions are of a short-term nature. As the prevalence of malaria in a given area is reduced by interventions, people lose (generally within 12 months) their acquired immunity to the parasite. As a result, if such interventions are discontinued without achieving full eradication of the parasite from the affected region, the population is left in a more vulnerable state than when the intervention first began (Garrett 1994: 443; Webb 2009: 33, 163).

More than a fever: The true costs of malaria

It is a given that malaria poses an ongoing challenge to individual health. Not only must one endure (as well as survive) the physical burden of the disease, one must also endure its associated socioeconomic burdens. Obtaining appropriate healthcare for proper diagnosis and treatment is necessary for full recovery; however, for many such care is neither readily available nor affordable, especially for those living in rural areas within malaria-endemic regions, particularly within Africa (de Castro & Fisher 2012; Worrall et al. 2005). Even where treatment is available, the costs can affect entire families – especially when an afflicted individual is a primary or supplementary income earner. Family resources are further strained when, in addition to one's normal work or family obligations, one must care for afflicted family members, as well as assist with traveling to and from health care facilities (Chima et al. 2003: 20–23; Sachs & Malaney 2002: 682).

There is also the likelihood that malaria's effects may linger far longer than its symptoms. In terms of cognitive development, malaria's symptoms (including cerebral malaria and anemia) risk impeding the intellectual development of children, with lasting socioeconomic consequences (Chima et al. 2003: 26). Furthermore, recent research has given additional credence to the notion that the disease impedes long-term intellectual development (Eppig et al. 2010). In short, as children's brains require large amounts of metabolic energy in order to properly develop, diseases like malaria impede intellectual development by interfering with metabolic processes. This line of research indeed observes an association between infectious disease and levels of measured intelligence (Eppig et al. 2010: 3803–3805), and furthermore finds that illnesses tend to exhibit stronger effects on intelligence than other commonly associated socioeconomic indicators, including income, education, and climate.

However, there are additional, less widely known consequences of malaria beyond the level of the individual sufferer. The indirect costs of malaria – such as the loss of work and productivity of those afflicted by the disease – have indeed been noted by others (Asante & Asenso-Okyere 2003; Chima et al. 2003; Gallup & Sachs 2001) and thus serve as a means for explaining how this disease has wider effects than the afflicted individual. Such aggregated effects challenge state capacity, including the state's ability to effectively finance and deliver public services. Malaria-related mortality, public costs of treatment, and the loss of productivity accrue and place increased demands on state resources that otherwise could have been utilized for other purposes. In other words, malaria imposes an opportunity cost. The argument is relatively straightforward: as individuals become ill they are unable to work and/or attend school, and they furthermore require professional medical treatment (financed either by the patient, the state, or a combination of both). The productivity losses and financial costs of treating the disease contribute to the continuation of a vicious circle that increasingly challenges the state's ability to provide for the safety and security of those residing within its borders. As previously highlighted, such impacts have been observed to negatively affect state economies by average decreases of 1% of GDP, reaching as high as 1.3% (Sachs & Malaney 2002: 682). While such losses may initially appear relatively small, it is important to consider that such losses are compounded for every year in which malaria remains endemic (that is, losses from one year carry over and add to losses in subsequent years). Researchers have also noted a correlation between levels of malaria and global rates of GDP per capita (Sachs & Malaney 2002) and have furthermore suggested one explanation as to how and why malaria affects state productivity. Positing the "quality-quantity dilemma," where families in malaria endemic regions are effectively compelled to ration their limited resources among their children because of the ever-present threat of their children dying from malaria, such uncertainties compel families to have more children as a type of risk management strategy. Sachs and Malaney (2002: 681–683) note that the combined presence of poverty, disease, and high fertility, accounts for an average 10% loss of income in countries with malaria, with losses reaching as high as 18% in highly endemic countries.

In addition to the financial costs and losses it imposes on states, malaria's pernicious effects have been noted in other contexts, with more direct implications for state security. Historically, malaria was famously a huge hindrance to the construction of the Panama Canal, as seen not only in France's initial attempt – and subsequent failure – to build the canal, but also in the United States' later successful effort, achieved only after acquiring knowledge of malarial transmission through mosquitoes (Garrett 1994: 47–48; McCullough 1977; Packard 2010: 120–121; Shah 2010: 149–151, 185).[6] Malaria again demonstrated its significance in both world wars as all sides fought over control of quinine and other malarial remedies for purposes of maintaining combat-ready regiments (Webb 2009). In particular, following the Japanese attack on Pearl Harbor in 1941, Japanese forces seized the Dutch East Indies, with particular interest in the cinchona plantations on the island of Java (Webb 2009: 157). Unable to procure sufficient amounts of quinine, between October 1942 and April 1943 Allied forces in the Southwest Pacific suffered 10 casualties from malarial illness for every one casualty caused by combat injury (Webb 2009: 157; see also Hays 2000: 49). Moreover, as Allied forces advanced through the Italian peninsula in 1944, German troops intentionally destroyed Italian bonification pumps – designed to pump out water from the Pontine marshes and remove the mosquito's breeding habitat – in order to impede Allied advances through Italy by not only compelling Allied forces to travel through rough terrain but also by subjecting them to an intentionally created malaria epidemic (Snowden 2006: 191–197). While this strategy largely failed in halting Allied progress, it unfortunately succeeded in bringing about the intended epidemic, afflicting more than 40% of the local population with malaria.

Indeed, malaria in World War II was of such significance that the United States created the Office of Malaria Control in War Areas (MCWA) in 1942, an agency charged with controlling malaria in and around U.S. military bases (CDC 2010). Of primary concern for the Office was the spread of malaria among U.S. soldiers stationed within malarial areas around the world, including the Southeastern United States. Indeed, the threat of malaria was of such importance that even after World War II, the MCWA continued its mission of malaria control and would later be expanded and become more widely known as the U.S. Centers for Disease Control and Prevention.

While malaria's role in times of war has waned since its peak in WWII, its danger to international security nevertheless remains significant. First, in considering the threat of state failure and/or collapse, malaria burdens states by placing additional stress on their health infrastructure and fiscal resources. Indeed, the U.S. National Intelligence Council has recognized that diseases like malaria can contribute to the decay and collapse of fragile and/or weak states, undermine the legitimacy of government, foment social unrest from the poor quality of life, and impede the readiness of security forces to respond in times of crisis (USNIC 2000, 2008).

Second, while it would be problematic to conceive of malaria as a direct cause of conflict, malaria nevertheless serves to potentiate its consequences. Ghobarah, Huth, and Russett (2004a: 85) note how "wars continue to kill people well after the shooting stops," particularly as conflict tends to increase the spread of disease, not only through the collapse of medical infrastructure in conflict-ridden regions but also through the exodus of refugees, the consequential rise of refugee camps, and the costs such camps place on neighboring countries and relief organizations (Ghobarah et al. 2004b; see also Smith, chapter 12 in this volume).

Moreover, just as diseases like malaria exacerbate the effects of conflict, so too do they risk spreading conflict and instability to other regions. As refugees from malaria-endemic areas risk spreading epidemics into other areas, such mass migrations pose additional challenges to their host countries through the resources required to not only accommodate such groups, but to also provide the medical care necessary to prevent any potential epidemics from occurring (McInnes & Lee 2006: 16). In other words, while malaria does not start wars, it nevertheless threatens to exacerbate and spread them through mechanisms of destabilization, increased burdens on state capacity, and increased human suffering from death and morbidity.

This discussion will likely be familiar to those acquainted with the literature on HIV/AIDS and security, as both diseases threaten international security through many of the same mechanisms. For instance, just as HIV/AIDS threatens the readiness and capability of state security forces (Singer 2000), as well as impedes processes of economic development, foreign aid, and international diplomacy (Youde 2005), so too does malaria reasonably fall within these concerns. To be sure, while the relationship between diseases like HIV/AIDS and state security is more complex than a simple causal argument (McInnes & Rushton 2010), there is reason to believe that diseases like AIDS and malaria contribute to state decay and collapse through a threshold effects model (Pierson 2004: 83–87) whereby, in adding to the state's overall burden, these diseases increase the difficulty for the state to function and fulfill its obligations to those residing within its borders.

In sum, the costs of malaria are experienced at all levels of society and continue to impose burdens on the state in terms of both traditional and nontraditional conceptualizations of security. Treating malaria as a security threat does not require an intellectual leap of faith: such impacts may be reasonably conceived as threats by impeding the ability of the state to defend itself from war and foreign threats, as well as in broader (human security) terms of threatening to place afflicted individuals within life-determining situations of poverty and illness (Booth 2007; Walt 1991). Furthermore, malaria's placement in this type of discussion easily fits within many of the established research programs within International Relations, in much the same manner as HIV/AIDS did in the past (Youde 2005). This section has highlighted the various ways in which malaria negatively impacts the state's ability to provide for the welfare and security of its inhabitants. In one way or another, malaria's effects can be seen at all levels of analysis and are experienced by everyone residing within such endemic zones. While malaria has traditionally been recognized mostly as a threat to public health, thus residing within the area of "low politics," such a conception only accounts for a small portion of the total threat posed by this disease, and risks underestimating its true costs.

Dynamics of affliction: Africa's distinct burden

It should come as no surprise that the African continent suffers a heavier burden from malaria than other regions. Not only are more cases reported within Africa than in any other endemic region, the continent furthermore bears the highest share of deaths from the disease, reaching as high as 90% of all cases around the world (WHO 2013: 1). While such burdens may only be partially explained by the levels of state capacity and financial resources available among African countries in these endemic zones, there are additional factors that must be considered in order to fully account for malaria's burden in Africa. In contrast to other regions of the globe, Africa generally possesses multiple environmental factors that make malaria's impact more severe than elsewhere. This section addresses these factors, showing how the combined presence of climate, type of vector, and type of parasite make the burden of malaria in Africa distinct.

First, the African continent is generally situated in a climate conducive to both malaria development and transmission, as much of the sub-Saharan portion resides between the Tropics of Cancer and Capricorn (Sachs & Malaney 2002: 681). These tropical regions experience increased rainfall – facilitating mosquito breeding habitats – and additionally possess year-round temperatures conducive to the development and survival of the malaria parasite (Anderson & May 1991; Cook & Zumla 2003; Gilles & Warrell 2002; Oaks et al. 1991; Sachs & Malaney 2002: 680). In other words, unlike other areas of the world experiencing malaria within more temperate regions, the African continent is largely predisposed to year-round endemicity.

However, geography alone does not explain everything. After all, other regions of the world similarly reside within tropical zones and also experience a year-round threat of malaria. What makes the African continent further distinct is the second feature concerning the *type* of malaria parasite endemic to the continent. While other continents possess different strains of malaria, Africa largely harbors the more severe *falciparum* strain (Hay et al. 2009, 2010; Webb 2009: 13). Although *plasmodium falciparum* is not exclusive to Africa, the pervasiveness and geographical extent to which this strain is found within Africa nevertheless makes it a distinct feature. As previously highlighted, unlike other strains, *falciparum* attacks red blood cells indiscriminately and does so with more voracity, infecting up to 80% of a victim's red blood cells (Packard 2007: 23; Sallares 2002: 25; Shah 2010: 27). Of further significance is the fact that the *falciparum* parasite appears to be the most difficult strain for the human immune system to naturally resist without the aid of medical intervention (Kwiatkowski 2005; Shah 2010: 27).

Third, Africa is also host to a particularly potent vector of malaria. The *anopheles gambiae*, a mosquito largely endemic to Africa, is considered to have evolved to exclusively feed on human populations, taking up to 100% of its blood meals from humans (Packard 2007: 25; Shah 2010: 25–26).[7] In addition, unlike other species of anopheles mosquitoes, the *gambiae* mosquito possesses a higher rate of susceptibility to the malaria parasite, thus increasing the likelihood that the parasite will be transmitted to other individuals. Recent research additionally suggests that the presence of the *falciparum* parasite within an infected *gambiae* actually induces the mosquito to feed more often than it otherwise would, thus further increasing the probability of malaria transmission onto other human hosts (Koella et al. 1998; Sinka et al. 2012).

In sum, the African continent possesses three features that make malaria particularly problematic, and thus a particularly significant threat to the security of the state. Through the conjunctural presence of a climate generally conducive to year-round endemicity, a virulent strain of the malaria parasite, and a species of mosquito highly apt in spreading the disease, Africa's experience and burden with malaria remains distinct, and furthermore serves to provide the highest rate of stable malaria transmission of any region in the world (Kiszewski et al. 2004). This is not intended to discount the threat of malaria as it is experienced elsewhere around the globe or to argue that malaria in other endemic areas does not constitute a threat to security. Africa has been and continues to be the region with the highest burden imposed by this disease. Even during the last Malaria Eradication Campaign (1955–1969), Africa was largely omitted from interventions because the region was then considered to have been too difficult for eradication efforts (Gramiccia & Beales 1988; Packard 2007: 154; Shah 2010: 205; Webb 2009: 167).

Turning a vicious circle into a virtuous one

Up to this point this chapter has shown the ways in which malaria impacts the state and society. While these insights are contributory to understanding the relationship between disease and state security, they are limited by the ways in which one conceptualizes that overall relationship. Despite examples highlighting malaria's negative effects, there remains an issue concerning the interrelationship between this disease and the community in which it resides: does malaria cause increased insecurity or is it instead a consequence of other prior factors, such as a given state's level of capacity?

In short, the answer is that it is both, and disentangling the relationship remains a challenge. While social scientists often like to think within logical frameworks of causality – that is, that distinct causes bring about distinct outcomes – such lines of thinking can be problematic when conceptualizing the role of diseases like malaria and their effects on the state. Nevertheless, it is possible to conceptualize this relationship and to additionally show how malaria's vicious circle of insecurity and decline may be transformed into a virtuous one instead. Utilizing an adapted model from Price-Smith's argument concerning disease and state capacity (2002: 23), Figure 14.1 highlights the complex interrelationship between malaria and its effects on the state and society.

Beginning with malaria's basic form (as an undifferentiated parasite), its potency is augmented by various intervening variables, including species of parasite, climate, as well as type and prevalence of mosquito vector. At the same time, however, state capacity – defined as the ability of the state to provide for the well-being of its inhabitants – acts to mitigate the disease's impacts through empowering the state and those living in its territory to resist and/or adapt to the disease's effects. This can range from the availability of medical services, to accessibility of preventive measures (such as insecticide-treated bed nets), to even gaining acquired immunity from repeated exposure over time. Furthermore, adaptability and state capacity may be additionally influenced by exogenous inputs, such as foreign aid, health interventions, and advances in medical technology. What is important to note, however, is that while diseases like malaria threaten to pull endemic countries into vicious circles of deteriorating capacity and instability, such outcomes are not deterministic, and may additionally be reversed through positive improvements in state capacity, medical knowledge, and availability of international health assistance.

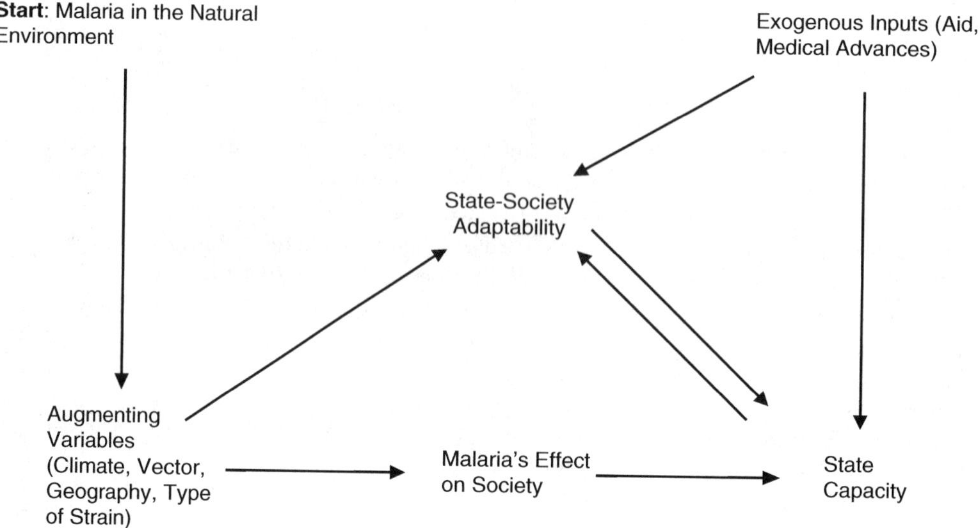

Figure 14.1 Malaria and State Capacity
Adapted from Price-Smith 2002: 23.

In sum, although the relationship between malaria, the state, and security is complex, it is nevertheless within our ability to grasp and illuminate this underexplored area of health security. Through highlighting the relationship between disease and the state in this fashion, we advance our understanding of how malaria continues to impact the security of the state and its inhabitants, and we furthermore contribute to preexisting research by building upon previous insights. For example, research on state building and development has emphasized factors including population density (Herbst 2000) and colonial inheritance (Kohli 2004; Young 1994). The inclusion of malaria into such analyses has the potential to further illuminate the reasons as to why some states have been more successful than others and to do so while providing richer explanations without sacrificing parsimony.

Conclusion

It is both ironic and tragic that malaria has continued to thrive for thousands of years despite possessing what may be considered a complex life cycle. After all, as noted above, malaria transmission generally requires a female anopheles mosquito to consume the blood of one infected individual, to ingest both male and female *gametocytes*, to have the parasite successfully undergo sexual reproduction within the mosquito host's life span, and to have the infected mosquito pass on the parasite to another individual through another blood meal – all the while avoiding hazards to its own life, such as insecticides and predators. It is difficult to comprehend how such a combination of factors came together to make malaria so pervasive and resilient, especially within Africa. It is also ironic that well-intentioned, albeit inconsistently applied, interventions appear to have increased the difficulty in eradicating malaria, either through allowing the parasite to develop resistance to antimalarial medications, by allowing mosquitoes to develop resistance to insecticides, or by temporarily reducing a local population's acquired resistance to the disease (Garrett 1994: 440–442; Webb 2009: 176–177).

Despite inherent limitations on accurate and reliable data on malaria prevalence throughout history, we do have enough information to understand how this disease has been a pervasive threat to the security of people and the states in which they reside. Not only has this disease existed for over a millennia (Packard 2007; Webb 2009), it has been credited with nothing less than altering the course of human evolution to cope with its deleterious consequences (Packard 2007: 29–31; Shah 2010: 21–27). Whether viewed through the lens of traditional or nontraditional definitions of security, malaria has been and remains a distinct threat. From the individual afflicted with the disease, to the economic consequences of having a significant proportion of society both unable to work and requiring medical care at any given moment, even to threats of state collapse and regional instability, malaria and its associated effects meet the criteria for being considered a threat to both human and national security.

Malaria constitutes more than a risk to public health. In terms of providing security, facilitating economic growth, and delivering public goods, malaria and its associated consequences undermine the execution of all these traditional functions and responsibilities of the state. While the purpose of this chapter has been to survey how malaria's impacts are felt across society, this is not to suggest that research on this issue has become exhausted. Indeed, there exist multiple avenues for further inquiry, including case studies of malaria's impacts on state development, the burden it imposes on national budgets, and its impact on the domestic workforce. Future analyses might also investigate the reasons why past efforts at global eradication failed, as well as the ongoing difficulties with regard to establishing international cooperation on malaria control among endemic countries. In addition, future research might inquire into malaria's particular role in periods of conflict and war, including whether its role as a conflict potentiator serves to prolong or reduce the length of combat between warring groups. Future research could even provide a service by obtaining improved assessments on the depth and breadth of malaria prevalence in affected countries: as a paradox of malaria, obtaining reliable data on its prevalence presupposes a sufficient level of state capacity to observe and document instances within a given country.

As a means of introducing this subject for a wide audience, this chapter has not only explained the difficulty in treating malaria in a broad fashion (as its burden depends on a variety of factors, including the species of parasite and vector of transmission), it has additionally shown how malaria has constituted a significant threat to the state and society, with particular emphasis on its distinct burden on the African continent. In drawing upon insights from within and outside international relations, this chapter serves as a platform for others that may be interested in further inquiry on this subject. As the subject of disease and its relationship to state building and security offers new avenues for further research, the horizon looks promising. Incorporating malaria into narratives of state security and development is not intended to not mean that malaria acts as a singular cause of poverty and insecurity throughout the world; rather, its incorporation into such areas of inquiry serves to further scholarly research by increasing our understanding of the real world and its inherently complex nature. What makes this issue further significant is that such insights may be utilized for providing both valuable and practical contributions towards improvement of the lives of people afflicted by this disease. In sum, until the wider implications of malaria are considered, the true costs of the disease are likely to remain underestimated. By addressing and including the pervasiveness of this disease within accounts of security, we may not only better understand the challenges that states confront, we may also better understand the ways in which those challenges may be overcome.

Notes

1 Although the following is only a summary description of the plasmodium parasite life cycle, for additional details on this subject see Warrell and Gilles (2002: 85–106).

2 To be sure, however, different species of anopheles possess differing levels of susceptibility to the parasite.

3 Differences in temperature affect the length of development within the mosquito's gut, with higher temperatures reducing the length of time to less than 10 days, and colder temperatures lengthening it to more than 30 days (Warrell & Gilles 2002: 91).

4 The use of insecticides in malaria endemic areas has also been employed as an additional means of controlling the spread of the disease. In addition, humans may also obtain acquired immunity to the malaria parasite from experiencing multiple infections in their lifetime.

5 For example, chloroquine was once regularly prescribed for any suspected cases of malaria, and was additionally distributed prophylactically among endemic populations (Webb 2009, 176–177). However, in 2010 the WHO revised its treatment guidelines to include diagnosis of malaria prior to disbursement of antimalarial medicines, with exceptions permitted in contexts where diagnostic testing remains unavailable (WHO 2010).

6 Though to be sure, the United States did not eradicate malaria from Panama. It has also been argued that the collapse of the French Third Republic was, in part, attributed to the amount of debt and loss incurred as a result of France's initial attempt at constructing the Canal (McCullough 1977: 221–223; see also Shah 2010, 151).

7 In contrast, other types of anopheline mosquitoes take around 50% of their total blood meals from humans (Packard 2007: 25).

References

Anderson, R.M. and May R. (1991) *Infectious Diseases of Humans: Dynamics and Control*, New York: Oxford University Press.

Asante, F.A. and Asenso-Okyere, K. (2003) *Economic Burden of Malaria in Ghana: A Technical Report Submitted to the World Health Organization (WHO), African Regional Office (AFRO)*. Institute of Statistical, Social and Economic Research, Legon: University of Ghana.

Booth, K. (2007) *Theory of World Security*, New York: Cambridge University Press.

CDC. (2010) 'CDC's origins and malaria'. Online. Available HTTP: <http://www.cdc.gov/malaria/about/history/history_cdc.html> (accessed 20 April 2013).

CDC. (2012a) 'Anopheles mosquitos'. Online. Available HTTP: <http://www.cdc.gov/malaria/about/biology/mosquitoes/> (accessed 4 May 2013).

CDC. (2012b) 'Malaria'. Online. Available HTTP: <http://www.cdc.gov/malaria/> (accessed 17 April 2013).

Chima, R.I., Goodman, C.A. and Mills, A. (2003) 'The economic impact of malaria in Africa: a critical review of the evidence', *Health Policy*, 63: 17–36.

Cook, G.C. and Zumla, A.I. (eds.) (2003) *Manson's Tropical Diseases*, 21st ed., Philadelphia: W.B. Saunders.

de Castro, M.C. and Fisher, M.G. (2012) 'Is malaria illness among young children a cause or a consequence of low socioeconomic status? evidence from the United Republic of Tanzania', *Malaria Journal*, 11: 161.

Eppig, C., Fincher C.L. and Thornhill R. (2010) 'Parasite prevalence and the worldwide distribution of cognitive ability', *Proceedings of the Royal Society B*, 277: 3801–3808.

Gallup, J.L. and Sachs J.D. (2001) 'The economic burden of malaria', *American Journal of Tropical Medicine and Hygiene*, 64: 85–96.

Garrett, L. (1994) *The Coming Plague: Newly Emerging Diseases in a World Out of Balance*, New York: Penguin.

Ghobarah, H.A., Huth, P. and Russett, B. (2004a) 'Comparative public health: the political economy of human misery and well-being." *International Studies Quarterly*, 48: 73–94.

Ghobarah, H.A., Huth, P. and Russett, B. (2004b) 'The post-war public health effects of civil conflict', *Social Science and Medicine*, 59: 869–884.

Gilles, H.M. and Warrell, D.A. (2002) *Bruce-Chwatt's Essential Malariology*, Boston: Arnold.

Gramiccia, G. and Beales, P.F. (1988) 'The recent history of malaria control and eradication', in W.M. Werndorfer and Sir I. McGregor (eds.) *Malaria: Principles and Practices of Malariology*, Vol. 2, New York: Churchill Livingstone: 1335–1378.

Hay, S.I., Guerra C.A., Gething, P.W., Patil, A.P., Tatem, A.J., Noor, A.M., Kabaria, C.W., Iqbal, C.M., Elyazar, R.F., Brooker, S., Smith, D.L., Moyeed, R.A. and Snow, R.W. (2009) 'A world malaria map: *Plasmodium falciparum* endemicity in 2007', *PLoS Medicine*, 6. Online. Available HTTP: <http://www.plosmedicine.org/article/info%3Adoi%2F10.1371%2Fjournal.pmed.1000048> (accessed 13 April 2013).

Hays, C.W. (2000) 'The United States Army and malaria control in World War II', *Parasitologia*, 42: 47–52.

Herbst, J. (2000) *States and Power in Africa: Comparative Lessons in Authority and Control*, Princeton: Princeton University Press.

Kiszewski, A., Mellinger, A., Spielman, A., Malaney, P., Sachs, S.E. and Sachs, J. (2004) 'A global index representing the stability of malaria transmission', *American Journal of Tropical Medicine and Hygiene*, 70: 486–498.

Koella, J.C., Sorensen, F.L. and Anderson, R.A. (1998) 'The malaria parasite, *Plasmodium falciparum*, increases the frequency of multiple feeding of its mosquito vector, *Anopheles gambiae*', *Proceedings of the Royal Society of London*, 265: 763–768.

Kohli, A. (2004) *State-Directed Development: Political Power and Industrialization in the Global Periphery*, Cambridge: Cambridge University Press.

Kwiatkowski, D.P. (2005) 'How malaria has affected the human genome and what human genetics can teach us about malaria', *American Journal of Human Genetics*, 77: 171–192.

McCullough, D. (1977) *The Path Between the Seas: The Creation of the Panama Canal, 1870–1914*, New York: Simon & Schuster.

McInnes, C. and Lee, K. (2006) 'Health, security, and foreign policy', *Review of International Studies*, 32: 5–23.

McInnes, C. and Rushton S. (2010) 'HIV/AIDS and security: where are we now?" *International Affairs*, 86: 225–245.

Oaks, S.C., Mitchell, V.S., Pearson, G.W. and Carpenter, C.C.J. (eds.) (1991) *Malaria: Obstacles and Opportunities*, Washington DC: National Academy Press.

Packard, R.M. (2007) *The Making of a Tropical Disease: A Short History of Malaria*, Baltimore: Johns Hopkins University Press.

Pierson, P. (2004) *Politics in Time: History, Institutions, and Social Analysis*, Princeton: Princeton University Press.

Price-Smith, A.T. (2002) *The Health of Nations: Infectious Disease, Environmental Change, and Their Effects on National Security and Development*, Cambridge: MIT Press.

Sachs, J. and Malaney, P. (2002) 'The economic and social burden of malaria', *Nature*, 415: 680–685.

Sallares, R. (2002) *Malaria and Rome: A History of Malaria in Ancient Italy*, New York: Oxford University Press.

Service, M.W. and Townson, H. (2002) 'The *Anopheles* vector', in D.A. Warrell and H.M. Gilles (eds.) *Essential Malariology*, 4th ed., London: Arnold: 9–84.

Shah, S. (2010) *The Fever: How Malaria Has Ruled Humankind for 500,000 Years*, New York: Sarah Crichton Books.

Singer, P.W. (2000) 'AIDS and international security', *Survival*, 44: 145–158.

Sinka, M.E., Bangs, M.J., Manguin, S., Rubio-Palis, Y., Chareonviriyaphap, T., Coetzee, M., Mbogo, C.M., Hemingway, J., Patil, A.P., Temperley, W.H., Gething, P.W., Kabaria, C.W., Burkot, T.R., Harbach, R.E. and Hay, S.I. (2012) 'A global map of dominant malaria vectors', *Parasites and Vectors*, 5. Online. Available HTTP: <http://www.parasitesandvectors.com/content/5/1/69> (accessed 16 May 2013).

Snow, R.W. and Gilles, H.M. (2002) 'The epidemiology of malaria', in D.A. Warrell and H.M. Gilles (eds.) *Essential Malariology*, 4th ed., London: Arnold: 85–106.

Snowden, F.M. (2006) *The Conquest of Malaria: Italy, 1900–1962*, New Haven, CT: Yale University Press.

USNIC. (2000) *The Global Infectious Disease Threat and Its Implications for The United States*, NIE-99–17D, Washington, DC. Online. Available HTTP: <http://www.dni.gov/files/documents/infectiousdiseases_2000.pdf> (accessed 31 July 2013).

USNIC. (2008) *Strategic Implications of Global Health*, ICA 2008–10D, Washington, DC. Online. Available HTTP: <http://www.dni.gov/files/documents/Special%20Report_ICA%20Global%20Health%202008.pdf> (accessed 31 July 2013).

Walt, S.M. (1991) 'The renaissance of security studies', *International Studies Quarterly*, 35: 211–239.

Webb, J.L.A., Jr. (2009) *Humanity's Burden: A Global History of Malaria*, Cambridge: Cambridge University Press.

WHO. (2010) *Guidelines for the Treatment of Malaria. Second Edition*, Geneva: World Health Organization Press.

WHO. (2012) *World Malaria Report 2012*, Geneva: World Health Organization Press.

WHO. (2013) 'Child mortality: distribution of causes by WHO region', *Global Health Observatory Data Repository*. Online. Available HTTP: <http://apps.who.int/gho/data/view.main.1461?lang=en> (accessed 9 April 2013).

Worrall, E., Basu, S. and Hanson K. (2005) 'Is malaria a disease of poverty? A review of the literature', *Tropical Medicine and International Health*, 10: 1047–1059.

Youde, J. (2005) 'Enter the fourth horseman: health security and international relations theory'. *Whitehead Journal of Diplomacy and International Relations*, 6: 193–208.

Young, C. (1994) *The African Colonial State in Comparative Perspective*, New Haven, CT: Yale University Press.

15

NONCOMMUNICABLE DISEASE AS A SECURITY ISSUE

Christopher Benson and Sara M. Glasgow[1]

Examining the place of noncommunicable diseases (NCDs) on the health security agenda is fundamentally a diagnosis of absence. Despite claims that the threats posed by infectious disease are distinct from traditional state-based enemies, the construction of disease as a security threat in the discourse does little to validate this argument. Rather, as this analysis demonstrates, it is the compatibility of infectious diseases with the traditional security paradigm that makes them a more conducive object of securitization than NCDs. In this chapter, we develop this argument by illustrating how such compatibility exists in three dimensions: the potential for infectious disease to be a catalyst for sociopolitical and economic transformation; the fact that it derives from organisms that may be targeted for eradication; and its immediacy as a public health threat. Such concerns mean that infectious disease fits comfortably within a traditional state-centric understanding of security. More puzzling is the fact that those who have taken a human security-based approach have exhibited a similar prioritization. By documenting the analytical and praxiological privilege that infection enjoys in the human security discourse, we demonstrate how this discourse has occluded NCDs. In so doing, we set the stage for a political critique to be articulated – specifically that there must be greater scholarly and policy urgency lent to the challenge of NCDs. While securitization is one means by which that urgency might be communicated, we do not claim this process is inevitable or even desirable; after all, the analytical tools that have framed the infectious disease threat in ways compatible with a traditional security paradigm are inappropriate for a categorically different form of illness.

Walking a path of critique necessitates an accounting of the conditions that enable one to begin upon it in the first place. The conditions germane to the critique here center on a prominent feature of the contemporary security discourse: a lack of engagement with the political implications of NCDs and the strategies developed to prevent them. Even amongst those who have focused on issues of health security, NCDs such as cancer, diabetes, and cardiovascular disease (CVD) are off the proverbial radarscope.

As McInnes highlights in this volume (chapter 1), those who have approached health security as a national/international security threat have focused largely on infectious diseases. More surprisingly, however, the human security literature has similarly focused much of its attention on infectious diseases. Human security scholars have addressed the threats posed by the human immunodeficiency virus (HIV) and severe acute respiratory syndrome (SARS), despite the fact that NCDs such as heart disease, diabetes, and cancer are the leading source of global mortality and nearly 80% of the NCD burden occurs in low- and middle-income countries (World Health Organization 2011). Moreover, if current trends continue, the relative toll exacted by NCDs vis-à-vis infections will only get worse: by 2030, projections indicate that mortality distribution will shift dramatically "from communicable, maternal, perinatal and nutritional (Group I) causes to non-communicable disease (Group II) causes" (Mathers & Loncar 2005: 2). Indeed, NCDs are expected to account for nearly 70% of the global mortality burden by 2030 (Mathers & Loncar 2005: 2).

We are thus presented with a conundrum: a human security agenda that could easily accommodate NCDs, yet has remained largely silent on the issue – even as these far outpace infection as a source of global morbidity and mortality. But before we can ascertain the extent to which NCDs could be viewed as a security threat (and we are not convinced that they should), we must attend to this conundrum as a clinician, engaging in that most fundamental of analytical exercises: diagnosis. Specifically, the purpose of this analysis is to diagnose and critically explore the reasons why the health security community, which seems to have no trouble addressing the general problem of disease, has had such analytical blinders on with regard to NCDs.

Conceptual issues

While disease has been omnipresent across human history, it has only relatively recently become part of the security studies literature as an issue other than its ramifications as a weapon, or the implications of war for population health. The post-Cold War era has been marked by a disciplinary reflection about what "security" means in theoretical and practical terms. The tropes of the traditional security discourse, however, remain relevant: the protection of a territory and population bounded to a sovereign or semisovereign state from an external military threat. This conventional definition delimits those issues that are analytically salient under such a conceptualization – e.g., military expenditures, weapons research and development, and proliferation issues. But this Westphalian notion of "security" has difficulty with some of the most pressing sources of human vulnerability, sources that do not respect territorial borders and are not wedded to the modern state apparatus.

Thus, the literature interrogating what "security" means in the contemporary threat environment is marked by a heightened diversification in themes and topics addressed, from the critical assessment of the discourse and practice of security (Krause & Williams 1997a, 1997b), to the call for an expanded agenda that addresses nontraditional, transborder threats (Myers 1989; Tuchman Matthews 1989; United Nations Development Program 1994).

In focusing on transborder problems, scholars identify two dimensions that make such problems perplexing for traditional security studies. The first concerns a shift in the object of security, in that individual welfare, not the state, becomes the object to be secured, and the second pertains to the inadequacy of a territorially bounded state to address and redress these problems. With regard to the first dimension, Krause and Williams (1997a) argue that shifting the focus from state survival as the object of security to the survival of the individual paradoxically facilitates an engagement with the "broadest global threats" (Krause and Williams 1997a: 45). In addition to a shift in the object of security, other scholars have articulated the functional incapacity of the state to address transborder issues due to domains of activity and inadequate infrastructure (Cusimano 2000: 32).

From such a perspective, a more encompassing "human security" approach has emerged (see also Caballero-Anthony & Amul, chapter 3 in this volume). As Paris (2001) has noted, multiple definitions of the phrase abound, but the United Nations Development Program's (UNDP) definition remains the 'most widely cited and the "most authoritative" definition of the term'

(Paris 2001: 90). The definition refers to "safety from chronic threats such as hunger, disease and repression" as well as the protection of people's everyday lives from "sudden and hurtful disruptions" (United Nations Development Program 1994: 23). These disruptions take many forms, but what is salient for this chapter is that we see a clear place for issues of disease on the human security agenda.

As understood here, "disease" refers to a condition that compromises the normal functioning of human biophysiology or mental capacity. However, its forms require clarification. This analysis bifurcates the categories of illness: "infectious diseases" induced by the presence of an organism capable of replication in or between human hosts; and "noncommunicable diseases" that are not transmissible and are the product of behavioral choices, genetic predisposition, environmental stressors, and other factors. The distinction between these categories becomes central for analyzing disease as a human security issue. For despite the claim from human security scholars that threats posed by transnational problems like disease are fundamentally distinct from traditional enemies, in practice the health issues that are most akin to traditional enemies have dominated the health security agenda. Thus, we argue here, it is the compatibility of *infectious* diseases with the traditional security paradigm that has made them a more conducive object of securitization than NCDs.

Before broaching how and in what ways NCDs have been overlooked on the human security agenda, it is worth demonstrating that such exclusion is consonant with a wider disciplinary disengagement with the issue. In a recent search of the JSTOR database, restricted to more recent political science articles (2000–present), we entered the following pairs of search terms in order to evaluate the relative emphasis of these two broad illness categories in the security literature. In order to be as comprehensive as possible, we searched titles, abstracts, and full text. The first search, for "noncommunicable disease" and "security" returned 72 results, while a second search for "infectious disease" and "security" yielded 3,512 results – nearly 50 times as many as the first. Furthermore, of articles that did address NCDs and security, examples disproportionately came from the policy literature, as opposed to the academic, and tended to use "security" in a more generic way. Thus there are comparatively few sources that allude to the idea of NCDs as a security threat. And while we are not arguing that NCDs should be securitized, there is no doubt that their global burden is of sufficient urgency to demand increased scholarly and policy attention in a more general sense.

Closer examination of these results indicate that in the vast majority of the 72 articles mentioning "noncommunicable disease" and "security" the connection between the two is ancillary – dealing not with NCDs as a substantive problem for security studies but rather the connections between NCDs and social policy issues, such as the provision of Social Security in the United States. While this phenomenon also occurred with the second search, far more direct and substantive links between infection and security have been drawn, particularly with regard to HIV/AIDS – as we shall shortly demonstrate. While not meant to be an exhaustive demonstration of the relative lack of attention paid to NCDs, it does at least suggest that a close analysis of them as a political phenomenon has historically not been a priority for the discipline.

The analytical primacy of infectious disease

If NCDs are not an analytical priority in the broader political science literature, we might expect to see a similar theme in a more detailed assessment of the security discourse. One way we can ascertain the relative exclusion of NCDs from this discourse is to highlight how ill-health has typically been approached – as argued here, by ascertaining the threat that infectious diseases pose to the security and stability of states and populations, while simultaneously overlooking the entrenched problem of NCDs. Thus we illuminate not only the premise that infectious diseases are favored in the security discourse on health, but also why their features, as opposed to those of NCDs, have made them more conducive to inquiry *even within human security-based approaches to health.*

To develop this argument, we must establish the prioritization of infectious diseases. To the extent that health and disease are objects of analysis in the literature, they are approached in a narrow context that emphasizes the dangers posed by "re-emerging" diseases like tuberculosis and cholera (Lee & Dodgson 2000), emerging infections like H7N9 avian flu (Glynn 2013), SARS (Curley & Thomas 2004; Tan 2003), and the entrenched pandemic of HIV.

Indeed, this latter dimension commands the most attention in the literature. Burkhalter (2004) and Poku et al. (2007), for example, provide macro-level policy perspectives on the connection between HIV and human security in the African region, while Ostergard (2002) focuses more specifically on how HIV reduces defense capacity and preparedness in the region, as well as prospects for economic stability and development. This connection between development and security in the context of the HIV crisis is further explored, again against the backdrop of Africa, by Boutayeb (2009), who concludes that the crisis constitutes a threat to both human development and human security. Other scholars emphasize the processes and normative frameworks by which infectious disease has become securitized, again with specific reference to HIV (McInnes 2006; McInnes & Rushton 2010). And even macro-level studies, such as those by Price-Smith (2001) and Glasgow and Pirages (2001) that reference general threats posed by infectious disease to state capacity and economic performance, often make liberal reference to the specific challenge of the HIV epidemic. This is not to say that such references are inappropriate but simply to clarify how dominant a theme it is in the health security discourse.

As objects of analysis, infectious diseases dominate the literature, and are the prototypical examples used to illustrate the concept of "health security." Consider Murphy's (2001) call for the expansion of the disciplinary teaching and research agendas to focus on a new "global health politics." He characterizes this issue in terms that reify infectious diseases as the privileged objects of analysis by focusing his examples on cross-border transmission of drug-resistant tuberculosis, cholera, and HIV/AIDS (352).

Even recognizing that HIV and other infections devastate many countries, far more people die annually of NCDs than AIDS, tuberculosis, cholera, or SARS. Yet these infectious diseases dominate the human security discourse on health. How might we account for this phenomenon? Three reasons suggest themselves: that sudden, violent, and widespread infectious disease epidemics can be a powerful catalyst for sociopolitical change; that the agents responsible for infectious disease can often be targeted and contained or eliminated; and that there is an immediacy to them that necessitates response. In conjunction, these reasons illuminate how the "novel" threat of infection is compatible with traditional security constructs and hence how infectious disease has come to overshadow NCDs as the dominant object of analysis in the health security discourse.

Infectious disease as a catalyst for transformation

To assert that infectious diseases are favored in this discourse is to recognize that they, more than NCDs, are compatible with existing modes of conceptualizing and providing for security. There are multiple ways in which this is manifest; one is that infectious diseases have historically demonstrated transformative power capable of restructuring modes of political and economic organization. But in order to radically transform – and even destroy – the political structures and economies of entire societies, diseases have to be capable of replication, usually in and between human hosts. Thus, scholars such as Cartwright (1972), Crosby (1986), Hobhouse (1989), and McNeill (1977) overwhelmingly turn their attention to infectious diseases: the plagues of classical society, bubonic plague, and smallpox, just to name a few.

In addition to privileging infection, the discourse also emphasizes epidemics that are broad in scope. Transformation cannot be achieved through isolated outbreaks with limited mortality. Thus the literature has tended to focus on referencing history's "great plagues" – high mortality events including the aforementioned outbreaks that besieged both ancient Greece and Rome, the Black Death, and the introduction of smallpox to Amerindian populations in the 16th and 17th centuries. In such cases, epidemics often persisted between one and three years, typically with high morbidity and mortality rates. It is estimated, for example, that the plague of Justinian claimed at its height 5,000 victims per day (McNeill 1977: 104). The Black Death was even more devastating, with mortality estimates ranging from between one quarter and one third of the entire European population (Hobhouse 1989: 16; McNeill 1977: 149).

With these great historical plagues as a referent, the contemporary health security discourse has turned its attention to modern illnesses that share similar characteristics. The diseases analyzed, therefore, are infectious – the product of "vast attacks on humans by a vast army of 'phantom warriors' – viruses, bacteria, and parasites" (Fox, 1997/1998: 121). Furthermore, the examples most often cited as threats are regional epidemics or global pandemics. To that end, Pirages and Runci assess the HIV epidemic in Africa and Asia, cholera in Latin America, and malaria worldwide (2000: 183). Additionally, Chow (1996) discusses the national security implications of the resurgence of tuberculosis, which has become a tremendous regional problem in areas such as the former Soviet republics.

Finally, a transformative disease is characterized by a high degree of intensity, as evidenced by morbidity and mortality. Two frequently analyzed diseases in the security discourse thus reflect high morbidity and/or mortality: HIV/AIDS, a phenomenon for which treatments are limited and expensive and no cure is available (Pirages & Runci 2000: 183–84) and tuberculosis, a resurgent disease that in some cases no longer responds to conventional antibiotics (Chow 1996: 63–65).

Having assessed the discursive practices pertaining to the framing of disease, we are left with a fundamental question: how does this particular conceptualization of disease – infectious, large-scale, often with high morbidity and/or mortality – facilitate its construction as a conventional security threat? In other words, how does framing disease in this manner serve to present it as a threat in terms compatible with the security of the sovereign or semisovereign state? The consequences of these transformative episodes suggest a potential answer to these questions.

Although many historians have analyzed the social construction of disease, it is also a biological process that derives its transformative power from its physical interaction with humanity – through its power to kill and to depopulate. In so doing, it also serves an important ecological function in controlling population growth rates where population density is significant enough to facilitate widespread transmission, morbidity, and mortality. In light of its transformative power, the altering of governmental apparati, patterns of political or economic relations, and societal composition are the tangible means by which change is signified. In the case of Athens, for example, an epidemic raged between 430–429 B.C.E. that had profound consequences along these lines, and "may have much to do with the failure of Athenian plans for the defeat of Sparta and the Peloponnesian League. Had Athens won that war, how different the subsequent political history would have been!" (McNeill 1977: 94).

In another case, the plague that raged during the reign of Justinian not only undermined the power and reach of the Roman state, but also comparatively shifted the locus of world power from the Mediterranean regions to continental Europe (McNeill 1977: 113). One thousand years later, the Black Death transformed economic and political practice, including the decline of serfdom and the manor system, changes in patterns of land tenure and inheritance, and an increase in technological innovation to mitigate the decline in the labor supply, among others (Hobhouse 1989: 15–21).

While such episodes predate the emergence of the national security state, they are useful in that they demonstrate the logic that is employed in contemporary analyses that frame disease as a threat to national security. More specifically, analytical priority is focused on widespread epidemics capable of producing disruptive effects in both sociopolitical and economic spheres that are still (at least partially) organized in accordance with the architecture of the modern state. By this, we do not mean to discount the forces of economic globalization or politico-economic regionalization. Statist patterns of organization are still relevant, however, and individual countries continue to pursue national economic and social policies.

Thus, when scholars speak of the breakdown of "national security" along this microbial dimension, they frequently frame it in terms of such disruptive effects, and with reference to these grand transformative experiences. Pirages and Runci, for example, emphasize historical episodes where the introduction of a disease into a previously unexposed population leads to the destruction of the prevailing authority structure and government (2000: 178). Additionally, Price-Smith (2002) focuses on the consequences of infectious diseases such as HIV and tuberculosis for state capacity and economic development. But it is Ostergard who best illuminates this principle through his treatment of the negative impact of HIV/AIDS in sub-Saharan Africa on military performance, recruiting, and experienced leadership (2002: 344).

What is salient with regard to Ostergard's analysis, as with Price-Smith's and others', is that he approaches it from a human security perspective – one that focuses on nonterritorially delimited, nonmilitary threats that target individuals as opposed to states, and in so doing are conceived as categorically different from traditional security threats. Yet, the framing of the critical danger posed by the pandemic is consistent with more traditional models emphasizing institutional survival and organizational capacity. In so doing, one simultaneously achieves the objective of exploring a "novel" object of analysis while garbing that analysis in tropes that have achieved longstanding legitimacy in international security.

We argue that emphasizing the threats diseases pose to the state is consistent with more conventional approaches to security. The norms and conventions of political practice – those lingering ghosts of the Cold War that whisper of "threats" and what it is we are to secure – offer a partial account of why the discourse frames the threat of disease in the way that it does. They also demonstrate how the logic of structuration within the security discourse can encompass a problem such as infection, while at the same time overlooking the more diffuse origins and consequences of chronic disease. But there are other relevant dimensions to the privileging of infectious disease over NCDs; it is to these dimensions that our reading now turns.

Infectious disease as a target for containment or eradication

While some may have the power to transform society, infectious diseases are the products of and are transmitted by identifiable organisms, and thus can be targeted for containment or eradication. NCDs, however, have historically been framed – even within the public health and medical communities – as a product of the confluence of behavioral and structural factors that problematize isolation and treatment (Marks & McQueen 2001). Thus, they are often framed in terms of management as opposed to cure (World Health Organization 1997: 4). In framing disease as a security threat, an agent that can be identified and targeted for containment and possible eradication fits far better into the security establishment's existing modes of conceptualizing and countering threat.

Although the framing of *unintended* epidemics as a security threat has emerged only in the last two decades, the security establishment has long cast a wary eye toward the dangers of biological weapons. Moreover, with contemporary political concerns with terrorism and bioweapons proliferation, the implications of disease for national security concerns are readily apparent. The potential for biological warfare, or "the deliberate spread of disease among an adversary's population, livestock, or plant life" (Center for Strategic and International Studies 2000: 36), has prompted defense doctrine seeking to counter in multiple ways the microbes responsible for such illnesses as anthrax, plague, botulism, and viral encephalitis. Eppright (1998) notes that these strategies, which include detection, avoidance, protection (in the form of vaccines, treatments, and containment), and decontamination, provide an excellent template for a broader "medical defense" that can counter a general security threat posed by unintended epidemics.

Thus, the strategies suggested to deal with infectious disease are already intrinsically linked with a previous framework for countering biological weapons: they focus on the agents themselves, not the structural conditions (poverty, malnutrition, environmental factors) that facilitate the emergence of the infectious disease. As a result, the most oft-suggested means by the security community to counter the infectious disease threat include global surveillance networks, vaccinations, and eradication campaigns, all of which are predicated upon coopting the public health institutions and infrastructure capable of preventing and/or responding to biological attacks into the national security architecture (Nunn 2002: 203).

A number of other studies (Carter 2004; Leitenberg 2003; O'Neil 2003; Wright 2002) have also pointed to biological weapons proliferation and bioterrorism in particular. In this context, the development of capabilities for containment and especially eradication are especially salient. A late 1990s hearing held by the U.S. House Committee on International Relations on the general threat of infectious disease to national security focused extensively on this last strategy. A series of questions submitted by committee members to a representative of the WHO targeted the possibilities for eradicating a number of infectious diseases, and inquired as to candidate agents, timelines, and projected investment costs (*Threat to the United States from Emerging Infectious Diseases* 1997). As Chairman Benjamin Gilman optimistically noted: "we have a world without smallpox. Let's try to imagine a world without leprosy or measles and we can do that. . . . I suggest we can do even more. We are fully capable of eliminating whole classes of diseases from our planet' (*Threat to the United States from Emerging Infectious Diseases* 1997: 3).

While Gilman's optimism is not universally shared, the example illustrates how the general problem of infectious disease lends itself to securitization: a preexisting framework designed to address biological weapons is already in place and the strategies employed there are perceived as useful for monitoring and containing potential epidemics. Thus we witness a lingering perception, demonstrated above, that the existing technologies and procedures developed for defensive bioweapons applications can and should be coopted for dealing with the more general human security threat of infection. Therein exists the tension in construing infectious disease as a "novel" security issue when the framework used to respond to it derives from traditional security thinking.

Moreover, in the military security arena, no such framework exists with regard to NCDs. Their perceived causes, as previously indicated by Marks and McQueen (2001), are framed as diffuse and largely the product of individual behavior and genetic predisposition; as a consequence, they do not lend themselves to intervention as readily as infectious agents. Thus we are able to once again witness how the structures and modes of analysis in the security discourse are able to conceptualize the threat of infection, while remaining ill-equipped to consider NCDs in similar terms.

The immediacy of infectious disease

The final reason why infectious disease is more compatible with preexisting analytical and praxiological dimensions of security is its immediacy. Put simply, infectious disease is a tremendous problem *now*, in many areas of the world. It accounts for approximately a third of all global mortality, and whereas, for example, HIV accounted for only 2% of global infectious disease deaths in 1990, by 2001 it accounted for 44% – an astounding jump in a relatively short time frame (Mathers et al. 2006). Currently, the sub-Saharan region is the most adversely affected, accounting for 69% of the global HIV burden with 23.5 million infected (UNAIDS 2012: 2). While overall HIV/AIDS-related deaths have decreased in the region by 32% since 2005 (UNAIDS 2012: 1), a number of countries continue to experience high prevalence rates, including Swaziland (25.9%), Botswana (24.8%), and Lesotho (23.6%) (UNAIDS 2010).

Because infectious diseases such as HIV pose a tremendous contemporary challenge, they are compatible with a security framework that is focused on immediate and present challenges to the state, one that is ill-equipped to deal with forward projections of a dynamic threat environment. Dalby has pointed to the difficulty that security analysts have with addressing threats outside their immediate field of vision, due to a preoccupation with control, predictability, and permanence (1992: 98). Such an overwhelming emphasis on these issues does not lend itself to internalizing awareness of threats not yet or only tangentially on the horizon. Thus, as noted by a number of scholars (Gaddis 1992/1993; Mearsheimer 1995; Waltz 1995; Wyn Jones 1999), the inability of security analysts to predict the fall of the Soviet Union and the end of the Cold War has remained a testament to the pervasive focus on the immediate threat environment that has so characterized the security establishment.

If infectious disease can be conveniently encompassed within a security framework that is designed to respond to imminent threats, NCDs have been invisible to the majority of those political scientists analyzing the political and economic dimensions and consequences of ill health. But even for those who recognize the additional burdens that NCDs place on health delivery systems, the very concept of an epidemiological transition – a shift in disease patterns away from infectious and toward noncommunicable illnesses – implies that NCDs may be deferred as a future scenario, put off until immediate problems of infectious disease can be dealt with. Bearing this in mind, infectious disease is prioritized because it is compatible, in multiple ways, with the conventional modes for conceptualizing and providing for security, and hence for countering threat: it is capable of generating sudden, dramatic, and indeed transformational change that can threaten the integrity or capacity of the state; it is linked to identifiable agents that can be targeted – microscopic, but still corporeal, entities than can be contained or killed; and finally, it is highly visible in its immediacy, all conditions that fit especially well with national security frameworks dominant during the Cold War.

NCDs, on the other hand, have neither the sudden transformative impact on social organization nor are construed as having origins in a source other than the nebulous web of lifestyle choice, genetic predisposition, and other factors. Finally, in a discipline that fetishizes the existential crisis – such as the prospect of mutually assured destruction – the slow, diffuse nature of the threat posed by NCDs simply fails to arouse the interest and sensibility of security studies. Hence, noncommunicable illnesses have remained an elusive object of political analysis in that realm.

NCDs: A human security threat?

While the major focus of this analysis is to demonstrate how the health security discourse analytically privileges infectious disease over NCDs, despite clear epidemiological trends that speak to a growing NCD burden, and to explain why this favor is consonant with a more traditional state-security paradigm, a few remarks are in order about the role of NCDs as a security threat. These remarks are preliminary, but it is possible to theorize two broad tracks by which such a threat could exist.

One would be to consider the implications of NCD morbidity and mortality on traditional security issues such as force readiness. For example, Grósz et al.(2007) report that cardiovascular disease accounts for approximately 10% of all military pilot groundings – a phenomenon that certainly has security implications. Additionally, Ruble et al. point out that while the overall proportion of U.S. Army Reservists declared medically nonavailable for deployment to Iraq in 2003 was relatively low, "most of the conditions leading to non-deployable troops were attributable to chronic disease," including asthma, diabetes, and cardiac problems (2005: 443–445). Thus, even from a conventional security perspective, it is possible to envision how NCDs can impact force availability and readiness.

The challenges posed by NCDs are not limited to force readiness, however; combat operations are increasingly affected by the presence of underlying NCDs in personnel. Sullenberger and Gentlesk (2008) point out that: "Historically, infectious diseases were the greatest medical threat to military personnel in combat operations. With advances in microbial therapy, however, *cardiovascular disease has overtaken infectious disease as the most likely cause for medical admission to a combat support hospital*" (2008: 193, emphasis added).

These examples represent only a small slice of how one *could* conceptualize NCDs as constituting a security threat. However, if the injunction of human security is to go beyond traditional concepts and models, then we must cautiously guard against falling into the trap that has led to the discursive framing of infectious disease in accordance with that traditional paradigm – despite the claim of novelty by many human security scholars. If security analysts treat NCDs in the same manner, looking narrowly at their implications for force readiness or combat operations, the risk remains of obscuring their more widespread and systemic consequences. As life expectancy continues to increase in many parts of the world, for example, populations surviving and living longer with managed (as opposed to curable) NCDs like heart disease or diabetes will find themselves confronting medical systems that must reconfigure to keep pace with these epidemiological trends, and social insurance programs that must do the same. The manner in which medical systems and infrastructure – as well as social and private insurance institutions – adjust to these pressures thus becomes a salient area of inquiry in terms of the human security implications of NCDs.

Additionally, to the extent that a general human security perspective considers the issue of macroeconomic shock relevant, then the economic consequences of NCDs are also important. For example, the WHO reports that for 2005 alone, the estimated national income losses due to cancer, stroke, and diabetes amounted to "18 billion dollars in China, 11 billion dollars in the Russian Federation, 9 billion dollars in India and 3 billion dollars in Brazil" (2005: 78). Certainly, as NCDs continue to comprise a greater share of the global morbidity and mortality burden, not only the direct costs of treatment but also concomitant income loss will be significant challenges.

The question then becomes whether such challenges to economy and society are sufficient to warrant the securitization of NCDs. Saying that they are areas of *inquiry* for human security is one thing; advocating the securitization of chronic disease is quite another. Given the global morbidity and mortality burden of NCDs, and their disproportionately heavy impact on lower income countries, we would argue for prioritizing NCDs as a global policy issue. But given the aforementioned predilection of the security discourse toward threats that are compatible with traditional assumptions and constructs, it is not reasonable to assume that that discourse can readily accommodate NCDs – perceived as they are to largely arise out of the confluence of individual choice and genetic predisposition or to be just the unfortunate consequence of aging societies.

Recently, however, there have been signs of greater prioritization of NCDs, even as they have resisted securitization. Indeed, it is the rapidly growing global burden posed by NCDs that led the United Nations to convene a High-Level Meeting on them in September 2011. The NCD Summit, like the June 2010 resolution of the General Assembly (United Nations General Assembly 2010) that called for it, attempted to extend analytical and policy primacy to the economic development burdens posed by NCDs; it also attempted to prioritize interventions (mostly behavioral) to prevent, or at least delay, NCD onset (United Nations General Assembly 2011). However, none of the documents produced by the plenary sessions and roundtables ever explicitly framed NCDs as a security threat; nor are they construed in such terms in the Political Declaration passed by the General Assembly.

This is not to say that NCDs do not pose significant challenges to economy and society, nor that these consequences could not be framed by a restructured and expanded security agenda. Rather, it suggests that their diffuse nature, perceived behavioral origins, and lack of cataclysmic, destabilizing institutional impact have thus far made them resistant to securitization, even as they have rightfully been elevated as a policy priority by institutions such as the United Nations.

Conclusion

If a seat remains at our disciplinary table for problems of illness, health security scholars must bear in mind two things. First, they must recognize that the current analytical and policy emphasis on problems of infection occludes a deserved attention paid to the challenges posed by NCDs; even though they do not strike suddenly or spectacularly, they exact not only a significant human toll but also function as a general stressor on the economy as well as public health, medical infrastructure, and social insurance. Moreover, the economic and cultural processes that facilitate the flourishing of NCD behavioral risks (e.g., poor diets, physical inactivity, and tobacco consumption) are central to the contemporary globalized environment that *is* a key element of the human security analytical agenda. This link to a contemporary globalized environment also provides a possible means to prioritize NCDs – to assess them as a consequence of structural changes in the global political economy – without having to awkwardly graft them on to the traditional security problematique. Thus, even if NCDs do not lend themselves as easily to securitization as infection, they are nonetheless the products of more than the behavioral choices and genetic predispositions of "at-risk" individuals. They are, in part, produced by the structural economic and sociopolitical conditions that allow such behaviors to flourish in the first place. And while it is beyond the scope of this analysis to delve into the particulars of such structures and processes, it is worth noting that they are manifold: transnational commodities industries pertaining to tobacco, processed foods, illicit drugs, and other consumption goods; urbanization and changing employment structures that may contribute to sedentary lifestyles; and economic reform agendas that curtail the public health expenditures necessary to respond adequately to these NCD challenges.

The second issue that human security scholars must come to terms with is that infectious disease is anything but a novel threat: rather, it enables analysts to graft "new" problems onto long-standing conceptual and praxiological security frameworks. These two blind-spots so currently rife in the literature are the twin sides, the Janus faces, of a longstanding problem of military planning: the tendency to prepare for future battle with the weapons and strategic vision of the past. Calling to mind the lessons and legacies of the past is appropriate, but arming oneself for future battle by preparing to fight the last war is not. And while the challenges posed by infectious disease may not in and of themselves constitute an obsolete war in the realm of human security, it is clear that they are no longer the only one: the times, and the trajectory of battle, are changing.

Note

1 The authors gratefully acknowledge permission of the *Journal of Human Security* to reprint material from the following article: Glasgow, S. (2008) 'Fighting the Last War: Human Security, Infection, and the Challenge of Noncommunicable Disease', *Journal of Human Security*, 4: 21–35.

References

Boutayeb, A. (2009) 'The impact of HIV/AIDS on human development in African countries', *BMC Public Health*, 9: 1–10.

Burkhalter, H. (2004) 'The politics of AIDS', *Foreign Affairs*, 83: 8–14.

Carter, A.B. (2004) 'How to counter WMD', *Foreign Affairs*, 83: 72–85.

Cartwright, F. (1972) *Disease and History*, New York: Barnes and Noble.

Center for Strategic and International Studies. (2000) *Contagion and Conflict: Health as a Global Security Challenge*, Washington, DC: Center for Strategic and International Studies.

Chow, J.C. (1996) 'Health and international security', *The Washington Quarterly*, 19: 63–77.

Crosby, A. (1986) *Ecological Imperialism: The Biological Expansion of Europe, 900–1900*, New York: Cambridge University Press.

Curley, M. and Thomas, N. (2004) 'Human security and public health in Southeast Asia: the SARS outbreak', *Australian Journal of International Affairs*, 58: 17–32.

Cusimano, M. (2000) 'Beyond sovereignty: the rise of transborder problems', in M. Cusimano (ed.) *Beyond Sovereignty: Issues for a Global Agenda*, New York: Bedford/St. Martin's.

Dalby, S. (1992) 'Security, modernity, ecology: the dilemmas of post-Cold War security discourse', *Alternatives*, 17: 95–134.

Eppright, C.T. (1998) 'The US as "hot zone": the necessity for medical defense', *Armed Forces and Society*, 25: 37–58.

Fox, W.C. (1997/1998) 'Phantom warriors: disease as a threat to US national security', *Parameters*, 27: 121–136.

Gaddis, J.L. (1992/1993) 'International relations theory and the end of the Cold War', *International Security*, 17: 5–58.

Glasgow, S. and Pirages, D. (2001) 'Microsecurity', in A.T. Price-Smith (ed.) *Plagues and Politics: Infectious Disease and International Policy*, New York: Palgrave.

Glynn, S. (2013) 'A new vaccine to protect against multiple strains of H7N9 bird flu virus', *Medical News Today*. Online. Available HTTP: <http://www.medicalnewstoday.com/articles/260467.php> (accessed 24 May 2013)

Grósz, A., Tóth, E. and Péter, I. (2007) 'A 10-year follow-up of ischemic heart disease risk factors in military pilots', *Military Medicine*, 172: 214–219.

Hobhouse, H. (1989) *Forces of Change: An Unorthodox View of History*, New York: Little, Brown and Company.

Krause, K. and Williams, M. (1997a) 'From strategy to security: foundations of critical security studies', in K. Krause and M. Williams (eds.) *Critical Security Studies: Concepts and Cases*, Minneapolis: University of Minnesota Press.

Krause, K. and Williams, M. (eds.) (1997b) *Critical Security Studies: Concepts and Cases*, Minneapolis: University of Minnesota Press.

Lee, K. and Dodgson, R. (2000) 'Globalization and cholera: implications for global governance', *Global Governance*, 6: 213–236.

Leitenberg, M. (2003) 'Distinguishing offensive from defensive biological weapons research', *Critical Reviews in Microbiology*, 29: 223–257.

Marks, J.S. and McQueen, D.V. (2001) 'Chronic diseases', in C.E. Koop (ed.) *Critical Issues in Global Health*, San Francisco: Jossey Bass.

Mathers, C.D. and Loncar, D. (2005) *Updated Projections of Global Mortality and Burden of Disease, 2002–2030: Data Sources, Methods and Results*. Evidence and Information for Policy Working Paper, Geneva: World Health Organization.

Mathers, C.D., Lopez, A.D. and Murray, C.J.L. (2006) 'The burden of disease and mortality by condition: data, methods, and results for 2001', in A.D. Lopez, C.D. Mathers, M. Ezzati, D.T. Jamison and C.J.L. Murray (eds.) *Global Burden of Disease and Risk Factors*, New York: Oxford University Press: 45–93.

McInnes, C. (2006) 'HIV/AIDS and security', *International Affairs*, 82: 315–326.

McInnes, C. and Rushton, S. (2010) 'HIV, AIDS and security: where are we now?' *International Affairs*, 86: 225–245.

McNeill, W. (1977) *Plagues and Peoples*, New York: Doubleday.

Mearsheimer, J.J. (1995) 'Back to the future: instability in Europe after the Cold War', in M. Brown et al. (eds) *The Perils of Anarchy: Contemporary Realism and International Security*, Cambridge, MA: MIT Press.

Murphy, C. (2001) 'Political consequences of the new inequality', *International Studies Quarterly*, 45: 347–356.

Myers, N. (1989) 'Environment and security', *Foreign Policy*, 74: 23–41.

Nunn, S. (2002) 'The future of public health preparedness', *Journal of Law, Medicine, and Ethics*, 30: 202–209.

O'Neil, A. (2003) 'Terrorist use of weapons of mass destruction: how serious is the threat?' *Australian Journal of International Affairs*, 57: 99–112.

Ostergard, R.L. (2002) 'Politics in the hot zone: AIDS and national security in Africa', *Third World Quarterly*, 23: 333–350.

Paris, R. (2001) 'Human security: paradigm shift or hot air?' *International Security*, 26: 87–102.

Pirages, D. and Runci, P. (2000) 'Ecological interdependence and the spread of infectious disease', in M. Cusimano (ed.) *Beyond Sovereignty: Issues for a Global Agenda*, New York: Bedford/St. Martin's.

Poku, N.K., Renwick, N. and Porto, J.G. (2007) 'Human security and development in Africa', *International Affairs*, 83: 1155–1170.

Price-Smith, A.T. (ed.) (2001) *Plagues and Politics: Infectious Disease and International Policy*, New York: Palgrave.

Price-Smith, A.T. (2002) *The Health of Nations: Infectious Disease, Environmental Change, and Their Effects on National Security and Development*, Cambridge, MA: MIT Press.

Ruble, P., Silverman, M., Harrell, J., Ringenberg, L., Fruendt, J., Walters, T., Christiansen, L., Llorente, M., Barnett, S.D., Scherb, B., Lumpkin, E. and Mitchell, D. (2005) 'Medical and physical readiness of the US Army Reserve for Noble Eagle/Enduring Freedom/Iraqi Freedom: recommendations for future mobilizations', *Military Medicine*, 170: 443–450.

Sullenberger, L. and Gentlesk, P.J. (2008) 'Cardiovascular disease in a forward military hospital during operation Iraqi freedom: a report from deployed cardiologists', *Military Medicine*, 173: 193–197.

Tan, P. (2003) 'SARS brings out Taiwan's sovereignty issue', *Asia Pacific Biotech News*, 7: 444–447.

Threat to the United States from Emerging Infectious Diseases: Hearing before the Committee on International Relations, (1997). House of Representatives, 105th Congress, 1st Sess.

Tuchman Matthews, J. (1989) 'Redefining security', *Foreign Affairs*, 68: 162–177.

UNAIDS. (2010) *Global Report: UNAIDS Report on the Global AIDS Epidemic 2010*. Online. Available HTTP: <http://www.unaids.org/globalreport/documents/20101123_GlobalReport_full_en.pdf> (accessed 5 August 2013).

UNAIDS. (2012) *Regional Fact Sheet: 2012*. Online. Available HTTP: <http://www.unaids.org/en/media/unaids/contentassets/documents/epidemiology/2012/gr2012/2012_FS_regional_ssa_en.pdf> (accessed 5 August 2013).

United Nations Development Program. (1994) *Human Development Report 1994*, New York: Oxford University Press.

United Nations General Assembly (2010, May 20) *Prevention and control of non-communicable diseases, A/RES/64/265*. Online. Available HTTP: <http://esango.un.org/event/documents/ARES64265.pdf> (accessed 14 May 2014).

United Nations General Assembly. (2011) *Political Declaration of the High-level Meeting of the General Assembly on the Prevention and Control of Non-communicable Diseases*, New York: United Nations.

Waltz, K. (1995) 'The emerging structure of international politics', in M. Brown et al. (eds) *The Perils of Anarchy: Contemporary Realism and International Security*, Cambridge, MA: MIT Press.

World Health Organization. (1997) *The World Health Report 1997*, Geneva: World Health Organization.

World Health Organization. (2005) *Preventing Chronic Diseases: A Vital Investment*, Geneva: WHO. Online. Available HTTP: <http://www.who.int/chp/chronic_disease_report/full_report.pdf?ua=1> (accessed 14 May 2014).

World Health Organization. (2011) *Global Status Report on Noncommunicable Diseases 2010*, Geneva: World Health Organization

Wright, S. (ed.) (2002) *Biological Warfare and Disarmament: New Problems/New Perspectives*. Lanham: Rowan and Littlefield.

Wyn Jones, R. (1999) *Security, Strategy, and Critical Theory*, Boulder: Lynne Rienner.

PART III

Responses

16

HEALTH, SECURITY, AND DIPLOMACY IN HISTORICAL PERSPECTIVE

Adam Kamradt-Scott

It has been periodically suggested that health-related diplomacy (now commonly described as "global health diplomacy") is a new phenomenon (Adams et al. 2008; Feldbaum & Michaud 2010). It has also been suggested that the explicit linkages drawn in recent years between national/international security and health are somehow a novel development (see Aldis 2008). What these claims fundamentally fail to appreciate, however, is that there is in fact an extraordinarily long historical association between health and security. Moreover, diplomacy has often been the tool governments have employed to address these concerns. Indeed, the association between health, security, and diplomacy dates back to well before the signing of the Treaty of Westphalia in 1648 C.E. that established the modern state system. The aim of this chapter is therefore to situate the contemporary interest in health security, and the response to health security threats, in historical context. To that end, the chapter commences by examining some of the initial diplomatic efforts to protect local, national, and international communities from threats to human health before examining more contemporary endeavors. While the narrative presented here is by no means intended to be all-inclusive, it hopefully serves to provide the reader with a fuller understanding of how health security and health diplomacy should be seen as enduring features of international politics.

Health security from antiquity to 1948

For millennia, humans suffered and died from disease with no knowledge or understanding of the aetiological cause. From time to time historians such as Herodotus and Thucydides recorded wars and conflicts where infectious disease outbreaks played a prominent role, but for centuries the microbial agents responsible for these mass casualty events were attributed to vengeful gods, meteorological conditions, spiritual and moral depravity, inclement weather, and foul-smelling mists (Porter 1999). At the same time, other threats to human health – such as lead poisoning arising from the metal's use in lining water pipes – habitually went unnoticed, even though they have also been attributed to the fall of entire civilizations (e.g. the Roman Empire) (Waldron 1973). This is not to suggest, however, that our forebears were oblivious or somehow unaware of the prevalence of disease – far from it. In fact, although their attempts to mitigate the impacts of disease were often misguided (i.e., sacrificing animals to appease gods, the practice of using leeches to bleed influenza sufferers), it is the trial and error of past generations to develop measures and systems intended to prevent, treat, or cure disease that ultimately contributed to the level of medical knowledge we now benefit from. Moreover, several historical approaches to combating disease – such as the quarantine practices of the late 14th century onwards – proved so effective that we continue to utilize equivalent methods today.

For a time, following the collapse of the Roman Empire the trend was for people to avoid settling in urban environments. By the 12th century, however, this began to reverse as people sought sanctuary and security in walled towns and cities. This move towards increased urbanization also brought with it greater risk of disease (Porter 1999; Reyerson 2000). In 1377 the city-state of Venice, which had been severely affected by the Black Death as it spread across Europe, introduced quarantine arrangements for the first time. Observing that the disease appeared to have arrived on ships carrying trade goods, the Venetian authorities mandated that all newly arriving vessels be prevented from unloading cargo or passengers for a period of 40 days, purportedly on the basis that it was the same length of time Christ and Moses had spent isolated in the desert (Delich & Carter 1994; Goodman 1952). Ships' captains were also required to report whether any passengers displayed signs or symptoms of illness – a practice that eventually gave rise to vessels carrying a "Bill of Health" that indicated whether the port of departure was free of disease (Stock 1945). These procedures initially proved controversial for the disruption they caused to trade; but given that they were instituted to protect people, and proved somewhat effective in reducing the frequency of plague outbreaks, other city-states soon followed Venice's lead, and not only ports. Genoa, Milan, Marseilles, Majorca, and Florence all introduced similar protocols to protect their respective populations. Even so, due to the rudimentary level of knowledge about disease, the measures were often applied inconsistently, which in turn added to the confusion about the nature of infectious diseases and the responses required to prevent their spread.

Aside from giving rise to quarantine practices, the Black Death also had a number of wider social implications for European society at the time. Indeed, the death of approximately a third of Europe's entire population contributed to major political, economic, and social changes, creating a new demand for labor that raised the value of the human body and encouraged greater mobility (Porter 1999). With the signing of the Treaty of Westphalia in 1648 that established the modern state system, countries became even more cognizant of the importance of the human body in providing economic and physical security to guarantee state sovereignty. Accordingly, public health campaigns coordinated by civilian authorities gained new significance as the health of the citizen became increasingly associated with the strength and security of the state.

As a result, the majority of European countries instituted some form of seaport- or land-based quarantine system to protect their populations from external disease threats while continuing to build domestic capacities to improve public health. Travelers, merchandise, even letters arriving from an area known to be affected by disease were isolated and disinfected (via fumigation), irrespective of whether they carried a health certificate from their port of departure or not. In most cases the isolation period lasted 40 days to distinguish between acute and chronic diseases, with people and goods isolated in either land-based *lazarettos* (quarantine stations) or boats anchored in the harbor. In cases where people had become infected or had been in close contact with someone who was infected, it was not uncommon for European authorities to impose an additional isolation period or "convalescence" (Cipola 1981). Moreover, these developments were not restricted to Europe. As Lee (2009) highlights, throughout the early 19th century authorities in Constantinople, Morocco, Egypt, and Persia instituted various quarantine measures overseen by councils and governing boards. Critically, however, while medical knowledge gradually improved over the years, even by the mid-19th century many questions remained unanswered over how diseases were transmitted.

In 1851 the first International Sanitary Convention was convened in Paris, France, in an attempt to formalize international quarantine arrangements. The meeting, which had been prompted by the introduction of yet another novel disease to Europe – this time in the form of cholera – brought together representatives from 12 states. Reflecting the increasingly close cooperation between economic and foreign policy interests and health, each country was represented by a medical doctor and a diplomat. Yet even though the negotiations lasted a full 6 months, including some 48 plenary sessions and multiple committee meetings, the convention failed in its objective of developing a uniform system of quarantine, principally due to ongoing differences in opinion over how cholera was transmitted (Goodman 1952; WHO 1958). Between 1851 and 1944, a further 14 international sanitary meetings were held, all primarily instigated in response to the notable impact that disease outbreaks were having on population health and international trade (Fidler 1999, 2001). At these meetings various disease control frameworks were tabled; but while agreement was reached in 1907 on the need to establish a new international organization in the form of the Office International d'Hygiène Publique (OIHP) to facilitate data collection and to alert the international community to disease outbreaks (Howard-Jones 1978), consensus on an international legal framework proved elusive.

The outbreak of hostilities in 1914 understandably hindered international cooperation on health issues for a time, but in the immediate aftermath of World War I multilateral efforts resumed with renewed vigor. Indeed, the interwar period witnessed the proliferation of international health initiatives and diplomacy (such as the Geneva Protocol of 1925 that banned the use of biological and chemical weapons in warfare) as well as prompting the creation of a new international health agency – the League of Nations' Health Organization – but this trend also had its drawbacks as institutions competed for resources and relevance (Fidler 1999; Howard-Jones 1978). The commencement of World War II again disrupted international health cooperation, but even before the conflict officially concluded in 1945 diplomats were considering the shape of the post-war world order and proposals were being advanced to create a new universal health agency that would subsume all the existing institutions into one. In 1946, an interim commission was formed to make these plans a reality, and negotiations began immediately to incorporate the various existing international and regional health organizations into a single new agency – the World Health Organization – which was officially created 2 years later on 7 April 1948. As testament to the links between health, security, and diplomacy, the constitution of the new WHO boldly declared, "The health of all peoples is fundamental to the attainment of peace and security and is dependent upon the fullest co-operation of individuals and States" (WHO 2006: 1).

Post-WWII, international security, and the new WHO

The general consensus of the international community in the immediate post-war period was that it had been led into a second major conflict largely because of the unfair conditions imposed on post-war Germany in 1919 by the Treaty of Versailles. The treaty's penalties had exacerbated already difficult social conditions, which in turn led to widespread discontent that the Nazi Party exploited to gain power. To prevent a repeat of these circumstances, it was proposed that some of the functions of government should be divested to new purpose-built international organizations. In so doing, theorists such as David Mitrany – who was a key figure in the post-war reconstruction efforts – suggested that nationalist tendencies and jealousies that led to conflict could be avoided, as people progressively saw themselves less as citizens of individual countries and more as "citizens of the world" (Mitrany 1944). Addressing social conditions, inequalities, and needs thus became an important focus of the post-WWII period, and health was initially considered one of several critically important areas.

With an explicit mandate to serve as the "directing and co-ordinating authority on international health work," the WHO was not surprisingly at the forefront of post-war developments in health and the key forum in which health diplomacy took place (WHO 2006: 1). As the first specialized agency of the United Nations, in many respects the WHO was the epitome of Mitrany's functionalist theory with the constitution outlining 22 functions or duties that can be broadly categorized into: directing and coordinating; normative; and research and technical assistance (Burci & Vignes 2004). Given the history of international health cooperation and the impact of past pandemics, the WHO was expected to play a strong role in preventing, controlling, and eradicating infectious diseases (see below). At the same time, the organization was also expected to establish new international standards and guidelines, assist member states (upon request) with any technical matter relating to human health, and provide leadership in fulfilling its primary objective of enabling the world's population to attain the "highest possible level of health." To that end, the new international health agency launched a variety of programs addressing a wide range of health issues from basic hygiene and sanitation practices, to chronic diseases such as cancer and diabetes, and maternal and child health. In addition, new expert working groups were formed to develop protocols and standards on topics ranging from the safety, quality, and efficacy of pharmaceuticals, to nutrition and food safety. Arguably, however, combatting epidemics and pandemics remained the WHO's foremost responsibility.

By 1948 and the creation of the WHO, the threat that infectious diseases posed to the international community was extremely well recognized. At the end of WWI one of the most devastating epidemiological events in recorded human history occurred in the form of the 1918 Spanish Influenza pandemic that killed approximately 40 million people worldwide. Moreover, several major epidemics of typhus, typhoid, malaria, cholera, and yellow fever had a demonstrable impact on military forces throughout WWII and at the time of the WHO's establishment were hampering the post-war reconstruction efforts (WHO 1948). The security implications of such events – both in terms of the loss of human life and the potential economic damage that ensued – were clear, and as such, the founders of the WHO imbued the organization with the constitutional authority to use any means at its disposal to combat epidemics and pandemics. In addition, one of the first tasks assigned to the WHO was to succeed where the International Sanitary Conventions of the 19th century had failed in developing a framework for international cooperation for controlling infectious diseases. In 1951 the supreme decision-making body of the organization – the World Health Assembly (WHA) – endorsed the International Sanitary Regulations (ISR) to "ensure maximum security against the international spread of diseases with a minimum interference with world traffic" (WHO 1983: 5).

Highlighting the importance attached to the new framework, and in contrast to standard international treaty-making protocols, once adopted the ISR were automatically binding on all WHO member states. The basis of the regulatory framework was an expectation that governments would report to the WHO outbreaks of six specific infectious diseases (cholera, typhoid, yellow fever, plague, smallpox, and typhus) because they were highly contagious, caused widespread human suffering, and had proven to be particularly disruptive to international trade. Information about outbreaks could also be disseminated to other countries, allowing governments to institute measures at their borders to protect their populations and (in principle) halt the disease's international spread. Thus the ISR were designed to increase both national and collective security in a context of increasing interconnectedness whilst at the same time avoiding unnecessary interference with international travel and trade.[1] Yet, despite the fact that the obligations on member states were binding and relatively straightforward, in practice, even immediately after the ISR's adoption, governments frequently failed to report outbreaks over concerns they would suffer embargos on their people and goods (Cash & Narishman 2000; Delon 1975). Compliance with the rules on reporting outbreaks of these diseases was intermittent at best, to the extent that the regulations and the need to cooperate in eradicating infectious diseases eventually came to be seen as largely irrelevant.

Further compounding this, it was not long before other, more conventional security considerations intervened, reducing the significance of health as a foreign policy/security issue. Social medicine, for example, which emphasized the need to consider how social and economic conditions adversely affected health, had been growing in prominence throughout the interwar period and arguably aligned well with many countries' post-war objectives. The rise of communism though, and the subsequent Cold War that erupted between the United States and Soviet Union, led some in the West to view the social medicine movement as a form of socialism to be resisted (Lee 2009). As the Cold War progressed, attention and resources were increasingly diverted to strengthening national defensive capabilities (e.g., military forces, nuclear arsenals, etc.) whilst advancements in science and medicine encouraged a sense of optimism that infectious disease outbreaks and other threats to human health no longer presented the hazard they once did.

Of course, not all of the impacts of the Cold War were negative. Indeed, the rivalry between the two superpowers resulted in the Soviet Union and United States donating significant resources in an effort to "outbid" each other in eradicating smallpox, which was successfully achieved in the late 1970s (Siddiqi 1995). Though contested, new targets and objectives such as "Health For All by the Year 2000" and the essential medicines list were developed; and at the same time, considerable diplomatic effort was expended in promoting initiatives such as the "Primary Health Care" movement and in developing new international treaties such as the Biological Weapons Convention (BWC) (Fidler 1999; Lee 2009; WHO 2008). Diplomacy was essential to all these efforts, not only in terms of developing the original targets and objectives but also in mitigating the worst excesses of the Cold War and other geopolitical events such as the 1978 oil crisis that threatened to divert attention from health.

The (re)discovery of health as a security issue and global health security

Two sets of circumstances in the 1980s led to closer attention once again being paid to health issues and their implications for national and international security. The first was the emergence of a new disease in the form of HIV/AIDS that demonstrated an ability to adversely affect Western countries as easily as it was affecting low-income countries. For approximately 50 years the majority of high-income, industrialized countries had enjoyed considerable success in eliminating infectious diseases as a public health menace. The development of antibiotics and vaccines from the late 1940s onwards had even led some to reportedly declare that the "war" against infectious diseases would soon be over.[2] This, combined with purpose-built infrastructure to improve water, sanitation, and healthcare, and improved food quality standards, had arguably led to a sense of complacency and immunity in many high-income countries that the emergence of HIV then shattered.

The second set of circumstances to have a notable impact was the progressive de-escalation of Cold War hostilities. By the late 1980s the Soviet Union and United States had entered into several confidence-building discussions to reduce tensions. These, combined with the Soviet policies of *glasnost* and *perestroika* aided in lessening threat perceptions amongst both countries' leaders, but also provoked those responsible for strategic planning and security to begin thinking about new potential threats (Krause & Williams 1996). From this juncture, the revision of the post-Cold War security agenda proceeded along two principal trajectories. The first was a *broadening* of the notion of security away from a narrow focus on traditional military concerns to include other issues such as ethnic conflict and environmental degradation. The second was a *deepening* of the security concept that witnessed the primacy of states as the sole referent of security being challenged, with some even advocating that the focus should shift to the individual human level (Krause & Williams 1996). Within this new analytical framework, emerging and reemerging infectious diseases (ERIDs) were actively promoted by security analysts, academics, and public health experts alike as a new "threat" that warranted significant national and international attention (McInnes & Lee 2006).

Accordingly, by the mid-1990s a new awareness had begun to emerge of the threat infectious diseases posed to the international community. In response, in 1995 the 48th WHA requested the WHO Director-General to revise and update the IHR (now renamed 'International Health Regulations') at the same time as updating the organization's policies and procedures for responding to disease outbreaks of international concern. The Assembly's decision reflected concerns over several disease-related events such as the reappearance of cholera in Latin America in 1991; the resurgence of tuberculosis and the emergence of new strains that were resistant to all known forms of treatment; a plague outbreak in 1994 in India that caused over U.S. $2 billion worth of economic damage to the national economy; and an outbreak of Ebola Hemorrhagic Fever (EHF) – one of the most lethal diseases to ever infect humans – in Zaire in 1995.

Outside the WHO, other developments elevating the connections between health and security were also underway. For example, the discovery in 1991 of stockpiles of biological and chemical weapons in the first Iraq war; the admission in 1992 that the now-former Soviet Union had maintained an offensive biological weapons program throughout the entire duration of the Cold War; and the discovery in 1995, after a terrorist attack on a Tokyo subway using sarin gas (a chemical weapon), that the cult responsible was also well-advanced in experimenting with biological weapons, added to concerns that health-related emergencies may not always be "naturally occurring" (Fidler 2005; Tucker 1999). In 1994 the United Nations Development Programme released a report advocating that human security replace state-centric notions of security and explicitly argued for the first time that "health security" should form part of this new way of viewing the world (UNDP 1994; see also Caballero-Anthony & Amul, chapter 3 in this volume). This call resonated strongly with plans to establish new multilateral institutions such as the Joint United Nations Programme on HIV/AIDS (UNAIDS) that aligned itself with academics and policy makers arguing that diseases like HIV/AIDS not only presented a direct threat to human health, national economic interests, and development, but that they also directly threatened national security interests via their impact on military forces (UNAIDS 1998). An outbreak of H5N1 avian influenza in Hong Kong in 1997 raised the specter of another influenza pandemic similar to the 1918 Spanish Flu, which many public health experts were warning was well overdue (see, for example, Webster 1994); while the discovery in 1999 of the West Nile virus in New York, and its progressive geographic spread throughout the United States, demonstrated that even highly developed countries were no longer invulnerable.

In response to these and other events, diplomacy was once again utilized to gain consensus on how best to mitigate the threats. Importantly, however, the WHO was no longer viewed as the only – or indeed the best – institution to progress this agenda. Multiple new fora began to emerge, many of which included an expanded array of global health actors (such as civil society organizations) that had often been previously excluded from official health-related diplomacy. At the same time, health began to be more directly addressed by other nonhealth intergovernmental institutions such as the World Bank and the World Trade Organization. Perhaps the most notable and explicit example of this dynamic was the United Nations Security Council's decision in 2000 to pass resolution 1308 that identified HIV/AIDS as a threat to international peace and security (Feldbaum, Lee & Patel 2006). This action, combined with the release the same year of the U.S. National Intelligence Council's report that identified emerging infectious diseases as a direct threat to U.S. domestic and foreign interests served to markedly elevate the security discourse around naturally occurring disease outbreaks (U.S. National Intelligence Council 2000). This message was again powerfully reinforced in early 2001 when, despite the fact that the IHR revision process remained incomplete, the WHO Secretariat submitted a report to the 54th WHA that outlined the need to strengthen epidemic outbreak alert and control measures to ensure "global health security" (WHO 2001). The unanimous passage of the accompanying resolution (WHA54.14) demonstrated that there was widespread in-principle diplomatic support; yet regrettably, less than 4 months later the 2001 anthrax letter attacks in the United States also revealed that the threat of terrorists using biological agents was far from hypothetical. Here again diplomacy was used as a means to strengthen countries' capacities to respond to such threats, prompting the creation of forums like the *Global Health Security Initiative* (GHSI) and the *G8 Global Partnership Against the Spread of Weapons and Materials of Mass Destruction*, as well as generating new momentum to strengthen the protocols of preexisting arrangements such as the 1972 Biological Weapons Convention (McInnes & Lee 2006; Thornton 2002).

The outbreak of a novel coronavirus named Severe Acute Respiratory Syndrome (SARS) in 2003 underscored again the need for rapid and transparent outbreak reporting. More specifically, the Chinese government's actions in attempting to purposefully conceal the existence of the disease permitted the virus to spread to Hong Kong, from where it was carried internationally to infect over 8,000 people, cause approximately 800 deaths, and result in over U.S. $30 billion in economic damage to the Asia-Pacific region alone. Indeed, the outbreak so captured international attention that new impetus was given to conclude the IHR revision process, and a series of intergovernmental meetings was convened between 2004 and 2005 to finalize the framework and the principles that would guide interstate cooperation. In May 2005, the revised IHR were endorsed by the 58th WHA ending the decade-long revision process. The new framework officially entered into force 2 years later in June 2007 to become binding on all 194 WHO member states. To coincide with the new framework's commencement, the WHO Director-General released the 2007 World Health Report that defined global public health security as "the activities required, both proactive and reactive to minimize vulnerability to acute public health events that endanger the collective health of populations living across geographical regions and international boundaries" (WHO 2007: ix).

This was a clear sign that the WHO had fully embraced the use of the concept of security to advance its public health objectives, generate greater political commitment, and secure additional resources (Davies 2008). Furthermore, it was not just the WHO that engaged in such rhetoric. By 2007 and the release of the WHO's World Health Report various institutions, political leaders and prominent officials had been talking up the threats arising from specific pathogens and using the language of security to advocate for additional resources (McInnes & Rushton 2013; Obama & Lugar 2005). This is a trend that has also continued (see, for example, David Nabarro's comments in Kamradt-Scott & McInnes 2012: S102), even to the extent whereby entities such as the G8 and the Asia-Pacific Economic Cooperation (APEC) that have traditionally concerned themselves only with economic and/or "hard" security matters were seen to convene high-level consultations, release communiqués, and commit themselves to achieving various health security-related objectives.

"New" global health diplomacy and security

In fact, at the start of the 21st century global health enjoyed unprecedented levels of investment and attention, and saw a proliferation of actors (Williams & Rushton 2011), much of which can be attributed to the (re)identification of health as a national/international security issue. Within this context, and as the above narrative attests, the overwhelming majority of diplomatic attention and resources has focused on the prevention and control of infectious diseases and the threat of bioterrorism (Chan et al. 2008; Fidler 2005). For example, following the re-emergence of the H5N1 avian influenza virus in late 2003 and the WHO's declaration that pandemic influenza was "the most feared security threat" (WHO 2007: 45), approximately U.S. $4.3 billion of new financial aid was allocated to strengthening global pandemic preparedness (UNSIC and World Bank 2010). It also prompted an intense 4-year diplomatic effort to reform the technical cooperation arrangements surrounding influenza surveillance and response to provide a more equitable distribution of benefits and pharmaceutical treatments for low-income countries (Fidler & Gostin 2011). Likewise, the UN Security Council's declaration that HIV/AIDS was a threat to international security, combined with the UN Millennium Development Goals' explicit focus on combatting HIV, brought the allocation of billions of dollars in new financial aid, in addition to the creation of new initiatives such as the Global Fund for HIV/AIDS, TB and Malaria and the President's Emergency Plan For AIDS Relief (PEPFAR). As Labonté and Gagnon (2010: 4) have observed, the significance attached to containing these two specific diseases even resulted in the French government designating two "thematic ambassadors" to coordinate regional diplomatic efforts.

Considerable diplomatic effort and financial resources have also been expended in reducing the threat of bioterrorism. Between 2001 and 2011, for instance, the U.S. government increased its civilian biodefense spending from U.S. $633 million to U.S. $6.48 billion "to improve biodefense, but also to improve preparedness and response more broadly" with a significant proportion of these funds allocated to strengthening international surveillance and response capacities (Franco & Sell 2010: 146). As noted above, the European Union, Mexico and the G7 (United States, United Kingdom, France, Germany, Canada, Italy, and Japan) established the GHSI in 2001 to combat the "threat of international biological, chemical and radio-nuclear terrorism" (GHSI 2013); while renewed emphasis and importance has been placed on the Biological Weapons Convention (BWC) negotiations as a "forum" for increased interstate dialogue, planning and preparedness (Koblentz 2012). In response to all this activity, however, some analysts have since highlighted that the effort and resources devoted to such endeavors reflects the fact that diseases like pandemic influenza threaten the interests of high-income countries, while those diseases that only threaten the poor (e.g., neglected tropical diseases) are relatively ignored (Aldis 2008; Feldbaum, Patel et al. 2006; Rushton 2011).

Taken to their logical conclusion, the implication of these criticisms – if accurate – is that the recent level of investment and diplomatic effort in global health as a consequence of its identification with national and international security concerns is in some way morally bankrupt as it only serves the interests of the most powerful. While some commentators advocate the dissolution of the health/security nexus, others have argued that low-income countries (and particularly those in Africa) need to engage more robustly in diplomatic fora and the global health security discourse to obtain more benefits and ensure their most pressing health needs are adequately addressed (Hwenda et al. 2011). Indeed, it could be argued the level of attention and resources directed towards strengthening global preparedness since 2003 reflected the perceived imminent and existential threat to the *entire* international community (see, for example, Abraham 2011), and that as such, the response could be viewed as both entirely proportional and appropriate. That health issues such as infectious diseases thereby (re)entered the realm of "high politics" was at least predictable in that, like the perceived threat of nuclear annihilation during the Cold War, the very nature of highly mobile virulent infectious diseases necessitate a rapid and robust response. Further, responding forcefully to such threats conceivably benefits everyone, not just those in wealthy nations.

Irrespective of which view is taken, what is abundantly clear is that health and security are likely to remain intimately connected now and well into the foreseeable future. Moreover, diplomacy will remain critical to addressing the challenges that emerge. For instance, the current level of global interconnectedness in travel and trade will ensure that naturally occurring disease outbreaks in one part of the world have the potential to spread internationally very quickly. Based on a long history of precedents it is likely that such incidents will cause human suffering as well as disrupt economies, perhaps even severely. Continued diplomatic engagement in forums such as (but notably, not exclusively) the World Health Assembly will thus be important to reduce the adverse impacts, strengthen surveillance and response capacities, and prevent avoidable deaths. Added to this, as some of the chapters in the rest of this volume explore, technological advances in synthetic biology and genetic manipulation are presenting a raft of new and hitherto unforeseen health-related security challenges (see Enemark, chapter 11 in this volume). Any attempt to mitigate these threats, either via elimination or regulation, without unduly hampering scientific knowledge will require diplomatic engagement at the highest level. Finally, although admittedly rare events, the intentional use of pathogens either by terrorists or state-based actors would inevitably have serious ramifications for the international community, potentially even leading to more conventional forms of conflict. Strengthening frameworks like the BWC via the improvement of confidence building and verification mechanisms thus represent important milestones – milestones that can only be reached via effective diplomatic engagement.

Given such realities, rather than withdraw from the discussion it perhaps behooves policymakers, health professionals, and academics to engage more fully with politicians in the debate surrounding health and security. If, for example, as has been suggested, the correlations drawn between health and security only serve to benefit those living in high-income countries, via diplomacy there is scope to address such an imbalance and broaden the agenda. In this respect, calls for low-income countries to withdraw from discussions conceivably do a greater disservice and do not redress the identified problems and funding gaps. Rather, what is required is an escalation of diplomatic engagement to reframe – and thereby reshape – the dialogue and ensure that those issues of particular concern to low-income countries are included and reflected in the broader health security agenda. Here, the work of Ingram (2013) and McInnes and Rushton (2013), amongst others, may offer some insights into how actors can engage in this debate.

Conclusion

As can be seen, therefore, while it may be tempting to view health security and health diplomacy as recent phenomena, in fact the historical connections between health, security, and diplomacy stretch back centuries. For much of this time, attention has quite reasonably focused on the threat that infectious diseases pose to the physical and economic interests of countries. Given the frequency of disease outbreaks and their demonstrable impact on population health – even, periodically, decimating entire civilizations – when compared to other health threats this preoccupation can perhaps be somewhat forgiven; and indeed, it has in turn provoked the emergence of various public health measures from the quarantine practices of the 14th century to the innovations in synthetic biology today, as well as prompting considerable international cooperation and collaboration in the form of purpose-built international organizations and multiple international agreements, regulatory frameworks, and standards.

For a time during the 20th century, the attention paid to health as a security issue was overshadowed by ideological enmity and the threat of nuclear annihilation, but in the mid-1990s the political landscape once again changed allowing for a broadening and deepening of the security concept. Many initially lauded this "new" development for the significant political capital and financial resources that were invested into strengthening cooperation frameworks and capacities to better respond to adverse health events. Some actors, such as the World Health Organization, embraced the change, actively seeking to fuse the language and concept of security with health to political advantage, while others have staunchly resisted the trend and openly questioned the consequences and implications. It thus remains to be seen what the long-term outcome will be of this latest (re)discovery and whether the current level of interest in the connections between health, security, and diplomacy remains intact. What is unfortunately guaranteed if history is any guide, however, is that adverse health events will continue to visit humanity and diplomacy remains one of our best tools to address them.

Notes

1 In 1969 the WHA determined that the framework warranted updating. Alongside renaming the ISR the "International Health Regulations" (IHR), two diseases – typhus and typhoid – were removed from the list of reportable diseases as, while they were still prevalent in some areas, they had been virtually eliminated by most industrialized countries. The IHR were then revised again in 1981 following the successful eradication of smallpox, reducing the overall scope of the framework to three diseases: cholera, plague, and yellow fever.

2 This statement has often been attributed to U.S. Surgeon-General Dr. William H. Stewart, but as Spellberg (2008) observes, no record of this statement has ever been located.

References

Abraham, T. (2011) 'The chronicle of a disease foretold: pandemic H1N1 and the construction of a global health security threat', *Political Studies*, 59: 797–812.

Adams, V., Novotny, T. and Leslie, H. (2008) 'Global health diplomacy', *Medical Anthropology*, 27: 315–323.

Aldis, W. (2008) 'Health security as a public health concept: a critical analysis', *Health Policy and Planning*, 23: 369–375.

Burci, G.L. and Vignes, C.H. (2004) *World Health Organization*, The Hague: Kluwer Law International.

Cash, R.A. and Narasimhan, V. (2000) 'Impediments to global surveillance of infectious diseases: consequences of open reporting in a global economy', *Bulletin of the World Health Organisation*, 78: 1358–1367.

Cipola, C.M. (1981) *Fighting Plague in Seventeenth-Century Italy*, Madison: University of Wisconsin Press.

Chan, M., Støre, J.G. and Kouchner, B. (2008) 'Foreign policy and global public health: working together towards common goals', *Bulletin of the World Health Organization*, 86: 498.

Davies, S.E. (2008) 'Securitizing infectious disease', *International Affairs*, 84: 295–313.

Delich, S. and Carter, A.O. (1994) 'Public health surveillance: historical origins, methods and evaluation', *Bulletin of the World Health Organization*, 72: 285–304.

Delon, P.J. (1975) *The International Health Regulations: A Practical Guide*, Geneva: World Health Organization.

Feldbaum, H., Lee, K. and Patel, P. (2006) 'The national security implications of HIV/AIDS', *PLoS Medicine*, 3(6): e171. doi:10.1371/journal.pmed.0030171

Feldbaum, H., Patel, P., Sondorp, E. and Lee, K. (2006) 'Global health and national security: the need for critical engagement', *Medicine, Conflict and Survival*, 22: 192–198.

Feldbaum, H. and Michaud, J. (2010) 'Health diplomacy and the enduring relevance of foreign policy interests', *PLoS Medicine*, 7(4): e1000226. doi:10.1371/journal.pmed.1000226

Fidler, D.P. (1999) *International Law and Infectious Diseases*, Oxford: Clarendon Press.

Fidler, D.P. (2001) 'The globalization of public health: the first 100 years of international health diplomacy', *Bulletin of the World Health Organization*, 79: 842–849.

Fidler, D.P. (2005) 'From international sanitary conventions to global health security: the new International Health Regulations', *Chinese Journal of International Law*, 4: 325–392.

Fidler, D.P. and Gostin, L.O. (2011) 'The WHO pandemic influenza preparedness framework: a milestone in global governance for health', *Journal of the American Medical Association*, 306: 200–201.

Franco, C. and Sell, T.K. (2010) 'Federal agency biodefense funding, FY2010-FY2011', *Biosecurity and Bioterrorism*, 8: 129–149.
Goodman, N. (1952) *International Health Organization and Their Work*, Blakiston: New York.
Global Health Security Initiative (GHSI). (2013) *GHSI Background: Overview: Global Health Security Initiative (GHSI)*. Online. Available HTTP: <http://www.ghsi.ca/english/background.asp> (accessed 3 September 2013).
Howard-Jones, N. (1978) *International Public Health between the Two World Wars – The Organizational Problems*, World Health Organization, Geneva.
Hwenda, L., Mahlathi, P. and Maphanga, T. (2011) 'Why African countries need to participate in global health security discourse', *Global Health Governance*, 4: 1–24.
Ingram, A. (2013) 'After the exception: HIV/AIDS beyond salvation and scarcity', *Antipode*, 45: 436–454.
Kamradt-Scott, A. and McInnes, C. (2012) 'The securitization of pandemic influenza: framing, security and public policy', *Global Public Health*, 7: s95-s110.
Koblentz, G.D. (2012) 'From biodefence to biosecurity: the Obama administration's strategy for countering biological threats', *International Affairs*, 88: 131–148.
Krause, K. and Williams, M.C. (1996) 'Broadening the agenda of security studies: politics and methods', *Mershon International Studies Review*, 40: 229–254.
Labonté, R. and Gagnon, M.L. (2010) 'Framing health and foreign policy: lessons for global health diplomacy', *Globalization and Health*, 6. doi:10.1186/1744-8603-6-14
Lee, K. (2009) *The World Health Organization*, New York: Routledge.
McInnes, C. and Lee, K. (2006) 'Health, security and foreign policy', *Review of International Studies*, 32: 5–23.
McInnes, C. and Rushton, S. (2013) 'HIV/AIDS and securitization theory', *European Journal of International Relations*, 19: 115–138.
Mitrany, D. (1944) *A Working Peace System: An Argument for the Functional Development of International Organization*, Oxford: Oxford University Press.
Obama, B. and Lugar, R. (2005, June 6) 'Grounding a pandemic', *The New York Times*. Online. Available HTTP: <http://www.nytimes.com/2005/06/06/opinion/06obama.html> (accessed 8 July 2013).
Porter, D. (1999) *Health, Civilization and the State: A History of Public Health from Ancient to Modern Times*, Routledge: London.
Reyerson, K. (2000) 'Medieval walled space: urban development vs. defense', in J. Tracy (ed.) *City Walls: The Urban Enceinte in Global Perspective*, Cambridge: Cambridge University Press.
Rushton, S. (2011) 'Global health security: security for whom? Security from what?', *Political Studies*, 59: 779–796.
Siddiqi, J. (1995) *World Health and World Politics: The World Health Organization and the UN System*, Columbia: University of South Carolina Press.
Spellberg, B. (2008) 'Dr. William H. Stewart: mistaken or maligned?', *Clinical Infectious Diseases*, 47: 294.
Stock, P.G. (1945) 'The International Sanitary Convention of 1944', *Proceedings of the Royal Society of Medicine*, 38: 309–316.
Thornton, C. (2002) 'The G8 global partnership against the spread of weapons and materials of mass destruction', *The Non-Proliferation Review*, 9: 135–152.
Tucker, J.B. (1999) 'Historical trends related to bioterrorism: an empirical analysis', *Emerging Infectious Diseases*, 5: 498–504.
UNAIDS. (1998) *AIDS and the Military*, Geneva: UNAIDS. Online. Available HTTP: <http://www.unaids.org/en/media/unaids/contentassets/dataimport/publications/irc-pub05/militarypv_en.pdf> (accessed 7 July 2013).
UNDP. (1994) *Human Development Report 1994: New Dimensions of Human Security*, New York: Oxford University Press.
UNSIC and World Bank. (2010) *Fifth Global Progress Report 2010: A Framework for Sustaining Momentum*, Bangkok: World Bank.
U.S. National Intelligence Council. (2000) *The Global Infectious Disease Threat and Its Implications for the United States, National Intelligence Estimate NIE99–17D*, Washington, D.C.: United States Government. Online. Available HTTP: <http://www.wilsoncenter.org/sites/default/files/Report6–3.pdf> (accessed 7 July 2013).
Waldron, H.A. (1973) 'Lead poisoning in the ancient world', *Medical History*, 17: 391–399.
Webster, R. (1994) 'While awaiting the next pandemic of influenza A', *British Medical Journal*, 309: 1179–1180.

WHO. (1948) *Official Records of the World Health Organization, No. 9: Report of the Interim Commission to the First World Health Assembly: Part I Activities*, New York: World Health Organization Interim Commission.

WHO. (1958) *The First Ten Years of the World Health Organization*, Geneva: World Health Organization.

WHO. (1983) *International Health Regulations (1969)*, 3rd annotated ed., Geneva: World Health Organization.

WHO. (2001) *WHA54.14 Global Health Security: Epidemic Alert and Response*. Online. Available HTTP: <http://apps.who.int/gb/archive/pdf_files/WHA54/ea54r14.pdf> (accessed 8 July 2013).

WHO. (2006) *Basic Documents*, 45th ed., Geneva: World Health Organization.

WHO. (2007) *The World Health Report 2007: A Safer Future: Global Public Health Security in the 21st Century*, Geneva: World Health Organization.

WHO. (2008) *The Third Ten Years of the World Health Organization: 1968–1977*, Geneva: World Health Organization.

Williams, O.D. and Rushton, S. (2011) 'Are the "good times" over? Looking to the future of global health governance', *Global Health Governance*, 5: 1–16.

17

PREPAREDNESS AND RESILIENCE IN PUBLIC HEALTH EMERGENCIES

Rebecca Katz & Erin Sorrell

> *A secure and resilient nation with the capabilities required across the whole community to prevent, protect against, mitigate, respond to, and recover from the threats and hazards that pose the greatest risk.*
>
> – *U.S. National Preparedness Goal (U.S. Department of Homeland Security 2011)*

As long as humans have existed, there have been disasters and emergencies and as long as there have been disasters and emergencies, there have been people who have responded to them and communities that have recovered and returned to normal living. Our world today, however, is presented with ever evolving threats from war, terrorism, natural disasters, and novel diseases with pandemic potential. Along with these threats is the growing knowledge that large-scale catastrophes and public health emergencies can not only affect the health of populations but also impact the economic, social, and security foundations of nations (Katz 2012).

Only in the past 10 years has the public health community endeavored to define public health emergency preparedness and identify the specific steps that nations, regions, and communities must take to identify, prepare for, respond to, contain, and recover from emergencies. In 2007, a group at the RAND Corporation offered the following definition of public health emergency preparedness:

> the capability of the public health and health care systems, communities, and individuals, to prevent, protect against, quickly respond to, and recover from health emergencies, particularly those whose scale, timing, or unpredictability threatens to overwhelm routine capabilities. Preparedness involves a coordinated and continuous process of planning and implementation that relies on measuring performance and taking corrective action.
>
> (Nelson et al. 2007: S9)

Public health preparedness includes a capable health care system, transparent communication mechanisms, human capacity, tools, and protocols in place to prevent, protect, and quickly respond to and recover from public health emergencies. Capacity does not equate to preparedness;

preparedness involves continuous assessments and improvements to plans, communication strategies, training, and gap analysis.

Events that can overwhelm routine public health capabilities fit into four basic categories: intentional or accidental release of chemical, biological, radiological, or nuclear agents; natural epidemics or pandemics; natural disasters; and man-made disasters. Most of these events, however, can be addressed through two broad functional requirements. The first is the basic function of a public health system, including event-based surveillance and broad diagnostic laboratory capacity. The second is the training, standard operating procedures, leadership, laws and regulations, and plans in place for cooperation and implementation of strategies to address the emergency (Levi et al. 2011).

Supporting the basic functions of public health systems requires developing and sustaining strong epidemiologic capacity to identify, investigate, and assess disease events in the community. This can be accomplished in part through strong biosurveillance systems, which provide a baseline assessment of routine public health events in order to quickly identify emergencies. Basic functions also include the need for community, regional, and national laboratories with diagnostic capacity that can communicate effectively with each other, move isolates safely and efficiently, and rapidly feed diagnostic results back to both the clinical and public health communities. Importantly, these basic epidemiologic and laboratory functions require a sustained, skilled workforce at the local, state, and national level.

The second broad area of public health preparedness builds on the basic core functions of the public health system to specifically address the possibility of emergencies and requires cohesive integration with a variety of sectors across all levels of government and health services. This includes the development of laws, regulations, plans, procedures, and training that bring together public health professionals, first responders, and emergency care professionals. By bringing these communities together for planning, training, and exercises, individuals and organizations begin to understand their roles and responsibilities, as well as the resources and actions available to them during crises. Each planning and training exercise is followed by an assessment in order to develop a lessons-learned approach for all sectors involved in preparing and responding to public health emergencies.

Establishing the capabilities, plans, and procedures to prepare for, respond to, contain, and recover from public health emergencies, requires an extensive range of actions. The U.S. Centers for Disease Control and Prevention defines 15 major capabilities for public health preparedness, essential for detection, response, management, and recovery from emergencies. These 15 capabilities, found in Table 17.1, span the domains of biosurveillance, incident management, information management, surge management, countermeasures and mitigation, and community resilience.

Much of public health emergency preparedness focuses on the ability to detect, assess, and respond to events. Recovery from these events – particularly at the community level, however, is also an essential function, and is captured by the term "resilience." The U.S. National Health Security Strategy defines community resilience as "the sustained ability of communities to withstand and recover- in both the short and long terms- from adversity, such as an influenza pandemic or terrorist attack" (U.S. Department of Health and Human Services 2009: 5). The U.S. Federal Emergency Management Administration (FEMA) takes a wider range approach to defining resilience. FEMA (2011) defines disaster-resilient communities as "communities that function and solve problems well under normal conditions. By matching existing capabilities to needs and working to strengthen these resources, communities are able to improve their disaster resiliency."

While determining when, in fact, a community is resilient and what that means in the wake of a disaster is complicated, community resilience has become an integral part of public health

Table 17.1 Public Health Preparedness Capabilities, as Defined by the U.S. Centers for Disease Control and Prevention

Capability	*Domain*
1. Community Preparedness	Community resilience
2. Community Recovery	Community resilience
3. Emergency Operations Coordination	Incident management
4. Emergency Public Information and Warning	Information management
5. Fatality Management	Surge management
6. Information Sharing	Information management
7. Mass care	Surge management
8. Medical Countermeasure Dispensing	Countermeasure and mitigation
9. Medical Materiel Management and Distribution	Countermeasures and mitigation
10. Medical surge	Surge management
11. Non-pharmaceutical interventions	Countermeasures and mitigation
12. Public health laboratory testing	Biosurveillance
13. Public health surveillance and epidemiologic investigation	Biosurveillance
14. Responder safety and health	Countermeasures and mitigation
15. Volunteer management	Surge management

Source: Centers for Disease Control and Prevention 2011

preparedness and overall health security. The framework for the U.S. National Health Security Strategy identifies both community resilience and basic and emergency health response systems as the cornerstones for achieving national health security (U.S. Department of Health and Human Services n.d.). These two integrated goals rely upon the nation's ability to meet 10 core objectives, all of which reiterate the six core domains identified by CDC in Table 17.1.

In this chapter, we will present how the United States has addressed public health preparedness and emergency response, focusing on the legal and regulatory framework and multisectoral approaches. We will then present the international plans and agreements pertaining to public health emergency preparedness and resilience and finish with a discussion of challenges for building prepared and resilient societies.

U.S. public health preparedness and emergency response

The US government should lead efforts to detect and conquer emerging infectious disease with the same energy it devoted to tackling polio in this country during the last century.
– The Trust for America's Health, 2008 – Germs Go Global: Why Infectious Diseases Are a Threat to America (Hamburg et al. 2008: 2)

Since the September 11, 2001, terrorist attacks and the delivery of anthrax letters in the weeks following, the United States has been faced with a series of public health emergencies, including devastating hurricanes, deadly tornados, mass shootings, and a novel influenza virus. On April 15, 2013, the United States faced another challenge when two improvised explosive devices were detonated at the Boston Marathon, killing three on site, and injuring an additional 264 individuals. Those who were injured received immediate aid, were triaged, and were rapidly transported to one of eight local hospitals. Of the patients transported to a hospital, including 20 who sustained critical injuries, all survived (Biddinger et al. 2013). The medical response was enabled in part by emergency preparedness programs, the advancement of disaster medicine, and mass casualty exercises supported by federal, state, and local entities that brought together multiple sectors to work collaboratively in the face of emergencies. One Boston emergency medicine physician said, "I cannot over-emphasize the importance of training . . . whether it's city-wide disaster drills or mock codes, the work we did together was the key to preparing us for this event" (Robert Wood Johnson Foundation 2013).

Dr. Atul Gawande, a physician at Boston's Brigham and Women's Hospital wrote, "Talking to people about that day, I was struck by how ready and almost rehearsed they [clinicians at the Boston hospitals] were for this event. A decade earlier, nothing approaching their level of collaboration and efficiency would have occurred. We have, as one colleague put it to me, replaced our pre-9/11 naïveté with post-9/11 sobriety. Where before we'd have been struck dumb with shock about such events, now we are almost calculating about them" (Gawande 2013).

The readiness of the Boston first responders and health care providers was in part the result of a decade of investments made by the federal government. Between 2003 and 2007, the Department of Homeland Security alone awarded over $27 billion in preparedness grants to state and local governments (Local, State, Tribal, and Federal Preparedness Task Force 2010). In addition, the Centers for Disease Control and Prevention Public Health Emergency Preparedness cooperative agreement has provided approximately $9 billion to public health departments since 2002, supporting a broad range of emergency preparedness activities within public health communities (Centers for Disease Control and Prevention 2013). There are a total of 62 cooperative agreements that provide support to all 50 states, four major metropolitan areas, and eight U.S. territories (Centers for Disease Control and Prevention 2013). The Hospital Preparedness Program, managed by the Department of Health and Human Services Assistant Secretary for Preparedness and Response, supports hospitals across the country, building surge capacity, safeguarding infrastructure, and supporting planning and training for large-scale emergencies. In 2012, the Hospital Preparedness Program provided over $350 million to strengthen hospital preparedness in US states and territories (U.S. Department of Health and Human Services 2012).

In addition to the federal funding supporting public health emergency preparedness and resilience, the last decade has seen a proliferation of laws, regulations, and best practices designed to support national efforts to detect, assess, respond, and recover from events. The first piece of contemporary legislation directly addressing public health emergencies was the Public Health Improvement Act of 2000. After the September 11, 2001 terrorist attacks, however, a string of new legislation was passed in rapid succession, followed by 10 years of new laws, regulations, executive orders, and directives (see Table 17.2).

In addition to these laws, regulations, and strategies, the United States developed a series of national planning documents. These national documents include event-specific planning guidance, such as pandemic flu plans that exist at both the federal and state level. The overarching national preparedness documents, however, are part of the National Response Framework (NRF), which evolved out of a Federal Response Plan, first put in place in 1992. Included in the NRF are annexes that address specific public health events. These include the Biological Incident Annex, which provides policy guidance for responding to intentional biological events. More broadly, Emergency Support Function #8 (ESF8) of the NRF addresses any public health or medical emergency, delineating which agencies are in charge of activities during an emergency. These plans are exercised regularly at all levels of government.

Table 17.2 Select Legislation and Presidential Directives in Support of Public Health Emergency Preparedness and Resilience in the United States

Year	*Legislation*	*Directive*
2000	*Public Health Improvement Act of 2000 (Public Law 106-505)*	
2001	*USA PATRIOT Act of 2001 (Public Law 107-56).*	
2002	*Public Health Security and Bioterrorism Preparedness and Response Act of 2002 (Public Law 107-188).*	
2004	*The Project Bioshield Act of 2004 (Public Law 108-276)*	*Biodefense for the 21st Century: National Security Presidential Directive 33/Homeland Security Presidential Directive 10*
2005	*Public Readiness and Emergency Preparedness (PREP) Act of 2005 (Division C of the Department of Defense Emergency Supplemental Appropriations; Public Law 109-148)*	
2006	*Pandemic and All-Hazards Preparedness Act of 2006 (Public Law 109-417).*	
2007	*Implementing Recommendations of the 9/11 Commission Act of 2007 (Public Law 110-53)*	*Medical Countermeasures Against Weapons of Mass Destruction: Homeland Security Presidential Directive 18*
		Public Health and Medical Preparedness: Homeland Security Presidential Directive 21
2009		*National Strategy for Countering Biological Threats, Presidential Policy Directive 2*
		Establishing Federal Capability for the Timely Provision of Medical Countermeasures Following a Biological Attack, Executive Order 13527
		National Health Security Strategy
2011		*National Preparedness Presidential Policy Directive 8*
2012		*National Biosurveillance Strategy*
2013	*Pandemic and All Hazards Preparedness Reauthorization Act of 2013 (Public Law 113-5)*	

Community resilience

National-level plans are essential for public health preparedness; and yet, no matter the breadth, all disasters are local. Therefore, preparedness planning and community resilience are most important at the local level. The Florida Department of Health's (2013) Community Resilience Unit provides an example of the range of activities public health departments must engage in in order to promote public health preparedness and resilience, including programs in readiness, neighborhood emergency preparedness, children's disaster preparedness, disaster behavioral response, and special needs sheltering.

This single example of community resilience programs at the state level demonstrates the wide range of activities public health departments support to promote public health preparedness and resilience. The Public Health Ready Program works with local health departments in the state to assess capacity for detecting and responding to public health emergencies. The Cities Readiness Initiative is a federal program to ensure that localities are prepared to distribute medical countermeasures, should they be needed in an emergency. The Neighborhood Emergency Preparedness Program works with small neighborhood teams to increase preparedness capacity. The Children's Preparedness Program works to ensure the safety and security of children during an emergency. The Vulnerable Populations Program ensures that all disaster planning addresses the needs of the most vulnerable members of society. Disaster Behavioral Health Teams are available to help populations deal with the emotional and physical effects of disasters. Lastly, the Special Needs Sheltering program assists localities with planning and execution of emergency shelters that can provide for special needs populations, including those requiring specific medical assistance (Florida Department of Health 2013).

These programs and others like them throughout the country are designed to provide resources and support so that communities are able to identify and outline their requirements for preparedness, plan accordingly, and work with the population, community leaders, and the private sector to ensure that they can recover as quickly as possible following an emergency. Community resilience programs, as well as local and national preparedness plans, are essential for a nation to be ready to address public health emergencies. As demonstrated in the next section, however, public health emergencies are not always contained within national borders. Our interconnected world makes global cooperation and coordination essential for the protection of populations around the world.

Going global: Public health preparedness at the international level

At the international level, public health emergency preparedness and resilience requires an array of infrastructure, capacity, and plans for approaching an event. Mounting an effective response to an international incident requires a coordinated effort that includes the same core competencies and planning on the national level, with the addition of coordination and cooperation of the incident-case country with its immediate neighbors and the global community, all while dealing with different languages, priorities, and cultures. Preparing for, detecting, responding to, and recovering from public health emergencies are ongoing concerns that must evolve to meet the needs of the international community. Infectious disease epidemics, natural disasters, terrorism, and major events like the nuclear incident in Fukushima, Japan, pose serious challenges to a nation's public health preparedness and response plans and illustrate the diverse and complex forms threats to public health can assume. No country is immune to large-scale public health emergencies. Over the past 12 years, there has been a range of global events. In the United States alone, there have been 11 major natural disasters, one large-scale man-made disaster, three major terrorist events, and five emerging infectious disease events (Lurie et al. 2013). These events, combined with major public health emergencies from around the world during this same time period, provide an indication of what we may expect in the future.

Public health emergency preparedness and response on an international scale includes detection systems, skilled and properly equipped personnel, authorities, methods, and tools to coordinate different governing bodies, which possess varying levels of preparedness, capacity, and resources in a timely manner to prevent additional events. Communication and transparency of information during an emergency enables comprehensive analysis of the event and its possible consequences, allowing for a harmonized approach by affected governments, organizations, and communities on disease control and other mitigation strategies. National resilience is crucial to reducing disease spread and morbidity and mortality internationally. The faster nations are able to rebound and again reach pre-event conditions, the less burdened the public health system will be. This resilience, however, requires mobilization of people and equipment and an understanding of the needs and challenges of affected populations. Sustainable capacity building relies on the long-term availability and commitment of effective resources. An international response relies on national and subnational capacities; capacities that require sustained commitments, in the form of budget and policy, from international organizations, national leaders, and from within the health sector.

International agreements and networks for international preparedness and response

The international public health emergency preparedness and response system is linked to every nation in the world. Many low- and lower-middle income countries carry heavy infectious disease burdens and are challenged by an ever-changing environment. Despite a new global emphasis on health systems strengthening as an agenda for preparedness to public health emergencies, many initiatives have focused on detecting and responding to a single disease at a time, creating obstacles in many countries to surveillance of and response to high-priority endemic diseases. Countries must therefore consider and prioritize initiatives internally as well as based on donor nation assistance and interests. The requirement for these nations to build capacity, sustain skilled personnel, and maintain a public health system capable of preparing for and responding to public health emergencies is a huge expectation. Therefore, it is of interest to every nation to assist and prepare for public health emergencies and do so with a global approach.

An event, whether it be a disease outbreak, natural disaster, or terrorist attack in one country can spread globally in a matter of days and become a public health event of international concern. These events require local, regional, and global preparedness, alert, and response mechanisms. Most nations, however, face substantial shortfalls in biosurveillance and early warning systems and diagnostic and forensic capacities, as well as law enforcement-public health collaboration. In particular, with an international incident and response there are legal barriers to information sharing, based on proprietary and national security interests. This can lead to possible delayed or under-reporting, inconsistent sampling and transport standards that complicate and/or delay diagnostics, and inconsistent licensing standards among nations that can delay or restrict approvals of capacities in an emergency. Complicated mechanisms for stockpiling and distribution of medical countermeasures lack central command structures that assign responsibilities. However, there are several global frameworks and entities that are at work to address these weaknesses and build capacity around the world.

International Health Regulations (2005)

The International Health Regulations (IHR) are a legally binding international agreement that govern the roles of the World Health Organization (WHO) and all of its Member States in identifying, sharing information on, and responding to any event that may constitute a public health emergency of international concern (PHEIC) that includes events of any origin, whether biological, chemical, radiological, nuclear, or other disasters. IHR (2005) (World Health Organization 2008) contributes to public health preparedness by obligating its Member States to build public health capacity. The eight core capacities identified by the WHO for IHR implementation include national legislation and policy, coordination and National Focal Point communication, surveillance, response, preparedness, risk communication, human resources and laboratories. Countries must also have capacity to detect and respond to events at Points of Entry, and to be able to address zoonotic events, food safety, chemical safety, and radiation emergencies, all categorized as "other hazards." These core capacities outline the operational meaning of each state party's obligation to detect, assess, report and respond to potential public health emergencies (World Health Organization 2011a). IHR (2005) provides a global framework for preparedness in its fifth core capacity, Preparedness.

Preparedness in the IHR (World Health Organization 2008) context includes the development of national, intermediate, and community level public health emergency response plans for relevant biological (including zoonotic and foodborne), chemical, radiological, and nuclear hazards. These plans must consider cross-cutting issues such as human resources, infrastructure, mobilizing relevant resources, transportation, and monitoring and evaluation. The legal authority required to address the PHEIC and to authorize the guidelines in the preparedness plan must also be considered. Table 17.3 outlines the checklist and indicators for meeting the preparedness capacity as provided by the WHO. Indicators in determining whether countries meet core capacity 5 include whether a multihazard national public health emergency preparedness and a response plan are developed and whether primary public health risks and resources are mapped.

Although IHR implementation has faced challenges, there has been success in developing national capacities including the development and implementation of public health emergency plans, the prioritization of these plans as an area of focus among nations, improved communication networks between and among nations, and increased reporting of potential emergencies to the WHO. The IHR framework assumes that Member States will build their core capacities on the foundations of functional health systems. Member States lacking the capacity to develop and/or implement preparedness plans can request assistance through Article 44 of the Regulations. Article 44 encourage states to share technical cooperation and assistance, logistical support, and financial resources through bilateral and multilateral channels in order to develop, strengthen, and maintain public health capacities (World Health Organization 2008).

Global Outbreak Alert and Response Network (GOARN)

The Global Outbreak Alert and Response Network (GOARN) is a network of individuals, laboratories, and organizations that link technical and human resources to rapidly identify, confirm, and respond to disease outbreaks of international concern. GOARN provides an operational framework to alert the international community to the threat of disease outbreaks and supports countries responding to outbreaks. The network specifies standards through its Guiding Principles for International Outbreak Alert and Response and operational protocols to standardize epidemiological, laboratory, clinical management, research, communications, logistics support, security, evacuation, and communications systems. The Guiding Principles focus on improving the delivery of international assistance in support of local efforts by GOARN partners. GOARN has become an essential aspect of global preparedness and response. Since its establishment GOARN and WHO have responded to over 50 global events with over 400 subject matter experts providing field support to 40+ countries. GOARN utilizes technical and operational expertise from scientific institutions in WHO Member States, medical and surveillance initiatives, regional technical and laboratory networks, United Nations organizations, and international humanitarian nongovernmental organizations (World Health Organization n.d.).

Table 17.3 Checklist and Indicators for Monitoring Progress in Meeting Capacity on Preparedness

Core Capacity 5: *Preparedness*[1]

Component of Core Capacity	*Country Level Indicator*	*Development of IHR Core Capacities by Capability Level*			
		Foundational	*Inputs and Processes*	*Outputs and Outcomes*	*Additional Achievements*
Public health emergency preparedness and response	Public health emergency preparedness and response	Assessment[2] of the ability of existing national structures and resources to meet IHR core capacity requirements (Annex 1A Paragraph 2) A national plan to meet IHR core capacity requirements has been developed (Annex 1A Paragraph 2)	National public health emergency response plans[3] developed. National public health emergency response plans in-corporate IHR related hazards and PoE Procedures, plans or strategy in place to reallocate or mobilize resources from national and sub-national levels to support action at community/primary response level	The national public health emergency response plan(s) is tested in actual emergency or simulation exercises and updated as needed Surge capacity[4] to respond to public health emergencies of national and international concern is available and tested through an exercise or actual event (e.g., as part of the response plans)	Country experiences and findings on emergency response and in mobilizing surge capacity, are documented and shared with the global community
Risk and resource management for IHR preparedness	Priority public health risks and resources are mapped	A directory of experts in health and other sectors to support a response to the IHR related hazards is available	A national risk assessment[5] has been conducted to identify potential "urgent public health events" and the most likely sources of these events National plan[7] for management and distribution[8] of stockpiles in place	National resources have been mapped[6] for IHR relevant hazards and priority risks Stockpiles (critical stock levels) for responding to priority biological, chemical, and radiological events and other emergencies are accessible	The national risk profile and resources are assessed regularly to accommodate emerging threats Contributes to international stockpiles

[1]Preparedness for development of public health emergency systems including implementation of the IHR.

[2]i.e., mapping of local infrastructure, PoE, health facilities, major equipment and supplies, staff, funding sources, experts, equipment, laboratories, institutions, NGOs to assist with community-level work, and transport.

[3]As appropriate for country context (federal vs. central government).

[4]Surge capacity: the ability of the health system to expand beyond normal operations to meet a sudden increased demand. (Health Care at the Crossroads: Strategies for Creating and Sustaining Community-wide Emergency Preparedness Strategies. JCAHO 2003).

[5]The risks are not only due to the source, but also the vulnerabilities and the absence or presence of capacities. This risk assessment should include the mapping of various hazards, disease outbreaks patterns, local disease transmission patterns, contaminated food or water sources, etc., as well as possible hazard sites or facilities which could be the source of a chemical, radiological, nuclear, or biological public health emergency of international concern, vulnerable populations.

[6]i.e., mapping of local infrastructure, PoE, health facilities, major equipment and supplies, staff, funding sources, experts, equipment, laboratories, institutions, NGOs to assist with community-level work, and transport.

[7]Could include management of international resources if needed.

[8]This includes the rotation of stocks in respect to their expiry dates, proper storage conditions for various drugs, logistic requirements, and distribution to pharmacies and hospitals around the country.

Adapted from: Checklist and Indicators for Monitoring Progress in the Development of IHR Core Capacities in States Parties (World Health Organization 2011a).

Global Early Warning System (GLEWS)

The Global Early Warning System (GLEWS) is a joint system that combines and coordinates alert and disease intelligence from the World Organisation for Animal Health (OIE), the United Nations Food and Agriculture Organization (FAO), and WHO to assist in prediction, prevention, and control of threats, including zoonoses, through sharing of information, epidemiological analysis, and joint risk assessment. Information gathered from GLEWS provides a direct feed to OIE, FAO, and WHO, providing each the ability to respond to and cover a wider range of public health emergencies. In addition to the support of WHO, FAO, and OIE, GLEWS is supported by international reference laboratories, national authorities, nongovernmental organizations, laboratory networks, and epidemiology networks. Sharing of information on disease alerts avoids unjustified duplication of efforts and combines the verification processes of OIE, FAO, and WHO, providing rapid, efficient, and coordinated assistance to affected nations (Global Early Warning System n.d.).

Global Health Security Initiative (GHSI)

The Global Health Security Initiative (GHSI) is an international partnership established in 2001 by Ministers/Secretaries of Health of Canada, France, Germany, Italy, Japan, Mexico, the United Kingdom, the United States, and the Health Commissioner of the European Union to address issues of protecting public health and security globally. GHSI calls for concerted global action to strengthen public health preparedness and response to the threat of international biological, chemical, and radio-nuclear terrorism as well as pandemic influenza. The Initiative is not intended to replace or duplicate existing organizations or networks; however, the GHSI works to protect public health and security globally, focusing on many issues related to preparedness and response including supporting WHO, information sharing and cooperation in developing plans, countermeasures, risk communication, regulatory frameworks, and surveillance and laboratory linkages. This informal partnership allows like-minded, resourced nations to align policies and actions related to public health preparedness and response on an international scale (Global Health Security Initiative n.d.). At the time this chapter went into print the U.S., in partnership with other national governments and international organizations launched the Global Health Security Agenda to promote progress on preventing epidemics, detecting biological threats, and rapidly responding to disease outbreaks, whether they be natural, intentional or accidental.

U.S. government engagement in global public health emergency preparedness and response

> *To stop disease that spreads across borders, we must strengthen our systems of public health. We will continue the fight against HIV/AIDS, tuberculosis and malaria. We will focus on the health of mothers and children. And we must come together to prevent, detect, and fight every kind of biological danger – whether it is a pandemic like H1N1, a terrorist threat, or a treatable disease. This week, America signed an agreement with the World Health Organization to affirm our commitment to meet this challenge. Today, I urge all nations to join us in meeting the WHO's goal of making sure all nations have core capacities to address public health emergencies in place by 2012. That is what our commitment to the health of our people demands.*
>
> *– President Obama's Address to the United Nations General Assembly, September 22, 2011 (The White House Office of the Press Secretary 2011)*

The United States has many strategies outlined for engaging in public health emergency preparedness and response. As the largest financial contributor to global health assistance, many U.S. government agencies include international policies and regulations, like IHR (2005), in developing their preparedness and response plans for public health emergencies. Fifteen federal agencies, plus the American Red Cross, are identified within the National Planning Frameworks (NPF) as involved in public health emergency preparedness. Of these 15 federal agencies, over half (8) are involved with supporting international engagements. These agencies include the Departments of Agriculture, Defense, Energy, Homeland Security/Federal Emergency Management Agency, State, Health and Human Services, USAID, and the Environmental Protection Agency.

However, proper preparedness and resilience plans are constantly evolving strategies that must be assessed and adapted to meet the array of public health emergency threats that may impact both domestic and international communities. The United States has evolved its policies and plans to address public health preparedness and emergency response through regulatory frameworks and multisectoral approaches with a focus on building capacity, collaboration, and outreach.

Lessons in public health emergency preparedness and resilience

Lessons learned: pH1N1 – first declared PHEIC by WHO Director-General under IHR (2005)

The 2009 H1N1 influenza A virus pandemic (pH1N1) was the first PHEIC declared by the WHO Director-General under the revised IHR (2005). In March, Mexican health officials detected a large number of influenza-like illness cases. On April 11, Mexican authorities began discussions with officials from the Pan American Health Organization (PAHO – the regional office of WHO). On April 18, the US National Focal Point (NFP) notified PAHO that southern California confirmed two cases of novel influenza, followed shortly by Mexico formally notifying PAHO of a potential PHEIC. In response, the WHO Director-General convened the IHR Emergency Committee, and declared pH1N1 a PHEIC on April 25, setting in motion WHO's pandemic influenza plan and issuing temporary recommendations under the IHR (2005) (Fischer & Katz 2010; Katz 2009). Mexico and the United States' quick response and reporting of the pH1N1 to WHO acted as an early warning allowing other countries to implement their pandemic plans and prepare for the potential spread within their borders. A majority of reports indicate that the overall response under the IHR (2005) was efficient, particularly when compared to the response to the SARS outbreak of 2002 (World Health Organization 2011b).

The 2009 pH1N1 highlights the importance of preparedness and local capacity, both in response and risk communication. Fortunately, both Mexico and the United States had these systems in place to act relatively quickly. However, as with any public health emergency there are lessons learned. The major problems identified include delays in disease confirmation from laboratory testing in Mexico and the recommendation by many countries against travel to North America, even quarantining North American citizens regardless of exposure, as well as banning pork imports from North America, even with reports that contracting pH1N1 was not associated with eating properly cooked pork (Katz 2009). WHO's Report of the Review Committee on the Functioning of the International Health Regulations (2005) and on Pandemic Influenza A (H1N1) 2009 noted that even with success in this first PHEIC, "the core national and local capacities called for in the IHR are not yet fully operational and are not now on a path to timely implementation worldwide" (World Health Organization 2011b). Had the pH1N1 initiated in a region less prepared and capable, or if the virus itself had been more lethal, the impact not only to the region of origin but to the global community could have been great. It will be critical moving forward to implement mechanisms so WHO Member States will be capable of detecting and responding to public health emergencies quickly.

Preparing for the unknown: Challenges to implementing public health emergency preparedness and resilience plans at the national and international levels

As previously mentioned in this chapter, public health emergencies require proper planning in order to minimize morbidity and mortality and to enhance community resilience. The role of globalization in the rapid dissemination of infectious disease and access to susceptible populations is indisputable. It is impossible to predict the exact nature of the next public health emergency, where it will emerge, and what its magnitude will be. Early detection, rapid public health response, and all-hazards coordination are more important now than ever. That is why it is essential that preparedness plans focus on establishing strong basic capacities that can adapt, regardless of the public health emergency. These plans must span from local to global communities, affording the best possible public health emergency preparation and enhancing the ability to respond and recover.

Progress has been achieved in both national and international preparedness and response planning in the last decade. However, more remains to be done, particularly improving linkages between domestic and global health systems and the response time in resourced countries and international organizations assisting low to middle-resourced countries. It is imperative that we expand upon lessons learned, sharing information among international networks and organizations to prevent a public health emergency in one region of the world from spreading globally in a matter of days. As we enter an era of budget cutting and global austerity, we are at risk of losing ground. Progress can be stalled if local, national, and international authorities do not invest in preparedness planning and assessment for emerging threats to public health. It will take a concerted effort and participation of all community sectors, and it will require strong political leadership.

Similar challenges exist at both the national and international levels for planning and preparedness. National preparedness plans require a trained and skilled workforce capable of development and implementation if and when that plan is necessary. This workforce includes skilled epidemiologists trained in both human and veterinary health as well as laboratory technicians capable of rapidly diagnosing cases the epidemiologist or clinical teams report. Without laboratory capacity, biosurveillance is unsuccessful. Challenges to sustaining this workforce include budgetary constraints for state and local health systems and loss of highly skilled personnel to private companies and nongovernmental organizations. As limited as the public health sectors are in many nations, the veterinary services are even worse off, leading to delays in disease detection, reporting, and risk communication in cases of zoonotic diseases. For example, only after the human cases of H7N9 were confirmed did the Ministry of Agriculture of the People's Republic of China expand and enhance surveillance in live bird markets, poultry farms, swine farms, and slaughterhouses for H7N9 surveillance. The first human cases presented in February 2013 and were confirmed as H7N9 in March, and the first avian isolates were characterized in April (World Health Organization 2013). A recent study concluded that H7N9 viruses had circulated in the animal reservoir in Asia for several months prior to their detection in humans and animals (Jonges et al. 2013). As approximately 75% of all emerging diseases are zoonotic, the need for an integrated animal/human health system is ever more important.

A major challenge for both high and low-resourced countries is the lack of available funding to support and sustain preparedness activities. Within the current fiscal environment it is difficult to justify and prioritize funding preparedness activities – including preparedness plans for natural disasters or nonendemic diseases – to a state or national budget committee. However, lack of preparation may have grave consequences. Preparedness and resilience plans must be regularly tested to assess and adapt to ever-evolving threats. In order for public health systems to advance and improve on preparedness and resilience plans there must be objectives, goals, and measurable targets. Metrics are imperative to demonstrate the value of a state and/or federal government's past, present, and future investment. Major challenges include determining what and how to measure. What constitutes a successful investment? How do you calculate return on investment? How do you measure success if being prepared means that you may not have as many public health emergencies to respond to or that you do not have to request assistance outside of your local community or country because you have effective rapid response teams? How do you measure something you were able to prevent or contain? In these instances success lies in not having to activate response and resilience plans. This type of success is very hard to quantify in budget negotiations at the regional, national and international level. Yet, public health professionals need to be ready to make a business case for preparedness and reliance planning and be able to deftly describe the costs and benefits, both in monetary figures and in lives saved.

Public health emergencies impact many entities; political will and support outside the health and veterinary sectors including agriculture, tourism, trade, finance, law enforcement, and defense is critical. As we have seen over the last decade, every nation is susceptible to multiple events capable of leading to public health emergencies. We have also seen that some of the most low-resourced nations have the most resilient populations. Not every country will have the resources available to develop, test, and refine all-hazards preparedness plans that engage multiple sectors, yet all nations must act. The scope of planning and exercising can vary, but it is necessary for every country and community to develop basic planning documents and outreach. At the end of the day, every citizen has a responsibility to be prepared. It is only then that lives will be saved, economic burdens decreased, and life returned to normal following public health emergencies.

References

Biddinger, P.D., Baggish, A., Harrington, L., d'Hemecourt, P., Hooley, J., Jones, J., Kue, R., Troyanos, C. and Dyer, K.S. (2013) 'Be prepared – the Boston Marathon and mass-casualty events', *New England Journal of Medicine*, 368: 1958–1960.

Centers for Disease Control and Prevention. (2011) *Public Health Preparedness Capabilities: National Standards for State and Local Planning*. Online. Available HTTP: <http://www.cdc.gov/phpr/capabilities/dslr_capabilities_july.pdf> (accessed 30 July 2013).

Centers for Disease Control and Prevention. (2013) *Funding and Guidance for State and Local Public Health Departments*. Onlinc. Available HTTP: <http://www.cdc.gov/phpr/coopagreement.htm> (accessed 30 April 2013).

Federal Emergency Management Agency (FEMA). (2011) *A Whole Community Approach to Emergency Management: Principles, Themes, and Pathways for Action*. Online. Available HTTP: <https://www.fema.gov/media-library/assets/documents/23781> (accessed 14 May 2014).

Fischer, J. and Katz, R. (2010) "The revised International Health Regulations: a framework for global pandemic response", *Global Health Governance*, 3(2).

Florida Department of Health. (2013) *Community Resilience*. Online. Available HTTP: <http://www.doh.state.fl.us/demo/BPR/community.htm> (accessed 26 July 2013).

Gawande, A. (2013) 'Why Boston's hospitals were ready', *The New Yorker*. Online. Available HTTP: <http://www.newyorker.com/online/blogs/newsdesk/2013/04/why-bostons-hospitals-were-ready.html> (accessed 25 July 2013).

Global Early Warning System. (n.d.) *About Glews*. Online. Available HTTP: <http://www.glews.net/about-glews/> (accessed 30 July 2013).

Global Health Security Initiative. (n.d.) *Global Health Security Initiative*. Online. Available HTTP: <http://www.ghsi.ca> (accessed 26 July 2013).

Hamburg, M.A., Levi, J., Elliot, K. and Williams, L. (2008) *Germs Go Global: Why Emerging Infectious Diseases Are a Threat to America*, Trust for America's Health. Online. Available HTTP: <http://healthyamericans.org/assets/files/GermsGoGlobal.pdf> (accessed 30 July 2013).

JCAHO (Joint Commission on Accreditation of Healthcare Organizations). (2003) *Health Care at the Crossroads: Strategies for Creating and Sustaining Community-Wide Emergency Preparedness Systems*. Online. Available HTTP: <http://www.jointcommission.org/assets/1/18/emergency_preparedness.pdf> (accessed 14 May 2014).

Jonges, M., Meijer, A., Fouchier, R.A., Koch, G., Li, J., Pan, J.C., Chen, H., Shu, Y.L. and Koopmans, M.P. (2013) 'Guiding outbreak management by the use of influenza A(H7Nx) virus sequence analysis', *Eurosurveillance*, 18(16).

Katz, R. (2009) 'Use of revised International Health Regulations during influenza A (H1N1) epidemic, 2009', *Emerging Infectious Diseases*, 15: 1165–1170.

Katz, R. (2012) 'Public health preparedness policy', In J.B. Teitelbaum and S.E. Wilensky (eds.) *Essentials of Health Policy and Law*, 2nd ed. Sudbury, MA: Jones and Bartlett Learning: 231–248.

Levi, J., Segal, L.M., Lieberman, D.A. and St. Laurent, R. (2011) *Ready or Not? Protecting the Public's Health from Diseases, Disasters, and Bioterrorism*, Trust for America's Health. Online. Available HTTP: <http://www.tfah.org/assets/files/TFAH2011ReadyorNot_09.pdf> (accessed 25 July 2013).

Local, State, Tribal, and Federal Preparedness Task Force. (2010) *Perspective on Preparedness: Taking Stock Since 9/11*. Online. Available HTTP: <http://www.calema.ca.gov/PlanningandPreparedness/Pages/Documents%20and%20Publications.aspx> (accessed 25 July 2013).

Lurie, N., Manolio, T., Patterson, A.P., Collins, F. and Frieden, T. (2013) 'Research as a part of public health emergency response', *New England Journal of Medicine*, 368: 1251–1255.

Nelson, C., Lurie, N., Wasserman, J. and Zakowski, S. (2007) 'Conceptualizing and defining public health emergency preparedness', *American Journal of Public Health*, 97: S9-S11.

Robert Wood Johnson Foundation. (2013) *Lessons from Boston: Providing Trauma Care. An RWJF Clinical Scholar shares lessons from the Brigham and Women's ER on the day of the Boston Marathon bombing*. Online. Available HTTP: <http://www.rwjf.org/en/about-rwjf/newsroom/newsroom-content/2013/04/lessons-from-boston--providing-trauma-care.html> (accessed 25 July 2013).

U.S. Department of Health and Human Services. (n.d.) *Framework for the NHSS*. Online. Available HTTP: <http://www.phe.gov/Preparedness/planning/authority/nhss/Pages/framework.aspx> (accessed 25 July 2013).

U.S. Department of Health and Human Services. (2009) *National Health Security Strategy of the United States of America*. Online. Available HTTP: <http://www.phe.gov/preparedness/planning/authority/nhss/strategy/documents/nhss-final.pdf> (accessed 25 July 2013).

U.S. Department of Health and Human Services. (2012) *Hospital Preparedness Program (HPP) Budget Period 1 (Fiscal Year 2012) Funding*. Online. Available HTTP: <http://www.phe.gov/Preparedness/planning/hpp/Documents/hpp-2012-funding.pdf> (accessed 26 July 2013).

U.S. Department of Homeland Security. (2011) *National Preparedness Goal*. Online. Available HTTP: <http://www.fema.gov/national-preparedness-goal> (accessed 14 May 2014).

The White House Office of the Press Secretary. (2011) *Remarks by President Obama in Address to the United Nations General Assembly*. Online. Available HTTP: <http://www.whitehouse.gov/the-press-office/2011/09/21/remarks-president-obama-address-united-nations-general-assembly> (accessed 30 July 2013).

World Health Organization. (n.d.) *Global Outbreak Alert and Response Network*. Online. Available HTTP: <http://www.who.int/csr/outbreaknetwork> (accessed 26 July 2013).

World Health Organization. (2008) *International Health Regulations (2005)*, 2nd ed. Geneva: World Health Organization, 30. Online. Available HTTP: <http://www.who.int/ihr/IHR_2005_en.pdf> (accessed 26 July 2013).

World Health Organization. (2011a) *IHR Core Capacity Monitoring Framework: Checklist and Indicators for Monitoring Progress in the Development of IHR Core Capacities in States Parties*. Online. Available HTTP: <http://www.who.int/ihr/IHR_Monitoring_Framework_Checklist_and_Indicators.pdf> (accessed 26 July 2013).

World Health Organization. (2011b) *Report of the Review Committee on the Functioning of the International Health Regulations (2005) in Relation to Pandemic (H1N1) 2009*. Online. Available HTTP: <http://apps.who.int/gb/ebwha/pdf_files/WHA64/A64_10-en.pdf> (accessed 26 July 2013).

World Health Organization. (2013) *Overview of the Emergence and Characteristics of the Avian Influenza A(H7N9) Virus*. Online. Available HTTP: <http://www.who.int/influenza/human_animal_interface/influenza_h7n9/WHO_H7N9_review_31May13.pdf> (accessed 26 July 2013).

18

MEDICAL COUNTERMEASURES AND SECURITY

Kendall Hoyt

One week after terrorists crashed passenger jets into the World Trade Center and the Pentagon, two senators and several news media outlets began to receive deadly anthrax letters instructing them to "Take Penacilin Now" (*sic*). What if these letters had contained no warning? What if this strain of anthrax had been resistant to antibiotics? What if anthrax had been aerosolized in a subway or from a plane over New York City? What if, instead of anthrax, terrorists unleashed a highly contagious disease? These were the questions that ran through the minds of U.S. health officials, emergency planners, and politicians in the fall of 2001.

George W. Bush announced in his 2002 State of the Union address that the United States needed new vaccines 'to fight anthrax and other diseases." Civilian biodefense initiatives boomed in the following months. While the overall budget to fight terrorism doubled after 2001, the bioterrorism budget quadrupled (Office of Management and Budget 2003).[1] Referring to White House budget requests, President Bush explained, "It's money that we've got to spend. It's money that will enable me to say we're doing everything we can do to protect America" (Connolly 2002: A03).

This "fund first, ask questions later" approach to civilian biodefense led to many missteps and midcourse corrections. The Bipartisan Weapons of Mass Destruction Research Center observed that "since 2001, the U.S. government has spent $65 billion on biodefense, and yet it has done so without an end to end strategic assessment of the nation's bio response capabilities" (The Bipartisan WMD Terrorism Research Center 2011). In the previous year, the Center awarded the nation an F for its ability to "rapidly recognize, respond, and recover from a biological attack." In particular, they noted the "lack of priority given to development of medical countermeasures-the vaccines and medicines that would be required to mitigate the consequences of an attack" (The Bipartisan WMD Terrorism Research Center 2011).

Health and Human Services (HHS) Secretary Kathleen Sibelius had, in fact, ordered a comprehensive review of the federal medical countermeasure enterprise in 2010. This review acknowledged that, "filling the discovery and developmental pipeline with needed product candidates . . . has been slower and more costly than anticipated' (HHS 2010: 5) Even so, Nicole Lurie, HHS Assistant Secretary for Preparedness and Response, maintained that the enterprise had added 11 products to the emergency stockpile with 80 more in the development pipeline (Schneidmiller 2013). While 11 products sounds like progress, on closer inspection, HHS has struggled to procure novel medical countermeasures (MCMs) that fill critical gaps in preparedness.

Building the U.S. strategic national stockpile

The Centers for Disease Control (CDC) began to stockpile items in 1999 as part of an HHS Bioterrorism Initiative to build public health preparedness for biological and chemical attacks on U.S. soil. This stockpile is designed to provide therapeutics, vaccines, and medical equipment anywhere in the United States within 12 hours of a request. The CDC deployed its first push-pack to New York City on September 11, 2001, and its second in response to the anthrax letter attacks. Funding for the stockpile, renamed the Strategic National Stockpile (SNS) in 2003, increased dramatically after these events and the newly formed Department of Homeland Security (DHS) assumed joint responsibility for the stockpile with the CDC.

Initially, the CDC sought countermeasures for anthrax, smallpox, plague, tularemia, botulism, and viral hemorrhagic fevers like Ebola. They prioritized these so-called category A agents because they can be easily disseminated or transmitted from person-to-person, have a high mortality rate, are likely to cause high levels of public panic, and/or require "special action" for public health preparedness.

In 2003, the CDC and DHS made a list of new MCMs that they would like to add to the stockpile. This list prioritized:

1 A next-generation smallpox vaccine that incorporates the modified vaccinia Ankara (MVA) strain for higher risk populations with compromised immune systems or skin conditions.
2 A recombinant protective antigen (rPA) anthrax vaccine that would require fewer doses per person and may serve as an effective post exposure prophylactic treatment.
3 The production of more botulinum antitoxin.
4 A botulism vaccine.
5 A monoclonal antibody botulism therapeutic.
6 A plague vaccine.
7 An Ebola vaccine.

Over the next 10 years, DHS identified over a dozen additional material threats to national security for which it sought countermeasures. These included cyanide, emerging infectious diseases such as pandemic flu, gram-negative pathogens (such as glanders, meliodosis, and typhus), multidrug resistant anthrax, nerve agents (such as sarin), and exposure to radiological and nuclear events.

Since the CDC initiated a stockpiling program in 1999, the FDA has licensed just one new vaccine against Category A threats, an updated version of the smallpox vaccine using cell culture techniques (ACAM 2000). In 2010, Bavarian Nordic began to deliver a MVA smallpox vaccine to the stockpile and in 2013, Siga Technologies began to produce a smallpox antiviral (Arestvyr) as well. While the FDA has not licensed these countermeasures, they have authorized them for emergency use.

A fast-acting, next-generation anthrax vaccine has been a top priority for the U.S. government since the first Gulf War, but 20 years and a billion dollars later, this vaccine remains elusive. Soon after the 2001 anthrax attacks, the FDA relicensed a 1970s version of the anthrax vaccine. This vaccine is ill suited to emergency use since it requires five shots over an 18-month period to build immunity. It also requires annual boosters to retain immunity. Two anthrax antitoxins, a botulinum antitoxin, and some radionuclide chelators have been added to the stockpile, but no other novel vaccines or therapeutics have been approved for the remaining category A threats.[2]

The U.S. MCM development enterprise struggles to overcome poor market incentives, an uncertain regulatory path for novel countermeasures, decentralized mission authority, and disjointed project management. More disturbingly, the SNS offers little protection against surprise attacks with engineered bioweapons, emerging infectious diseases, or fast moving epidemics such as SARS. MCM development programs are still searching for an effective way to redirect their efforts from a fixed-defense stockpiling strategy to more adaptive methods that will allow them to respond to these scenarios. To date, these strategies seek to incorporate broad-spectrum therapeutics and rapid MCM development capabilities.

Early efforts to mobilize research and development for biodefense

After the 2001 attacks, the U.S. government had a unique window of opportunity to enlist the help of large, experienced drug development firms. Concerned that the next attack could involve smallpox, pharmaceutical executives rushed to Washington to offer their assistance. Companies such as Merck, GlaxoSmithKline, American Home Products, and Baxter International submitted proposals to produce a smallpox vaccine (Agovino 2001). Gail Cassell, a vice president at Eli Lilly and Company, was among those who was determined to help the government obtain a smallpox drug. She "tore through paperwork that normally would have taken months, put samples of the drugs on a plane and flew them to government laboratories in the Washington area to be tested against smallpox" (Gillis 2001). Should one of those drugs prove effective, Cassell announced, Lilly would initiate a crash development program: "we are absolutely willing to do that. I would emphasize that we would do it for the good of the country, not for the good of Lilly" (Gillis 2001).

Unfortunately, no one federal agency or administrator seized this moment to create a central clearinghouse for these extramural research and development (R&D) initiatives. Private sector enthusiasm soon turned to frustration. Executives testified that they had workable proposals but that they did not know where to send them or to whom they should talk. Worse still, they noted that the agencies themselves often did not know where to direct their calls (House Government Reform Committee, Veterans Affairs, and International Relations Subcommittee 2001).

The majority of biodefense R&D is scattered among a collection of programs within HHS and the Department of Defense (DOD). In addition to these programs, the CDC, the Department of Energy (DOE), the Environmental Protection Agency (EPA), the Food and Drug Administration (FDA), and DHS also own pieces of the biodefense research agenda. R&D efforts in each of these departments and agencies reflected a wide range of constituent interests and agency missions rather than a nationally coordinated program.

As months wore on with no further attacks, the public's sense of urgency subsided and it became increasingly difficult for HHS to persuade large biopharmaceutical companies to develop MCMs. Given the high cost and risk of development, companies prefer to invest in drug and vaccine candidates with large, well-defined markets and a clear regulatory path. Many biodefense therapeutics, and nearly all biodefense vaccines, offer neither. Unlike seasonal flu or pediatric vaccines, for example, biodefense vaccines have irregular, low volume demand from a single buyer – the government. Since they are manufactured for a stockpile, they have limited production runs, which raises their unit cost of production. As the only buyer, the government also has an unfair advantage in negotiating prices.

Licensure is not straightforward either. It is difficult to conduct human efficacy trials for novel MCMs because they counteract uncommon pathogens. To circumvent this problem, the FDA introduced the animal efficacy rule in 2002, which allows companies to submit evidence from animal studies in lieu of human efficacy data. While this rule removed a practical hurdle, it introduced a new scientific and regulatory challenge to find appropriate animal models for human diseases. To date, the FDA has approved only one novel product using the animal rule, a monoclonal antibody to treat inhalational anthrax (National Research Council 2011).[3]

Recognizing these market and regulatory challenges, the Bush Administration initiated several push and pull programs to incentivize new MCM development. The primary beneficiary of programs to push early stage research through the development pipeline was the National Institute of Allergy and Infectious Diseases (NIAID), a division of the National Institutes of Health (NIH). In 2003, the NIAID received $1.7 billion for biodefense research. According to NIAID director, Anthony Fauci, this was "the biggest single-year request for any discipline or institute in the history of the NIH" (Miller 2002). The institute continued to receive comparable sums in subsequent years, allowing the NIH to overtake the DOD as the federal lead for biodefense R&D.

While this was a thrilling windfall for any institute director, Vannevar Bush, former director of the Office of Scientific Research and Development during World War II and a seasoned veteran of federal R&D mobilization efforts, would have cautioned against any approach that involved too much money and too little coordination. As federal R&D budgets swelled during the Cold War, Bush warned that, "If the country pours enough money into research, it will inevitably support the trivial and the mediocre. The supply of scientific manpower is not unlimited" (Hotelling 1963: 1623). The key to success, he argued, lies not in the sum of money, but in "the form of the organization" and the ability of "military officers, scientists, and engineers [to work] together effectively in partnership" (Bush 1970: 68).

Historically, vaccine development projects were most effective when they took advantage of the type of collaboration that Bush described. More specifically, their projects employed integrated research practices. Integrated research is managed from the top down, coordinated across disciplines and developmental phases, and conducted in an environment that facilitates the free exchange of knowledge (Hoyt 2012). Integrated research practices, which had their roots in prewar industrial settings like Bell Labs and General Electric, blossomed during World War II when the military, industry, and academia joined forces to mobilize research and development. These practices were honed during the war and carried over into many mid-century vaccine development projects. When Tommy Francis developed the first flu vaccines during World War II, he employed integrated research practices. So too did Jonas Salk when he developed the first polio vaccines and Maurice Hilleman when he developed a number of new vaccines, including the adenovirus, measles, mumps, rubella, meningococcal meningitis, and hepatitis B vaccines.[4]

Typically, one project director had end-to-end responsibility for individual vaccine candidates. It was not unusual for a director to follow a candidate as it traveled between the field, the lab, the clinic, and the manufacturing facility. Project directors ensured that their development teams also understood the upstream and downstream requirements of each product. At the Walter Reed Army Institute of Research (WRAIR), for example, epidemiologists worked closely with lab scientists, and lab scientists worked closely with clinicians, manufacturers, and regulators. Integrating R&D in this fashion facilitated lab-to-industry hand offs because it allowed project directors to design products that could be manufactured and evaluated more easily, enhanced situational awareness, expedited go/no-go decisions, and facilitated technology transfer.

NIH intramural and extramural grant programs excel at generating new knowledge in a bottom-up fashion through investigator-initiated research, but they do not support the type of integrated research practices that promote product development. NIH-funded investigators often operate independently until it is time to hand-off a project to the next disciplinary silo or developmental phase. Because they reap professional rewards for publications (not products) they tend to be highly specialized and poorly coordinated, resulting in methods and technologies that do not always transfer well from one group to another. Over the years, awkward hand offs have contributed to the rising cost, time, and failure rate of drug and vaccine development. Since the NIAID took the lead for biodefense research in 2003 numerous publications, but few licensed MCMs, have emerged from these research initiatives.

In addition to funds to push new biodefense vaccines through the research phase, in 2004, the Bush Administration initiated a $5.6 billion program to pull MCMs through commercial development. This program – Project BioShield – guaranteed funding for a 10-year period to procure seven MCMs to fight five pathogens; it authorized the FDA to make countermeasures under development available to the public in an emergency; and it bolstered NIH resources to hire personnel, expedite peer review, and procure laboratory materials on short notice (White House Press Office 2003).

BioShield was intended to encourage pharmaceutical companies to assume the risk of development in exchange for a government guarantee to purchase licensed (or soon to be licensed) MCMs for the SNS. This entrepreneurial model, as originally conceived, carried many advantages. First, it would provide a strong market guarantee that circumvented the appropriations process by allowing for direct payments from the U.S. treasury. This would allow companies to calculate their investment risk in a manner consistent with traditional business practices. Second, it offered a hands-off approach that allowed industry to pursue their own development strategy. And third, it didn't put the government in a position of trying to choose winners. Congress objected, however, to the concept of an "indefinite mandatory authorization" to fund this initiative because it would bypass the annual appropriations process. They opted instead for a Special Reserve Fund that would provide $5.6 billion over 10 years to procure medical countermeasures for the SNS (Kadlec 2010: 103).

In practice, $5.6 billion was inadequate to pull seven MCMs onto the market. According to the Congressional Budget Office, it would cost approximately $8.1 billion to develop seven MCMs over 10 years, a 45% increase over the original White House estimate (Congressional Budget Office 2003). Subsequent estimates have been far higher, citing $14 billion through FY 2015 to pull eight MCMs through licensure with a 90% chance of success (Matheny et al. 2008: 981).[5]

These rising estimates reflect the high failure rate of drug development and account for the need to fund multiple companies simultaneously to assure one successful outcome. Failure rates are not an independent variable, however. The relatively small size of BioShield awards invites a higher failure rate because they fail to attract larger companies with a strong record for new drug and vaccine approvals.

Originally, legislators did not think that they would have to pay premium prices to engage competent manufacturers. The 2004 BioShield legislation was designed to lure these manufacturers with market guarantees, tax incentives, liability protections, accelerated regulatory review, and NIH-subsidized early-stage R&D. Because the government is in a position to reduce the cost and risk of MCM development in this way, officials assumed they could negotiate lower contract prices.

To meet the manufacturing requirements of biodefense contracts, however, large companies would have to displace product lines with viable commercial markets or build new facilities. To date, these firms have been unwilling to do either because the opportunity costs are too high. BioShield margins are fixed at 10% by Federal Acquisition Regulations and sales volumes are low because MCMs are purchased for a stockpile. Firms like Merck and Sanofi-Aventis command margins closer to 26% to 31% for commercial drugs with high sales volumes (Smith et al. 2003: 197).

Instead, BioShield contracts appeal to small, inexperienced biotechnology companies with lower opportunity costs. While smaller companies carry lower upfront costs to the government, they generate hidden costs and inefficiencies. HHS discovered the challenges of working with smaller biotechnology companies in 2004 when they awarded VaxGen (a small California-based company) $877 million to deliver a next-generation recombinant protective antigen (rPA) anthrax vaccine. This contract required VaxGen to bring a Phase II candidate through licensure within two years. When VaxGen ran into technical difficulties for which it had no in-house expertise, it had to outsource the work. After a 2-year extension, VaxGen was unable to resolve a technical problem with the vaccine. Under pressure from lobbyists working for VaxGen's rival – Emergent BioSolutions – HHS canceled the contract, setting back the target date for a next-generation anthrax vaccine indefinitely (Lilly 2010). HHS underestimated the complexity of vaccine development and overestimated the late stage development and manufacturing capabilities of small companies.

HHS's protracted struggle to develop a next-generation anthrax vaccine illustrates how MCMs, and vaccines in particular, can fall into the "valley of death." This term refers to the frequency with which promising candidates fail in late stage development, less for scientific or technical reasons than for financial or managerial ones. Early stage funding is well-supported through the NIH or small business innovation research (SBIR) grants and end-stage procurement grants are available through BioShield. Late-stage development has little support, however. This funding gap occurs at the most expensive and risky phase of development. Approximately 60% to 75% of the overall development costs are incurred during clinical trials and the start-up of the manufacturing phase (Monath 2000). Only 20% of all drugs entering Phase 1 clinical trials are ever approved for commercial distribution (Monath 2000). Small biotechnology companies rarely have the financial resources, expertise, or infrastructure to overcome these late-stage development and manufacturing challenges on their own. They often have to contract out for these capabilities to fill government orders. Furthermore, few of these companies have much experience with the FDA and they require significant assistance to navigate the regulatory process.

Midcourse corrections: First wave

In an effort to bridge the valley of death, Congress passed the Pandemic and All-Hazards Preparedness Act (PAHPA: PL 109–417) in 2006. This legislation created the Biomedical Advanced Research and Development Authority (BARDA) to provide managerial oversight and financial support with milestone grants for mid- and late-stage MCM development activities. This legislation also created the Public Health Emergency Medical Countermeasures Enterprise (PHEMCE) Governance Board to serve as an interagency body to coordinate and communicate MCM priorities and the National Biodefense Science Board (NBSB) to provide outside expert advice. In support of this legislation, congress removed $884 million from BioShield's Special Reserve Fund in 2009, placing $304 million into NIAID research programs and $580 million with BARDA to manage late-stage development programs and to award milestone grants (Gottron 2010: 9).

Milestone grants allowed BARDA to award up to 50% of the final contract when companies achieve prespecified development objectives. These grants offered an immediate solution to some of the challenges facing small biotechnology companies trying to cross the valley of death. Ultimately, however, they compounded the problem. These transfers further undercut BioShield's original entrepreneurial appeal by weakening its market guarantee and by shifting managerial responsibilities onto BARDA to coordinate the late stage development, manufacturing, and licensure activities of smaller companies.

Vaccine development is not a straightforward engineering and manufacturing problem. Unlike building a new tank or consumer electronic device, it does not lend itself to a modular development approach because the type of knowledge required can be "sticky." Sticky information is "costly to acquire, transfer and use in a new location" (von Hippel 1994: 429). The procedures required to grow a pathogen in one lab, for example, may not work well in another lab, or at a different volume. This information can be tacit and therefore difficult to reduce to a "blueprint." It is difficult for a third party (such as BARDA) to delegate and coordinate vaccine development in a piecemeal fashion. Outsourcing through arm's-length contracts – with the government as an intermediary – disrupts the integrated R&D processes and working relationships that permit sticky information to transfer effectively from one development phase to the next (Hoyt 2012).

BioShield suffers from an additional problem that is more fundamental than its struggle to attract competent manufacturers or to coordinate product development. BioShield is predicated on a fixed-defense stockpiling strategy. With approximately 50 pathogens and toxins already on the CDC's select agent list, and new pathogens emerging at a regular rate, the sheer number of possible threats will outstrip our drug development resources. Vaccines and drugs can take over a decade to develop, costs range from U.S. $800 million to U.S. $1 billion per licensed countermeasure, and 80% of the candidates that make it into clinical trials fail (DiMasi et al. 2003; Gronvall et al. 2013: 32; Monath 2000).

The time, cost, and risk of development is daunting, but predicting which MCMs will be needed is harder still. Biothreat predictions are notoriously unreliable. Military and civilian populations were not adequately prepared for anthrax in 2001, SARS in 2003, or H1N1 in 2009. Conversely, large-scale immunization programs against botulinum toxin in World War II, swine flu in 1976, anthrax prior to the first Gulf War, and smallpox prior to the second Gulf War, all addressed threats that failed to materialize (Hoyt 2006: A23).

Given the multitude of existing threats and the difficulty of predicting future threats, stockpiling should target a small set of high-risk pathogens such as smallpox and anthrax. Over time, new evidence or advances may argue for the addition or exclusion of MCMs, but it will be prudent to keep this set small. It makes more sense to invest our limited resources in building the research tools and infrastructure that will allow us to catch up to novel threats, even if it is not possible to predict them.

To build this capability, HHS needs to scrutinize every step – from the moment it identifies a new pathogen to the moment it administers a safe and effective countermeasure – for opportunities to shorten development times. Accelerating development times is critical. When the world was confronted with an unfamiliar virus, like SARS, the U.S. MCM apparatus never caught up. If SARS had continued to collect victims at the same rate that it had in 2003, we would be asking ourselves, "Why haven't we devised an emergency pathway for drug/vaccine development that allows us to respond to these surprises?"

While it is unlikely that we will ever develop real-time capabilities, the ability to react within months (rather than years) would limit the number of casualties from emerging infectious diseases and pandemics. In some respects, this capability is already within reach. We have platforms and protocols that allow us to generate new flu vaccines on a 6- to 8-month timeline. These development times were possible even before BARDA began to work with industry to develop valuable time saving techniques such as cell cultures, reverse genetics, and flu gene synthesis. Even if a vaccine is not widely available for the first wave of infection (as was the case for the 2009 H1N1 pandemic), health care workers still have time to mitigate a second and third wave with a vaccine.

Faster reaction times could also limit the damage from an attack with a biological weapon. Deliberate attacks with unknown pathogens are especially challenging because they can be difficult to detect and most MCMs work best if they are administered within the first 24 hours. Chances are, first responders would miss the first wave of infection. However, once responders have identified the cause and obtained an effective MCM, they can mitigate, and maybe even deter, subsequent attacks with the same pathogen. Eventual access to MCMs could also allow officials to lift travel restrictions and/or permit civilians to re-enter broadly contaminated areas.

Midcourse corrections: Second wave

The PHEMCE implementation plan under PAPHA recognizes the strategic limitations of BioShield's fixed-defense approach and aspires to a more flexible defense strategy, calling for "broad spectrum solutions" such as multiuse therapeutics, technologies, and processes that reduce the cost and time of development (HHS 2007). As part of this initiative, in June of 2009, BARDA solicited proposals to accelerate drug development tasks ranging from rapid diagnostics to new methods of bioprocess development and manufacturing, vaccine stabilization, and delivery.

By 2010, HHS identified a new wave of initiatives in their end-to-end review, many of which elaborated flexible defense strategies (HHS 2010). These included: 1) a proposal to establish a Concept Acceleration Program at NIAID to expedite the identification and development of MCM candidates 2) a nonprofit Strategic Investor to provide financial capital and business advice to companies with promising MCM technologies, 3) three U.S.-based Centers for Innovation in Advanced Development and Manufacturing (ADMs) to provide facilities and expertise for BARDA-sponsored developers to make investigational vaccine lots and to provide surge capacity in the event of a pandemic, and 4) investments in regulatory science, procedures, and policy that would facilitate FDA review of MCMs. Separately, the DOD and HHS have launched an Integrated Portfolio Initiative to leverage resources and programs across BARDA, the NIH, and the DOD to develop medical countermeasures for chemical, biological, and radiological threats.

These initiatives could alleviate many of the problems that have beset civilian MCM programs over the past decade, ranging from poor market incentives and an uncertain regulatory path, to decentralized mission authority. Accelerating development times is more complicated, however. If the United States intends to build an MCM program that can respond to novel and emerging threats, three things need to happen. First, it must shift the strategic focus from fixed to flexible defenses. Second, it must support this shift with long-term R&D outlays and programmatic support. And third, it must promote integrated research practices within this accelerated MCM program.

Securing steady funds over a period of 10 or more years will be a challenge going forward. BARDA operates under an exceedingly constrained budget, which limits its ability to pursue both fixed and flexible strategies simultaneously. The Special Reserve Fund, which expired in FY 2013, contained $5.6 billion. This sum was insufficient (by several billion dollars) to accomplish BioShield's original objective, which was to pull seven countermeasures through development in ten years. In addition to BARDA's new mission to pursue flexible defenses, the PHEMCE implementation plan now calls for a longer list of pathogen-specific MCMs as well. While the mission has expanded, the budget has not; Congress reauthorized legislation that would allow BARDA and BioShield to operate at roughly the same level of funding for the next five years ($2.8 billion from FY 2014 to FY 2018).

Sustained federal support is critical because private sector incentives are not aligned with the public need to build an accelerated path for MCM development. While markets drive the development of some component technologies that enable faster development times, the private sector is unlikely to implement many process improvements without federal encouragement. The private sector is especially unlikely to integrate functions both before and after traditional drug development tasks such as a surveillance, detection, diagnosis, and distribution.

While private sector incentives are misaligned, public sector methods are maladapted to the task of engineering a MCM superhighway. HHS has indicated that the NIH will take the lead for flexible defense research because they have a "long term focus on platform technologies and broad-spectrum medical countermeasures that will allow for the rapid introduction of additional response capabilities for emerging infectious agents" (Gronvall 2008: 1e3). In 2011, the NIH also introduced a new center, the National Center for Advancing Translational Sciences (NCATS) to stimulate early-stage research in new drug and diagnostic development. While the NIH may be on the leading edge for flexible defense research, the bottom-up discovery processes that govern NIH projects will complicate efforts to knit new methods and flexible defense technologies into an accelerated development pathway. NIH director Francis Collins explicitly stated that NCATS will "avoid a top-down management approach" (Collins 2011: 90cm17).

BARDA, on the other hand, operates much like a Lead System Integrator, outsourcing MCM development to a changing cast of contractors, who in turn subcontract portions of their work. This arrangement makes it difficult for BARDA to synthesize new findings, transfer information effectively, and to train and retain a workforce with an intuitional memory for lessons learned. NCATS, NIAID's proposed Concept Acceleration Program, and BARDA are all designed to usher new candidates out of the lab and across the valley of death, but these efforts will fail unless HHS is able to reintroduce the type of integrated research practices that fueled mid-century levels of vaccine innovation.

Public private product development partnerships (PPPs), and/or government-backed consortia may provide the best opportunity to nurture integrated research practices. HHS's newly funded ADMs are structured as a PPP. As such, ADMs could provide a stable environment for more productive forms of industry/government collaboration. To succeed, HHS will have to resist the tendency to manage ADMs like a traditional contract manufacturing organization and instead invest in them as a long-term development partner. Ideally, an ADM can provide the stability required to train and retain a highly skilled interdisciplinary workforce. ADMs can also foster more efficient technology transfer by implementing top-down project management and by facilitating collaborative problem solving, site visits, and training fellowships. ADMs must also be able to attract talent, build a reputation as a dynamic learning environment, and become early adopters of new manufacturing technologies and research tools. To facilitate early adoption, it would be useful to embed a technology watch team within ADMs, or to liaison with the NIAID's Concept Acceleration Program and NCATS.

Promoting innovation in late stage development and manufacturing is important, but ultimately it is just one link in the chain of capabilities required to generate safe and effective MCMs in emergencies. Over time, HHS should link ADMs into an end-to-end system that includes detection, early stage research, clinical research, and regulatory science. For example, it will be important to work with the NIH to develop new methods to rapidly detect and characterize unknown pathogens with an eye towards having these methods link directly into early stage MCM discovery and preclinical development platforms. It will also be important for ADMs to work with the FDA to develop rapid evaluation tools. As ADMs begin to generate MCM candidates, it may also be possible to collaborate with NIH-sponsored Vaccine Treatment and Evaluation Units at academic research centers to devise clinical trial designs that can evaluate MCM candidates more rapidly than we do today.

Tremendous gains in speed and efficiency can come from the way new diagnostic, discovery, testing, manufacturing, and delivery methods are linked together. When timeliness becomes the goal, scientists, engineers, clinicians, and regulators will begin to visualize and solve MCM development problems in new ways. For example, rather than developing environmental detection devices and diagnostics in isolation, they might ask, "Is it possible to develop detectors that offer critical diagnostic information?" "Is it possible to develop diagnostics that facilitate the search for drug targets?" Or, "Can we develop target-agnostic vaccine scaffolds and drug development platforms that accelerate development times, lower cost, and facilitate regulatory review?"

Different types of vaccines, antimicrobials, monoclonal antibodies, and antivirals will each rely on different platforms with a diverse set of components, but over time, the U.S. program should have a set of integrated platforms and emergency pathways in use.

In sum, HHS must make a sustained commitment to flexible defenses and take advantage of the new ADM framework to begin to integrate the programs and tools required to build accelerated MCM development capabilities. To accomplish these goals more efficiently, HHS must invest in ADMs as a long-term development partner and reintroduce integrated research practices. If HHS can pursue these objectives, over time the U.S. MCM enterprise will discover new ways to catch up to fast moving pandemics, emerging infectious diseases, and bioterrorism.

Notes

1 The Bush administration requested $45 billion to fight terrorism and $5.9 billion to fight bioterrorism in fiscal year 2003. This request reflects an estimated 230% and 420% increase, respectively, over pre-9/11 spending levels.

2 Antitoxins confer rapid passive immunity and can be used to prevent post-exposure illness. Anthrax antitoxins may be particularly useful if populations are attacked with an antibiotic-resistant strain of anthrax. Chelators, such as Calcium and Zinc DTPA (diethylenetriaminepentaacetate) formulations, reduce internal exposure to radiation by binding to radionuclides so they can be eliminated from the body.

3 The FDA approved Raxibacumab to treat inhalational anthrax in December 2012.

4 Maurice Hilleman developed and/or improved over 25 vaccines over the course of his career. For a record of his remarkable contributions to vaccine development, see Offit (2007). For a more detailed description of how these scientists employed integrated research practices, see Hoyt (2012) and Oshinsky (2005).

5 Subsequent studies have used more conservative measures, estimating the actual cost to be between $6.3 billion and $11.6 billion for 2009–2015 (Klotz & Pearson, 2009: 698).

References

Agovino, T. (2001, November 1) 'Drug firms consider smallpox vaccine', *Associated Press.*

The Bipartisan WMD Terrorism Research Center. (2011) *Bioresponse Report Card*, Washington: WMD Center. Online. Available HTTP: <http://www.wmdcenter.org/wp-content/uploads/2011/10/bio-response-report-card-2011.pdf> (accessed 22 January 2014).

Bush, V. (1970) *Pieces of the Action*, New York: William Morrow and Company.

Collins, F. (2011) 'Reegineering translational science: the time is right', *Science Translational Medicine*, 3. doi:10.1126/scitranslmed.3002747

Congressional Budget Office. (2003) *CBO Cost Estimate, S. 15, Project BioShield Act of 2003*, Washington, DC: CBO.

Connolly, C. (2002, February 6) 'Bush promotes plans to fight bioterrorism', *Washington Post.*

DiMasi, J.A., Hansen, R.W. and Grabowski, H.G. (2003) 'The price of innovation: new estimates of drug development costs', *Journal of Health Economics*, 22: 151–185.

Gillis, J. (2001, November 8) 'Scientists race for vaccines: drug companies called key to bioterror fight', *Washington Post.*

Gottron, F. (2010) *Project BioShield: Authorities, Appropriations, Acquisitions, and Issues for Congress*, Washington: Congressional Research Service. Online. Available HTTP: <http://fpc.state.gov/documents/organization/137280.pdf> (accessed 22 January 2014).

Gronvall, G. (2008) 'Biodefense countermeasures: the impact of Title IV of the U.S. Pandemic and All-Haz ards Preparedness Act', *Emerging Health Threats Journal*, 1: e3. doi:10.3134/ehtj.08.003

Gronvall, G.K., Rambhia, K.J., Adalja, A., Cicero, A., Inglesby, T. and Kadlec, R. (2013) *Next-Generation Monoclonal Antibodies: Challenges and Opportunities*, Baltimore: UPMC Center for Biosecurity. Online. Available HTTP: <http://www.upmchealthsecurity.org/our-work/pubs_archive/pubs-pdfs/2013/2013-02-04-next-gen-monoclonal-antibodies.pdf> (accessed 14 May 2014).

HHS. (2007) *PHEMCE Implementation Plan for Chemical, Biological, Radiological, and Nuclear Threats.* Online. Available HTTP: <http://www.phe.gov/Preparedness/mcm/phemce/Documents/2007-phemce-implementation.pdf> (accessed 14 May 2014).

HHS. (2010) *The Public Health Emergency Medical Countermeasures Enterprise Review: Transforming the Enterprise to Meet Long-Range National Needs.* Online. Available HTTP: <http://www.phe.gov/preparedness/mcm/enterprisereview/Pages/default.aspx> (accessed 14 May 2014).

Hotelling, H. (1963) 'Vannevar Bush speaks', *Science*, 142: 1623.

House Government Reform Committee, Veterans Affairs, and International Relations Subcommittee. (2001) *Congressional Testimony: Bioterrorism Vaccines*, 23 October 2001.

Hoyt, K. (2006, March 3) 'Bird flu won't wait', *New York Times.*

Hoyt, K. (2012) *Long Shot: Vaccines for National Defense*, Cambridge: Harvard University Press.

Kadlec, R. (2010) 'Case studies of HHS chemical, biological, radiological, and nuclear medical countermeasure development programs, executive summary,' in T. Wizemann, C. Stroud and B.M. Altevogt (eds.) *The Public Health Emergency Medical Countermeasures Enterprise: Innovative Strategies to Enhance Products from Discovery Through Approval*, Washington: National Academies Press. Online. Available HTTP: <http://www.nap.edu/catalog/12856.html> (accessed 14 May 2014).

Klotz, L. and Pearson, A. (2009) 'BARDA's budget', *Nature Biotechnology*, 27: 698–699.

Lilly, S. (2010) 'Getting rich on Uncle Sucker: should the federal government strengthen efforts to fight profiteering?' Center for American Progress, 20 October. Online. Available HTTP: <http://www.americanprogress.org/issues/2010/10/pdf/unclesucker.pdf> (accessed 14 May 2014).

Matheny, J., Mair, M. and Smith, B, (2008) 'Cost/success projections for U.S. biodefense countermeasure development', *Nature Biotechnology*, 26: 981–983.

Miller, J. (2002, February 4) 'Bush to request a major increase in bioterror funds', *New York Times.*

Monath, T. (2000, April) 'Industry involvement in federal vaccine development and procurement efforts', presentation at the Second Meeting of the Institute of Medicine Committee on a Strategy for Minimizing the Impact of Naturally Occurring Diseases of Military Importance: Vaccine Issues in the U.S. Military, Washington, DC.

National Research Council. (2011) *Animal Models for Assessing Countermeasures to Bioterrorism Agents*, Washington DC: National Academies Press.

Office of Management and Budget. (2003) *Annual Report to Congress on Combating Terrorism*, Washington, DC: U.S. Government Printing Office.

Offit, P. (2007) *Vaccinated: One Man's Quest to Defeat the World's Deadliest Diseases*, Washington: Smithsonian Books.

Oshinsky, D. (2005) *Polio: An American Story*, New York: Oxford University Press.

Schneidmiller, C. (2013, March 1) 'Q&A: BioShield program successful after "rocky start," HHS Preparedness Chief says', *Global Security Newswire.*

Smith, B., Inglesby, T. and O'Toole, T. (2003). 'Biodefense R&D: anticipating future threats, establishing a strategic environment', *Biosecurity and Bioterrorism: Biodefense Strategy, Practice, and Science*, 1: 193–202.

von Hippel, E. (1994) '"Sticky information" and the locus of problem solving: implications for innovation', *Management Science*, 40: 429–439.

White House Press Office. (2003, February 3) 'President details Project BioShield'. Online. Available HTTP: <http://georgewbush-whitehouse.archives.gov/news/releases/2003/02/20030203.html> (accessed 14 May 2014).

19

INTERNET SURVEILLANCE AND DISEASE OUTBREAKS

Sara E. Davies

In March 2013, the People's Republic of China (hereafter referred to as China) reported to the World Health Organization (WHO) that it had detected three human cases of a novel bird flu strain. Two of them proved fatal (Lancet 2013). The spread of the strain appeared to be limited to instances of direct contact between poultry and humans. WHO announced the new strain, H7N9, to the world the following day, including on Twitter. That same day, WHO's original tweet, which linked to a press announcement in Geneva, generated 100–200 retweets per hour. Over the next four days, retweets rose to 500 per hour (Norris 2013). It is clear that the Internet has become an important mechanism for reporting information about disease outbreaks. What is less clear is what sort of mechanism it is.

Prior to the publication of the H7N9 case history in the *New England Journal of Medicine* on 24 April 2013 (Li et al. 2013), discussion about H7N9 in the social media was facilitated by communications from the Chinese Ministry of Health, and primarily the Chinese National Influenza Centre (Butler & Cyranoski 2013). There were expressions of genuine surprise about the openness of the Chinese government – to the extent that one WHO official observed, "I almost wonder if we are missing something, their [the Chinese government] disclosure is so complete" (Interview with Author 2013b). However, whilst some expressed surprise and praised China's openness (Nature 2013), others pointed to anomalies regarding China's public disclosures (Garrett 2013). One assessment noted that, as with national surveillance in general, transparent reporting and responsiveness to outbreaks was not consistent across the country (Huang 2013).

This case, and others like it, exemplifies how global disease reporting has changed in the Internet age, and why for some global surveillance by technical providers – called Internet surveillance response programs (ISRPs) – is vital for detecting, analyzing, and reporting outbreak events around the world (Chan et al. 2010). ISRPs scour the Internet for signs of disease reports and then alert their subscribers independently of government authorities. Their proponents argue that ISRPs are uniquely able to penetrate the state to identify conversations, behaviors, and local reports in order to alert the international community to disease outbreaks – even when a state may wish to keep an outbreak within its borders secret.

In this chapter, I explore the growth of ISRPs that have, over the last two decades, increasingly mapped and reported disease outbreaks around the world. ISRPs are mostly open-source platforms that are widely seen as being vital for maintaining transparent lines of communication and reporting during infectious disease outbreaks (Brownstein et al. 2008). The proliferation of ISRPs has prompted some to argue that it is now futile for states to try to cover up outbreaks of disease because global detection cannot be avoided (Shkabatur 2011). Yet while ISRPs have certainly changed practices in relation to the reporting of outbreak events, their capacity to gather and analyze information remains contingent on a number of factors external to technology. In particular, political and media freedoms, government structures, Internet coverage, and the diagnostic capacity of the ISRP itself, all influence ISRPs' capacity to reveal – and a state's capacity to conceal – outbreaks. Further, questions remain over how well ISRPs actually advance outbreak reporting rather than simply amplifying traditional surveillance activity (Huang 2013).

This chapter examines both the capacity of ISRPs to challenge states' response to disease outbreak events – by virtue of transparent communication – and their limits in three parts. First, I set out the types of ISRPs, their integration into the global disease surveillance system, and the various ways in which they seek to differentiate between "rumours" and "real time intelligence" (Wilson & Brownstein 2009). Second, I discuss limitations to ISRP data collection, particularly in relation to the claim that disease intelligence may be gleaned "in spite" of a state's wishes or gained "prior" to a state's knowledge (Brownstein et al. 2008). Finally, I consider how these limitations should be taken into consideration in understanding why states have agreed to allow the WHO to collect unverified information from "unofficial" non-state sources under the 2005 revised International Health Regulations (IHR).

The presumption that ISRPs make a positive contribution to global disease surveillance is especially interesting given broader debates in political science and international relations around the transformation of the relationship between politics and technology (i.e., Fung et al. 2013; Singh 2013). Internet surveillance cannot compel states to report disease outbreaks in an open and transparent fashion, especially when they are willing to risk the consequences of not reporting. However, past inaction (or conspiracy theories) should not lead us to misinterpret the desire of many states to overcome the limitations of ISPR technology to improve their own surveillance, alert, and response functionality. Many states (democratic or not) want to control the message during an (outbreak) crisis to limit damage. The analytical dilemma faced by ISRPs and the wider international community is knowing when the message is being controlled in an attempt to conceal an outbreak and when it is being controlled in order to positively manage risk communication.

ISRPs, WHO, and the International Health Regulations

More than 60% of WHO's Alert and Response Operations first outbreak reports come from "unofficial informal sources," which includes electronic media, discussion sites, and social media (WHO 2014). The proliferation of social media (e.g., Twitter, Facebook, Weibo) has led many ISRPs (e.g. BioCaster, PULS) to rely primarily upon "ontology software" for text mining and language translation to detect early reports or "rumours" of novel disease outbreaks. Others, such as GPHIN (Global Public Health Intelligence Network), rely on a combination of software and human analysts. Within GPHIN, analysts with language proficiency in Arabic, Farsi, English, Spanish, Russian, Chinese, Portuguese, and French sift through thousands of reports produced daily to determine which ones need to be placed on the subscriber-only alert page (which can also be emailed to subscribers).

Established in 1996, GPHIN was one of the first real-time surveillance networks to be created, having been developed in cooperation with WHO Headquarters and the Public Health Agency of Canada. Until the past year, its reports were primarily issued to fee-paying subscribers and therefore were not publicly accessible to those not affiliated with a subscribing government, international organization, or defense and security organization.

HealthMap, by contrast, has always been a free access Internet surveillance network that analyses media reports on a scale similar to GPHIN and also collates reports from other Internet surveillance providers such as MedISys (an EU joint research centre project) and ProMED Mail (PMM), which is now partnered with HealthMap. Presently, much focus is on improving text and string searches of blogs and social media sites to produce real-time alerts of disease outbreaks with color codes indicating source reliability (which entails "last minute" human moderation prior to posting), contextual use, and geographic location (Castillo-Salgado 2010; Collier 2010).

Since 2005, international responses to disease outbreaks, including verification, containment, and alert procedures, have been guided by the revised International Health Regulations (IHR) (see also Heymann & West, chapter 8, and Hoffmann, chapter 20, in this volume). Under the revised IHR, both state and non-state actors may communicate to WHO outbreak events that meet the IHR "Public Health Emergency of International Concern" (PHEIC) criteria. Under Article 9, the WHO may take into account "sources other than [state, formal] notifications or consultations" and "assess these reports according to established epidemiological principles and then communicate information on the event to the State Party in whose territory the event is allegedly occurring" (WHO 2005: Article 9.1). States are expected to respond to WHO communications based on non-state reports within 24 hours, while the *source* of the report is permitted to remain confidential. Confidentiality may not be of paramount importance for ISRPs such as GPHIN or BioCaster (depending of course on the ISRP's own source, which could be the media or an individual informant), but for some individuals, non-governmental organizations, and religious organizations who may also inform WHO of outbreak events, confidentiality can be critical.

The significance of Article 9 was best explained by WHO's (then) Director of IHR Coordination, Dr Guénaël Rodier:

> *In today's information society, you cannot ignore or hide a problem for very long.* You can perhaps ignore or hide an event for a day or two, but after a week it's virtually impossible. *WHO and its partners have a powerful system of gathering intelligence that will pick anything up immediately. Today, events are often initially reported, not by a Member State, but by non-official sources such as the media, NGOs (nongovernmental organizations), our network of collaborating centres, laboratory networks and partners in the field. . . .* One of the incentives for countries to report such events is that these will already have been reported via the electronic highway. We will be in a much better position to help if we have been involved early on by the affected country. The fear of being named and shamed by the media and other countries concerned by the situation is in itself an incentive.
>
> (Rodier 2007: 429, emphasis added)

The added value provided by ISRPs is their analytical capability, which allows them to separate the "signal from the noise" (Brownstein et al 2008: 1019). Picking up the signal does not just alert WHO but, in many cases, also the affected state itself that an outbreak is occurring. However, Article 9 is also seen as providing a coercive tool that makes states aware of the real possibility of being "named and shamed" if they fail to report in a timely fashion. This observation is, arguably, supported by earlier cases in which early alerts enabled WHO to seek further information from first-affected member states, as in the SARS outbreak in China (2002–2003),[1] the H5N1 Avian Influenza strain's emergence in Thailand and Vietnam, the human infections of H5N1 in Indonesia, and, more recently, the H1N1 "Swine Flu" outbreak in Mexico in early 2009. Initial alerts for these outbreaks came from PMM, GPHIN, and HealthMap (Brownstein et al. 2009; Madoff & Woodall 2005).

Much attention has been devoted to the comparative efficiency of ISRPs (Castillo-Salgado 2010; Collier 2010; Hitchcock et al. 2007), their ability to push states towards transparency (Fidler 2004; Heymann & Rodier 2004; Madoff & Woodall 2005), and the need for greater interoperability to improve their surveillance and alert performance (Hartley et al. 2010). GPHIN, for example, has been essential to WHO's capacity to identify disease events and provide direct assistance to states, sometimes prior to those states and neighboring states being aware of the extent of the outbreak themselves (Mykhalovskiy & Weir 2006). As Pat Drury, head of Global Outbreak Alert and Response Network (GOARN) based at WHO Headquarters, argued to the United Kingdom's Intergovernmental Organizations Select Committee in 2008, such "sources of information" help the WHO special operations center identify which media and incident reports need to be assessed for risk to the local and international community, which in turn leads to recommendations for the country and the WHO to take appropriate action (United Kingdom Parliament 2008: 211).

SARS is often seen as a landmark case that convinced states that in the future they would be unable to prevent the leakage of information about disease outbreaks:

> [P]erhaps the greatest legacy of SARS, disease reporting changed almost overnight from being approached with hesitancy and preoccupation with concern about the potential economic fallout from such transparency, to something that was simply expected and respected.
>
> (Heymann et al. 2013: 780)

During the H1N1 "Swine Flu" outbreak in 2009, it has been argued that the value of Article 9 [in revised IHR (2005)] in assisting with real time intelligence gathering on disease outbreaks was effectively demonstrated:

> During the 2009 H1N1 influenza pandemic, non-traditional surveillance sources such as Internet news sources provided new public health data. Collectively, these sources overcame certain limitations of traditional surveillance systems, including reporting delays, inconsistent population coverage, and a poor sensitivity to detect emerging diseases.
>
> (Brownstein et al. 2010: 1733)

> Surveillance of pandemic (H1N1) 2009 serves as an example of the real time capability of identifying emerging disease events in general, particularly events that may be evident in local media in the regional vernacular. Other event-based biosurveillance systems have demonstrated the effectiveness of extracting relevant information from Internet media sources as a means for detecting and monitoring disease events. Internet media reporting provides an emerging resource for early detection of new events and for providing situational awareness of evolving events, particularly when official sources may not be available.
>
> (Nelson et al. 2012: 12)

Article 9 clearly articulates both the right of ISRPs to report an event to WHO and the authority for WHO to receive these alerts and to then seek verification from the state(s) concerned.

Surveillance for action: The possibilities and limitations of ISRPs

Two rationales were at work in driving the adoption of Article 9 in the revised IHR, which opened the door to a formal role for Internet disease surveillance. First, it was not just WHO Headquarters that wanted to know about outbreaks that could pose a risk to health and trade. All states wanted this information, because they have a keen interest in knowing about diseases that might arise in their neighborhood. Second, whilst states certainly wanted to know about other states' outbreaks, they still believed that they could control information flows and that they have a sovereign right to do so. As a result of this second consideration, the revised IHR still requires WHO to consult the affected state before publicly announcing an outbreak event identified by an ISRP. Therefore, states agreed to Article 9 because, while there *is* some inevitability regarding information leakage, there also remained the possibility of them controlling the flow of information (at least initially) to manage the risk associated with an outbreak within their borders.

It is not always the case, however, that states are attempting to cover up outbreaks. In some cases, especially where public health capacity is weak, rumors may be the only source of information available about a particular outbreak. The question is, what do the revised IHR allow WHO to do with such information? In a 2008 article entitled "Surveillance sans frontières," the developers of HealthMap noted the multidimensional contribution of ISRPs in environments where states had not yet reached their IHR core capacity requirements.[2] It was argued that in these situations of compromised capacity, ISRPs effectively provide a communication service for many countries that do not have their own adequate communication-based health infrastructure. In that regard, it is worth noting that some ISRPs like GPHIN, until recently, provided a members-only platform to facilitate communication amongst members without public alerts. This reporting format allowed for the WHO to follow local outbreak information in real time and to assist with a state's verification process (Brownstein et al. 2008: 1020). Therefore, states and ISRPs do not necessarily exist in tension with one another. ISRPs can be a useful tool for states themselves.

However, ISRPs are only as useful as the information that they can glean. This problem is magnified if we take into account the fact that not all ISRPs operate in the same way. Some (such as HealthMap) are wholly reliant on open-source material, some (e.g., ProMED) rely on a combination of open-source and anonymous communications, and some (e.g., GPHIN) have both membership-only platforms and open-source platforms – which means that reports are not always shared across the open and closed platforms. These complications create the potential for confusion, duplication, breaches of confidentiality, and competition amongst ISRPs (Hartley et al. 2010). This informed the creation of the Global Health Security Action Group (GHSAG) under the Global Health Security Initiative (created in 2001), which is led by Ministers/Secretaries/Commissioners of Health from Canada, the European Commission, France, Germany, Italy, Japan, Mexico, the United Kingdom, the United States, and the World Health Organization. The GHSAG has been working for the last decade to promote movement towards a common global reporting platform shared by all ISRPs and managed by WHO. In the meantime, there have been annual discussions on the development of shared procedures around text analysis, alert and reporting procedures, and handling of controversial information (GHSI 2011: 4). The development of a shared platform by HealthMap and ProMED has been identified as a future example of how multiple ISRPs can combine to address these challenges (Barboza et al. 2013).

There are, however, other problems that affect ISRPs as well as more traditional reporting systems that are rarely discussed in the field (Brownstein et al. 2008: 1021–1022; see also Castilo-Salgado 2010; Hartley et al. 2010; Katz & Fischer 2010; Schmidt 2012). As such, in the rest of this section I will briefly examine the political implications of the limitations that Brownstein and his colleagues note, particularly problems associated with the reporting sources, surveillance "black holes," and report differentiation between suspected and confirmed outbreak events. These limitations suggest that states have retained more control over information flows than is often presumed, and that they might still be able to decide what they will allow to be reported publicly (and when), affecting in turn the timeliness claims of (some) ISRPs and the capacity of WHO to generate a timely response. Indeed, the fact that some ISRPs do not distinguish between suspected and confirmed reports might allow some recalcitrant states to create the appearance of compliance with the IHR without actually engaging in prompt, timely, and comprehensive reporting.

Sources

ISRPs' search functionality relies primarily on local reporting of disease events. The process for HealthMap, MedISys, and GPHIN involves text mining technology and access to large news aggregation sites such as FACTIVA. Human moderation steps in at various points to filter reports: GPHIN almost from the beginning, HealthMap in the middle, and Biocaster and MedISys literally prior to posting. Naturally the focus is on quality reporting – delivering real alerts with valid source credentials – as well as on posting relevant alerts of interest to the reader. Systems that can search for both naturally occurring diseases and other types of outbreak event (e.g., accidental or deliberate release of chemical or biological agents that are listed in the Annex 2 attached to the revised IHR) have a relatively high degree of added value, but the same tools can also generate results that are not relevant. Sifting through these reports to determine which is which is a complex technical task for these providers (Linge et al. 2009). Naturally these systems will produce a lot of search results or "rumours," as Grein and his colleagues famously termed them (Grein et al. 2000), and thus they are almost bound to produce at least one accurate report of an outbreak. However, the importance and nature of the source itself is often overlooked in relation to these semantic and text mining searches.

To understand the efficiency, effectiveness and coverage of surveillance technologies – whether at the national or global level – we need to understand more about the political systems in which these technologies are operating. A quick scan of HealthMap's output for 30 days, for example, will show a lot of news media sources, but the vast majority of their content has been informed by public health officials releasing outbreak news. In other words, these media reports are more often than not sourced from the government itself. This was noted by Brownstein and his colleagues (Brownstein et al. 2008: 1022), and again by Blench (Blench 2010: slide 19), when he showed that the quantity of verified official report sources is virtually equal to that of news media report sources. But this basic fact – that at least half of all "non-official" reports actually come from the government itself – has not yet penetrated discussion about the utility of ISRPs in promoting government transparency.

Identifying governments as a significant (even if indirect) source for ISRPs is important for two reasons. First, failure to acknowledge this fact feeds into the notion that states are not cooperating with the release of health information – when in fact they may be cooperating more than is recognized. Second, this neglect of the government's role as a source of information inflates the "intelligence" capacity of ISRPs when in fact they may only be as good as they are in large part because governments generally make this information available. Therefore, what is new and needs to be emphasized is the search tool that ISRPs provide and the promotional impact of this information. The ISRPs themselves are probably generating much less information that is genuinely "new" or "non-governmental" than is commonly thought.

In some instances, governments are providing both the first suspect report and the subsequent official confirmation, but this is not identified as an important trend (Chan et al. 2010; Collier et al. 2008; Rotureau et al. 2007). Instead the focus is often on how such surveillance networks encourage reluctant states to engage in more transparent behavior (Shkabatur 2011). We cannot know precisely to what extent ISRPs are ahead of states until there is a clearer distinction made in ISRP reporting between sources that have some level of associated government input and those that are wholly "independent." This is a particular problem in this field, because most countries' health sectors have a significant state component and some are wholly state-run.

Another complication that arises from the ISRPs' lack of clarity about official involvement in the first outbreak report is that it is sometimes difficult to follow up on outbreak reports, i.e., to keep track of which "alert" was then "verified" as an actual outbreak (Rotureau et al. 2007). As such, deeper examination of the actual source of suspected outbreak reports and the level of "official" association should become standardized in ISRP alerts. Media agencies in a number of countries are state-owned, and media reporting and Internet usage are not without government interference in many parts of the world (O'Malley et al. 2009). This raises the need for more sensitive text mining, including free media and Internet ratings (for example, usage access in a country) and the introduction of (admittedly costly) human analysis that may be sensitive to these political contexts. Such a change goes against those ISRPs trending towards automated text processing algorithms, but the clarity gained by more sensitive text mining would enable the international community to have the tools to examine which states are progressing in meeting their IHR core capacities and which are not. This potentially uncaps the real transformative potential of ISRPs on state behavior.

Black holes

Noting the source limitations of ISRPs also allows us to realistically understand the contribution that they can make to shedding light on those places where the freedom to report is constrained, whether by politics or technology. HealthMap has argued that while 85% of its reports come from news media sources, there is a "clear bias towards increased reporting from countries with higher numbers of media outlets, more developed public health resources, and greater availability of electronic communication infrastructure" (Brownstein et al. 2008: 1021). HealthMap thus not only acknowledges an information bias, but a coverage bias towards the diseases that will pique public interest, reflected in media outlets' choice to publish some outbreak–related stories and not others (Brownstein et al. 2008: 1022; Collier 2010: 12). The French Institute for Public Health Surveillance has noted similar concerns about the coverage gaps that their server has in particular geographic locations, and GPHIN has also referred to such coverage gaps (Blench 2008; Rotureau et al. 2007). What is the significance of these surveillance "black holes"?

Communication deficiencies in various locations and an inability to secure the local news for global consumption are the primary causes of surveillance "black holes" (Brownstein et al. 2008; Hartley et al. 2010). Less frequently discussed obstacles for Article 9 to reach its full potential are limits on the freedom of the Internet, the press and independent actors to report outbreaks that they deem to be a potential PHEIC. As Madoff and Woodall (2005: 729) argue, one of the most transformative aspects of PMM has been its provision of a portal for those in autocratic regimes to report disease outbreaks that they felt were being ignored, misdiagnosed or posed a risk of international spread, often at a cost to their own liberty.

A recent example of surveillance "black holes" compromising early knowledge on the location and spread of an outbreak has been the suspected novel coronavirus (MERS-CoV) in the Middle East. In the early stages following the virus' identification in 2012, there was little information coming from the Middle East region, the suspected origin of MERS-CoV. Most information at this early stage came from affected individuals upon return to the United Kingdom, Europe, and Asia, after the 2012 Hajj pilgrimage (Branswell 2013a). For over a year, there had been concerted efforts by WHO Headquarters and the WHO Middle East North African (MENA) Regional Office to gain access to countries that had reported small numbers of MERS-CoV cases (Ball 2013; Branswell 2013b; Cyranoski 2013). Surveillance technology was, for the most part, struggling to overcome political (control of Internet freedom and press) and cultural obstacles (normalization of sharing biodata) to gain access to reports of the outbreak from within the region itself (Interview with Author 2013a). The desire (at least originally) for the outbreak to be verified "discreetly" led to bilateral (as opposed to multilateral) virus-sharing arrangements between research laboratories and the affected states. However, these bilateral arrangements allegedly compromised WHO Headquarters' promotion of a multilateral framework for sharing outbreak reports to facilitate global level alerts (Ball 2013). WHO Headquarters has continued to insist on dialogue, multipartner engagement and increased awareness of the purpose of *global* surveillance and reporting mechanisms with MENA states (WHO 2013).

Given the obstacles encountered, without such concerted engagement efforts by WHO Headquarters – and in spite of the surveillance tools available – knowledge of MERS-CoV would still be quite poor and "murky"; indeed, some still regard this to be the case (Ball 2013; Branswell 2013b; Cyranoski 2013). For now, WHO intervention has (somewhat) alleviated the surveillance black hole that threatened MERS-CoV-related information flows (Interview with Author 2013a). But the black hole was a significant problem in 2012, and may have delayed the world's response, as shown by the time lag between the suspected onset of cases reported in the first ISRP report and communicated in WHO's report (see Figure 19.1, Mackay 2013). This case shows that states still play a vital role in disease outbreak reporting that WHO and ISRPs will struggle to bypass if they rely upon the provisions of Article 9 of the revised IHR.

In cases where rumor generation (through news, social media, etc.) is poor, the last option is for individuals to provide alerts. However, the provision of anonymity under Article 9 does not make it easier for NGOs or public health officials in countries where they are strictly bound to memoranda of understanding with their host government (i.e., North Korea) and where access to the Internet is limited, monitored, or regulated. There is little that ISRPs or WHO can do about these problems, but heightened awareness of the potential human rights implications of "early reporting" and the individual risks taken by those supplying such early warnings is important.

Technical concerns

The existence of ISRPs has certainly forced states to respond with better domestic surveillance and more prompt reporting, as indeed have the IHR revisions that allowed ISRPs and other communications to freely come to WHO outside of state control under Article 9. The technical revolution, the power of news media, and the pressure it can exert upon states is thus not to be underestimated, but its power to name and shame is reliant upon two important caveats: efficiency and accuracy (Keller et al. 2009).

As mentioned above, it is difficult to track country reporting performance between first report of an event and first government confirmation (i.e., lab-confirmed diagnosis). Not every country reports in the same fashion. When an ISRP publishes summaries or actual lab reports from some countries, this is often the first public knowledge of an outbreak, while other states have regular outbreak reports of suspected events and then sometimes follow up with lab diagnostics (Rotureau et al. 2007: 1591). Obviously timeliness and quality are not the same in these two examples. In countries where most laboratory reports are the first reports to emerge of a disease outbreak, it is impossible to know with surety when the state identified the first cases or how many cases prior to the one reported were either never tested or were hushed up. Alternatively, where states provide a high volume of information on suspect outbreak investigations, it can be difficult to trace those

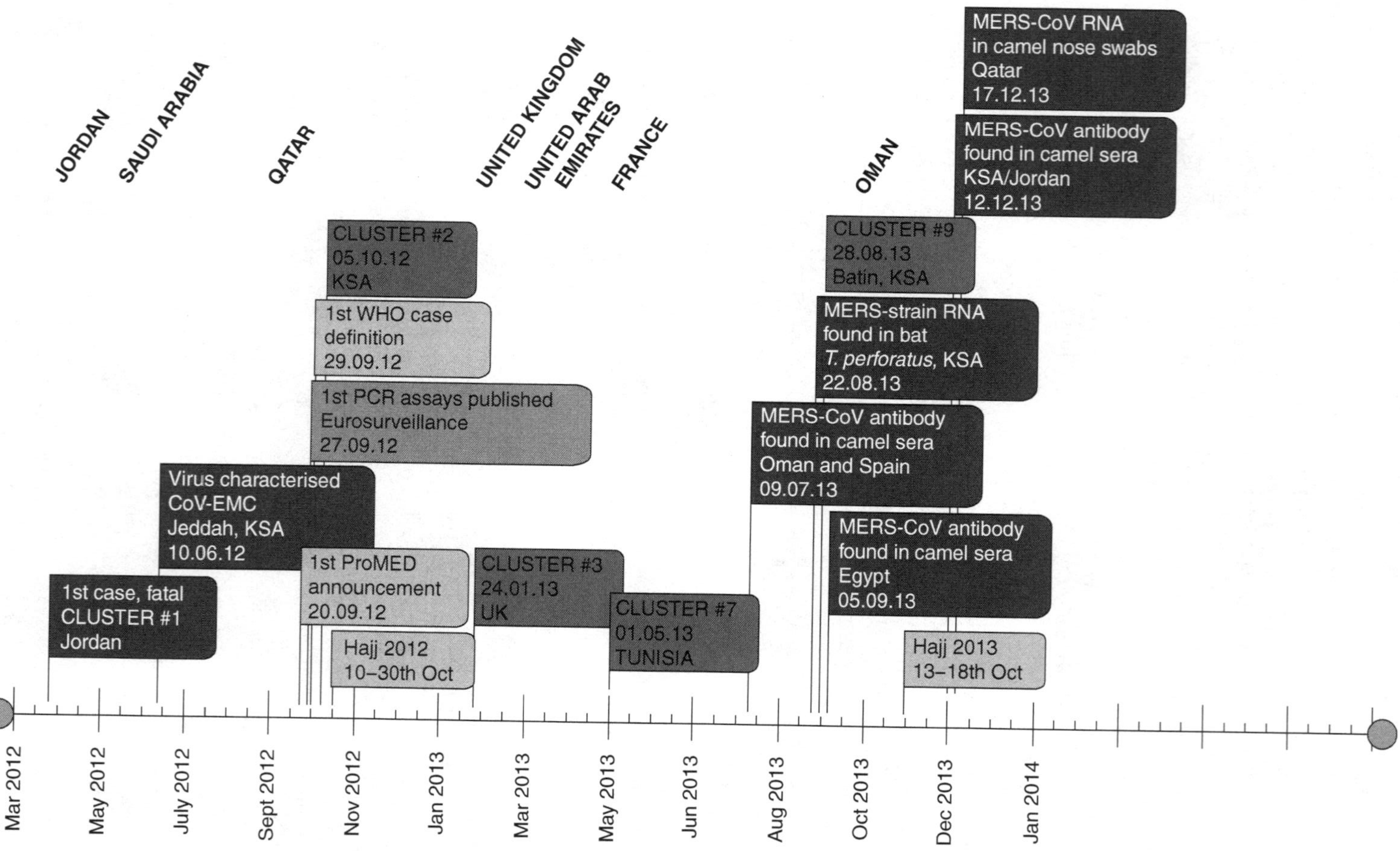

A timeline showing some key events starting from the first retrospectively confirmed human case of infection by the Middle East Respiratory Syndrome Coronavirus in June 2012.

Figure 19.1 Timeline of Key Events in MERS-CoV Outbreak, June 2012

Source: Mackay 2013.

that were followed up with lab diagnostics versus those that were not. Essentially, the world knows a lot about the diseases it is most interested in or that it knows to be on the "look out for" (Collier 2010: 14–15). But ISRPs may not make us any better at predicting the unknown. This, arguably, compromises transparency promises, responsiveness, and most of all reveals the limitations of what this intelligence can deliver without the necessary political, social and economic reform (Lancet 2007: 2763; O'Malley et al. 2009).

Technology will be continually adapted in the attempt to overcome the limitations states seek to put on open reporting, but there will remain important political, institutional, cultural, social, and economic limitations on the freedom of individuals to engage in these technologies and to use them for the purpose of preventing and containing a PHEIC.

Conclusion

There can be no doubt that the emergence of non-state based information about suspected disease outbreaks and the communication of this information to WHO heralds an important development in the field. But we need to understand both its transformative potential and its limitations. Three key points warrant emphasis in this regard.

First, there remain profound limitations to the communication of information in despotic and autocratic regimes that do not respect the basic political or civil freedoms needed to facilitate free communication. This in turn limits the capacity of institutions and individuals within the country to act freely under Article 9 without fearing any repercussions. The fact that there has been such little discussion of this, and especially the practical implications of the confidentiality clause under IHR (2005), remains a cause for concern (O'Malley et al. 2009).

Second, we need to acknowledge the role of the state in implementing Article 9 and how it influences the work of ISRPs specifically. The claims made for ISRPs are that they can locate outbreak events in spite of a state's effort to cover them up (Castillo-Salgado 2010: 104; Grein et al. 2000: 348), and that they can assist public health officials in detecting an event of which they were previously unaware (Shkabatur 2011: 428). Rarely is it acknowledged that an ISRP may have "found" an outbreak that the state already knew existed, or that an ISRP found it *only because the state reported the event*. As such, the promise that the public airing of the "signal" creates the impetus for states to act is a problematic claim because in many cases the state is itself involved in generating the signal in the first instance.

Finally, differentiating between who is giving the signal, what the signal entails, and the political context in which the signal exists, remains important. If ISRPs ultimately come to share a common surveillance platform – where reporting and verification reports are coordinated to have universal impact – we may see an entity emerge that has significant capacity to generate compliance (Grein et al. 2001). At present the multiple ISRPs place different emphases on sources, as well as employ different alert and report methods. A shared global surveillance platform would highlight gaps in coverage, making it easier to identify states and regions that have hitherto eluded surveillance. Yet even in these circumstances, a state's capacity to meet the core reporting requirements of the IHR (2005) will remain critical since compliance failures can be as much about incapacity as political choice.

Notes

1 WHO used "Web-based systems trawling for unusual health events" to seek clarification on the "rumours" of higher than usual pneumonia outbreaks in Southern China over 2002–2003 that turned out to be SARS (Heymann 2013).

2 Under the revised IHR, states agreed to meet eight core capacity conditions by 1 July 2012 in the fields of national legislation, policy and financing, creation and coordination of National Focal Point (NFP) communications, surveillance, response, preparedness, risk communication, and human resources and laboratories. It was widely presumed that not all member states would achieve these eight capacities by agreed timeframe (1 July 2012) but that they would identify areas where they needed assistance in order to map a timeframe for achievement of these core capacities with extensions granted on a case-by-case basis by the WHO Director-General.

References

Ball, J. (2013, June 23) 'New Mers-Coronavirus continues to smoulder', *BBC News*. Online. Available HTTP: <http://www.bbc.co.uk/news/health-23003837>.

Barboza, P., Vaillant, L., Mawudeku, A., Nelson, N.P., Hartley, D.M, Madoff, L.C., Linge, J.P., Collier, N., Brownstein, J.S., Yangarber, R. and Astagneau, P. (2013) 'Evaluation of epidemic intelligence systems integrated in the early alerting and reporting project for the detection of A/H5N1 influenza events', *PLoS One*, 8. Online. Available HTTP: <http://www.plosone.org/article/info:doi/10.1371/journal.pone.0057252> (accessed 24 August 2013).

Blench, M. (2008) 'Global Public Health Intelligence Network (GPHIN)', 8th AMTA Conference, Hawaii, 21–25 October. Online. Available HTTP: <http://www.mt-archive.info/AMTA-2008-Blench.pdf> (accessed 14 May 2014).

Blench, M. (2010) Global Public Health Intelligence Network (GPHIN), Global Risk Forum Davos. Online. Available HTTP: <http://www.slideshare.net/GRFDavos/idrcdavosmediumppt> (accessed 10 October 2011).

Branswell, H. (2013a, May 22) 'Canadian expert says Saudi coronavirus outbreak "complex" but reporting pending', *Global News*. Online. Available HTTP: <http://globalnews.ca/news/580906/canadian-expert-says-saudi-coronavirus-outbreak-complex-but-report-pending/> (accessed 14 May 2014).

Branswell, H. (2013b, June 7) 'Saudi silence on deadly MERS virus frustrates world health experts', *Scientific American*. Online. Available HTTP: <http://www.scientificamerican.com/article.cfm?id=saudi-silence-on-deadly-mers-virus-outbreak-frustrates-world-health-experts>.

Brownstein, J.S., Freifeld, C.C., Chan, E.H., Keller, M., Sonricker, A.L., Mekaru, S.R. and Buckeridge, D.L. (2010) 'Information technology and global surveillance of cases of 2009 H1N1 influenza', *New England Journal of Medicine*, 362: 1731–1735.

Brownstein, J.S., Freifeld, C.C. and Madoff, L.C. (2009) 'Digital disease detection – harnessing the web for public health surveillance', *New England Journal of Medicine*, 360: 2153–2157.

Brownstein, J.S., Freifeld, C.C., Reis, B.Y. and Mandl, K.D. (2008) 'Surveillance sans frontières: internet-based emerging infectious disease intelligence and the HealthMap Project', *PLoS Medicine*, 5: 1019–1024.

Butler, D. and Cyranoski, D. (2013) 'Flu papers spark row over credit for data; rush to publish on H7N9 avian flu upsets Chinese scientists', *Nature*, 497: 14–15.

Castillo-Salgado, C. (2010) 'Trends and directions of global public health surveillance', *Epidemiologic Review*, 32: 93–109.

Chan, E.H., Brewer, T.F., Madoff, L.C., Pollack, M.P., Sonricker, A.L., Keller, M., Freifeld, C.C., Blench, M., Mawudeku, A. and Brownstein, J.S. (2010) 'Global capacity for emerging infectious disease detection', *PNAS*, 107: 21701–21706.

Collier, N. (2010) 'What's unusual in online disease outbreak news?' *Journal of Biomedical Semantics*, 1: 1–18.

Collier N., Doan, S., Kawazoe, A., Goodwin, R.M., Conway, M., Tateno, Y., Ngo, Q.H., Dien, D., Kawtrakul, A., Takeuchi, K., Shigematsu, M. and Taniguchi, K. (2008) 'BioCaster: detecting public health rumors with a Web-based text mining system', *Bioinformatics*, 24: 2940–2941.

Cyranoski, D. (2013, May 17) 'Scientists look to Saudi Arabia for coronavirus clues', *Nature*. Online. Available HTTP: <http://www.nature.com/news/scientists-look-to-saudi-arabia-for-coronavirus-clues-1.13000> (accessed 14 May 2014).

Fidler, D.P. (2004) 'Germs, governance, and global public health in the wake of SARS', *Journal of Clinical Investigation*, 113: 799–804.

Fung, A., Russon Gilman, H. and Shkabatur, J. (2013) 'Six models for the internet + politics', *International Studies Review*, 15: 30–47.

Garrett, L. (2013, April 24) 'The big one? Is China covering up another flu pandemic – or getting it right this time?' *Foreign Policy*. Online. Available HTTP: <http://www.foreignpolicy.com/articles/2013/04/23/the_big_one> (accessed 14 May 2014).

Global Health Security Initiative (GHSI). (2011) 'Ten years of collaborative action'. Online. Available HTTP: <http://www.ghsi.ca/Documents/AnniversaryPublicationFinal.pdf> (accessed 24 August 2013).

Grein, T.W., Kande-Bure, K.O., Rodier, G., Plant, A.J., Bovier, P., Ryan, M.J., Ohyama, T. and Heymann, D.L. (2000) 'Rumors of disease in the global village: outbreak verification', *Emerging Infectious Diseases*, 6: 97–102.

Hartley, D., Nelson, N., Walters, R., Arthur, R., Yangarber, R., Madoff, L., Linge, J., Mawudeku, A., Collier, N., Brownstein, J., Thinus, G. and Lightfoot, N. (2010) 'The landscape of international event-based biosurveillance', *Emerging Health Threats Journal*, 3: e1–8. doi:10.3134/ehtj.10.003

Heymann, D.L. (2013, March 15) 'How SARS was contained', *New York Times*.

Heymann, D.L., Mackenzie, J.S. and Peiris, M. (2013) 'SARS legacy: outbreak reporting is expected and respected', *The Lancet*, 381: 779–781.

Heymann, D.L. and Rodier, G.R. (2004) 'Global surveillance, national surveillance, and SARS', *Emerging Infectious Diseases*, 10: 173–175.

Hitchcock, P., Chamberlain, A., Van Wagoner, M., Inglesby, T.V. and O'Toole, T. (2007) 'Challenges to global surveillance and response to infectious disease outbreaks of international importance', *Biosecurity and Bioterrorism: Biodefense Strategy, Practice, and Science*, 5: 206–227.

Huang, Y. (2013, May 23) 'Responding to disease outbreaks: is China's move toward greater transparency irreversible?' *Asia Unbound*. Online. Available HTTP: <http://blogs.cfr.org/asia/2013/05/23/responding-to-disease-outbreaks-is-chinas-move-toward-greater-transparency-irreversible/>

Interview with Author. (2013a, April 12) Internet Surveillance Response Program Official (via Skype), New York.

Interview with Author. (2013b, April 14) UNSIC official, New York.

Katz, R. and Fischer, J. (2010) 'The revised International Health Regulations: a framework for global pandemic response', *Global Health Governance*, 3: 1–18.

Keller, M., Blench, M., Tolentino, H., Freifeld, C.C., Mandl, K.D., Mawudeku, A., Eysenbach, G. and Brownstein, J.S. (2009) 'Use of unstructured event-based reports for global infectious disease surveillance', *Emerging Infectious Diseases*, 15: 689–695.

Koblentz, G.D. (2010) 'Biosecurity reconsidered: calibrating biological threats and responses', *International Security*, 34: 96–132.

The Lancet. (2007) 'International Health Regulations – the challenges ahead', *The Lancet*, 369: 1763.

The Lancet. (2013) 'From SARS to H7N9: will history repeat itself?', *The Lancet*, 381: 1333.

Li, Q., Zhou, L., Zhou, M., Chen, Z., Li, F., Wu, H., Xiang, N., Chen, E., Tang, F., Wang, D., Meng, L., Hong, Z., Tu, W., Cao, Y., Li, L., Ding, F., Liu, B., Wang, M., Xie, R., Gao, R., Li, X., Bai, T., Zou, S., He, J., Hu, J., Xu, Y., Chai, C., Wang, S., Gao, Y., Jin, L., Zhang, Y., Luo, H., Yu, H., He, J., Li, Q., Wang, X., Gao, L., Pang, X., Liu, G., Yan, Y., Yuan, H., Shu, Y., Yang, W., Wang, Y., Wu, F., Uyeki, T.M. and Zijian Feng, U. (2014) 'Epidemiology of human infections with Avian Influenza A(H7N9) Virus in China', *New England Journal of Medicine*, 370: 520–532.

Linge, J.P., Steinberger, R., Weber, T.P., Yangarber, R., Van der Goot, E., Al Khudhairy, D.H. and Stilianakis, N.I. (2009) 'Internet surveillance systems for early alerting of health threats', *Eurosurveillance*, 14: 1–2.

Mackay, I.M. (2013, June 26) 'Middle East Respiratory Syndrome Coronavirus (MERS-CoV)', *Virology Down Under*. Online. Available HTTP: <http://www.uq.edu.au/vdu/VDUMERSCoronavirus.htm> (accessed 14 May 2014).

Madoff, L.C. and Woodall, J.P. (2005) 'The internet and the global monitoring of emerging diseases: lessons from the first 10 years of ProMED-mail', *Archives of Medical Research*, 36: 724–730.

Mykhalovskiy, E. and Weir, L. (2006) 'The Global Public Health Intelligence Network and early warning outbreak detection: a Canadian contribution to global public health', *Canadian Journal of Public Health*, 97: 42–44.

Nature. (2013) 'The fight against bird flu', *Nature*. Online. Available HTTP: <http://www.nature.com/news/the-fight-against-bird-flu-1.12850> (accessed 14 May 2014).

Nelson, N.P., Yang, L., Reilly, A.R., Hardin, J.E. and Hartley, D.M. (2012) 'Event-based internet biosurveillance: relation to epidemiological observation', *Emerging Themes in Epidemiology*, 9: 1–13. Online. Available HTTP: <http://www.ete-online.com/content/pdf/1742-7622-9-4.pdf> (accessed 14 May 2014).

Norris, B. (2013) 'Tracking influenza A H7N9 through social media', *Social Heath Insights*, Online. Available HTTP: <http://socialhealthinsights.com/2013/04/tracking-influenza-a-h7n9-through-social-media/> (accessed 14 May 2014).

O'Malley, P., Rainford, J. and Thompson, A. (2009) 'Transparency during public health emergencies: from rhetoric to reality', *Bulletin of the World Health Organization*, 87: 614–618.

Rodier, G.R. (2007) 'New rules on international public health security', *Bulletin of the World Health Organization*, 85: 428–430.

Rotureau, B., Barboza, P., Tarantola, A. and Paquet, C. (2007) 'International epidemic intelligence at the Institut de Veille Sanitaire, France', *Dispatch*, 13: 1590–1592.

Schmidt, C.W. (2012) 'Trending now: using social media to predict and track disease outbreaks', *Environmental Health Perspectives*, 120: a30–a33.

Shkabatur, J. (2011) 'A global panopticon? The changing role of international organizations in the information age', *Michigan Journal of International Law*, 33: 159–214.

Singh, J.P. (2013) 'Information technologies, meta-power, and transformations in global politics', *International Studies Review*, 15: 5–29.

United Kingdom Parliament. (2008, July 21) 'Diseases know no frontiers: how effective are intergovernmental organisations in controlling their spread?' *Volume II: Evidence, Select Committee on Intergovernmental Organizations*, House of Lords, 1st Report Session of 2007–2008, HL Paper 143–II.

WHO. (2005) *International Health Regulations*, Geneva: World Health Organization.

WHO. (2013, June 26) 'Middle East respiratory syndrome coronavirus (MERS-CoV) – update', *Global and Alert Response*. Online. Available HTTP: <http://www.who.int/csr/don/2013_06_26/en/index.html> (accessed 14 May 2014).

WHO (2014) 'Epidemic Intelligence – Systematic Event Detection'. Online. Available HTTP: <http://www.who.int/csr/alertresponse/epidemicintelligence/en/> (accessed 14 May 2014).

Wilson, K. and Brownstein, J. (2009) 'Early detection of disease outbreaks using the internet', *Canadian Medical Association Journal*, 180: 829–831.

20

MAKING THE INTERNATIONAL HEALTH REGULATIONS MATTER

Promoting compliance through effective dispute resolution

Steven J. Hoffman

Recent pandemic outbreaks like Severe Acute Respiratory Syndrome (SARS) in 2002 and A(H1N1) influenza in 2009 highlight the central importance of the International Health Regulations (IHR) in maintaining global health security. Adopted through the governing bodies of the World Health Organization (WHO), the IHR establish a rule-based system for preventing and responding to acute health risks of international concern. They have the force of international law, empower WHO to coordinate pandemic responses, and impose a range of obligations on states. For example, the IHR oblige its 194 state parties to maintain surveillance and response capacities and to enforce minimum requirements at points of entry. The IHR also require governments to report certain enumerated public health events and tolerate declarations of emergencies and recommendations from WHO's secretariat. Developed countries are further legally obligated to assist developing countries in achieving the core capacities required by this agreement (Baker & Forsyth 2007; Fidler & Gostin 2006; McDougall & Wilson 2007; World Health Organization 2006).

The IHR represent the latest mechanism through which states have coordinated their response to infectious disease outbreaks. Since quarantine was first used by European ports in the 14th century, the world has seen a successive series of regimes governing global health security, moving from unilateral measures (1377–1851) to international conferences (1851–1892) to institutionalized coordination (1892–1946) to having a single global health security hegemon – WHO – that has been the most important actor in this regime complex ever since (Hoffman 2010). The IHR were revised in 2005 following the SARS outbreak to further expand the WHO secretariat's authority, strengthen its global alert response network, and elevate states' reporting obligations (Fidler & Gostin 2006).

Although the revised IHR were lauded by many as ground breaking, pragmatically, many countries did not meet the June 2012 implementation deadline and requested a two-year extension to continue scaling-up national capacity for pandemic preparedness (Ijaz et al. 2012). It has become apparent that many countries do not have adequate research, workforce, laboratory, or surveillance capacity to support broad-spectrum pandemic responses. Neither does WHO, which currently has an estimated influenza budget of U.S. $7.7 million, an amount equivalent to less than one-third of what New York City dedicates to public health emergencies (Economist 2013; Hoffman & Røttingen 2014). The 2011 Review Committee on the Functioning of the IHR overall concluded that the world is "ill-prepared to respond to a severe influenza pandemic or to any similarly global, sustained and threatening public-health emergency", and that despite existing arrangements in support of pandemic responses, health systems at all levels are currently inadequately equipped to cope with the burdens of serious pandemics (WHO 2011a; see also Edge & Hoffman in press). The G20 Leaders' Declaration in September 2013 noted this capacity challenge and called on countries to comply with their IHR obligations (G20 2013).

Structurally, the IHR are criticized as often as they are praised. The new regulations are said to narrowly define health security (Lancet 2007), fail to specify how national governments are actually supposed to collaborate with one another (Bhattacharya 2007), emphasize surveillance to the exclusion of other essential elements like information sharing (Lancet 2004), rely upon peer pressure and public knowledge for compliance (Wise 2008), and contain no legal enforcement mechanism (Sturtevant et al. 2007). They also depend upon national governments' acquiescence to new global health responsibilities (Merianosa & Peiris 2005), provide opportunities for the politicization of epidemic responses (Suk 2007), and rely on surveillance networks in developing countries that may not be optimally functioning (Wilson et al. 2008).

However, the most stinging criticism of the IHR – and the one that exacerbates all other criticisms – is that an effective dispute resolution mechanism is absent from their provisions. Whereas most criticisms are centered around particular issues of compliance or fears of noncompliance, this last criticism highlights the fundamental absence of any formal mechanism that can be expected to promote compliance. The centrality of dispute resolution is further underscored by the fact that most criticisms of the IHR may eventually lead to disputes between state parties that need to be resolved. The other criticisms could also mostly be mitigated if only there were reliable and effective dispute resolution mechanisms in place for when disagreements inevitably arise.

This is a problem. In a globalized world where the actions of one state affect every other, the consequences of disagreements and noncompliance with international laws can be devastating. The Indonesian virus-sharing dispute brings the depth of these concerns to the fore (Hoffman 2010). Starting in late 2006, Indonesia refused to share H5N1 virus samples despite their significance to global disease surveillance efforts. The country hoped to leverage its virus samples to obtain tangible benefits, particularly technology transfers and vaccine provisions (Enserink 2007). Supported by most developing countries, Indonesia demanded guaranteed access to future vaccines for poorer states that carry a disproportionate burden of the relevant disease and justified these demands by invoking the principles of sovereignty over biological materials, transparency of the global health system, and equity between developed and developing nations (Sedyaningsih et al. 2008).

In this case, virus sharing resumed following a provisional compromise (WHO 2007a), and disagreement was mostly resolved with the World Health Assembly's adoption of the Pandemic Influenza Preparedness Framework for the Sharing of Influenza Viruses and Access to Vaccines and Other Benefits in May 2011 (WHO 2011b). However, this dispute – which spanned six calendar years – highlights how unresolved disagreements can delay or prevent global action during health security emergencies, which can be dangerous, possibly leading to unnecessary death, environmental damage, illness, or financial collapse, in addition to the economic, psychological, and social costs associated with uncertainty and fear. Disagreements over IHR compliance could also affect friendly relations among states and could even lead to armed intervention if a state's health security interests were perceived to be sufficiently threatened (Bonventre et al. 2009; Feldbaum 2009; Peterson 2002). The world is perhaps particularly vulnerable during pandemic outbreaks, when states are likely to disagree on issues like disease origin, travel advisories, trade bans, border closings, vaccine provision, and proper treatment of foreign nationals.

Table 20.1 Goals for IHR Dispute Resolution

Goal	*Significance*
1. Guaranteed resolution	• Ensures the dispute will eventually be resolved • Eliminates uncertainty and reduces fear • Encourages parties to meaningfully participate in other voluntary resolution processes such as mediation or negotiation
2. Quick process (or fast-track option)	• Limits amount of time for inaction among parties • Prevents delay in responding to public health emergency of international concern • Considers potentially rapid evolution of pandemic situations
3. Transparent and fair	• Enhances credibility in and legitimacy of the process • Encourages parties to meaningfully and fully participate • Promotes buy-in, trust, and compliance
4. Authoritative	• Ensures decisions are final and accepted by all parties • Encourages participation and compliance • Diminishes impact, relevance, and persuasiveness of post-hoc complaints concerning legitimacy of the process
5. Maintains friendly relations	• Ensures parties can continue working together on global communicable disease control as is necessary • Prevents the eruption of secondary, more serious conflicts in other arenas (e.g., armed intervention) • Promotes the underlying values and principles of WHO, UN, and the entire multilateral international system
6. Realistic implementation	• Encourage adoption of the revised dispute resolution process • Increases traction and lessens barriers for reform • Fewer roadblocks to success

For international laws like the IHR to really matter, they must provide parties with confidence that their obligations will be fulfilled universally, and that if they are not, mechanisms promoting compliance are available (Hoffman & Røttingen 2012). They must provide parties with a quick, transparent, and fair way to articulate their concerns and protect their interests. An effective dispute resolution process is essential to this confidence as it provides parties a method through which to interpret legal obligations, complain of noncompliance, and resolve other disagreements as necessary. Indeed, since disputes are a normal part of law and politics, the strength of international legal and political institutions can at least be partially evaluated on the way in which disputes are managed (see Table 20.1).

Dispute resolution in the International Health Regulations

Fortunately, dispute resolution is not entirely absent in the IHR. Governed by Article 56 of its provisions, two types of disputes are recognized with different processes for resolution. For disagreements between states, the parties "shall seek in the first instance to settle the dispute through negotiation or any other peaceful means of their own choice, including good offices, mediation or conciliation." If a resolution is not attained, the parties "may agree to refer the dispute to the [WHO] Director-General, who shall make every effort to settle it." Binding arbitration is then possible if the dispute is among states that have voluntarily accepted it "as compulsory with regard to all disputes concerning the interpretation or application of these Regulations."

Disagreements between a state and WHO are referred to the World Health Assembly for resolution (WHO 2006).

At first glance, the approach to dispute resolution that is outlined in the IHR seems rather progressive. It recognizes the limitations, costs, and consequences of formal litigation and promotes alternative processes such as negotiation, mediation, conciliation, and arbitration. Reference to the World Health Assembly, WHO's highest governing body, ensures that all state parties affected by the dispute have an important role in solving it.

However, while the parties may be legally required to *attempt* settling the dispute, there is no guarantee or requirement that they actually resolve it. Negotiation and conciliation are strictly voluntary, as is mediation with the Director-General. This lack of any obligatory mechanism compelling the disputing parties to participate means that it will be power and political influence, rather than law and legal norms, that determine the resolution process and outcome. The absence of a guaranteed final settlement also unnecessarily extends uncertainty and provides little incentive for rapid resolution. While binding arbitration as outlined in the IHR would address many of these concerns, its use is possible only in disputes between members that have voluntarily accepted this additional obligation. As of now, despite heightened awareness for the IHR's importance following the SARS and H1N1 pandemics, not a single country has done so (Gian Luca Burci, WHO Legal Counsel, email communication, 24 February 2014). This means these arbitration provisions are not in reality having any effect. Finally, reference to the World Health Assembly in disputes between WHO and state parties is essentially a majority rule system that prioritizes politics and national self-interest over legal and scientific considerations. International realities and structural barriers to equal participation dictate that some states will be more influential before this governing body than others (Hoffman 2012).

In light of this voluntariness, there are currently few incentives for states to ever resolve their disputes and no mechanism to ensure a timely settlement. Politics is allowed to reign supreme – which historically has been detrimental to progress in public health (Howard-Jones 1975; Lancet 1892; Suk 2007) – with weaker states left particularly disadvantaged and all states left vulnerable. In the realm of quickly evolving communicable diseases, the world is in danger when disputes are unresolved or are addressed too slowly. Poorly monitored airports, for example, can lead to the needless spread of disease between continents, and noncompliance with reporting obligations could delay worldwide pandemic response efforts resulting in exponentially worse outcomes (WHO 2007b).

The dearth of strong dispute resolution mechanisms is not unique to public health. With some clear exceptions for trade (e.g., World Trade Organization) and conflict (e.g., UN Security Council), too often states are left without effective mechanisms to authoritatively interpret international laws, define their rights and obligations under them, or adjudicate allegations of transgression. States have few legal options to confront parties that may unwittingly be in violation of a certain provision or who are purposely refusing to fulfill an obligation for leverage or coercion. Political solutions to complex disputes may require too much time or may not be possible at all. There may also be times when it is desirable to shield decisions from the ordinary influence of politics and power, such as in technical disputes or emergencies where decisions may be better if informed primarily by scientists and research evidence (Suk 2007). Moreover, in the absence of a rational and effective dispute resolution process, disagreements can be left unresolved or managed through irrational processes such as dominance through economic strength, political clout, or even the use of force (Emond 1989; Hoffman 2012).

The aforementioned Indonesian virus-sharing dispute highlights how ambiguity, voluntariness, and political considerations continue to challenge the IHR's dispute resolution process and real-world effectiveness. It also highlights the existing divisions among developed, developing, and emerging countries that no doubt serve as a destabilizing force and a likely source for future disputes. Indeed, deliberations at WHO meetings following this particular dispute's passing showed that there is not even consensus among states for the conceptualization of virus sharing as a health security issue that would be covered by the IHR (Aldis 2008). This example demonstrates that the existing dispute resolution process has not been entirely successful and that strategies for strengthening it are necessary for a healthy future.

Alternative dispute resolution processes

There are two broad classes of dispute resolution mechanisms from which state parties could draw in their efforts to enhance IHR effectiveness and compliance with them.

Advisory mechanisms

Advisory bodies can help conflicting state parties to increase the likelihood of a negotiated settlement. Such a resolution is ideal given its potential to be quick and harmonious. One opportunity to strengthen negotiation may be to involve an independent legal expert early in the process so that he/she can provide an initial opinion on the matters in dispute and provide at least one neutral perspective on legal ambiguities. Such a mechanism could be particularly useful for situations where there is a dispute over differing interpretations of the IHR or legal issues involving the agreement's implementation. The role of neutral legal expert could possibly be served by WHO's Chief Legal Officer if the dispute is among states or by the UN's Chief Legal Officer if the dispute involves WHO.

If independent negotiations fail, facilitative or evaluative mediation can be used to help the parties identify their core concerns and craft creative solutions. The use of this process is envisioned by the IHR, which essentially nominates WHO's Director-General to serve as mediator in disputes among states. Mediation in this context could be strengthened by making it a compulsory activity, using professional mediators with advanced training and expanding its application to include disputes between states and WHO. These changes can be made in various ways. For example, an independent group such as the UN Mediation Standby Team could neutrally facilitate this process with great success given their extensive training and experience (United Nations 2008). A special dispute review board with legal and health experts could alternatively be constituted on a permanent or ad-hoc basis to provide an early evaluation of the dispute and make authoritative recommendations. If that is not desirable, a "mini-trial" could be conducted to further enhance these efforts given it lets high-level decision-makers make their best case in front of a panel and hear one group's take on the merits of their core arguments.

More formal political and legal mechanisms could also be incorporated as part of the dispute resolution process of the IHR. Policy commissions or special inquiry panels could be established to investigate disputes and assess proposals that could later be implemented to resolve them (e.g., European Community's Badinter Commission on the dissolution of Yugoslavia). Another common mechanism is the expert supervisory committee that continually and systematically assesses compliance by the relevant parties and makes authoritative rulings on legal issues. This device is commonly relied upon in human rights treaties and includes various bodies such as the Committee Against Torture, Committee on the Elimination of Discrimination against Women, Committee on the Elimination of Racial Discrimination, Committee on the Rights of the Child, Committee on Economic, Social and Cultural Rights, and the Human Rights Committee overseeing the International Covenant on Civil and Political Rights. While these groups of experts mostly accept reports from countries and make recommendations, some of them can entertain complaints or "communications" from states about others (e.g., Committee against Torture and the Human Rights Committee). Their rulings are not binding but are generally viewed, like advisory opinions of the International Court of Justice, as one of the most authoritative interpretations possible about the obligations imposed by the relevant treaty (McGoldrick 1991). A similarly constituted expert committee focused on the IHR could perhaps be equally effective in advising the resolution of disputes.

Overall, advisory mechanisms are best suited to empower disputing parties to develop their own solutions. They are flexible, prioritize integrative resolutions, reflect the concerns of the disputants, and encourage compliance. Advisory processes also help to preserve continuing relations that are critically important in the international sphere. These advantages, however, assume that a resolution is possible. None of the advisory mechanisms described above can compel meaningful participation, bind parties' future action, induce settlements, or guarantee compliance (Kanowitz 1986). If an internal expert or permanent review board leads the mediation or evaluation process, the process may lack independence and due process safeguards. The use of external professional mediators or commissioners, on the other hand, may not be ideal either because they will likely lack important technical knowledge on the science of communicable disease prevention and control.

Adjudicative mechanisms

Dispute resolution processes can alternatively involve more formalized adjudication where a specific resolution is developed or imposed by an independent body after the conflicting parties have presented their cases. The decisions of these bodies are final, except for appeals, and are meant to go well beyond just advising the parties on their respective positions or facilitating negotiation.

Adjudicative bodies in the context of the IHR could be structured in many ways. For example, WHO could create a special judicial organ that would be tasked with arbitrating disputes of all varieties and issue formal binding decisions across WHO's legal frameworks. This approach has been adopted by other international organizations including the Benelux, Organization for Security and Cooperation in Europe, Economic Community of Western African States, Organization of Central American States, and Organization of Arab Petroleum Exporting Countries.

Alternatively, WHO could form a specialized IHR Dispute Resolution Board that would concern itself exclusively with the interpretation and implementation of this legal instrument. It could emulate existing administrative bodies that resolve staff complaints or adjudicate disputes arising from treaties. For example, the International Tribunal of the Law of the Sea, created by the 1982 Law of the Sea Convention, adjudicates conflicts between states, gives advisory opinions, and can order interim measures even when the main proceedings are being heard in a different adjudicative forum (Klabbers 2009). Past success with such dispute resolutions boards is particularly convincing. As a requirement for World Bank-funded projects valued at over U.S. $10 million, they have been extensively utilized around the world (World Bank 2007). Their potential use in resolving conflicts among parties in ongoing relationships is recognized internationally (e.g., International Chamber of Commerce 2004).

The creation of ad-hoc bodies to resolve specific issues is also not without precedents. WHO has in the past empowered temporary commissioners to investigate and report on certain issues of pressing concern (e.g., WHO Commission on Intellectual Property Rights, Innovation and Public Health 2006; WHO Commission on Macroeconomics and Health 2001; WHO Commission on Social Determinants of Health 2008) and contracting parties to the old GATT regime used to hastily convene multiparty panels to resolve conflicts when they arose (Klabbers 2009;

Klabbers & Vreugdenhil 1986). The UN Security Council has even created temporary international criminal tribunals for Rwanda and the former Yugoslavia. Given the nexus between communicable diseases and global health security, it is not entirely inconceivable for the UN Security Council to form a similar body in the context of disputes arising from the IHR. (Rubin & Arroyo 2007).

Dispute resolution under the IHR could also include reference to the International Court of Justice, the judicial organ of the UN. In keeping with Article 36 of the court's constituting statute, states could voluntarily accept the jurisdiction of the International Court of Justice for all future disputes among themselves concerning the IHR (International Court of Justice 1945). Decisions of the court for such matters would then be final, legally binding, and enforceable via reference to the UN Security Council.

The use of this mechanism for disputes between states and WHO is a bit more complicated. While Article 96(2) of the UN Charter already lets the organization "request advisory opinions of the Court on legal questions arising within the scope of their activities" (United Nations 1945), these decisions technically have no binding force and can be granted or denied at the discretion of the court (International Court of Justice 1950). Advisory opinions, however, are perhaps as authoritative a statement as is possible on international law and can be made legally binding if parties to the IHR accept them as so for disputes that WHO refers to the court for resolution. The strategy of accepting the binding nature of advisory opinions via collateral agreements has been incorporated within many international treaties, including the General Convention on Privileges and Immunities of the UN (United Nations 1946). It is not inconceivable that states would accept advisory opinions related to the IHR as binding as a condition of joining, for example, a broader trade agreement.

The discretionary nature of advisory opinions issued by the court, however, is also probably not a great concern. Whereas the former Permanent Court of International Justice demonstrated hesitance to issue such nonbinding opinions to settle disputes without explicit state authorization (Permanent Court of International Justice 1923), the current International Court of Justice almost always accepts them and has stated that requests for them "in principle, should not be refused" (International Court of Justice 1950). Ironically, the only request for an advisory opinion that was ever rejected by the court actually came from WHO when it asked the court to rule on the legality of nuclear weapons. The International Court of Justice refused to provide an advisory opinion on principle, explaining that "none of the functions of the World Health Organization is dependent upon the legality of the situations upon which it must act," which means it does not have the ability to request the opinion (International Court of Justice 1996). There can be no doubt that global communicable disease control is of central (if not of the most central) importance to WHO's core functions and that advisory opinions on legal concerns involving this topic would almost surely be welcomed. The only certain problem that remains is that international organizations have no standing before the International Court of Justice other than through advisory opinions (International Court of Justice 1945). This means that states have no ability to initiate proceedings against WHO even if so desired. This explains why most claims by states against international organizations have historically been resolved through arbitration or independent commissions (Arsanjani 1981).

Overall, like advisory mechanisms, adjudicative processes are also not perfect. While they may provide for final decisions that are imposed on the parties, resolutions may be suboptimal given that they are not developed by the parties themselves and their implementation could inadvertently serve to harm friendly relations among them (Kanowitz 1986). The decisions of these bodies are also not necessarily legally binding depending on the status and provisions of its constituting instrument, and the disputing parties may have to rely on "political massaging" and rhetorical persuasion to encourage compliance no matter their legal status (Klabbers 2009).

Table 20.2 Advisory and Adjudicative Dispute Resolution Processes

	Mechanisms	*Strengths*	*Weaknesses*
Advisory Bodies	1. Initial legal opinion 2. Mandatory mediation 3. Dispute review board 4. Mini-trial 5. Special inquiry panels 6. Expert supervisory committee	• Empower disputing parties to develop their own solutions • Prioritize integrative resolutions • Guidance from technical experts or professional facilitators • Reflect concerns of disputants • Preserve existing relationships • Encourage compliance	• Voluntary process • No guaranteed resolution • No mechanism to ensure compliance • May lack independent or due process safeguards • Professional facilitators may not have necessary technical knowledge
Adjudicative Bodies	7. Formal judicial organ 8. Dispute resolution board 9. Ad-hoc tribunal 10. International court of justice	• Provide final authoritative decisions • Guarantee resolution to dispute • Compel participation • Formal procedures • Likely to have transparent and fair process	• Can issue suboptimal resolutions • Limited participation in developing resolution by the disputing parties • Potentially antagonistic • Can harm friendly relations • May lack necessary technical knowledge

Again, depending on how they are structured, adjudicative bodies may lack independence and/or technical knowledge on communicable disease control (see Table 20.2).

Mandatory multitiered dispute resolution for promoting compliance with the International Health Regulations

Given no single dispute resolution process is perfect, a multitiered process is likely the best route forward. Successful past use of hybrid processes show that the creativity and innovation invested in their design will often yield better results than the stringent use of single mechanisms (Brown & Marriott 1993; Emond 1989). They can also help isolate particular conflicts without disrupting broader collaborations and can offer provisional resolutions when delayed action would otherwise lead to enormous consequences.

Multitiered dispute resolution systems generally start with a process that can be applied very quickly for emergency situations but allows appeals to eventually achieve an authoritative judgment. Early mechanisms would be binding on the parties until the decisions reached are replaced by a voluntary settlement or a later sanctioned process. Parties would be expected to implement early resolutions while waiting for the results of any appeals they may initiate. This provides for a stop-gap measure and allows the international community to move forward in the interim until the next process concludes.

Specifically, in the context of the IHR, it is possible to envision a three-tiered dispute resolution system that starts with an 1) *initial legal opinion,* which, if unsatisfactory to one of the parties, could be appealed to an 2) *advisory body,* which, if also unsatisfactory to one of the parties, could be appealed to an 3) *adjudicative body* for final resolution. The initial legal opinion could be given, for example, by a neutral legal expert, and the advisory body could be a permanent dispute review board. Final pleadings could then be made to an adjudicative body such as an arbitration panel that would issue a last and binding judgment. In this system, the initial legal opinion would be binding and implemented until (and unless) the dispute review board recommends a conflicting resolution. This recommendation would then be binding and implemented until (and unless) the arbitration panel issues its final decision. The three tiers could involve three different dispute resolution bodies or as little as one body operating in a different capacity at each of the three stages but with necessary independence between them. If just one body is preferred, an expert supervisory committee like those used in human rights treaties may be particularly effective, especially as part of a larger system where this committee continually assesses compliance, accepts reports, hears complaints, and makes rulings on legal issues. Regardless of the specific mechanism responsible for each of the three tiers, a negotiated or mediated voluntary settlement among the parties that is reached prior to the final adjudicative body's ruling would replace whatever opinions or recommendations had already been issued and implemented (see Figure 20.1).

An initial legal opinion may be a particularly effective first step given the speed in which one could be issued (e.g., as few as 2–5 days). If provided by a neutral expert such as the Chief Legal Officer of WHO (for disputes among states) or the UN (for disputes involving WHO), it could

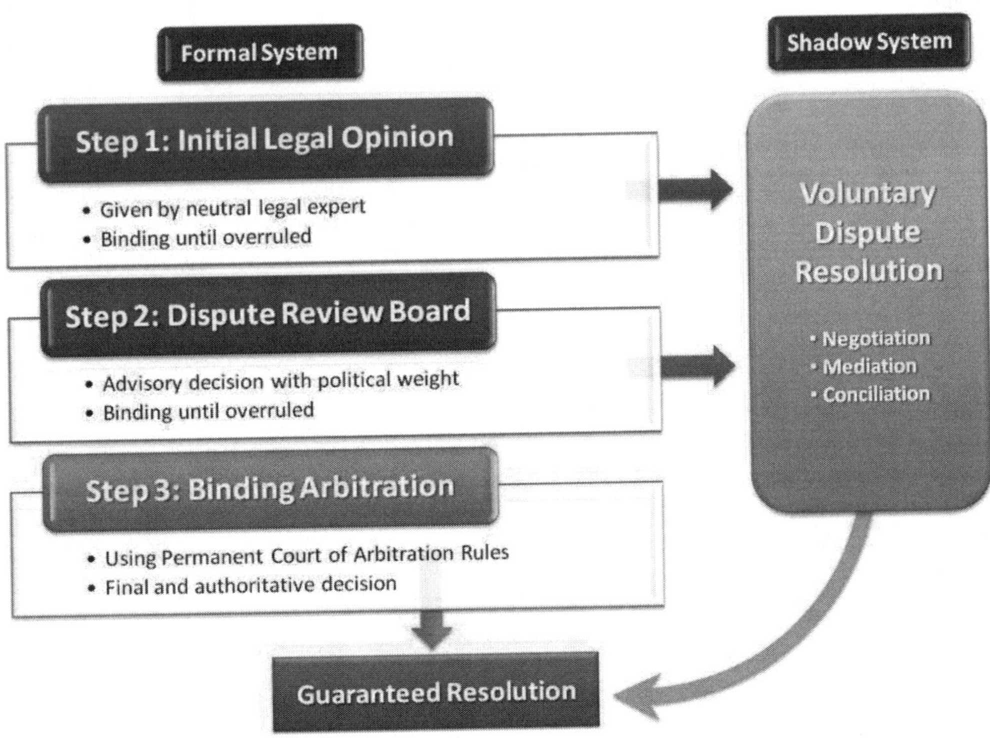

Figure 20.1 Proposed Multitiered IHR Dispute Resolution Process and its Shadow System

carry sufficient authority commensurate with the requirement for temporary implementation. It could also serve as a valuable input to negotiation, mediation, and conciliation efforts by clarifying the legal issues involved in the dispute. Similar provisional mechanisms involving other types of experts contributed successfully to the multitiered dispute resolution processes employed in constructing Hong Kong's International Airport and The Netherland's Maeslant Water Barrier (Bosch 2001; Lewis 2002; Sandborg 1999).

An advisory body such as a permanent dispute review board is well-suited to be the second step of this multitiered process given it can more extensively review any dispute's details over a few weeks and offer guidance to the parties in a form that would carry significant political weight. Again, any recommendations issued by this body would dually serve as both binding orders until overruled and as extremely valuable input to help resolve the dispute through voluntary processes.

Finally, adjudicative bodies such as a binding arbitration panel is ideally structured to offer final decisions on conflicts as the third step of the proposed dispute resolution process. An arbitration panel's work can be completed within a couple of months and would leave the disputants with an authoritative and final resolution.

While multitiered dispute resolution systems are themselves designed to promote compliance, perhaps the most important benefit to be obtained from them is the "shadow system" of voluntary collaborative dispute resolution that they support. So long as there are no mandatory steps that must be followed, the more powerful or less affected conflicting party will have little incentive to engage in more collaborative forms of dispute resolutions such as negotiation, mediation, and conciliation. However, if mandatory processes exist, it will be within parties' own self-interest to actively seek out acceptable settlements rather than leave the resolution to others who will impose one on them – possibly without considering their priorities or interests. In the domestic context, this need for a less advantageous process is met by the judicial system that forces disputants to participate in a thoroughly and universally unpleasant and costly process. No such last-resort system exists under most international laws, including the IHR, to encourage disputants to pursue more collaborative ways of coming to resolution. The proposed multitiered model, however, fulfills the necessary requirements, requiring steps that go from the participative to authoritative thereby gradually increasing pressure among the parties to find a mutually agreeable solution. The more meaningful participation that the mandatory system is intended to elicit for voluntary mechanisms has been shown in other contexts to yield better results (Brown & Marriott 1993; Ginsburg & McAdams 2004).

Conclusion

Recent events have highlighted the vital importance of the IHR to global health security, yet their various weaknesses remain untouched with little debate among researchers, national decision makers, and global health leaders on how to improve them. This chapter explains why the existing system for resolving disputes is one of the greatest limitations of the IHR and identifies practical ways in which it can be strengthened. Specifically, a multitiered process that guarantees a quick and final resolution would enhance confidence in the global communicable disease control regime, prevent inaction when there is a conflict, and reduce the role of politics in technical health security decisions. It could also help promote state parties' compliance with the treaty, an especially important issue since 2012 when requirements for core surveillance and response capacities came into effect. Additionally, a mandatory system would provide incentives for parties to engage with more participatory mechanisms that together constitute perhaps the most productive integrated system for dispute resolution.

Change will not be easy but it is also not impossible. Several recent events may have opened windows of opportunity for progress, such as the sobering findings of WHO's 2011 IHR Review (WHO 2011a), the World Economic Forum listing pandemics as a top global risk (World Economic Forum 2013), outbreak of Middle East Respiratory Syndrome in Saudi Arabia in 2012 (Chan 2013), outbreak of A(H7N9) influenza in China in 2012 (Harada et al. 2013), and launch of the US-led Global Health Security Agenda in February 2014 to boost global coordination and elevate capacity in developing countries (US Department of Health & Human Services 2014).

Better models for resolving disputes under the IHR can be implemented within existing structures and without formal changes to WHO's constitution or any other international treaty. Politicization, noncompliance, and power conflicts need not be inherent flaws of international laws such as the IHR as some have described them. Practical solutions exist and are ready for implementation.

References

Aldis, W. (2008) 'Health security as a public health concept: a critical analysis', *Health Policy and Planning*, 23: 369–375.

Arsanjani, M.H. (1981) 'Claims against international organizations: ouis custodiet ipsos custodes', *Yale Journal of World Public Order*, 7: 131–176.

Baker, M.G. and Forsyth, A.M. (2007) 'The new International Health Regulations: a revolutionary change in global health security', *New Zealand Medical Journal*, 120: e1–8.

Bhattacharya, D. (2007) 'An exploration of conceptual and temporal fallacies in international health law and promotion of global public health preparedness', *Journal of Law, Medicine and Ethics*, 35: 588–598.

Bonventre, E.V., Hicks, K.H. and Okutani, S.M. (2009) *U.S. National Security and Global Health: An Analysis of Global Health Engagement by the U.S. Department of Defense*, Washington DC: Center for Strategic and International Studies.

Bosch, J. (2001) 'The role of ADR in the construction of the Hong Kong Airport and the Maeslant Water Barrier', *Construction Law Journal*, 17: 498–506.

Brown, H.J. and Marriott, A.L. (1993) *ADR Principles and Practice*, London: Sweet & Maxwell.

Chan, M. (2013) *WHO Director-General addresses the Sixty-Sixth World Health Assembly*, Geneva: World Health Organization.

Economist. (2013, April 20) 'Coming, ready or not: despite progress, the world is still unprepared for a new pandemic disease', *Economist*. Online. Available HTTP: <http://www.economist.com/news/leaders/21576390-despite-progress-world-still-unprepared-new-pandemic-disease-coming-ready-or-not> (accessed 25 February 2014).

Edge, J.S. and Hoffman, S.J. (in press) 'Strengthening national health systems' capacity to respond to future global pandemics', in S.E. Davies and J. Youde (eds.) *The Politics of Disease Outbreak Surveillance: The New Frontier for States and Non-State Actors*, Aldershot: Ashgate Publishing.

Emond, D.P. (1989) 'Alternative dispute resolution: a conceptual overview', in D.P. Emond (ed.) *Commercial Dispute Resolution*, Toronto: Canada Law Book.

Enserink, M. (2007) 'Avian influenza: Indonesia earns flu accord at World Health Assembly', *Science*, 316: 1108.

Feldbaum, H. (2009) *U.S. Global Health and National Security Policy*, Washington DC: Center for Strategic and International Studies.

Fidler, D.P. and Gostin, L.O. (2006) 'The new International Health Regulations: an historic development for international law and public health', *Journal of Law, Medicine and Ethics*, 34: 85–94.

G20. (2013) *G20 Leaders' Declaration*. September. Online. Available HTTP: <https://www.g20.org/sites/default/files/g20_resources/library/Saint_Petersburg_Declaration_ENG.pdf> (accessed 25 February 2014).

Ginsburg, T. and McAdams, R. (2004) 'Adjudicating in anarchy: an expressive theory of international dispute resolution', *William and Mary Law Review*, 45: 1229–1339.

Harada, N., Alexander, N. and Olowokure, B. (2013) 'Avian influenza A(H7N9): information-sharing through government web sites in the Western Pacific Region', *Western Pacific Surveillance and Response Journal*, 4: 44–46.

Hoffman, S.J. (2010) 'The evolution, etiology and eventualities of the global health security regime', *Health Policy and Planning*, 25: 510–522.

Hoffman, S.J. (2012) 'Mitigating inequalities of influence among states in global decision making', *Global Policy Journal*, 3: 421–432.

Hoffman, S.J. and Røttingen, J.-A. (2012) 'Assessing implementation mechanisms for an international agreement on research and development for health products', *Bulletin of the World Health Organization*, 90: 854–863.

Hoffman, S.J. and Røttingen, J.-A. (2014) 'Split WHO in two: strengthening political decision-making and securing independent scientific advice', *Public Health*, 128: 188–194.

Howard-Jones, N. (1975) *The Scientific Background of the International Sanitary Conferences, 1851–1938*, Geneva: World Health Organization.

Ijaz, K., Kasowski, E., Arthur, R.R., Angulo, F.J. and Dowell, S.F. (2012) 'International Health Regulations – what gets measured gets done', *Emerging Infectious Diseases*, 18: 1054–1057.

International Chamber of Commerce. (2004) *Dispute Board Rules*, Paris: International Chamber of Commerce.

International Court of Justice. (1945) *Statute of the International Court of Justice*, New York: United Nations.

International Court of Justice. (1950) 'Interpretation of peace treaties: advisory opinion', *I.C.J. Reports* (30 March): 65–119. The Hague: International Court of Justice.

International Court of Justice. (1996) 'Legality of the use by a state of nuclear weapons in armed conflict: advisory opinion', *I.C.J. Reports* (8 July): 66–85. The Hague: International Court of Justice.

Kanowitz, L. (1986) *Cases and Materials on Alternative Dispute Resolution*, St. Paul: West Publishing Company.

Klabbers, J. (2009) *An Introduction to International Institutional Law*, 2nd ed., Cambridge: Cambridge University Press.

Klabbers, J. and Vreugdenhil, A. (1986) 'Dispute settlement in GATT: DISC and its successor', *Legal Issues of Economic Integration*, 1: 115–138.

Lancet. (1892) 'The Venice Sanitary Conference', *Lancet*, 139: 95.

Lancet. (2004) 'Public-health preparedness requires more than surveillance', *Lancet*, 364: 1639–1640.

Lancet. (2007) 'WHO fails to address health security', *Lancet*, 370: 714.

Lewis, D. (2002) 'Dispute resolution in the new Hong Kong International Airport Core Programme Projects – postscript', *International Construction Law Review*, 19: 68–78.

McDougall, C.W. and Wilson, K. (2007) 'Canada's obligations to global public health security under the revised International Health Regulations', *Health Law Review*, 16: 25–32.

McGoldrick, D. (1991) *The Human Rights Committee: Its Role in the Development of the International Covenant on Civil and Political Rights*, Oxford: Oxford University Press.

Merianosa, A. and Peiris, M. (2005) 'International Health Regulations (2005)', *Lancet*, 366: 1249–1251.

Permanent Court of International Justice. (1923) *Status of the Eastern Carelia: Advisory Opinion: PCIJ, Series B*, No. 5, 23 July. The Hague: Permanent Court of International Justice.

Peterson, S. (2002) 'Epidemic disease and national security', *Security Studies*, 12: 43–81.

Rubin, H. and Arroyo, A. (2007) *The International Compact for Infectious Diseases*, Philadelphia: Institute for Strategic Threat Analysis and Response at the University of Pennsylvania.

Sandborg, D.L. (1999) 'Multistep ADR gets creative at Hong Kong's new airport', *Alternatives to the High Cost of Litigation*, 17: 41–61.

Sedyaningsih, E.R., Isfandari, S., Soendoro, T. and Supari, S.F. (2008) 'Towards mutual trust, transparency and equity in virus sharing mechanism: The avian influenza case of Indonesia', *Annals Academy of Medicine of Singapore*, 37: 482–488.

Sturtevant, J.L., Anema, A. and Brownstein, J.S. (2007) 'The new International Health Regulations: considerations for global public health surveillance', *Disaster Medicine and Public Health Preparedness*, 1: 117–121.

Suk, J.E. (2007) 'Sound science and the new International Health Regulations', *Global Health Governance*, 1: 1–4.

United Nations. (1945) *Charter of the United Nations*, New York: United Nations.

United Nations. (1946) *Convention on the Privileges and Immunities of the United Nations: Adopted by the General Assembly of the United Nations on 13 February 1946*, New York: United Nations.

United Nations. (2008, March 5) 'Top UN mediation team now on call for crises around the world'. Online. Available HTTP: <http://www.un.org/apps/news/story.asp?NewsID=25866&Cr=diplomacy&Cr1#.Uwzy4nmmE6I> (accessed 25 February 2014).

US Department of Health & Human Services. (2014) *Global Health Security Agenda: Toward a World Safe and Secure from Infectious Disease Threats*, Washington DC: US Department of Health & Human Services. Online. Available HTTP: <http://www.globalhealth.gov/global-health-topics/global-health-security/GHS%20Agenda.pdf> (accessed 25 February 2014).

WHO Commission on Intellectual Property Rights, Innovation and Public Health. (2006) *Public Health, Innovation and Intellectual Property Rights*, Geneva: World Health Organization. Online. Available HTTP: <http://www.who.int/intellectualproperty/documents/thereport/ENPublicHealthReport.pdf> (accessed 25 February 2014).

WHO Commission on Macroeconomics and Health. (2001) *Macroeconomics and Health: Investing in Health for Economic Development*, Geneva: World Health Organization.

WHO Commission on Social Determinants of Health. (2008) *Closing the Gap in a Generation: Health Equity through Action on the Social Determinants of Health: Final Report of the Commission on Social Determinants of Health*, Geneva: World Health Organization.

Wilson, K., Tigerstrom, B. and McDougall, C. (2008) 'Protecting global health security through the International Health Regulations: requirements and challenges', *Canadian Medical Association Journal*, 179: 44–48.

Wise, J. (2008) 'UK steps up its global health security', *Lancet Infectious Diseases*, 8: 350.

World Bank. (2007) *Standard Bidding Documents: Procurement of Works and User's Guide*, Washington DC: World Bank.

World Economic Forum. (2013) *Global Risks 2013: Eighth Edition*, Geneva: World Economic Forum. Online. Available HTTP: <http://www3.weforum.org/docs/WEF_GlobalRisks_Report_2013.pdf> (accessed 25 February 2014).

World Health Organization (WHO). (2006) *International Health Regulations (2005)*, Geneva: World Health Organization.

World Health Organization (WHO). (2007a, March 27) 'Indonesia to resume sharing H5N1 avian influenza virus samples following a WHO meeting in Jakarta'. Online. Available HTTP: <http://www.who.int/mediacentre/news/releases/2007/pr09/en/> (accessed 25 February 2014).

World Health Organization (WHO). (2007b) *World Health Report 2007: A Safer Future: Global Public Health Security in the 21st Century*, Geneva: World Health Organization.

World Health Organization (WHO). (2011a) *Report by the Director-General – Implementation of the International Health Regulations (2005): Report of the Review Committee on the Functioning of the International Health Regulations (2005) in relation to Pandemic (H1N1) 2009*, A64/10 ed, Geneva: World Health Organization.

World Health Organization (WHO). (2011b) *Pandemic Influenza Preparedness Framework for the Sharing of Influenza Viruses and Access to Vaccines and Other Benefits*, Geneva: World Health Organization. Online. Available HTTP: <http://whqlibdoc.who.int/publications/2011/9789241503082_eng.pdf> (accessed 25 February 2014).

21

BIOSECURITY EDUCATION FOR LIFE SCIENTISTS

The missing past, inadequate present, and uncertain future

Malcolm Dando

It is not difficult to find concerns about the hostile misuse of advances in the modern life sciences today. For example the report on *Global Strategic Trends-Out to 2040* published by the UK Ministry of Defence's Development, Concepts and Doctrine Centre (DCDC) pointed out that:

> The CBRN [Chemical, Biological, Radiological and Nuclear] threat from state and non-state actors is *likely* to increase, facilitated by lowering of some entry barriers, dual purpose industrial facilities and the proliferation of technical knowledge and expertise. Terrorist attacks using chemical, biological and radiological weapons are *likely*, as are mass-casualty attacks using novel methods.
>
> (DCDC 2010:15, italics emphasis in original)

"Likely" in this text indicates an assumed probability of between 60% and 90%.

To guard against the danger of the misuse of advances in the life sciences the international community has developed what can be called a web of preventive policies – good intelligence, international agreements nationally implemented, export controls, sensible defense, and an expected response to deviations from the norm of nonuse of chemical and biological weapons – that together are expected to persuade anyone considering such misuse that it is not worth doing. Central to this web is the 1925 Geneva Protocol that prohibits the use of such weapons, the 1975 Biological and Toxin Weapons Convention (BTWC), and the 1997 Chemical Weapons Convention (CWC).

As State Parties to the CWC have been largely concerned with the formidable task of destroying the huge lethal chemical weapons stockpiles built up during the Cold War period of the second half of the last century, they have only recently begun to turn their attention to the awareness and education of scientists as an essential component of the in-depth national implementation of the Convention. Therefore, there is much more information about and experience of this issue in relation to the BTWC than the CWC. Thus for the purposes of this chapter the main focus will initially be on this longer standing international agreement and its national implementation by State Parties.

The BTWC does not have a major international organization to take care of its operation so its development has been steered by a series of five-yearly Review Conferences. This Convention also does not have an effective system of verifying that its members are living up to their obligations. In an attempt to correct this deficiency the 1986 (Second) and the 1991 (Third) Review Conferences agreed a system of annual declarations that were designed to increase the confidence in compliance, but these politically binding Confidence-Building Measures (CBMs) have never been submitted by enough states and in full enough form to achieve that objective. So in 1991, and throughout the following decade, an effort was made to agree a legally binding instrument of declarations, visits, and inspections that would form, in effect, a Verification Protocol. This effort was unsuccessful and the 2001–2002, 2006, and 2011 Review Conferences agreed instead on a series of three Inter Sessional Processes (ISPs) – annual meetings at Expert and then at State Party levels – on topics that might be more easily managed by States Parties and lead to a strengthening of the Convention.

Despite this difficult history, the BTWC forms a major barrier to the hostile misuse of the modern life sciences. Article I, in part, states that:

> Each State Party to this convention undertakes never in any circumstances to develop, produce, stockpile or otherwise acquire or retain:
>
> (1) Microbial or other biological agents, or toxins whatever their origin or method of production, of types and in quantities that have no justification for prophylactic, protective or other peaceful purposes.
>
> (United Nations 1972)

So biological agents and toxins can only be used for peaceful purposes. It should also be understood that the word "toxin" here has a wider meaning than scientists might usually understand. As the World Health Organization (WHO) noted:

> In the sense of the Biological and Toxin Weapons Convention, "toxin" includes substances to which scientists would not normally apply the term. For example, there are chemicals that occur naturally in the human body that would have toxic effects if administered in large enough quantity. Where a scientist might see a bioregulator, say, the treaty would see a poisonous substance produced by a living organism, in other words a toxin – nor is this unreasonable.
>
> (World Health Organization 2004: 216)

Therefore there is an overlap between the BTWC and the more recent Chemical Weapons Convention in that both cover what have been called "mid-spectrum agents" such as toxins and bioregulators. The CWC prohibition ranges from classical lethal chemical agents such as the nerve gases through to these agents, and the BTWC prohibition ranges from the mid-spectrum agents through to traditional biological agents and genetically modified biological agents.

Protection against such a formidable threat cannot just rest on an international-level agreement. Therefore Article IV of the BTWC requires that:

> Each State Party to the Convention shall, in accordance with its constitutional processes, take any necessary measures to *prohibit and prevent* the development, production, stockpiling, acquisition or retention of the agents, toxins, weapons, equipment and means of delivery specified in Article I of the Convention, within the territory of such State, under its jurisdiction or under its control anywhere.
>
> (emphasis added)

The meaning of "prohibit" here is obvious. State Parties are required to be sure that laws are in place to enact the prohibition of the nonpeaceful use of biological agents and toxins. However, "prevention" *comes before* the act that is prohibited, and could imply for example, the use of oversight systems or codes of conduct for scientists. Moreover, at the Second Five-Year Review Conference of 1986, State Parties agreed, under Article IV, that:

> The Conference notes the importance of . . .
>
> - Inclusion in textbooks and medical, scientific and military educational programmes of information dealing with the prohibition of bacteriological (biological) and toxin weapons and the provisions of the Geneva Protocol.
> - And believes that such measures which States might undertake in accordance with their constitutional processes would strengthen the effectiveness of the Convention.
>
> (United Nations 1986: 5)

This surely makes sense as oversight systems of regulation or codes of conduct are unlikely to be successful if the need for such measures is not well understood. Moreover, it is not just important that scientists understand their responsibilities under the Convention but also that they are able to contribute their expertise to maintaining and developing the prohibition against chemical and biological weapons at a time of rapid scientific and technological change (Petro et al. 2003: 161–168). It is not surprising, therefore, that similar statements about education of scientists assisting in the strengthening of the Convention can be found in the outcome of subsequent review conferences.

The missing past

What is surprising is that 25 years later, in a Working Paper for the Seventh Five-Year Review Conference in 2011, eleven states, including the UK and USA Depositary States, reported that:

> While the existence of a well-developed sense for aspects related to (bio-) safety among students and practising life scientists has been repeatedly confirmed, there is, in general, a limited level of awareness of the risk of malevolent misuse of the biological sciences.

and:

> Existing curricula and/or training at university or research facilities do often contain references to aspects related to (bio-)safety, but rarely contain any aspects related to (bio-)security.
>
> (Australia et al. 2011: 3)

The work of our group at Bradford over the last 10 years has led us to reach the same conclusions and to try to contribute to the process of correcting this deficiency in the biosecurity education of life scientists. Biosafety is concerned with scientists working safely in the laboratory and biosecurity can also apply in the laboratory (for example in ensuring that dangerous materials are not stolen), but biosecurity also extends beyond the laboratory, for example in scientists being careful that their benignly intended work cannot easily be misused by others for hostile purposes.

In 2005 State Parties had the content, promulgation, and adoption of codes of conduct for scientists as part of their agenda for the Intersessional Meetings. In preparation for these meetings, in cooperation with Brian Rappert at the University of Exeter, we conducted a series of interactive seminars with practicing life scientists in UK universities and concluded that:

> There is little evidence from our seminars that participants:
>
> a. regarded bioterrorism or bioweapons as a substantial threat;
> b. considered that development in life sciences research contributed to biothreats;
> c. were aware of the current debates and concerns about dual-use research; or
> d. were familiar with the BTWC.
>
> (Whitby & Dando 2010: 2–3)

Subsequent work involving over 90 seminars in 16 different countries confirmed that this lack of awareness was pervasive around the world.

There could, of course, be a variety of reasons for this deficiency, but it seemed to us that such a deficiency would be unlikely if biosecurity was well taught at university level. So we did a series of surveys of what was being taught in different countries and regions. We began by looking at courses in Europe with colleagues in Italy and the results were startling in that only 3 out of 57 universities sampled had a biosecurity module and all of these were optional (Mancini & Revill 2008: 4).

Subsequent studies with colleagues in Japan and Israel showed a similar picture of lack of education on biosecurity in universities in Japan, the Asia-Pacific region, and Israel. When we asked lecturers why biosecurity was not taught we were given a number of reasons, including that they lacked sufficient expertise and necessary resources (Whitby & Dando 2010: 5). These seemed to us to be cogent reasons that we might be able to assist in addressing.

The inadequate present

When State Parties to the BTWC met in the 2008 Intersessional Process one of their agenda topics was "Oversight, education, awareness raising and adoption and/or development of codes of conduct with the aim of preventing misuse in the context of advances in bio-science and bio-technology research with the potential of use for purposes prohibited by the Convention." In regard to education they came to clear-cut decisions as to what was required:

> State Parties agreed on the value of education and awareness programmes:
>
> (i) Explaining the risks associated with the potential misuse of the biological sciences and biotechnology;
> (ii) Covering the moral and ethical obligations incumbent on those using the biological sciences;
> (iii) Providing guidance on the types of activities that could be contrary to the aims of the Convention and relevant laws and regulations and international law;
> (iv) Being supported by accessible teaching materials, train-the-trainer programmes, seminars, workshops, publications and audio-visual materials.
>
> (United Nations 2008: 7)

The State Parties had thus given guidance as to both the content and the means by which biosecurity education might be delivered.

We took this guidance as our starting point and, in cooperation with colleagues in Italy and Japan, designed and produced a 21-lecture internet-based open source Education Module Resource (EMR). Following the introductory lecture, lectures 2–10 cover the threat of biowarfare and bioterrorism and the development of the non-proliferation regime, lectures 11–18 cover the responsibilities of scientists, lectures 19–20 national implementation of the BTWC, and lecture 21 the building of a "a web of prevention." Because we were working with scientists and medical doctors we were well aware of the need to tailor the political and ethical material for our intended audience. Therefore, in the first section on the history of biological warfare the agents weaponized were discussed using the most recently available information on the pathogens and toxins and how the diseases they caused might best be treated, and in the later sections ethical issues were discussed in the context of the need to expand our understanding of the responsible conduct of research. Each lecture consists of PowerPoint slides with direct access to the references used via the Internet and a set of questions that might be used for essay topics or seminars (Espona 2013: 155–173).

We thought it unlikely, given the constraints on the life sciences timetable, that anyone would use the whole of the module. However, we tested out whether lecturers would be able to use various parts of the EMR to fit into their courses. This "no one size fits all" approach has proved to be successful and the module has now been translated into a number of languages and used in a variety of different institutions.

While the EMR was a reasonable first step it was clearly not sufficient. We therefore designed an associated Train-the-Trainer course that would assist lecturers and other researchers to use and build on the EMR. This program is entirely based on distance learning using the Internet as a virtual classroom that can be created for participants from many different countries using PowerPoint presentations, webcam and audio equipment. We currently run a 20-credit course at UK master's degree level of 12 lectures and 12 seminars over a 12-week period and a shorter certificated course. The course is financed by the U.S. State Department's Biosecurity Engagement Program and several sets of students have completed the course over recent years.

A further step has been to develop a short course of five lectures based on the EMR but designed for specific countries that is much more fully supported by guidance on how the lectures should be used. Again, this approach has been tested out with colleagues, for example in Ukraine, and is being used in former Soviet States and the Middle East with support from the UK's Defence Science and Technology Laboratories. The approach here, however, goes well beyond just making educational material available and is intended to provide both a basis, and continuing support, for the development of networks of lecturers in a country and region who will take the awareness-raising and education process forward. By assisting with such processes in different countries and reporting back to meetings of BTWC State Parties it is hoped that a contribution can also be made to the development of models of best practice.

With colleagues at the University of Manchester, we are now asking how material might be developed for various sections of the modern life sciences and how ethical issues might be better approached to interest scientists. It is clear that one of the sections of modern biology that has been misused in the past is microbiology/immunology, and to make the EMR as interesting as possible for scientists the first section on the threat mixes material on the history of offensive biological weapons programs, particularly in the 20th century, with the most recent information on the traditional biological agents such as anthrax and smallpox. However, as the sciences of chemistry and biology increasingly converge (United Kingdom 2012: 1–5) it is more and more necessary to think of the need for the CWC and BTWC prohibition regimes to be considered as a whole. The potential misuse of modern neuroscience, for example, needs to be considered by both conventions (Poland 2011: 1–4) given the subject's misuse in the development of both deadly lethal nerve agents and incapacitants in the last century. Thus, in the UK, we have set up a network project involving neuroscientists, neuroethicists, and security specialists to look at how an open-source module might be designed and developed for neuroscientists. Over the period 2012–2013 we have assessed the present state of neuroethics teaching for neuroscientists in the UK and elsewhere (Walther 2013: 343–351), agreed on the ideal state we would like a module to achieve, and discussed some of the detailed components. We intend to finish the module later in the year. This will provide the basis for a phase of testing out the use of the module in various courses.

There is a well-known difficulty of teaching the *social* implications of science to practicing scientists. Even though we are getting much better at teaching about the internal aspects of responsible conduct of science (for example, data falsification and plagiarism), we are still developing a means of successfully transmitting ideas about the responsibility scientists have for the external aspects of science – for example, in regard to the problem of hostile misuse of benignly-intended work (Carlson & Frankel 2011: 1–3). Furthermore, it is even more difficult to engage scientists, who are trained to look for a correct answer to a problem, with ethical discussions of social issues where there are unlikely to be any clear-cut, single, correct answers (Jones 2011: 192–213). One way to deal with these difficulties is to use an "active" mode of teaching where students are required to discuss issues and to formulate their own views within their group (Novossiolova et al. 2013: 10–11) and we are therefore seeking to apply this process of active learning to the content that we are developing for neuroscientists.

Yet on any reasonable assessment, the small-scale, "bottom-up" efforts that we, and other civil society groups, are making to improve the biosecurity education of biologists and associated scientists just does not match up to the scale of the problem. While we are providing useful models that might be extensively used by others, what is being done is surely quite inadequate as a response to the need for security education for the life and associated sciences community worldwide.

The H5N1 issue in 2012–2013

The implications of the lack of biosecurity education became very clear in the chaotic response of the scientific community to the experiments that made lethal H5N1 bird influenza transmissible in mammals (see Enemark, chapter 11 in this volume).

State Parties to the BTWC agreed, at the Sixth Review Conference in 2006, that part of the agenda for the 2008 meetings in the Intersessional Process should be:

> Oversight, education, awareness-raising, and adoption and/or development of codes of conduct with the aim of preventing misuse.
>
> (United Nations 2008: 1)

and in regard to oversight it was agreed that State Parties should:

> Ensure that oversight measures are balanced and proportional to the risk, to avoid creating undue restrictions on scientific research, development, publication and biotechnology.
>
> (United Nations 2008: 14)

Anyone who believed that it would be easy to achieve consensus about that balance between risk and benefits should have paused for thought when the then editor of *Science* stated, after the US National Scientific Advisory Board for Biosecurity (NSABB) approved the publication about the recreation of deadly Spanish influenza in 2005, "So would I . . . have published the paper even if the NSABB had voted otherwise? Absolutely" (Novossiolova et al. 2012: 41).

These concerns, about legal oversight, can only have been increased by the international handling of the publication of the papers on mammalian-transmissible deadly H5N1 influenza in 2012. In the United States dual-use research of concern has become defined as:

> life sciences research that, based *on current understanding*, can be *reasonably anticipated* to provide knowledge, information, products or technologies *that could be directly misapplied* to pose *a significant threat* with *broad potential consequences* to public health and safety, agricultural crops and other plants, animals, the environment, materiel, or national security.
>
> (Office of Science Policy 2012: 1, emphasis added)

Experts could surely be expected to disagree about those sections of the definition that are italicized. This conclusion was borne out when the NSABB decided that it was acceptable to publish the work done on H5N1 in The Netherlands by Fouchier's group on a split 12–6 vote, and the dissenters stated, in part, that:

> **The data in the newly-revised Fouchier manuscript are immediately and directly enabling.** As currently written, the revised Fouchier manuscript provides information that would enable the near-term misuse of the research in ways that would endanger public health or national security
>
> (National Institutes of Health 2012: 4, bold emphasis in original)

The virologists involved in what have become known as these "Gain of Function" experiments agreed to call a moratorium on their work, but then decided amongst themselves to end the moratorium in early 2013 (Fouchier et al. 2013: 520) much to the consternation of some other eminent virologists (Wain-Hobson 2013: 411) and the U.S. government, which issued new requirements for receiving federal funding for such research (Malakoff & Enserink 2013: 1025). We have yet to see how this and other problems with legal oversight are dealt with in the details of the new U.S. legislation but it seems unlikely that such an approach will be taken up by many other states. Yet, whatever system is eventually chosen by states, it will have to involve scientists and it is hard to see how they can be useful participants if they have no biosecurity knowledge.

The uncertain future

The 2011 Seventh Review Conference of the BTWC was well prepared for with numerous meetings, studies, and reports. As we have seen in regard to education and awareness raising, one important outcome of these preparations was a Working Paper by 11 States Parties, including the UK and the United States. The paper described the various experiences of these States Parties in engagement with their scientific communities and noted the lack of biosecurity education in university courses (Australia et al. 2011: 3).

The net result was also noted: "Life scientists do not often consciously consider the possibility that their specific work could be of relevance to a biological weapons programme or otherwise misused to cause harm." Logically, therefore, the paper concluded that:

> the frequent lack of awareness of aspects related to biosecurity and the obligations of the Convention among life scientists has to be addressed more urgently, strategically, and comprehensively.
>
> (Australia et al. 2011: 4)

The paper went on to list again the series of steps contained in the 2008 report of the Meeting of States Parties.

As a result of such input the issue of education and awareness-raising was prominent in the Standing Agenda Items (SAIs) agreed for the Third Intersessional Process of 2012–1015 (United Nations 2012b: 23–24). Under the "Review of developments in the field of science and technology related to the Convention" the subitem (e) on education and awareness raising about risks and benefits of life sciences and biotechnology was quite specific and subitems under the other SAIs included the issue of education of scientists as well. Overall, however, many people judged the outcome of the Review Conference as disappointing in relation to the efforts and expectations beforehand and even in regard to Article IV two serious commentators noted that:

> the loss of the first sentence of paragraph 14 of the *Final Declaration* of The Sixth Review Conference stating that "*The conference urges the inclusion in medical, scientific and military education materials and programmes of information on the Convention and the 1925 Geneva Protocol*" is a retrograde step in the light of the surveys of education that have shown the widespread absence of information on the Convention and the 1925 Geneva Protocol.
>
> (Pearson & Sims 2012a: 69, italics emphasis in original)

These commentators continued:

> It has become all too evident in recent years that there is an abysmal level of knowledge and awareness of the Convention and its obligations in those engaged in the life sciences. The failure to address this effectively under Article IV is a serious omission.
>
> (Pearson & Sims 2012a: 69)

The relevant section of the Seventh Review Conference declaration reads: "promote the development of training and education programmes for those granted access to biological agents and toxins relevant to the Convention" (Pearson and Sims 2012a: 40) and certainly does not suggest the same urgent need to include relevant material as did the 2006 Sixth Review Conference. So effective consideration of education and awareness-raising was by no means assured in the third ISP.

Education did figure strongly in the papers, statements, presentations and side events of the July 2012 Meeting of Experts. The United Kingdom, for example, strongly endorsed the first recommendation of the UK Royal Society report, *Neuroscience, conflict and security*, in its paper, *The Convergence of Chemistry and Biology: Implications of Developments in Neurosciences*, stating:

> Action is required to generate: a renewed effort by appropriate professional bodies to inculcate the awareness of the dual-use challenge among neuroscientists at an early stage of their training: and, greater levels of awareness among scientists of the obligations arising from the CWC and BTWC and the potential malign applications of their research.
>
> (United Kingdom 2012: 2)

The working paper also referred to a follow-up round table meeting at the Royal Society on its report and the view that:

> A number of complementary interventions could be exploited in addition to working through scientific societies including, for example, law enforcement outreach to scientists and insertion of relevant materials in core texts for science courses.
>
> (United Kingdom 2012: 3)

The UK paper continued:

> The UK shares the view that it is important to look at how the issue of dual-use can be assimilated within broader professional training for scientists in the university curricula in a holistic and sustainable manner both at home and abroad.
>
> (United Kingdom 2012: 3)

This hints at a growing awareness of many concerned with the biosecurity education of life scientists that a much broader and comprehensive approach is needed.

A number of the proposals made at the Meeting of Experts, for example those made by the UK on insertion of relevant material into core texts for science courses and assimilating material on the Convention into the broader professional training of scientists at university, were included in the Chairman's synthesis paper from the meeting (Chairman 2012: 7). What was clearly missing was the kind of proposal such as that State Parties should agree to provide annual reports on the steps they have taken to improve biosecurity education that would open up the possibility of substantial and cumulative improvements and the development of best practices (Whitby et al. 2011: 139).

Again, education featured in the preparations for, and at, the 2012 December Meeting of States Parties. In an interesting innovation, for example, one of the Vice-Chairs set up an e-group with the stated aim "of exchanging views between the scientific community and policy makers on ideas of how to deal with dual use issues." A paper was then prepared by the e-group and this suggested, in part, that:

> (a) increased efforts be made nationally, regionally and internationally to ensure that all those engaged in the life sciences are aware of the Convention and its prohibitions and obligations.
>
> (Poland 2012: 2);

and:

> (e) States Parties be requested to advise subsequent Meetings of States Parties of the steps they have taken in regard to the above so that the experience gained and best practices can be shared for the benefit of all States Parties.
>
> (Poland 2012: 2)

So the idea of gaining substantial cumulative progress in education and awareness raising was not entirely lost during the year.

In the report of the meeting, however, while "States Parties reiterated the importance of measures . . . to increase awareness among scientists, academia and industry of the Convention and related laws and regulations" they merely "recognised the value of pursuing various national measures." These included:

> (b) Strengthening linkages between biosafety and biosecurity training and broader issues of responsible conduct; and
> (d) Supporting the inclusion of relevant material in professional training courses.
>
> (United Nations 2012a: 7)

This could leave the impression that little advance has been made since 2008, but that might be a false impression because of events outside of the BTWC itself.

In October 2011 a Working Paper for the Seventh Review Conference of the BTWC addressed the issue of the convergence of chemistry and biology and raised some important questions such as:

> (a) As biology, chemistry and enabling technologies are converging, what are the consequences for the international system of disarmament and non-proliferation?
>
> (Poland 2011: 2)

Because of this convergence, the paper argued that the development of effective bio-security measures was a priority, In this regard it suggested that:

> The BTWC and CWC [Chemical Weapons Convention] review mechanisms should seek and engage actively the relevant stakeholders engaged in the building of national bio-chemical safety and security measures. The BTWC and CWC review mechanisms should further combine their potential to develop the roles of the BTWC/CWC as a platform for raising awareness, disseminating best practices and training in the areas of bio-chemical safety and security.
>
> (Poland 2011: 3)

So biochemical security education for both chemists and biologists, in this view, has now become a priority for both the BTWC and CWC.

In its review of the operation of the CWC since the last Review Conference, in preparation for the 2013 Third Review, the OPCW (Organisation for the Prohibition of Chemical Weapons) Technical Secretariat drew attention to the awareness levels of chemists that closely mirrored what is known of the awareness of biologists:

> Given the acknowledged low levels of awareness about the Convention among some key stakeholders, the OPCW needs to identify target audiences and develop approaches specific to each of them. Such approaches could include educational materials for secondary and tertiary level students.
>
> (Technical Secretariat 2012: 20)

It then noted that:

> Some work has already been conducted in this area by the OPCW and IUPAC [International Union of Pure and Applied Chemistry], and the temporary working group on education and outreach, recently established by the SAB [Scientific Advisory Board] . . . will make recommendations on how to take this work forward.
>
> (Technical Secretariat 2012: 21)

Now, therefore, given the greater resources available to the OPCW and IUPAC, they are increasingly likely to take over the leading role in the education and awareness-raising from the BTWC InterSessiononal Process.

Furthermore, in his response to the report of the 19th Session of the Scientific Advisory Board in late 2012, the OPCW Director-General indicated that there were much wider educational linkages to be explored:

> The Director-General encourages the TWG [Temporary Working Group] to explore potential cooperation with other relevant international organisations and regimes, for

> example, with the Preparatory Commission for the Comprehensive Nuclear-Test-Ban Treaty Organisation (CTBTO), the International Atomic Energy Agency (IAEA). . . . his cooperation could include participation in events, meetings, networks, and joint projects.
>
> (Director General 2012: 3)

The mention of the IAEA is of particular interest because of the resources that have been applied to nuclear security education over the last decade.

A paper titled *Biosecurity Education for the Life Sciences: Nuclear Security Education Experiences as a Model* prepared for the 2012 BTWC Meeting of Experts, explained that:

> to enhance nuclear security, the International Atomic Energy Agency (IAEA) has developed and launched three successive Nuclear Security Plans for the periods 2002–2005, 2006–2009, and 2010–2013.
>
> (Novossiolova & Pearson 2012: 4)

In regard to education the paper noted that a study guide titled *Educational Programme in Nuclear Security* had been prepared in 2010 (Novossiolova & Pearson 2012: 5).

The guide acknowledged the low level of nuclear security knowledge among relevant stakeholders and the lack of available university-level education courses. Thus it pointed out that:

> the IAEA stands ready to assist, upon request, in increasing lecturers' knowledge pertaining to nuclear security and in developing adequate textbooks and other teaching material in cooperation with its Member States.
>
> (Novossiolova & Pearson 2012: 5)

The guide also describes a model of a master's degree and a certificated program in nuclear security in order to provide States with a comprehensive strategy for the implementation of nuclear security education.

The paper goes on to describe how the Nuclear Security Plan for 2010–2013 placed increasing emphasis on education, including the founding of the International Nuclear Security Education Network (INSEN) under the auspices of the IAEA. Then, reflecting on what has been done in the nuclear area to deal with education, the authors of the paper suggest what would be required for a serious program to deal with the biosecurity education deficit:

> First and foremost, there is a need for *state-led* initiatives, commitment and cooperation at the international and regional level in the field of biosecurity education. . . . Secondly, there is a need for a synchronised and coordinated approach that builds upon the existing expertise in the field. . . . Thirdly, the implementation of a comprehensive biosecurity education plan will require adequate financial support. It is essential that funds be specifically allocated for purposes of human resource development, education and awareness-raising in order to ensure continuity and sustainability.
>
> (Novossiolova & Pearson 2012: 15)

Finally, the authors argue that a serious biosecurity education plan "should include short-term, mid-term and long-term goals and that corresponding milestones be defined" and that "Periodic reviews of the progress made at every stage of implementation need to be conducted" (Novossiolova & Pearson 2012: 16).

Conclusion

Despite the constructive criticisms that have been made of the third ISP of the BTWC (Pearson & Sims 2012b: 1–14; South Africa 2012: 1–3), it seems very unlikely that it can be rapidly transformed into an instrument that can, for example, design and implement an International Biosecurity Education Network (IBSEN). We should, perhaps, not be too pessimistic about that conclusion because, as the INSEN becomes better known and the OPCW and CTBTO press on with their education plans, the biosecurity education deficit will stand out ever more clearly. Moreover, as comprehensive analyses begin to be undertaken, it will be obvious that the present unsatisfactory state of biosecurity education – in an area where rapid convergent advances are very likely to offer major opportunities for hostile misuse – cannot be allowed to continue. Then, if the BTWC/IPS remains in its present semimoribund state, the international community could find other instruments to deal with the problem.

The Third Review Conference of the CWC in April 2013 concluded that serious attention must be given to the awareness levels and education of scientists, stating, in part, that it:

> Encouraged the Secretariat, in concert with the SAB temporary working group on education and outreach, to assist State Parties, upon request, in implementing education and outreach activities, including by demonstrating materials, conducting workshops and regional meetings.
>
> (Organisation for the Prohibition of Chemical Weapons 2013: 20)

Yet the outcome in regard to the adequate security education of chemists, and particularly biologists, worldwide must remain in doubt. "Bottom-up" activities by civil society and some "top-down" activities by states are likely to continue, and perhaps accelerate, but the question that still has to be asked is whether this will in any way match the scale of the security problems likely to be thrown up by the continuing scope and pace of advances in the life and associated sciences in coming decades.

References

Australia et al. (2011, December 1) *Revised: Possible Approaches to Education and Awareness-Raising Among Life Scientists*, BWC/CONF.VII/WP.20/Rev.1, Geneva: United Nations.

Carlson, R. and Frankel, M. (2011) 'Reshaping responsible conduct of research', *Professional Ethics Report*, 24: 1–3.

Chairman. (2012, October 1) *Synthesis of Considerations, Lessons, Perspectives, Recommendations, Conclusions and Proposals Drawn From the Presentations, Statements, Working Papers and Interventions on the Topics Under Discussion at the Meeting of Experts*. BWC/MSP/2012/L.1, Geneva: United Nations.

Development, Concepts and Doctrine Centre (DCDC). (2010) *Global Strategic Trends – Out to 2040*, London: Ministry of Defence.

Director-General. (2012, November 5) *Response to the Report of the Nineteenth Session of the Scientific Advisory Board*. EC-71/DG.1, OPCW, The Hague: Organisation for the Prohibition of Chemical Weapons.

Espona, M.J. (2013) 'Biosecurity and dual-use issues: the education module resource', in M.L. Gross and D. Carrick (eds.) *Military Medical Ethics for the 21st Century*, Burlington: Ashgate.

Fouchier, R.A.M., Garcia-Sastre, A. and Kawaoka, Y. (on behalf of 40 co-authors) (2013) 'Transmission studies resume for avian flu', *Science*, 339: 520.

Jones, J. (2011) 'Teaching ethics to science students: challenges and a strategy', in B. Rappert (ed.) *Education and Ethics in the Life Sciences*, Canberra: Australian National University Press.

Malakoff, D. and Enserink, M. (2013) 'New U.S. rules increase oversight of H5N1 studies, other risky science', *Science*, 339: 1025.

Mancini, G. and Revill, J. (2008) *Fostering the Biosecurity Norm: Biosecurity Education for the Next Generation of Life Scientists*, London: Network-Centro Volta and University of Bradford.

National Institutes of Health. (2012, April 20) *Statement by NIH Director Francis Collins, M.D., Ph.D. on the NSABB Review of Revised H5N1 Manuscripts*, Washington DC: National Institutes of Health: 5. See *National Science Advisory Board for Biosecurity Findings and Recommendations, 29–30 March 2012* attached to the Statement.

Novossialova, T., Minehata, M. and Dando, M.R. (2012) 'The creation of a contagious H5N1 influenza virus: implications for the education of scientists', *Journal of Terrorism Research*, 3: 39–51.

Novossilova, T.A., Mancini, G. and Dando, M. (2013) *Effective and Sustainable Education for those in the Life Sciences: The Benefits of Active Learning*, Briefing Paper No. 7 (Third Series), University of Bradford, June.

Novossiolova, T.A. and Pearson, G.S. (2012, October) *Biosecurity Education for the Life Sciences: Nuclear Security Education Experience as a Model*, Briefing Paper No. 5 (Third Series), Bradford, UK: University of Bradford.

Office of Science Policy. (2012, March 29) *United States Government Policy for Oversight of Life Sciences Dual Use Research of Concern*, Washington, DC: US National Institutes of Health.

Organisation for the Prohibition of Chemical Weapons. (2013, April 19) *Report of the Third Special Session of the Conference of the State parties to Review the Operation of the Chemical Weapons Convention*, RCR-3/3, OPCW, The Hague: Organisation for the Prohibition of Chemical Weapons.

Pearson, G.S. and Sims, N.A. (2012a, March) *The BTWC Seventh Review Conference: A Modest Outcome*, Review Conference Paper No. 31, Bradford, UK: University of Bradford.

Pearson, G.S. and Sims, N.A. (2012b, November) *Maximizing the Potential of the BTWC Intersessional Process*, Briefing Paper No. 6 (Third Series), Bradford, UK: University of Bradford.

Petro, J.B., Plasse, T.R. and McNulty, J,A. (2003) 'Biotechnology: impact on biological warfare and biodefense', *Biosecurity and Bioterrorism*, 1: 161–168.

Poland. (2011, October 11) *Strengthening Biosafety and Security while Convergence of Biology and Chemistry Has Increased: Building Joint Responses between the BTWC and CWC Regimes against Misuse of Biological and Chemical Agents*, BWC/CONF.VII/WP.4, Geneva: United Nations.

Poland. (2012, November 22) *The Crucial Role of Life Scientists in the Effective Implementation of the BTWC*, BWC/MSP/2012/WP. 2, Geneva: United Nations.

South Africa. (2012, December 5) *The Intersessional Process: Comments and Proposals*, BWC/MSP/2012/WP.7, Geneva: United Nations.

Technical Secretariat. (2012, October 5) *Review of the Operation of the Chemical Weapons Convention since the Second Review Conference*, WGRC-3/S/1, OPCW, The Hague: Organisation for the Prohibition of Chemical Weapons.

United Kingdom. (2012, July 12) *The Convergence of Chemistry and Biology: Implications of Developments in Neurosciences*, BWC/MSP/2012/MX/WP.1, Geneva: United Nations.

United Nations. (1972) *Convention on the Prohibition of the Development, Production, and Stockpiling of Bacteriological (Biological) and Toxin Weapons and on their Destruction.* Online. Available HTTP: <http://www.un.org/disarmament/WMD/Bio/pdf/Text_of_the_Convention.pdf> (accessed 14 May 2014).

United Nations. (1986) *The Second Review Conference of the States Parties to the Convention on the Prohibition of the Development, Production and Stockpiling of Bacteriological (Biological) and Toxin Weapons and on their Destruction, Final Document*, BWC/CONF.11/13/11, Geneva: United Nations.

United Nations. (2008) *Report of the Meeting of State Parties*, BWC/MSP/2008/5, Geneva: United Nations.

United Nations. (2012a, December 19) *Report of the Meeting of States Parties.* BWC/MSP/2012/5, Geneva: United Nations. Online. Available HTTP: <http://daccess-dds-ny.un.org/doc/UNDOC/GEN/G13/600/47/PDF/G1360047.pdf?OpenElement> (accessed 15 May 2014).

United Nations. (2012b, January 13) *Seventh Review Conference of the States Parties to the Convention on the Prohibition of the Development, Production and Stockpiling of Bacteriological (Biological) and Toxin Weapons and on their Destruction, Final Document*, BWC/CONF.VII/7, Geneva: United Nations.

Wain-Hobson, S. (2013) 'H5N1 viral-engineering dangers will not go away', *Nature*, 495: 411.

Walther, G. (2013) 'Ethics in neuroscience curricula: a survey of Australia, Canada, Germany, the UK, and the US', *Neuroethics*, 6: 343–351.

Whitby, S., Bollaert, C. and Dando, M.R. (2011, September) 'Article IV: national implementation, education, outreach and codes of conduct', in G.S. Pearson, N.A. Sims and M.R. Dando (eds.) *Key Points for the Seventh Review Conference*, Bradford, UK: University of Bradford.

Whitby, S. and Dando, M.R. (2010) *Effective Implementation of the BTWC: The Key Role of Awareness Raising and Education*, Review Conference Paper No. 26, Bradford, UK: University of Bradford.

World Health Organization. (2004) *Public health response to biological and chemical weapons: WHO guidance*, Geneva: WHO.

22
HEALTH SECURITY AND FOREIGN POLICY

Joshua Michaud

Foreign policy has recently become more focused on issues of health. The traditional concerns of foreign policy such as national security, military, and economic power continue to drive and shape how countries engage internationally, but in recent years health has become a more prominent component of this engagement. The trend is the result of a combination of factors. For one, it is now conventional wisdom among policy makers and political leaders that health issues can and do impact the traditional security and economic concerns that are the focus of foreign policy. In addition, the ongoing process of globalization, trade liberalization, and international migration have contributed to a growing global interdependence, which has meant countries are increasingly vulnerable to threats that emerge elsewhere, including health threats. These links have perhaps been most vividly illustrated through the actions and reactions to a number of high-profile infectious disease outbreaks in the recent past, but the overlap between health and foreign policy extends beyond simply worrying about the next outbreak and now encompasses security and military engagements, trade and economic policy, and many other areas. In addition to using foreign engagement to address perceived threats, many countries are using overseas health engagement as a tool to create and take advantage of foreign policy opportunities, in areas such as conflict resolution, stabilization, counterterrorism, and others. Still, given the growing overlap, there remain concerns that linking health with foreign policy can lead to unresolvable tensions and can actually undermine global efforts to improve health. There remains an open question about which set of objectives – global public health objectives or self-centered states' foreign policy objectives – should drive such engagement and should take precedence when tension arises between the two.

This chapter examines this topic by first defining foreign policy and diplomacy and highlighting their links in a historical perspective. Then, the chapter reviews recent examples of foreign policy engagement on a set of key issue areas, including countries' use of development assistance for health, and the links between international trade, health, and foreign policy. The chapter then reflects on these examples and describes how a few key countries have decided to strike the balance between their traditional foreign policy objectives and the objective of promoting global public health.

Defining foreign policy and diplomacy

In the study of international relations, states are considered to be the primary actors in the international system (Walt 1998). While different international relations theories view state motivations in different ways, all theories assume each state has a set of interests they wish to pursue through external engagement (Snyder 2004). Whether it be protecting or amplifying military and economic power, spreading democracy, or pushing forward a set of societal ideals and values, states and other actors engage internationally with an agenda for action. States frame and pursue their international interests through *foreign policy*, which can be defined as the "substance, aims and attitudes of a state's relations with others" and the "activity whereby state actors act, react and interact" between the "internal or domestic environment and an external or global environment" (Evans & Newnham 1998: 128). Therefore, a state's foreign policy is the international agenda and set of actions that are generated from its domestic politics and societal views.

Foreign policy objectives can be pursued in many ways: a "hard power" extreme of offensive military action for conquest and colonization, economic dominance, or coercion, changing terms of international trade and commerce, formal and informal diplomatic negotiations, or a more "soft power" approach such as cross border partnerships and cultural norm-setting (Nye 2011). While approaches can be different, the objective for these tools is the same: influencing the behavior of others (other states, individuals, organizations, non-state entities, etc.) to move the international system toward outcomes the state wants.

Changing conceptions of health and security in foreign policy

For most of modern history, international engagement between states only rarely dealt with issues of health. During the rise of the nation-state and growth in international transit and commerce in the 18th to 19th centuries, the preeminent focus of attention for states' foreign policies were traditional security and economic issues, reflecting to a large degree the realist conceptualization of states' interests. Pursuit of influence through military power and economic expansion were the key objectives for states, with those of Western Europe, for example, exerting power through annexation of overseas colonies in the poorer, weaker areas in the continents of Asia, Latin America, and Africa.

Health issues, when part of international engagements at all, usually arose as because they directly affected states' core military or economic interests. As has been discussed extensively in the health diplomacy literature, the first international diplomatic conferences focused on health were organized due to Western European states' concerns about cross-border communicable disease spread – in particular the scourges of cholera, yellow fever, plague, and smallpox – that created difficulties for the growing international traffic of goods and persons (Fidler 2001; see also Kamradt-Scott, chapter 16 in this volume). In particular, concern about diseases carried aboard trading ships had led to a patchwork of different quarantine and inspection requirements at international ports, and international negotiations in part were undertaken to standardize processes at points of entry. These discussions were also influenced by the spread of understanding of the biological basis for disease, especially the growing acceptance of the germ theory of disease and the resulting need for scientifically defensible trade restrictions and quarantine requirements where issues of disease were concerned.

For much of the 20th century, links between foreign policy and health remained mostly confined to direct communicable disease threats to the economic and national security interests of states. The International Sanitary Conventions, brought under the auspices of the WHO after 1945 and later renamed the International Health Regulations, were designed with the dual purpose of protecting the health of states through reducing the international spread of disease – in fact, restricted to the same four diseases that had concerned the colonial powers a century earlier – while at the same time minimizing interference with international travel and trade. This narrow conceptualization began to change in the 1980s and 1990s as academics and policymakers increasingly highlighted a link between health and core security interests. For example, the U.N. Security Council and the U.S. intelligence community declared HIV (and later, emerging infectious diseases in general) a national security threat (Feldbaum et al. 2006; National Intelligence Council 2000; United Nations Security Council 2000). The terrorist attacks of September 11, 2001, and the deadly anthrax bioterrorism attacks in the United States the same year also had a transformative effect on the foreign policies of the United States and other Western countries (Heyman 2002). For the first time, many high-level national security policymakers began to draw clear lines between poor health conditions abroad and the stability of states and the international system as a whole, making the case that core national security interests could be jeopardized anywhere poor health conditions fueled instability, extremism, and state failure (Congressional Research Service 2008; National Intelligence Council 2008; Patrick 2006;).

Current issues and debates in health and foreign policy

Referring to the current "era of globalization and interdependence" that the global community faces, some countries have pushed for a greater formal recognition of the links between foreign policy and health. In 2007, the Ministries of Foreign Affairs of Brazil, France, Indonesia, Norway, Senegal, South Africa, and Thailand issued a joint statement known as the Oslo Ministerial Statement on Global Health and Foreign Policy, in which they called on all governments to "broaden the scope of foreign policy" to incorporate health goals to a greater extent. These countries declared they would make health "a point of departure and a defining lens that each of our countries will use to examine key elements of foreign policy and development strategies" (Foreign Policy and Global Health Group 2013; Global Health and Foreign Policy Initiative 2007). Elsewhere, Switzerland has a formal global health foreign policy strategy (Swiss Federal Department of Foreign Affairs 2012), and the UK has published a cross-government strategy on promoting health through foreign policy called "Health is Global" (UK Department of Health 2011). In 2009 the UN General Assembly adopted resolution 63/33 on the same topic, in which member states recognized a "transformation of health from a specialized, technical area into a political and economic concern central to Governments and societies" (UN General Assembly 2009).

These statements reflect the more expansive and inclusive vision of the links between health security and foreign policy. Health threats are now defined very broadly by governments, and many governments also see more opportunities to use engagement on health to address traditional foreign policy objectives (Frist 2007; Hotez & Thompson 2009; Labonte & Gagnon 2010). Some commentators have gone so far as to claim health has become a primary component and driving force for foreign policy, with Richard Horton stating that health can "move foreign policy away from a debate about interests to one about global altruism" (Horton 2007: 807). Fidler has called the growth of foreign policy relevance of health issues a "revolution," stating that that "nothing in the prior history of national and international efforts on public health compares to the political status public health has reached today" (Fidler 2004).

While there is widespread recognition that health and foreign policy are increasingly linked, there is an ongoing debate about how and when (or even if) health shapes foreign policy and vice versa. Is foreign policy driven by *increased interest in achieving health goals* or is there increasing use of *health as an instrument to achieve traditional foreign policy goals* such as economic growth and national security? Further, do these opposing theoretical views have implications for the real-world practice of foreign policy and health engagement?

To shed some light and offer some conclusions the remainder of the chapter will examine recent actions of states in several key areas. First, development assistance for health and trade policy and health are examined, with an emphasis on the United States and other high-income countries. Then, key links between health and foreign policy in other countries are reviewed.

Health and development assistance

Development assistance has long been framed as serving dual functions: an attempt to address humanitarian needs and a means to further the foreign policy objectives of the donor country (Lancaster 2006). This inherently creates a tension, as foreign policy by definition is about serving a country's interests while a key humanitarian principle is independence from political interest (Theiren 2007).

When founding the U.S. Agency for International Development (USAID) in 1961, President Kennedy stated that its purpose was a humanitarian one, but with clear links to U.S. foreign policy interests. In particular, Kennedy argued that USAID could combat the potential spread of hostile ideologies such as communism and prevent the collapse of states, which "would be disastrous to our national security, harmful to our collective prosperity, and offensive to our conscience" (Kennedy 1961). Such sentiments have been echoed by the U.S. government ever since as a rationale for maintaining foreign assistance, up to and including the current USAID Administrator. Other major donors, from the UK to Germany and Japan, have used similar language and logic to explain their support for development assistance for health.

Overall, health has been an expanding component of aid. From 1990 to 2001 assistance for health almost doubled from $5.7 billion to $10.8 billion, and after 2001 there was an even more rapid expansion of health assistance; by 2010 donors had provided an estimated $28.2 billion in such assistance. More recently, there has been a plateauing of assistance amounts at roughly the 2010 level, a trend ascribed to the continuing effects of the global economic downturn that began in 2008 (Institute for Health Metrics and Evaluation 2013).

Domestic politics and global strategic interests have clearly played a role in shaping how and where assistance (including health assistance) is directed. During the conservative Thatcher (UK) and Reagan (United States) administrations in the 1980s, funding for family planning and social services overseas was cut sharply, reflecting those governments' views. The President's Emergency Plan for AIDS Relief (PEPFAR), the largest bilateral health aid program in history, was both a moral priority for President George W. Bush but also a response to lobbying from the President's political base. Much development assistance for health has been justified on the basis of intangible benefits provided, such as increased goodwill or trust-building. PEPFAR has been touted as promoting positive views of the United States on the African continent and serves as a vehicle for creating political leverage and increased influence with the governments of recipient countries (Frist 2007). This view is not universally held. Some commentators have expressed doubt about the links between aid and leverage over recipient governments. Some have gone even further, arguing that there can be an overall reduction in leverage, with donor countries locked into supporting authoritarian and corrupt regimes in recipient countries because to withdraw support for life-saving medications would produce a massive political liability and backlash for donors (Easterly 2010; Lyman & Wittels 2010).

Reflecting the reality that strategic interests drive assistance trends, the top six recipients of total U.S. assistance (health and nonhealth) in 2012 were: Israel, Afghanistan, Pakistan, Iraq, Egypt, and Jordan. However, Table 22.1 also demonstrates that the list of the top recipients of bilateral health assistance from the United States the same year was dominated by major African recipients of HIV/AIDS funds through the PEPFAR program, as well as Afghanistan.

While some authors have noted a growing correlation between development assistance for health and the distribution of actual disease burden (Institute for Health Metrics and Evaluation 2013),

Table 22.1 Top Recipients of U.S. Bilateral Foreign Assistance, Fiscal Year 2012

Ranking	*Total Bilateral Assistance*		*Bilateral Health Assistance*	
	Country	*Assistance*	*Country*	*Assistance*
1	Israel	3,075,000,000	Nigeria	579,247,000
2	Afghanistan	2,327,462,000	Kenya	556,910,000
3	Pakistan	2,101,908,000	South Africa	479,969,000
4	Iraq	1,683,345,000	Tanzania	430,139,000
5	Egypt	1,556,500,000	Ethiopia	390,589,000
6	Jordan	675,950,000	Uganda	378,059,000
7	Kenya	652,200,000	Zambia	343,636,000
8	Nigeria	625,388,000	Mozambique	331,669,000
9	Ethiopia	580,405,000	Afghanistan	181,500,000
10	Tanzania	531,179,000	Haiti	174,980,000

Source: www.foreignassistance.gov

other studies have shown there remains a continuing disconnect between aid and the burden of health conditions (Glassman et al. 2012). Many of the most important health issues for low and middle income countries are simply not addressed in any significant way by donors: noncommunicable diseases, road traffic accidents, and mental health issues barely register where aid has been directed. Finally, under the current system of heavily donor-dictated funding for projects of interest, "global public goods" have been underfunded, such as building country capacity for emerging infectious disease surveillance and response (Michaud 2010).

Health and international trade

With an increasingly interconnected and globalizing world where economic inputs and activities from goods, services, human resources, investments, knowledge, and supply chains often cross borders, trade has become an ever more important component of foreign policy. Support for trade liberalization has been on the rise, with free trade negotiations and agreements greatly expanding in number in recent decades, as countries seek to promote economic development through closer and more open ties with trading partners (McMahon 2006).

Trade policy's link to health has been recognized as critical (McDonald & Horton 2009; McGrady 2012). For one, trade in health-related goods and services is a rapidly growing segment of international trade, and many high-income and some middle-income countries have large domestic and export markets in this sector. This section discusses one component of this sector, pharmaceuticals, and how countries have approached international trade negotiations as part of foreign policy related to intellectual property and patents for pharmaceuticals.

Intellectual property rights and access to medicines

The Trade-related Aspects of Intellectual Property (TRIPS) Agreement of the World Trade Organization (WTO) "harmonizes the national patent laws of WTO members by establishing minimum standards for the protection of patent rights" (Condon & Sinha 2008: 154). The agreement asks WTO member countries to strike a balance between the need for incentivizing innovation through international coordination of patent protections and the desire for widespread access to potentially life-saving products, such as pharmaceuticals and medical devices. All WTO members, including developing countries, are required to ratify the TRIPS Agreement upon entrance to the organization, although developing countries have been given transition periods to allow them to bring their national intellectual property legislation into compliance with TRIPS standards. All except the poorest countries were required to have TRIPS-compliant national intellectual property protection laws enacted by 2005. The poorest countries (those with a per capita Gross Domestic Product of less than U.S. $750 a year) have been given an extension until 2016 to become TRIPS-compliant. Under the normal imposition of patent protection under TRIPS, countries are not permitted to allow the duplication of patented goods such as pharmaceuticals.

Even as countries are expected to provide such patent protection, under the agreement member states are allowed certain "flexibilities" in the case where certain pharmaceuticals may be needed to address a critical public health issue. For example, countries can issue "compulsory licenses" for domestic generic production of critical medicines or import cheaper generic medicines in order to reduce costs when addressing a critical public health need. Even though these flexibilities have been touted as removing the "final patent obstacle to cheap drug imports" (World Trade Organization 2003), there is limited capacity in developing states to actually implement the available flexibilities and despite the explicit legal basis for these flexibilities, countries have only rarely utilized them to circumvent patent protections on pharmaceuticals. There has been significant political pressure put on countries seeking to use the flexibilities, for example through including generic medicine promoting countries on the office of the U.S. Trade Representative (USTR) "special 301" list of countries violating or in danger of violating patent protections (U.S. Trade Representative 2013a). Such states are further restricted due to a growing number of bilateral and regional trade agreements that stipulate protections on pharmaceutical patents that are stricter than those in the TRIPS agreement (these are known as "TRIPS-plus" measures) (World Health Organization 2009).

Several ongoing trade negotiations, including for the Trans-Pacific Partnership (TPP) trade agreement (a regional trade negotiation among countries including the United States, Australia, Malaysia, Vietnam, Peru, and Chile), and the European Union–India FTA negotiations, have drawn attention due to their potential impact on intellectual property and access to medicines. The USTR released a statement in 2012 upholding that the United States seeks to incorporate language in the TPP negotiation that would "deploy the tools of trade policy to promote trade in, and reduce obstacles to, access to both innovative and generic medicines, while supporting the innovation and intellectual property protection that is vital to developing new medicines" (U.S. Trade Representative 2013b)." But commentators have worried that public health will again take a back seat to corporate interests and that strict intellectual property controls will be a feature of these new agreements should they be enacted (McDermott 2013; Wallach & Beachey 2013). Yet another agreement that has drawn attention for its potential to have a negative public health impact is the Anti-Counterfeiting Trade Agreement (ACTA), to which a number of countries have already agreed (Medicines sans Frontieres 2012).

Countries' efforts to control international intellectual property rights have also impacted health security during global epidemics and pandemics, as patents on medicines, vaccines, and even the disease agents themselves can get tangled up in negotiations over patents and patentability. In 2007 the Indonesian government famously declared "viral sovereignty" over H5N1 influenza virus samples taken from that country, precipitating a diplomatic crisis that led to multiple rounds of tense bilateral and multilateral negotiations (Lange 2011; see also Aldis & Soendoro, chapter 26 in this volume). In a more recent example, Canadian laboratories have claimed that Dutch scientists' patent controls over the so-called Middle-Eastern Respiratory Virus (MERS) have slowed their research into this emerging viral disease (Canadian Broadcasting Corporation 2013; Kupferschmidt 2013).

Trade agreements and tobacco

Another important aspect of trade and health is the broader population health impact trade policies can have, particularly through the effect that trade liberalization can have on markets for global "bads" such as alcohol, tobacco, and unhealthy and unsafe foods. While trade agreements have been pursued for economic development reasons, an important public health impact of trade liberalization has been the growth of demand for and use of tobacco products, especially in populations in low- and middle-income countries. Evidence indicates that liberalization generally leads to reduced tariffs and taxes and increased competition on tobacco products, which reduces prices and stimulates demand (World Health Organization 2012). Also, free trade agreements and international investment agreements have often been structured in such a way as to allow multinational tobacco companies to dispute public health control and preventive measures put in place by governments aimed at curbing tobacco use. The legal disputes claim that restrictions are a violation of the agreements, amounting to unfair control of a traded good. For example, Uruguay, which for its own domestic reasons has decided to enact some of the strictest tobacco control measures anywhere, has been targeted by tobacco companies with legal action. Likewise, the government of Norway has been the subject of lawsuits for its restrictions on tobacco. The Framework Convention on Tobacco Control, while providing a framework and suggested process for increased tobacco control measures by WHO member states, lacks any real enforcement mechanisms and global efforts to control tobacco have shown previous little progress, especially in lower income countries.

The ongoing trade negotiations around the Trans-Pacific Partnership (TPP) and the European Union–India FTA negotiations both have featured language relevant for tobacco. The USTR initially introduced language into the TPP negotiations to carve out exceptions for domestic tobacco control measures implemented in support of public health, but has decided to hold off promoting this tobacco-specific exception (New York Times 2013). This has led to disappointment among public health proponents and tobacco control advocates, who have worried that public health will again take a back seat to corporate interests, especially the interests of tobacco companies (Kenny 2012).

If it were the case that foreign policy were driven by public health concerns instead of traditional self-interested domestic economic concerns, one would expect evidence that health objectives would shape negotiations on such critical health issues as intellectual property and tobacco. This not the case, though. The evidence reviewed here suggests countries' economic interests, whether protection of the domestic pharmaceutical industry or domestic tobacco production and export, have typically trumped public health concerns.

Approaches to health and foreign policy outside the United States and Europe

China

China's foreign policy as it relates to health has transformed in the last several decades. Previously, the country was inward-looking, and espoused a policy of noninterference in the domestic affairs of other countries through its foreign engagements. The Chinese government tended to demonstrate a lack of transparency and reluctance for engagement with international partners, as evidenced by its failure to work with the WHO and other external partners during the 2002–2003 SARS epidemic. China's reluctance to engage during that time was widely seen as contributing to further spread of the disease and a greater numbers of cases and deaths. The lessons from SARS seem to have turned China toward greater engagement and there has been a notable increase in collaborative research and epidemiological investigation on communicable disease issues since that time (Chan et al. 2010; see also Huang, chapter 7 in this volume).

China has also transformed its international health engagement through its foreign aid and development assistance for health. Long a major recipient of health assistance, China is now a net donor (Huang 2013). While China has provided assistance through health projects in other countries (in Africa and Asia primarily) since as far back as 1963, there has been a marked increase in the number and magnitude of these engagements in the recent past (Youde 2007). From 2007 to 2011, China committed $757.1 million in health assistance to Africa alone, though even this represents just a small proportion (16%) of U.S. health assistance to the region over the same period. China has highlighted several key principles for its foreign aid, such as political noninterference and responding to the needs and demands of recipient countries, but has also expressed a strategic interest in providing aid, which is in part intended to "strengthen [recipient countries'] state power, which in turn undermines the power of imperialism" (Huang 2013). China's engagement on health has been "driven by a foreign policy agenda that focuses on expanding international influence while improving international image" – language that would not be out of place when discussing many Western countries' approach to health as an element of foreign policy (Huang 2013).

India

India has increased its development assistance for health as well, though the country remains a significant recipient of aid rather than a net donor. India's small overseas aid program for health is more regionally focused than is China's, and its top recipients of aid include Bhutan, Nepal, and Afghanistan, though small amounts are provided to other regions such as Africa. Despite the country espousing a noninterference policy similar to that of China, commentators have noted that economic and strategic priorities have often trumped the country's stated ideals and moral discourses about its assistance (Huang 2013).

A key area of engagement for India has been on pharmaceuticals. India was long a champion for flexibility on compulsory licensing for pharmaceuticals, and the country has grown to become a global market force in generic medicines. For example, Indian companies now produce more than 80% of all donor-funded HIV/AIDS drugs globally. India's pro-generics stance has been an effective way to promote its economic development in this area, though the country has come under increasing pressure to adopt stricter intellectual property controls.

South Africa

As the most economically powerful sub-Saharan African nation, often included among the so-called BRICS emerging economic powers, and the only African nation that is part of the G20, South Africa has not yet moved forcefully on health issues through its foreign engagements. Instead, it has adopted a more inward-looking focus when it comes to health (Cooke 2010). Despite being the country with the greatest number of people living with HIV, South Africa has not made any visible efforts to take a leadership role on this critical health issue through foreign policy engagement. While still a major recipient of donor assistance from abroad, South Africa has made efforts to take ownership of financing health programs internally and has even announced an intention to set up a foreign assistance program of its own.

It is worth noting that while there has been little evidence of engagement and influence on health issues coming from South Africa's government, nongovernmental organizations from South Africa have had an enormous effect on health governance around the world. For example, it was the activism of the Treatment Action Campaign based in South Africa that catalyzed the global movement to reduce the price and increase access to antiretroviral medications for HIV/AIDS. This activism had a hand in transforming the global economics of HIV treatment. Such an impact could be seen as a reflection of the constructivist viewpoint that international influence can be achieved through the power of ideas, not only through the military or economic power of a state.

Brazil

Since the 1960s, Brazil has been providing assistance to other countries, though most of its work in health has only begun in the last decade. Brazil's constitution states that health is a human right, and its technical and monetary assistance is directed to pursuing that ideal at an international level. The country has sought to reach out to other developing countries through a South–South exchange in order to provide lessons learned from its own efforts to provide health equity and access to health care to its own population, which have been seen for the most part as highly successful (Gomez 2009). The country provided an estimated $4 billion in foreign assistance in 2010 (Economist 2010).

The country has seemingly pursued these humanitarian health goals quite vigorously, sometimes in a way that goes against its own economic interests and domestic political considerations. For example, Brazil was an early and enthusiastic supporter of the Framework Convention on Tobacco Control, despite the fact that the country is a major exporter of tobacco and the tobacco industry pressured the government not to support it (Lee et al. 2010). Still, the Brazilian government also supports external engagement on health as a means for stimulating Brazilian-based companies and industries, contributing to the country's economic growth. Many commentators have remarked on Brazil's support for increased flexibility for pharmaceutical manufacturing under TRIPS. This has been linked to its support for health (and access to medicines) as a human right but also to its desire to boost the country's own emerging biotechnology and pharmaceutical sectors.

Cuba

The small island nation of Cuba has been a prime example of the links between health and foreign policy and how health engagement can lead to influence. Since 1961 the socialist country has famously "exported" its doctors and other health professionals for short- and long-term assignments in other countries. By one count, the country sent over 130,000 medical personnel to 107 different countries over the last 50 years. In one year alone (2008) approximately 30,000 Cuban doctors were engaged in external health engagements (Feinsilver 2010).

Just as with many other countries, Cuba's use of "health diplomacy" has served humanitarian and self-interest purposes. The Cuban government has expressed a desire to support health equity and promote the Cuban revolution's principle of health as a human right; on the other hand these engagements often provide tangible benefits to the Cuban government (Werlau 2011). Cuba has sent medical professionals to Venezuela for years in exchange for preferential pricing on Venezuelan oil and other subsidies. This translated into an estimated $9.4 billion in overall subsidies to Cuba from Venezuela in 2008 alone. Further, Cuba uses these medical engagements as a method to promote export of products from its biotechnology sector. In addition, there has been a symbolic effect of Cuba's medical diplomacy, "a way to project Cuba's image abroad as increasingly more developed and technologically sophisticated . . . righteous, just, and morally superior because it is sending doctors rather than soldiers to far-flung place around the world" (Feinsilver 2010).

Conclusion

Adherents to any branch of international relations theory would have some evidence to point to support their views in the area of health and foreign policy. Realists might point to the self-interested focus of trade policies pursued by many countries as evidence of the supremacy of economic self-interest for states. Liberals could point to the lasting institutions built to promote health security, from the expansion of the IHR regime to the Doha Declaration emphasizing the right of countries to produce and purchase generic medicines for public health needs. Constructivists could highlight the power that ideas and norms have had in shaping the foreign policy stances of countries on health, from the advocacy on access to HIV/AIDS medications brought by the South African Treatment Action campaign, to the international reproach directed at China that led to a change in that country's cooperation and transparency following SARS.

Despite theoretical differences, what has unified almost all recent work on the subject of health and foreign policy is a view that the two are increasingly linked, and will continue to be so. Views on which health issues constitute matters of national interest have broadened far beyond simply control of infectious diseases at countries' borders. Health issues, far from being an afterthought of foreign policy, are now commonly considered highly relevant to national interests; practitioners of foreign policy and supporters of global public health can both benefit from increased communication and understanding, though a delicate balance is sometimes required between the two.

References

Canadian Broadcasting Corporation. (2013, May 28) 'Saudi coronavirus work stymied at Canadian lab'. Online. Available HTTP: <http://www.cbc.ca/news/health/saudi-coronavirus-work-stymied-at-canadian-lab-1.1322426> (accessed 30 May 2013).

Chan, L., Chen L. and Xu, J. (2010) 'China's engagement with global health diplomacy: was SARS a watershed?' *PLoS Medicine*, 7: e1000266.

Condon, B.J. and Sinha, T. (2008) *Global Lessons from the AIDS Pandemic: Economic, Financial, Legal, and Political Implications*, Berlin: Springer-Verlag.

Congressional Research Service. (2008) *Weak and Failing States: Evolving Security Threats and U.S. Policy*, Washington, DC: Government Printing Office.

Cooke, J. (2010) 'South Africa and global health: minding the home front first', in K. Bliss (ed.) *Key Players in Global Health: How Brazil, Russia, India, China, and South Africa Are Influencing the Game*, Washington, DC: Center For Strategic and International Studies.

Easterly, W. (2010, November 25) 'Aid for scoundrels', *New York Review of Books*.

Economist. (2010, July 15) 'Brazil's foreign aid programme: speak softly and carry a blank cheque', *The Economist*.

Evans, G. and Newnham, J. (1998) 'Foreign policy', *The Penguin Dictionary of International Relations*, London: Penguin.

Feinsilver, J.M. (2010) 'Fifty years of Cuba's medical diplomacy: from idealism to pragmatism', *Cuban Studies*, 41: 85–104.

Feldbaum, H., Lee, K. and Patel, P. (2006) 'The National security implications of HIV/AIDS', *PLoS Medicine*, 3: e171.

Fidler, D.P. (2001) 'The globalization of public health: the first 100 years of international health diplomacy', *Bulletin of the World Health Organization*, 79: 842–849.

Fidler, D.P. (2004) 'Caught between paradise and power: public health, pathogenic threats, and the axis of illness', *McGeorge Law Review*, 35: 45–104.

Foreign Policy and Global Health Group. (2013) 'Our common vision for the positioning and role of health to advance the UN development agenda beyond 2015', *Lancet*, 381: 1885–1886.

Frist, W. (2007) 'Medicine as a currency for peace through global health diplomacy', *Yale Law and Policy Review*, 26: 209–229.

Glassman, A., Duran, D. and Sumner, A. (2012) *Global Health and the New Bottom Billion: How Funders Should Respond to Shifts in Global Poverty and Disease Burden*, Washington: Center for Global Development.

Global Health and Foreign Policy Initiative. (2007) 'Oslo Ministerial Declaration-global health: a pressing foreign policy issue of our time', *Lancet*, 369: 1373–1378.

Gomez, E. (2009) 'Brazil's public option: what Obama can learn from Lula about universal health care'. *Foreign Policy*. Online. Available HTTP: <http://www.foreignpolicy.com/articles/2009/09/02/brazils_public_option>.

Heyman, D. (2002) *Lessons from the Anthrax Attacks: A CSIS Report on a National Forum on Biodefense*, Washington: Center for Strategic and International Studies.

Horton, R. (2007) 'Health as an instrument of foreign policy', *Lancet*, 369: 806–807.

Hotez, P. and Thompson, T. (2009) 'Waging peace through neglected tropical disease control: a US foreign policy for the bottom billion', *PLoS Neglected Tropical Diseases*, 3: e346.

Huang, Y. (2013) *Enter the Dragon and Elephant: China and India's Participation in Global Health Governance*, New York: Council on Foreign Relations.

Institute for Health Metrics and Evaluation. (2013) *Financing Global Health 2012: The End of the Golden Age?* Seattle: Institute for Health Metrics and Evaluation.

Kennedy, J.F. (1961, March 22) 'Special Message to the Congress on Foreign Aid' speech delivered to U.S. Congress, Washington, DC. Online. Available HTTP: <http://www.presidency.ucsb.edu/ws/?pid=8545>.

Kenny, C. (2012) 'In the war against smoking, America is on the wrong side', *Business Week Small World Blog*. Online. Available HTTP: <http://www.businessweek.com/articles/2012–07–02/in-the-war-against-smoking-america-is-on-the-wrong-side>.

Kupferschmidt, K. (2013) 'As outbreak continues, confusion reigns over virus patents', *ScienceInsider*, Online. Available HTPP: <http://news.sciencemag.org/scienceinsider/2013/05/as-outbreak-continues-confusion-.html>.

Labonte, R. and Gagnon, M.L. (2010) 'Framing health and foreign policy: lessons for global health diplomacy', *Globalization and Health*, 6. doi:10.1186/1744-;8603-;6-14

Lancaster, C. (2006) *Foreign Aid: Diplomacy, Development, and Domestic Politics*, Chicago: University of Chicago Press.

Lange, J. (2011) 'Negotiating issues related to pandemic influenza preparedness: the sharing of influenza viruses and access to vaccines and other benefits', in E. Rosskam, I. Kickbusch (eds.) *Negotiating and Navigating Global Health: Case Studies in Global Health Diplomacy*, Singapore: World Scientific.

Lee, K., Chagas, N. and Novotny, T. (2010) 'Brazil and the Framework Convention on Tobacco Control', *PLoS Medicine*, 7.

Lyman, P. and Wittels, S.B. (2010) 'No good deed goes unpunished: the unintended consequences of Washington's HIV/AIDS programs', *Foreign Affairs*, 89: 74–84.

McDermott, J. (2013, May 31) 'Worlds apart: making sure trade policies improve global health', *Roll Call*. Online. Available HTTP: <http://www.rollcall.com/news/worlds_apart_making_sure_trade_policies_improve_global_health_commentary-225237-1.html>.

McDonald, R. and Horton, R. (2009) 'Trade and health: time for the health sector to get involved', *Lancet*, 373: 273–274.

McGrady, B. (2012) *Trade and Public Health*, Cambridge: Cambridge University Press.

McMahon, R. (2006) *The Rise in Bilateral Free Trade Agreements*, New York: Council on Foreign Relations.

Medicine sans Frontieres. (2012) 'Blank cheque for abuse: ACTA and its impact on access to medicines'. Online. Available HTTP: <http://www.msfaccess.org/sites/default/files/MSF_assets/Access/Docs/Access_Briefing_ACTABlankCheque_ENG_2012.pdf>.

Michaud, J. (2010) 'Governance implications of emerging infectious disease surveillance and response as global public goods', *Global Health Governance*, 3.

National Intelligence Council. (2000) *The Global Infectious Disease Threat and Its Implications for the United States*, National Intelligence Estimate, Washington, DC: National Intelligence Council.

National Intelligence Council. (2008) *Strategic Implications of Global Health: Intelligence Community Assessment 10-D*, Washington, DC: National Intelligence Council.

New York Times. (2013, August 31) 'The hazard of free-trade tobacco', *New York Times*: SR10.

Nye, J. (2011) *The Future of Power*, New York: Public Affairs.

Patrick, S. (2006) *Weak States and Global Threats: Assessing Evidence of "Spillovers"*, Washington, DC: Center for Global Development.

Snyder, J. (2004) 'One world, rival theories', *Foreign Policy*, 145: 52–62.

Swiss Federal Department of Foreign Affairs. (2012) *Swiss Health Foreign Policy*. Online. Available HTTP: <http://www.news.admin.ch/NSBSubscriber/message/attachments/26254.pdf>.

Theiren, M. (2007) 'Health and foreign policy in question: the case of humanitarian action', *Bulletin of the World Health Organization*, 85: 218–224.

U.S. Trade Representative. (2013a) *Special 301 Report*, Washington, DC: USTR. Online. Available HTTP: <http://www.ustr.gov/sites/default/files/05012013%202013%20Special%20301%20Report.pdf>.

U.S. Trade Representative. (2013b) *Trans-Pacific Partnership Trade Goals to Enhance Access to Medicines*, Washington, DC: USTR. Online. Available HTTP: <http://www.ustr.gov/webfm_send/3059>.

UK Department of Health. (2011) *Health Is Global: An Outcomes Framework for Global Health 2011–2015*, London: HM Government.

UN General Assembly. (2009) 'Global health and foreign policy: strategic opportunities and challenges', 64th session, agenda item 123.

United Nations Security Council. (2000) *Resolution 1308 on the Responsibility of the Security Council in the Maintenance of International Peace and Security: HIV/AIDS and International Peacekeeping Operations*. Online. Available HTTP: <http://daccess-dds-ny.un.org/doc/UNDOC/GEN/N00/536/02/PDF/N0053602.pdf?OpenElement>.

Wallach, L. and Beachy, B. (2013, June 2) 'Obama's covert trade deal', *New York Times*.

Walt, S. (1998) 'One world, many theories', *Foreign Policy*, 110: 29–46.

Werlau, M.C. (2011) 'Cuba's business of humanitarianism: the medical mission in Haiti', *Cuba in Transition*, 21: 194–212.

World Health Organization. (2009) *Public Health Related TRIPS-Plus Provisions in Bilateral Trade Agreements*, Geneva: World Health Organization.

World Health Organization. (2012) *Confronting the Tobacco Epidemic in a New Era of Trade and Investment Liberalization*, Geneva: World Health Organization.

World Trade Organization. (2003) 'Decision removes final patent obstacle to cheap drug imports'. Online. Available HTTP: <http://www.wto.org/english/news_e/pres03_e/pr350_e.htm>.

Youde, J. (2007) 'Why look east? Zimbabwean foreign policy and China', *Africa Today*, 53: 3–19.

23

NGOs AND HEALTH SECURITY

Securing the health of people living with HIV/AIDS[1]

Amy S. Patterson

While numerous studies have investigated the relationship between health and security, few have questioned how NGOs understand this linkage (Orbinski 2007). This chapter addresses this gap. It asserts that NGOs that address AIDS in sub-Saharan Africa have not utilized what William Aldis (2008) terms the "health and security" paradigm, which asserts that diseases with high morbidity and mortality rates may threaten state security. While NGOs have rejected this AIDS "securitization," they have only partially embraced the human security perspective, despite the concept's focus on non-state actors and its promotion of socioeconomic and political development. International NGOs have been more likely than local African NGOs working on AIDS to accept human security's assertion that health is only one of many threats to individual security. Instead, many local NGOs have adopted a globalist viewpoint that investigates health at the individual level, and they use security-derived language to connect AIDS to food security, domestic violence, and stable access to AIDS treatment. In their arguments, they assert that the links between AIDS and other insecurities threaten the AIDS response itself.

Globally, thousands of NGOs advocate for the rights of people living with HIV (PLHIVs) and provide AIDS-related services such as HIV prevention, care, support, and antiretroviral therapy (ART). This chapter concentrates on international and grassroots NGOs that work in sub-Saharan Africa because the region has two-thirds of the world's PLHIVs. In 2011, approximately 24 million Africans were HIV positive, 1.2 million died of AIDS, and 1.8 million became newly infected with HIV. Two-thirds of the continent's AIDS funding comes from bilateral and multilateral donors and international NGOs, a fact that makes a comparison between the AIDS-security perspectives of local NGOs and these global funders pertinent (UNAIDS 2012). The diverse NGO world includes international NGOs, Africa-specific NGOs, faith-based organizations (FBOs), and community-based organizations (CBOs). Some NGOs engage in advocacy, while others focus on service delivery. To simplify the analysis, I refer to all of these as NGOs, though when appropriate, the chapter specifies NGO type.

The chapter proceeds as follows. In the next section, I briefly describe my methodology. In the third section, I demonstrate how NGOs have rejected the AIDS securitization paradigm prevalent during the early 2000s because it potentially could stigmatize PLHIVs and because it reflected the interests of the Global North. The fourth section investigates the uneven acceptance of the human security paradigm by NGOs. The fifth section argues that local NGOs have embraced a globalist perspective as they argue that food insecurity, domestic violence, and unstable treatment access affect individual health and the AIDS response itself. The final section questions the implications of the local NGO perspective for the health-security debate and for NGOs themselves.

Methodology

My findings are based on over 120 open-ended interviews, 60 focus groups, and an examination of websites of 40 international NGOs working on AIDS. I identified interviewees based on organizational roles and through snowball sampling. In 2005, I interviewed policy makers, policy analysts, and NGO representatives in Washington, DC, about the U.S. President's Emergency Plan for AIDS Relief (PEPFAR) and security. Between 2007 and 2011, I interviewed African NGO and FBO leaders and international donors in Ghana, Zambia, and the United States. I questioned how these actors framed AIDS and how they perceived national and international AIDS policies.

I held focus groups with organizations of PLHIVs in poor neighborhoods in seven Zambian cities in 2011. I asked about these groups' activities, challenges, and relations with donors, state officials, and community elites. Groups were affiliated with the Network of Zambian People Living with HIV and AIDS (NZP+), AIDS clinics, and religious institutions. All interviews and focus groups were transcribed, read for accuracy, and coded in NVivo using terms such as security, violence, terrorism, human rights violations, and stability. All interviewees and focus group members were assured of personal and organizational anonymity in published materials.

Finally, my research assistant examined the websites of NGOs working on AIDS.[2] These NGOs had consultative status at the World Health Organization or the UN Economic and Social Council[3] or they had been included on the University of Pennsylvania's "NGOs and Community Health Organizations in Africa" website.[4] Mission statements and program descriptions were checked for security-related terms.

Health and security: The securitization of AIDS

During the early 2000s, "HIV/AIDS [was] increasingly being portrayed by a range of international organizations, national governments, non-governmental organizations and scholars of international relations as having important security implications"(Elbe 2006: 121; see also Fourie, chapter 9 in this volume). Securitization first emerged in the 1990s among U.S. government agencies and foreign policy analysts, though it gained dominance during the early 2000s. The International Crisis Group (2001), the U.S. Institute for Peace (2001), the Center for Strategic and International Studies (2002), and the U.S. National Intelligence Council (2000) asserted that AIDS could decimate African economies and weaken militaries. Assumed high HIV rates among security personnel would make it difficult for African states to protect their borders. Warring parties could intentionally use HIV infection against their enemies (Elbe 2002; Feldbaum et al. 2006; Ostergard 2002; Sagala 2006). Large numbers of AIDS deaths in strategically important states such as Ethiopia, Nigeria, India, China, and Russia could threaten global stability (USNIC 2000). Securitization was solidified in the UN Security Council's 2000 sessions on AIDS and the resulting Resolution 1308, which said "that the HIV/AIDS pandemic, if unchecked, may pose a risk to stability and security" (McInnes & Rushton 2010; UN Security Council 2000). Securitization meant that AIDS was no longer just a public health or development challenge but also a global phenomenon with security consequences for states and the international system.

Securitization is a subjective, contentious act. Political actors choose to elevate an issue to the security realm in order to benefit their interests. In doing so, they identify securitizing agents, referent objects (i.e., groups threatened), existential threats, and emergency measures to counter threats (Buzan et al. 1998: 24; Elbe 2006). In hindsight, it appears that AIDS was only partly securitized. Most Security Council members did not fully support Resolution 1308, although it was politically difficult for them to publicly oppose it. Securitization benefited UN agencies (such as UNAIDS) that gained funding and influence, a process that demonstrates how international institutions play politics to achieve their own goals (Barnett & Finnemore 2004). Securitization also motivated the United States, which had been the central proponent of securitization in the UN, to create the President's Emergency Plan for AIDS Relief (PEPFAR) in 2003.

While most NGOs rejected securitization, a few coupled securitization language with human rights and development concepts in their AIDS advocacy. One international NGO official linked U.S. efforts against AIDS to the war on terror, but he did not ignore the relationship between poverty and AIDS (interview, Washington, DC, 24 February 2005). The International HIV/AIDS Alliance and the International Council of AIDS Service Organizations participated in securitization (Vieira 2007), yet they also rooted their demands for AIDS treatment access in human rights paradigms. And the website for Africa Action, a U.S.-based advocacy organization, stated that "the HIV/AIDS pandemic is the greatest global threat in the world today." However, it also highlights human rights challenges in Congo and Zimbabwe and economic concerns like African debt.[5]

Most international and African NGOs, however, ignored securitization to focus on other frameworks. For example, the Advocacy Network for Africa (a U.S. consortium of FBOs and NGOs that work in Africa), Human Rights Watch, Amnesty International, World Vision, American Friends Committee, and Africare emphasized development and human rights concepts when they discussed AIDS. One international NGO official stated, "For NGOs the security argument has not been one around which to mobilize" (interview, Washington, DC, 21 March 2005). At the local level, one African NGO representative referred to AIDS as a security concern, but this was only a vague reference to HIV rates among soldiers (Zambian NGO official, interview, Kabwe, 18 April 2011). And in places where one might anticipate securitization – African military institutions – the securitization framework was absent. In two discussions with PLHIVs at Zambian military facilities, no one linked AIDS to military preparedness (focus group, Lusaka, 5 May 2011; focus group, Lusaka, 9 May 2011).

There were several reasons that securitization did not appeal to NGOs. First, securitization could exacerbate the AIDS stigma since it tended to portray PLHIVs as faceless entities that could destabilize states. Securitization compounded the view that "HIV-positive people are not human beings" (Zambian NGO official, interview, Lusaka, 5 May 2011; focus group, Lusaka, 12 March 2011). Second, securitization reflected the power imbalance between the Global North and Global South; as such, it held few benefits for African NGOs (Orbinski 2007). Third, because they feared that securitization would lead to greater military involvement in the Global South, "most NGOs tend to dislike the security focus or framework for any issue" (international NGO official, interview, Washington, DC, 21 March 2005). Securitization could require NGOs to cooperate with Western militaries, a trend that might harm NGOs' legitimacy if these militaries had historically ignored human rights violations (Bristol 2006).

As a political act, securitization pointed to potential flaws in state agencies – the military and police – and it questioned the ability of African states to meet the most basic requirements of statehood – the protection of territory and the promotion of order. While global powers could point out these possible deficiencies, NGOs that hoped to work in some African states could not. Development-oriented NGOs often avoid political questions about power and representation, as these NGOs emphasize technical solutions to problems (Ferguson 1990; Uvin 1998). African NGOs feared that being "too political" could hamper the state recognition they needed for funding access (Michael 2004; multilateral donor, interview, Accra, 8 October 2008). These patterns led international and local NGOs to avoid securitization.

NGOs, as well as policymakers, recognized that securitization had positive and negative effects on resource allocation (Ingram 2007). On the one hand, even NGOs that did not utilize securitization still benefited from the attention and funding that securitization generated. For example, PEPFAR, a policy partly resulting from securitization, funneled considerable sums through international NGOs and their African partners (Patterson 2006). On the other hand, AIDS was no longer relegated solely to health ministries; instead, the multisectoral approach meant a variety of ministries and NGOs implemented AIDS-related programs (UNAIDS 1998). This was positive for "new players" in AIDS, but for long-standing health and development NGOs, these new players were potentially threatening; they did not "know the terrain," yet they received funding (U.S. policy maker, interview, Washington, DC, 15 April 2005; multilateral donor, interview, Lusaka, 23 February 2011). Some grassroots PLHIV groups had to compete with CBOs that emerged after securitization, and they complained that the new groups "don't even have PLHIVs in their leadership" (Zambian NGO official, interview, Ndola, 23 May 2011).

NGO reactions to securitization reinforce the point that securitization was never the dominant AIDS paradigm (Rushton 2007). Even among securitizing agents, the AIDS-security rhetoric waned by the late 2000s. Between 2005 and 2011, the Security Council did not discuss AIDS, and in 2011 when it passed Resolution 1983, the document focused on HIV in peacekeeping missions not AIDS as a destabilizing force (UN Security Council 2011). The decline of AIDS securitization reflected rigorous questions about its assumptions (Barnett & Prins 2006) and nuanced investigations of the multifaceted, complex ways that security and AIDS may or may not be linked (Aginam & Rupiya 2012; Iqbal & Zorn 2010). Perhaps most condemning, by the 2010s securitization's dire predictions about Africa's economic decline and military demise had not come true. In 2013, the World Bank predicted that Africa's annual economic growth rate would be over 5%, outpacing the global average (BBC News 2013), and African militaries took on increased responsibilities in Somalia and Mali.

Uneven application of the human security perspective: International versus local NGOs

The 1994 *Human Development Report* introduced the human security concept, describing it as freedom from "chronic threats such as hunger, disease and repression" and "protection from sudden or hurtful disruptions in the pattern of life" (UNDP 1994: 23). The report listed seven types of threats to human security: economic, food scarcity, health, environment, personal, community, and politics. While the UN Commission on Human Security (2003: 4) asserted that human security and national security are interrelated, human security has been associated with individuals' vulnerabilities not state vulnerabilities (Chandler 2008). As such it "is concerned with reducing and – when possible – removing the insecurities that plague human lives" (Sen 1999: 8).

Because of its broad definition of threats, human security has been closely linked to the "multiple challenges of development" (Poku et al. 2007: 1155). While theoretically the state provides the public good of human security, in some cases states either cannot or will not do so. Non-state actors, particularly NGOs, become crucial in fostering human security (Ward 2007). The goals of development NGOs – to alleviate poverty, combat injustice, improve the quality of life for the poor, provide health care to all people, and realize human rights[6] – are to mitigate threats to human security.

Even though human security sees a crucial role for NGOs, links security to development, and focuses on individuals, relatively few NGOs working on AIDS used the concept, and those that did tended to be international NGOs not African NGOs or CBOs. International NGOs asserted that AIDS leads to hunger and rural poverty, since it kills farm workers and depletes rural household resources (international NGO official, phone interview, 14 April 2005). They described how

AIDS makes children less secure: AIDS orphans are more likely to drop out of school, to lack proper nutrition, and to suffer from abuse (international NGO official, interview, Lusaka, 14 August 2007; international NGO official, interview, Washington, DC, 16 March 2005). Some international FBOs maintained that AIDS puts undue stress on religious institutions as it kills their members and saps organizational resources (international FBO official, interview, Lusaka, 6 August 2007; Patterson 2011). For all of these organizations, AIDS was viewed as a causal variable that impedes some aspect of human development and security.

Local NGOs did not dispute these claims, but they were less likely to use the human security framework to discuss AIDS. This hesitancy partly reflects five broad challenges with the concept itself. First, human security is "sweeping and open-ended" (Paris 2001: 91); its breadth allows actors to choose how it may benefit them (Chandler 2008). In practical terms, this meant a variety of development NGOs worked on AIDS, even if they lacked public health or AIDS experience (Morfit 2011). This was troublesome for local NGOs with established AIDS efforts (Zambian NGO, interview, Lusaka, 7 March 2011; Ghanaian NGO, interview, Accra, 18 November 2008). Second, human security does not prioritize threats. But local NGOs viewed AIDS as an exceptional threat, one that should be prioritized (Ghanaian FBO official, interview, Accra, 29 August 2008). Third, although human security created space for NGOs, it was often only international NGOs that had the resources to utilize this space. Local NGOs and groups of PLHIVs complained about their marginal role in the AIDS response. International NGOs, in conjunction with donors and state officials, made AIDS policies with minimal representation from PLHIV groups (Zambian NGO official, interview, Lusaka, 7 March 2011; focus group, Kabwe, 18 April 2011). Fourth, as human security elevates NGOs, it often downplays the role of the state (Chandler 2008). But African NGOs have demanded more state involvement on AIDS (Patterson 2006). For example, groups of PLHIVs in southern Africa have mobilized for better state management of ART programs.[7]

Finally, as its critics have indicated, the human security concept is historically situated in the post-cold war period before 9/11 (Tadjbakhsh 2005). Similarly, the concept's application to AIDS was better suited to the pre-ART access period. During that period, HIV infection was a paramount threat to individual security because it led to certain death, and AIDS deaths negatively affected agricultural production, household poverty, and children's education. Yet between 2000 and 2011, the percentage of African PLHIVs with ART access grew from 1% to 56%. By 2011, over 80% of PLHIVs in Namibia, Swaziland, Zambia, Rwanda, and Botswana could access ART (UNAIDS 2012). AIDS treatment reduces the infected person's HIV level so that opportunistic infections such as tuberculosis do not cause mortality; it has contributed to the decline in AIDS deaths in Africa since 2005 (Brown 2011). Treatment lowered the AIDS threat to individual security: PLHIVs now farm, care for their children, and contribute to society.

NGOs and the language of security: Connecting AIDS to other vulnerabilities

While local NGOs working on AIDS have rejected securitization and human security frameworks, they have tended to emphasize what Sara Davies (2010) terms a "globalist" vision of health, in which the referent object is the individual, threats to the individual's health are broadly understood, and the focus is on people most vulnerable to disease. This globalist view has the advantage of focusing on individual health, not population health. Unlike the human security paradigm, it treats health as a dependent variable, not one of many independent variables that affect an individual's security. It also contrasts with the global health security paradigm, which investigates the factors that "threaten the health of people internationally" and that increase the risk of morbidity and mortality for a state's population (WHO 2007). While the global health security concept has brought together the foreign policy and public health camps, it has increasingly divided the Global North and Global South. It has led to policies that seek to protect populations in the Global North from deadly epidemics that emerge abroad, and it has facilitated international regulations that increase the burden on poor states to report and contain such epidemics (Miller & Dowell 2012; Rushton 2011; Youde 2011).

Using the globalist perspective in the context of AIDS in Africa, NGOs have stressed how food insecurity, gender-based violence, and unstable access to ART endanger the health of PLHIVs. They carry the individual-level of analysis further, however, to assert that if these three insecurities are not mitigated then the entire AIDS response will be jeopardized. Even though they reject the securitization paradigm, they "utilize security language strategically in an attempt to secure greater political attention (and resources)" (Rushton 2011: 779). They use security terms (e.g., security, threat, violence, and instability) alongside human rights, development, and religious jargon (e.g., justice, equality, compassion, and rights), and they reframe problems with security-related phrases. For example, hunger is *food insecurity*, relationship abuse equals *gender-based violence*, and ART shortages become *instability in treatment*.

Food insecurity

The World Food Summit of 1996 defined food security as the condition "when all people at all times have access to sufficient, safe, nutritious food to maintain a healthy and active life" (FAO 1996). On their websites, international NGOs such as the Regional AIDS Initiative of Southern Africa, Africare, the Carter Center, and World Vision mention food security as a programmatic focus. Over half of interviewees and all focus group discussions brought up food insecurity. AIDS and food security "are linked," with food security "certainly being a mitigating factor for the spread of AIDS" (international NGO official, interview, Washington, DC, 18 March 2005). Three-quarters of Zambian focus groups also reported that the lack of food was the biggest challenge their members faced.

NGO officials asserted that food insecurity affects an individual's health in numerous ways. First, malnutrition makes HIV-negative people vulnerable to HIV infection (Stillwaggon 2006: 47). The malnourished, HIV-negative partner of someone with HIV is at a higher risk of contracting the virus than the adequately nourished HIV-negative partner. Second, hunger may cause the most marginalized people in society to risk HIV infection for food. Women who lack resources may have sex without a condom or sex with a partner whose HIV status is unknown in order to get food (Siplon 2005: 24). Third, food insecurity negatively affects the health of HIV-positive people, since hungry people on ART may quit taking their medications. PLHIVs described how ART made them ill without food (focus group, Lusaka, 23 March 2011; focus group, Kitwe, 19 May 2011; focus group, Livingstone, 27 June 2011). AIDS clinic workers explained how difficult it was to get their hungry clients to take their medication when it made them ill (Zambian clinic worker, interview, Lusaka, 2 March 2011). Fourth, malnutrition accelerates the progression of HIV to AIDS in the body, making HIV-positive individuals sick more quickly (Gillespie & Kadiyala 2005). One PLHIV said, "Some of our members quit taking their drugs, and they got very sick. So sick we had to carry them to the clinic. Some even died" (focus group, Kabwe, 18 April 2011).

Food insecurity also negatively affects emotional health and communal relationships. An HIV-positive Zambian who provides care to other HIV-positive people explained:

> The biggest challenge we [caregivers] have is food. Look at the situation if the caregiver is an HIV positive person. They go to visit a fellow positive person who has no food.

> That means they [the caregiver] have to share from the resources they have. You cannot just dress someone and leave them without any food. We [caregivers] have found ourselves in situations whereby we are forced to share the little that we have.
>
> (focus group, Lusaka, 7 April 2011)

Food insecurity caused stress and it led to distrust between clients and caregivers (focus group, Lusaka, 22 March 2011). Clients sometimes suspected that their caregivers hoarded food that aid organizations had provided for HIV-positive clients (Zambian FBO official, interview, Lusaka, 5 May 2011; focus group, Lusaka, 10 March 2011). Caregivers became angry that clients expected them to "go into their pockets" to buy food for them (focus group, Chingola, 20 May 2011).

Yet food security was not just a factor that affected individual health: it also harmed the global AIDS response. One Zambian FBO leader explained:

> If people don't have food, they won't take the ARVs or they will just vomit them up. And it says right on the package, "Take with food." So the entire treatment agenda is in danger if we don't look at the larger poverty issues.
>
> (interview, Lusaka, 20 August 2007)

If thousands of hungry PLHIVs quit therapy, AIDS deaths would not continue to decline. If hungry people took their drugs erratically, HIV could become resistant. ART efficacy would be compromised (AIDS clinic officer, interview, Lusaka, 1 March 2011; focus group, Lusaka, 12 March 2011). Donors might shy away from AIDS treatment if such failures emerged.

The AIDS response also could be undermined if food insecurity challenges the interpersonal trust needed for collective action against AIDS. The AIDS response depends on thousands of volunteers who provide care, educate community members about HIV prevention, and ensure ART adherence. As one international NGO officer said, "The AIDS response would be nothing without all these volunteers, many of whom are HIV positive" (interview, Lusaka, 8 June 2011). According to international and local NGOs, the security of the AIDS response itself depends on the health of HIV-positive people, a factor greatly shaped by food insecurity.

Gender-based violence

Surveys and anecdotal evidence suggest that many African women are subject to violence. For example, one in six women in South Africa is in an abusive relationship (Walker et al. 2004: 17), and over 60% of women and 48% of men in Zambia believe wife beating is acceptable for reasons such as child neglect (Central Statistics Office, Ministry of Health, Tropical Disease Research Centre, & University of Zambia 2009). International NGOs have highlighted how sexual violence makes HIV-negative women vulnerable to HIV infection, since it tears cervical tissues and makes them vulnerable to HIV penetration (international NGO official, interview, Washington, DC, 11 March 2005; Human Rights Watch 2003). Gender-based violence also endangers the health of HIV-positive women since it may prevent them from accessing needed medical and social services. Fearing abuse, women may hide their AIDS medications from their partners or skip clinic appointments (Twebaze 2009).

Despite these challenges, far fewer PLHIV groups brought up gender-based violence than food insecurity, a surprising outcome since the vast majority of group members were women (NGO official, interview, Lusaka, 21 March 2011). This finding did not mean that gender-based violence was unimportant for these women. Rather, it demonstrated how these groups often lacked power, and thus, could not easily challenge traditional hierarchies and gender norms through public discussion of violence (Siplon 2005). If NGOs raise these issues, local women often wish to avoid them, as one Ghanaian FBO official explained:

> We try to educate women about their rights and domestic violence. But when we do, they say, "It is my husband; he is the breadwinner. If I complain to the police, they will take him away and what will I do? I have a child." So they will take what you have to say with a grain of salt.
>
> (interview, Accra, 4 December 2008)

Because of women's marginal position, "at the local level, these issues get lost" (international FBO official, interview, Grand Rapids, Michigan, 21 May 2008).

Additionally, global dynamics heightened the attention that international NGO officials placed on gender-based violence. Diplomatic attention and widespread media coverage led the number of global policy actions that address domestic violence to increase from 80 in 2000 to 260 in 2010 (Pierotti 2013). Funding has followed diplomatic attention and policy reforms. For example, when former U.S. Secretary of State Hilary Clinton visited the Democratic Republic of Congo in 2009 to highlight sexual violence in the country's war, she also pledged funding for victims of violence. And in 2012, PEPFAR announced $3 million in grants to NGOs that work on gender-based violence (U.S. Department of State 2012). International NGOs, as well as some of their African counterparts, have capitalized on these opportunities. In 2007, one Zambian NGO that provides legal aid to HIV-positive people who face workplace discrimination contemplated expanding its clientele to victims of domestic violence (Zambian NGO official, interview, Lusaka, 20 August 2007). And after Mrs. Clinton's funding announcement in Congo, many NGOs took up the issue of sexual violence (Autesserre 2012).

Regardless of their reasons for addressing violence, both international and local NGOs said the problem could undermine the AIDS response. Women feared abuse, the end of a marriage, and the loss of children if they disclosed their HIV positive status to their partners (international NGO official, interview, Lusaka, 15 August 2007). These fears were not unfounded, as one AIDS counselor at a Zambian clinic described the likelihood of marital stability if a wife was HIV positive:

> I'd say that in seventy-five percent of marriages I see the couple supports each other. But the challenge comes when the man is negative. . . . Women have not left marriages. . . . I can think of only two or three cases where a man has come and said my wife ran away because she cannot stay with a man who is positive. But for positive women, no; it is different.
>
> (interview, Lusaka, 18 March 2011)

HIV-positive women's secrecy hampered the prevention of HIV transmission and the promotion of HIV testing, both essential for long-term success against AIDS.

Additionally, gender-based violence hampered AIDS activism. When some women in Zambia publicly spoke about their HIV status and formed local organizations to address AIDS, their husbands and male relatives beat them. One group leader explained, "When you come out in the open [about your HIV status], you will save a lot of people. But [the men] will just say, 'That one, she has too much courage.' And they will just violate you. They will abuse you physically, emotionally and spiritually" (focus group, Lusaka, 12 April 2011). Such abuse hindered AIDS education efforts and HIV testing. For many NGO officials, the security of the AIDS response partially rested on the physical security of African women.

Unstable access to ART for people living with HIV/AIDS

In 2011, dozens of Zambian PLHIVs described how ART had "brought them back to life," helped them "rise up out of their beds," and made them "fit" (focus group, Lusaka, 14 April 2011; focus group, Livingstone, 27 June 2011; focus group, Kitwe, 19 May 2011). These miraculous recoveries were possible because of the establishment of the Global Fund to Fight AIDS, Tuberculosis and Malaria in 2002 and PEPFAR in 2003. As of 2012, PEPFAR directly supported 5.1 million people on ART, while the Global Fund supported 4.2 million (Global Fund 2012; PEPFAR 2012). As of 2013, these two programs covered most ART costs in sub-Saharan Africa, except in South Africa. Yet, the 2008 global recession and subsequent Euro crisis and U.S. deficit raised concerns among NGOs, public health officials, and AIDS activists about how much longer donors would pay these costs (Garrett 2013). These fears were not unfounded: PEPFAR experienced cuts for fiscal years 2012 and 2013, raising questions about how the program would reach its target of 6 million people on ART by the end of 2013 (Aziz 2013; Mazzotta 2011). In 2011, the Global Fund suspended new grants until 2014 (McNeil 2011).[8]

In response to funding decreases, international NGOs such as AIDS Healthcare Foundation, World Vision, and World Relief expressed concern about stable access to ART (Kaiser Daily Global Health Policy Report 2013a, 2013b). One Zambian NGO official questioned the "sustainability" of donors' commitment (interview, Lusaka, 17 March 2011), and two others voiced their "fears" for ART security (interview, Lusaka, 30 March 2011; interview, Lusaka, 31 May 2011). While African NGO officials and PLHIV groups did not mention ART stability as often as food insecurity, they did worry about long-term treatment access. PLHIVs understood that their survival depended on lifelong access to ART and that if AIDS medications were not free, most PLHIVs would be unable to afford them (focus group, Lusaka, 22 March 2011; focus group, Ndola, 21 May 2011).

As early as 2009, donor shortfalls had affected the health security of some PLHIVs. Some Zambian clinics began to provide clients with a two-week supply of ART, instead of a month supply, forcing clients to incur greater transportation costs as they returned more frequently to clinics. These costs led clients to miss dosages (Zambian AIDS clinic officer, interview, Lusaka, 7 June 2011). Funding shortfalls prevented clinics from providing several months' supply of drugs to rural populations who could not reach clinics on impassable roads during the rainy season (Zambian NGO official, interview, Mpika, 4 July 2011). Clinics in Zambia, Burundi, and Uganda reported drug shortages, which NGOs said led to several PLHIV deaths (IRIN 2009; IRIN 2011; Lusaka Times 2013; Zambian Watchdog 2013).

Some AIDS clinics in Zambia became more selective about the clients they accepted. One clinic did not offer ART to individuals unless they were the spouses of current clients (Zambian NGO official, interview, Lusaka, 9 May 2011), while another quit giving ART to migrants. An NGO official explained:

> If people don't have an address, a place they live, we just won't accept them. These Zimbabweans and Congolese. . . . They are here and then gone. They don't adhere [to ART] and then we can't find them. We can't use resources on them.
>
> (interview, Lusaka, 12 March 2011)

Such rationing was a matter of survival for both clients who faithfully adhered to ART and the NGOs themselves. If clinics wasted resources on high-risk clients, more responsible PLHIVs might be harmed. More broadly, clients who disappeared could negatively affect a clinic's aggregate adherence rates, which had to be reported monthly to donors. If these rates dropped below 90%, organizations could lose funding (Zambian NGO official, interview, 7 June 2011). Lost resources meant fewer staff members, reduced salaries, and less program development (Zambian NGO official, interview, Lusaka, 26 May 2011). In this rationing process, NGO survival could triumph over the health security of "risky" PLHIVs.

Both local and international NGOs, as well as PLHIV groups, also pointed out that the instability in ART access that resulted from uncertain funding endangered the global AIDS response. For local NGO clinics, declines in donor support necessitated that they serve fewer clients, implement user fees, and/or utilize means tests for services (NGO clinic official, interview, Lusaka, 29 March 2011). NGO officers and PLHIV groups expressed concern that if clinics tested individuals for HIV but could not offer ART, few people would take the test (NGO official, interview, Kitwe, 20 May 2011). Without HIV testing, prevention is difficult. Researchers also have discovered that ART itself is a form of prevention, since early treatment makes PLHIVs 96% less likely to infect others with HIV (CDC 2013). At the 2012 International AIDS Conference, NGO officials, activists, and policymakers stressed that "treatment is prevention," and that widespread ART access is essential to secure the health of PLHIVs and the broader AIDS response (International AIDS conference, author observations, Washington, DC, 22–27 July 2012). For all NGOs, the security of the global AIDS response required stability in ART provision.

Conclusion

NGOs that work on AIDS have rejected securitization because of its focus on militaries and state stability, and they have only partially embraced human security, seeing its focus as too broad and its application in a post-ART access environment as too limited. Instead, NGOs, particularly at the local level, have adopted a globalist perspective: they emphasize individual not population health, they view health to be a dependent variable, and they question how factors such as food insecurity, gender-based violence, and unstable ART access affect the health security of PLHIVs. In the process, they adopt the security language to link individual health security with the survival of the global AIDS response.

The NGO approach raises four broader points. First, it elucidates the need for grassroots examinations of culture, politics, economics, and society to better understand how local-level variables make individuals more (or less) vulnerable to poor health. Such investigations provide a necessary counter to the global health security paradigm that focuses on international factors such as migration or trade and state-level variables such as state spending or health system structures that affect the health of a state's population. Second, the local NGO perspective presents a Global South angle on health, one often ignored in the global health security literature and among policymakers in the Global North. Global health security has concentrated on disease surveillance and control for global epidemics, and it has pushed the costs of global health security onto poor countries at the expense of local health and development concerns (Rushton 2011). The NGO perspective, particularly as found among African NGOs and PLHIVs, highlights the complex factors affecting health in the Global South. Resulting policy responses should move beyond surveillance and control to foster institutions and sustainable funding mechanisms for health in the Global South (Garrett 2013).

Third, the NGO use of security-derived language to increase attention to socioeconomic problems demonstrates both the power of security frameworks and the difficulty in defining security. Global funding for prevention of gender-based violence and alleviation of hunger has increased in the post-2000 period. While the use of security frames is not the only reason for this outcome, the security language has enabled NGOs and advocates to link these long-term development challenges to the interests of states in the Global North. But in the process, their frameworks challenge traditional definitions of security and therefore, may have only temporary influence. As scholars continue to clarify definitions of security, they should also investigate how NGO securitization of health-related issues may promote or hamper particular policy or program outcomes.

Finally, the NGO perspective challenges NGOs themselves, particularly those that focus solely on AIDS. As mentioned above, many of these groups have viewed AIDS to be an exceptional issue, one that requires its own institutions, programs, and budgets (Morfit 2011). Yet, as NGOs specify the factors that negatively affect the health security of PLHIVs, they connect AIDS with broader development objectives.[9] Socioeconomic and political development is essential to improve agricultural production for food security, to promote the gender equality that limits gender-based violence, and to establish sustainable funding mechanisms that ensure drug access for PLHIVs. The AIDS and development viewpoint, not the AIDS exceptionalism embedded in some NGOs' approaches, has the best possibility to secure health not only for PLHIVs in Africa but also for all people in the Global South.

Notes

1 Funding for fieldwork for this article was provided by the U.S. Fulbright Scholar Program and Calvin College in Grand Rapids, Michigan. I am grateful to Jeremy Youde and Simon Rushton for helpful comments and to Harold Smith, University of the South student, for research assistance.
2 Several of these NGOs work globally on a variety of health and development issues.
3 These lists are available at http://www.who.int/civilsociety/relations/NGOs-in-Official-Relations-with-WHO.pdf and http://csonet.org/content/documents/E2011INF4.pdf (accessed 17 March 2013).
4 This list is available at http://www.africa.upenn.edu/health/ngos_org.htm (accessed 17 March 2013).
5 See http://www.africa.upenn.edu/Urgent_Action/apic-12303.html (accessed 17 May 2013).
6 The websites for the international NGOs Africare (http://www.africare.org), Doctors without Borders (http://www.doctorswithoutborders.org), World Vision International (http://www.wvi.org), Care International (http://www.care-international.org), American Jewish World Service (http://ajws.org), Oxfam (http://www.oxfam.org), and Caritas Internationalis (http://www.caritas.org) illustrate these objectives (all accessed 20 May 2013).
7 See the Stop Stock-Outs Campaign, a movement started in 2009 and supported by Oxfam, several southern African PLHIV groups, Health Action International, and the Open Society Institute. Information available at: <http://stopstockouts.org/stop-stock-outs-campaign/> (accessed 25 May 2013).
8 The Global Fund did allow some funding allocations between 2011 and 2014, but only for invited applicants.
9 See Woodling et al. (2012) on the resurgence of the AIDS-development framework.

References

Aginam, O. and Rupiya, M. (eds.) (2012) *HIV/AIDS: The Security Sector in Africa*, New York: United Nations University Press.

Aldis, W. (2008) 'Health security as a public health concept: a critical analysis', *Health Policy and Planning*, 23: 369–375.

Autesserre, S. (2012) 'Dangerous tales: dominant narratives on the Congo and their unintended consequences', *African Affairs*, 111: 202–222.

Aziz, R. (2013, March 26) 'Congress finalizes FY 2013 budget with PEPFAR cuts, boost to Global Fund', *Science Speaks: HIV & TB News*. Online. Available HTTP: <http://sciencespeaksblog.org/2013/03/26/congress-cuts-pepfar-boosts-global-fund-as-fy-2013-finalized> (accessed 24 May 2013).

Barnett, M. and Finnemore, M. (2004) *Rules for the World: International Organizations in Global Politics*, Ithaca: Cornell University Press.

Barnett, T. and Prins, G. (2006) 'HIV/AIDS and security: fact, fiction and evidence – a report to UNAIDS', *International Affairs*, 82: 359–368.

BBC News. (2013, April 15) 'Africa's economic growth to outpace average', *BBC News Business*. Online. Available HTTP: <http://www.bbc.co.uk/news/business-22156755> (accessed 17 April 2013).

Bristol, N. (2006) 'Military incursions into aid world anger humanitarian groups', *The Lancet*, 367: 384–386.

Brown, D. (2011, November 21) 'AIDS deaths and new infections continue to fall in most parts of the world', *Washington Post*. Online. Available HTTP: <http://articles.washingtonpost.com/2011–11–21/national/35282015_1_hiv-last-year-antiretroviral-therapy-infections> (accessed 20 May 2012).

Buzan, B., Wæver, O. and de Wilde, J. (1998) *Security: A New Framework for Analysis*, Boulder: Lynne Rienner Publishers.

Center for Disease Control and Prevention (CDC). (2013) 'Prevention benefits of HIV treatment'. Online. Available HTTP: <http://www.cdc.gov/hiv/prevention/research/tap> (accessed 15 May 2013).

Center for Strategic and International Studies (CSIS). (2002) *The Second Wave of the HIV/AIDS Pandemic*, Washington, DC: CSIS. Online. Available HTTP: <http://csis.org/files/media/csis/pubs/021003_secondwave.pdf> (accessed 5 May 2005).

Central Statistics Office, Ministry of Health, Tropical Disease Research Centre, and University of Zambia. (2009) *Zambia: Demographic and Health Survey 2007*. Online. Available HTTP: < http://dhsprogram.com/pubs/pdf/FR211/FR211[revised-05-12-2009].pdf > (accessed 14 May 2014).

Chandler, D. (2008) 'Review essay: human security: the dog that didn't bark', *Security Dialogue*, 39: 427–438.

Davies, S.E. (2010) *Global Politics of Health*, Cambridge: Polity.

Elbe, S. (2002) 'HIV/AIDS and the changing landscape of war in Africa', *International Security*, 27: 159–177.

Elbe, S. (2006) 'Should HIV/AIDS be securitized? The ethical dilemmas of linking HIV/AIDS and security', *International Studies Quarterly*, 50: 119–144.

Feldbaum, H., Lee, K. and Patel, P. (2006) 'The national security implications of HIV/AIDS', *PLoS Medicine*, 3. Online. Available HTTP: <http://www.plosmedicine.org/article/info:doi/10.1371/journal.pmed.0030171> (accessed 21 May 2013).

Ferguson, J. (1990) *The Anti-Politics Machine: 'Development', Depoliticization, and Bureaucratic Power in Lesotho*, Cambridge: Cambridge University Press.

Food and Agriculture Organization (FAO). (1996) *Rome Declaration on World Food Security*, report from the World Food Summit, Rome, 13–17 November. Online. Available HTTP: <http://www.fao.org/docrep/003/w3613e/w3613e00.htm> (accessed 15 May 2013).

Garrett, L. (2013, May 22) 'The survival of global health"- part two: the future of global health funding'. Online. Available HTTP: <http://lauriegarrett.com/blog/2013/5/22/v2g06vzw590xhleqoevmfd2ri3gacg> (accessed 25 May 2013).

Gillespie, S. and Kadiyala, S. (2005) 'HIV/AIDS and food and nutrition security: interactions and response', *American Journal of Agricultural Economies*, 87: 1282–1288.

Global Fund. (2012) 'End-year Results for 2012', media release. Online. Available HTTP: <http://www.theglobalfund.org/en/blog/30906/> (accessed 24 May 2013).

Human Rights Watch. (2003) *Just Die Quietly: Domestic Violence and Women's Vulnerability to HIV in Uganda*, New York: Human Rights Watch. Online. Available HTTP: <http://www.hrw.org/sites/default/files/reports/uganda0803full.pdf> (accessed 4 June 2004).

Ingram, A. (2007) 'HIV/AIDS, security and the geopolitics of US-Nigerian relations', *Review of International Political Economy*, 14: 510–534.

International Crisis Group. (2001) *HIV/AIDS as a Security Issue*, Brussels: International Crisis Group. Online. Available HTTP: <http://www.crisisgroup.org/~/media/Files/africa/HIV-AIDS%20as%20a%20Security%20Issue.ashx> (accessed 15 October 2001).

Iqbal, Z. and Zorn, C. (2010) 'Violent conflict and the spread of HIV/AIDS in Africa', *Journal of Politics*, 72: 149–162.

IRIN. (2009, July 31) 'Uganda: government inquiry launched as ARV shortages blamed for deaths', *IRIN News*. Online. Available HTTP: <http://www.irinnews.org/Report/85526/UGANDA-Government-inquiry-launched-as-ARV-shortages-blamed-for-deaths> (accessed 7 March 2013).

IRIN. (2011, September 5) 'Deaths reported as ARV shortage continues', *IRIN News*. Online. Available HTTP: <http://www.irinnews.org/Report/93657/BURUNDI-Deaths-reported-as-ARV-shortage-continues> (accessed 7 March 2013).

Kaiser Daily Global Health Policy Report. (2013a, May 20) 'AIDS Healthcare Foundation lobbying Congress to reauthorize PEPFAR'. Online. Available HTTP: <http://kff.org/daily-news/may-20–2013/> (accessed 21 May 2013).

Kaiser Daily Global Health Policy Report. (2013b, May 17) 'Members of faith community, U.S. legislators, PEPFAR leadership meet to discuss U.S. foreign aid, global AIDS response'. Online. Available HTTP: <http://kff.org/news-summary/members-of-faith-community-u-s-legislators-pepfar-leadership-meet-to-discuss-u-s-foreign-aid-global-aids-response/> (accessed 22 May 2013).

Lusaka Times. (2013, July 27) 'A critical shortage of ARVs hits most facilities around the country', *Lusaka Times*. Online. Available HTTP: <http://www.lusakatimes.com/2013/07/27/a-critical-shortage-of-arvs-hits-most-health-facilities-around-the-country/> (accessed 8 August 2013).

Mazzotta, M. (2011, December 16) 'PEPFAR takes a hit in 2012 funding; military HIV research program sustains funding after close call', *Science Speaks: HIV & TB News*. Online. Available HTTP: <http://sciencespeaksblog.org/2011/12/16/pepfar-takes-a-hit-in-2012-funding-bill-military-hiv-research-program-sustains-funding-after-close-call/> (accessed 24 May 2013).

McInnes, C. and Rushton, S. (2010) 'HIV, AIDS and security: where are we now?' *International Affairs*, 86: 225–245.

McNeil, D. (2011, November 23) 'Global Fund will pause new grants and seek new manager', *New York Times*. Online. Available HTTP: <http://www.nytimes.com/2011/11/24/health/global-aids-fund-cancels-fund-raising-and-seeks-new-manager.html?_r=0 > (accessed 2 January 2012).

Michael, S. (2004) *Undermining Development: The Absence of Power among Local NGOs in Africa*, Bloomington, IN: Indiana University Press.

Miller, R. and Dowell, S. (2012) *Investing in a Safer United States: What is Global Health Security and Why Does it Matter?* Washington, DC: CSIS. Online. Available HTTP: <http://csis.org/files/publication/120816_Miller_InvestingSaferUS_Web.pdf> (accessed 21 May 2013).

Morfit, N.S. (2011) '"AIDS is money": how donor preferences reconfigure local realities', *World Development*, 39: 64–76.

Orbinski, J. (2007) 'Global health, social movements and governance', in A. Cooper, J. Kirton and T. Schrecker (eds.) *Governing Global Health*, Aldershot: Ashgate Publishing.

Ostergard, R. (2002) 'Politics in the hot zone: AIDS and national security in Africa', *Third World Quarterly*, 23: 333–350.

Paris, R. (2001) 'Human security: paradigm shift or hot air?' *International Security*, 26: 87–102.

Patterson, A. (2006) *The Politics of AIDS in Africa*, Boulder: Lynne Rienner Publishers.

Patterson, A. (2011) *The Church and AIDS in Africa: The Politics of Ambiguity*, Boulder: FirstForum Press.

Pierotti, R. (2013) 'Increasing rejection of intimate partner violence: evidence of global cultural diffusion', *American Sociological Review*, 78: 240–265.

Poku, N., Renwick, N. and Porto, J.G. (2007) 'Human security and development in Africa', *International Affairs*, 83: 1155–1170.

Rushton, S. (2007) 'Securizing HIV/AIDS: pandemics, politics and SCR 1308', paper presented at the International Studies Association Conference, Chicago, 28 February–3 March.

Rushton, S. (2011) 'Global health security: security for whom? Security from what?' *Political Studies*, 59: 779–796.

Sagala, J.K. (2006) 'HIV/AIDS and the military in Sub-Saharan Africa: impact on military organizational effectiveness', *Africa Today*, 53: 53–77.

Sen, A.K. (1999) *Development as Freedom*, Oxford: Oxford University Press.

Siplon, P. (2005) 'AIDS and patriarchy: ideological obstacles to effective policy making', in A. Patterson (ed.) *The African State and the AIDS Crisis*, Aldershot: Ashgate Publishing.

Stillwaggon, E. (2006) *AIDS and the Ecology of Poverty*, London: Oxford University Press.

Tadjbakhsh, S. (2005) 'Human security: the seven challenges to operationalizing the concept', paper delivered at UNESCO conference entitled 'Human Security: 60 Minutes to Convince', Paris, 13 September.

Twebaze, J. (2009) 'Disclosures and silences: challenges to marital relationships in the era of ART in Uganda', paper presented at the conference of the International Research Network on AIDS and Religion in Africa, Lusaka, Zambia, 13–15 April.

UNAIDS. (1998) *Expanding the Global Response to HIV/AIDS through Focused Action*, Geneva: UNAIDS. Online. Available HTTP: <http://whqlibdoc.who.int/publications/1998/a62533.pdf > (accessed 14 May 2014).

UNAIDS. (2012) *Regional Fact Sheet 2012*. Online. Available HTTP: <http://www.unaids.org/en/media/unaids/contentassets/documents/epidemiology/2012/gr2012/2012_FS_regional_ssa_en.pdf> (accessed 14 May 2014).

UN Commission on Human Security. (2003) *Human Security Now: Protecting and Empowering People.* Online. Available HTTP: <http://www.unocha.org/humansecurity/chs/finalreport/index.html> (accessed 25 April 2012).

UN Development Program (UNDP). (1994) *Human Development Report: New Dimensions of Human Security*, New York: Oxford University Press. Online. Available HTTP: <http://hdr.undp.org/en/reports/global/hdr1994/chapters/> (accessed 18 May 2010).

UN Security Council. (2000) 'Resolution 1308', S/RES/1308 (2000). Online. Available HTTP: <http://daccess-dds-ny.un.org/doc/UNDOC/GEN/N00/536/02/PDF/N0053602.pdf?OpenElement> (accessed 20 May 2013).

UN Security Council. (2011) 'Resolution 1983', S/RES/1983 (2011). Online. Available HTTP: <http://www.unaids.org/en/media/unaids/contentassets/documents/document/2011/unsc/20110607_UNSC-Resolution1983.pdf> (accessed 22 May 2013).

U.S. Department of State. (2012) 'Ambassador Verveer announces grants to address gender-based violence as part of the global HIV response'. Online. Available HTTP: <http://www.state.gov/r/pa/prs/ps/2012/11/201095.htm> (accessed 14 May 2013).

U.S. Institute of Peace. (2001) *AIDS and Violent Conflict in Africa*, Washington, DC: United States Institute of Peace. Online. Available HTTP: <http://www.usip.org/files/resources/sr75.pdf> (accessed 4 January 2002).

U.S. National Intelligence Council (USNIC). (2000) *National Intelligence Estimate: The Global Infectious Disease Threat and Its Implications for the United States*, Washington, DC: National Intelligence Council. Online. Available HTTP: <http://www.wilsoncenter.org/sites/default/files/Report6–3.pdf> (accessed 15 February 2013).

U.S. President's Emergency Plan for AIDS Relief (PEPFAR). (2012) 'Latest results'. Online. Available HTTP: <http://www.pepfar.gov/funding/results/index.htm> (accessed 19 May 2013).

Uvin, P. (1998) *Aiding Violence: The Development Enterprise in Rwanda*, West Hartford, CT: Kumarian Press.

Vieira, M. A. (2007) 'Southern Africa's response(s) to international HIV/AIDS norms: the politics of assimilation', paper presented at the International Studies Association Conference, Chicago, 28 February–3 March.

Walker, L., Reid, G. and Cornell, M. (2004) *Waiting to Happen: HIV/AIDS in South Africa (The Bigger Picture)*, Boulder: Lynne Rienner Publishers.

Ward, T. (2007) 'The political economy of NGOs and human security', *International Journal of World Peace*, 24: 43–64.

Woodling, M., Williams, O. and Rushton, S. (2012) 'New life in old frames: HIV, development, and the "AIDS Plus MDGs" approach', *Global Public Health*, 7: S144–S158.

World Health Organization (WHO). (2007) *World Health Report 2007: A Safer Future: Global Public Health Security in the 21st Century*, Geneva: World Health Organization. Online. Available HTTP: <http://www.who.int/whr/2007/en/> (accessed 17 May 2013).

Youde, J. (2011) 'Mediating risk through the International Health Regulations and bio-political surveillance', *Political Studies*, 59: 813–830.

Zambian Watchdog. (2013, May 13) 'ARV shortage hits Western Province'. Online. Available HTTP: <http://www.zambianwatchdog.com/arv-shortage-hits-western-province/> (accessed 19 May 2013).

PART IV

Controversies

24

HEALTH SECURITY AND/OR HUMAN RIGHTS?

Joseph J. Amon

How does "health security" relate to human rights? Are they in opposition? Synergistic? Unrelated? In other words, should the title of this chapter be "Health Security *and* Human Rights" or "Health Security *or* Human Rights"?

Advancing "health security" is not inherently in conflict with the respect and protection of human rights. In fact, as Colin McInnes describes in an earlier chapter, the development of the concept of "human security" by the UN Development Program (UNDP 1990, 1994) and others (Chen 2004; Chen et al. 2003; Ogata & Cels, 2003; Ogata & Sen, 2003; Sen 2000; Thomas 2000) was very much grounded in human rights. Similarly, the World Health Organization (WHO) identified as the goal of health security minimizing "vulnerability to acute public health events" (WHO 2007: ix) – a goal consistent with human rights treaties recognizing the right to the highest attainable standard of health.

Yet, the "securitization" of health, and its martial overtones, can be fairly understood as suggesting a tension, if not a conflict, between definitions of health security that focus on the way in which health issues threaten the security of the *state*, and with the human rights obligations of the state to respect, protect, and fulfill individual rights. This chapter will explore this relationship, first by examining the foundations of health and human rights and discussing when derivations on individuals' rights are permissible in the context of public health emergencies and threats to state security under international human rights law and then through three diverse case studies. While much of the literature on the relationship of health security and human rights has centered on global infectious disease threats such as HIV/AIDS and SARS, the tension between health security and human rights is evident in a much broader range of issues. Specific case studies in this chapter will examine extremely drug-resistant tuberculosis (XDR-TB), drug dependency, and lead poisoning. Each, in distinct ways, has been defined as a "security" threat, and each allows an opportunity to explore how the "health security" framing of public health concerns can result in rights-restricting state responses.

Understanding the relationship between health and human rights

Acknowledgement of a right to the "highest attainable standard of health" as a normative standard was first articulated in the preamble to the 1946 Constitution of the World Health Organization. In the following decades this right was reiterated and further defined, in both international instruments such as the Universal Declaration of Human Rights (UDHR 1948) and the International Covenant on Economic, Social and Cultural Rights (ICESCR 1966), and in more than 120 constitutions worldwide (OHCHR and WHO n.d.).

A "right to health" does not, however, guarantee an individual a healthy life. Rather, it identifies specific obligations of governments: to *respect* the rights of individuals and to refrain from interfering with their access to prevention or treatment; to *protect* individuals through positive steps to expand access to care and from harm; and to *fulfill* the right to health through national planning and implementation of public health programs. Recognizing the many "determinants" of health, international treaties addressing the right to health frequently emphasize the importance of related rights, such as the right to information and education, to water and sanitation, to food and housing, to a healthy environment, and to be free from violence.

The expansive nature of the right to health is balanced, however, by the recognition that states may progressively realize their obligations in regard to the right to health, according to available resources. However, while states "move as expeditiously and effectively as possible towards the full realisation of [the right]" (CESCR 2000), they must also guarantee certain core obligations. These include ensuring nondiscriminatory access to health facilities; providing essential medicines; ensuring equitable distribution of health facilities, goods, and services; and taking measures to prevent, treat, and control epidemic disease.

Central to the development of the right to health has been the development of accountability mechanisms to ensure that the right is not wholly aspirational. Accountability can include simple reporting of health indicators (e.g., progress towards Millennium Development Goals), reporting to treaty monitoring bodies, or more formal judicial, quasi-judicial, and administrative review. Lawsuits seeking access to medicines is one example of judicial review (Biehl et al. 2012), while quasi-judicial review might involve complaints filed with a patients' rights commission. Pressure from nongovernmental organizations investigating health-related human rights abuses and demanding redress form another type of accountability (Amon et al. 2012).

Restrictions on liberty in the name of "health security"

Rights to life, liberty, and security of person and the right to equal protection of the law also have an impact on health, and health status can impact upon the realization of these rights. While the International Covenant on Economic, Social and Cultural Rights is understood as central to the right to health, the International Covenant on Civil and Political Rights (ICCPR) is understood to protect civil and political rights such as the right to liberty and freedom from arbitrary arrest or detention (ICCPR 1966). It holds that a detention may be "arbitrary" and in violation of the right to liberty and security, even if it is in accordance with local or national laws, if it is random or capricious or disproportionate (Human Rights Committee 1994). This provision is applicable to all forms of deprivations of liberty, including those related to threats to public health (Human Rights Committee 2003).

Elaboration of the requirements for and scope of restrictions on any rights protected by the ICCPR can be found in two key sources: first, in the Siracusa Principles, a nonbinding document developed by nongovernmental organizations and adopted by the UN Economic and Social Council in 1984, and second, in the authoritative interpretations of the United Nations Human Rights Committee (HRC) – the body charged with overseeing state implementation of the ICCPR.

The Siracusa Principles state that restrictions on human rights under the ICCPR must meet standards of legality, evidence-based necessity, proportionality, and gradualism. Specifically, limitations on rights must be, among other provisions, strictly "necessary," meaning that the limitations respond to a pressing public or social need and proportionately pursue a legitimate aim and are the least restrictive means required for the achievement of the purpose of the limitation. Additional protections include that the restriction is provided for and carried out in accordance with the law, that it is not discriminatory, and that the burden of justifying a limitation upon a right lies with the state seeking to impose the limitation (Amon et al. 2009). While the Siracusa Principles broadly address restrictions on rights in times of insecurity, they also explicitly note: "Public health may be invoked as a ground for limiting certain rights in order to allow a State to take measures dealing with a serious threat to the health of the population or individual members of the population. These measures must be specifically aimed at preventing disease or injury or providing care for the sick and injured" (United Nations Economic and Social Council 1985).

In 1999, the HRC published General Comment No. 27 specifically related to freedom of movement, which includes an analysis of the criteria for justifiable limitations on movement, including for public health reasons. The General Comment, like the Siracusa Principles, stresses the need for restrictions to be provided for by law, demonstrably necessary, consistent with other rights in the ICCPR, and nondiscriminatory. The Committee particularly dwells on the necessity of the proposed restriction: "It is not sufficient that the restrictions serve the permissible purposes; they must also be necessary to protect them. Restrictive measures must conform to the principle of proportionality; they must be appropriate to achieve their protective function; they must be the least intrusive instrument amongst those which might achieve the desired result" (Human Rights Committee 1999).

However, while these documents provide guidance to states on when and how restrictions on liberty in the name of public health threats may be implemented, neither addresses disease transmission, treatment, or public health risks in depth. For example, the Human Rights Committee in General Comment No. 27 only briefly mentions public health amidst consideration of the "national security, public order (ordre public), public health or morals and the rights and freedoms of others." Neither the Siracusa Principles nor General Comment No. 27 address the fact that public health threats can *stem* from state actions, and neglect. While the World Health Organization's International Health Regulations (IHR; WHO 2005) are an additional authority for considering how human rights relate to public health threats, the IHR primarily address disease surveillance and notification related to transnational infectious disease threats (Todrys et al. 2013).

XDR-tuberculosis

In 2006, the emergence of a multidrug-resistant strain of tuberculosis, dramatically labeled "extremely drug resistant tuberculosis," or XDR-TB, led to widespread media attention and fears of an untreatable, fatal, and potentially pandemic illness. These fears also led to the detention of patients in the name of health security.

In many regards XDR-TB was a new and truly scary disease: in Tugela Ferry, a town in Kwa-Zulu-Natal, an XDR-TB outbreak in HIV-positive patients killed 52 of 53 people infected (Altman 2007). But in other ways, the emergence of XDR-TB was less sudden than it initially seemed: the WHO had estimated that there were 14,034 drug-resistant TB cases in South Africa in 2006 (WHO 2008), and a 2006 study in KwaZulu-Natal found high rates of drug resistant and XDR-TB (Gandhi et al. 2006). HIV was also highly prevalent in the country and TB was a leading cause of death among those infected. Rather than something completely new, XDR-TB could be understood as the continuation of long-standing failures to effectively treat both TB and HIV in South Africa.

Under South African law, as is true under public health laws in many countries, authorities may detain an individual suffering from an infectious disease until the disease ceases to present a public health risk. With this authority, government policy guidelines called for the isolation of all MDR- and XDR-TB patients in a specialist facility for a minimum of six months (Republic of South Africa 2004). However, South Africa had little ability to identify, isolate, and treat tens of thousands of drug-resistant TB patients. The result was, predictably, arbitrary treatment. Some individuals with XDR-TB were detained for as long as 2 years (Masie 2008). Others were discharged after 6 months to "make room for new patients" (Duggar 2008). In both cases no assessment of infectiousness was made (Andrews et al. 2007), and patients newly diagnosed with drug-resistant tuberculosis (a process that can take many weeks, during which time the patient is in the community and infectious) were typically not isolated immediately, due to long waiting lists for in-patient beds. The problem was large: in March 2009, the AIDS Law Project reported that approximately 1,700 people, including children, were being detained in TB isolation facilities, many of them in sub-standard conditions that violated South African constitutional rights and national health legislation (AIDS Law Project 2009). Patients repeatedly attempted to escape confinement, citing isolation from families, loss of income, and lack of access to effective treatment.

The case of XDR-TB in South Africa is typical in many ways of the conflicts that can emerge between security concerns and human rights in the context of new, emerging, poorly understood, and feared infectious disease threats. There is, at the base, a real threat to health, and often life, for some individuals. At the same time, the media often sensationalizes health security threats and inaccurately promotes them as indiscriminately threatening all individuals. With little evidence, emerging diseases are often portrayed in terms of a threat – both physical and moral – to the integrity of the state. The lack of complete understanding of disease transmission, and the absence of effective treatment and/or prevention strategies, results in the frequent desire by political leaders to adopt high profile actions that have more symbolic value than public health effectiveness: in short, to "do something." Framing the health crisis as one of national security, and framing those who are infected as threatening the integrity of the state, makes it easy for that "something" to be the detention of individuals infected, at-risk, or believed to be infected. The protections envisioned in the Siracusa Principles and General Comment No. 27 are often forgotten.

Drug dependency

Drug use, and drug dependency, presents a different kind of health, and national, security threat. However, there are many similarities to that of emerging infectious disease threats. Particularly when drug use is increasing, or when new drugs (again, often poorly understood) are introduced, sensationalistic media accounts, and fears of the public health and "moral" consequences to the population can create a demand that governments respond to the threat with rights restrictive measures.

In 2012 it was estimated that more than 235,000 people were detained in over 1,000 compulsory drug "treatment" centers in East and South East Asia (Lewis 2012). Individuals in these centers are held for periods of months to years and can experience a wide range of human rights abuses, including violation of the rights to freedom from torture and cruel, inhuman, and degrading treatment; freedom from arbitrary arrest and detention; a fair trial; privacy; the highest attainable standard of health; and freedom from forced labor (Amon et al. 2013).

The history of compulsory drug rehabilitation and the number of individuals in detention in the region is varied. In China and Vietnam, compulsory drug detention is historically grounded in a decades-old system of "re-education through labor" (RTL) that has also detained peaceful dissidents, activists, and others deemed threats to national security or public order (Human Rights Watch 2010, 2011a). By contrast, drug detention centers are a more recent phenomenon in countries such as Cambodia and Lao PDR and were developed in part through the support of international donors, operating within an explicit security framework of the international "war" on drugs (Amon et al. 2013b).

Yet, despite a reliance on detention, drug use is primarily recognized by governments in the region as an administrative infraction and drug users are frequently referred to – in both official documents, and by politicians – as "patients." For example, in Lao PDR, the national drug law states that "[d]rug addicts are to be considered as victims" (Human Rights Watch 2011b), and Chinese law requires that drug users be rehabilitated (Liu et al. 2010; State Council of the People's Republic of China 1995). Thailand's Narcotic Addict Rehabilitation Act, like others in the region, officially considers "drug addicts" as "patients" (Human Rights Watch 2007).

The expansion of compulsory drug 'treatment' centers coincides with fears of an "epidemic" of drug use that, like XDR-TB, is said to threaten public health and state security. While drug users are supposedly understood as patients not criminals, detained drug users are denied access to evidence-based health care, and long-term detention and the incorporation of compulsory exercise and forced labor in many centers betray an approach to drug use that more closely resembles the response to a "moral panic" than a health security threat. At its base, the response by these governments is founded upon establishing social order and meting out punishment. Again, the protections of the Siracusa Principles and General Comment No. 27 are absent.

Environmental health

In the last 15 years, China's gross domestic product has increased ten-fold (World Bank 2009). Economic growth has helped lift 200 million people out of absolute poverty since 1978, but undertaken without appropriate accompanying safeguards, it has also exacted a steep environmental price: widespread industrial pollution that has contaminated water, soil, and air and put the health of millions of people – likely even hundreds of millions – at risk. Currently, 20 of the world's 30 most polluted cities are in China (World Bank 2010).

One specific environmental health problem is lead poisoning. Lead poisoning is among the most common pediatric health problems in China (Shen et al. 2001), and while the lack of comprehensive data makes it difficult to determine the full extent of the epidemic, media accounts and research studies suggest that acute and chronic lead poisoning is a public health emergency affecting whole communities (Asia News 2009; Associated Press 2010; Li et al. 2004; Xingxin & Qian 2009).

What has been the response to this health threat? From the grassroots, there has been an unprecedented uprising: In the past few years it has been estimated that more than 100,000 "mass incidents" (protests) have occurred in China, many of which are related to pollution, land access, and environmental degradation. The Chinese government has been forced to respond and acknowledge environmental degradation and access to health care as threats to "social harmony" (Cohen & Amon 2012). In this context, environmental health was first defined by the people, and then by the state, as a security threat.

Once environmental health was understood as a health security issue, the Chinese government implemented legal reforms and increased intimidation. In the last few years a wide range of laws, regulations, and action plans promoting rigorous new standards for coal-fired plants designed to cut mercury, sulfur dioxide, and nitrogen oxide emissions, and encourage more environmentally friendly industries have been adopted (Ministry of Environmental Protection, The People's Republic of China 2012). The Chinese government's response to environmental protests also included ordering projects to be terminated and factories to be shut down (Reuters 2012). But at the same time, in many places enforcement of environmental regulations remains lax, and research on lead poisoning conducted by Human Rights Watch in four Chinese provinces found frequent reports of intimidation and the arrest of parents seeking access to information and treatment for lead poisoning (Cohen & Amon 2012). In one case, in Hunan Province, a busload of parents who were on their way to the provincial capital was stopped by the police (Watts 2010). The parents, after encountering hostility from local officials in their villages, were planning to request help and information from provincial authorities. Individuals interviewed in the community where this incident occurred reported that several people were arrested, and, at the time of the research, more than 6 months afterwards, one of the people arrested was still in jail (Cohen & Amon 2012).

Attempts by journalists to report on pollution have also been undermined by intimidation and threats. Journalists who reported on lead poisoning said that police had followed them or forced them to leave the area when attempting to interview people. A journalist who had been to a site in Hunan said that after he left the area police had questioned the people he had interviewed. A journalist who had been reporting on lead poisoning in Shaanxi was forced to leave the province. In one province, a government official told Human Rights Watch: "Journalists are not allowed to come here and not allowed to go into villages to talk to people." In another province, government officials said that individuals could only be interviewed about pollution if the local propaganda department (宣传部) cleared the questions in advance (Cohen & Amon 2012). Here too, rights were restricted in violation of international human rights law, including those of journalists and civil society seeking to respond to and expand understanding of a health security risk.

Considering rights restrictions

In these three cases, fears of a "new" disease (XDR-TB), of a "moral" crisis (drug dependency), or of social unrest due to the health consequences of environmental degradation (lead poisoning), contributed to the framing of a health issue as a security one and led to a response by the state based upon restricting liberty rather than promoting a public health, or human rights, approach. In each case, the state's response relied upon detention and either ignored or undermined evidence-based public health alternatives.

In the case of XDR-TB in South Africa, the substantive and procedural safeguards prescribed by Siracusa were clearly lacking. The government regulation applied to detaining XDR-TB cases entirely omits routine procedural protections that should be afforded patients: to challenge their detention in the courts, at regular intervals, and to be provided with legal representation. As a result, health care workers were in the position of making ad hoc decisions on patient isolation without procedural or legal guidance. Some detainees did go to court to mount challenges to their detention as inconsistent with the rights granted by the South African Constitution, but such challenges were ineffective (two of an original four patients in one such suit died pending a final outcome). No rapid review procedure was in place, and the burden of challenging the detention was on the patient. By contrast, international law requires that the review of detention should be automatic, and the burden of proof in each hearing should be on the authorities to justify the need for continuing detention (African Charter on Human and Peoples' Rights 1981; ICCPR 1966).

Secondly, limitations are only permissible if strictly necessary to achieve a given objective. Ambulatory and community-based treatment models for MDR-TB and XDR-TB have been successfully implemented in a number of settings – ranging from Lesotho to Latvia, Estonia, Georgia, Peru, the Philippines, Nepal, and the Russian Federation – without having to resort to extraordinary measures that infringe on a patient's human rights (Amon et al. 2009). Since the patients detained in South Africa were not generally refusing treatment and since ambulatory or community-based treatment programs provide a viable alternative to wholesale forced isolation, their forced isolation could not be seen as strictly necessary to achieve public health goals.

Thirdly, the design and implementation of the South African program was counter-productive to the goal of advancing public health. As is true with HIV, SARS, or drug dependency, incarcerating the sick discourages individuals from coming forward voluntarily for screening and treatment. Since determining an individual's drug-resistant TB diagnosis can take up to 8 weeks (during which time no treatment measures are undertaken), followed by a wait for an isolation ward bed of 4 to 6 additional weeks, the South African system created the potential for widespread infection prior to isolation. Holding MDR-TB and XDR-TB patients in over-crowded hospitals with inadequate ventilation increased the risk of nosocomial disease transmission and cross-infection. Because only patients who enter the public health system faced the risk of incarceration, those who turned to private sector providers for TB care were not placed in isolation.

In the example of compulsory drug detention centers in China, Vietnam, Lao PDR, and Cambodia, the same shortcomings in relationship to the Siracusa Principles are seen. The en masse detention of individuals without due process protections and without individualized determination of dependency violates both protections against arbitrary detention and deprivation of liberty, and the absence of effective drug dependency treatment violates claims that detention is strictly necessary. Claims that such detention is undertaken in the name of health security (Wu 2013) are contradicted, as with TB, by the fact that research, and authoritative health agencies such as WHO and UNODC, support community-based alternatives as more effective and rights-respecting. Compulsory detention for drug users is counter-productive to the idea of "low threshold" treatment of what is best understood as a chronic and relapsing condition, driving individuals who may otherwise seek care away from it.

While government laws and rhetoric emphasize an approach of addressing the "epidemic" of drug use by treating drug users as patients, it is not difficult to see that the attitude of officials is often plainly taking advantage of fears of drug users to justify harsh punishment. For example, the commander of a "treatment" center run by the military police in Cambodia described to the press how detainees at his center were forced to stand in the sun or "walk like monkeys" as punishment for attempting to escape (Smith 2010). Similarly, a Cambodian Interior Ministry spokesperson suggested to a reporter that those in drug "treatment" "need to do labor and hard work and sweating – that is one of the main ways to make drug-addicted people become normal people" (Deutsche Press-Agentur 2010).

In China, the "securitization" of environmental health concerns is neither in response to a new and deadly infectious disease nor to a "moral panic." Instead, it is a reflection of the threat presented by environmental and health activists organizing "mass incidents" (protests). Restrictions of due process and liberty, as with XDR-TB and drug detention, are again prominent.

However, in this case, protests about access to health care and treatment are also about corruption, lack of accountability, participation, and transparency (Xiaoyun 2012). Framing health threats as "security" issues, and then responding to them as such, will inevitably result in counter-protests, highlighting the need for information, participation, and accountability. Protests related to pollution and environmental health, which affect whole communities and transcend socioeconomic strata, mark a departure from previous health-related activism in China, such as around HIV or SARS. While the civil society response to HIV and SARS were similarly sparked by government denial and neglect, protests in response to environmental health threats have achieved a much broader and larger constituency (Amon 2008). Heavy-handed government responses, trying to stem citizen unease around environmental degradation, have galvanized local communities, turning small scale upset into large and sometimes violent uprisings.

In the case of air pollution and lead poisoning, the health security threat is not easily addressed: there is no vaccine or treatment that will quickly turn the tide of the significant health consequences that China faces from environmental degradation. As mentioned, in some cases, the government has increased enforcement. In others, communities have been bought off: offered financial remediation and relocation. To truly address the problem, however, broader, rights-based protections will be necessary, including engagement with civil society.

Conclusion

The Siracusa Principles emphasize the need for state responses to public health crises to be proportionate and gradual. While protecting the public from drug-resistant TB, treating individuals who are dependent upon drugs, and addressing widespread environmental health risks are legitimate and important public health objectives, freedom of movement is a fundamental individual right. Intimidation and detention in the name of public health security, when less intrusive and restrictive measures have been proven feasible and effective, are not consistent with human rights principles.

Human rights norms are essential for the protection of both individuals and communities in times of public health emergencies, and participation of civil society is critical to an effective response (Commission to Investigate the Introduction and Spread of SARS in Ontario 2006; Gostin 2006; Tarantola et al. 2009). This cooperation requires a sense of trust of the government that is fostered by respect for human rights and eroded by a lack of information. Health threats such as emerging infectious diseases, drug dependency, and lead poisoning pose a crisis of legitimacy for government officials. Uncertainties about the effectiveness of control strategies and competing interests across government actors complicate the assessment of the legitimacy of rights limiting measures and highlight the importance of transparent decision-making processes.

The lack of detailed guidance in human rights law specific to public health threats, and the lack of a clear definition and understanding of "health security" more generally, allows states to adopt rights-limiting actions under broad claims of poorly defined threats to public health or order. The human rights implications of rights-restricting measures in the case of a public health threat are undoubtedly different than threats to national security and suggest the need for new international standards related to rights-restricting measures and threats to public health. Effective treatment for certain diseases can last months or years (or be unknown or unavailable), and the risks to the public of any health security threat vary greatly according to the manner and ease of transmission, the severity of disease, and the availability of treatment.

A General Comment from the Human Rights Committee or a set of principles from an independent body of experts could give broader authority to the WHO to more specifically define criteria for rights-restricting measures in the face of public health threats and ensure that national laws and practices recognize and comply with existing obligations not to commit arbitrary deprivations of liberty or limit freedom of movement excessively. New standards at the international level clearly specifying how rights-limiting steps should be employed could help states' development and reform of laws and policies related to rights-restricting measures for TB patients, individuals who use drugs, or those simply seeking information and treatment for environmental health threats. New standards could also help define an understanding of "health security" in harmony with the respect for, and protection of, human rights.

References

African Charter on Human and Peoples' Rights. (1981) OAU Doc. No. CAB/LEG/67/3 rev. 5, reprinted in *International Legal Materials* (1982) vol. 21. Online. Available HTTP: <http://www1.umn.edu/humanrts/instree/z1afchar.htm> (accessed 5 July 2013).

AIDS Law Project. (2009) *Human Rights in the Response to TB in South Africa: State and Individual Responsibilities*. Unpublished report.

Altman, L.K. (2007, March 20) 'Rise of a deadly TB reveals a global system in crisis', *The New York Times*. Online. Available HTTP: <http://www.nytimes.com/2007/03/20/health/20docs.html?pagewanted=alland_r=0> (accessed 28 June 2013).

Amon, J.J., (2008) 'High hurdles to health in China', in M. Wordon (ed.), *China's Great Leap: The Beijing Games and Olympian Human Rights Challenges*, New York: Seven Stories Press.

Amon, J.J., Buchanan, J., Cohen, J. and Kippenberg, J. (2012) 'Child labor and environmental health: government obligations and human rights.' *International Journal of Pediatrics*, 2012. Online. Available HTTP: <http://dx.doi.org/10.1155/2012/938306> (accessed 5 July 2013).

Amon, J.J., Girard, F. and Keshavjee, S. (2009) 'Limitations on human rights in the context of drug-resistant tuberculosis: a reply to Boggio et al', *Health and Human Rights*, 11. Online. Available HTTP: <http://www.hhrjournal.org/2009/10/07/limitations-on-human-rights-in-the-context-of-drug-resistant-tuberculosis-a-reply-to-boggio-et-al/> (accessed 5 July 2013).

Amon, J.J., Schleifer, R., Pearshouse, R. and Cohen, J.E. (2013a) 'Compulsory drug detention in East and Southeast Asia: evolving government, UN and donor responses', *International Journal of Drug Policy*, (July). doi:10.1016/j.drugpo.2013.05.019

Amon, J.J., Schleifer, R., Pearshouse, R. and Cohen, J.E. (2013b) 'Compulsory drug detention centers in China, Cambodia, Vietnam and Lao PDR: health and human rights abuses', *Health and Human Rights*, 15:124–137.

Andrews, J., Basu, S., Scales, D., Maru, D. S.-R. and Subbaraman, R. (2007) 'XDR-TB in South Africa: theory and practice', *PLoS Medicine*, 4. doi: 10.1371/journal.pmed.0040163

Asia News. (2009, August 11) 'Hundreds of children with blood poisoning in Shaanxi', *Asia News*. Online. Available HTTP: <http://www.asianews.it/news-en/Hundreds-of-children-with-blood-poisoning-in-Shaanxi-16019.html> (accessed 14 May 2014).

Associated Press. (2010, March 17) 'China investigating child lead poisoning cases', *Associated Press*. Online. Available HTTP: <http://www.thestreet.com/story/10705008/1/china-investigating-child-lead-poisoning-cases.html> (accessed 28 June 2013).

Biehl, J., Amon, J.J., Socal, M.P. and Petryna, A. (2012) 'Claiming the right to health in Brazilian courts: results from a database of lawsuits for medicines in the State of Rio Grande do Sul', *Health and Human Rights*, 14: 36–52.

CESCR (Committee on Economic, Social, and Cultural Rights). (2000) *General Comment No. 14, The Right to the Highest Attainable Standard of Health*, UN Doc. E/C.12/2000/4. Online. Available HTTP: <http://www1.umn.edu/humanrts/gencomm/escgencom14.htm> (accessed 14 May 2014).

Chen, L.C. (2004) 'Health as a human security priority for the 21st century', paper for Helsinki Process Human Security Track III. Online. Available HTTP: <http://citeseerx.ist.psu.edu/viewdoc/download?doi=10.1.1.176.681&rep=rep1&type=pdf> (accessed 14 May 2014).

Chen, L.C., Leaning, J. and Vasant, N. (eds.) (2003) *Global Health Challenges for Human Security*, Cambridge: Harvard University Press.

Cohen, J.E. and Amon, J.J. (2012) 'China's lead poisoning crisis', *Health and Human Rights*, 14: 74–86.

Commission to Investigate the Introduction and Spread of SARS in Ontario. (2006) *The SARS Commission, Final Report*, Ottawa: SARS Commission. Online. Available HTTP: <http://www.archives.gov.on.ca/en/e_records/sars/report/index.html> (accessed 18 May 2009).

Deutsche Press-Agentur. (2010, 26 January) 'Human rights body says Cambodia's drug rehab centres must close', *The Nation (Baangkok)*. Online. Available HTTP: <http://www.nationmultimedia.com/2010/01/26/regional/Human-rights-body-says-Cambodia&039;s-drug-rehab-c-30121185.html> (accessed 15 May 2014).

Duggar, C. (2008, March 25) 'TB patients chafe under lockdown in South Africa', *New York Times*. Online. Available HTTP: <http://www.nytimes.com/2008/03/25/world/africa/25safrica.html?pagewanted=all&_r=1&> (accessed 14 May 2014).

Gandhi, N.R., Moll, A., Sturm, A.W., Pawinski, R., Govender, T., Lalloo, U., Zeller, K., Andrews, J. and Friedland, G. (2006) 'Extensively drug-resistant tuberculosis as a cause of death in patients co-infected with tuberculosis and HIV in a rural area of South Africa', *The Lancet*, 368: 1575–1580.

Gostin, L.O. (2006) 'Public health strategies for pandemic influenza: ethics and the law', *Journal of the American Medical Association*, 295: 1700–1704.

Human Rights Committee. (1994) 'Communication No. 458/1991 A. W. Mukong v. Cameroon'. UN doc. CCPR/C/51/D/458/1991.

Human Rights Committee. (1999) 'International Covenant on Civil and Political Rights, general comment no. 27, Freedom of movement (Art.12)', UN Doc. No. CCPR/C/21/Rev.1/Add.9. 1999. Available HTTP: <http://hasbrouck.org/documents/UNHRC-general-comment-27.pdf> (accessed 14 May 2014).

Human Rights Committee. (2003) 'International Covenant on Civil and Political Rights, general comment no. 8, rights to liberty and security (Art.9)', U.N. Doc. HRI/GEN/1/Rev.6 at 130. Online. Available HTTP: < http://www1.umn.edu/humanrts/gencomm/hrcom8.htm > (accessed 15 May 2014).

Human Rights Watch. (2007) *Deadly Denial: Barriers to HIV/AIDS Treatment for People who Use Drugs in Thailand*, New York: Human Rights Watch. Online. Available HTTP: <http://www.hrw.org/sites/default/files/reports/thailand1107.pdf> (accessed 5 July 2013).

Human Rights Watch. (2010) *"Skin on the Cable": The Illegal Arrest, Arbitrary Detention, and Torture of People who Use Drugs in Cambodia*, New York: Human Rights Watch. Online. Available HTTP: <http://www.hrw.org/reports/2010/01/25/skin-cable-0> (accessed 28 June 2013).

Human Rights Watch. (2011a) *The Rehab Archipelago: Forced Labor and Other Abuses in Drug Detention Centers in Southern Vietnam*, New York: Human Rights Watch. Online. Available HTTP: <http://www.hrw.org/reports/2011/09/07/rehab-archipelago-0> (accessed 28 June 2013).

Human Rights Watch. (2011b) *Somsanga's Secrets: Arbitrary Detention, Physical Abuse, and Suicide inside a Lao Drug Detention Center*, New York: Human Rights Watch. Online. Available HTTP: <http://www.hrw.org/reports/2011/10/11/somsanga-s-secrets-0> (accessed 28 June 2013).

ICCPR (International Covenant on Civil and Political Rights). (1966) *G.A. Res. 2200A (XXI)*. Online. Available HTTP: <http://www.ohchr.org/en/professionalinterest/pages/ccpr.aspx> (accessed 18 April 2012).

ICESCR (International Covenant on Economic, Social and Cultural Rights). (1966) *G.A. Res. 2200A (XXI)*, U.N. Doc. A/6316.

Lewis, G. (2012) 'Opening Remarks', speech delivered to the Second Regional Consultation on Compulsory Centres for Drug Users, Kuala Lumpur, Malaysia, 1–3 October.

Li, S., Zhenyia, Z., Lon, L. and Hanyun, C. (2004) 'Preschool children's lead levels in rural communities of Zhejiang Province, China' *International Journal of Hygiene and Environmental Health*, 207: 437–440.

Liu, Y., Liang, J., Zhao, C. and Zhou, W. (2010) 'Looking for a solution for drug addiction in China: exploring the challenges and opportunities in the way of China's new drug control law', *International Journal of Drug Policy*, 21: 149–154.

Masie, D. (2008, April 11) 'Tuberculosis: sick of loneliness', *Financial Mail*: 18.

Ministry of Environmental Protection, The People's Republic of China. (2012) 'Emission standard of air pollutants for thermal power plants'. Online. Available HTTP: <http://english.mep.gov.cn/standards_reports/standards/Air_Environment/Emission_standard1/201201/t20120106_222242.htm> (accessed 5 July 2013).

Ogata, S. and Cels, J. (2003) 'Human security – protecting and empowering the people', *Global Governance*, 9: 273–282.

Ogata, S. and Sen, A. (2003) *Human Security Now: Commission on Human Security*, New York: Commission on Human Security.

OHCHR and WHO. (n.d.) *The Right to Health, Fact Sheet No. 31*, Geneva: Office of the United Nations High Commissioner for Human Rights. Online. Available HTTP: <http://www.who.int/hhr/activities/Right_to_Health_factsheet31.pdf> (accessed 5 July 2013).

Republic of South Africa. (2004) 'National Health Act, No. 61 of 2003' (2004) sec. 7; Republic of South Africa: Regulations Relating to Communicable Diseases and the Notification of Notifiable Medical Conditions, Government Notice No. R2438.

Reuters. (2012, July 30) 'China paper blames poor government decision making for violent protest', *Reuters*. Online. Available HTTP: <http://www.reuters.com/article/2012/07/30/us-china-environment-protest-idUSBRE86T04N20120730> (accessed 28 June 2013).

Sen, A. (2000) 'Why human security?', text of presentation at the International Symposium on Human Security. Online. Available HTTP: <http://sicurezzaambientale.gruppi.ilcannocchiale.it/mediamanager/sys.group/447/filemanager/Sen2000.pdf> (accessed 5 July 2013).

Shen, X. Wu, S. and Yan, C. (2001) 'Impacts of low-level lead exposure on development in children: recent studies in China', *Clinical Chimica Acta*, 313:217–220.

Smith, P. (2010, January 25) 'Southeast Asia: Human Rights Watch charges torture, rape, illegal detentions at Cambodian drug rehab centers; demands they be shut down', *Washington Post*.

State Council of the People's Republic of China. (1995) 'Methods for Forced Detoxification, Art. 2' (in Chinese), Beijing: Government of the People's Republic of China.

Tarantola, D., Amon, J., Zwi, A., Gruskin, S. and Gostin, L. (2009) 'H1N1, public health security, bioethics, and human rights', *Lancet*, 373: 2107–2108.

Thomas, C. (2000) *Global Governance, Development, and Human Security: The Challenge of Poverty and Inequality*, London: Pluto Press.

Todrys, K.W., Howe, E. and Amon, J.J. (2013) 'Failing Siracusa: governments' obligations to find the least restrictive options for tuberculosis control', *Public Health Action*, 3: 7–10.

UDHR (Universal Declaration of Human Rights). (1948) G.A. Res. 217A (III), U.N. Doc. A/810 at 71 (1948), Article 17.

United Nations Development Programme (UNDP). (1990) *Human Development Report 1990*, New York: Oxford University Press. Online. Available HTTP: <http://hdr.undp.org/en/reports/global/hdr1990> (accessed 5 July 2013).

United Nations Development Programme (UNDP). (1994) *Human Development Report: New Dimensions of Human Security*, New York: Oxford University Press.

United Nations Economic and Social Council UN Sub-Commission on Prevention of Discrimination and Protection of Minorities. (1985) 'The Siracusa Principles on the Limitation and Derogation Provisions in the International Covenant on Civil and Political Rights', Section I.A.12 U.N. Doc. E/CN.4/1985/4, Annex. Online. Available HTTP: <http://www.unhcr.org/refworld/docid/4672bc122.html> (accessed 13 March 2012).

Watts, J. (2010, March 16) 'China defends detention of lead poisoning victims who sought medical help', *The Guardian*. Online. Available HTTP: <http://www.guardian.co.uk/environment/2010/mar/16/china-lead-poison-victims> (accessed 5 July 2013).

World Bank. (2009) *From Poor Areas to Poor People: China's Evolving Poverty Reduction Agenda, An Assessment of Poverty and Inequality in China*, Beijing: World Bank. Online. Available HTTP: <https://openknowledge.worldbank.org/bitstream/handle/10986/3031/473490SR0CN0P010Disclosed0041061091.pdf?sequence=1> (accessed 5 July 2013).

World Bank. (2010) 'Data: China'. Online. Available HTTP: <http://web.worldbank.org/WBSITE/EXTERNAL/COUNTRIES/EASTASIAPACIFICEXT/CHINAEXTN/0,,contentMDK:20680895~pagePK:1497618~piPK:217854~theSitePK:318950,00.html> (accessed 28 June 2013).

World Health Organization (WHO). (2005) *International Health Regulations*, Geneva: World Health Organization. Online. Available HTTP: <http://whqlibdoc.who.int/publications/2008/9789241580410_eng.pdf> (accessed 18 April 2012).

World Health Organization (WHO). (2007) *The World Health Report 2007 – A Safer Future: Global Public Health Security in the 21st Century*, Geneva: World Health Organization.

World Health Organization. (2008) *Guidelines for the Programmatic Management of Drug-Resistant Tuberculosis: Emergency Update 2008*, Geneva: World Health Organization. Online. Available HTTP: <http://whqlibdoc.who.int/publications/2008/9789241547581_eng.pdf> (accessed 15 May 2014).

Wu, Z. (2013) 'Arguments in favour of compulsory treatment of opioid dependence', *Bulletin of the World Health Organization*, 91: 142–145.

Xiaoyun, P. (2012, July 30) 'Public needs say in decisions about local environment', *Global Times*. Online. Available HTTP: <http://www.globaltimes.cn/content/724172.shtml> (accessed 28 June 2013).

Xingxin, Z. and Qian, W. (2009, September 28) 'Tests confirm widespread lead poisoning', *China Daily*. Online. Available HTTP: <http://www.chinadaily.com.cn/china/2009–09/28/content_8743836.htm> (accessed 28 June 2013).

25

REEVALUATING HEALTH SECURITY FROM A COSMOPOLITAN PERSPECTIVE

Garrett Wallace Brown & Preslava Stoeva

Over the last two decades there have been intense policy debates about what is commonly called the "securitization of health." Many scholars have argued that there is an inherent tension between policies that prioritize state security interests and those that promote human health and wider health obligations, particularly when those obligations evoke duties of justice beyond national borders. Many scholars have also suggested that this tension is systemic and irresolvable, since the current national and international order is intrinsically state-centric where domestic and foreign health policies prioritize short-term domestic needs over more long-term policies that could deliver greater longitudinal benefits to a wider population. As an interjection into this debate, this chapter posits that existing arguments about health security are obsolete and no longer fit for purpose because they focus too narrowly on responding to isolated symptoms of poor health versus mitigating wider causes. Traditional ways of thinking about health and security are problematic in how they conceptualize security and fail to take into account broader structural conditions that drive poor health in the first place. Namely, traditional views define the problems of ill-health and insecurity in narrow strategic terms, which are overly state-centric (despite their desire to break free from realist theoretical thinking) and which promote an ethos of security over an ethic of care. This ontology in turn helps to predetermine the scope of available policy options and skews political responses in a way that ignores the structural conditions of inequality and power differentials, which greatly underpin health-based insecurity.

The discussion of the relationship between health and security is taking place at a time when the field of security studies is itself undergoing a significant self-evaluation and redefinition. While this could be seen as a complication, it is also an opportunity to seek a richer understanding of the relationship between ill-health and security. The idea of health itself is an elusive goal and there are a number of different approaches to achieving good health and to understanding what a condition of health security would entail (Brown et al. 2014). To add to this emerging area of study, this chapter proposes that a cosmopolitan approach to health should be taken because it is not confined to the strategic interests of powerful states and actively promotes an ethic of care over an ethos of security. In doing so, it will be argued that health is the key component to human beings living minimally decent lives and that any reasonable conception of health security must prioritize this normative concern by focusing on alleviating the long-term causes of ill-health globally instead of pursuing current ad hoc state-centric policies that are targeted narrowly to infectious diseases, provide weakened security for only a few, and which ultimately leave a vast majority of human beings vulnerable to what in most cases are preventable health risks.

Health, security, foreign policy: What are the links?

Conceptualizations of the relationship between health and security range from those maintaining a strong link between the two disciplines to those denying that there is sufficient evidence to suggest that health is a security concern.[1] While there are a number of good overviews of the health security debate (Aldis 2008; Ban 2003; Ingram 2004; Lee & McInnes 2003; Rushton 2011), they often refer solely to each other and thus reinforce a particularly insular conceptualization of health security, one that does not engage with the full spectrum of theories of security. Authors have approached questions of health and security from different disciplinary backgrounds, making it difficult to classify these approaches into distinct categories. This literature review will, therefore, be structured around the three main problems that, we argue, plague the health security literature (broadly defined), namely that the literature: a) narrowly defines security in state-centric terms as "security from"; b) promotes "an ethos of security over an ethic of care"; and c) defines the threat to security posed by ill-health in narrow terms – primarily as infectious diseases and bioterrorism.

Much of the literature on health and security, especially the earlier studies, has tended to focus on the relationship between health, foreign policy and national security. The exploration of the relationship between health and foreign policy, for example, is typified by the works of Fidler (2004, 2005, 2007, 2009), Fidler and Drager (2009), and Katz and Singer (2007). Works interrogating health, foreign policy, and security include Lee and McInnes (2003), Ingram (2004), McInnes and Lee (2006), and Coupland (2007), while a more narrow investigation of health as a national security priority can be found in Fidler (1998, 2003), Peterson (2002), Feldbaum et al (2006), and Evans (2010). These works approached the question of health as a security and foreign policy concern – a significant broadening of the security agenda – but they often used the terms security and national security interchangeably. Clearer distinctions ought to have been drawn. While realist and neorealist IR scholars believe that national security interests are fixed, threats stem from "outside" the boundaries of the sovereign state and tend to be military in nature (Morgenthau 1954; Walt 1991; Waltz 1954, 1979), scholars like Booth (1991, 2005, 2007), Buzan (1991b), Terriff et al. (1999), Tickner (1995), Baldwin (1997), and others have argued (for different reasons) that the concept of security is bigger and more complex than the pursuit of national security. While these critical works offer a rich debate on questions including the referent object of security, the nature of security, the relevance of gender, and the range of nonmilitary threats to security, the health security literature has failed to adequately explore these various approaches to security thinking. Instead it has relied predominantly on the securitization theory framework presented by Buzan (1991b), Waever (1995), and Buzan et al. (1997). As we discuss below, whilst it is able to accommodate an expansion in the range of threats to security, this mode of analysis itself tends to be state-centric in terms of the referent object of security.

In a critical analysis of the concept of health security, William Aldis (2008: 371) emphasized the continued lack of agreement on the definition, scope and implementation of "health security,", and the concerns raised by developing states in response to the pursuit of ill-defined "global health security." Aldis implicitly reveals the centrality of state authority in his discussion of the involvement of military units in public health interventions and the importance of local and national responses based on a viable health system (2008: 374, citing Watts 2005). Rushton (2011: 782) disagrees that "uncertainty about the *meaning* of health security is . . . really the root of the problem." He further concludes that the "narrow conceptualisation [of health security] dominates the mainstream policy agenda" (793), where the narrow conceptualization refers to a state-centric definition of security, where infectious diseases and bioterrorism are the main threats.

Hoffman (2010) presented an historical overview of the global governance of health and its relationship to the security lexicon. He highlighted an important consideration in the discussion of health governance and security, which is often overlooked – the role of different actors beyond states and intergovernmental organizations, which is an issue examined extensively in the global political economy and governance strands of the global health literature (Kay & Williams 2009; Poku 2002; Rushton & Williams 2011; Yach & Bettcher 1998), but which remains largely left out of health security debates. The different layers of this literature are yet to crystallize into a theoretically informed, generalizable framework of analysis, from which to act as a basis for a coherent theory of health security.

The current literature also promotes an ethos of security over an ethic of care, simply because traditional understandings of security as "security from" external threats inhibits an ethic of positive care. They are grounded in traditional theories of international relations, which assume duality in the moral standards that apply to individuals and to states (Morgenthau 1954; Viotti & Kauppi 2010: 42–117). This is so, due to the assumed raison d'être of states, which authorizes the use of any means to achieve the overriding aim of the preservation of the state. Thus, for example, Ban (2003: 21, italics emphasis in original) argues that not all threats posed by health are security challenges and classifies these as "*direct* or *indirect*," distinguished by the degree of risk they pose to (state) security. The result of this – apparent in the conclusion that the main threats to national security are posed by infectious diseases and bioterrorism – are endemic in the literature (Lee & McInnes 2003; McInnes & Lee 2012; NIC 2000; Rushton 2011; and others discussed in the next section).

The third shortcoming of the literature on health security relates to the narrow definition of the security risks posed by ill-health with a focus on infectious diseases – either as a whole (Brower & Chalk 2003; Elbe 2011; Fidler 1997, 1998; Garrett 1996; Lederberg 1996; NIC 2000; Population Council 1996) or individually – e.g., HIV/AIDS and pandemic influenza. Early U.S.-based studies of communicable diseases as a threat to security were part of a quest for finding the next big security challenge after the end of the Cold War. Their tone is quite alarmist and the solutions that they offer are narrowly focused and usually inadequate. The impact of HIV/AIDS on security was extensively debated over the last decade. Discussions were prompted by the exponential growth in the number of people infected with HIV/AIDS and a concern that high mortality rates would threaten the stability of already volatile states (Elbe 2002; ICG 2001; McInnes & Rushton 2010; Ostergard 2002; Prins 2004; Rushton 2010; Singer 2002). These concerns were validated by the debate on the impact of HIV/AIDS on peace and security in Africa held in 2000 at the UN Security Council (UNSC). The debate culminated in the adoption of Resolution 1308 on HIV/AIDS and International Peacekeeping Operations, which confirmed the link between HIV/AIDS and international security and discussed the need for cooperation among states, UN bodies, and the broader community in monitoring and containing the pandemic. The link drawn by UNSC between highly infectious communicable disease and national and international security set an important precedent, which paved the way for studies of other communicable diseases and their potential to disrupt stability and security, including influenza, TB and malaria. Reflecting on the high mortality of the 1918 influenza epidemic and the threat posed by the rapid spread of different viruses, scholars discussed the potential of flu pandemics to threaten national security and international stability and the steps that can be taken to contain a potential epidemic (Abraham 2011; Curley & Herington 2011; Ingram 2008; Kamradt-Scott & Lee 2011; Pereira 2008; Smith 2006). Yet, such a focus on infectious diseases represents a very narrow view of the potential threats to human health, and one that is the preference of richer countries with well-developed health systems. The same can be said about bioterrorism, which refers to the risks posed by the illicit production and use of biological weapons or pathogens (by state and non-state actors) (Feldbaum & Lee 2004; Lee & McInnes 2003; Rushton 2011). There is limited evidence from mortality statistics, however, that these are indeed the most significant threats to human as well as state security.

Security debates in international relations

Searching for the causes of insecurity

The flaws in the health security literature, as identified in the previous section, reflect broader debates in the field of security studies in particular, and the discipline of international relations in general. Debates about peace, war, and security are at the very heart of the study of international relations, which emerged in part to seek answers to the question about the causes of war. The dominant security paradigm in international relations has been premised on the assumption that the state is the sole referent object of security, that security is best achieved through the acquisition of power, and that national security takes precedence over all other concerns. These assumptions are shared by classical realists, neorealists, pluralist English School scholars, and many conventional constructivists. To a greater or lesser degree, they all agree with the premise expressed by Lippmann (1943: 51) that "a nation is secure to the extent to which it is not in danger of having to sacrifice core values, if it wishes to avoid war, and is able, if challenged, to maintain them by victory in such a war." Their positions vary, however, with regard to the scope of security threats – namely, whether security is defined solely in military-strategic terms (Bull 1977; Morgenthau 1954; Waever 1995; Walt 1991; Waltz 1954), or whether security threats include political, societal, economic and ecological factors (Buzan, 1991a, 1991b).

A plethora of studies published in the aftermath of the Cold War sought to demonstrate through empirical examples that conflicts and insecurity were caused by factors other than states' strategic considerations. These included military threats from non-state actors, social identity, environmental degradation, resource scarcity/abundance, violations of human rights, transnational crime, poverty, underdevelopment, international trade, migration, and others (Brainard & Chollet 2007; Collier 2008; Crawford 1995; Duffield 2007; Hough 2004; Kaldor 2007; Klare 2008; Klare & Chandrani 1998; Terriff et al. 1999; etc.). While these studies demonstrated the need to widen the security agenda, they did not necessarily mount a more fundamental and theoretically informed challenge against traditional security analysis.

Revolution or evolution: Challenging securitization theory

Securitization theory is one attempt to offer a new theoretical framework for analysis of security. It was developed by the Copenhagen School of Security Studies to bridge traditionalist security and wider security approaches (Buzan et al. 1997: 2–4). Securitization theory that, as we noted above, has been the theoretical framework of choice for most studies of health security, argues that security is about survival (Buzan et al. 1998: 21) but also that it is "the move that takes politics beyond the established rules of the game . . . requiring emergency measures and justifying actions outside the normal bounds of political procedure" (Buzan et al. 1998: 23–24). Buzan, Waever, and de Wilde present a securitizing move as a speech act designating an existential threat (1998: 26). In other words, securitization theory proponents accept the possibility of a widening security agenda, without having to promote any radical changes to traditional security assumptions, as advocated by peace studies, feminist, postcolonial, or critical security studies.

While enabling the expansion of security agendas, securitization theory overlooks the main question plaguing post-Cold War security studies – the centrality of the state to security analysis. Ontologically, the theory is premised on state centrism and a narrow understanding of what the security agenda comprises, who can affect it, and how. Waever, considered the first proponent of securitization, starts his analysis from the premise that the very concept of security refers to the state, and security, therefore "has to be read through the lens of *national* security" (Waever 1995: 49), which is often linked to military power and "special rights" for states (Buzan et al. 1998: 23–24; Waever 1995: 54). Such a position corresponds to the assumptions of both neorealism/ structuralism (see Waltz 1979, 1990) and Wendtian constructivism (see Wendt 1999) – for which Buzan et al. express a preference (1998: 34). These two theories profoundly disagree, however, on the question of the relationship between agents and structures (Wendt 1992) and can therefore not be synthesized. Despite the fact that proponents of securitization theory often suggest that their theory is inclusive of actors beyond the state and includes issues other than military-strategic concerns, their framework does not manage to sufficiently depart from a state-centric focus on security, which has implications for how the health–security nexus fits in the framework and how it is studied. Furthermore, the critiques from critical security scholars who have suggested that securitization theory promotes a restrictive understanding of security as a negative value, as militarized, zero-sum, confrontational, and state-centric (Booth 2007: 165), have also not been addressed. Critics also share concerns about the neglect of questions about marginalized groups, gender, the role of power and interests – private and public, political and economic – as well as questions of normativity, which should not be seen as arising solely in the aftermath of a crisis (Booth 2005; McDonald 2008; Peoples & Vaughan-Williams 2010).

The epistemological and methodological assumptions underwriting securitization theory are also seemingly incompatible. On the one hand, securitization theorists criticize the postpositivist epistemology of critical security studies (Buzan et al. 1998: 34–35), while on the other, they rely on postpositivist discourse analysis and its emphasis on language in the process of granting issues an "exceptional status of security threat." Critical constructivists who study language (see Weldes 1996), however, reject the positivist epistemology accepted by conventional constructivists such as Wendt, Checkel, Kratochwil, Finnemore, and others, which is the substance of "the third great debate" in the discipline of international relations (see Smith et al. 1996).

Whether health analysts agree or disagree with the premises and usefulness of the securitization approach, it is important to recognize that it cannot possibly apply to every study of "health security." At most, securitization theory is relevant only to a narrow segment of the policy debate, namely to the discussion preceding agreement that health is a security concern. Following closure of this debate,[2] securitization theory provides little help in analyzing most policies related to health and therefore other theories need to be considered. As a result, the securitization discourse does not provide an adequate framework in which to address many of the concerns plaguing health security analysis – i.e., the challenges to the state being the sole relevant referent object of security, the expanding nature of existential threats that face humanity (including communicable and noncommunicable diseases, environmental change, challenges to food production, etc.), and/ or the policies required to address the health threats that pose a risk to individual and societal security (however that is defined).

Focusing on the human: Human security and critical security studies

Approaches that take the individual as a referent object of security include human security and critical security studies. The term "human security" was first introduced in the UNDP *Human Development Report* in 1994 and was defined broadly as "freedom from fear and freedom from want" (UNDP 1994: 24), focusing attention on the security of individuals, in contrast to traditional security studies that favor the state. There are disagreements in academic circles, however, about the scope, usefulness, and traction of the concept of human security, as some argue that it attempts to encapsulate too many things and is rendered too general in the process (Chandler & Hynek 2011; Khong 2001; Mack 2005; Paris 2001).

Critical security scholars, also referred to as the Welsh School, agree that the meaning of security needs to be reconceptualized so that security is understood in relation to individuals, as a process of *emancipation* (Booth 1991, 2007: 110; Peoples & Vaughan-Williams 2010: 17; Wyn Jones 1995, 1999, 2004). With this starting point in mind, there are a number of different routes that can be taken, as critical approaches can include post-structuralist, feminist, gender, and post-colonial perspectives. All of these insist, however, on questioning the status quo, particularly the role of authority, knowledge, and power relationships, and on challenging the established state-centric international order. Critical security theorists also share an opposition to: a) the militarization of security; b) the inside/outside dichotomies created by state-centric politics; c) the omission of structural factors in the analysis of violence, poverty and underdevelopment by traditional IR approaches; and d) to the use of positivist, objectivists approaches (Booth 2007: 4, 22–26; Krause & Williams 1997: 49; Peoples & Vaughan-Williams 2010: 20–21). These scholars drive home the message that security has real meaning to individuals and societies, a meaning that is not abstract, elusive, or shrouded in the mystery of high politics. Security, they argue, is about improving human well-being, empowering individuals, and addressing inequalities and marginalizations. It is about freedom from threats, and not just about survival, because survival does not guarantee security as it does not eliminate threats (Booth 2007: 106). Debates about the reconceptualization of security are pertinent in a world where the number of armed conflicts and conflict-related deaths is steadily declining (Human Security Report Project 2011), and where other security threats like health become more significant for everyday life.

While critical security studies outline the need for, and the potential benefit of, a significant and fundamental rethinking of security politics, they often fall short of offering a way of amending the current political order. As a response, it might be useful to think of security as having both a negative (security from) and a positive (security to) aspect (Gjørv 2012: 836). This attempt to find a middle ground between the Copenhagen and the Welsh schools recognizes traditional security concerns and the role of the state and military, while also providing space to reflect on a broader spectrum of relevant actors, on the epistemological foundations of security practices, and on the way these are often entangled with politics in other social realms. Through empirical case studies, Gjørv demonstrates that the pursuit of security is a dialogue with many stakeholders (2012: 859), not a speech act as suggested by Waever (1995: 55). He also raises questions about distributive justice and normative principles, which critical security scholars have struggled with, but which are central to the cosmopolitan approach outlined later in this chapter.

The trouble with health and the security challenges posed by ill-health

Thinking of "health" as a cause of insecurity is ontologically significant, because "health" is delivered through the existing government-run infrastructures of public health. This then means that the state is automatically envisaged as the primary center of authority and the source of solutions to a particular crisis and the evaluation of other non-state entities or structures is deemed unnecessary because states are perceived to have sovereign control over their territories and people. In dealing with ill-health/disease, however, any political authority will have to work with a wide array of actors – the medical professional community, local authorities, pharmaceutical companies, civil society organizations, intergovernmental organizations, private–public partnerships, private foundations, etc. All of these actors contribute to a much more complex political process, which not only cannot be reduced to state leadership and authority but can also have a direct impact on the ability of states to deliver security to their citizens, something that is not sufficiently reflected in the current literature.

Furthermore, security challenges are posed by a great variety of conditions of ill-health. The focus of the existing health security literature is therefore indefensibly narrow, as discussed by Ban (2003), McInnes and Lee (2006), and Rushton (2011) and leaves out a plethora of concerns such as neglected tropical diseases, infectious diseases prevalent in low and middle income countries (which pose little risk to developed states), and noncommunicable diseases, which have killed more than two and a half times as many people as all wars and political violence in the 20th century combined (McCandless 2013; World Health Organization 2011; see also Benson & Glasgow, chapter 15 in this volume). Health sociologists further warn us that, as a result of modern technological change, the boundaries of illness have become blurred and that the "expansion" of the health agenda, or the medicalization of health, do not always provide satisfactory solutions (Blaxter 2010; Conrad 1992, 2007).

Health, in other words, is rather complex and the rigid divisions between individual-focused medicine and society-oriented public health ignore a whole spectrum of concerns for the individual as part of the whole. It is important to acknowledge also that the concepts of health and disease are asymmetrical rather than simply opposites, in that the absence of disease is part of health, but health is more than the absence of disease (Blaxter 2010: 19). "Health security," therefore, is something of a misnomer, which may be partly responsible for the resulting lack of conceptual clarity in the field (McInnes & Lee 2006: 23). To use a health analogy, health security discussions have overwhelmingly focused on addressing the symptoms, rather than the causes, of insecurity. They have largely failed to take into account underlying determinants of health – particularly complex structural problems like environmental degradation, poverty, underdevelopment, access to food, etc., which have been left out of security-driven solutions. It is, therefore, important to explore new theoretical approaches to global health that can help to respond to many of the lacunas that exist in contemporary health security debates.

A cosmopolitan approach to the nexus of ill-health and security

Whereas traditional debates around health security have focused on the security of the state resulting in a tendency to prioritize transborder infectious diseases (Peterson 2002; Rushton 2011), a cosmopolitan approach to health can be seen to be more closely aligned to aspects of *critical security studies* as outlined above. This is because cosmopolitans maintain a strict focus on individual health, demand ethical duties for health beyond state borders, and seek to draw attention to the structural causes of poor health versus simply focusing on the securitization of existing symptoms. In particular, a cosmopolitan approach to health defends three normative principles that contradict many popular approaches to contemporary health security.

First, cosmopolitans maintain that human beings are the primary unit of moral concern, not states, and argue that the structural conditions (economic, political, social) that determine the security of one's health would need to intonate with the ethical priorities of the individual. To be clear, this does not mean that the state or its long-term security is unimportant. Most cosmopolitans would suggest that well constituted states have an important instrumental role to play in securing the quality of human wellbeing (Brown 2011). Nevertheless, unlike most traditional scholars of security, cosmopolitans do believe that the state does not, in and of itself, have an intrinsic worth where its *raison d'etat* can be pursued regardless of the effects it has on human beings, whether they are citizens or noncitizens. For cosmopolitans, state-centric security perspectives over fetishize the status quo and often treat states as self-reliant and fully self-determining entities that act independently of their citizens. When contextualized in relation to increased globalization and the globalized nature of public health, the cosmopolitan argues that if there are proven causal pathways between geopolitical and economic structures that clearly impact on social determinants of health (Braveman et al. 2011; Brown & Labonte 2011; Labonte et al. 2009; WHO 2008), then there is significant ethical motivation (as well as motivations related to state security) to rethink current global governance structures and the normative priorities that should underwrite them (Benatar & Brock 2011; Brown & Paremoer 2014; Friel & Marmot 2011; Pogge 2004; Sen 2000; Venkatapuram 2011).

Second, cosmopolitanism argues that all individuals have an equal moral status where state-centric security maximizations should be preceded and trumped by the demands of justice. As an alternative to traditional conceptualizations of security, a focus on global health justice refers to the idea that individuals ought to receive treatment that is fitting to them as dignified human beings as well as the assignment of corresponding rights and duties necessary to create an equitable distribution of benefits and burdens within a social order. This translates into a reconceptualization of health security in both moral and institutional terms where the determination of "who gets what why" must meet the bar of justice and where all states have global responsibilities toward alleviating global health inequalities (Brown 2012). In terms of the relation between justice and security, as with many prescriptions made throughout the history of political thought – including Aristotle, Machiavelli, Kant, and Rawls – cosmopolitans suggest that the best way to secure the long-term security/stability of any political organization is by establishing mutually consistent and fair conditions of justice. The idea being that if globalization has broadened the scope of health security relationships beyond state borders (as even a statist position on global health admits), then the state loses its boundedness in favor of new political formulations that can better capture the interrelations that exist in a globalized world and their impacts on human health. This also suggests that – if health is a key component to living a minimally decent life, and if security means to "secure" this minimal threshold, and if globalization has broadened the scope of interdependency when securitizing health, and if the key to providing security rests on more than targeted short-term self-interest – then for the cosmopolitan, it is crucial to underwrite global health policy with long-term principles of global justice that can start to address the structural causes of ill-health versus simply focusing on symptoms that affect wealthier states.

Third, cosmopolitanism moves beyond state-centric paradigms further by arguing that human beings have equal status universally, regardless of where they live and regardless of other communal particularities (such as race, ethnicity, religion, citizenship, nationality, gender, or place of birth). As a result, cosmopolitans argue that any scheme of health security that is based exclusively on state citizenship (Daniels 2008) is morally arbitrary when it comes to formulating its distributive principles (Caney 2005). This is because it is simply a matter of happenstance whether a person is born in one place versus another. In fact, where a person is born is purely a matter of luck and as many cosmopolitans argue, it is ethically untenable to determine the quality of one's health solely on the good fortune of birth alone. As a result, the requirement of communal membership as an overriding precondition for prioritizations in health security is dubious and thus weakens the normative appeal of state-centric approaches. As an alternative, most cosmopolitans adopt a minimal rights-based approach to global health and argue that because all human beings are entitled to basic health satisfaction, richer states (as well as the state in which a person resides) have minimal corresponding duties of justice (not just security) in order to advance the fulfilment of those rights. As has been argued above, there are intuitive reasons to suggest that altering unjust systems would create the background conditions necessary for the long-term health of a greater number of people, not just those fortunate enough to have been born into an affluent community.

These basic cosmopolitan principles generate several implications in relation to global health security. First, given its focus on the deontological worth of human beings and its focus on global justice as a key guarantor of health security, cosmopolitanism can generate broadened normative recommendations for reforming the current institutional health architecture. In line with Pogge, cosmopolitans suggest that even if our duties of justice are only minimal, in that we are obligated to restrict systematic violations of negative rights, and if there is evidence of a systemic perpetuation of health inequalities that affect negative rights as a result of current global structures, then we have a moral obligation to reform these institutional structures in light of more equitable cosmopolitan concerns. Because national interests are often prioritized within existing health policy and thus represent a form of *microbialpolitik* (Fidler 1999: 19), there is a propensity to give a prioritized focus to the securitization of transborder infectious diseases while ignoring other health related emergencies or determinants (Rushton 2011; Youde 2005). One consequence of this is that normative appeals to security become most suitable for addressing acute crisis, but often remain inadequate for addressing the underlying causes of infectious diseases, be they political, economic, social, or cultural (McInnes & Lee 2006; Youde 2005). In further response below, a cosmopolitan approach seeks to mitigate the underlying causes before they require the type of securitization necessary in situations of acute crisis.

Second, unlike the statist approach, and in relation to the above, cosmopolitanism prioritizes the socioeconomic aspects that affect the quality of human health. As a result, a cosmopolitan approach links nicely to debates about the social determinants of health and draws attention to correcting failures that continue to perpetuate key social inequalities and large disparities in individual health. In this regard, the cosmopolitan approach resonates with a growing body of literature that suggests that a greater focus on the social determinants of health (with a call for more radical deliberative and distributive reforms) is necessary in order to construct more equitable global health policies within state communities as well as between states (Putland et al. 2011; WHO 2008). As is often argued, there is considerable evidence to suggest that current global socioeconomic practices can have considerable negative externalities on health systems. For example, Ted Schrecker (2014) has examined existing structural "conditionalities" within financial markets and showed that these limit the health policy options available to lower middle income countries (LMICs). In addition, the built-in financial ability for mass elite capital flight from LMICs countries adversely reduces available social resources and intensifies economic inequality. In both cases, argues Schrecker, these global market forces impinge upon local socioeconomic conditions and thus have a significant detrimental effect on health. As highlighted above, these underlying factors are crucially in need for reform – reforms that should be underwritten by cosmopolitan principles of global justice (Lenard & Straehle 2012).

Third, unlike the statist approach, and related to the two implications above, cosmopolitanism seeks to force policy makers to recognize that Western states are actually culpable for perpetuating structures that underwrite existing health inequalities and therefore have duties to alter unjust systems. As Susan Peterson (2006) and Simon Rushton (2011) have suggested, if the normative argument about global health is framed solely in terms of security, then most Western countries will not face the same threats as most of the world's population and they will therefore dedicate insufficient resources to those most in need. Since this distribution can be rationalized within existing security paradigms, it will assist in "relieving Westerners of any moral obligation to respond to health crisis beyond their own national borders" (Peterson 2006: 46). As an alternative, the cosmopolitan argues that this is inherently unjust, since it will not only affect who we think we have duties of justice to but also, it will significantly limit the range of factors we think we have relational responsibility for. This is not only shortsighted in that Western states may be ignoring health security threats that will come to affect them in the unforeseen future, but it is also shortsighted in that it helps to sustain the conditions that create ill-health and thus make even agreed security risks more difficult to defend against.

Conclusion

The phrase "an ounce of prevention is worth a pound of cure" – a common saying coined by Benjamin Franklin – suggests that it is often easier to prevent trouble at first sight than to wait until problems become difficult to mitigate. In many ways the cosmopolitan approach to human security advocated in this chapter posits a similar view. Namely, if health security is important, and if it matters because it represents the fundamental interests of human beings, and if the social determinants of health at the global level can greatly affect the quality of an individual's long-term health; then a more expanded and cosmopolitan conceptualization of health security is required. A reconceptualization that resists symptom based state-centric prioritizations and that alternatively responds to the structural socioeconomic causes that buttress ill-health. Although this will to a large extent require something of a paradigm shift from the current approaches outlined in this chapter, making this shift will not necessarily require traditional security scholars to stray too far from their usual ontological "playbook." This is because the logic for this shift can be easily found in realism itself. For as the realist Machiavelli says in *The Prince* (1961: 12), "disorders can be quickly healed if they are seen well in advance (and only a prudent ruler has such foresight); yet when, for lack of a diagnosis, they are allowed to grow in such a way that everyone can recognise them, remedies are often far too late." If we agree with this basic realist insight, as many cosmopolitans do, then when it comes to global health, perhaps it is now time for traditional security scholars to get real.

Notes

1 Some scholars argue that the link between health and security is evidenced by the cooperation of states in Europe seeking to address the spread of some infectious diseases, starting from the 19th century – Fidler (2001), Szreter (2003). Scholars like Peterson (2002), McInnes (2009), McInnes and Lee (2012), and Rushton (2011), on the other hand base their work on the discrepancy between theoretical projections and practical developments.

2 One could argue that political closure was marked by UNSC Resolution 1308 – for a further discussion of political closure, see Preslava Stoeva, *New Norms and Knowledge in World Politics: Protecting People, Intellectual Property and the Environment*, London: Routledge, 2010: 31–33

References

Abraham, T. (2011) 'The chronicle of a disease foretold: pandemic H1N1 and the construction of a global health security threat', *Political Studies*, 59: 797–812.

Aldis, W. (2008) 'Health security as a public health concept: a critical analysis', *Health Policy and Planning*, 23: 369–375.

Baldwin, D. (1997) 'The concept of security', *Review of International Studies*, 23: 5–26.

Ban, J. (2003) 'Health as a global security challenge', *Seton Hall Journal of Diplomacy and International Relations*, 4: 19–28.

Benatar, S. and Brock, G. (eds.) (2011) *Global Health and Global Health Ethics*, Cambridge: Cambridge University Press.

Blaxter, M. (2010) *Health*, 2nd ed. Cambridge: Polity.

Booth, K. (1991) 'Security and emancipation', *Review of International Studies*, 17: 313–326.

Booth, K. (2007) *Theory of World Security*, Cambridge: Cambridge University Press.

Booth, K. (ed.) (2005) *Critical Security Studies and World Politics*, Boulder: Lynne Rienner.

Brainard, L. and Chollet, D. (eds) (2007) *Too Poor for Peace?: Global Poverty, Conflict, and Security in the 21st Century*, Washington, DC: Brookings Institution Press.

Braveman, P., Egerter, S. and Williams, D. (2011) 'The social determinants of health: coming of age', *Annual Review of Public Health*, 32: 381–398.

Brower, J. and Chalk, P. (2003) *The Global Threat of New and Reemerging Infectious Diseases – Reconciling U.S. National Security and Public Health Policy*, Santa Monica: RAND Corporation. Online. Available HTTP: <http://www.rand.org/pubs/monograph_reports/MR1602> (accessed 4 October 2013).

Brown, G.W. (2011) 'Bringing the state back into cosmopolitanism: the idea of cosmopolitan responsible states', *Political Studies Review*, 9: 53–66.

Brown, G.W. (2012) 'Distributing who gets what and why: four normative approaches to global health', *Global Policy*, 3: 292–302.

Brown, G.W. and Labonte, R. (2011) 'Globalization and its methodological discontents: contextualizing globalization through the study of HIV/AIDS', *Globalization and Health*, 7: 1–12.

Brown, G.W. and Paremoer, L. (2014) 'Global health justice and a right to health,' in G. W. Brown, G. Yamey and S. Wamala (eds.) *Global Health Policy*, London: Willey-Blackwell.

Brown, G.W., Yamey, G. and Wamala, S. (eds.) (2014) *Global Health Policy*, London: Willey-Blackwell.

Bull, H. (1977) *The Anarchical Society: A Study of World Order in Politics*, London: Macmillan.

Buzan, B. (1991a) 'New patterns of global security in the twenty-first century', *International Affairs*, 67: 431–451.

Buzan, B. (1991b) *People, States and Fear: An Agenda for International Security Studies in the Post-Cold War Era*, 2nd ed. London: Harvester Wheatsheaf.

Buzan, B., Waever, O. and de Wilde, J. (1997) *Security: A New Framework for Analysis*, Boulder: Lynne Rienner.

Caney, S. (2005) *Justice Beyond Borders*, Oxford: Oxford University Press.

Chandler, D. and Hynek, N. (eds.) (2011) *Critical Perspectives on Human Security – Rethinking Emancipation and Power in International Relations*, Oxon: Routledge.

Collier, P. (2008) *The Bottom Billion: Why the Poorest Countries Are Failing and What Can Be Done About It*, Oxford: Oxford University Press.

Conrad, P. (1992) 'Medicalization and social control', *Annual Review of Sociology*, 18: 209–232

Conrad, P. (2007) *The Medicalization of Society: On the Transformation of Human Conditions into Treatable Disorders*, Baltimore: John Hopkins University Press.

Coupland, R. (2007) 'Security, insecurity and health', *Bulletin of the World Health Organization*, 85: 181–183.

Crawford, B. (1995) 'Hawks, doves, but no owls: international economic interdependence and construction of the new security dilemma', in R. Lipschutz (ed.) *On Security*, New York: Columbia University Press.

Curley, M. G. and Herington, J. (2011) 'The securitisation of avian influenza: international discourses and domestic politics in Asia', *Review of International Studies*, 37: 141–166.

Daniels, N. (2008) *Just Health: Meeting Health Needs Fairly*, Cambridge: Cambridge University Press.

Duffield, M. (2007) *Development, Security and Unending War*, Cambridge: Polity.

Elbe, S. (2002) 'HIV/AIDS and the changing landscape of war in Africa', *International Security*, 27: 159–177.

Elbe, S. (2011) 'Pandemics on the radar screen: health security, infectious disease and the medicalisation of insecurity', *Political Studies*, 59: 848–866.

Evans, J. (2010) 'Pandemics and national security', *Global Security Studies*, 1: 100–109.

Feldbaum, H. and Lee, K. (2004) 'Public health and security' in A. Ingram (ed.) *Health, Foreign Policy and Security: Towards a Conceptual Framework for Research and Policy*, UK Global Health Programme, Working Paper No.2, London: The Nuffield Trust.

Feldbaum, H., Patel, P., Sondorp, E. and Lee, K. (2006) 'Global health and national security: the need for critical engagement', *Medicine, Conflict and Survival*, 22: 192–198.

Fidler, D. (1997) 'The globalization of public health: emerging infectious diseases and international relations', *Indiana Journal of Global Legal Studies*, 5: 11–51.

Fidler, D. (1998) 'Microbialpolitik: infectious diseases and international relations', *American University International Law Journal*, 14: 1–53.

Fidler, D. (1999) *International Law and Infectious Diseases*, Oxford: Clarendon Press.

Fidler, D. (2001) 'The globalisation of public health: the first 100 years of international health diplomacy', *Bulletin of the World Health Organisation*, 79: 842–849.

Fidler, D. (2003) 'Public health and national security in the global age: infectious diseases, bioterrorism and realpolitik', *George Washington International Law Review*, 35: 787–856.

Fidler, D. (2004) 'Fighting the axis of illness: HIV/AIDS, human rights, and U.S. foreign policy', *Harvard Human Rights Journal*, 17: 99–136.

Fidler, D. (2005) 'Health as foreign policy: between principle and power', *Whitehead Journal of Diplomacy and International Relations*, 6: 179–194.

Fidler, D. (2007) 'Reflections on the revolution in health and foreign policy', *Bulletin of the World Health Organization*, 85: 243–244.

Fidler, D. (2009) 'Health and foreign policy: vital signs', *The World Today*, 65: 27–29.

Fidler, D. and Drager, N. (2009) *Global Health and Foreign Policy: Strategic Opportunities and Challenges*, Draft Background Paper for the Secretary-General's Report on Global Health and Foreign Policy. Geneva: World Health Organization. Online. Available HTTP: <http://www.who.int/trade/events/UNGA_Back ground_Rep3_2.pdf > (accessed 19 July 2013).

Friel, S. and Marmot, M. (2011) 'Action on the social determinants of health', *Annual Review of Public Health*, 32: 225–36.

Garrett, L. (1996) 'The return of infectious disease', *Foreign Affairs*, 75: 66–79.

Garrett, L. (2007) 'The challenge of global health', *Foreign Affairs*, 86: 14–38.

Gjørv, G.H. (2012) 'Security by any other name: negative security, positive security, and a multi-actor security approach', *Review of International Studies*, 38: 835–859.

Hoffman, S. (2010) 'The evolution, etiology and eventualities of the global health security regime', *Health Policy and Planning*, 25: 510–522.

Hough, P. (2004) *Understanding Global Security*, Oxon: Routledge.

Human Security Report Project. (2011) *Human Security Report 2009/2010: The Causes of Peace and the Shrinking Costs of War*, New York: Oxford University Press.

Ingram, A. (2008) 'Pandemic anxiety and global health security' in R. Pain and S.J. Smith (eds.) *Fear: Critical Geopolitics and Everyday Life*, Aldershot: Ashgate.

Ingram, A. (ed.) (2004) *Health, Foreign Policy and Security: Towards a Conceptual Framework for Research and Policy*, UK Global Health Programme, Working Paper No.2, London: The Nuffield Trust.

International Crisis Group (ICG). (2001) *HIV/AIDS as a Security Issue*. Online. Available HTTP: <http:// www.crisisgroup.org/en/regions/africa/001-hiv-aids-as-a-security-issue.aspx> (accessed 15 July 2013).

Kaldor, M. (2007) *Human Security: Reflections on Globalization and Intervention*, Cambridge: Polity.

Kamradt-Scott, A. and Lee, K. (2011) 'The 2011 Pandemic Influenza Preparedness Framework: global health secured or a missed opportunity?', *Political Studies*, 59: 831–847.

Katz, R. and Singer, D. (2007) 'Health and security in foreign policy', *Bulletin of the World Health Organization*, 85: 233–234.

Kay, A. and Williams, O.W. (eds) (2009) *Global Health Governance: Crisis, Institutions and Political Economy*, London: Palgrave Macmillan.

Khong, Y. (2001) 'Human security: a shotgun approach to alleviating human misery?', *Global Governance*, 7: 231–236.

Klare, M. (2008) *Rising Powers, Shrinking Planet: How Scarce Energy Is Creating a New World Order*, New York: Metropolitan Books.

Klare, M. and Chandrani, Y. (eds) (1998) *World Security: Challenges for a New Century*, 3rd ed. New York: St Martin's Press.

Krause, K. and Williams, M. (eds) (1997) *Critical Security Studies: Concepts and Strategies*, Oxon: Routledge.

Labonte, R., Schrecker, T., Packer, C. and Runnels, V. (eds) (2009) *Globalization and Health: Pathways, Evidence and Policy*, New York: Routledge.

Lederberg, J. (1996) 'Infectious disease – a threat to global health and security', *Journal of the American Medical Association*, 276: 417–419.

Lee, K. and McInnes, C. (2003) Health, Foreign Policy and Security – a Discussion Paper, London: The Nuffield Trust. Online. Available HTTP: <http://www.nuffieldtrust.org.uk/sites/files/nuffield/publi cation/health-foreign-policy-and-security-apr03.pdf> (accessed 7 Apr 2012).

Lenard, P. and Straehle, C. (eds.) (2012) *Health Inequalities and Global Justice*, Edinburgh: Edinburgh University Press.

Lippmann, W. (1943) *U.S. Foreign Policy: Shield of the Republic*, Boston: Little, Brown.

Machiavelli, N. (1961) *The Prince*, London: Penguin.

Mack, A. (2005) *Human Security Report 2005: War and Peace in the 21st Century*, New York: Oxford University Press.

McCandless, D. (2013, March 18). 'Information is Beautiful on How We Die', *The Guardian*. Online. Available HTTP:<http://www.guardian.co.uk/news/datablog/2013/mar/18/information-beautiful-how-we-die> (accessed 27 March 2013).

McDonald, M. (2008) 'Securitization and the construction of security', *European Journal of International Relations*, 14: 563–587.

McInnes, C. (2009) 'National security and global health governance' in A. Kay and O. Williams (eds.) *Global Health Governance – Crisis, Institutions and Political Economy*, Basingstoke: Palgrave Macmillan.

McInnes, C. and Lee, K. (2006) 'Health, security and foreign policy', *Review of International Studies*, 32: 5–23.

McInnes, C. and Rushton, S. (2010) 'HIV, AIDS and security: where are we now?', *International Affairs*, 86: 225–245.

Morgenthau, H.J. (1954) *Politics among Nations – The Struggle for Power and Peace*, New York: McGraw.

National Intelligence Council (NIC). (2000) *The Global Infectious Disease Threat and Its Implications for the United States*, National Intelligence Estimate NIE99–17D. Online. Available HTTP: <http://www.fas.org/irp/threat/nie99-17d.htm> (accessed 15 May 2014).

Ostergard, R. (2002) 'Politics in the hot zone: AIDS and national security in Africa', *Third World Quarterly*, 23: 333–350.

Paris, R. (2001) 'Human security: paradigm shift or hot air?', *International Security*, 26: 87–102.

Peoples, C. and Vaughan-Williams, N. (2010) *Critical Security Studies: An Introduction*, Oxon: Routledge.

Pereira, R. (2008) 'Processes of securitisation of infectious diseases and Western hegemonic power: a historical political analysis', *Global Health Governance*, 2: 1–15.

Peterson, S. (2002) 'Epidemic disease and national security', *Security Studies*, 12: 43–81.

Pogge, T. (2004) 'Relational conceptions of justice: responsibilities for health outcomes', in S. Anand, F. Peter and A. Sen (eds.) *Public Health, Ethics, and Equity*, Oxford: Oxford University Press.

Poku, N. (2002) 'The Global AIDS Fund: context and opportunity', *Third World Quarterly*, 23: 283–298.

Population Council. (1996) 'The National Science and Technology Council on emerging and re-emerging infectious diseases', *Population and Development Review*, 22 : 175–183.

Prins, G. (2004) 'AIDS and global security', *International Affairs*, 80: 931–952.

Putland, C., Baum, F. and Ziersch, A. (2011) 'From causes to solutions – insights from lay knowledge about health inequalities', *BMC Public Health*, 11: 1–11.

Rushton, S. (2010) 'AIDS and international security in the United Nations system', *Health Policy and Planning*, 25: 495–504.

Rushton, S. (2011) 'Global health security: security for whom? Security from what?', *Political Studies*, 59: 779–796.

Rushton, S. and Williams, O.D. (eds.) (2011) *Partnerships and Foundations in Global Health Governance*, Basingstoke: Palgrave Macmillan.

Schrecker, T. (2014) 'The exterritorial reach of money: global finance and the social determinants of health' in G.W. Brown, G. Yemay and S. Wamala (eds.) *Global Health Policy*, London: Wiley-Blackwell.

Sen, A. (2000) *Development as Freedom*, New York: Anchor Books.

Singer, P.W. (2002) 'AIDS and international security', *Survival*, 44: 145–158.

Smith, R.D. (2006) 'Responding to global infectious disease outbreaks: lessons from SARS on the role of risk perception, communication and management', *Social Science and Medicine*, 63: 3113–3123.

Smith, S., Booth, K. and Zalewski, M. (eds.) (1996) *International Theory: Positivism and Beyond*, Cambridge: Cambridge University Press.

Stoeva, P. (2010) *New Norms and Knowledge in World Politics – Protecting People, Intellectual Property and the Environment*, London: Routledge.

Szreter, S. (2003) 'Health and security in historical perspective', in J. Chen and V. Narasimhan (eds.) *Global Health Challenges for Human Security*, Cambridge: Harvard University Press.

Terriff, T., Croft, S., James, L. and Morgan, P. (1999) *Security Studies Today*, Cambridge: Polity Press.

Tickner, J.A. (1995) 'Re-visioning security' in K. Booth and S. Smith (eds.) *International Relations Theory Today*, Cambridge: Polity Press.

United Nations Development Programme (UNDP). (1994) *New Dimensions of Human Security, Human Development Report*. Online. Available HTTP: <http://hdr.undp.org/en/reports/global/hdr1994/> (accessed 28 January 2014).

Venkatapuram, S. (2011) *Health Justice*, Cambridge: Polity Press.

Viotti, P. and Kauppi, M. (2010) *International Relations Theory*, 4th ed. London: Pearson.

Waever, O. (1995) 'Securitization and desecuritization', in R. Lipschuz (ed.) *On Security*, New York: Columbia University Press.

Walt, S. (1991) 'The renaissance of security studies', *International Studies Quarterly*, 35: 211–239.

Waltz, K. (1954) *Man, the State and War: A Theoretical Analysis*, New York: Columbia University Press.

Waltz, K. (1979) *Theory of International Politics*, New York: McGraw Hill.

Waltz, K. (1990) 'Realist thought and neorealist theory', *Journal of International Affairs*, 44: 21–37.
Weldes, J. (1996) 'Constructing national interests', *European Journal of International Relations*, 2: 275–318.
Wendt, A. (1992) 'Anarchy is what states make of it: the social construction of power politics', *International Organization*, 46: 395–425.
Wendt, A. (1999) *Social Theory of International Politics*, Cambridge: Cambridge University Press.
World Health Organization (WHO). (2008) *Closing the Gap in a Generation: Health Equity through Action on the Social Determinants of Health*, Geneva: WHO.
World Health Organization (WHO). (2011). *The Top 10 Causes of Death.* Online. Available HTTP: <http://who.int/mediacentre/factsheets/fs310/en/> (accessed 27 March 2013).
Wyn Jones, R. (1995) '"Message in a bottle"? Theory and praxis in critical security studies', *Contemporary Security Policy*, 16: 299–319.
Wyn Jones, R. (1999) *Security, Strategy, and Critical Theory*, Boulder: Lynne Rienner Publishers.
Wyn Jones, R. (2004) 'On emancipation: necessity, capacity, and concrete utopias', in K. Booth (ed.) *Critical Security Studies and World Politics*, Lynne Rienner Publishers Inc.
Yach, D. and Bettcher, D. (1998) 'The globalization of public health, I: threats and opportunities', *American Journal of Public Health*, 88: 735–744.
Youde, J. (2005) 'Enter the fourth horseman: health security and international relations theory', *Whitehead Journal of Diplomacy and International Relations*, 6: 193–208.

26

INDONESIA, POWER ASYMMETRY, AND PANDEMIC RISK

The paradox of global health security

William L. Aldis & Triono Soendoro

In late 2006 the world was on the brink of a catastrophic pandemic due to the avian influenza ("bird flu") virus H5N1. It was essential to conduct genetic studies of new viral strains isolated from human cases and to get a head start on vaccine development for those strains that appeared to have the highest pandemic potential. At this critical moment there was a breakdown in the global system for sharing of virus isolates.[1] Indonesia, without access to vaccines and antiviral medications and acting in desperation, suspended sharing of viral isolates with the World Health Organization (WHO) and its Collaborating Centers. International reaction was harsh and immediate.

Here we analyze Indonesia's position. We argue that the virus sharing episode, not fully resolved 7 years after it erupted into a global crisis, has implications for health security far beyond sharing of viruses and benefits. If the geopolitical issues surrounding this episode are not properly understood and resolved, we can expect ominous consequences far beyond avian influenza. We will see that embedded in the geopolitics of virus and benefit sharing there is a paradox: when countries pursue security on their own narrowly defined terms while disregarding the vital interests of others, all countries become less secure.

We will give special attention to issues of ownership, specifically ownership of biological materials and derivatives; and with it, rights to the products of that ownership. Central to these concerns are material transfer agreements, or terms and conditions of transfer, in the context of a market-based political economy (Chan & de Wildt 2007: 1–6). While only a small part of this complex story, these issues and their relationship to access, possession, and economic exploitation of knowledge can serve as an analytic frame or entry point to understand the events that precipitated Indonesia's decision to suspend sharing of H5N1 isolates with the global system in early 2007. Why did the key actors (nonindustrialized countries, the WHO, industrialized countries, and commercial interests) behave the way they did? And most important, what does this tell us about potential fracture lines in fragile global relationships that are essential to maintain global health security generally?

We will not attempt a detailed epidemiological account of the global H5N1 avian influenza outbreak or an exhaustive history of the continuing controversy over sharing of virus isolates and sequences and benefits thereof. Likewise we will not enter into the debate on how the International Health Regulations and the Convention on Biological Diversity apply to sharing of viruses and benefits. These issues have been well discussed elsewhere (Fidler, 2008; Irwin 2010;

Sedyaningsih et al. 2008; World Health Organization 2011a). Instead we will identify key contentious points that have general significance for global health security. After a review of the events leading up to Indonesia's decision to cease virus sharing, we will attempt to answer the following questions about this extraordinary situation:

1. Why did Indonesia take the extraordinary step of suspending transfer of H5N1 virus isolates to WHO? Could the crisis have been avoided or quickly resolved? If so, how?
2. What were the underlying issues, and what steps have been taken to resolve them?
3. What steps can be taken now to protect the vital interests of non-industrialized or low-income countries?
4. Are there wider implications for global health security? Could similar breakdowns occur for other pandemic risks, or unrelated global health threats?

Background to the crisis

Human disease associated with influenza A subtype H5N1 reemerged in January 2003 for the first time since an outbreak in Hong Kong in 1997. Three people in one family were infected after visiting Fujian province in mainland China and two died (Peiris et al. 2004: 617–619). By late 2006, there had been 263 human cases and 158 deaths in nine countries, with virological studies showing considerable genetic variation among strains isolated from human cases. The case fatality rate in Indonesia was an extraordinary 81% in 1995 and 1996 – among the highest death rates recorded for any human pathogen (Sedyaningsih et al. 2008: 484). However the virus was poorly transmissible between humans, with only rare cases of probable human-to-human spread (Olsen et al. 2005: 1799; Ungchusak et al. 2005: 333–340). Nevertheless virologists were aware that the genetically unstable H5N1 virus could, through genetic reassortment or mutation, transform into a strain with the lethality of H5N1 and the transmissibility of human Influenza A: the pandemic virus. Prompt genetic analysis of isolates from human cases was urgently required and, when appropriate, preparation of attenuated (weakened) seed viruses for vaccine production.

It was at this critical juncture that Indonesia suspended sharing of new H5N1 isolates with WHO's Collaborating Centers, where genetic analysis and production of attenuated seed strains for vaccine production were carried out.

The evolving virus sharing crisis

The international media reaction to Indonesia's decision to withhold viral isolates was intense, polarized, and revealing. In an editorial titled "Recipe for a Pandemic," the *Wall Street Journal* argued that "Supari (Indonesia's Minister of Health) asserts that Indonesian bird flu is a form of intellectual property, from which the country should benefit. By hoarding samples and trying to tinker with the financial incentives that drive pharmaceutical innovation, Indonesia is endangering everyone" (Wall Street Journal 2008). In an opinion piece published in the *Washington Post,* the respected U.S. diplomat Richard Holbrooke and the science journalist Laurie Garrett aggressively criticized Indonesia's claim to what they called "viral sovereignty." The authors described the idea that sovereign states could exercise ownership rights over samples of viruses found in their territory as "ludicrous" and "dangerous folly" (Holbrooke & Garrett 2008). The U.S. Secretary of Defense dismissed concerns raised by Indonesia's Minister of Health over the possible military use of H5N1 as "nutty" (United Press International 2008). (However, it was later revealed that the U.S. military did have an extensive system of influenza virus collection operating in parallel with WHO's influenza surveillance system in 56 countries, Hammond 2008a.)

In much of the negative international reaction there is an assumption that Indonesia's actions were arbitrary, inexplicable, or motivated by a desire for financial gain. The U.S. Secretary for Health and Human Services (equivalent to Minister of Health) was quoted as saying that the Indonesian Minister of Health's "bottom line appeared to be . . . share samples, get paid" (Associated Press 2008). Few of these negative stories presented Indonesia's position or acknowledged the fact that the country did have legitimate and urgent public health concerns that were not being addressed by the existing mechanisms for sharing viruses and accessing benefits including vaccines and antiviral drugs. Epidemiologists also recognized, of course, that the source country of an emergent pandemic pathogen would be the epicenter of an evolving pandemic and would face the highest mortality early on.

Other observers were more sympathetic to Indonesia's situation. An editorial in the respected British journal *The Lancet* noted that "To protect the global population, 6.2 billion doses of pandemic vaccine will be needed, but current manufacturing capacity can only produce 500 million doses . . . most developing countries would have no access to vaccine during the first wave of a pandemic and possibly throughout its duration. . . . Indonesia's move to secure an affordable vaccine supply for its population is understandable" (Lancet 2007: 532).

Why did Indonesia take the extraordinary step of suspending sharing of H5N1 isolates with WHO's Collaborating Centers? From mid-2006 onward, Indonesia received a series of shocks that led it to question the sincerity of WHO and the international community. In violation of WHO guidelines, studies on H5N1 strains from Indonesia were reported at international meetings without prior participation or consultation with Indonesian scientists (or in some cases with notification only hours before the presentation). Indonesian scientists were asked in a *pro forma* fashion to become coauthors on papers already written by international scientists, who, to the surprise of Indonesia's scientists, had been given access to viral isolates sent by Indonesia to WHO (Sedyaningsih et al. 2008: 485). This is not a trivial question of publication rights: Indonesian virologists and public health officials were left in the dark on scientific research on lethal viruses actively circulating in their country.

Then it was revealed in early 2007 that an Australian company had developed and patented a vaccine from an Indonesian H5N1 strain (Fidler 2008). More disturbing, officials in WHO's Regional Office for South-East Asia and in Indonesia subsequently discovered that WHO's 2005 guidelines on sharing of influenza isolates, titled "Guidance for the Timely Sharing of Influenza Viruses/Specimens with Potential to Cause Human Influenza Pandemics," had been mysteriously deleted from the WHO website. These guidelines required that "designated WHO Reference Laboratories will seek permission from the originating country/laboratory to co-author and/or publish results obtained from the analyses of relevant viruses/samples . . . there will be no further distribution of viruses/specimens outside the network of WHO Reference Laboratories without permission from the originating country/laboratory." (Although these guidelines have been deleted from WHO's public records, the authors have copies in their files that are available on request.)

Adding further to Indonesia's anxieties, WHO admitted that further patents had been sought on modified versions of influenza (H5N1) samples shared through the Global Influenza Surveillance Network (GISN) without the notification or consent of the countries that supplied the samples, contrary to the inexplicably deleted WHO guidelines (Fidler 2008: 88; Khor 2007b; Sedyaningsih et. al. 2008: 486). A flood of patents and patent applications on pandemic-prone influenza viruses isolated in Indonesia, Thailand, and Vietnam, first detected in 2007 (Hammond 2007), has accelerated since (Hammond 2011). Even the Centers for Disease Control in Atlanta, USA, a WHO Collaborating Center, was discovered to have claimed patents on vaccines containing gene sequences from H5N1 influenza viruses contributed to WHO by Indonesia (Hammond

2008b). Source countries and their scientists were, and remain, uninformed on the content and purposes of these patents and others taken by commercial enterprises (Novartis, GlaxoSmith-Kline, Temasek Life Sciences, & others) on materials that they donated to WHO with the understanding that they would be used for public health purposes.

Officials in Southeast Asian countries began to ask the obvious question: would affected countries be able to obtain vaccines produced from the isolates they submitted to WHO? When asked how countries could obtain vaccines from manufacturers, the response of the WHO Assistant Director General for Communicable Diseases was not reassuring: "That will be necessary for the countries to negotiate. WHO is not involved in financial negotiations, either in selling viruses or buying vaccines. Countries will negotiate bilaterally with vaccine manufacturers" (World Health Organization 2007a).

The cumulative effect of all of this was a loss of trust in the WHO secretariat by many of its member states. Loss of trust in WHO on this issue is not a trivial matter. In an extraordinary development, member states from nonindustrialized countries insisted that the record of the first intergovernmental meeting on sharing of viruses and access to benefits contained an acknowledgement that "there has been a breakdown of trust in this essential system of the international collaboration and collective action", and that "the current system does not deliver the desired level of fairness, transparency and equity" (Irwin 2010; World Health Organization 2007b). There are few if any other instances when a significant number of WHO member states concluded that the WHO secretariat had not acted in the best interests of the most vulnerable countries.

Indonesia's radical step in refusing to share H5N1 isolates had a specific objective: to ensure that the country would have access to a portion of the vaccines, antiviral drugs, and diagnostic technologies that would be derived from the viral isolates collected by Indonesian scientists and transmitted in good faith to WHO's Collaborating Centers. Contrary to incomplete reports in the international media, the country was willing to resume submission of specimens if they could be assured of access to some of the benefits.

Indonesia's position, stated early in the crisis in February 2007, was specific, consistent with current practice, and actionable:

> Indonesia will insist on a material transfer agreement (MTA) before sending the Indonesian strain of bird flu virus to foreign laboratories to prevent them from being used for commercial purposes. . . . We agree to send the virus to the WHO with new conditions or mechanisms approved by both parties as well as by other developing countries. Until then, we won't share the samples. . . . The organization [WHO] sometimes forgets the good of the people in general and we want to change that.
>
> (Khor 2007a)

If this proposal had been taken seriously, it would have had been a good starting point for resolving the crisis.

An MTA is a document that is signed by both provider and recipient of scientific or other materials. It sets out conditions of transfer, and usually includes provisions on how the material will be used, restriction on further transfer without prior notification of the provider, and limitations on commercial use. In essence it maintains control – de facto ownership – of the material in the hands of the provider. MTAs are routinely required for shipment of human biological materials or other hazardous materials in the United States and in Europe. In Indonesia, MTAs have been required in Indonesian law since 1995 (Ministry of Health Republic of Indonesia 1995; Ministry of Research and Technology Republic of Indonesia 2006) and were further reinforced by a 2006 provision that government officials who failed to comply with this and other domestic laws could face 13 years of imprisonment. Clearly there was an international precedent, indeed a requirement, for use of MTAs when transporting hazardous biological materials.

Indonesia's analysis of the situation facing the populations of nonindustrialized countries, and their rationale for demanding an MTA, was clearly stated in international meetings convened to resolve the problem (Republic of Indonesia 2007). These statements were routinely ignored in the international media. Several member states, led by the United States, vigorously opposed Indonesia's proposal to apply a material transfer agreement (Irwin 2010). This refusal is revealing. Industrialized countries argued that applying an MTA was inappropriate in an evolving pandemic situation and would slow the process of developing a vaccine. This was clearly a false argument, since WHO Collaborating Centers and commercial vaccine producers *required* MTAs for all further transfer of isolates and seed viruses (Sedyaningsih et al. 2008: 487).

There is little argument about rights of ownership of biological materials. The only question is *ownership by whom.*

We will never know what form a transparently negotiated MTA would have taken, had it been negotiated at this point. Certainly it would have contained guarantees that the source country and other nonindustrialized countries would have access to vaccines and other benefits. Indeed, the WHO MTAs (redesignated as standard material transfer agreements or SMTAs) that emerged after 6 years of often bitter argument, and over the resistance of several industrialized countries, contained some of the features that should have been negotiated in early 2007 (World Health Organization 2011b: 30–36).

Six years of meetings and rancorous negotiations followed the industrialized countries' refusal to accept Indonesia's proposal to negotiate a material transfer agreement. The issue was debated in intergovernmental meetings, at WHO's Executive Board and World Health Assemblies, in high-level technical meetings, and in open-ended working groups. The outcome was a Pandemic Influenza Preparedness Framework, a Partnership Agreement (a mechanism to fund WHO's influenza activities in part through industry contributions), and two "Standard Material Transfer Agreements": SMTA 1 and SMTA 2 (World Health Organization 2011b: 3–60; World Health Organization 2011c: 2–10; World Health Organization 2013: 1–10). While all of these products are important, we will restrict this discussion to the two SMTAs.

SMTA 1 is used for transfer of influenza viral isolates and other "PIP biological materials"[1] from originating countries to WHO and its Collaborating Centers and for all transfers within WHO's GISRS (Global Influenza Surveillance and Response System). For our purposes, a key clause in the SMTA 1 is in Article 6 (Intellectual Property Rights), which states: "Neither the Provider nor the Recipient should seek to obtain any intellectual property rights (IPRs) on the Materials." This is an interesting provision. While most MTAs are written to ensure that the originator (provider) of a substance or product retains ongoing control over its further use, commercial application and so forth, this MTA is intended to have the opposite effect.

SMTA 2 is used for transfers of materials to entities outside the WHO GISRS. These entities include vaccine manufacturers. Only one SMTA 2 has been negotiated so far, with the vaccine producer GlaxoSmithKline (WHO/GlaxoSmithKline 2013: 1). This SMTA contains many positive features, including commitments by GSK to donate a portion of its pandemic vaccine production to a WHO stockpile that is provided for in the Pandemic Influenza Preparedness Framework. However, there are several significant omissions. There are no limitations on patenting or use of materials or derivatives. There is a provision for "acknowledging the contributions of WHO laboratories in presentations and publications," but no requirement to involve national or WHO scientists in research, for example in field trials on vaccine efficacy, or to inform WHO or its member states of the existence of clinical trials or their findings. It is disappointing that WHO accepted an SMTA 2 that did not have provisions that are appropriately required for WHO's own affiliated laboratories (World Health Organization 2011b: 30–31).

Perhaps the most surprising feature of the GlaxoSmithKline/WHO SMTA is the dispute resolution process. Disputes that cannot be resolved between the parties will be referred to the commercially funded International Chamber of Commerce and presumably handled through the ICC's International Court of Arbitration. It is extraordinary that a United Nations agency would submit itself to binding arbitration by a private sector body, and it is far from certain that such a body will be capable of dealing with the critical public health issues likely to arise in disputes.[2]

Viewed from the perspective of nonindustrialized countries, especially those at the likely epicenter of an emerging pandemic, what has been gained and lost after 6 years of negotiation over sharing of viruses and benefits? While the WHO's Pandemic Influenza Preparedness Framework and standard material transfer agreements do contain provisions for antiviral and vaccine stockpiling of vaccines and other benefits (including, as an option, licensing for vaccine production in "developing" countries) there is no specific provision that the source countries of the original viral isolates (the epicenter for a pandemic) will receive sufficient vaccines and other supplies, and the quantities reserved for low-income nonindustrialized countries are low in proportion to their populations and their likely pandemic exposure.

A simple "thought experiment" illustrates the inequitable situations of industrialized and nonindustrialized countries on the virus and benefit sharing issue. Imagine this scenario:

> *An outbreak caused by a novel viral pathogen occurs in the United States, with many cases and deaths. A similar viral strain had been studied in a WHO Collaborating Center in China, and this laboratory has advanced knowledge and techniques relevant to this virus. The US is requested to forward virus isolates to the Chinese Collaborating Center without conditions and surrendering all intellectual property claims, as required by WHO's SMTA 1. The Chinese WHO CC would quickly produce a seed virus and transmit it to commercial producers of its choice in China or elsewhere, utilizing a WHO SMTA 2 transfer agreement. There would be no guarantee that the US would receive any vaccines.*

Would the United States agree to forward virus isolates to WHO under these conditions? Not likely. But these are the terms imposed on countries like Indonesia when they submit viral isolates to WHO under the SMTA 1.

Wider implications for global health security

The Erasmus episode

Whatever fragile level of trust may have been emerging after agreement on the Pandemic Influenza Framework was shaken at the 2013 World Health Assembly. The Health Minister of Saudi Arabia complained that Erasmus University in the Netherlands had obtained, sequenced, and developed a MTA for the virus responsible for the newly described (and highly lethal) Middle East Respiratory Syndrome (MERS). While Erasmus University had the legal right to proceed as they did, doing so without prior notification of the Saudi government (and, needless to say, without any consideration of sharing of benefits with the source country) was ethically questionable.

The virus that causes MERS is a coronavirus, not an influenza virus, and therefore not covered under the provisions of the WHO Pandemic Influenza Preparedness Framework. However, one would have hoped that the Erasmus laboratory, whose head is a longtime consultant to WHO and a member of WHO's strategic advisory group on influenza, would have behaved differently in this situation. The Erasmus group claims that the virus is being made freely available to researchers, but Erasmus University maintained tight control on further use of the virus through an MTA – "The provider retains ownership of the material" (Office of the University Counsel University of North Carolina/Erasmus University 2013: 2–6). There is little doubt that the interests of international researchers – and next in line, commercial interests – are better protected than those of vulnerable populations in the Middle East and elsewhere (Garrett & Builder 2013; Hammond 2013; Kupferschmit 2013).

Protecting the vital interests of nonindustrialized countries

Trust and transparency are rare commodities in the geopolitics of global health. Nonindustrialized countries at risk from global health threats should enter negotiations and agreements with their eyes open.

Hoffman (2012) analyzed the inequalities of influence between states in global decision making. More important, he proposed a series of steps that could be taken to remedy the problems. He starts with the observation that international organizations (including WHO):

> assert superordinate normative authority based on having egalitarian governance structures. However, when defining equality with respect to states' real-world influence in determining substantive outcomes, it is evident that there is an equality-influence gap between the rhetoric of parity among states and the reality of international politics. This is problematic because it undermines trust in those international institutions that falsely claim to embody equality among states when empirically they do not.

Hoffman then identifies three main causes of this disproportional influence among states in global decision making: (a) external imbalances in political capital; (b) internal economic barriers; and (c) surreptitious influence through non-state actors. All of these factors were operative in the Indonesian virus-sharing crisis.

Finally and most significant, Hoffman points to six initiatives as ways forward: 1) building capacity for leadership in global advocacy; 2) supporting global networks owned by developing countries; 3) equalizing multiparty partnerships; 4) facilitating evidence-informed global decision making; 5) enhancing accountability and independent evaluation; and 6) encouraging further discussion on institutional reforms (Hoffman 2012: 421–432).

Each of these six initiatives deserves further discussion, but here we will briefly explore the first and second, which are closely related and can be discussed together. For these two initiatives, nonindustrialized countries can operate independently of their more powerful neighbors and can expect immediate gains.

Building capacity for leadership in global advocacy and supporting global networks owned by developing countries

In global fora the industrialized countries are often in the lead. They are confident. They have skilled diplomatic, legal, and technical staff. They know how to network. Like-minded high-income countries come together to plan their moves and countermoves well in advance of important international meetings. Nonindustrialized countries have many of the necessary skills, but their qualified negotiators and technical experts are sometimes working in isolation. Although there are exceptions (the potent triangulation of Brazil, India, and South Africa on pharmaceutical trade negotiations is an example), there have also been many missed opportunities.

Nonindustrialized countries can mobilize on an ad hoc basis for a specific issue, as was attempted with some success in the Indonesia virus sharing episode; but a more structured caucus approach (e.g., the G-77 and the G-22 groups) provides more scope for policy, tactical synergy, and capacity building. For some issues, a different mix of countries or a different policy or technical orientation is needed. The treaty-based South Centre, an intergovernmental organization with 55 member states, is an example. The South Centre is respected for its strong intellectual and policy support to its members (South Centre 2013).

The paradox of global health security

The World Health Organization's member states have negotiated the issues of sharing of pandemic-potential viruses and benefits with great difficulty and uncertain results. The process was marked by an absence of trust and transparency.

Beyond pandemic preparedness, we encounter difficult questions at the intersection of public health and national security on the road to global health security. A healthy relationship between all nations (or at least between most nations, most of the time) is a precondition for global health security. While this will seem obvious to some, many global negotiations and transactions have been based on the implicit assumption that more powerful nation states are in a position to dictate terms to the less fortunate and should take advantage of the opportunity when it arises. This was attempted in the case of Indonesia and sharing of H5N1 isolates, with potentially catastrophic results.

This is the paradox of global health security. Countries that pursue their own narrowly conceived national security and commercial interests while disregarding the vital interests of other countries will weaken global – and their own – health security in the long run, a danger that was narrowly averted in the Indonesia virus sharing episode. The problems created by a narrow "securitized" approach to global health are not limited to influenza virus sharing: "A key lesson to emerge from the international virus sharing controversy is . . . that a securitized response to infectious disease management can also have unanticipated consequences in terms of further complicating international health cooperation" (Elbe 2010). While this lesson is obvious for a problem like pandemic disease, for which the entire world population is in a common risk pool, it applies equally to other problems such as nuclear safety, arms control, or any of many other security threats for which global cooperation and agreement are essential.

Notes

1 In this paper we refer to influenza viral isolates. WHO documents and agreements refer to a broader range of influenza related materials, collectively termed "PIP (pandemic influenza preparedness) materials." These include "human clinical specimens; virus isolates of wild type human H5N1 and other influenza viruses with human pandemic potential; and modified viruses prepared from H5N1 and/or other influenza viruses with human pandemic potential developed by WHO GISRS laboratories, these being candidate vaccine viruses generated by reverse genetics and/or high growth re-assortment."

2 By submitting to binding arbitration (dispute resolution) by a private body, WHO appears to have taken the extraordinary step of waiving protections guaranteed to it by the Convention (treaty) on the Privileges and Immunities of the Specialized Agencies approved by the General Assembly of the United Nations on November 21, 1947.

References

Associated Press. (2008) 'Indonesia says bird flu virus-sharing battle not about money', Online. Available HTTP: <http://www.thejakartapost.com/news/2008/04/23/indonesia-says-bird-flu-virussharing-battle-not-about-money.html> (accessed 5 February 2013).

Chan, C. K. and de Wildt, G. (2007) *Developing Countries, Donor Leverage, and Access to Bird Flu Vaccines*, New York: United Nations Department of Economics and Social Affairs.

Elbe, S. (2010) 'Haggling over viruses: the downside risks of securitizing infectious disease', *Health Policy and Planning*, 25: 476–485.

Fidler, D.P. (2008) 'Influenza virus samples, international law, and global health diplomacy', *Emerging Infectious Diseases*, 14: 88.

Garrett, L. and Builder, M. (2013) 'The Middle East plague goes global', *Foreign Policy*. Online. Available HTTP: <http://www.foreignpolicy.com/articles/2013/06/28/the_middle_east_plague_goes_global?page=0,0> (accessed 30 June 2013).

Hammond, E. (2007) *Some Intellectual Property Issues Related to H5N1 Influenza Viruses Research and Vaccines*, Penang: Third World Network. Online. Available HTTP: <http://www.twnside.org.sg/title2/IPR/pdf/ipr12.pdf> (accessed 6 June 2012).

Hammond, E. (2008a) *US Military Flu Virus Collection Parallels WHO Virus System*, Third World Network. Online. Available HTTP: <http://www.twnside.org.sg/title2/intellectual_property/info.service/2008/twn.ipr.info.081108.htm> (accessed 6 June 2010).

Hammond, E. (2008b) *WHO-linked Centre Lays Patent Claim Related to Bird Flu Virus*, Third World Network. Online. Available HTTP: <http://www.twnside.org.sg/title2/health.info/2008/twnhealthinfo20080804.htm> (accessed 12 December 2010).

Hammond, E. (2011) *An Update on Intellectual Property Claims Related to Global Pandemic Influenza Preparedness*, Penang: Third World Network. Online. Available: <http://www.ip-watch.org/weblog/wp-content/uploads/2011/04/PCT-PATENT-APPLICATIONS-FOR-INFLUENZA-VACCINES.pdf> (accessed 6 June 2012).

Hammond, E. (2013) *Sovereignty and Patents at the Fore in Debate over MERS virus*, Third World Network. Online. Available HTTP: <http://www.twnside.org.sg/title2/health.info/2013/health130510.htm> (accessed 1 June 2013).

Hoffman, S.J. (2012) "Mitigating inequalities of influence among states in global decision making', *Global Policy*, 3: 421–432.

Holbrooke, R. and Garrett, L. (2008, 10 August) '"Sovereignty" that risks global health', *Washington Post*. Online. Available HTTP: <http://articles.washingtonpost.com/2008–08–10/opinions/36864341_1_flu-outbreaks-bird-flu-siti-fadilah-supari> (accessed 16 September 2010).

Irwin, R. (2010) 'Indonesia, H5N1, and global health diplomacy', *Global Health Governance*, 3.

Khor, M. (2007a) 'Indonesia to share bird flu samples only if there is a new system', Third World Network. Online. Available HTTP: <http://www.twnside.org.sg/title2/health.info/twninfohealth078.htm> (accessed 15 March 2013).

Khor, M. (2007b) 'WHO admits patents taken on avian flu virus', *Third World Resurgence*, 201: 19.

Kupferschmit, K. (2013, May 28) 'As outbreak continues, confusion reigns over virus patents', *ScienceInsider*. Online. Available HTTP: <http://news.sciencemag.org/scienceinsider/2013/05/as-outbreak-continues-confusion-.html> (accessed 18 July 2013).

Lancet. (2007) 'Global solidarity needed in preparing for pandemic influenza', *Lancet* 369: 532.

Ministry of Health Republic of Indonesia. National Institute of Health Research and Development. (1995) *Government Regulation No 39, 1995 on Health Research and Development*. Republic of Indonesia.

Ministry of Research and Technology Republic of Indonesia. (2006) *Government Regulation No 41, 2006 on Permission to Conduct Research and Development Activities for Foreign Universities, Foreign Research and Development Institution, Foreign Organization and Foreigners*. Republic of Indonesia.

Office of the University Counsel University of North Carolina/Erasmus University. (2013) *Materials Transfer Agreement*, Online. Available HTTP: <http://www.twnside.org.sg/title2/intellectual_property/info.service/2013/ipr.info.130512/22227717951a47369b9515.pdf> (accessed 2 June 2013).

Olsen, S.J., Ungchusak, K., Sovann, L., Uyeki, T.M., Dowell, S.F., Cox, N.J., Aldis, W. and Chunsuttiwat, S. (2005) 'Family clustering of avian influenza A (H5N1)', *Emerging Infectious Diseases*, 11: 1799–1801.

Peiris, J., Yu, W., Leung, C., Cheung, C., Ng, W., Nicholls, J.A., Ng, T., Chan, K., Lai, S. and Lim, W. (2004) 'Re-emergence of fatal human influenza A subtype H5N1 disease', *The Lancet*, 363: 617–619.

Republic of Indonesia. (2007) *Remarks by Indonesian Delegation at Inter-Governmental Meeting for Pandemic influenza Preparedness*. Online. Available HTTP: <http://www.ip-watch.org/files/Indonesia_statement_WHO.pdf> (accessed 4 August 2013).

Sedyaningsih, E.R., Isfandari, S., Soendoro, T. and Supari, S.F. (2008) 'Towards mutual trust, transparency and equity in virus sharing mechanism: the avian influenza case of Indonesia', *Annals Academy of Medicine Singapore*, 37: 482–488.

South Centre. *Home Page*. Online. Available HTTP: <http://www.southcentre.int/>(accessed 1 December 2012).

Ungchusak, K., Auewarakul, P., Dowell, S.F., Kitphati, R., Auwanit, W., Puthavathana, P., Uiprasertkul, M., Boonnak, K., Pittayawonganon, C. and Cox, N. J. (2005) 'Probable person-to-person transmission of avian influenza A (H5N1)', *New England Journal of Medicine*, 352: 333–340.

United Press International (UPI). (2008, February 26) 'Gates: bird flu bio-weapon charge nutty'. Online. Available HTTP: <http://www.upi.com/Emerging_Threats/2008/02/26/Gates-Bird-flu-bio-weapon-charge-nutty/UPI-45241204071037/> (accessed 13 March 2008).

Wall Street Journal. (2008, April 18) 'Recipe for a pandemic', *Wall Street Journal*.

WHO/GlaxoSmithKline. (2013) *Standard Material Transfer Agreement 2*, Online. Available HTTP: <http://www.who.int/influenza/pip/benefit_sharing/gsk_smta2_dec_2012.pdf> (accessed 30 May 2013).

World Health Organization. (2007a) 'Indonesia to resume sharing H5N1 avian influenza virus samples following a WHO meeting in Jakarta', Online. Available HTTP: <http://www.who.int/mediacentre/news/releases/2007/pr09/en/> (accessed 12 January 2013).

World Health Organization. (2007b) *Interim Statement of the Intergovernmental Meeting on Pandemic Influenza Preparedness: Sharing of Influenza Viruses and Access to Vaccine and Other Benefits*. Online. Available HTTP: <http://apps.who.int/gb/pip/pdf_files/IGM_PIP-IntStatement-en.pdf> (accessed 15 December 2012).

World Health Organization. (2011a) 'H5N1 avian influenza: timeline of major events', Online. Available HTTP: <http://www.who.int/influenza/human_animal_interface/avian_influenza/H5N1_avian_influenza_update.pdf> (accessed 16 December 2012).

World Health Organization. (2011b) *Pandemic Influenza Preparedness Framework*, Geneva: World Health Organization.

World Health Organization. (2011c) *Questions and Answers: Pandemic Influenza Preparedness Framework*, Online. Available HTTP: <http://www.who.int/influenza/pip/PIP_FQA_Nov_2011.pdf> (accessed 11 August 2012).

World Health Organization. (2013) *Partnership Contribution Standard Operating Procedures*, Online. Available HTTP: <http://www.who.int/influenza/pip/benefit_sharing/pc_sop_may_2013.pdf> (accessed 15 May 2013).

27

HEALTH SECURITY AND THE DISTORTION OF THE GLOBAL HEALTH AGENDA

Michael A. Stevenson & Michael Moran

In the late 1990s, the World Health Organization (WHO) sought to raise the profile of communicable diseases in world affairs by highlighting humanity's common vulnerability to pathogens with pandemic potential (Davies 2008: 297). To mitigate such threats, proponents of what would become known as *health security* advocated that states embrace three general strategies. First, to ensure early detection of serious, unexpected public health emergencies with the potential to impede global travel and trade, the criteria for health events reportable under international law would require updating (Rodier et al. 2007: 1147). Second, linkages between national disease surveillance programs would have to be strengthened, and states would need to commit to curtailing health threats within their borders while ensuring transparency of process (Katz & Fischer 2010: 8). Finally, governments would need to secure access to sufficient quantities of relevant preventative and therapeutic health technologies such as vaccines and antiviral medications in the event of a global health emergency (Kamradt-Scott 2012: S111).

All three of these strategies have been acted upon. Since 1997 WHO has played host to the Global Outbreak Alert and Response Network (GOARN), which links over 120 national surveillance and response programs and which has been credited with identifying and marshalling the global response to the 2003 Severe Acute Respiratory Syndrome (SARS) outbreak (Heymann 2004: 1127). Moreover in 2005, the International Health Regulations (IHR) were revised to constitute a global legal framework that compels WHO member states to invest in their public health systems and notify the world when potential global threats emerge (Rodier et al. 2007: 1447). Furthermore, with the support of WHO, public–private partnerships aimed at developing and delivering essential medicines to populations with limited purchasing power have proliferated (Buse & Waxman 2001: 748–754), and those countries with the financial wherewithal, have made multibillion dollar advanced market commitments to purchase vaccine and antiviral drugs as part of their pandemic influenza planning (Kamradt-Scott & McInnes 2012: S95–S110).

There is little doubt that the concept of health security has played an important role in public health and particularly communicable disease control rising in importance in international affairs, moving health from its traditional domain of low politics to a concern of foreign affairs. Yet the communicable (Black et al. 2003) and noncommunicable diseases (NCDs) (Mathers & Loncar 2006) accounting for the majority of global deaths and disability-adjusted life-years (DALYs) do not meet the criteria for securitization (see also Benson & Glasgow, chapter 15 in this volume). Neither a measles epidemic in Chad nor an increase in the overall prevalence in type II diabetes in China has relevance to either GOARN or the IHR, despite the significant human and economic costs associated with each scenario.

Moreover some segments of the public health community have suggested the embrace of health security within international policy arenas has led to other proven public health models such as primary care being marginalized and questioned its actual impact on reducing global health disparities (Aldis 2008). The IHR revisions for example have led to new commitments from low-income countries to strengthen long atrophied health systems, but have not produced any new dedicated funds to assist governments to do so.

Finally, health security has done little to alleviate the socioeconomic disparities giving rise to unequal access to pharmaceuticals produced in the free market (Widdus 2001: 713). Despite industry-initiated drug donation schemes, and a proliferation of product development partnerships (PDPs) driving new pharmaceuticals at discount prices for developing countries, there remains a persistent lack of access across the South to essential medications due to limited supply as well as cost and distribution challenges (Cameron et al. 2009), which has been particularly evident as countries have sought to secure access to flu vaccines and antivirals (Mounier-Jack et al. 2007).

Consequently this chapter argues the rise to prominence of the health security paradigm in international relations has created three significant distortions to the global health agenda.

The most obvious distortion is a focus on a handful of emerging pathogens that have caused little morbidity and mortality, compared to more ubiquitous communicable and noncommunicable diseases such as malaria and diabetes that account for the overwhelming global burden of disease. This in turn serves to illustrate the ongoing neglect of health systems in low and lower middle income countries (LMICs) that has not been improved by better early warning systems, changes to international health laws, or greater inter-state dialogue on preparing for acute public health emergencies. Instead securitization has led to a distortion in funding priorities, which has meant that a large group of countries neither have the capacity nor the resources to safeguard the health of their own populations. Finally the state-centric health security paradigm ignores the fact that much of whether disease can be prevented and treated is dictated by firms' commercial interests. This is because the majority of the world's states have left it to the private sector to ensure the development of preventative and therapeutic health technologies employed in public health protection as well as for the development of new drugs for biodefense. This creates dual vulnerabilities. On the one hand, the reliance on the private sector leads to a lack of secure access to drugs for diseases disproportionately affecting the South. On the other, a core pillar of health security, the threat from bioterrorism, is left largely unaddressed by the major developers of new products, multinational pharmaceutical companies.

Health security in practice: Broad concept, narrow focus

Early proponents of health security envisioned that the concept would serve to catalyze government investments in public health broadly defined. In practice, however, its impact has been largely restricted to reinvigorating global systems for detecting and reacting to acute viral epidemics with pandemic potential.

Pathogens that affect the north

International collaboration on influenza detection began in 1950 when WHO began linking national laboratories engaged in influenza surveillance under the auspices of the Global Influenza Surveillance Network (GISN) (Kamradt-Scott 2012: S113). Such vigilance was justifiable for in the 20th century alone three influenza pandemics claimed over 40 million lives. While GISN would eventually involve over one hundred countries, the salience of pandemic preparedness as an international policy issue grew exponentially in the wake of two comparatively much smaller epidemics. The first was the 1997 H5N1 avian influenza outbreak in Hong Kong, which produced only 18 human cases, but was marked by a 33% case-fatality rate, and was only arrested after the island's entire poultry stock was destroyed (Kamradt-Scott 2012: S113–114). Six years later, multiple outbreaks of the novel SARS coronavirus produced over 8,000 cases and over 900 deaths (WHO 2003: 75) and caused over $30 billion in economic damage in the Asia-Pacific region alone (Kamradt-Scott & McInnes 2012: S102; see also Heymann, chapter 8 in this volume).

As noted by Fidler (2004: 801), avian influenza and SARS demonstrated to states just how vulnerable integrated economies are to pathogens when diagnostic, preventative, and therapeutic technologies are lacking. Clearly states are taking such threats seriously. Between 2005 and 2009, for example, approximately $4.3 billion was made available by governments to mitigate the threat of pandemic influenza alone (Kamradt-Scott & McInnes 2012: S102). What is disconcerting to some public health practitioners, however, is that while such pathogens constitute serious public health threats, the spending targeted towards them is not proportionate to the global burden of disease. Consequently, questions have been raised as to whether the shift in policy priorities and reallocation of finite financial resources associated with the advancement of the concept of health security are sufficiently justifiable (Aldis 2008: 373).

Evidence gives weight to such criticism. The majority of annual deaths attributed to communicable diseases are caused not by emerging zoonoses, but by a ubiquitous set of enteric and respiratory pathogens that disproportionately affect the world's poor. In the same year SARS emerged, more than 10 million impoverished children died from one of a small number of communicable diseases that included diarrhea, pneumonia, measles, malaria, and HIV/AIDS, and in over half of these deaths, under nutrition was a contributing factor (Black et al. 2003: 2226–2234). Indeed 57% of these deaths were deemed to have been preventable, provided universal coverage of relatively simple evidence-based interventions was achieved in low-income countries. These include breastfeeding, the administration of oral-rehydration therapy, micronutrients, basic antibiotics and vaccinations, and access to insecticide-treated materials, sanitation, clean water, and skilled birth attendants (Jones et al. 2003: 68). Yet, of these common diseases only HIV/AIDS and malaria have really been prioritized in terms of global health funding, and only HIV/AIDS has been widely viewed as a security threat.

Omission of NCDs in LMICs

Even more significant is the toll NCDs are taking on global health. At the dawn of the new millennium, NCDs such as ischemic heart disease, cerebrovascular disease, chronic obstructive pulmonary disease, lung/tracheal cancers, and diabetes mellitus were the cause of almost 54% of deaths in LMICs, and 87% of deaths in high-income countries (HICs) (Mathers & Loncar 2006: 2022). Current projections suggest that the balance will shift further as diseases of lifestyle become more prevalent in LMICs. Tobacco-related diseases for example are expected to cause 50% more deaths in 2015 than HIV/AIDS, with the total number of tobacco-related disease deaths expected to double between 2005 and 2030 in LMICs (from 3.4 to 6.8 million people) (Mathers & Loncar 2006: 2011). Furthermore, over 1 billion people are currently estimated to be overweight (Hossain et al. 2007: 213–215), which increases their risk of mortality due to high cholesterol, blood pressure, and type II diabetes. Developing countries presently carry 70% of the global diabetes burden (Jamison et al. 2006) and the global incidence of this disease is expected to double between 2000 and 2030 (Wild et al. 2004: 1047–1053). Overall, the proportion of global deaths due to NCDs is projected to rise from 59% in 2002 to 69% in 2030 (Mathers & Loncar 2006: 2011).

Mirroring the majority of global deaths attributed to communicable diseases, much of the present NCD-driven mortality is preventable: not because of cutting edge science-enabled innovation, but because the behavioral and physiological risk factors underpinning many of these diseases are well understood. Up to 40% of all cancers and 80% of premature diabetes and cardiovascular disease could be prevented through dietary changes, sufficient exercise, and smoking abatement (Magnusson 2010: 490).

The revised IHR do little to call attention to the rise of NCDs. Only those caused by radiological or chemical agents circulated inadvertently via international trade will be detected (Fidler & Gostin 2006: 86). Moreover GOARN was clearly not designed to raise alarms over those pathogens responsible for the majority of deaths. By design, GOARN thus inadvertently reinforces the tendency of the health security paradigm to pay a disproportionate amount of attention to a small set of infectious diseases, while neglecting others and effectively ignoring NCDs altogether.

The observation that global health spending priorities are unrepresentative of the global burden of disease is not novel. As articulated by Shiffman in relation to SARS, "when a disease is perceived to be a threat to the peoples of rich countries, donors are more likely to pay attention" (Shiffman 2006: 418). The danger, as noted by Davies (2008: 2), is that in championing the health security concept, WHO has run the risk of becoming locked into a single approach to detecting and responding to public health threats, which obscures other viable options. Moreover, the promotion of health security also places the organization charged with protecting global society's most vulnerable in the awkward position of shifting the basis for investing in disease surveillance programs from humanitarian grounds towards safeguarding national security and international trade. Consequently, say critics of the concept, health security has been perceived by some developing countries as a vehicle through which the national interests of wealthy Northern states have become institutionalized within the international heath architecture (Aldis 2008: 371–373) and national security prioritized over global public health (Kamradt-Scott & McInnes 2012: S103).

Health security and health systems: Whose priorities?

The nexus between functioning national health systems and health security is clear. First, at the most basic level health systems are the first line of defense – "even [a] deterrent" – against the use of biological weapons such as smallpox (McInnes & Lee 2006: 8). Second, without adequate human resources and workforce capacity the principles of surveillance, prevention, control and response to disease outbreaks – whether intentional release or zoonotic – are constrained and compromised (Rodier et al. 2007). Third, even with sound international surveillance, for the IHR to operate effectively they require a commensurate response at the national and subnational level (Nsubuga et al. 2010: 2). In short, weak national capacities constitute a serious risk to global health security.

WHO's *World Health Report 2006: Working Together* recognized this linkage and delineated a dire situation regarding the continuing "crises" of workforce capacity in many LMICs and the implications for national health systems. Some 57 countries, mostly in sub-Saharan Africa and Asia, were experiencing a "critical shortage" of "doctors, nurses and midwives" (WHO 2006: xxiii) with "many national health systems . . . weak, unresponsive, inequitable – even unsafe" (WHO 2006: xv). The theme was followed-up in the *World Health Report 2007: A Safer Future*, which turned its attention to issues of "global public health security." This report also identified weak systems as the principal barrier to health security and argued that strengthening health systems was "essential not only to assure the best possible public health of national populations, but also to assure global public health security" (WHO 2007: 57).

That this evidence has been a catalyst for change is contested. The G8's 2008 Toyako Summit produced a pledge to take action to strengthen health systems in LMICs (Reich & Takemi 2009: 508). Moreover the major global health initiatives (GHIs) – from the GAVI Alliance to the US President's Emergency Plan for AIDS Relief – have ostensibly refocused their efforts around health system strengthening (HSS). Yet critics argue that much of what is often claimed to be HSS efforts are "in fact selective, disease-specific interventions" that may "undermine progress towards the long-term goal of" an "inclusive health system" (Marchal et al. 2009: 1). From this perspective, the international community's attention to strengthening health systems in LMICs has been seen by critics as wholly inadequate.

The North–South divide: Definitions, responsibilities and donor priorities

In theory securitization should provide a strong impetus for a focus on strengthening national capacity but in practice some argue that it has exposed a disconnection between the interests of HICs and many (but not all) LMICs. This schism has manifested as a series of tensions over global health priorities including over definitions, responsibilities, and the implications of donor-driven demands.

First, for many the term "health security" remains vague and ill-defined. On one hand, it is perceived as a descriptor of health problems in LMICs that may "threaten" the "vital interests" of HICs (Ollila 2005: 3). In contrast, Elbe (2011: 221) has observed that health security in many LMICs is conceived of less in terms of the threat posed by a select few highly infectious diseases and "armed conflict or bioterrorism," and more in terms of "the absence of more effective and affordable health care." As a result of this disconnect, tension remains over what health security is and in whose interests the term is deployed. Aldis (2008: 373) has argued the concept has been used to justify a "re-assignment of policy priorities and a re-allocation of resources." This has meant for example that the resource mobilization and political attention that has been coupled with framing health security as an "existential threat" (Elbe 2010: 478) has prioritized a select group of pathogens over the lack of access to primary care, despite the latter having been identified as an important problem by many LMICs (Ollila 2005: 3).

Second, one of the fundamental responsibilities implicit in the revised IHR is that all states must construct the necessary "public health infrastructure in the name of mutual protection" (Katz & Fischer 2010: 9). Yet this remains beyond the present capability of many national health systems struggling to provide even selective primary care. It can therefore be perceived "as an enormous obligation" on LMICs "primarily to protect the populations" of HICs (Katz & Fischer 2010: 9; Davies 2008).

Third, the narrow definition of health security has been mirrored in the focus of the major GHIs, which many perceive as equivalent distortions of global health priorities. As with health security, GHIs have played an integral role in bringing new resources to bear on communicable and neglected diseases and are "seen as essential mechanisms for achieving health security" (Hoffman 2010: 515). However the sheer number of new actors, agencies, and initiatives – the majority of which have a disease-specific focus rather than a broader health systems mandate – has led to the emergence of an increasingly fragmented and uncoordinated system. This places additional strain on national capacity while diverting potential "financial and human resources away from government agencies" and, albeit unintentionally, further "contributing to weakness in health systems" (Reich & Takemi 2009: 508). The effect is therefore to undermine health security as well as reinforce the assumption that the relatively narrow focus on communicable diseases that may threaten the wellbeing of HICs reflects donor rather than recipient priorities (Elbe 2011: 221).

Health as human security

Interestingly, some have observed that the incorporation of health into a security paradigm had its genesis in the UNDP's *Human Development Report 1994: New Dimensions of Human Security*, which used the post-Cold War context to reframe security in multidimensional terms and beyond the narrow confines of conflict (and the nation-state) (Aldis 2008: 371; Curley & Thomas 2004: 18; see also Caballero-Anthony & Amul, chapter 3 in this volume). However it has been argued that over time the term has been co-opted by a range of interests, most successfully the security community, and, as noted, framed in more narrow terms. While the concept of human security has also been criticized for being equally as fuzzy and nebulous, Elbe (2011: 221) has suggested that it in fact it might offer a less risky alternative "security card" for cementing the prominence of health in key policy-making circles. By framing health as a human security problem, Elbe (2011: 221) posits that the term can appeal equally to public health professionals and thereby avoid alienating a key constituency. Indeed as Reich and Takemi (2009: 512) have noted, conceptualizing health as human security involves the twin strategies of "protection" – or shielding "people from crucial and pervasive threats" – and "empowerment" – or enabling "people the capacity to cope with difficult situations." Broadening the agenda may serve as a rallying point around which key actors and agencies can think about strengthening health systems in LMICs rather than in narrow sectional or national interests.

Public sector capacity and essential pharmaceuticals: What role for global health security?

Market failure and the rise of product development partnerships

Since vaccines and drugs are widely considered to be essential tools for preventing and treating disease, pharmaceuticals form a central plank of the health security approach (Kamradt-Scott 2012). Ensuring that pharmaceuticals are accessible to those who need them most however is a significant challenge, due in no small part to well-entrenched divisions of labor existing between public and private sectors within liberal market economies. While the public sector usually plays a role in the funding discovery-stage research, with few exceptions it is the private sector that develops and produces pharmaceuticals (Widdus 2001: 713). This arrangement allows governments to focus finite resources elsewhere, but creates vulnerabilities when firms' need for profit cannot be met. Proponents of health security have not offered a plan for mitigating this vulnerability.

The dangers of states relying exclusively on business to provide essential public health tools is well illustrated by the fact that less than 1% of the pharmaceuticals brought to market in the final 25 years of the 20th century were for so-called "tropical diseases" such as tuberculosis and lymphatic filariasis that predominantly affect populations in poor countries with limited purchasing power (Trouiller & Olliaro 1999: 61–63). That the Special Program for Research and Training in Tropical Diseases (TDR) was established in 1975 as a joint initiative of WHO, the United Nations Development Program (UNDP), and the World Bank to work informally with industry for of the world's poor, demonstrated that multilateral organizations recognized this vulnerability early in this crisis (Croft 2005: 3), but were ill equipped to address it autonomously. Consequently the first public-private product development partnerships (PDPs) functioned as targeted capital funds

(Wheeler & Berkley 2001: 730) explicitly seeking to overcome market failure by lowering the financial risk for industry to engage in high-cost research and development, beginning with the International AIDS Vaccine Initiative (IAVI) in 1996, and followed by similarly structured initiatives for diseases such as malaria, tuberculosis, and dengue fever among others.

Initially, these arrangements were championed not by international organizations, but by private philanthropic foundations, most notably the Rockefeller Foundation (Moran & Stevenson 2013: 132), which underwrote efforts to convert discoveries in basic science into novel health technologies providing immediate value to the world's most vulnerable populations. PDPs have been able to capitalize on both the resources of multiple companies concurrently (Wheeler & Berkley 2001: 729), and on the volition of public sector regulators to see needed products developed, which has effectively reduced the time urgently needed pharmaceuticals spend within the research and development pipeline (Croft 2005). Indeed PDPs have been credited with dramatically increasing the number of novel preventative, diagnostic, and treatment options in existence for diseases disproportionately affecting the poorest populations of LMICs (Moran 2005: e302).

Because firms' responsibilities to shareholders previously worked against the development of pharmaceuticals for pressing (although relatively unprofitable) public health challenges, it has been argued that despite its many successes, the partnership model must be considered an ongoing social experiment that may yet prove unsustainable (Buse & Waxman 2001: 751). There are examples, such the Malaria Genome Project, of successful PDPs (Bond 2001: 522) that have not involved for-profit entities. Moreover multinational pharmaceutical companies' willingness to offer discounted prices to poor countries and, in some cases, provide products at no cost (such as Merck's longstanding Mectizan Donation Program), illustrate that business can still play an important role in alleviating pressing global health problems in the absence of profit (Asante & Zwi 2007: 178). Yet numerous examples also exist to show that there will always be potential conflict between shareholder interests and the public good. A case in point was Abbott Laboratories' challenge of Thailand's patent infringement of its cardiac drug *Plavix*, which the country justified under the World Trade Organization's Agreement on Trade-Related Aspects of Intellectual Property Rights (TRIPS) flexibility provision for securing access to medicines essential to protecting public health (Asante & Zwi 2007: 178–179). Moreover most of the funds sustaining PDPs come from public and philanthropic coffers (Nwaka 2005: S22), and even proponents of health partnerships have noted that as a general rule, "under the social venture capital model, private firms must be able to earn a profit if product production is to be sustainable" (Wheeler & Berkley 2001: 731).

States need to reacquire the capacity to manufacture essential pharmaceuticals

The long-term viability of the partnership model to provide governments with needed pharmaceuticals must be questioned, for even after 20 years of PDPs, approximately one-third of the global population lacks access to essential medicines (United Nations Millennium Project 2005) and pricing remains a significant constraint on availability (Cameron et al. 2009). Even when production is carried out by Southern firms that are able to reduce end costs through economies of scale, poor coverage rates of essential pharmaceuticals associated with high pricing persist to the detriment of public health. India, for example produces approximately half of the generic antiretroviral (ARV) drugs purchased for use in developing countries, yet only 6% to 15% of Indians living with HIV have access to ARVs themselves (Asante & Zwi 2007: 176). This is a systemic dilemma that is not confined to the global South. Drug shortages reported in the United States for example increased almost threefold between 2005 and 2010, to the point that 178 drugs used for the treatment of common infections and cancers, and anesthetics employed in surgery, ceased being produced because they were deemed to be generating insufficient profit for producers (Wilson 2012: 263–264).

Historically, production of influenza vaccine generated low returns on investment that, combined with the harmonization and heightening of regulatory standards and rising insurance premiums, gradually reduced the number of producers to the point where now almost 90% of global influenza vaccine is manufactured by only four multinational corporations: GlaxoSmithKline, Merck, Sanofi (Aventis AG), and Pfizer (Sheridan 2005: 1359). In the wake of the first H5N1 outbreak, mounting concerns within governments over an unchecked influenza pandemic created a surge in demand for influenza vaccine, which producers capitalized upon by increasing prices. Through advanced market commitments, an estimated 60 countries have secured access to a finite supply of influenza vaccine (Waldie & Robertson 2012). However the fact that over 100 countries still lack such access is a testament to the dangers of states totally divesting themselves of the capacity to develop and produce essential pharmaceuticals.

To meet demand and reduce drug prices, individual LMICs have the option of considering domestic production as opposed to importing from established generic producers such as Brazil and India (Wilson et al. 2012). This is typically not a viable option for vaccines however, given the prohibitive costs of carrying out basic research, building factories, conducting clinical trials, and manufacturing and distributing end products. In most instances it will be more cost-effective for the private sector to lead research and development efforts. However the only ways poor countries are going to ensure essential pharmaceuticals – including vaccines – are available on demand in times of crisis is to prioritize public sector capacity building in pharmaceutical research and development.

Brazil serves as a case in point. While the Brazilian pharmaceutical industry currently accounts for over 15% of the global market share for generic drugs (Sorte 2012: 1062) the country has maintained public sector capacity to run the full pharmaceutical gauntlet for the production of therapeutic drugs. Rio de Janeiro's Institute for Technology in Pharmaceuticals (Farmanguinhos) is one of several public labs in Brazil supplying the Brazilian National Public Health System with drugs for neglected diseases such as Hansen's disease, high-incidence diseases such as ischemic heart disease, and high-cost diseases such as HIV/AIDS (Sorte 2012: 1064). This capacity is critical to Brazil meeting its constitutional obligation of providing universal pharmaceutical care to its population (Naves & Silva 2005: 224), which was illustrated by the fact that the country was the sole emerging economy G20 member which succeeded in meeting the MDG HIV/AIDS treatment target of 80% coverage by 2007 (Garrett & Alavian 2010: 7). Not only are Brazil's public laboratories critical to ensuring high-volume production of essential medicines, they also serve to stimulate private sector interest in new areas relevant to the country's needs, and reduce the trade deficit by reducing the need to purchase high-cost drugs on the international market (Sorte 2012: 1076).

The reliance of government on industry to provide essential medicines is a problem in all realms of health security. For example, the small markets created by national biodefense programs are of little interest to multinational pharmaceutical firms (see Hoyt, chapter 18 in this volume). This is because there is in effect only one purchaser, the U.S. government, placing producers in a weak position to negotiate prices. The consequence of "market uncertainties" is that multinational pharmaceutical firms have not substantively engaged in drug development in any "meaningful way" (Bolken & Hruby 2008: 3). Large firms see an opportunity cost in directing resources to the development of drugs for a "market that will never materialize" (Gillfillan et al. 2004: 325). This in turn means governments must turn to small startup biotechnology firms, which have lacked the capacity and experience to deliver on their commitments and move drugs to late stage development, passing the "crucial middle-stage" in what in venture capital is termed the "valley of death" (Bolken & Hruby 2008: 3). States are therefore further vulnerable by virtue of their relinquishment of development and on their reliance on the private sector for a critical and arguably traditional component of health security.

Conclusion

Many have attributed the expansion of resources for global health that has occurred since the late 1990s, and the movement of health from the periphery of the international agenda toward the center, to the strategic framing of health as a security issue. There is little doubt that global health has received a level of political attention and resource mobilization that is largely unprecedented. Securitization has played a key role in this realignment of the global agenda, buttressed by a strengthened international regulatory regime through the IHR, which have been tested by outbreaks of highly pathogenic influenza strains including H5NI and more recently H1NI. Moreover the number and range of disease-specific GHIs that have emerged concurrently to tackle health problems in LMICs is at least in part attributable to health's newfound salience as a strategic priority.

Yet the continuing focus on a relatively narrow selection of pathogens and direct security threats such as bioterrorism has led some to ask: in whose interest is securitization (see also DeLaet, chapter 28 in this volume)? Thus far in practice, health security appears to largely reflect the agenda of HICs understandably concerned about the potential impact of disease outbreaks on their populations and economies. To be an effective metastrategy for reducing global health risks, the health security agenda needs to be reframed to reflect the health needs of the majority of the world's population who do not reside in rich countries. To do so, greater emphasis must be placed on mitigating those communicable and noncommunicable diseases that account for the majority of global deaths, strengthening weak health systems in LMICs, and building public sector capacity to produce essential pharmaceuticals to offset the potential of market-failure.

References

Aldis, W. (2008) 'Health security as a public health concept: a critical analysis', *Health Policy and Planning*, 23: 369–375.

Asante, A. and Zwi A. (2007) 'Public-private partnerships and global health equity: prospects and challenges', *Indian Journal of Medical Ethics*, 4: 176–180.

Black, R., Morris, S. and Bryce, J. (2003) 'Where and why are 10 million children dying every year?', *The Lancet*, 371: 2226–2234.

Bolken, T.C. and Hruby, D.E. (2008) 'Discovery and development of antiviral drugs for biodefense: Experience of a small biotechnology company', *Antiviral Research*, 77: 1–5.

Bond, E.C. (2001) 'Public/private sector partnership for emerging infections', *Emerging Infectious Diseases*, 7: 522–525.

Buse, K. and Waxman, A. (2001) 'Public–private health partnerships: a strategy for WHO', *Bulletin of the World Health Organization*, 79: 748–754.

Cameron, A., Ewen, M., Ross-Degnan, D., Ball, D. and Laing, R. (2009) 'Medicine prices, availability, and affordability in 36 developing and middle-income countries: a secondary analysis', *The Lancet*, 373: 240–249.

Croft, S. (2005) 'Public-private partnership: from there to here', *Transactions of the Royal Society of Tropical Medicine and Hygiene*, 99(Suppl): S9–14.

Curley, M. and Thomas, N. (2004) 'Human security and public health in Southeast Asia: the SARS outbreak', *Australian Journal of International Affairs*, 58: 17–32.

Davies, S.E. (2008) 'Securitizing infectious disease', *International Affairs*, 84: 295–313.

Elbe, S. (2010) 'Haggling over viruses: the downside risks of securitizing infectious disease', *Health Policy and Planning*, 25: 476–485.

Elbe, S. (2011) 'Should health professionals play the global health security card?', *The Lancet*, 378: 220–221.

Fidler, D.P. (2004) 'Germs, governance, and global public health in the wake of SARS', *The Journal of Clinical Investigation*, 113: 799–804.

Fidler, D.P. and Gostin, L.O. (2006) 'The new International Health Regulations: an historic development for international law and public health', *Journal of Law, Medicine & Ethics*, 34: 85–94.

Garrett, L. and Alavian, E.H. (2010) 'Global health governance in a G-20 world', *Global Health Governance*, 4: 1–14.

Gilfillan, L., Smith, B.T., Inglesby, T.V., Kodulkla, K., Schuler, A., Lister, M. and O'Toole, T. (2004) 'Taking the measure of countermeasures: leaders' views on the nation's capacity to develop biodefense countermeasures', *Biosecurity and Biodefense*, 2: 320–327.

Heymann, D.L. (2004) 'The international response to the outbreak of SARS in 2003', *Philosophical Transactions of the Royal Society B*, 359: 1127–1129.

Hoffman, S.J. (2010) 'The evolution, etiology and eventualities of the global health security regime', *Health Policy and Planning*, 25: 510–522.

Hossain, P., Kawar, B. and Nahas, M. (2007) 'Obesity and diabetes in the developing world: a growing challenge', *New England Journal of Medicine*, 356: 213–215.

Jamison, D.T., Breman, J.G. and Measham, A.R. (2006). 'Cost-effective strategies for noncommunicable diseases, risk factors, and behaviors', in D.T. Jamison (ed.), *Priorities in Health*, Washington, DC: World Bank.

Jones, G., Stekeetee, R., Black, R.E., Bhutta, Z. and Morris, S. (2003) 'How many child deaths can we prevent this year?', *Lancet*, 362: 65–71.

Kamradt-Scott, A. (2012) 'Evidence-based medicine and the governance of pandemic influenza', *Global Public Health*, 7: S111–S126.

Kamradt-Scott, A. and McInnes, C. (2012) 'The securitisation of pandemic influenza: Framing, security and public policy', *Global Public Health*, 7: S95–S110.

Katz, R. and Fischer, J. (2010) 'The revised International Health Regulations: a framework for global pandemic response', *Global Health Governance*, 3: 1–18

Magnusson, R.S. (2010) 'Global health governance and the challenge of chronic, non-communicable disease', *Journal of Law, Medicine & Ethics*, 38: 490–507.

Marchal, B., Cavalli, A. and Kegels, G. (2009) 'Global health actors claim to support health system strengthening: is this reality or rhetoric?', *PLoS Medicine*, 6: 1–5.

Mathers, C. and Loncar, D. (2006) 'Projections of global mortality and burden of disease from 2002 to 2030', *PLoS Medicine*, 3: 2011–2030.

McInnes, C. and Lee, K. (2006) 'Health, security and foreign policy', *Review of International Studies*, 32: 5–23.

Moran, M. (2005) 'A breakthrough in R&D for neglected diseases: new ways to get the drugs we need', *PLoS Medicine*, 2: e302.

Moran, M. and Stevenson, M. (2013) 'Illumination and innovation: what philanthropic foundations bring to global health governance', *Global Society*, 27: 117–37.

Mounier-Jack, S., Jas, R. and Coker, R. (2007) 'Progress and shortcomings in European national strategic plans for pandemic influenza', *Bulletin of the World Health Organization*, 85: 923–929.

Naves, J.O.S. and Silver, L.D. (2005) 'Evaluation of pharmaceutical assistance in public primary care in Brasília, Brazil', *Revista de Saúde Pública*, 39: 223–230.

Nsubuga, P., Nwanyanwu, O., Nkengasong, J.N., Mukanga, D. and Trostle, M. (2010) 'Strengthening public health surveillance and response using the health systems strengthening agenda in developing countries', *BMC Public Health*, 10: 1–5.

Nwaka, S. (2005) 'Drug discovery and beyond: the role of public-private partnerships in improving access to new malaria medicines' *Transactions of the Royal Society of Tropical Medicine and Hygiene*, 99: S20–S29.

Ollila, E. (2005) 'Global health priorities: priorities of the wealthy?', *Globalization and Health*, 1: 1–5.

Reich, M.R. and Takemi, K. (2009) 'G8 and strengthening of health systems: follow-up to the Toyako summit', *The Lancet*, 373: 508–515.

Rodier, G., Greenspan, A.L., Hughes, J.M. and Heymann, D.L. (2007) 'Global public health security', *Emerging Infectious Diseases*, 13: 1447–1452.

Sheridan, C. (2005) 'The business of making vaccines', *Nature Biotechnology*, 23: 1359–1366.

Shiffman, J. (2006) 'Donor funding priorities for communicable disease control in the developing world', *Health Policy and Planning*, 21: 411–420.

Sorte, W.F., Jr. (2012) 'The production and R&D structure of the Brazilian pharmaceutical industry: the role of public procurement and public drug production', *Global Public Health*, 7: 1062–1079.

Trouiller, P. and Olliaro, P. (1999) 'Development output from 1975 to 1996: what proportion for tropical diseases?', *International Journal of Infectious Diseases*, 3: 61–63.

United Nations Development Program (UNDP). (1994) *Human Development Report 1994: New Dimensions of Human Security*, New York: Oxford University Press.

United Nations Millennium Project. (2005) *Prescription for Healthy Development: Increasing Access to Essential Medicines: Report of the Task Force on HIV/AIDS, Malaria, TB, and Access to Medicines, Working Group on Access to Essential Medicines*, London: Earthscan.

Waldie, P. and Robertson, G. (2012, August 23) 'How vaccines became big business', *Globe and Mail*. Online. Available HTTP: <http://m.theglobeandmail.com/life/health-and-fitness/health/conditions/how-vaccines-became-big-business/article572731/?service=mobile> (accessed 26 June 2013).

Widdus, R. (2001) 'Public–private partnerships for health: their main targets, their diversity, and their future directions', *Bulletin of the World Health Organization*, 79: 713–720.

Wild, S., Roglic, G., Green, A., Sicree, R. and King, H. (2004) 'Global prevalence of diabetes estimates for the year 2000 and projections for 2030', *Diabetes Care*, 27: 1047–1053.

Wilson, D. (2012) 'Deepening drug shortages', *Health Affairs*, 31: 263–266.

Wilson, K.R., Kohler, J.C. and Ovtcharenko, N. (2012) 'The make or buy debate: considering the limitations of domestic production in Tanzania', *Global Health*, 8: 20.

Wheeler, C. and Berkley, S. (2001) 'Initial lessons from public–private partnerships in drug and vaccine development', *Bulletin of the World Health Organization*, 79: 728–734.

World Health Organization (WHO). (2003) *The World Health Report 2003: Shaping the Future*, Geneva: World Health Organization.

World Health Organization (WHO). (2006) *The World Health Report 2006: Working Together for Health*, Geneva: World Health Organization.

World Health Organization (WHO). (2007) *The World Health Report 2007: A Safer Future*, Geneva: World Health Organization.

28

WHOSE INTERESTS IS THE SECURITIZATION OF HEALTH SERVING?

Debra L. DeLaet

In an age when national security concerns continue to dominate both the domestic and foreign policy agendas of many states, securitization has become an increasingly common phenomenon. Securitization involves the practice of constructing and framing specific phenomena as national security issues (Waever 1995: 57–58). Securitization dynamics have shaped a wide range of policy arenas, including issues like "terrorism" and immigration (with its connections to border control) that purportedly have fundamental associations with traditional national security concerns. More interestingly, states and other actors are increasingly securitizing policy areas that traditionally have been conceptualized as existing outside of the realm of national security, including human rights and the environment. Global health initiatives have not been resistant to this trend, and international organizations, states, and nongovernmental organizations increasingly frame global health challenges as potential national security issues (Fidler 2007: 41–66). The logic of securitization suggests that policy areas will accrue benefits, namely increased saliency, prioritization, and funding, via being framed as national security issues. The successful securitization of HIV/AIDS as a global health challenge is a prominent case in point. The priority status of HIV/AIDS on the global health agenda is due, in part, to the fact that this issue has been successfully framed as a threat to security at both the national and global levels.

Although it has potential benefits, health securitization also risks producing significant costs. Securitization tends to activate state-centric policy responses that shift scarce resources away from public health actors and initiatives towards already well-funded security institutions and programs. Additionally, even though successful health securitization efforts have led to increases in absolute spending on global health issues, it has diverted funds away from critical, poverty-related health challenges and solutions towards single, securitized illnesses, most prominently HIV/AIDS, in ways that do not reflect the global burden of disease. In examining the relative costs and benefits of health securitization, this chapter illuminates whose interests are – and are not – being served by the securitization of global health. The chapter ultimately suggests that securitization has been shaped more by the interests of relatively privileged populations, especially in developed countries, whereas the costs are more likely to be borne by marginalized groups in both developed and developing countries.

Health securitization: National security or human security?

The securitization debate – in global health as in other issue areas – implicates fundamental questions about the nature and meaning of security in world politics. Discussions of the relative advantages or disadvantages of securitization often proceed without a clear conceptualization of the nature of the "security" that undergirds the securitization of global issues (Aldis 2008: 370–372). Likewise, questions regarding whether health securitization represents a rational response to specific health challenges that genuinely threaten national security or whether it has been pursued primarily as a political strategy to raise the profile of particular global health initiatives too often go unexamined. Given these complexities, it makes sense to begin this chapter with an exploration of the contested meanings of – and rationales for – the concept of security in the health securitization debate.

Traditionally, the discipline of International Relations has focused on *national security*, conceptualized as state security from external military threats. Conversely, *human security* is a conception of security that focuses on the well-being of *individual* human beings. Unlike national security, the concept of human security encompasses internal as well as external threats to human well-being and seeks to detach the concept of security from militarization. In 1994, the United Nations Development Programme (UNDP) put human security prominently on the international policy agenda. The UNDP offered a very broad conception of security as being primarily concerned with individual human beings rather than states and as encompassing economic, health, and social well-being rather than simply freedom from violence (United Nations Development Programme 1994: 22).

An examination of the relative influence of national security versus human security paradigms on health securitization is revealing. In terms of the number and quality of human lives at stake, health challenges are, first and foremost, threats to *human security* rather than *national security*. Nevertheless, health securitization has proceeded largely within a national security paradigm. The disconnect between health as a challenge that primarily implicates human security and securitization as a state-centric response grounded in considerations of national security raises serious questions about the effectiveness of securitization as a tool for advancing the promotion of health.

Across the globe, preventable infectious diseases, in terms of sheer numbers, threaten far more people than war or other forms of militarized conflict. In both developing and developed countries, disease is the greatest threat to human life. In fact, "infectious disease morbidity and mortality far exceed war-related death and disability in human history" (Fidler 2003: 807). Communicable illnesses, especially upper respiratory infections, diarrhea, and tuberculosis, kill an average of 17 million people in the developing world each year (United Nations Development Programme 1994: 27–28). This number far outweighs annual war-related deaths across the globe. Notably, most of these deaths are preventable, many of them striking children under 5 years of age. Low-income populations, in the developed as well as developing world, are also more likely to die from these treatable diseases.

Similarly, noncommunicable illnesses represent a large and growing percentage of the global burden of disease (see also Benson & Glasgow, chapter 15 in this volume). Even in low-income countries, noncommunicable illnesses have become leading causes of morbidity and mortality. For instance, heart disease has emerged as the second leading cause of death in low-income countries, causing a higher percentage of deaths than diarrheal illnesses and behind only lower respiratory infections (World Health Organization 2008: 12.) As in the case of communicable illnesses, noncommunicable diseases cause far more morbidity and mortality than militarized conflict.

To be sure, evidence of potential linkages between global health and national security exists. Price-Smith asserts that the Spanish Influenza epidemic of 1918–1919 helped contribute to the defeat of Austria and Germany in World War I, largely because the disease had higher prevalence and mortality rates among Austrian and German troops and thereby contributed to the capitulation of these powers (Price-Smith 2009: 33–56). In a similar vein, some scholars have asserted that the staggering HIV prevalence rates in many southern African countries may undermine the military preparedness and combat effectiveness of the armed forces in these countries (Elbe 2002: 159–177; Heinecken 2001: 7–17). These examples suggest that the invocation of health as a national security concern may be warranted in some cases.

However, health challenges primarily threaten national security in indirect ways – by displacing people across borders, by depleting a state's material resources, or by undermining state capacity. Epidemic disease can contribute to state collapse and violent conflict within a country just as political violence can serve to amplify the spread of communicable illnesses that further undermine political stability with potential national security consequences (Fidler 2003: 787–856). Furthermore, public health challenges also clearly affect the interests of states; because a state's military power is fundamentally shaped by its material resources, any public health challenge that depletes those resources has the potential to undermine the state's security interests. According to Price-Smith, high prevalence of communicable illnesses in countries and regions reduces state capacity by increasing poverty, contributing to state failure, and generating instability within countries and regions (Price-Smith 2009: 16–17). Notably, the mechanisms by which health challenges may come to threaten national security tend to be more prominent in low-income, less-developed countries (Price-Smith 2009: 179). Similar dynamics involving the deterioration of state capacity, the displacement of populations across territorial borders, and epidemic disease outbreaks in refugee camps, are common in war-affected regions, suggesting that a public health/national security linkage may be the norm rather than the exception in zones of conflict (Price-Smith 2009: 179).

In contrast to the largely indirect linkages between health and national security, health challenges are a clear and direct threat to human security. Despite this, the preponderance of the evidence suggests that the global discourse of health securitization has largely proceeded within a national security paradigm. The concept of human security has been invoked in the securitization debate in global health. Nevertheless, Simon Rushton contends that the dominant global discourse on health security actually represents a significant consensus in which a national security model prevails and in which rapidly spreading infectious diseases, HIV/AIDS, and biological weapons/bioterrorism represent the primary threats (Rushton 2011: 782).

Both historical and contemporary examples indicate that health securitization has foundations in traditional, state-centric conceptions of security. For instance, 19th century European powers, concerned that "tropical" diseases might threaten their imperial power and commercial interests abroad, set up centers and programs for the treatment of tropical illnesses. These centers represent state-led responses to health challenges conceptualized as potential national security threats (Fidler 2003: 848–849). Also in the 19th century, European militaries were at the forefront of national efforts to promote sanitary reforms because they saw such measures as necessary to ensure military preparedness (Fidler 2003: 848–849). These historical examples suggest a process of health securitization with deep roots in a national security paradigm.

More recently, in the United States, the Central Intelligence Agency's National Intelligence Council identified infectious diseases as potential threats to national security in its report, issued in January 2000, titled *The Global Infectious Disease Threat and its Implications for the United States*. In a similar development that same month, the UN Security Council took up the issue of the HIV/AIDS crisis in sub-Saharan Africa. The UN Charter gives the Security Council the primary responsibility for the maintenance of international peace and security, but this body does not have charter-based authority over nonsecurity issues in international affairs. Thus, the fact that the

Security Council dealt with the issue of HIV/AIDS (and passed Resolution 1308 on the subject in July 2000) signals that the international community frames important global health challenges, like HIV/AIDS, as national security issues. A number of nongovernmental organizations, including the Center for Strategic and International Studies and the International Crisis Group, also have issued reports that have identified global health challenges as potential threats to national security (Fidler 2003: 793–794).

Given the prominence of health challenges as threats to the human life, health securitization grounded in the concept of human security arguably has a compelling logic. However, as Davies (2010: 1189) notes, securitization that does not invoke statist concerns has not gained traction, and the dominant global discourses on health security have primarily been undergirded by national security concerns, including a preoccupation with biological weapons, HIV/AIDS, and specific types of infectious diseases – namely, those diseases perceived to have the greatest risk of crossing borders and causing regional or global pandemics. Poverty-related infectious diseases that constitute a high proportion of the burden of disease but are perceived as more readily containable within specific territories – for example, diarrheal diseases – have not risen to the level of securitized health challenges (Rushton 2011: 782–783). In this regard, critics contend that health securitization may really be about "the protection of Western states from exogenous disease threats" rather than improving the health and quality of life of particularly vulnerable populations (Rushton 2011: 788). This raises questions over whether securitization is the best instrument for increasing the saliency, prioritization, and funding of health as a public policy priority.

Securitization and the global health agenda

Because it has been grounded primarily in a national security framework, health securitization may distort the global health agenda in inappropriate ways (see also Stevenson & Moran, chapter 27 in this volume). The successful securitization of a particular illness results in increased funding and a prioritized position on domestic and global policy agendas. To the extent that such increased funding and prioritization leads to positive health outcomes in the targeted area, it may be difficult to argue that health securitization is problematic. Yet, the process by which some diseases are securitized and others are not is a product of the political interests, strategic calculations, and influence of key actors in global health rather than a reflection of an objective assessment of where the most critical health needs exist.

The successful securitization of HIV/AIDS provides the most prominent example of this dilemma. In recent decades, HIV/AIDS funding has increased significantly in comparison to other important global health funding categories. Global funding for HIV/AIDS initiatives increased from approximately 6% of all global health aid in 1998 to roughly half of total global health funding in 2007 (Shiffman et al. 2009: S45). The sheer magnitude and scale of the global AIDS crisis help to explain why global spending on this issue has increased so dramatically. Yet, spending on HIV/AIDS is disproportionate to its contribution to the global burden of disease, and spending on other global health problems that constitute a larger portion of the global burden of disease is much lower. The dramatic increase in funding for HIV/AIDS was paralleled by a significant decrease in the proportionate funding for other prominent global health issues. For instance, funding for health systems declined from roughly 62% to 26% of total health aid during this period. Similarly, funding for population and reproductive health declined from 26% to 12% of total health aid between 1998 and 2007 (Shiffman et al. 2009: S45).

In terms of absolute numbers, the gulf between spending on HIV/AIDS and other global health initiatives is vast. Global health aid directed towards HIV/AIDS rose from U.S. $300 million in 1996 to U.S. $15.6 billion in 2008 (Joint United Nations Programme on HIV/AIDS and the Henry J. Kaiser Family Foundation 2009: 3). This figure includes aid from national governments, multilateral funding organizations, most prominently the Global Fund to Fight AIDS, TB, and Malaria, and the private sector. Development funds for health initiatives to fight tuberculosis and malaria were smaller but still significant. In 2007, global donors spent U.S. $0.6 billion on tuberculosis programs and U.S. $0.7 billion on malaria programs (Institute for Health Metrics and Evaluation 2009: 25). Notably, HIV/AIDS received much higher levels of funding than either tuberculosis or malaria despite the fact that both of these diseases account for a higher percentage of the burden of disease in low and middle income countries.

Supporters of increased spending on HIV/ AIDS contend that it may have spillover benefits in other issue areas and may contribute to the development of health systems within recipient countries by raising the profile of public health as a policy priority, strengthening public health infrastructure, and expanding access to primary health care services as vulnerable populations participate in HIV treatment programs (Shiffman et al. 2009; Yu et al. 2008). Moreover, due to the dire demographic and social consequences of HIV/AIDS in "hyper-endemic" countries, some scholars argue that disproportionate levels of global health aid are warranted (Smith et al. 2011: 345–356).

However, critics argue that disproportionate spending on HIV/AIDS has inappropriately diverted global health aid from larger priorities in recipient countries (Poku & Whitman 2012: 146–161). According to this perspective, disproportionate funding for HIV/AIDS undermines the development of strong national health systems by crowding out funding for general health care and other critical health priorities (Lordan et al. 2011: 351–355; Shiffman et al. 2009). According to critics, global health aid directed at HIV/AIDS not only inappropriately diverts funding from other health priorities but also draws critical health care personnel away from work in key sectors of the health care system for more lucrative positions with HIV/AIDS programs (Yu et al. 2008).

A consideration of the effects of increased global spending on HIV/AIDS on global women's health initiatives is instructive. Women constitute a majority of the HIV-infected population in many countries with high HIV prevalence rates and are among the primary beneficiaries of the increase in global health aid for HIV/AIDS. Indeed, funding for maternal and child health has actually increased in tandem with the growth in HIV/AIDS funding. For example, development assistance for maternal and child health increased by 105% between 2003 and 2008 (Pitt et al. 2010: 1485–96). Notably, this increase has come about largely because a significant portion of global health aid in this area is channeled through HIV/AIDS programs. In this regard, the increase in maternal/child health funding in recent decades has primarily been a vehicle for targeting health challenges associated with HIV/AIDS rather than distinct maternal/child health problems, including neonatal infections, birth asphyxia and trauma, prematurity/low birth weight, and diarrheal diseases (one of the leading causes of child morbidity and mortality in developing regions).

Despite the fact that global health aid for maternal/child health programs has increased in conjunction with the dramatic growth in spending on HIV/AIDS, it is significantly lower in absolute terms than global health aid for HIV/AIDS (Pitt et al. 2010: 1485–96). Furthermore, the correspondence between spending and the global burden of disease is highly distorted in the case of maternal/child health. Maternal/child health problems constitute a large proportion of the burden of disease for women in countries with high HIV prevalence rates that is significantly disproportionate to the amount of aid directed towards these problems. As in the case of HIV/AIDS, the pernicious economic, social, and political consequences of inadequate attention to women's health issues might warrant levels of spending higher than those suggested by the burden of disease alone. Yet, even with an increase in funding in recent decades, global health aid for maternal/child health remains well below what would be proportionate given burden of disease indicators.

The successful securitization of HIV/AIDS, then, has resulted in higher levels of spending that surely have produced improved health outcomes in targeted countries. However, similar levels of spending in other priority areas may have produced even better health outcomes and more sustainable long-term solutions in recipient countries. On this point, some scholars have noted that global HIV/AIDS initiatives have not been integrated with existing health programs and structures to the same degree as reproductive or maternal health programs. As a result, it might be argued that increased funding for reproductive and maternal health would be more likely to generate spillover benefits than HIV/AIDS initiatives that typically have been implemented as vertical, crisis-driven programs (Windisch et. al 2011).

The distorting effects produced by the securitization of HIV/AIDS – a process driven significantly by the United States and the Joint United Nations Program on HIV/AIDS (Viera 2007: 146) – are illustrative of the ways in which health securitization is primarily defined and driven by the interests of key non-state and state actors, primarily located in high-income, developed countries. Specifically, the illnesses most likely to cross borders and to threaten the interests of populations in developed countries – such as HIV/AIDS – have been constructed as security threats whereas many poverty-related illnesses that cause greater morbidity and mortality in developing countries have not (Labonté & Gagnon 2010: 4–5). To this end, securitization functions as a containment strategy and has parallels with state responses to more traditional, militarized threats to national security.

Not surprisingly, governing elites in developing countries often articulate dramatically different perspectives about health priorities and have resisted the securitization of global health because of the ways in which it limits their ability to direct health aid towards the health priorities that they define for themselves and instead shifts public policy debates and spending towards those health challenges perceived as exogenous threats to the national security of developed countries. Thus, the securitization of health represents a state-centric response to health governance. Like the prevailing state-centric modes of international interactions, health securitization "privileges the protection of the most powerful states in the international system" and "heightens unease about 'whose security' really counts" (Rushton 2011: 791, 780).

The risks of securitization for marginalized groups

Not only does a state-centric vision of the nexus between global health and security risk privileging the interests of the powerful, it also generates discriminatory effects that harm marginalized groups and that produce resistance to public health initiatives among these groups. Because health securitization has been grounded largely in a national security paradigm, it tends to activate two types of responses: surveillance and emergency response (Rushton 2011: 784). In both cases, securitized responses focus on containing the risks of outbreak rather than addressing root causes of health challenges (Rushton 2011: 784). Such containment strategies typically emphasize the identification and isolation of at-risk groups. Because marginalized groups are particularly vulnerable to many illnesses due to a complicated array of socioeconomic factors, securitized responses often target minority populations as a first line of defense. In turn, the discriminatory elements of public health initiatives have commonly lead marginalized groups to develop a rational suspicion of public health endeavors.

In general, public health measures can produce discriminatory and repressive effects among marginalized populations, and health securitization is likely to amplify such effects. The use of quarantines to control epidemic outbreaks, aggressive vaccination programs that integrate security personnel in implementation strategies, and disease surveillance activities targeted at particularly vulnerable (often minority) populations are all examples of the kinds of securitized public health responses that may be implemented in discriminatory ways and that may violate civil liberties (see also Amon, chapter 24 in this volume).

Michael Willrich has identified the "turn-of-the-century war against smallpox" in the United States as "one of the most important civil liberties struggles of the twentieth century" (Willrich 2011: 24). Central to this struggle were fundamental questions about compulsory vaccination, privacy, bodily integrity, and freedom of religion as it related to questions of medical practices. Resistance to compulsory vaccination led many "antivaccinationists" to withdraw from the public sphere when faced with smallpox, ultimately undermining public efforts to eradicate the disease (Willrich 2011: 39). The practice of forcibly quarantining sick individuals and "suspects" believed to have been exposed to the disease in overcrowded and squalid pesthouses where their basic needs were neglected not only contributed to the resistance to public health initiatives but also likely exacerbated the spread of the disease (Willrich 2011: 60). The racial dimension of this problem – most of the people quarantined in destitute pesthouses were African American, and local authorities sometimes tried to contain smallpox by quarantining entire African American neighborhoods – underscores the discriminatory effects of securitized public health measures (Willrich 2011: 102).

The complicated intersections between securitization and public health as they relate to migration effectively illustrate the exclusionary and discriminatory dimensions of health securitization. Public health initiatives have long served as mechanisms for racial exclusion among migrant populations (Horton & Barker 2009: 784–785). Discussing an historical example of the medical screening of Mexican migrants in the early 20th century, Stern argues that the convergence of medicalization and militarization "worked to create a regime of eugenic gatekeeping on the U.S.-Mexican border that aimed to ensure the putative purity of the 'American' family-nation while generating long-lasting stereotypes of Mexicans as filthy, lousy, and prone to irresponsible breeding" (Stern 2005: 58–59). Over time, public health has become increasingly entangled with border control in the United States. In particular, the increased militarization of the U.S.–Mexican border has been accompanied by more aggressive public health interventions targeted at migrant populations. Heightened border patrol efforts have involved expanded medical screenings that have been deployed with discriminatory profiling. In turn, militarized and medicalized border patrol efforts give weight to a view of Mexican migrants as "inferior" and threatening. In the end, such dynamics reinforce perceptions that migrants are a threat to both health and national security and that health securitization is an appropriate and critical response.

Aggressive global vaccination campaigns also demonstrate the potential pitfalls of health securitization. The World Health Organization's pursuit of an assertive vaccination campaign aimed at the eradication of smallpox in the 1970s is illustrative. After recognizing the persistence of the disease in countries plagued by civil conflict and natural disasters, the WHO adopted more aggressive methods involving surveillance and containment. The WHO encouraged governments to adopt methods involving active surveillance of villages and remote areas for signs of the disease. WHO and local health workers worked together to quickly isolate infected individuals and vaccinate populations in areas where they found active cases of infection, and national militaries, paramilitaries, and local police forces used force to counter opposition to the vaccination campaign in some instances (Bhattacharya 2008: 911–912).

Although global vaccination campaigns are among the most successful public health initiatives, the legacy of such campaigns also includes cultural resistance to vaccination programs, especially in developing countries. For example, some political and religious groups in various Indian and Pakistani communities assert that the WHO polio vaccination campaign is actually a hidden family planning campaign, targeted particularly at Muslim families (Salim 2012: 96–97). As a result, many families in these communities have refused to allow their children to be vaccinated against polio; notably, cases of polio subsequently have surged in these areas. Similarly, members of target communities in southern Africa have been reluctant to participate in HIV vaccination trials due to fear that the HIV/AIDS epidemic is, in fact, a result of a "Western conspiracy" to infect local populations with the deadly disease (Sivela 2012: 55–57).

The risks of discrimination and repression associated with health securitization are heightened in a context where securitization as a general phenomenon has become one of the defining features of contemporary politics and governance. Due to its growing importance, securitization infuses almost every aspect of politics. In the case of health, the multifaceted nature of securitization means that not only are public health responses themselves securitized but also that public health actors and medical personnel are increasingly called upon to contribute to national security initiatives.

The effort to integrate public health actors and medical personnel in the creation of Homeland Security Fusion Centers (created under the authority of the U.S. Department of Homeland Security and the U.S. Department of Justice) is a striking example of this phenomenon. The role of public health and medical personnel in these centers is to gather, analyze, and share health information, "including health security risks, associated with the detection of suspicious biological or chemical agents within a community to law enforcement agencies" (Lenart et al. 2012: 174). Many states and cities have adopted fusion centers as a strategy for responding to potential terrorist threats, including threats with explicit connections to health, such as the intentional release of biological agents. According to proponents of this approach to "homeland security," "The ability to respond effectively to threats or events that place the country at risk is greatly enhanced when collection, analysis, synthesis and dissemination of public health and medical information and intelligence are included in the national network of anti-terrorism fusion centers" (Lenart et al. 2012: 175). However, such centers redirect scarce resources away from actual health programs, and public health personnel whose work is securitized will be more likely to pursue implementation strategies that isolate and discriminate against minority populations most likely to be perceived as potential security threats.

Ultimately, the fundamental goals of national security and public health are at odds. Successful public health initiatives require removing stigma associated with illness to invite the participation of vulnerable and medically underserved populations. When fused with national security concerns, the public health dimension of the project is likely to be diminished by intelligence gathering and surveillance. The racialized and exclusionary history of public health initiatives suggests that, when overlain with security imperatives, public health initiatives may be directed towards identifying "enemy others." An adversarial model of security is likely to render marginalized groups suspicious and threatening and, in this way, diminish their participation in public health initiatives. Unfortunately, when the goals of the competing projects of public health and securitization come into conflict, it is likely that a security logic will triumph.

Conclusion

Despite potential benefits in the form of increased political saliency and the generation of greater resources for global health initiatives, health securitization generates a number of costs that raise questions about its appropriateness as a political strategy for addressing important global health challenges. The securitization of health risks generating state-centric policy responses that shift scarce resources away from public health initiatives and empower police, intelligence, and military actors rather than public health or medical personnel. In a similar vein, the securitization of health risks distorting global health spending priorities by benefiting securitized diseases over other critical public health challenges in ways that do not necessarily reflect the burden of disease. The risks of the securitization of health are especially acute for marginalized populations, whom the state is more likely to perceive as potential security threats.

To be sure, increased spending on securitized illnesses, most notably HIV/AIDS, has saved lives. Nevertheless, the question remains whether more lives might be saved with fewer downside risks if the resources poured into securitized responses to health challenges were instead used to build public health infrastructure and national health care systems designed to address the poverty-related health challenges that are the greatest cause of preventable morbidity and mortality across the globe. A public health approach (while itself fraught with a history of exclusionary and discriminatory effects) would be less likely to generate counterproductive stigma and "othering" that undermines the effectiveness of public health endeavors in the long-run.

Unfortunately, because a national security paradigm remains the foundation of health securitization, it is likely to distort the global health agenda in ways that privilege the containment of specific high-profile illnesses over the poverty-related health challenges that constitute the highest percentage of the global burden of disease. State-centric, security-oriented solutions to global health challenges have led to narrow, vertical, single-disease approaches to health promotion rather than more broad-based, horizontal, and sustainable solutions intended to address the root causes of poverty-related health challenges. As a result, the process of health securitization is most likely to serve the interests of relatively privileged populations in developed countries while failing to address the most critical health needs of low-income populations, especially in developing countries. In the process, the costs of health securitization are most likely to be borne by marginalized populations everywhere.

References

Aldis, W. (2008) 'Health security as a public health concept: a critical analysis', *Health Policy and Planning*, 23: 369–375.

Bhattacharya, S. (2008) 'The World Health Organization and global smallpox eradication', *Journal of Epidemiology and Community Health*, 62: 909–912.

Davies, S.E. (2010) 'What contribution can international relations make to the evolving global health agenda?', *International Affairs*, 86: 1167–1190.

Elbe, S. (2002) 'HIV/AIDS and the changing landscape of war in Africa', *International Security*, 27: 159–177.

Fidler, D.P. (2003) 'Public health and national security in the global age: infectious diseases, bioterrorism, and realpolitik', *The George Washington International Law Review*, 35: 787–856.

Fidler, D.P. (2007) 'A pathology of public health securitism: approaching pandemics as security threats,' in A.F. Cooper, J.J. Kirton and T. Schrecker (eds.) *Governing Global Health*, Burlington: Ashgate Publishers.

Heinecken, L. (2001) 'Living in terror: the looming security threat to southern Africa,' *African Security Review*, 10: 7–17.

Horton, S. and Barker, J.C. (2009) '"Stains" on their self-discipline: public health, hygiene, and the disciplining of undocumented immigrant parents in the nation's internal borderlands', *American Ethnologist*, 36: 784–798.

Institute for Health Metrics and Evaluation. (2009) *Financing Global Health 2009: Tracking Development Assistance for Health*, Seattle: University of Washington. Online. Available HTTP: <http://www.healthmetricsandevaluation.org/publications/policy-report/financing-global-health-2009-tracking-development-assistance-health> (accessed 20 June 2013).

Joint United Nations Programme on HIV/AIDS (UNAIDS) and the Henry J. Kaiser Family Foundation. (2009) *Financing the Response to AIDS in Low- and Middle-Income Countries: International Assistance from the G8, European Commission, and Other Donor Governments in 2008*. Online. Available HTTP: <http://kaiserfamilyfoundation.files.wordpress.com/2013/01/7347–052.pdf> (accessed 20 June 2013).

Labonté, R. and Gagnon, M. (2010) 'Framing health and foreign policy: lessons for global health diplomacy', *Globalization and Health*, 6: 1–22.

Lenart, B., Albanese, J., Halstead, W., Schlegelmilch, J. and Paturas, J. (2012) 'Integrating public health and medical intelligence gathering into Homeland Security Fusion Centers', *Journal of Business Continuity and Emergency Planning*, 6: 174–179.

Lordan, G., Ki Tang, K. and Carmignani, F. (2011) 'Has HIV/AIDS displaced other health funding priorities? Evidence from a new dataset of development aid for health', *Social Science & Medicine*, 73: 351–355.

Poku, N. and Whitman, J. (2012) 'Developing country health systems and the governance of international HIV/AIDS funding', *International Journal of Health Planning and Management*, 27: 146–161.

Pitt, C., Greco, G., Powell-Jackson, T. and Mills, A. (2010) 'Countdown to 2015: assessment of Official Development Assistance to maternal, newborn, and child health between 2003–2008', *Lancet*, 376: 1485–96.

Price-Smith, A.T. (2009) *Contagion and Chaos: Disease, Ecology, and National Security in an Era of Globalization*, Cambridge: MIT Press.

Rushton, S. (2011) 'Global health security: security for whom? Security from what?' *Political Studies*, 59: 779–796.

Salim, F. (2012) 'Culture, politics, and religion: exploring resistance to vaccinations in South Asia', *Human Welfare*, 1: 91–104.

Shiffman, J., Berlan, D. and Hafner, T. (2009) 'Has aid for AIDS raised all funding boats?' *Journal of Acquired Immune Deficiency Syndromes*, 52: S45-S48.

Sivela, J. (2012) 'Infected condoms and pin-pricked oranges: an ethnographic study of AIDS legends in two townships in Cape Town', *Cultural Analysis*, 11: 45–66.

Smith, J., Ahmed, K. and Whiteside, A. (2011) 'Why HIV/AIDS should be treated as exceptional: arguments from Sub-Saharan Africa and Eastern Europe', *African Journal of AIDS Research*, 10: 345–356.

Stern, A.M. (2005) *Eugenic Nation: Faults and Frontiers of Better Breeding in Modern America*, Berkeley: University of California Press.

United Nations Development Programme. (1994) *Human Development Report 1994*, New York: Oxford University Press.

Viera, M.A. (2007) 'The securitization of the HIV/AIDS epidemic as a norm: a contribution to constructivist scholarship on the emergence and diffusion of international norms', *Brazilian Political Science Review*, 1: 137–181.

Waever, O. (1995) 'Securitization and desecuritization,' in R.D. Lipschutz (ed.) *On Security*, New York: Columbia University Press.

Willrich, M. (2011) *Pox: An American History*, New York: Penguin Press.

Windisch, R., De Savigny, D., Onadia, G., Somda, A., Wyss, K., Sié, A. and Kouyaté, B. (2011) 'HIV treatment and reproductive health in the health system in Burkina Faso: resource allocation and the need for integration', *Reproductive Health Matters*, 19: 163–175.

World Health Organization. (2008) *The Global Burden of Disease: 2004 Update*, Geneva: World Health Organization.

Yu, D., Souteyrand, Y., Banda, M.A., Kaufman, J. and Perriens, J.H. (2008) 'Investment in HIV/AIDS programs: does it help strengthen health systems in developing countries?' *Globalization and Health*, 4. Online. Available HTTP: <http://www.globalizationandhealth.com/content/pdf/1744-8603-4-8.pdf> (accessed 20 June 2013).

SELECT BIBLIOGRAPHY

Aaltola, M. (2012) *Understanding the Politics of Pandemic Scares: An Introduction to Global Politosomatics*, London: Routledge.

Abraham, T. (2011) 'The chronicle of a disease foretold: pandemic H1N1 and the construction of a global health security threat', *Political Studies*, 59: 797–812.

Aginam, O. and Rupiya, M. (eds.) (2012) *HIV/AIDS: The Security Sector in Africa*, New York: United Nations University Press.

Aldis, W. (2008) 'Health security as a public health concept: a critical analysis', *Health Policy and Planning*, 23: 369–373.

Alibek, K. (1999) *Biohazard*, London: Arrow.

Altman, D. (2003) 'HIV and security', *International Relations*, 17: 417–427.

ASCI [AIDS, Security and Conflict Initiative] (2009) *HIV/AIDS, Security and Conflict: New Realities, New Responses*, New York: Social Science Research Council. Online. Available HTTP: <www.ssrc.org/workspace/images/crm/new_publication_3/%7Be2090d2b-72a8-de11-9d32-001cc477ec70%7D.pdf> (accessed 20 January 2014).

Ban, J. (2003) 'Health as a global security challenge', *Seton Hall Journal of Diplomacy and International Relations*, 4: 19–28.

Barnett, T. (2006) 'A long-wave event. HIV/AIDS, politics, governance and "security": sundering the intergenerational bond?', *International Affairs*, 82: 297–313.

Barnett, T. & Prins, G. (2006) 'HIV/AIDS and security: fact, fiction and evidence – a report to UNAIDS', *International Affairs*, 82: 359–368.

Bashford, A. (ed.) *Medicine at the Border: Disease Globalization and Security from 1859 to the Present*, Basingstoke, UK: Palgrave Macmillan.

Beigbeder, Y. (1998) 'The World Health Organization and peacekeeping', *International Peacekeeping*, 5: 31–48.

Benatar, S. (2005) 'The HIV/AIDS pandemic: a sign of instability in a complex global system', in A. Van Niekerk and L. Kopelman (eds.) *Ethics and AIDS in Africa: The Challenge to Our Thinking*, Claremont: David Philip Publishers.

Bonventre, E.V., Hicks, K.H. and Okutani, S.M. (2009) *U.S. National Security and Global Health: An Analysis of Global Health Engagement by the U.S. Department of Defense*, Washington DC: Center for Strategic and International Studies.

Brower, J. and Chalk, P. (2003) *The Global Threat of New and Re-emerging Infectious Diseases: Reconciling US National Security and Public Health*. Santa Monica, CA: RAND Corporation.

Brundtland, G.H. (2003) 'Global health and international security', *Global Governance*, 9: 417–423.

Caballero-Anthony, M. (2005) 'SARS in Asia: crisis, vulnerabilities and regional responses', *Asian Survey*, 45: 475–495.

Caballero-Anthony, M. (2006) 'Combating infectious diseases in East Asia: securitization and global public goods for health and human security', *Journal of International Affairs*, 59: 105–127.

Caceres, S.B. (2011) 'Global health security in an era of global health threats', *Emerging Infectious Diseases*, 17: 1962–1963.

Carus, W.S. (2001) *Bioterrorism and Biocrimes: The Illicit Use of Biological Agents in the 20th Century*, Washington, DC: National Defense University.

Center for Strategic and International Studies (2000) *Contagion and Conflict: Health as a Global Security Challenge*, Washington, DC: Center for Strategic and International Studies.

Chan, M., Støre, J.G., and Kouchner, B. (2008) 'Foreign policy and global public health: working together towards common goals', *Bulletin of the World Health Organization*, 86: 498.

Chen, L.C. (2004) 'Health as a human security priority for the 21st century', paper for Helsinki Process Human Security Track III. Online. Available HTTP: <http://citeseerx.ist.psu.edu/viewdoc/download?-doi=10.1.1.176.681&rep=rep1&type=pdf> (accessed 27 June 2013).

Chen, L.C., Leaning, J. and Narashimhan, V. (eds.) (2003) *Global Health Challenges for Human Security*, Cambridge, MA: Harvard University Press.

Chen, L.C. and Narasimhan, V. (2003) 'Human security and global health', *Journal of Human Development and Capabilities*, 4: 181–190.

Chow, J.C. (1996) 'Health and international security', *The Washington Quarterly*, 19: 63–77.

Collier, S.J. and Lakoff, A. (eds.) (2008) *Biosecurity Interventions: Global Health and Security in Question*, New York: Columbia University Press.

Commission on Human Security. (2003) *Human Security Now: Protecting and Empowering People*, New York: Commission on Human Security.

Coupland, R. (2007) 'Security, insecurity and health', *Bulletin of the World Health Organization*, 85: 181–183.

Curley, M.G., and Herington, J. (2011) 'The securitisation of avian influenza: international discourses and domestic politics in Asia', *Review of International Studies*, 37: 141–166.

Curley, M. and Thomas, N. (2004) 'Human security and public health in Southeast Asia: the SARS outbreak' *Australian Journal of International Affairs*, 58: 17–32.

Davies, S.E. (2008) 'Securitizing infectious disease', *International Affairs*, 84: 295–313.

Davies, S.E. (2010) *Global Politics of Health,* Cambridge: Polity Press.

Elbe, S. (2002) 'HIV/AIDS and the changing landscape of war in Africa', *International Security*, 27: 159–177.

Elbe, S. (2006) 'Should HIV/AIDS be securitized? The ethical dilemmas of linking HIV/AIDS and security', *International Studies Quarterly*, 50: 119–144.

Elbe, S. (2009) *Virus Alert: Security, Governmentality and the AIDS Pandemic*, New York: Columbia University Press.

Elbe, S. (2010) 'Haggling over viruses: the downside risks of securitizing infectious disease', *Health Policy and Planning,* 25: 476–485.

Elbe, S. (2010) *Security and Global Health: Towards the Medicalization of Insecurity*, Cambridge: Polity Press.

Elbe, S. (2011) 'Pandemics on the radar screen: health security, infectious disease and the medicalisation of insecurity', *Political Studies*, 59: 848–866.

Elbe, S. (2011) 'Should health professionals play the global health security card?', *The Lancet*, 378: 220–221.

Enemark, C.P. (2010) 'Law in the time of anthrax: biosecurity lessons from the United States', *Journal of Law and Medicine*, 17: 748–760.

Epstein, P.R. (2005) 'Climate change and human health', *New England Journal of Medicine*, 353: 1433–1436.

Evans, J. (2010) 'Pandemics and national security', *Global Security Studies*, 1: 100–109.

Feldbaum, H. (2009) *U.S. Global Health and National Security Policy*, Washington DC: Center for Strategic and International Studies.

Feldbaum, H., Lee, K. and Patel, P. (2006) 'The national security implications of HIV/AIDS', *PLoS Medicine,* 3. doi:10.1371/journal.pmed.0030171

Feldbaum, H., Patel, P., Sondorp, E., and Lee, K. (2006) 'Global health and national security: the need for critical engagement', *Medicine, Conflict and Survival*, 22: 192–198.

Fidler, D.P. (1998) 'Microbialpolitik: infectious diseases and international relations', *American University International Law Journal*, 14: 1–53.

Fidler, D.P. (2003) 'Public health and national security in the global age: infectious diseases, bioterrorism and realpolitik', *George Washington International Law Review*, 35: 787–856.

Fidler, D.P. (2004) 'Germs, governance, and global public health in the wake of SARS', *Journal of Clinical Investigation*, 113: 799–804.

Fidler, D.P. (2005) 'From International Sanitary Conventions to global health security: the new International Health Regulations', *Chinese Journal of International Law,* 4: 325–392.

Fidler, D.P. (2007) 'A pathology of public health securitism: approaching pandemics as security threats', in A.F. Cooper, J.J. Kirton and T. Schrecker (eds.) *Governing Global Health: Challenge, Response, Innovation*, Aldershot, UK: Ashgate.

Fidler, D.P. and Gostin, L. (2008) *Biosecurity in the Global Age: Biological Weapons, Public Health and the Rule of Law*, Stanford, CA: Stanford University Press.

Fischer, J. and Katz, R. (2010) 'The revised International Health Regulations: a framework for global pandemic response', *Global Health Governance*, 3(2), pp. 1–18.

Fourie, P. (2009) 'The relationship between the AIDS pandemic and state fragility' in P. Fourie, S. Maclean and S. Brown (eds.) *Health for Some: The Political Economy of Global Health Governance*, New York: Palgrave Macmillan.

Fourie, P. and Schönteich, M. (2002) 'Africa's new security threat', *African Security Review*, 10: 29–44.

Fox, W.C. (1997/1998) 'Phantom warriors: disease as a threat to US national security', *Parameters*, 27: 121–136.

Frenk, J. (2009) 'Strengthening health systems to promote security', *The Lancet*, 373: 2181–2182.

Frist, W. (2007) 'Medicine as a currency for peace through global health diplomacy', *Yale Law and Policy Review*, 26: 209–229.

Gallup, J.L. and Sachs, J.D. (2001) 'The economic burden of malaria', *American Journal of Tropical Medicine and Hygiene*, 64: 85–96.

Garber, R. (2002) 'Health as a bridge for peace: theory, practice, and prognosis – reflections of a practitioner', *Journal of Peacebuilding and Development*, 1: 69–84.

Garrett, L. (1994) *The Coming Plague: Newly Emergent Diseases in a World out of Balance*, New York: Farrar, Straus and Giroux.

Garrett, L. (2005) *HIV and National Security: Where Are The Links?* New York: Council on Foreign Relations.

Gayer, M., Legros, D., Formenty, P. and Connolly, M. A. (2007) 'Conflict and emerging infectious diseases', *Emerging Infectious Diseases,* 13: 1625–1631.

Ghobarah, H.A., Huth, P., and Russett, B. (2004) 'The post-war public health effects of civil conflict', *Social Science and Medicine*, 59: 869–884.

Guillemin, J. (2005) *Biological Weapons*, New York: Columbia University Press.

Gutlove, P. (1998) 'Health bridges for peace: integrating health care with community reconciliation', *Medicine, Conflict and Survival,* 14: 6–23.

Harman, S. (2012) *Global Health Governance*, New York: Routledge.

Heinecken, L. (2001) 'Living in terror: the looming security threat to southern Africa,' *African Security Review*, 10: 7–17.

Hoffman, S.J. (2010) 'The evolution, etiology and eventualities of the global health security regime', *Health Policy and Planning*, 25: 510–522.

Hoyt, K. (2012) *Long Shot: Vaccines for National Defense*, Cambridge: Harvard University Press.

Huang, Y. (2013) 'Global Health, Civil Society and Regional Security', in R. Sukma and J. Gannon (eds.) *A Growing Force: Civil Society's Role in Asian Regional Security*, Tokyo: Japan Center for Economic Research.

Ingram, A. (ed.) (2004) *Health, Foreign Policy and Security: Towards a Conceptual Framework for Research and Policy*, UK Global Health Programme, Working Paper No.2, London: The Nuffield Trust.

Ingram, A. (2007) 'HIV/AIDS, security and the geopolitics of US-Nigerian relations', *Review of International Political Economy*, 14: 510–534.

Ingram, A. (2008) 'Pandemic anxiety and global health security' in R. Pain and S.J. Smith (eds.) *Fear: Critical Geopolitics and Everyday Life.* Aldershot, UK: Ashgate.

Ingram, A. (2011) 'The Pentagon's HIV/AIDS programmes: governmentality, political economy, security', *Geopolitics,* 16: 655–674.

Iqbal, Z. and Zorn, C. (2010) 'Violent conflict and the spread of HIV/AIDS in Africa', *Journal of Politics,* 72: 149–162.

Irwin, R. (2010) 'Indonesia, H5N1, and global health diplomacy', *Global Health Governance*, 3, pp. 1–21.

Kamradt-Scott, A. and Lee, K. (2011) 'The 2011 pandemic influenza preparedness framework: global health secured or a missed opportunity?' *Political Studies*, 59: 831–847.

Kamradt-Scott, A. and McInnes, C. (2012) 'The securitisation of pandemic influenza: Framing, security and public policy', *Global Public Health*, 7: S95–S110.

Karlen, A. (1996) *Man and Microbes: Diseases and Plagues in History and Modern Times,* New York: Touchstone.

Katz, R. and Singer, D. (2007) 'Health and security in foreign policy', *Bulletin of the World Health Organization,* 85: 233–234.

Kelle, A. (2007) 'Securitization of international public health: implications for global health governance and the biological weapons prohibition regime', *Global Governance*, 13: 217–235.

King, N.B. (2002) 'Security, disease, commerce: ideologies of postcolonial global health', *Social Studies of Science*, 32: 763–789.

Koblentz, G.D. (2009) *Living Weapons: Biological Warfare and International Security*, Ithaca: Cornell University Press.

Koblentz, G.D. (2010) 'Biosecurity reconsidered: calibrating biological threats and responses', *International Security*, 34: 96–132.

Koblentz, G.D. (2012) 'From biodefence to biosecurity: the Obama administration's strategy for countering biological threats', *International Affairs*, 88: 131–148.

Koblentz, G.D. and Tucker, J.B. (2010) 'Tracing an attack: the promise and pitfalls of microbial forensics', *Survival*, 52: 159–186.

Kruk, M.E., Freedman, L.P., Anglin, G.A., Waldman, R.J. (2010) 'Rebuilding health systems to improve health and promote statebuilding in post-conflict countries: a theoretical framework and research agenda', *Social Science and Medicine,* 70: 89–97.

Labonte, R. and Gagnon, M.L. (2010) 'Framing health and foreign policy: lessons for global health diplomacy', *Globalization and Health*, 6. doi:10.1186/1744-8603-6-14.

Lafferty, K.D. (2009) "The ecology of climate change and infectious diseases', *Ecology*, 90: 888–900.

Lederberg, J. (1996) 'Infectious disease – a threat to global health and security', *Journal of the American Medical Association*, 276: 417–419.

Lederberg, J., Shope, R.E. and Oaks, S.C. (eds.) (1992) *Emerging Infections: Microbial Threats to Health in the United States*, Washington, D.C.: National Academy Press.

Leitenberg, M. and Zilinskas, R.A. (2012) *The Soviet Biological Weapons Program: A History*, Cambridge: Harvard University Press.

MacQueen, G. and Santa Barbara, J. (2000) 'Peace building through health initiatives', *British Medical Journal,* 321: 293–296.

McInnes, C. (2006) 'HIV/AIDS and security', *International Affairs,* 82: 315–326.

McInnes, C. (2009) 'National security and global health governance' in A. Kay and O. Williams (eds.), *Global Health Governance – Crisis, Institutions and Political Economy*, Basingstoke, UK: Palgrave Macmillan.

McInnes, C. (2011) 'HIV, AIDS and conflict in Africa: why isn't it (even) worse?' *Review of International Studies,* 37: 485–509.

McInnes, C. and Lee, K. (2006) 'Health, security and foreign policy', *Review of International Studies*, 32: 5–23.

McInnes, C. and Rushton, S. (2010) 'HIV, AIDS and security: where are we now?', *International Affairs*, 86: 225–245.

McInnes, C. and Rushton, S. (2011) 'HIV/AIDS and securitization theory', *European Journal of International Relations*, 19: 115–138.

McNeill, W. (1976) *Plagues and Peoples*, New York: Anchor Press.

Miller, R. and Dowell, S. (2012) *Investing in a Safer United States: What is Global Health Security and Why Does it Matter?* Washington: CSIS. Online. Available HTTP: <http://csis.org/files/publication/120816_Miller_InvestingSaferUS_Web.pdf> (accessed 21 May 2013).

Murray, C.J.L., King, G., Lopez, A.D., Tomijima, N., and Krug, E.G. (2002) 'Armed conflict as a public health problem', *British Medical Journal,* 324: 346–349.

National Intelligence Council (2000) *The Global Infectious Disease Threat and Its Implications for the United States*, National Intelligence Estimate. Washington: National Intelligence Council.

National Intelligence Council (2008) *Strategic Implications of Global Health: Intelligence Community Assessment 10-D*, Washington: National Intelligence Council.

Ogata, S. and Cels, J. (2003) 'Human security – protecting and empowering the people', *Global Governance*, 9: 273–282.

Ogata, S. and Sen, A. (2003) *Human Security Now: Commission on Human Security*, New York: Commission on Human Security.

O'Keefe, M. (2012) 'Lessons from the rise and fall of the military AIDS hypothesis: politics, evidence and persuasion', *Contemporary Politics*, 18: 239–253.

O'Manique, C. and Fourie, P. (2010) 'Security and health in the twenty-first century', in M. Duan Cavelty and V. Mauer (eds.) *The Routledge Handbook of Security Studies*, New York: Routledge: 243–253.

Ostergard, R. (2002) 'Politics in the hot zone: AIDS and national security in Africa', *Third World Quarterly*, 23: 333–350.

Ostergard, R.L. (ed.) (2007) *HIV/AIDS and the Threat to National Security*, New York: Palgrave Macmillan.

Ouagrham-Gormley, S.B. (2012) 'Barriers to bioweapons: intangible obstacles to proliferation', *International Security*, 36: 80–114.

Peterson, S. (2002/2003) 'Epidemic disease and national security', *Security Studies*, 12: 43–81.

Petro, J. B., Plasse T.R. and McNulty J.A. (2003) 'Biotechnology: impact on biological warfare and biodefense', *Biosecurity and Bioterrorism*, 1: 161–168.

Poku, N., Renwick, N. and Porto, J.G. (2007) 'Human security and development in Africa', *International Affairs*, 83: 1155–1170.

Price-Smith, A.T. (ed.) (2001) *Plagues and Politics: Infectious Disease and International Policy*. New York: Palgrave.

Price-Smith, A.T. (2002) *The Health of Nations: Infectious Disease, Environmental Change, and Their Effects on National Security and Development*, Cambridge, MA: MIT Press.

Price-Smith, A.T. (2009) *Contagion and Chaos: Disease, Ecology, and National Security in the Era of Globalization*, Cambridge, MA: MIT Press.

Prins, G. (2004) 'AIDS and global security', *International Affairs*, 80: 931–952.

Rodier, G.R. (2007) 'New rules on international public health security', *Bulletin of the World Health Organization*, 85: 428–430.

Rodier, G., Greenspan, A.L., Hughes, J.M. and Heymann, D.L. (2007) 'Global public health security', *Emerging Infectious Diseases*, 13: 1447–1452.

Rosebury, T. (1949) *Peace or Pestilence: Biological Warfare and How to Avoid It*, New York: McGraw-Hill.

Rosenau, W. (2001) 'Aum Shinrikyo's biological weapons program: why did it fail?' *Studies in Conflict and Terrorism*, 24: 289–301.

Rushton, S. (2010) 'AIDS and international security in the United Nations system', *Health Policy and Planning*, 25: 495–504.

Rushton, S. (2011) 'Global health security: security for whom? Security from what?', *Political Studies*, 59: 779–796.

Sachs, J. and Malaney P. (2002) 'The economic and social burden of malaria', *Nature* 415: 680–685.

Sagala, J.K. (2006) 'HIV/AIDS and the military in Sub-Saharan Africa: impact on military organizational effectiveness', *Africa Today*, 53: 53–77.

Seckinelgen, H., Bigirumwami, J. and Morris, J. (2010) 'Securitization of HIV/AIDS in context: gendered vulnerability in Burundi', *Security Dialogue*, 41: 515–535.

Semenza, J.C. and Menne, B. (2009), 'Climate change and infectious diseases in Europe', *Lancet Infectious Diseases*, 9: 365–375.

Singer, P. W. (2002) 'AIDS and international security', *Survival*, 44: 145–158.

Smallman-Raynor, M.R. and Cliff, A.D. (2004) *War Epidemics: An Historical Geography of Infectious Diseases in Military Conflict and Civil Strife, 1850–2000*, Oxford, UK: Oxford University Press.

Smith, B., Inglesby, T., and O'Toole, T. (2003). 'Biodefense R&D: anticipating future threats, establishing a strategic environment', *Biosecurity and Bioterrorism: Biodefense Strategy, Practice, and Science*, 1: 193–202.

Tarantola D., Amon J., Zwi A., Gruskin S., Gostin L.(2009) 'H1N1, public health security, bioethics, and human rights', *Lancet*, 373: 2107–2108.

Tucker, J.B. (1999) 'Historical trends related to bioterrorism: an empirical analysis', *Emerging Infectious Diseases*, 5: 498–504.

Tucker, J.B. (ed.) (2000) *Toxic Terror: Assessing Terrorist Use of Chemical and Biological Weapons*, Cambridge, MA: MIT Press

Tucker, J.B. (2001) *Scourge: The Once and Future Threat of Smallpox*, New York: Atlantic Monthly Press.

Vogel, K.M (2013) *Phantom Menace or Looming Danger? A New Framework for Assessing Bioweapons Threats*, Baltimore, MD: Johns Hopkins University Press.

Watts, S. (1997) *Epidemics and History: Disease, Power and Imperialism*, London: Yale University Press.

Weir, L. (2012) 'A Genealogy of global health security', *International Political Sociology*, 6: 322–325.

Weir, L. and Mykhalovskiy, E. (2010) *Global Public Health Vigilance: Creating a World on Alert*, New York: Routledge.

Whiteside, A., de Waal, A., and Gebre-Tensae, T. (2006) 'AIDS, security, and the military in Africa: a sober appraisal', *African Affairs*, 105: 201–218.

WHO (2007) *The World Health Report 2007 – A Safer Future: Global Public Health Security in the 21st Century*, Geneva: WHO.

Wilson, K, Von Tigerstrom, B. and McDougall, C. (2008) 'Protecting global health security through the International Health Regulations: requirements and challenges', *Canadian Medical Association Journal*, 179: 44–48.

Wright, S. (ed.) (2002) *Biological Warfare and Disarmament: New Problems/New Perspectives*. Lanham: Rowan and Littlefield.

Youde, J. (2005) 'Enter the fourth horseman: health security and international relations theory', *Whitehead Journal of Diplomacy and International Relations*, 6: 193–208.

Youde, J. (2012) *Global Health Governance*. Cambridge: Polity Press.

Yuk-Ping, C.L. and Thomas, N. (2010) 'How is health a security issue? Politics, responses and issues', *Health Policy and Planning*, 25: 447–453.

Zacher, M.W. and Keefe, T.J. (2008) *The Politics of Global Health Governance: United by Contagion*, Houndmills, UK: Palgrave Macmillan.

INDEX

9/11 13, 22, 53, 108, 109, 110, 113, 125, 127, 129, 203, 204, 215, 216, 267, 281

Abbot Laboratories 334
abortion 52
accountability 33, 37, 114, 294, 299, 324
adenovirus 218
Advocacy Network for Africa 279
Afghanistan 127, 128, 147, 148, 268, 269, 272
aflatoxin 120, 122
Africa Action 279
Africare 279, 282
Agreement on Trade-Related Aspects of Intellectual Property Rights (TRIPS) 269–70, 273, 334
AIDS Healthcare Foundation 285
AIDS *see* HIV/AIDS
AIDS Society of Asia and the Pacific (ASAP) 42
Al Qaeda 127–8
al-Zawahiri, Ayman 127
American Friends Committee 295
American Home Products 217
American Red Cross 211
Amnesty International 279
Annan, Kofi 12
anthrax 13–4, 22, 73, 119, 122, 125, 126–7, 133–4, 181, 195, 203–4, 215, 216, 218, 220, 221, 256, 267
Anti-Counterfeiting Trade Agreement (ACTA) 270
antibiotics 77, 102, 126, 130, 131, 135, 179, 193, 330 *see also* antimicrobial resistance
antimicrobial resistance 20, 39, 41, 102, 115, 135, 155, 165, 170, 178, 194, 215, 216, 283, 293, 295–6, 299, 300
antiretroviral therapy (ART) 78, 79, 94, 114, 147, 273, 277, 283, 285–6, 334
antivirals 77, 78, 84, 130, 216, 224, 318, 320, 321, 323, 328, 329
APT Partnership Laboratories 41
arbovirus 20
Argentina 25
armed conflict 7, 9, 32, 34, 38, 48, 50–1, 53–7, 67, 85, 111, 131, 141–9, 159, 167, 171, 189, 191, 193, 197, 242, 265, 307, 309, 332, 333, 340, 341, 345
Armed Forces Health Surveillance Centre (AFHSC) 102
army *see* military
artemisinin combination therapy (ACT) 181
ASEAN 39, 43; Institutes of Strategic and International Studies (ASEAN ISIS) 34
ASEAN Plus Three 34, 36, 40, 41
Asia Pacific Alliance for Sexual and Reproductive Health and Rights (APA) 42
Asia Pacific Observatory on Health Systems and Policies (APO) 42, 43
Asia Partnership on Emerging Infectious Diseases Research (APEIR) 42
Asia-Pacific Economic Cooperation (APEC) 35, 195
Asian Development Bank (ADB) 99
Asian Financial Crisis 1997 34
Asian-Pacific Resource and Research Centre for Women (ARROW) 42
Aum Shinrikyo 125–6
austerity 48, 51, 212
Australia 14, 40, 93, 122, 135, 270, 320
Australia Group 124
Austria 341
Axworthy, Lloyd 12

Bavarian Nordic 216
Baxter International 217
Belgium 86
Bell Labs 218

Bill and Melinda Gates Foundation 76
bin Laden, Osama 127
BioCaster 227, 228, 231
biodefense 63, 76, 120, 127, 128, 130, 131–3, 134, 138, 196, 215–24, 329, 335 *see also* biosecurity
biological weapons 13, 14, 18, 20–4, 60, 63, 74, 76, 88, 118–29, 130–8, 142, 181, 191, 194, 196, 215, 216, 222, 231, 252, 253–9, 307, 331, 341, 342, 346
Biological Weapons Convention 1972 (BWC) 122, 123–4; 131–3, 138, 193, 196–7, 252–62; Confidence-Building Measures 124, 193, 197, 253
Biomedical Advanced Research and Development Agency (BARDA) 220–3
Biopreparat 121–2, 131
Bioregulators 118, 120, 253
biosecurity 7, 13–4, 15, 36, 74–6, 130, 133–5, 138, 252–63; *see also* biodefense
biotechnology 57, 120, 121, 123, 128, 129, 130, 132, 135, 137, 138, 220, 255, 257, 259, 273, 335
bioterrorism 7, 8, 10, 11, 13, 14, 60, 62, 63, 75, 76, 78, 79, 83, 118–29, 133, 134, 137, 142, 181, 195–7, 202, 210, 224, 252, 255, 256, 267, 305, 306, 307, 329, 332, 336, 341
Bipartisan Weapons of Mass Destruction Center 215
Bolivia 25
Boston marathon 203–4
Botswana 147, 182, 281
botulinum *see* botulism
botulism 119, 120, 122, 181, 216, 221
Bovine Spongiform Encephalopathy (BSE) 93, 94
Brazil 25, 183, 267, 272, 325, 335
Bubonic Plague *see* plague
Burundi 54, 285
Bush, George W. 53, 109, 133, 215, 218–9, 268
Butler, Thomas 134

Cambodia 42, 84, 297, 299
Canada 19–21, 26, 74, 88, 94, 95, 97, 196, 210, 227, 230
cancer 53, 168, 175, 183, 192, 330, 331, 335
cardiovascular disease 175, 183
Carter Center 282
Centers for Disease Control and Prevention (CDC) (United States) 14, 24, 107, 202, 203, 204, 216, 217, 221, 320
Central Intelligence Agency (CIA) (United States) 8, 111, 112, 341
cerebrovascular disease 330
Chad 158, 328
Chemical Weapons Convention (CWC) 124, 252–3, 256, 259, 261, 263
Chen, Lincoln 12
Chernobyl 11
Chikungunya fever 155
child health 52, 163, 165, 166, 192, 205–6, 210, 281, 296, 330, 340, 343, 344, 346
Chile 25, 270
China, People's Republic of 38, 41, 42, 74, 85, 87, 88, 97, 122, 132, 145, 147, 183, 212, 226, 228, 249, 271–2, 274, 278, 296, 297, 299–30, 319, 323, 329
cholera 8, 21, 23, 76, 99, 101, 102, 106, 144, 178, 179, 191, 192, 194, 266
chronic diseases *see* non-communicable diseases
chronic obstructive pulmonary disease (COPD) 330
civil society organizations (CSOs) 42, 194, 257, 309
class 49, 50, 57, 110, 111
climate change 1, 32, 151–61, 164
Cold War 7, 32, 56, 64, 85, 89, 111, 121, 180, 182, 193, 194, 196, 218, 252, 306, 307
Colombia 25
Commission on Human Security 12, 33, 35, 280
Comprehensive Test Ban Treaty (CTBT) 124, 262
conflict *see* armed conflict
Convention on the Prohibition, Development, Production, and Stockpiling of Bacteriological (Biological) and Toxin Weapons and on their Destruction 1972 *see* Biological Weapons Convention 1972
Copenhagen School 62, 109, 307, 309 *see also* securitization
Council for Security Cooperation in the Asia Pacific (CSCAP) 34
counterinsurgency 54, 79, 122
counterterrorism 54, 265, 346 *see also* terrorism, War on Terror
crime 7, 32, 86, 307
Cuba 273
cybercrime *see* crime

Darfur 159
Daschle, Thomas 126, 127
Defence Science and Technology Laboratories (DSTL) (United Kingdom) 256
Defence Trade Controls Act 2012 (Australia) 135
degenerative diseases 35
Democratic Republic of Congo (DRC) 55, 279, 284, 285
dengue fever 41, 155, 334
Department of Agriculture (United States) 211
Department of Defense (DoD) (United States) 54, 132, 133, 211, 217
Department of Energy (United States) 211
Department of Health and Human Services (United States) 60, 202, 204, 211
Department of Homeland Security (United States) 132, 204, 205, 211, 216, 346
Department of Justice (United States) 134, 346
Department of State (United States) 110, 132, 256, 284
development *see* development assistance for health; economic development; human development

development assistance for health (DAH) 40, 167, 169, 265, 267, 268–9, 272, 342–4 *see also* economic development, human development
diabetes 53, 175, 183, 192, 329, 330, 331,
diarrheal illnesses 134, 144, 340, 342, 343
disability 35, 328, 340
disarmament, demobilization and reintegration (DDR) 55
discrimination 52, 86, 243, 284, 346 *see also* nondiscrimination, stigma
Doha Declaration 274
domestic violence 52, 277, 284 *see also* gender-based violence
drug use/abuse *see* narcotic use 52, 111, 143, 184, 298
dual-use 14, 27, 260
dysentery 8

East Asia Vision Group 34
Ebola Hamorrhagic Fever 10, 76, 93, 102, 119, 194, 216
economic development 13, 20, 33–43, 51, 56, 73, 107–8, 109, 146, 148, 153, 155–7, 160, 167, 170–1, 178, 180, 184, 194, 271, 278–82, 287, 307, 309 *see also* development assistance for health; human development
ectromelia virus 135–6, 13
Ecuador 25
Edgewood Chemical and Biological Center (United States) 132
Egypt 87, 95, 190, 234, 268, 269
Eli Lilly and Company 217
Emergent Biosolutions 220
emerging and reemerging infectious diseases *see* emerging infectious diseases
emerging infectious diseases (EID) 7, 10, 18–27, 39, 40–2, 62, 73, 76, 92–103, 178, 194, 206, 212, 216, 217, 221, 223, 224, 229, 267, 269, 296, 300, 329, 330
England *see* United Kingdom
environmental change *see* climate change
environmental degradation 32, 35, 38, 51, 159, 193, 297–8, 300, 307, 310
Environmental Protection Agency 211, 217
equity 37, 111, 273
Estonia 298
Ethiopia 269, 278
ethnicity 49, 50, 55, 57, 311
European Centre for Disease Prevention and Control (ECDC) 76
European Commission 60, 210, 230, 243
European Union 20, 26, 76, 196, 210, 270, 271
extremely drug-resistant tuberculosis (XDR-TB) 293, 295–6, 298, 299

faith-based organizations (FBOs) 277–9, 281
famine 9, 38, 115
Federal Bureau of Investigations (FBI) (United States) 13, 126–7
Federal Emergency Management Administration (FEMA) (United States) 202
flooding 38
Food and Agriculture Organization (FAO) 97, 156, 210, 282
Food and Drug Administration (FDA) (United States) 216–20, 222, 224
food security 156–9, 277, 282–3, 287
foreign policy 34, 42, 63, 75–6, 88, 110, 191, 193, 265–74, 278, 282, 305–7
Fort Detrick *see* United States Army Medical Research Institute for Infectious Diseases
Fouchier, Ron 136–8, 258
fragile states 51, 54, 113, 147, 167 *see also* state failure
Framework Convention on Tobacco Control (FCTC) 271, 273
France 86, 121, 160, 166, 191, 196, 210, 230, 235, 267
Francis, Tommy 218
Franklin, Benjamin 313
Fukushima 111, 206

G20 240
G8 195, 332
Gates Foundation *see* Bill and Melinda Gates Foundation
gender 48–57, 105, 115, 146, 283, 287, 305, 308, 309, 311
gender-based violence 55, 282, 283–4, 286–7 *see also* sexual violence, domestic violence
General Electric 218
Geneva Conventions 142
Geneva Protocol 1925 122, 191, 252, 254, 259
Georgia 298
Germany 86, 98, 121, 155, 191, 196, 210, 230, 268, 341
Gilman, Benjamin 181
glanders 119, 216
GlaxoSmithKline 217, 321, 322, 323, 335
Global Alliance for Vaccines and Immunization (GAVI Alliance) 41, 77, 78, 332
Global Early Warning System (GLEWS) 210
Global Fund to Fight AIDS, Tuberculosis and Malaria 41, 109, 196, 285, 343
global health diplomacy 36, 189, 195–6
global health governance 43, 62, 66, 68, 71, 106–7
Global Health Security Action Group (GHSAG) 230
Global Health Security Initiative (GHSI) 195, 196, 210
Global Influenza Surveillance and Response System (GISRS) 322
Global Influenza Surveillance Network (GISN) 320, 329–30

Global Outbreak Alert and Response Network (GOARN) 21–2, 76, 208, 229, 328–9, 331
global public goods 37, 269
Global Public Health Intelligence Network (GPHIN) 21, 227–32
governmentality 8
Gross Domestic Product (GDP) 87, 94, 99, 113, 163, 166, 270, 297

haemorrhagic fever 102
Haiti 143–4, 269 *see also* United Nations Stabilization Mission in Haiti
Hajj 232, 234
Health Action International Asia-Pacific (HAIAP) 42
health as a bridge for peace 67–8, 147–8
health diplomacy *see* global health diplomacy
health system strengthening 10, 27, 36–40, 43, 55, 207, 332–3, 336, 343
HealthMap 228, 230–2
heart disease *see* ischemic heart disease
hepatitis B 218
Hilleman, Maurice 218
HIV *see* HIV/AIDS
HIV/AIDS 1, 8, 9, 10, 14, 38, 39, 41, 42, 49, 51, 53–7, 73–4, 77, 78, 79, 83, 84, 92, 94, 105–15, 143–4, 145–7, 148–9, 167, 168, 177, 178, 179, 180, 182, 193, 194, 196, 268, 272–3, 274, 277–87, 293, 306, 330, 332, 334, 335, 339, 341–4, 346, 347
Holbrooke, Richard 111, 319
Hong Kong 74, 95, 97–100, 194, 195, 248, 319, 330
human development 37, 41, 110, 178, 278–82 *see also* development assistance for health (DAH); economic development
human granulocytic anaplasmosis 155
human monocytic ehrlichiosis 155
human rights 2, 12, 37, 52, 53, 57, 87, 105–11, 115, 233, 243, 247, 278, 279, 282, 293–300, 339
Human Rights Committee *see* United Nations Human Rights Committee
Human Rights Watch 279, 298
human security 1, 2, 7, 11–13, 32–43, 49, 51–2, 56, 60, 74–5, 77–9, 85, 87, 89, 109–11, 141, 159, 163, 167, 175–8, 180–4, 194, 277, 280–1, 286, 293, 308–9, 313, 333, 340–2
Hurricane Katrina 160

immigration *see* migration
India 86, 145, 183, 194, 270–1, 272, 278, 325, 334–5, 345
Indonesia 41, 42, 85, 88, 89, 240, 242, 267, 270, 318–25
inequality 35, 50, 51, 108, 158, 304, 312
influenza 2, 9, 10, 20, 38 42, 53, 60, 73, 83, 86–8, 94–7, 102, 130, 136–7, 146, 148, 189, 196, 202–3, 210–11, 240, 249, 306, 318–25, 328–30, 335; 'Asian flu' 1957; H1N1 'Swine Flu' 38, 78, 93, 210–11, 229, 239; H5N1 'Bird Flu' 38, 39, 194, 196, 228, 257–8, 318–22; H7N9 38, 93; highly pathogenic avian influenza (HPAI) 41, 336; 'Spanish flu' 1918 84, 146, 192, 257, 306, 340
Institute of Medicine (IoM) (United States) 19, 92
Institute of Ultra-Pure Biological Preparations (Soviet Union) 121
intellectual property rights 41, 165, 244, 269–72, 319, 322, 323
Intergovernmental Panel on Climate Change (IPCC) 152
International AIDS Vaccine Initiative (IAVI) 334
International Atomic Energy Agency (IAEA) 25, 124, 262
International Chamber of Commerce 323
International Committee of the Red Cross (ICRC) 142, 148
International Council of AIDS Service Organizations 279
International Court of Arbitration 323
International Court of Justice 244–6
International Covenant on Civil and Political Rights (ICCPR) 243, 294–5
International Covenant on Economic, Social and Cultural Rights (ICESCR) 52, 243, 294
international development *see* development assistance for health; economic development; human development
International Health Regulations (IHR) 18–9, 21–6, 27, 84, 93, 99–103, 106, 194–5, 207–11, 227–33, 235, 239–49, 266, 274, 295, 328–9, 331–2, 336
International HIV/AIDS Alliance 279
International Nuclear Security Education Network (INSEN) 262–3
International Sanitary Convention 101, 191
International Sanitary Regulations 101, 106 *see also* International Health Regulations
International Union of Pure and Applied Chemistry (IUPAC) 261
Internet surveillance response programs (ISRPs) 107, 226–35
Iran 25, 122, 124, 132
Iraq 24, 122, 124, 142, 148, 183, 194, 268–9
Iraq Survey Group 122
Ireland, Republic of 74, 98
ischemic heart disease 330, 335
Israel 255, 268–9
Italy 86, 166, 196, 210, 230, 255–6
Ivins, Bruce E. 13, 126–7, 133–4, 138

Jackson, Ron 136
Japan 11, 25, 34, 40, 42, 121, 125, 148, 166, 196, 206, 210, 230, 255–6, 268
Johnson, Lyndon 151

Joint United Nations Programme on HIV/AIDS (UNAIDS) 77, 109, 194, 279
Jordan 235, 268–9

Kamal, Hussein 122
Kawaoka, Yoshihiro 136–7
Kennedy, John F. 268
Kenya 94, 269
Kuan Yew, Lee 84

Lac Tremblant Declaration 1994 19–20
Lao PDR 41–2, 297, 299
Latvia 298
League of Nations Health Organization (LNHO) 191
Leahy, Patrick 126–7
Lederberg, Joshua 19
leprosy 64–5, 181
Lesotho 147, 182, 298
Lothar Salomon Test Facility 132
Lugar, Dick 83
Lurie, Nicole 215
lyme borreliosis 155

malaria 1, 9, 11, 19–20, 38–41, 73, 77, 143–4, 155–6, 163–71, 179, 192, 210, 285, 306, 329–30, 334, 343
Malaria Eradication Campaign (1955–69) 169
Malaria Genome Project 334
Malaysia 40, 94, 270
malnutrition 38, 56, 141, 158, 160, 181, 282, 330
Marburg virus 93
maternal health 52, 176, 192, 343–4
measles 144, 181, 218, 328, 330
Médecins sans Frontières 76
medical countermeasures 73, 77–9, 89, 120, 133, 202–3, 207, 215–24
medicalization 36, 71–9, 107, 310, 345
MedISys 228, 231
meliodosis 216
meningitis 76, 218
Merck 217, 219, 335; Mectizan Donation Program 334
Mexico 23, 87–7, 95, 102, 196, 210–11, 228, 230
Middle East respiratory syndrome coronavirus (MERS-CoV) 83, 102, 234, 249, 270, 323
migration 1, 9, 13, 32, 35–6, 63–4, 85, 159, 167, 265, 286, 307, 339, 345
military 7–9, 13–14, 34, 36, 49, 50, 53–6, 62–3, 72–5, 77, 79, 85–9, 105–15, 122, 124, 128, 131–3, 138, 141, 143–9, 176, 180, 181, 183, 192–4, 218, 221, 254, 259, 265–6, 273, 279, 280, 299, 305, 307–9, 319, 340–1, 346
Millennium Development Goals (MDGs) 37, 196, 294, 335
Ministry of Defence (United Kingdom) 252
mosquitos 155–6, 163–71
multi drug-resistant tuberculosis (MDR-TB) 296, 298–9
Multi-Country AIDS Program (MAP) (World Bank) 109
mumps 218
Myanmar 84

Namibia 281
narcotic use 52, 111, 143, 184, 298
National Biodefense Science Board (NBSB) (United States) 134, 220
National Center for Advancing Translational Sciences (NCATS) (United States) 223
National Health Security Strategy (United States) 60, 202–3, 205
National Institute of Allergy and Infectious Diseases (NIAID) (United States) 218–20, 222–3
National Institutes of Health (NIH) (United States) 218–20, 222–4
National Intelligence Council (United States) 8–9, 112, 167, 341
National Pandemic Flu Service (United Kingdom) 79
National Response Framework (NRF) (United States) 204
National Science Advisory Board for Biosecurity (NSABB) (United States) 134, 136, 257–8
National Security Council (United States) 77
National Security Strategy 2006 (United States) 112
Naval Medical Research Unit 2 (NAMRU-2) (United States) 88
neglected tropical diseases 196, 310
Nepal 144, 272, 298
Network of Zambian People Living with HIV and AIDS (NZP+) 278
New Zealand 40
Nigeria 269, 278
Nipah virus 93–4
Nixon, Richard M. 121–31
noncommunicable diseases 2, 35, 38–40, 42–3, 79, 175–84, 269, 308, 310, 328, 336, 340
nondiscrimination 37 *see also* discrimination, stigma
North Korea 122, 132, 161, 233
Norway 155, 271
Novartis 321
Nuclear Non-Proliferation Treaty (NPT) 124
nutrition 52, 157, 192, 281 *see also* malnutrition

Obama, Barrack 83, 210
obesity 73, 79
Office for the Coordination of Humanitarian Affairs (OCHA) 39
Office International d'Hygiene Publique (OIHP) 101
Office of Malaria Control in War Areas (MCWA) (United States) 167
Ogata, Sadako 12, 33

OIE *see* World Organization for Animal Health
One World, One Health 37
Organization for the Prohibition of Chemical Weapons (OPCW) 124, 261, 263

Pakistan 25, 268–9, 345
Pan American Health Organization (PAHO) *see* World Health Organization
Panama Canal 166, 172
Pandemic and All-Hazards Preparedness Act 2006 78, 205
Pandemic Influenza Preparedness Framework for the Sharing of Influenza Viruses and Access to Vaccines and Other Benefits 240, 322–3
pandemic influenza *see* influenza
Paraguay 25
peacekeeping 8–9, 144–5, 280, 306
People's Republic of China *see* China
PEPFAR *see* President's Emergency Plan for AIDS Relief
Peru 25, 270, 298
Pfizer 335
Philippines 40–1, 66, 298
plague 21, 23, 65, 76, 85–6, 99, 101–2, 106, 120–1, 134, 155, 179, 181, 190, 192, 194, 216, 266, 280 *see also* Plague of Athens; Plague of Justinian
Plague of Athens 86, 141, 143
Plague of Justinian 87, 179
police 115, 146, 279, 298–9, 345–6
poliomyelitis (polio) 20, 102, 218, 345–6
pollution 32, 64, 151–2, 297–300
poverty 9, 12–15, 32, 34–41, 51–2, 57, 108, 160, 166, 168, 171, 181, 279–83, 297, 307, 309–10, 339–44, 347
Powell, Colin 111
preparedness 23, 36, 39, 60, 74, 78, 134, 178, 196, 201–13, 215–6, 239–40, 279, 325, 330
President's Emergency Plan for AIDS Relief (PEPFAR) (United States) 78, 147, 196, 268, 278–80, 284–5, 332
product development partnerships (PDP) 223, 323–4
Project al-Zabadi 127
Project BioShield 79, 219, 220–2
ProMED Mail 20–1, 228, 230, 235
Public Health Agency of Canada 227
public health emergency of international concern (PHEIC) 25, 101–3, 207–8, 210–11, 228, 232, 235, 241
Public Health Improvement Act 2000 204–5
PULS 227

quarantine 36, 65, 88–9, 99, 190–1, 197, 239, 266, 344–5

race 49, 50, 311
Rajneesh, Bhagwan Shree 125 *see also* Rajneeshees
Rajneeshees 125
RAND Corporation 75, 201
Reagan, Ronald 268
refugees 55, 143–4, 148, 159, 167, 341
research and development (R&D) 78, 121, 133, 176, 217–24, 334–6
resilience 147, 160, 201–13
ricin 119, 120
Rift Valley fever 94, 155
risk communication 208, 210–12, 227
Rockefeller Foundation 334
Ross River virus 155
rubella 218
Russia 122, 132, 145, 155, 183, 227, 278, 298
Rwanda 148, 159, 245, 281

Salk, Jonas 218
Sanofi-Aventis 219, 335
sarin 126, 194, 216
Saudi Arabia 234, 323
saxitoxin 120
science diplomacy 147–8
Scientific Research Institute of Applied Microbiology 121
Scientific Research Institute of Molecular Biology 121
securitization 2, 36, 38, 43, 53–7, 61–4, 71–2, 85–9, 106–13, 115, 175–7, 183–4, 277–82, 286–7, 293, 299, 304–8, 312, 328–9, 336, 339–47
Sen, Amartya 12
Senegal 267
September 11 2001 attacks *see* 9/11
severe acute respiratory syndrome (SARS) 1, 9, 10, 23, 35–6, 38–9, 41, 63, 73–4, 76, 83–4, 86, 93–4, 97–9, 102–3, 106, 147, 175, 178, 195, 211, 217, 221, 228, 229, 239, 242, 271, 274, 293, 299–300, 328, 330–1
sexual violence 48, 50, 52, 54–6, 115, 143, 284 *see also* gender-based violence
sexuality 49–51, 111
sexually transmitted infections (STIs) 13
Shoko Asahara 125 *see also* Aum Shinrikyo
Shope, Robert 19
Sibelius, Kathleen 215
Siga Technologies 216
Singapore 40, 74, 84, 98
Siracusa Principles 294–300
smallpox 14, 85, 101–2, 120, 121, 134, 136, 142–3, 179, 181, 192–3, 216–7, 221, 256, 266, 331, 345
social determinants of health 36, 39, 48, 52–3, 55, 57, 107, 311–3
Somalia 94, 280
South Africa 114, 122, 147, 263, 269, 272–4, 283, 285, 295–6, 298–9, 325
South Centre 325
Southeast Asian Ministers of Education Organization (SEAMEO) 42

Southeast Asian Tobacco Control Alliance (SEATCA) 42
sovereignty 23, 43, 109, 110–11, 158, 190, 240
Soviet Union 64, 121–2, 131, 182, 193
Spain 95, 234
Special Program for Research and Training in Tropical Diseases (TDR) 333
Sri Lanka 142
state building 34, 163, 170, 171
State Department (United States) *see* Department of State
state failure 15, 54, 112–3, 146–7, 167, 267, 341 *see also* fragile states
stigma 52, 55, 111, 144, 277, 279, 346–7 *see also* discrimination, nondiscrimination
Strategic National Stockpile (United States) 79, 216–7
structural violence 48, 54, 57
Supari, Siti Fadilah 88–9, 319
Swaziland 281
Switzerland 267
synthetic biology 197
syphilis 143
Syria 122, 132

Tamiflu 77, 79
Tanzania 94, 134, 269
Temasek Life Sciences 321
terrorism 32, 53, 73, 76, 109, 110, 111, 112, 194, 201, 203, 204, 206, 207, 215, 278, 339, 346 *see also* bioterrorism, counterterrorism, War on Terror
Thailand 42, 84, 228, 267, 297, 320, 334
Thatcher, Margaret 268
tick borne encephalitis 155
tobacco 42, 184, 271, 273, 330
tourism 10, 41, 74, 87, 213
trade 10, 26, 41, 87–8, 92, 94–103, 190–2, 197, 213, 230, 240, 242, 245, 265–7, 269–71, 286, 307, 325, 328, 331
Trans-Pacific Partnership (TPP) 270–1
Treatment Action Campaign (TAC) (South Africa) 273–4
TRIPS *see* Agreement on Trade-Related Aspects of Intellectual Property Rights
tuberculosis (TB) 19–20, 38–41, 73, 77, 178–80, 194, 210, 281, 333, 334, 340, 343 *see also* multi drug-resistant tuberculosis (MDR-TB); extremely drug-resistant tuberculosis
tularemia 119, 155
typhus 143, 192, 216

United States Trade Representative (USTR) 270
Uganda 143, 269, 285
Ukraine 88, 256
ul Haq, Mahbub 33
UNAIDS *see* Joint United Nations Programme on HIV/AIDS
UNDP *see* United Nations Development Programme
UNICEF *see* United Nations Children's Fund
United Kingdom 75, 94, 147, 196, 210, 229, 230, 234, 259
United Nation Office of Drugs and Crime (UNODC) 299
United Nations Children's Fund (UNICEF) 77
United Nations Development Programme (UNDP) 11–13, 33, 85, 111, 176, 194, 280, 293, 308–9, 333, 340
United Nations Economic and Social Council 294
United Nations General Assembly 1, 111, 184, 267
United Nations Human Rights Committee (HRC) 243–4, 294–5, 300
United Nations Monitoring and Verification Commission (UNMOVIC) 122
United Nations Security Council 1, 8, 26, 53, 54, 77, 83, 110, 111, 143, 145, 194, 196, 245, 267, 278–80, 306, 341–2
United Nations Special Commission (UNSCOM) 122
United Nations Stabilization Mission in Haiti (MINUSTAH) 144
United States 8, 10, 18–25, 53, 60, 63–4, 74–5, 77–9, 83–4, 88, 92, 98, 109–12, 121–2, 124, 126, 128, 131–6, 148, 160, 166–7, 177, 193, 194–6, 201–13, 215–24, 230, 258, 267–8, 270, 279, 321–3, 334–5, 341, 345
United States Army Medical Research Institute for Infectious Diseases (USAMRIID) 126–7
Universal Declaration of Human Rights (UDHR) 294
universal health coverage 37–8
urbanization 1, 35, 152, 184
Uruguay 25, 271
USAID (United States Agency for International Development) 211, 268
USSR *see* Soviet Union

variant Creutzfeld-Jakob Disease (vCJD) 93, 94
VaxGen 220
Venezuela 25, 273
Vietnam 40, 41, 42, 74, 98, 228, 270, 296, 299, 320
viral encephalitis 119, 181
viral hemorrhagic fever *see* haemorrhagic fever

Walter Reed Army Institute of Research (WRAIT) (United States) 218
War on Terror 53, 74, 76, 108, 110, 115, 279 *see also* counterterrorism, terrorism
war *see* armed conflict
West Nile virus 10, 94, 155, 194
WHO Global Strategy for the Containment of Antimicrobial Resistance 102
World Bank 41, 43, 77, 94, 97, 109, 194, 244, 280, 333 *see also* Multi-Country AIDS Program

World Economic Forum 249
World Food Summit 1996 282
World Health Assembly 20–2, 25, 192, 197, 240, 242, 323
World Health Organization (WHO) 1, 10–11, 18–27, 37, 40–2 62, 74, 76, 77, 83, 87–8, 95–9, 101–6, 136, 147, 181, 183, 191–6, 198, 207–12, 226–35, 239, 242–9, 266, 271, 278, 293, 295, 200, 318–25, 328–9, 345, 347; collaborating centers 40, 228, 318–9, 320–3; constitution of 60; Eastern Mediterranean Regional Organization (EMRO) 23–5; Middle East and North Africa Regional Office (MENA) 233; Pan American Health Organization (PAHO) 101, 211; South-East Asia Regional Organization (SEARO) 22–5, 40; Western Pacific Regional Office (WPRO) 24–5, 40, 43
World Organization for Animal Health (OIE) 95, 210
World Relief 285
World Trade Organization (WTO) 41, 194, 242, 269–70, 334
World Vision 285
World War One 86, 121–2, 146, 191, 341
World War Two 66, 110–1, 121, 144, 167, 191, 218, 221

yellow fever 19, 21, 23, 76, 101–2, 155, 192, 266

Zambia 147, 269, 278–86
Zimbabwe 56, 279, 285
zoonoses 92–3, 160, 210, 212, 330–1
zoonotic diseases *see* zoonoses